De Gruyter Handbook of Disability and Management

De Gruyter Handbook of Disability and Management

Edited by
Joy E. Beatty, Sophie Hennekam and Mukta Kulkarni

DE GRUYTER

ISBN 978-3-11-162086-2
e-ISBN (PDF) 978-3-11-074364-7
e-ISBN (EPUB) 978-3-11-074373-9
ISSN 2748-016X
e-ISSN 2748-0178

Library of Congress Control Number: 2022948713

Bibliographic information published by the Deutsche Nationalbibliothek
The Deutsche Nationalbibliothek lists this publication in the Deutsche Nationalbibliografie;
detailed bibliographic data are available on the internet at http://dnb.dnb.de.

www.degruyter.com

De Gruyter Handbooks in Business, Economics and Finance

De Gruyter Handbook of Personal Finance
Edited by: John E. Grable and Swarn Chatterjee

De Gruyter Handbook of Entrepreneurial Finance
Edited by: David Lingelbach

De Gruyter Handbook of Organizational Conflict Management
Edited by: LaVena Wilkin and Yashwant Pathak

De Gruyter Handbook of Sustainable Development and Finance
Edited by: Timothy Cadman and Tapan Sarker

De Gruyter Handbook of Responsible Project Management
Edited by: Beverly L. Pasian and Nigel Williams

De Gruyter Handbook of Business Families
Edited by: Michael Carney and Marleen Dieleman

For more information, scan QR code below or visit https://www.degruyter.com/serial/dghbef-b/html

Contents

Part 1: Framing the Discussion

Part 2: Intersectionality

Part 3: **Social Reactions to Disability**

Part 4: **The Role of Context**

Part 5: Expanding Disability Definitions

Part 6: Research and Practice

List of Contributors

Muhammad Ali (PhD, Melbourne University) is an associate professor at the QUT Business School, Queensland University of Technology, Brisbane, Australia. His areas of research interest are managing diversity, work–life programs, and organizational effectiveness. He has published in journals such as *Human Resource Management*, *Journal of Construction Engineering and Management*, *Journal of Business Ethics*, *International Journal of Human Resource Management*, *Journal of Management in Engineering*, *International Journal of Project Management*, and *Human Resource Management Journal*. His research has been recognized nationally and internationally. He is a senior fellow of the Higher Education Academy, UK. He is currently serving as an associate editor of the *Australian Journal of Management* and an editorial board member of the *Human Resource Management Journal*.

Courtney L. Baker, PhD, is Assistant Professor of Industrial/Organizational Psychology at East Carolina University. She received her BS from Bradley University and her MA and PhD from Northern Illinois University. Dr. Baker's research focuses on a variety of issues relevant to the aging workforce, including the impact of disability, ageism, wellbeing, and selective mistreatment. She has published book chapters and articles in peer-reviewed journals on topics related to aging, quantitative methodologies, and workplace mistreatment.

Jana F. Bauer is a postdoctoral research associate at the Chair of Labor and Vocational Rehabilitation at the University of Cologne. In 2008 she received her diploma and in 2018 her PhD in Psychology from the University of Cologne. In her PhD thesis, she investigated the role of personal resources in student teachers' mental strain and health. She is in charge of the management of the third-party funded projects "PROMI – promoting inclusive doctoral studies" and "To tell or not to tell? Working with chronic health conditions". In her research, she strives toward a close connection between research and practice, the involvement of relevant stakeholders, and a focus on (personal and environmental) enabling factors and resources.

Miriam K. Baumgärtner is Head of Well-being, Switzerland and drives cultural transformation at PwC. She holds a master's degree in Psychology and a PhD in Strategy and Management. She worked as a researcher and scientific project leader at the University of St.Gallen, Switzerland for over 12 years. Her research projects with corporate partners centered around the topics of equality, diversity & inclusion, mental health, leadership, and new ways of working (or a combination thereof). She has published in top-tier journals and regularly presents at international scientific conferences and company events. For her concept of health-focused leadership, she won the Swiss Public Health Award and the University of St.Gallen Impact Award.

Lara Bellotti is currently a PhD student in Work and Organizational Psychology at the University of Bologna, Department of Psychology. Her research interests include managing diversity and inclusion at work (e.g., age diversity), aging at work and retirement processes and behaviors, and the work integration of people with mental disabilities. Her doctoral work specifically explores the effects of age-related stereotypes within the workplace and studies retirement precursors affecting the organizations' capacity to retain and engage older workers. She holds a Joint Master of Science degree in Work, Organizational, and Personnel Psychology (WOP-P) from the Universities of Bologna and Valencia with the support of the Erasmus+ Programme of the European Union.

https://doi.org/10.1515/9783110743647-203

Stephan A. Boehm is Associate Professor of Diversity Management and Leadership at the University of St.Gallen, Switzerland, where he also serves as the Director of the Center for Disability and Integration (CDI-HSG). His research focuses on leadership, diversity and HR management. He has a special interest in the vocational inclusion of employees with disabilities, health-focused leadership, as well as the management of digitalization and demographic change. Stephan has published in outlets such as *The Academy of Management Journal, Journal of Management, Personnel Psychology* or *Leadership Quarterly*. He has won various research prizes including the Journal of Organizational Behavior Best Paper Award, the Swiss Public Health Award, the Vontobel Award for Research on Aging and the AOM's Saroj Parasuraman Award for the Outstanding Publication on Gender and Diversity.

Silvia Bonaccio is the Ian Telfer Professor in Workplace Psychology at the University of Ottawa's Telfer School of Management. Her work focuses on the facilitators of positive work experiences for employees living with disabilities. She also conducts research on the influence of anxiety and emotions in personnel selection. She has published in leading management and applied psychology journals, such as the *Journal of Management, Organizational Behavior and Human Decision Processes, Human Resource Management*, and the *Journal of Organizational Behavior*. She serves on the editorial board of the *Journal of Business and Psychology* and the *Journal of Behavioral Decision Making*, and she is an associate editor at *Personnel Assessment and Decisions*. She is past Chair of the Canadian Society for Industrial and Organizational Psychology.

Christoph Breier, M.A., is a research associate and PhD student at the University of St.Gallen's Center for Disability and Integration (CDI-HSG) in Switzerland. His research focusses on career transitions and the inclusion of persons with disabilities in organizations. Previously he worked as a junior researcher for the Institute for Nonprofit and Public Management at the University of Applied Sciences and Arts Northwestern Switzerland (2015–2017). He has a bachelor's and master's degree in Politics and Administration from the University of Konstanz (2008–2014) in Germany.

Susanne M. Bruyère, PhD, CRC, is Professor of Disability Studies and Director, K. Lisa Yang and Hock E. Tan Institute on Employment and Disability, Cornell University's premier research, training, and technical assistance resource focusing on disability inclusion in employment, education, and community. In her role, Dr. Bruyère serves as Institute administrative and strategic lead, and also personally serves as the director/co-director of numerous research, dissemination, and technical assistance efforts focused on employment and disability policy and effective workplace practices for people with disabilities. She is the author of five books, many scholarly and practitioner articles, and online training programs and tools on workplace disability inclusion used by private and public sector organizations globally. She holds a doctoral degree in Rehabilitation Counseling Psychology from the University of Wisconsin-Madison and is a Fellow in the Society of Industrial and Organizational Psychologists and the Division of Rehabilitation Psychology of the American Psychological Association.

Camellia Bryan is an Elia Scholar and PhD Candidate in Organization Studies at the Schulich School of Business at York University, Ontario, Canada. Her research aims to promote the de-stigmatization of marginalized social identities in organizations through understanding how stigma holders resist stigmatization and how organizations can go about overcoming resistance to diversity on the part of employees belonging to dominant social identity groups.

Veronika Chakraverty was employed as a research associate at the Chair of Labor and Vocational Rehabilitation at the University of Cologne from 2017 to 2022, where she was part of the project "To tell or not to tell? Working with chronic health conditions". In her PhD project, she focuses on the subjective dimension of workplace inclusion in workers with long-term health conditions. From 2014 to 2016, she studied psychology at the University of Cologne (MSc) and worked as a research assistant with the Chair of Educational Psychology at the University of Cologne. Previously, she worked in the field of knowledge management for the Federal Ministry of Agriculture and Food in Germany where she conceptualized and designed government websites. In 2001, she received her diploma in communication design from the Bauhaus University in Weimar.

Catherine E. Connelly is a professor and Canada Research Chair at the DeGroote School of Business at McMaster University in Hamilton, Ontario. Her research focuses on the experiences of workers with disabilities, temporary foreign workers, gig workers, and leaders. Dr. Connelly's research has appeared in several outlets including the *Journal of Management*, the *Journal of Applied Psychology*, the *Journal of Organizational Behavior*, *Human Resource Management*, *Academy of Management Discoveries*, *Human Resource Management Review*, the *Journal of Management Information Systems*, and several others. She currently serves on the editorial boards of *Academy of Management Discoveries*, the *Journal of Organizational Behavior*, *European Management Journal*, *Human Resource Management*, *Human Resource Management Review*, and *Human Relations*, where she is also a former associate editor.

David J. G. Dwertmann is Associate Professor of Management at Rutgers University. He received his PhD in Strategy and Management from the University of St.Gallen in Switzerland. David is interested in the social and cognitive processes that result in feelings of otherness and how to overcome them. He has studied otherness in the form of people with versus without disabilities, immigrants versus non-immigrants, different levels of status and hierarchy, and more. He is particularly interested in how social norms, organizational climate, and leadership influence these processes. His work has been published in premier business journals such as the *Academy of Management Journal*, *Journal of Organizational Behavior*, and the *Journal of Management* among others. David has received local, national, and international awards for his work.

Cihat Erbil, PhD, is currently Assistant Professor in the Department of Business Administration at Ankara Haci Bayram Veli University in Ankara, Turkey. His research interests are in the areas of critical management studies, organisational sociology, and diversity. He uses the critical realism perspective in his works to reveal asymmetrical power relations and makes disadvantaged and underrepresented individuals and nonhumans visible by voicing them.

William E. Erickson, MS, is a researcher at the Yang Tan Institute on Employment and Disability at Cornell University. He has been actively involved with disability research for over 20 years and has extensive disability research experience in a variety of areas including employment, employer practices and policies, vocational rehabilitation, disability statistics, secondary data sources, survey design, web accessibility, and youth transition. He is the lead researcher in the production of the Annual Disability Status Report series and has expertise in the area of disability statistics and secondary data related to disability responding to thousands of Technical Assistance requests regarding disability statistics and related information for over 15 years through Cornell University's DisabilityStatistics.org.

Elisa S. M. Fattoracci is a third-year doctoral student in the Industrial-Organizational Psychology program in the Department of Psychological Sciences at Rice University. Her research interests include understanding identity-based adversity in the workplace. Currently, she is studying the effects of workplace microaggressions on employee outcomes and the influence of contested and invisible disabilities on the evaluative process. Ultimately, Elisa hopes to amplify and center the voices of employees with marginalized identities, as well as facilitate meaningful work for all employees. Elisa earned her BA in Psychology and Italian Studies from UC Berkeley in 2014.

Melissa Feigelson is a human capital analytics leader with experience developing corporate workforce analytics functions that deliver key talent insights and support strategic business initiatives. Melissa can set the strategy for analytics, lead cross-disciplinary review of analytics across HR functions, and drive the design and development of tools that enable HR professionals to transform big picture data into meaningful metrics. The common thread throughout Melissa's work is to give leaders greater insight into organizational trends and empower evidence-based decision making. Melissa earned a PhD in Industrial Organization Psychology from the State University of New York at Albany and holds a bachelor's degree in Psychology from Binghamton University.

Kayla B. Follmer is an associate professor of management at West Virginia University. Her research centers on understanding the work experiences of employees with stigmatized identities with particular emphasis on employees with mental illness. She also investigates the ways in which organizational factors impact serious psychological consequences such as suicidal ideation. Her research has been published in leading management journals including *Organizational Behavior and Human Decision Processes*, *Journal of Management*, *Group and Organization Management*, and *Journal of Organizational Behavior*.

Mirit K. Grabarski, PhD, is an assistant professor at the Faculty of Business Administration at Lakehead University, Canada. Her research interests are career development, positive organizational scholarship (empowerment and resilience), and diversity and inclusion. Her current projects explore organizational support for employee careers, and particularly career empowerment of new immigrants, as well as diversity programs that remove barriers for career development. She has specific interest in gender diversity and more recently in neurodiversity, using a social model perspective. Mirit earned her PhD in Organizational Behavior from the Ivey Business School at Western University, Canada and her MBA from the Open University of Israel.

Stefan C. Hardonk is associate professor at the Centre for Disability Studies, University of Iceland, Reykjavík, Iceland. His research expertise is situated within disability studies and he has studied employment participation and work inclusion from the perspectives of disabled people themselves, support professionals and employers. From 2018 to 2021 he was involved in the research project 'Rethinking work inclusion for people with intellectual disabilities' which was funded by the Research Council of Norway and included academic partners from Norway and Iceland. In his current research projects, he places emphasis on understanding how work, employment and labour market measures aimed at disabled people are given meaning within the context of the Nordic welfare state.

Mikki Hebl graduated with her BA from Smith College and PhD from Dartmouth College. She joined the faculty at Rice University in 1998, and is currently the Martha and Henry Malcolm Lovett Professor of Psychology with an additional appointment in the Jones School. Mikki's research focuses on workplace discrimination and the ways both individuals and organizations can remediate such discrimination and successfully manage diversity. She has approximately 175 publications, 21 teaching awards (including the most prestigious national award called the Cherry Award), research grants from NSF and NIH, and several gender-related research awards. In 2014, she was honored with the Academy of Management's Sage Award for lifetime achievement in research advancing knowledge of gender and diversity in organizations, and in 2018, she was selected as the Woman in Academia with Outstanding Career Award from the business school at the University of Lausanne, Switzerland.

Lana L. Huberty, PhD, Dean and Associate Professor, College of Kinesiology, Concordia, St. Paul, joined the faculty in the summer of 2013 with a PhD in Kinesiology from the University of Minnesota. She brought with her a wealth of industry practice in both private and public sport and recreation settings. Dr. Huberty's expertise in health and wellness includes 30+ years of group and individualized fitness training for which she holds numerous professional certifications including NETA, LMI, PHI, and YogaFit. Her research interests and publications focus on sport marketing and events, sport and recreation leadership, and gender, race, and ability diversity and inclusion.

Amit Jain is a faculty member with the Organization & Leadership Studies department at S.P. Jain Institute of Management and Research, Mumbai, India. He teaches courses in the field of organizational behaviour which includes courses such as Diversity at Workplace, Navigating Careers Now and in the Future, Management of Change, and Mental Wellbeing @Work. He also holds the position of Associate Program Head for the Post Graduate Management Programme for Women (PGMPW) a unique program by SPJIMR for women who have been on a career break and want to return to their professional career. His area of research interest is diversity and inclusion with specific focus on persons with disabilities. He was awarded the Swiss Government Excellence Scholarships (ESKAS) in 2019 to pursue his post-doctoral studies with the Center for Disability and Integration (CDI-HSG), University of St.Gallen.

Eline Jammaers is Assistant Professor at the Faculty of Business Economics from Hasselt University (Belgium) and guest lecturer at Université Catholique de Louvain (Belgium). She holds a PhD in business from Hasselt University (Belgium). Her research investigates the Othering processes related to diversity of gender, dis/ability and animals in the waged workplace and in the context of self-employment. Using a post-structuralist lens, she aims to deconstruct unhelpful taken-for-granted binaries in organizational thinking of agency/structure, body/mind and human/non-human. The broader aim of her research is to question dominant power relations and reflect on more egalitarian workplace alternatives. Her work has appeared in *Human Relations*, *Organization Studies*, *Organization*, *Entrepreneurship and Regional Development*, *Gender, Work and Organization* and *International Journal of Human Resource Management*.

Melanie Jones is Professor of Economics at Cardiff Business School, UK. Her research in empirical labour economics involves the quantitative analysis of large-scale secondary data.She has a particular expertise in labour market inequality, including relating to disability, and this work has been published in high quality international journals such as *Oxford Economic Papers*, *Economics Letters*, *Cambridge Journal of Economics*, *British Journal of Industrial Relations*, *Social Science and Medicine*, and *Work, Employment and Society*. Melanie is committed to translating her academic evidence into policy and practice, and she has acted as an expert advisor to government and given evidence at parliamentary select inquiries. She is a founding member of disability@work (www.disa bilityatwork.co.uk) which seeks to provide academic evidence on disability to a range of audiences.

Robert T. Keating is Assistant Teaching Professor in the Department of Psychology at Illinois Institute of Technology where he regularly teaches courses in industrial-organizational psychology and workplace diversity, equity, and inclusion. He is completing his doctoral training in the Social and I-O Psychology Program at Northern Illinois University. His primary research attempts to build clarity around the workplace inclusion concept, which has involved studies examining employees' felt experiences of inclusion, the features of the work environment that cue those feelings, and associated work-related and well-being outcomes. Robert and collaborators have extended this work toward understanding how organizations can improve the employment experiences of workers with stigmatized identities. This work has resulted in several conference presentations (SIOP, AOM) and peer-reviewed publications.

Maria H. Khan is a PhD candidate at the Faculty of Business and Law at Queensland University of Technology, Australia. Her research interests encompass social inclusion, social inequalities, decent work perspectives, gender diversity and leadership. Her current projects explore social and structural features of standard and non-standard working practices and their implications on marginalized and vulnerable groups. Maria completed her MPhil from QUT, Australia and MSc in Management from the University of Surrey, UK.

Douglas Kruse is Distinguished Professor in the School of Management and Labor Relations at Rutgers University, a Research Associate at the National Bureau of Economic Research (Cambridge, MA), and a Research Fellow at the IZA Institute for the Study of Labor (Bonn, Germany). Dr. Kruse served as Senior Economist at the White House Council of Economic Advisers in 2013–2014. He received an MA in Economics from the University of Nebraska-Lincoln and a PhD in Economics from Harvard University. His research has focused on the employment and earnings effects of disability, and the causes, consequences, and implications of employee ownership and profit sharing.

Koen Van Laer is Associate Professor at the Faculty of Business Economics of Hasselt University (Belgium), where he leads the research group SEIN – Identity, Diversity & Inequality Research. Drawing on critical perspectives, his work focuses on disability, ethnicity, sexual orientation and religion at work, on the way workplace experiences and careers are connected to power inequalities, and on the way 'difference' is managed and constructed in organizations. His work on diversity, inequality and inclusion has appeared in edited volumes as well as in international journals such as *Human Relations, Organization, Scandinavian Journal of Management, The International Journal of Human Resource Management, and Work, Employment and Society*. He serves on the editorial boards of *Organization* and *Human Relations*.

Isabelle Langlois has a bachelor's degree in Career Development and is a master's candidate in Career Counselling at the Université du Québec à Montréal (UQAM). She also holds a BA in International Studies (First Class Standing) from York University. Before working as a teaching and research assistant at UQAM and as a professional development counselor, she worked for nearly 15 years in feminist and community organisations with the aim of improving social justice. Her research and practice interests lie in addressing the reproduction of injustices and discrimination that arise from oppressions in the practice of career counselling.

Célia Lemaire is a full professor at *iaelyon*, Lyon 3 University, Magellan laboratory. Her research focuses on the organizational, managerial and control practices that facilitate the work of health and social care actors to improve the trajectories of the people cared for. Based on longitudinal studies rooted in the research field, she is interested in the attitude of actors towards management tools, the way they participate in their construction and the impacts that the tools have on the work of the actors. She approaches management as a "link factory", considering the double meaning of the term link, which can unite actors around projects or tighten them excessively; and looks for modalities that favor an optimization of systems to take into account the singularity of situations.

Kimberly M. Lukaszewski received her PhD from the University at Albany, State University of New York. She is currently Professor of Management at Wright State University. Her research is focused on electronic human resource management and diversity issues. Her work has been published in journals such as the *Human Resource Management Review*, the *Journal of Managerial*

Psychology, *Journal of Business and Psychology*, the *Journal of Business Issues*, the *Journal of the Academy of Business Education*, *AIS Transaction in Human-Computer Interactions* and *Communications of the Association for Information Systems*. She currently serves on the editorial boards of *Journal of Managerial Psychology*, *Research in Human Resource Management*, *Journal of Human Resource Education*, and served as a guest editor of a special issue of *Journal Managerial Psychology* on social issues, for three special issues of *Transactions on Human-Computer Interaction* on HRIS and e-HRM, and a research series in *Research in Human Resource Management*.

Brent J. Lyons is York Research Chair of Stigmatization and Social Identity and Associate Professor of Organization Studies at the Schulich School of Business at York University, Ontario, Canada. His research explores how processes of stigmatization and marginalization play a role in employees' work experiences, including how these processes disadvantage employees' access to power and resources in organizations, and how employees challenge and overcome these disadvantages. His research has been published in the *Academy of Management Review*, *Journal of Applied Psychology*, *Organizational Behavior and Human Decision Processes*, and the *Journal of Management*.

Jesus J. Martinez is currently working at McKinsey and Company as Research and Knowledge Fellow on the Organizational Science and Analytics team. At McKinsey, Jesus works with the Diversity, Equity, and Inclusion team. In this role, he conducts research on an inclusion assessment and supports the development of articles and blogs. Jesus is finishing his doctoral degree in Social-Industrial/Organizational Psychology at Northern Illinois University. His dissertation takes an intersectional lens to examine whether occupational fit explains discrimination in the field of engineering.

Kristie L. McAlpine is Assistant Professor of Management at Rutgers University. She received her PhD in Human Resource Studies from Cornell University. Kristie is interested in several themes associated with the changing nature of work, particularly changes stemming from advances in technology and demographic changes in the workforce. Specifically, she studies the individual and team outcomes of flexible work arrangements (e.g., telecommuting) and diversity, as well as how individuals and organizations navigate the work–family interface. Her research has been published in outlets such as the *Annual Review of Organizational Psychology and Organizational Behavior* and *Industrial and Labor Relations Review*. It has also been featured in *The New York Times*.

Megan R. McSpedon is a PhD student in Industrial and Organizational Psychology at Rice University. Her work explores motivation, shocks, and learning across the lifespan.

Mackenzie J. Miller is a PhD student in Management at West Virginia University. Mackenzie earned a bachelor's in Psychological Science and master's in Clinical Psychology from Ball State University. Broadly, her research is centered around studying diversity and equity in the workplace through an intersectional feminist lens. Mackenzie is particularly interested in unpaid/invisible labor, stigma and stigmatized work, as well as sexism and sexual harassment in the workplace. Additionally, her research focuses on examining the experiences of employees with concealable disabilities with the aim of improving accessibility and inclusivity in the workplace.

Katherine Moore holds qualifications in human resource management, management, disability and psychology. Katherine's research generally explores the employability of people with disabilities, and the organisational mechanisms that support sustainable employment outcomes for this group. She is also interested in the extent to which the changing landscape of work will impact on the employability of people with cognitive and neurological impairments; in particular, how organisational diversity practices impact on experiences of inclusion in workplaces of people with disabilities. Prior to her academic career, Katherine worked in the disability field for 20 years, primarily assisting people with moderate to high support requirements to find and maintain employment.

Katherine L. Moore is an attorney and independent researcher who writes scholarly articles and advocacy pieces that promote disability justice, awareness, and inclusion. She was Associate Professor and the Founder of the Health Justice Clinic at Seton Hall University School of Law, which she directed for five years, forging strategic relationships with medical partners of all sizes across New Jersey with a focus on services for veterans and people with disabilities. Prior to Seton Hall, she was Professor at New York University School of Law and Staff Attorney at the Bronx Defenders, where she practiced in family court fighting for the rights of parents with disabilities to retain custody over their children. She lives in New Jersey with her husband and two children.

Mark E. Moore is a faculty member in the Department of Kinesiology at East Carolina University, Greenville, North Carolina USA. His research interests relate to the examination of organizational and marketing theories as they apply to sport organizations. His work has been published in such journals as *Vocational Behavior*, *Gender in Management*, *Equality, Diversity and Inclusion: An International Journal*, *Sport Marketing Quarterly*, *Journal of Marketing Channels*, *Sport Management Education Journal* and *British Journal of Management*.

Mathilde Niehaus is a full professor at the University of Cologne. Since 2002, she is the Chair of the Unit for Labor and Vocational Rehabilitation. Previously, she was a full professor at the University of Vienna (Austria) and visiting professor at the Alpen-Adria University (Austria). She received her doctoral degree (in psychology, Dr. rer. nat.) from the University of Trier, and her habilitation (post-doctoral dissertation Dr. phil. habil.) from the University of Oldenburg. Her work has been published in more than 200 articles in academic journals of different disciplines. She has served on several scientific editorial and advisory boards.

Esra Odabaşi has worked in various divisions of the human resources departments of the international companies Imperial Tobacco, Boehringer Ingelheim, ABBOTT and EnerjiSA. Motivated by her own disability and limitations, in 2016, she set out to start the first company that provided consultancy services for the employment of the disabled in Turkey: ES Kariyer. ES Kariyer provides recruitment services and coaching and mentoring services in the same field in order to ensure its sustainability. As a TEDx speaker, Esra has been a finalist in the national Female Entrepreneur of the Year competition, organized by Garanti Bank, KAGİDER and Ekonomist. She holds a bachelor's degree in Business and has been coaching and mentoring professionally ever since.

Timothy A. Oxendahl is a doctoral student in Industrial/Organizational Psychology at Rice University. His research interests include individual differences, team dynamics, the aging workforce, and learning in the workplace, with a focus on technology-driven solutions for long-term workforce success. Prior to graduate school, he conducted research with organizations including Oregon Health and Science University, U.S. Center for SafeSport, and Portland State University. Timothy holds a BS from Portland State University.

Mustafa F. Özbilgin is Professor of Organisational Behaviour at Brunel Business School, Brunel University London. He also holds two international positions: Co-Chaire Management et Diversité at Université Paris Dauphine and Visiting Professor of Management at Koç University in Istanbul. His research focuses on equality, diversity and inclusion at work from transdisciplinary, international, comparative and relational perspectives. His research is supported by national and international grants and impacts policies and practices promoting equality in the UK and internationally. He is an engaged scholar, driven by values of workplace democracy, equality for all, and the humanisation of work. He is the founder of the international conference: Equality, Diversity, and Inclusion. He served as editor-in-chief of *Equality, Diversity, and Inclusion: an international journal*, *British Journal of Management* and *European Journal of Management*.

Ramona L. Paetzold is Professor in the Management Department at Texas A & M University. She holds a doctorate in statistics (minor area psychology), with other degrees in mathematics and law. Since the mid-1990s, she has been treated for Bipolar Disorder 1, and is therefore aware of the difficulties of navigating academia with a severe mental illness. Her management-related publishing has been related to sexual harassment and disability discrimination. Prior to that, she published extensively in the field of statistics, and currently, most of her publications are in social psychology. She has also taught at Carnegie-Mellon University and the University of Maryland.

Sarah Richard is Associate Professor at EM Strasbourg Business School. She defended her PhD on disability disclosure. Her research interests cover disability at the macro, the meso and the individual level. Her work focuses on disability policies in several countries; it also looks at individual choices depending on the disability and also explores the specific working environment of the adapted and the sheltered sector. She explores disability in general and the specific population of individuals with mental illnesses. Her work has been published in several French and international journals. She also teaches organizational behavior and human resource management and is the disability officer for Em Strasbourg Business School.

Yana van der Meulen Rodgers is Professor in the Department of Labor Studies and Employment Relations in the School of Management and Labor Relations at Rutgers University. She also serves as Faculty Director of the Center for Women and Work at Rutgers. Yana specializes in using quantitative methods to conduct research on women's health, labor market status, and well-being. She has worked regularly as a consultant for the World Bank, the United Nations, and the Asian Development Bank, and she was President of the International Association for Feminist Economics. She currently serves as an associate editor with the journals *World Development* and *Feminist Economics*. Yana earned her PhD in economics from Harvard University and her BA in economics from Cornell University.

Emily H. Rosado-Solomon is Assistant Professor at Babson College. She received her PhD from Rutgers University School of Management and Labor Relations, and has previously served on the faculty at California State University – Long Beach. Her research broadly focuses on the way that people engage with one another at work. Within that space she has three interrelated streams of research: interpersonal communication; mental illness and work; and diversity, equity, and inclusion. She is particularly interested in the experiences of those with mental health challenges and the ways they navigate their symptoms within the constraints and supports of various organizational contexts.

Matthew C. Saleh, PhD, JD, is Senior Research Associate and Lecturer at Cornell University. Matt's research focuses on career pathways for youth with disabilities and barriers to employment, such as justice involvement. At Cornell, Matt teaches undergraduate courses in disability studies and a course in the government department on mass incarceration in the United States. Matt is Principal Investigator (PI) on the U.S. Department of Health and Human Service's funded project "Improving VR Outcomes for Out-of-School Youth Involved in the Justice and/or Foster Care Systems" and PI on a pilot program called "*Pro Se*: Empowering Justice-Involved Youth and Young Adults through Speech, Debate, and Self-Advocacy Training," which provides a virtual certificate program in "Speech and Debate" to justice-involved youth, offered by Cornell undergraduate students.

Alecia M. Santuzzi is Professor in the Social-Industrial/Organizational Psychology Program and Director of Research Methodology Services at Northern Illinois University. She received her PhD in Psychological Sciences from Tulane University and completed postdoctoral training in Quantitative Methods at the University of Illinois, Urbana-Champaign. Dr. Santuzzi has over 20 years of experience designing and successfully executing research on the experience of social stigma from the target's perspective, with a particular emphasis on disability stigma and identity management decisions in the workplace. Her most recent work considers social and individual factors that contribute to a worker's decision to disclose a disability, and the costs and benefits of those decisions.

Frederike Scholz is Assistant Professor in HRM at the Department of Human Resource Studies at Tilburg University, in the Netherlands. Prior to that she undertook a postdoc at SEIN- Identity, Diversity & Inequality Research at Hasselt University, Belgium. She specialises in research on disability, labour market exclusion/inclusion, online recruitment, digital exclusion/inclusion, artificial intelligence, job crafting and active labour market policies. She is currently on the editorial board of *Gender, Work and Organization* and has published her work in *Human Relations*.

Sarah von Schrader is the Director of Research and Program Evaluation at Cornell University's Yang-Tan Institute (YTI) on Employment and Disability. Sarah's research focuses on employer practices related to recruiting, hiring, and advancing individuals with disabilities, working on topics like disability disclosure/self-identification, employment discrimination, workplace flexibility, and federal workplaces. Sarah received her doctorate in Education Measurement and Statistics from the University of Iowa and bachelor's degree in Mathematics from Colorado College.

Lisa Schur is Professor and past Chair of the Department of Labor Studies and Employment Relations at Rutgers University, where she teaches employment law and labor studies. She received a PhD in Political Science from the University of California-Berkeley and a JD from Northeastern University. Her research focuses on the economic, political, and social inclusion of people with disabilities, particularly their political participation and employment experiences and outcomes. In addition to publishing in peer-reviewed journals, she wrote an invited White Paper on Disability and Voting for the Presidential Commission on Election Administration, and co-authored the book *People with Disabilities: Sidelined or Mainstreamed?* published by Cambridge University Press.

Elisabeth R. Silver is a doctoral student and NSF Fellow in Industrial/Organizational Psychology at Rice University. She holds a BS in Biopsychology, Cognition, and Neuroscience from the University of Michigan and an MA in Industrial/Organizational Psychology from Rice University. Her research leverages traditional and computational methods to study when, why, and how people with privileged social identities uphold or resist inequalities in the workplace. Within the disability space, Elisabeth's work focuses on identifying and remediating discrimination based on neurodivergence.

Dianna L. Stone received her PhD from Purdue University, and serves on the faculties of the University of New Mexico, University at Albany, and Virginia Tech. Her research focuses on diversity and cross-cultural issues in organizations, unfair discrimination, electronic HR, privacy, and reactions to selection techniques. She has published over 100 articles, books, and book chapters, and results of her research have been published in the *Journal of Applied Psychology*, *Personnel Psychology*, *The Academy of Management Review*, *Journal of Management*, and *Human Resource*

Management Review. She is the former editor of the *Journal of Managerial Psychology*, and associate editor of *Human Resource Management Review*. At present, she is the editor of *Research in Human Resource Management* with James Dulebohn. She received the Scholarly Achievement Award and the Janet Chusmir Sage Service Award from the Gender and Diversity Division of the Academy of Management, and received the Trailblazer Award from the PhD Project. She is also a Fellow of the Society for Industrial and Organizational Psychology, the Association for Psychological Science, and the American Psychological Association.

Sasha Bolivar Trouwborst is originally from the Netherlands but moved to the United States in 2016. She graduated with a Masters of Science in Finance and is currently working as a financial analyst. She has lived in four different countries and traveled to more than 50 places throughout her lifetime. She herself has several learning and physical disabilities, and truly believes that it is critical to spread awareness of the different disabilities people may struggle with (especially within the workplace).

Patrizia Villotti obtained a PhD in Psychological Sciences and Education at the University of Trento in Italy, and held several postdoctoral positions in work psychology and mental health at work in different countries (Italy, Belgium, Canada). She has more than 10 years of experience in clinical, research, and teaching activities. She currently works as a professor at the Department of Education – Career Counselling at the Université du Québec à Montréal (UQAM) in Canada. She does research in organizational psychology, work disability prevention and management, and clinical psychology.

Sabrina D. Volpone is Associate Professor in the Organizational Leadership division at the University of Colorado, Boulder's Leeds School of Business. She is also the founder and director of the Diversity and Identity Management (DI&ID) Research Lab (https://diidmgmtresearchlab.com/). Dr. Volpone's research focuses on diversity management and identity management in organizations. Specifically, she uses both qualitative and quantitative methods to understand how organizations manage their diverse workforces and how diverse individuals flourish through the management of their identities at work. Her research has been published in peer-reviewed journals such as the *Academy of Management Journal, Journal of Applied Psychology, Journal of Management, Organizational Behavior and Human Decision Processes, and Personnel Psychology,* among others.

Victoria Wass is Professor Emerita at Cardiff Business School. Her teaching and research is at the intersection of labour economics and HRM and her publications span journals in both disciplines. She has a particular and continuing interest in measuring disability disadvantage in the workplace. She has a private practice working as an expert witness specialising in valuing claims for loss of future earnings. The basis of the claim is often post-injury disability-related employment disadvantage. In addition to advising in the context of litigation, she provides advice to government departments, parliamentary committees and organisations in the area of disability inclusion, with particular emphasis on measuring outcomes and progress. She is a founding member of disability at work (https://www.disabilityatwork.co.uk/) which provides research on disability in an accessible format.

Kevin Williams is Professor of Psychology and Dean of the Graduate School at the University at Albany, State University of New York. His current research interests include the psychology of security, where his work examines behavioral decision processes related to information security; human motivation and performance, where he studies the self-regulatory processes that guide goal strivings and goal revision over time; and employee assessment and appraisal, where his work seeks to identify best practices for assessing and evaluating employee aptitude and performance.

Sara Zaniboni, PhD, is Professor in Work and Organizational Psychology, University of Bologna. Her main research interests include diversity at work (e.g., age, disability, gender). She leads a research group that studies how to manage and enhance diversity at work. Her research in this domain has led to publications on refereed journals, participation in international research projects and in journal editorial boards. She is one of the main creators and organizers of the "Age in the Workplace Meeting", a bi-yearly conference series that brings together main experts from Europe, United States, Canada, Australia. She has been a visiting researcher at the University of Essex, University of Sherbrooke, and Portland State University, and since 2021 she is an adjunct/visiting professor at ETH Zurich.

Joy E. Beatty, Sophie Hennekam and Mukta Kulkarni

Introduction: Workplace Inclusion of Persons with Disabilities – Contemporary Assumptions, Definitions, and Concepts to Guide Research and Practice

The *De Gruyter Handbook of Disability and Management* aims to highlight current disability research from well-known global management scholars and features empirical studies, conceptual and theoretical developments, and practical suggestions for improving the workplace experiences of persons with disabilities. The *Handbook* includes contributions from authors from 12 countries: the United States of America, Canada, the United Kingdom, France, Germany, Switzerland, Italy, Belgium, the Netherlands, Turkey, Australia, and India. It has been a pleasure and an honor to work with this set of distinguished authors on the *Handbook*, and in this editorial introduction we would like to highlight some of the major themes that can be drawn collectively from this assembly of leading-edge work.

We first highlight broad and inter-related themes derived from the various contributions in this volume and then present an overview of each chapter. We conclude by drawing implications for practice.

Challenging Ableist Norms and Assumptions

The first theme that emerged from several chapters surrounds ableist norms and assumptions in the workplace. Individuals with disabilities often cannot conform to the prevailing norm of the ideal, unencumbered able-bodied worker, putting them at a disadvantage in the labor market. Consistent with existing literature on disability studies, several chapters in this volume challenge these ableist norms and assumptions and highlight that disabilities can be associated with functional differences across a range of contexts that can lead to positive outcomes both for employees with disabilities and the organizations themselves. For example, Dwertmann and McAlpine (Chapter 12 in this volume) argue that a disability can present both advantages and limitations and that this depends on the fit between the functional abilities of a person with a disability and the requirements of a specific job. Thus, rather than focusing on the impairments of the person with disability (PWD), a person–job fit lens

Joy E. Beatty, Eastern Michigan University
Sophie Hennekam, Audencia Business School, Nantes, France
Mukta Kulkarni, Indian Institute of Management - Bangalore

https://doi.org/10.1515/9783110743647-001

emphasizes the fit between the abilities of the worker and the demands of the job, challenging the need for PWD to comply with the ableist norms in the workplace (Hennekam et al., 2021). Further, Dwertmann and McAlpine show that performance advantages can result when there is a good fit between the two. Similarly, Lyons, Bryan, and Volpone (Chapter 17 in this volume) defy neurotypical and ableist norms by arguing that a neuroqueerness perspective allows us to uncover the exclusionary nature of these norms and call for more inclusionary practices and perspectives. They argue that a neuroqueerness lens could help organizations formulate alternative perspectives in their quest to depathologize neurodivergence and the identities of neurodivergent persons within their work environments. Their focus on the unique strengths of neurodiverse workers aligns with earlier research that emphasized the work-related strengths neurodiverse individuals can bring to the workplace. For instance, individuals with attention deficit hyperactivity disorder (ADHD) have been argued to possess characteristics that are a good fit with entrepreneurship (Wiklund et al., 2016), adults with dyslexia tend to be more creative than adults without dyslexia (Majeed et al., 2021), and individuals with autism spectrum disorder (ASD) are reported to be honest and dedicated employees (Cope & Remington, 2022). Similarly, Özbilgin, Erbil and Esra Odabaşı (Chapter 11 in this volume) investigate the emergence of leaders with disabilities and assess their standing in the boardroom. They show that the context, specifically whether disability is regulated or unregulated in the context of work, influences the way disability is managed in various countries. These chapters all move away from the medical model of disability, which argues that individuals are disabled because of their impairment or difference, and focus on the importance of the context and the potential advantages disability can bring to the workplace, aligning with a strengths-based perspective (Bakker & van Woerkom, 2018). A related approach comes from Follmer and Miller (Chapter 7 in this volume), who draw upon positive psychology to consider how disabilities can enrich employees' work experiences when accommodations are provided. They focus on individuals with concealable disabilities as they discuss the benefits of reasonable accommodations for both employees and employers and identify reasons for employees who require reasonable accommodations failing to request them at work. Further, they posit that an individual-centered approach is needed to enhance the inclusion of individuals with concealable disabilities. Finally, Paetzold and Beatty (Chapter 19 in this volume) suggest that individuals with serious mental illness, such as schizophrenia and bipolar disorder, can hold down jobs and perform well, despite the negative beliefs regarding their employability. They draw on the concept of sanism to explain the difficulties and exclusion experienced by these individuals in the context of work. Presenting the lived experiences of academics with serious mental illness as case studies, they argue for appropriate support for, and understanding of, these conditions to allow individuals with mental illness to live meaningful and satisfying lives.

Collectively, the authors in this volume point to the need to challenge ableist norms and assumptions and focus on an individual's abilities, instead of that person's impairments. Moving away from the medical model that focuses on what is "wrong" with an individual and how dysfunctional aspects can be removed, these chapters tend to align with the social model of disability, which posits that disability is the result of society's failure to meet the needs of PWD (Oliver, 1990, 2013). The social model was developed by individuals with disabilities themselves, as they felt that the medical model did not reflect or explain their experiences or enhance their labor market participation and inclusion (Barnes & Mercer, 2005). Indeed, the social model highlights what individuals need to be able to function fully and requires society to adapt to employees with disabilities rather than putting the burden wholly on the individuals themselves. Contextual factors, such as disability legislation, workplace accommodations, and demands–ability fit, are important to consider in order to challenge the social norms and structures that disadvantage individuals with disabilities and to create inclusive workplaces for all.

Questioning the Sufficiency of Legislation

The second theme that emerged collectively from several chapters is that legislation that protects individuals with disabilities from unfair treatment or that encourages organizations to hire workers with disabilities is not enough to enhance employment opportunities or workplace experiences. Rather, it seems that legislation is a starting point or a prerequisite condition to managing and increasing diversity and inclusion. Many countries have adopted anti-discrimination laws and disability quotas to increase the employment rate of persons with disabilities, yet their employment rate is still considerably lower than that of persons without a disability (World Health Organization, 2011). For example, 17.9% of individuals with disabilities in the United States were employed in 2020, compared with 61.8% of those without a disability, and median earnings of individuals with disabilities were $8,046 lower than those without disabilities (Bureau of Labor Statistics, 2021).

Unfortunately, there is a lack of data to assess the effectiveness of legal measures of disability legislation, which Wass and Jones (Chapter 4 in this volume) refer to as a *data deficit*. They underscore that more and better data regarding the employment of PWD is needed at both the organizational and national levels. They further outline that without comprehensive and accurate data to track the impact of legislation aimed at improving the employment situation of individuals with disability, we cannot know if the intended increase in inclusion is being achieved.

Legislation does not always lead to the intended outcome, and may paradoxically have unintended negative consequences (Richard & Hennekam, 2021). Stone, Lukaszewski, Feigelson, and Williams (Chapter 10 in this volume) suggest that legislation can lead managers to experience compliance, but also resistance and reactance, defined as an unpleasant form of motivational arousal that occurs when people perceive a threat to their own freedom. Stone and colleagues' empirical study explores managers' intentions to hire PWD when managers are exposed to a "Best Employer Award for Hiring People with Disabilities." They found that several of the hiring managers' beliefs were more positive after learning of the award than prior to it, even though their companies did not receive the award. Stone and colleagues then suggest that positive public recognition is a useful motivator to increase the employment of PWD.

Another example of unintended consequences is shown by Richard and Lemaire (Chapter 15 in this volume) and is related to alternative forms of employment in France to improve the integration of individuals with disabilities into the workforce. They suggest that sheltered employment presents a compassionate policy solution for PWD to participate in paid employment, but results in situations with poor person–job fit and underemployment for some employees. They outline the tensions that support staff in sheltered employment structures face and how the staff shape managerial practices toward employees with disabilities.

Thus, while legislation is important to improve the labor market position of individuals with disabilities, authors in this volume show that what is needed is to ensure the proper measurement of the efficacy of existing laws, to be aware of unintended negative consequences, and to consider managers' beliefs about employees with disabilities when aiming to increase the employment rate of this population.

Conceptualizing Disability

The third broad theme that we identify in this volume is the evolving understanding and conceptualization of the term *disability*. According to the United Nations Convention on the Rights of Persons with Disabilities (CRPD), persons with disabilities are defined as individuals with "long-term physical, mental, intellectual or sensory impairments which in interaction with various barriers may hinder their full and effective participation in society on an equal basis with others" (CRPD, 2006, Article 1). However, the boundary conditions of this notion, such as which conditions should be included and whether there is a threshold that determines at what point someone starts being considered disabled and at what point or moment someone is no longer disabled, are unclear and debatable. Several authors in this volume expand the boundaries of the term and point to the invisible and temporal character of some disabling conditions. For example, Scholz and Van Laer (Chapter 18 in this volume) suggest that psychological burnout, a condition that tends to be excluded from the disability fold, deserves greater attention from employers and Paetzold and Beatty (Chapter 19) suggest that people with serious mental illness be accommodated in organizations. The temporal nature of disability is highlighted by Rosado-Solomon, Bolivar Trouwborst, Schur, and Kruse (Chapter 13 in this volume). Drawing on the social model of disability, they explain that the temporal constraints of work and mental illness create tensions that form a barrier for individuals with mental illness as they navigate the world of work. Specifically, they remind us that fluctuating symptoms may create variability in functional performance and potentially awkward social situations if employees have to explain or justify their changing performance levels.

Several chapters in this volume focus on neurodiversity, an umbrella term that includes a range of neuro-cognitive developmental conditions (Singer, 1999), such as ASD, ADHD, dyslexia, dysgraphia, dyspraxia, dyscalculia, and Tourette syndrome. These neuro-cognitive differences influence how individuals perceive, think, and act. Although it has been estimated that around 15% to 20% of the population worldwide is neurodiverse and that this percentage is on the rise (Doyle, 2020), there is disagreement as to whether these conditions are considered disabilities or should be positioned as cognitive differences. Neurodiverse individuals seem to encounter a range of challenges when navigating the workplace (Krzeminska et al., 2019), such as difficulties with correctly interpreting non-verbal language for individuals with ASD (Patton, 2019), impulsivity for individuals with ADHD (Wiklund et al., 2016), or challenges in planning and organizing for individuals with dyslexia (Smith-Spark et al., 2016). However, the implications of the uniqueness of neurodiverse individuals in the context of work are not well understood. Khan, Ali, Grabarski, and K. Moore (Chapter 16 in this volume) focus on neurodiversity, using a human resource (HR) perspective, and identify challenges as well as the best practices HR personnel can adopt to create a more inclusive workplace.

Finally, several chapters focus on the concept of intersectionality, in which the outcomes of disability may vary according to the constellation of identities held by the person with disabilities. Individuals have multiple social identities that interact and intersect with one another, leading to qualitatively different experiences. Schur, van der Meulen Rodgers, and Kruse (Chapter 5 in this volume) explore the disparate effects of COVID-19 on workers with physical and mental disabilities, with an intersectional analysis by disability, race/ethnicity, and gender. Similarly, Bellotti, Zaniboni, Langlois, and Villotti (Chapter 6 in this volume) examine the intertwined issues related to age and mental disability at work and identify possible workplace accommodations and interventions to promote the integration and participation of both younger and older workers with mental disorders. Clearly, there are many other social identities, such as gender, sexual orientation, or class, which may intersect with one's identity as a person with disabilities. These conversations problematize the very ontology of disability, offering pathways to rethink our theorization and practice with regard to disability inclusion.

Attending to Socio-material Structures

The fourth theme refers to the socio-material structures that shape the experiences and inclusion of individuals with disabilities. Socio-material structures refer to the intersection of technology, organization, and work. This includes the way work is organized, HR management (HRM) practices, organizational culture, social structures, and networks, as well as technological advances that change the way work is being done. By examining the social and material aspects of work simultaneously, the impact of technology and the social organization of work on the workplace experiences of workers with disabilities become apparent. Several chapters in this volume point to the role of technology. For example, Bauer, Chakraverty, Greifenberg, and Niehaus (Chapter 21 in this volume) developed a science-based interactive online tool that supports employees with invisible disabilities in their decision to disclose their disability. This is an example of the effects of assistive technology, an emerging and promising line of research in disability studies and management (Nijs & Maes, 2021; Owuor et al., 2018). Drawing on technology and HR policies and practices, Saleh, Malzer, Erickson, von Schrader, and Bruyère (Chapter 20 in this volume) discuss practices in disability-inclusive online outreach and recruitment. The authors present results from three studies, in which they identify disability-related messaging and content that exists on employer career websites; provide employer perspectives on effective online recruitment practices and barriers; and ascertain the experiences of jobseekers with disabilities in online outreach and recruitment by employers. The importance of technology is also emphasized by Fattoracci, McSpedon, Hebl, Oxendahl, and Silver (Chapter 2 in this volume) as they mention that employees with disabilities who used to encounter resistance when requesting work-from-home accommodations have seen improvements in employer attitudes about remote work. As we go to press in 2023, three years into the global pandemic, the indicators are that organizations will continue to transform work structures to incorporate remote work technologies for employees with and without disabilities.

Inclusive HRM practices related to selection, recruitment, training, or career development have been argued to help employees with disabilities navigate the workplace (Beatty et al., 2019; Kulkarni, 2016; Schloemer-Jarvis et al., 2022). Building on this body of literature, Lefcoe, Bonaccio, and Connelly (Chapter 9 in this volume) provide a literature review of managers' reactions to individuals with disabilities during three key stages of the employment cycle: recruitment and selection, the provision of accommodations, and performance management. They identify contextual factors that may shape managers' attitudes toward individuals with disabilities. Indeed, although the role of specific workplace accommodations has been studied extensively (McDowell & Fossey, 2015; Santuzzi & Waltz, 2016), the role of organizational culture and the reactions of others at work have received less attention (von Schrader et al., 2014). In this volume, M. E. Moore and Huberty (Chapter 14) explore the role workplace culture has in equality, diversity, and inclusion strategies with a specific focus on individuals with disabilities, reminding us that organizational cultures can both help and hinder improvement efforts. These authors note that culture can be a driving force for diversity and inclusion since it encompasses and promotes organizational values.

Overview of the Volume

The chapters in this volume are organized into six broad sections, which we outline here. Part 1 includes a range of chapters on the ongoing debate regarding the conceptualization and definition of the term disability in the context of work. In Chapter 1, Jammaers and Hardonk discuss the different models that underlie contemporary research on disability: the medical model, the social model, and the extended social interpretation of disability model. They provide an overview of the various disability paradigms and note that the conceptual debates are far from settled. They call for more collaboration with practitioners, employees with disabilities, and other disciplines to enhance our understanding of how best to support PWD in the context of work. In a similar vein, Fattoracci and colleagues (Chapter 2) problematize our understanding of what exactly constitutes an impairment or a disability, who may identify this, who may be perceived as qualifying for legal protection, and subsequent workplace treatment of such individuals. Adding further to the conversation, in Chapter 3, K. L. Moore outlines how advances in technology and shifting notions of inclusion during times of uncertainty, such as during the COVID-19 pandemic, can change what it means to be disabled and how one may be accommodated at work. Moore explains the current legal requirements in the United States regarding reasonable accommodations for individuals with disabilities as part of the non-discrimination requirements of the Americans with Disabilities Act. Further, she describes some potential future innovations in law, policy, and practice. This chapter foretells new court challenges to the existing standard of reasonable accommodation as remote work norms have developed during the pandemic, and how these changes may further shape legislation. In Chapter 4, Wass and Jones affirm the importance of the accurate measurement of disability, as this will demonstrate the extent of disability inequality and the impact of employer practices implemented to address it. Drawing on the context in the United Kingdom, they provide a set of recommendations to promote organizational data collection on disability based on an approach that is useful, meaningful, and manageable for the organization, and that will benefit national policy development. They draw attention to how organizational data collection on disability can be enhanced (e.g., with standardized methods and definitions and reporting requirements) such that both individual employers and national policy can benefit.

Part 2 is titled "Intersectionality" and outlines the importance of considering other social identities in conjunction with disability. In Chapter 5, Schur and colleagues empirically demonstrate that the COVID-19 pandemic has erased many of the employment gains and exacerbated the employment disparity between persons with and without disabilities. Specifically, White and Black women with disabilities experienced greater employment losses during the pandemic compared to White men without disabilities. Whereas Schur and colleagues refer to gender and race, Bellotti and colleagues (Chapter 6) consider age as an important intersectional identity. They note the multiple biases that those with a disability and the elderly encounter, and critically review the existing literature on the age-differential effect of work-design factors on mental health. They suggest that work-design interventions, such as social support and increasing job autonomy, can aid such employees. In Chapter 7, Follmer and Miller refer to how employees with concealable disabilities may fare across different times and contexts, with minority employees suffering the most. Since disabilities may manifest uniquely across impairments and individuals, and disclosure is a necessary condition for receiving accommodations, the authors outline how an individual-centered approach may best support such employees.

Part 3 consists of chapters that focus on social reactions across the employment relationship. In Chapter 8, Santuzzi, Keating, Martinez, and Thomas delineate patterns of stereotypes and reactions to multiple differences, including invisible disabilities, mental illness, and neurodivergence. They suggest that these experiences must be viewed in light of the larger context of factors, on both the individual level (e.g., intersecting identities) and the organizational level (e.g., climate of inclusion), to better understand the variability in experiences among employees with disabilities. In Chapter 9, Lefcoe and colleagues focus on manager reactions to individuals with disabilities during key stages of the employment cycle: recruitment and selection, the provision of accommodations, and performance management. They outline ways to include those with a disability across these time periods fairly, for example by sensitizing managers to a more realistic image of PWD, and urge employers to view disability inclusion as more than "checking a box." Stone and colleagues (Chapter 10) examine the relation between a "Best Employer Award for Hiring People with Disabilities" and non-winning managers' beliefs and intentions to hire individuals with disabilities. They demonstrate that awards for hiring PWD lead hiring managers to report that those with disabilities have a higher level of skills and abilities, that they would be comfortable working alongside these employees, and that the costs of accommodations would be reasonable. The authors discuss the implications for enhancing managers' beliefs about individuals with disabilities and the potential for increasing the employment rate of PWD. In Chapter 11, Özbilgin and colleagues argue that in order for employees with disabilities to increase their representation in leadership positions, trust deficits regarding their leadership skills and potential must be overcome. Their three-phase intervention model proposes that creating a safe space, implementing structural changes in leadership succession and career policies, and recognizing the untapped leadership potential of PWD will help overcome the trust deficit.

Part 4 contains chapters on a variety of contexts or contextual factors that further influence the inclusion of individuals with disabilities. In Chapter 12, Dwertmann and McAlpine introduce a Disability Contingency Framework that has its roots in the person–job fit literature. The authors posit that individuals with disabilities have abilities that, if properly aligned with the demands of the job, can lead to positive outcomes for organizations. Rosado-Solomon and colleagues (Chapter 13) refer to an understanding of mental illness and the temporal context. They suggest that the temporal features of mental illness (fluctuations in ability) can be addressed by employers (e.g., by adjusting the temporal structures of tasks), which can aid the successful employment of individuals with mental illness. They argue that challenges for employees with mental illness can be improved by rethinking the way business is conducted, instead of sidelining employees because they accomplish their work differently from neurotypical peers. In Chapter 14, M. E. Moore and Huberty refer to the context of the overall organizational culture, outlining what we know about disability treatment. For example, we know that norms of respectful dialogue can lead to inclusion. They also identify areas that need further investigation with respect to the role of organizational culture in disability inclusion, such as collecting data to determine if weak cultures foster discriminatory attitudes. In Chapter 15, Richard and Lemaire refer to the French context, in which alternative employment forms, such as sheltered employment, enhance and facilitate the inclusion of workers with a disability, but also pose concerns that include difficulty in balancing the logic of performance alongside inclusion.

Part 5 outlines the expanding definitions of disability and which conditions or differences could or should be included under the umbrella of disability. In Chapter 16, Khan and colleagues outline the experiences of neurodiverse employees in Australia, noting issues of stigma and discrimination. They suggest that HR practices could help address these challenges, for example by improving communication practices and extending workplace accommodations to all employees. Lyons and colleagues (Chapter 17) refer to neuroqueerness, which highlights ways in which neurodivergent individuals can disrupt dominant notions of neurotypicality and neurodivergence. The authors suggest that autistic employees can "neuroqueer" organizational life to expand our thinking about who is a person with a disability and how they are included within workplaces. Scholz and van Laer (Chapter 18) further the idea of what disability means as they explore the experiences of individuals who have experienced burnout. Drawing on interview data from Belgium, they show that burnout can result in extended periods of inability to work even after employees return to the workplace. These authors reframe burnout, not as an individual failure, but as an organizational problem since overwhelming workplace economic systems are the source of burnout. Lastly, Paetzold and Beatty (Chapter 19) frame serious mental illnesses as compatible with productive employment, as they counter "sanism discrimination" by providing examples of well-known academics who have lived with serious mental illnesses while successfully navigating organizational and professional demands.

Part 6 outlines HR interventions that can strengthen the workplace inclusion of individuals with a disability. In Chapter 20, Saleh and colleagues suggest that employers must attend to the disability-related messaging and content of their online outreach and recruitment practices. Specifically, easy-to-implement practices, such as including images of employees with disabilities on organizational career webpages, can render recruitment more inclusive. Bauer and colleagues (Chapter 21) have outlined ongoing work in which stakeholders are co-developing tools that enable self-disclosure decisions based on employees' preferences for privacy, authenticity, and cost–benefit analysis of the disclosure decision, which can be utilized by both employees and administrators. Scholz (Chapter 22) suggests that online recruitment practices, an increasingly common way to reach and recruit employees, can be made more accessible through the use of universal accessibility guidelines and tools and by simplifying the design of online application processes. Finally, Baumgärtner, Boehm, Breier, and Jain (Chapter 23) outline how research–practice collaborations can lead to evidence-based inclusion. For example, they introduce the St. Gallen Inclusion Index, which represents the measurement of inclusion across individual and team/organizational dimensions, and suggest that team-based job crafting can help stakeholders shift focus from disability to ability management.

Future Research Directions

Several exciting avenues for future research emerged after reflecting on the contributions in this *Handbook*. These directions are outlined below in light of prior research and the chapters included in this volume.

Attending to the Macro-social Context(s)

As the chapters from various countries illustrate, there is a range of laws and policies that shape the approaches to disability and management. This presents an opportunity to engage in cross-cultural comparisons to evaluate the effectiveness of certain measures and approaches in increasing the labor market participation and enhancing the employment experiences of individuals with disabilities. Although country-specific laws and regulations are important, they are embedded in rich historical and cultural traditions, so it is unlikely that a country can simply take up another country's approach without any adaptations. Consequently, the study of country-specific measures, such as the disability-quota system in place in some countries, can help illuminate the circumstances in which such measures are (un)successful. Cultural values, such as religious beliefs and whether a culture tends to perceive diversity as a threat or an opportunity, have an impact on how disability is perceived and handled. Further, cultural norms and attitudes influence the extent to which disability is considered to be a stigmatizing attribute and thus how individuals deal with their identity as an employee with disabilities, for example in the disclosure decision and whether to ask for workplace accommodations. In addition to cross-cultural differences, the heterogeneity within the population of employees with disabilities needs more attention. For example, do existing HR policies and practices work for all employees with disabilities or do some sub-populations feel that their specific needs are not met by these policies? More tailored support that acknowledges the heterogeneous nature of this population is needed to attract and retain these individuals and develop their careers (Brzykcy et al., 2019; Kulkarni, 2016).

Broadening the Scope of Employment Contexts and Transitions

The chapters included in this *Handbook* focus on a wide range of relevant variables, and we argue that the field should continue to broaden the scope of disability and management research. For example, most existing research tends to focus on employed people with disabilities and the barriers to employment they encounter. However, underemployment, unemployment, or alternative forms of employment, such as social workplaces or sheltered employment, have received comparatively little scholarly attention, as outlined by Richard and Lemaire (Chapter 15). Similarly, there is much to be learned from the transition from school to work, and the transition from protected to mainstream sectors. How does the career of an individual with a disability unfold over time? This is likely to be a bumpy road with advances and setbacks that can only be uncovered through longitudinal data. In addition, sometimes, practice seems to be ahead of academia. An example is neurodiverse workers, who form an understudied population in the areas of management and organizational psychology (Doyle & McDowall, 2022; Krzeminska et al., 2019). Some large organizations have successfully launched inclusive HR policies and practices that have led to an increase in neurodiversity in their workforces. The success stories of Microsoft, SAP, Ford, and EY need to be examined to spur practice-based research. Scholars need to analyze what happens on the work floor in order to enhance our understanding of which policies, practices, and approaches lead to better career prospects and more pleasant work experiences for employees with disabilities, while also bringing positive outcomes such as enhanced levels of productivity and innovation to organizations. Finally, we encourage researchers to incorporate objective measures of effectiveness, such as the hiring levels (at the entry level or higher) and salaries of individuals with disabilities. These employment data are needed to establish the link between diversity and inclusion practices, such as diversity statements and HRM practices, and actual results. These data may be difficult to obtain but are important to show that organizational strategies or practices are more than just optics, and that they have a noticeable and positive impact on the experiences of employees with disabilities.

Expanding the Methodological Repertoire

We encourage disability researchers to adopt a wider range of methodological approaches. Although in-depth qualitative studies consisting of interviews or focus groups and quantitative studies aimed at testing hypotheses and models provide important insights, other methods, such as experimental designs, practice-based research, observations, and small-scale ethnographic case studies, could bring a different and complementary understanding of employment experiences. Studies *with* individuals with disabilities rather than *on* such individuals would in particular do justice to their voices and lived experiences; indeed, it serves us to remember the common slogan in the disability rights movement: "Nothing about us without us." Similarly, multilevel research is needed to bridge our knowledge of individual-, organizational-, and societal-level factors. As the experiences of individuals with disabilities are complex and affected by factors on all levels, research should aim to capture this complexity by showing the interrelated and intersectional nature of the issues involved. Our *Handbook* bridges management and disability studies, but more interdisciplinary research is needed to learn from other perspectives, theoretical angles, and research methods. It is precisely at the intersection of multiple disciplines and multiple methods that new insights can be gained. Finally, disability is not static. Individuals can encounter disabling conditions and they can also recover. The symptoms of their conditions often fluctuate and evolve in unpredictable ways. For this reason, longitudinal research designs would be helpful to capture the evolving nature of disability, as well as the reactions of others at work, the way it is managed, or its impact on someone's career. As stressed by Rosado-Solomon and colleagues (Chapter 13), there are temporal challenges related to disability that need further attention.

Enhancing Workplace Inclusion through Technology and Universal Design Principles

Many inclusion policies and practices target specific individuals at work. For example, explicit communication is often advocated for individuals with autism, as indirect implicit communication is challenging for this population. However, many small workplace changes, such as providing individuals with the possibility to work from home, a space in which people can relax, or standing desks, may benefit all employees, not just the individuals for whom the adaptations were initially designed. Universal design principles might help to make the workplace more inclusive to all (Lid, 2014), and technological advances may play a key role in making the employment cycle more inclusive (Kett et al., 2021). However, as some chapters suggest, technology utilization cannot always be equated with accessibility. For example, as Scholz suggests (Chapter 22), organizations are increasingly relying on online recruiting, but this may not mean increased access. Still, technology holds great potential for improving access to employment for individuals with disabilities, as Saleh and colleagues (Chapter 20) empirically demonstrate, especially when employers incorporate both instrumental and symbolic content and design that can reach and attract diverse talent pools.

Implications for Practice

An important contribution of this *Handbook* is in the HR implications and solutions proposed across the chapters. We anticipate that practitioners can gain new ideas on ways to improve their organizations to promote the employment, retention, and thriving of employees with disabilities.

Attending to HR Policies and Practices across the Employment Cycle

HR policies and practices are prominent in the recommendations of many chapters in this *Handbook*. For example, regarding the hiring stage, research has shown that job interviews disadvantage individuals with autism (Cooper et al., 2018). Thus, interviewing techniques as well as selection criteria need to be revised to facilitate more inclusive outcomes. Further, many chapters point to ongoing experiences of negative stereotypes and discrimination. This is relevant to HR professionals, who can provide training to change managers' and co-workers' beliefs about disability and improve inclusion and support to facilitate the working lives of employees with disabilities so that they can meet the demands of their job and develop their careers (Beatty et al., 2019). In addition, new tools are available to help individuals with disabilities reach their objectives and to function fully at work. For instance, scanning software, manual reading pens, and spell checkers for individuals with dyslexia or dictation and word prediction software for individuals with dysgraphia are simple tools that greatly reduce the perceived impairment related to these conditions. Regarding rewards and recognition, Stone and colleagues (Chapter 10) suggest that individual and group recognition systems can incentivize the employment of individuals with disabilities through awards and corporate gifts, highlighting successes with virtual walls of fame, and asking local TV or radio stations to feature the awards. Retention is another topic that is relevant to HR practitioners. Dwertmann and McAlpine (Chapter 12) show that allowing individuals to use their strengths and to find a good match between their abilities and the demands of the job leads to positive outcomes for both employees with disabilities and organizations. Thus, an individualized approach and possibly an inventory to identify one's strengths and capitalize on them might help employees with disabilities thrive and remain in the workplace. Finally, job design and flexible work options are other HR practices that are often helpful to optimize the contributions of all employees, including those with disabilities.

Creating an Inclusive Culture

The chapters in this *Handbook* collectively illustrate that several simple and inexpensive measures can be implemented to fashion more inclusive organizations. For example, the features of an organization's website can easily be made more accessible to individuals with disabilities. Saleh and colleagues (Chapter 20) point out that organizations should incorporate both instrumental and symbolic content and design on their websites, to show that there is real effort being made and awareness of the issues. The wording of job advertisements and an organization's mission and vision statements provide potential applicants with cues about the organizational culture. Explicitly mentioning disability or even disability sub-groups, such as individuals with neuro-cognitive differences, increases perceptions of inclusion. Having existing employees that function as role models and speak openly about their experiences in the organization can be another effective way to signal a disability-friendly or disability-inclusive culture. Providing individuals with a mentor on whom they can rely in case of questions or difficulties can be reassuring for employees with disabilities. As suggested by Santuzzi and colleagues (Chapter 8), employers can aim to develop mentoring cultures that delegate decision making to lower organizational levels. Paetzold and Beatty (Chapter 19) remind us that it is important that disability management and accommodation processes are distinct from disciplinary procedures and that organizations should adopt their disability practices in a systematic way that shows a disability strategy. Finally, as employers aim to develop inclusive cultures, the framing of the concept of inclusion comes into play. Most research conceptualizes inclusion as a property of the organization, and that organizations that adopt inclusive practices are *ergo* inclusive. A different view offered by Santuzzi and colleagues (Chapter 8) is that inclusion is a feeling experienced by the individual, referred to as "felt inclusion," instead of an organizational practice.

Focusing on Training

Although diversity awareness is increasing in organizations, Fattoraci and colleagues (Chapter 2) point to the lack of disability-related diversity training. They suggest that more development is needed around what "to deliver as content, how to best serve as an ally, how to ensure trust, and how to foster physically and psychologically safe environments for PWD to request accommodations. [43]" Indeed, training could increase awareness, reduce stigma, and give managers and co-workers the knowledge and tools to better support individuals with disabilities. Training interventions can also be used to promote a disability-inclusive culture, and these may be designed internally or in conjunction with government offices and advocacy organizations. For instance, Baumgärtner and colleagues (Chapter 23) review their efforts with *Inclusion Champions Switzerland*, in which they work with organizations and the Swiss Federal Office of the Equal Treatment of Persons with Disabilities. They outline a team-based job-crafting exercise that supports teams shifting to a strengths-based view instead of a disability- and deficit-focused view. Another example of a training approach is seen in Chapter 21, in which Bauer and colleagues outline an online self-assessment tool they developed in Germany that helps people with invisible disabilities to navigate their disclosure decision in the workplace. Their tool allows employees to assess the pros and cons of disclosing their disability, and then make their individual decision. The tool attends to privacy concerns because it is not associated with an employer and does not require registration or a login to use.

To sum up, in the aggregate, the authors and co-editors of this *Handbook* share the view that more can and should be done to support employees with disabilities. The underlying logic of this view is both ethical, to increase diversity, equity, and inclusion, and strategic, for organizations to benefit from the currently untapped or under-tapped pools of human resources. We are inspired by the state of scholarship in the disability field that is deepening and enriching research about what disability is; what disability means in legal, social, and organizational contexts; and how researchers and practitioners can work together toward the goal of improving the employment outcomes for persons with disabilities. We hope that this research compilation furthers this goal and supports the ongoing cross-disciplinary and international work.

References

Bakker, A. B., & van Woerkom, M. (2018). Strengths use in organizations: A positive approach of occupational health. *Canadian Psychology/Psychologie canadienne, 59*(1), 38–46. https://psycnet.apa.org/doi/10.1037/cap0000120

Barnes, C., & Mercer, G. (2005). Disability, work, and welfare: Challenging the social exclusion of disabled people. *Work, Employment and Society, 19*(3), 527–545. https://doi.org/10.1177%2F0950017005055669

Beatty, J. E., Baldridge, D. C., Boehm, S. A., Kulkarni, M., & Colella, A. J. (2019). On the treatment of persons with disabilities in organizations: A review and research agenda. *Human Resource Management, 58*(2), 119–137. https://psycnet.apa.org/doi/10.1002/hrm.21940

Brzykcy, A. Z., Boehm, S. A., & Baldridge, D. C. (2019). Fostering sustainable careers across the lifespan: The role of disability, idiosyncratic deals and perceived work ability. *Journal of Vocational Behavior, 112*, 185–198. https://psycnet.apa.org/doi/10.1016/j.jvb.2019.02.001

Bureau of Labor Statistics. (2021). *Persons with a disability: Labor force characteristics summary.* https://www.bls.gov/news.release/disabl.nr0.htm

Convention on the Rights of Persons with Disabilities, 2006. United Nations.

Cooper, E. R., Hewlett, A. K., Cooper, R., Jameson, M., Cooper, R., & Todd, R. (2018). *Neurodiverse voices: Opening doors to employment, achieve ability commission*. AchieveAbility. http://www.achieveability.org.uk/files/1516612947/wac-neurodiverse-voices-opening-doors-toemployment-report_2018_interactive.pdf

Cope, R., & Remington, A. (2022). The strengths and abilities of autistic people in the workplace. *Autism in Adulthood*, 4(1), 22–31. https://doi.org/10.1089/aut.2021.0037

Doyle, N. (2020). Neurodiversity at work: A biopsychosocial model and the impact on working adults. *British Medical Bulletin*, 135(1), 108–125. https://doi.org/10.1093/bmb/ldaa021

Doyle, N., & McDowall, A. (2022). Diamond in the rough? An "empty review" of research into "neurodiversity" and a road map for developing the inclusion agenda. *Equality, Diversity and Inclusion*, 41(3), 352–382. https://doi.org/10.1108/EDI-06-2020-0172

Hennekam, S., Follmer, K., & Beatty, J. E. (2021). The paradox of mental illness and employment: A person–job fit lens. *The International Journal of Human Resource Management*, 32(15), 3244–3271. https://doi.org/10.1080/09585192.2020.1867618

Kett, M., Holloway, C., & Austin, V. (2021). Critical junctures in assistive technology and disability inclusion. *Sustainability*, 13(22), 12744. https://doi.org/10.3390/su132212744

Krzeminska, A., Austin, R. D., Bruyère, S. M., & Hedley, D. (2019). The advantages and challenges of neurodiversity employment in organizations. *Journal of Management & Organization*, 25(4), 453–463. https://doi.org/10.1017/jmo.2019.58

Kulkarni, M. (2016). Organizational career development initiatives for employees with a disability. *The International Journal of Human Resource Management*, 27(14), 1662–1679. https://doi.org/10.1080/09585192.2015.1137611

Lid, I. M. (2014). Universal design and disability: An interdisciplinary perspective. *Disability and Rehabilitation*, 36(16), 1344–1349. https://doi.org/10.3109/09638288.2014.931472

Majeed, N. M., Hartanto, A., & Tan, J. J. (2021). Developmental dyslexia and creativity: A meta-analysis. *Dyslexia*, 27(2), 187–203. https://doi.org/10.1002/dys.1677

McDowell, C., & Fossey, E. (2015). Workplace accommodations for people with mental illness: A scoping review. *Journal of Occupational Rehabilitation*, 25(1), 197–206. https://doi.org/10.1007/s10926-014-9512-y

Nijs, S., & Maes, B. (2021). Assistive technology for persons with profound intellectual disability: A European survey on attitudes and beliefs. *Disability and Rehabilitation: Assistive Technology*, 16(5), 497–504. https://doi.org/10.1080/17483107.2019.1668973

Oliver, M. (1990). *The politics of disablement*. Macmillan.

Oliver, M. (2013). The social model of disability: Thirty years on. *Disability and Society*, 28(7), 1024–1026. https://doi.org/10.1080/09687599.2013.818773

Owuor, J., Larkan, F., Kayabu, B., Fitzgerald, G., Sheaf, G., Dinsmore, J., McConkey, R., Clarke, M., & MacLachlan, M. (2018). Does assistive technology contribute to social inclusion for people with intellectual disability? A systematic review protocol. *BMJ Open*, 8(2), e017533. http://orcid.org/0000-0002-7768-3116

Patton, E. (2019). Autism, attributions and accommodations: Overcoming barriers and integrating a neurodiverse workforce. *Personnel Review*, 48(4), 915–934. https://doi.org/10.1108/PR-04-2018-0116

Richard, S., & Hennekam, S. (2021). When can a disability quota system empower disabled individuals in the workplace? The case of France. *Work, Employment and Society*, 35(5), 837–855. https://doi.org/10.1177%2F0950017020946672

Santuzzi, A. M., & Waltz, P. R. (2016). Disability in the workplace: A unique and variable identity. *Journal of Management*, 42(5), 1111–1135. https://psycnet.apa.org/doi/10.1177/0149206315626269

Schloemer-Jarvis, A., Bader, B., & Böhm, S. A. (2022). The role of human resource practices for including persons with disabilities in the workforce: A systematic literature review. *The International Journal of Human Resource Management, 33*(1), 45–98. https://doi.org/10.1080/09585192.2021.1996433

Singer, J. (1999). 'Why can't you be normal for once in your life?' From a 'problem with no name' to the emergence of a new category of difference. In M. Corker & S. French (Eds.), *Disability discourse*. Buckingham: Open University Press.

Smith-Spark, J. H., Henry, L. A., Messer, D. J., Edvardsdottir, E., & Ziecik, A. P. (2016). Executive functions in adults with developmental dyslexia. *Research in developmental disabilities, 53–54*, 323–341. https://doi.org/10.1016/j.ridd.2016.03.001

von Schrader, S., Malzer, V., & Bruyère, S. (2014). Perspectives on disability disclosure: The importance of employer practices and workplace climate. *Employee Responsibilities and Rights Journal, 26*(4), 237–255. https://doi.org/10.1007/s10672-013-9227-9

Wiklund, J., Patzelt, H., & Dimov, D. (2016). Entrepreneurship and psychological disorders: How ADHD can be productively harnessed. *Journal of Business Venturing Insights, 6*, 14–20. http://dx.doi.org/10.1016/j.jbvi.2016.07.001

World Health Organization. (2011). *World report on disability: Summary, 2011*. http://www.who.int/disabilities/world_report/2011/report.pdf

Part 1: **Framing the Discussion**

Eline Jammaers and Stefan C. Hardonk

1 Overview of Disability Paradigms in Disability and Management Research

Abstract: This chapter discusses the different disability models that underlie contemporary research efforts in the field of management and organisation studies (MOS). It draws attention to the different emphases that result from this paradigmatic diversity in terms of knowledge building and praxis in human resource management. By classifying recent empirical research papers related to disability in various contexts of employment, we compare three broad categories, labelled as the 'medical model', 'social models' and 'extended social interpretations' of disability, highlighting their notable differences and similarities. We outline a number of enduring points of discussion identified within our domain and conclude on the strengths of different models. We end the chapter with a call for future researchers to collaborate, not only with human resources (HR) practitioners and disabled people themselves, forming meaningful alliances, but also with one another to transcend the emphases and limitations inherent to different sub-disciplines and create knowledge that has the potential to support disabled people's participation in work and employment.

Keywords: disability models, management and organization studies, research agenda

Introduction

The interdisciplinary field of disability studies developed in the late 1970s and paralleled the disability movement led by activists striving for independent living rights in different geographical regions from the 1960s onwards. As an academic field, it invested much of its time in clarifying the different concepts around disability (Goodley, 2011). Such theoretical clarity is often missing in studies on disability in the workplace discussed in disciplines of management, social psychology, sociology and rehabilitation psychology. This chapter engages with the question of what disability paradigms commonly underlie studies in the field of management and organisation studies (MOS) and what consequences this has for issues identified as causing disabled people's socio-economic disadvantage. We distinguish three broad categories: the medical model, social models and extended social interpretations of disability.

Eline Jammaers, Faculty of Business Economics, Hasselt University, Hasselt, Belgium
Stefan C. Hardonk, Faculty of Sociology, Anthropology and Folkloristics, University of Iceland, Reykjavík, Iceland

https://doi.org/10.1515/9783110743647-002

For each model, we discuss its theoretical underpinnings, including conceptual differences between impairment and disability, its geographical origins, and practical implications for inclusion policy and practice. To exemplify how different disability paradigms co-exist within our domain, we point to examples of recent empirical articles published in top-tier journals. It should be noted that such publications are not always explicit about their conceptual basis and they can be perceived to fit into more than one of the theoretical categories presented in this chapter. By providing examples, we aim to illustrate the different theoretical streams rather than provide a definitive classification. We conclude this chapter by describing some common critiques and uniting virtues of different models.

The Medical Explanation

The most fundamental conceptual distinction within disability studies is between the 'medical model of disability' as a point of reference on the one hand, and alternative social theories of disability on the other. The medical model explains disability – defined as a state in which a person who has an impairment experiences oppression, difficulty to participate in different domains of society and inequality – by pointing at impairments (Abberley, 1996; Goodley, 2011). In this model, individuals are categorised based on impairment, which is seen as 'any loss or abnormality of psychological, physiological, or anatomical structure or function' (Oliver, 1996, p. 31). Consequently, the medical model of disability assigns roles of expertise and power over disabled people's lives to health care professionals. Applied to the notion of work, the medical model focuses on impairments as the main barrier to participation in productive activities, because they are assumed to inevitably prevent a person from making a socially valued contribution to systems of production and value creation. Employability is thus dependent upon physical, mental or cognitive (dys)functioning (Hughes & Paterson, 1997) and can be regained through rehabilitation and retraining on the part of the individual to learn to adjust to new conditions and reintegrate into the (paid) labour market. For those who are unable to achieve such reintegration, exclusion from the labour market is considered acceptable. From a historical perspective, the medical model of disability developed during the Enlightenment period and industrialisation when the production of biomedical knowledge about what constitutes a 'normal' body/mind increased (Winance & Devlieger, 2009). In many respects, it still dominates thinking about disability today, even as alternative models have offered a counter-narrative. Indeed, the model continues to allocate legitimate decision-making over disabled people's working lives mainly to the medical profession which is tasked with categorising and defining individuals, sometimes resulting in disabled people's exclusion and devaluation in terms of work and beyond.

Empirical studies in MOS geared towards this paradigm consider work as therapeutic and essential for both the physiological survival and psychological well-being of disabled people in our societies. Typically, such research is concerned with finding methods on how to make people return to work (RTW) (Brendbekken et al., 2016), distinguishing individual and organizational factors that predict a successful re-integration in work (Villotti et al., 2021). For instance, it is acknowledged that prior job satisfaction as well as contact with employers while absent from work are associated with a more positive experience (Skaczkowski et al., 2021). Research typically also seeks clarification on who plays a vital role in creating a supportive RTW environment, like supervisors (Nastasia et al., 2021) or RTW coordinators (MacEachen et al., 2020). The studies aim to explore how people can be rendered productive again in as limited a time as possible to avoid that they pose a too large burden for society (de Vroome et al., 2015). Experiments with reasonable accommodations best suited to support a return to work are popular (Wong et al., 2021), as are the testing and comparing of more general RTW program effectiveness (Oakman et al., 2016), alongside personal strategies that help workers stay productive despite various impairments such as persistent pain conditions (Phillips et al., 2012).

The Social Models

During the 1960s, a movement led by disabled activists resisted the medical model and instead proposed radically different social approaches, which shifted the attention from individuals' impairments to the social environment and society's structure. This movement, which is reflected in scholarly work, developed into a 'minority model' in the USA whereas in the UK a 'social barrier model' became foregrounded – each with their own emphases.

The Minority Model Explanation

In this approach, the environment is conceptualised as permeated by attitudinal barriers and 'people with disabilities' are seen as occupying a minority position in society which results in their 'devaluation, stigmatisation, discreditation and being discounted' (Goodley, 2011, p. 13). The approach draws parallels with other minorities, such as African-Americans, who experience marginalization and peripheral membership in society. When majority members consider individuals belonging to a minority as undesirable deviation from the norm, stigma occurs and socio-economic disadvantage follows. Consequently, the minority model prioritises interventions such as increasing disability awareness in society and taking legal measures against discrimination (Shakespeare & Watson, 2001). It provides a strong foundation for the development of disability identity and a political movement emphasising disabled people's autonomy and their right to independent living (Schur, 1998).

Empirical studies in MOS departing from this paradigm are plentiful and have often turned to social psychology theories to explain the socio-economic disadvantage of disabled people. Processes of discrimination and exclusion are seen as 'resulting from intrapersonal and interpersonal cognitive processes' (Janssens & Steyaert, 2019, p. 520), with stereotyping and stigmatisation negatively impacting the careers of disabled people. Hiring intentions and attitudes of employers towards disabled people form an important cornerstone in this stream of literature (e.g., Ren et al., 2008). Once employed, disabled people are found to be less socially accepted by colleagues on average (Vornholt et al., 2013) and employers hold lower expectations regarding their performance (Bonaccio et al., 2020; Colella et al., 1998). Consequently, disabled people view treatment by management in more negative terms (Schur et al., 2017) and can even become discouraged workers enacting self-limiting career moves (Ali et al., 2011). Not asking for work-related help proactively (Kulkarni & Gopakumar, 2014; Kulkarni & Lengnick-Hall, 2011) or not requesting accommodations out of monetary and imposition costs or anxiety (Baldridge & Veiga, 2006; Bonaccio et al., 2020) again negatively affect career outcomes. Popular in this paradigm are investigations of how different types of impairments (in/visible, acquired/congenital, physical/cognitive) harness different types of reactions and prejudice in the workplace (Friedman, 2020; Santuzzi et al., 2019). Apart from better understanding where discrimination stems from, studies from a minority perspective have focused on which supportive workplace policies work well for including disabled people (Chan et al., 2010; Kulkarni, 2016; Schur et al., 2014) and the role of climate for inclusion (Dwertmann & Boehm, 2016), while others have focused on the effectiveness of more general HR policies, practices and values (e.g., Baumgärtner et al., 2015; Brzykcy et al., 2019).

The Social Barrier Explanation

The disadvantage in society that disabled people face (e.g., in terms of housing, living conditions, education and employment) in this approach is considered a purely socially created condition that results from barriers in society, with an emphasis on material structures (Oliver, 1996). Contrary to the medical model with its focus on the individual, the social barrier model thus calls for societal-level action through social, education and labour market policy (Winance & Devlieger, 2009). It argues that when buildings, for example, would be designed with wheelchair users in mind, including lifts and ramps, mobility impairment would not result in lack of opportunities for participation, i.e., disability. The social barrier explanation then provides a social theory to address oppression of disabled people as a social and political problem within exploitative capitalist societies that uphold a strong able-body/mind norm (Abberley, 1996, 2002; Barnes & Mercer, 2005; Finkelstein, 1981; Roulstone, 2002). This perspective explicitly relates disability to power by revealing how oppressive structural barriers prevent participation in society, and it gives disabled people voice within a movement with a common political objective.

Empirical studies in MOS inspired by this paradigm are more rare[1] and, for instance, link the rise of precariousness and austerity measures to shrinking resources for the support of disabled workers, who are evermore expected to be work-ready and able (Foster, 2018; Foster & Fosh, 2010; Richards & Sang, 2016), a cultural epoch referred to as 'neoliberal-ableism' (Goodley et al., 2014). For instance, research has shown how job descriptions designed around able-bodied norms make it impossible for disabled people to fill them in (Foster & Wass, 2013) whilst expectancies of working extremely long hours and (social) flexibility (Jammaers et al., 2019; Randle & Hardy, 2017) increasingly prevent disabled employees from mirroring the ideal worker image. The physical design of the office, too, has been shown to prevent full inclusion, hampering disabled people's productivity, social inclusion, independence and health and safety (Van Laer et al., 2020). Importantly, the '"designing-out" of otherwise motivated and qualified disabled people from meaningful work and participation in society' (Harpur & Blanck, 2020, p. 517) does not only occur through bricks and mortar, but increasingly through technology (Knights & Latham, 2020). Such studies conclude that the policies created for breaking down barriers in the social environment oftentimes are too reactive (Woodhams & Corby, 2007) and constitute little more than an 'empty shell' (Hoque et al., 2014; Hoque & Noon, 2004) while possibilities for reasonable accommodations are underutilised out of fear of bullying (Foster, 2007; Robert & Harlan, 2006) or lack of employers' willingness to adapt work practices (Harlan & Robert, 1998).

Extended Social Interpretations

Despite the importance of the minority and social barrier model for activism and scholarship, they have not remained without criticism, giving rise to several efforts globally in the past twenty years to provide conceptual additions and alternative social interpretations of disability (Corker & Shakespeare, 2002; Williams & Mavin, 2012). Drawing on feminist perspectives, scholars have questioned the binary approach of impairment-disability and the absence of individual experience and the body in social model theories (Thomas, 1999). This has resulted in approaches that treat the body as a complex site of cultural and corporeal production and acknowledge the effects that bodily variations may have on people's everyday lives (e.g., pain

---

1 Of the articles included in the review by Beatty et al. (2019), only 15% explicitly mention the social barrier model or an extended social approach to disability.

and fatigue) (Shakespeare, 2006; Shildrick, 2009; Thomas, 2007). Further emphasising the need for interdisciplinary collaboration in the production of knowledge about disability, some scholars in disability studies have turned to critical realism as a holistic approach (Danermark, 2002; Williams, 1999). Others pointed out how social models have traditionally not paid attention to diversity within the category of disability, which has led to the critique that intersectional approaches are needed to incorporate the role of different dimensions and contexts. In addition, efforts have been made to address the absence of language within the social models, drawing lessons from the linguistic turn in general social theory and leading to the adoption of a cultural approach that considers dis/ability as a sign system that differentiates and marks bodies and minds, producing abled ('normative') and disabled ('inferior') bodies (Davis, 1995; Goodley, 2011). Post-structural language-based approaches highlight how power relations develop from the linguistic constructions of disabled people as normal/abnormal workers. Such critical approaches have been advocated as a promising way to transcend conceptual disagreement in the field (Grue, 2011). Applied to work participation, extended social interpretations focus on deconstructing normalcy whilst recognising impairment in the workplace as a legitimate organising requirement (Williams & Mavin, 2012). This means that there is a space for recognising direct effects of impairments on the working lives of disabled people in addition to and interrelation with social and organisational factors.

Empirical studies in MOS relying on extended social interpretations of disability, for example, have pointed to grand and small discourses inside and outside organisations, and how they relegate disabled employees to subordinate positions of un-employability, removing them even further away from the labour market, instead of successfully reintegrating them (Holmqvist et al., 2013; Scholz & Ingold, 2021). Research into the perspectives of employed disabled people (Elraz, 2018; Jammaers et al., 2016) and their supervisors and colleagues (Dobusch, 2017; Jammaers & Zanoni, 2021; Mik-Meyer, 2016a,b) or even their service dogs (Jammaers, 2021b) shows how disability is persistently constructed in negative terms in relation to work. A recent study by Woods et al. (2019), for instance, argues how discourses around mental health as individual failure are used by organisations to divert attention away from workplace conditions, portraying disabled people as 'weak' and 'unable to cope' thereby exacerbating the social suffering caused. Even when disabled people craft a job for themselves through self-employment, discourses of dependence threaten to question their legitimacy in the eyes of stakeholders, turning them into 'unexpected' entrepreneurs (Jammaers & Williams, 2021b; Jammaers & Zanoni, 2020). Only on rare occasions are disabled people considered an asset to organisations due to the positive disability-related skills they bring to the workplace (Baldridge & Kulkarni, 2017; Maravelias, 2020). Turning to the importance of intersectional identities, a handful of studies have zoomed in on gendered experiences of disability. Practices such as joking at work (Sang et al., 2016) or overcompensation (Jammaers & Williams, 2021a) are found to originate in masculine ideas of humour, fitness and strength causing detriment to the lived workplace experiences of disabled men.

Uniting Strengths through Common Purpose

Notwithstanding the theoretical developments described in this chapter, the debate among scholars is far from settled as different critiques remain. For instance, it could be argued that many disability-related studies in MOS silence those who are being marginalised by prioritising the opinions of medical and clinical experts (Woods et al., 2019), or HR managers and students (Beatty et al., 2019). By excluding their voices from the research design (Gabel & Peters, 2004), or including them only superficially as a 'socio-demographic trait' (Janssens & Zanoni, 2021), disabled people are reduced to victims, destined to undergo the stereotypes and accept the negative decisions of managers. Related, studies that conceive of disability as static or fixed (Dwertmann, 2016), or treat disability in isolation from other meaningful intersecting identities (Meekosha & Shuttleworth, 2009), overlook its complexity and socially constructed nature (Harlan & Robert, 1998). It is argued disability is not ontologically independent of the broader socio-historical environment that shapes the economic, symbolic and legislative contexts in which disabled people work (Beatty et al., 2019; Jammaers et al., 2016). Similarly, organisations do not simply constitute a 'neutral background' against which interactions between diverse people take place (Janssens & Zanoni, 2021, p. 3). Consequently, the corporate world bears a great responsibility both for attenuating individual behaviour of organisational members (e.g., through anti-bias training and mentoring) as well as for addressing organisational structures proactively (e.g., through diversity plans and targets) in order to be inclusive.

Despite the different paradigmatic positions that empirical studies about disability in MOS are grounded in (medical, minority, social barrier, extended social interpretation), they are united by a common goal: to generate knowledge that may help to work against the socio-economic disadvantage of disabled people. This common ambition can act as a uniting force transcending issues related to epistemological and methodological difference and debate. By bringing together perspectives, scholarship can build on the strengths of different paradigms. Studies inscribed in a minority model often provide a managerial approach, inviting HR practitioners to 'join hands with researchers' to advance 'evidence based best practices in the field' and build more inclusive workplaces (Beatty et al., 2019, pp. 133–134). Such ready-to-use implications for HR practice are generally not offered by studies inspired by the social barrier model and extended social interpretations. Such studies make significant contributions through their demonstrated self-reflexivity about the role of conceptual choices in their approach to disability in the workplace (e.g., theory X or Y; intersecting or single identities; . . .) as well as researchers' own embodiment and relations to the research topic (e.g. similarity to or difference from respondents) in the process of data collection and analysis (Alvesson, 2010; Cunliffe, 2003). Such transparency with regard to researcher positionality is consistent with the 'nothing about us, without us' approach of the disability movement (Barnes, 2004; Danieli & Woodhams, 2005; Jammaers, 2021a; Stone & Priestley, 1996), which is also reflected in the United Nations Convention on the Rights of Persons with Disabilities (2006).

To advance the academic field of disability in MOS, researchers must avoid both under-theorisation as well as lack of practical usability that pose a threat to the maturing of our field. Therefore, we end this chapter with a call for ongoing dialogue both with disabled people and between scholars from different sub-disciplines. Such collaboration can (continue to) take various forms, such as the designing of multidisciplinary research projects together with disability organisations, the organising of disability symposia at key MOS conferences inviting scholars with different backgrounds, or the co-production of a scholarly research handbook offering practical guidance through various perspectives. While this may challenge traditional expectations of academic inquiry, which are often grounded in particular domains and research traditions, such collaborative development is likely to progress the quality of research and publications aimed at improving inclusive societies and organisations.

References

Abberley, P. (1996). Work, utopia and impairment. In L. Barton (Ed.), *Disability and society: Emerging issues and insights* (Chapter 4). Longman.

Abberley, P. (2002). Work, disability and European social theory. In C. Barnes, M. Oliver & L. Barton (Eds.), *Disability studies today* (pp. 121–38). Polity Press.

Ali, M., Schur, L., & Blanck, P. (2011). What types of jobs do people with disabilities want? *Journal of Occupational Rehabilitation*, *21*(2), 199–210. https://doi.org/10.1007/s10926-010-9266-0

Alvesson, M. (2010). *Interpreting interviews*. Sage.

Baldridge, D. C., & Kulkarni, M. (2017). The shaping of sustainable careers post hearing loss: Toward greater understanding of adult onset disability, disability identity, and career transitions. *Human Relations*, *70*(10), 1217–1236. https://doi.org/10.1177/0018726716687388

Baldridge, D. C., & Veiga, J. F. (2006). The impact of anticipated social consequences on recurring disability accommodation requests. *Journal of Management*, *32*(1), 158–179. https://doi.org/10.1177/0149206305277800

Barnes, C. (2004). Reflections on doing emancipatory disability research. In J. Swain, S. French, C. Barnes, & C. Thomas (Eds.), *Disabling barriers, enabling environments* (pp. 48–53). Sage.

Barnes, C., & Mercer, G. (2005). Disability, work, and welfare: Challenging the social exclusion of disabled people. *Work, Employment & Society*, *19*(3), 527–545. https://doi.org/10.1177/0950017005055669

Baumgärtner, M. K., Dwertmann, D. J., Boehm, S. A., & Bruch, H. (2015). Job satisfaction of employees with disabilities: The role of perceived structural flexibility. *Human Resource Management*, *54*(2), 323–343. https://doi.org/10.1002/hrm.21673

Beatty, J. E., Baldridge, D. C., Boehm, S. A., Kulkarni, M., & Colella, A. J. (2019). On the treatment of persons with disabilities in organizations: A review and research agenda. *Human Resource Management*, *58*(2), 119–137. https://doi.org/10.1002/hrm.21940

Bonaccio, S., Connelly, C. E., Gellatly, I. R., Jetha, A., & Ginis, K. A. M. (2020). The participation of people with disabilities in the workplace across the employment cycle: Employer concerns and research evidence. *Journal of Business and Psychology*, *35*, 135–158. https://doi.org/10.1007/s10869-018-9602-5

Brendbekken, R., Eriksen, H. R., Grasdal, A., Harris, A., Hagen, E. M., & Tangen, T. (2016). Return to work in patients with chronic musculoskeletal pain: Multidisciplinary intervention versus brief intervention: A randomized clinical trial. *Journal of Occupational Rehabilitation*, *27*, 82–91. https://doi.org/10.1007/s10926-016-9634-5

Brzykcy, A. Z., Boehm, S. A., & Baldridge, D. C. (2019). Fostering sustainable careers across the lifespan: The role of disability, idiosyncratic deals and perceived work ability. *Journal of Vocational Behavior*, *112*, 185–198. https://psycnet.apa.org/doi/10.1016/j.jvb.2019.02.001

Chan, F., Strauser, D., Maher, P., Lee, E.-J., Jones, R., & Johnson, E. T. (2010). Demand-side factors related to employment of people with disabilities: A survey of employers in the Midwest region of the United States. *Journal of Occupational Rehabilitation*, *20*(4), 412–419. https://doi.org/10.1007/s10926-010-9252-6

Colella, A., DeNisi, A., & Varma, A. (1998). The impact of ratee's disability on performance judgements and choice as partner: The role of disability–job fit stereotypes and interdependence of rewards. *Journal of Applied Psychology*, *83*(1), 102–111. https://psycnet.apa.org/doi/10.1037/0021-9010.83.1.102

Corker, M., & Shakespeare, T. (2002). *Disability/postmodernity: Embodying disability theory*. Continuum.

Cunliffe, A. L. (2003). Reflexive inquiry in organizational research: Questions and possibilities. *Human Relations*, *56*(8), 983–1003. https://doi.org/10.1177%2F00187267030568004

Danermark, B. (2002). Interdisciplinary research and critical realism: The example of disability research. *Alethia*, *5*(1), 56–64. https://doi.org/10.1558/aleth.v5i1.56

Danieli, A., & Woodhams, C. (2005). Emancipatory research methodology and disability: A critique. *International Journal of Social Research Methodology*, *8*(4), 281–296. https://doi.org/10.1080/1364557042000232853

Davis, L. J. (1995). *Enforcing normalcy: Disability, deafness, and the body*. Verso.

De Vroome, E., Uegaki, K., van der Ploeg, C., Treutlein, D., Steenbeek, R., de Weerd, M., & van den Bossche, S. (2015). Burden of Sickness Absence Due to Chronic Disease in the Dutch Workforce from 2007 to 2011. *Journal of Occupational Rehabilitation*, *25*(4), 675–684.

Dobusch, L. (2017). Gender, dis-/ability and diversity management: Unequal dynamics of inclusion? *Gender, Work & Organization*, *24*, 487–505. https://doi.org/10.1111/gwao.12159

Dwertmann, D. J. G. (2016). Management research on disabilities: Examining methodological challenges and possible solutions. *The International Journal of Human Resource Management*, *27*(14), 1477–1509. https://psycnet.apa.org/doi/10.1080/09585192.2015.1137614

Dwertmann, D. J. G., & Boehm, S. A. (2016). Status matters: The asymmetric effects of supervisor–subordinate disability incongruence and climate for inclusion. *Academy of Management Journal*, *59*(1), 44–64. https://psycnet.apa.org/doi/10.5465/amj.2014.0093

Elraz, H. (2018). Identity, mental health and work: How employees with mental health conditions recount stigma and the pejorative discourse of mental illness. *Human Relations*, *71*(5), 722–741. https://doi.org/10.1177%2F0018726717716752

Finkelstein, V. (1981). Disability and the helper/helped relationship: An historical view. In A. Brechin, P. Liddiard & J. Swain (Eds.), *Handicap in a social world* (pp. 58–65). Hodder and Stoughton.

Foster, D. (2007). Legal obligation or personal lottery? Employee experiences of disability and the negotiation of adjustments in the public sector workplace. *Work, Employment and Society*, *21* (1), 67–84. https://doi.org/10.1177%2F0950017007073616

Foster, D. (2018). The health and well-being at work agenda: Good news for (disabled) workers or just a capital idea? *Work, Employment and Society*, *32*(1), 186–197. https://www.jstor.org/ stable/26969785

Foster, D., & Fosh, P. (2010). Negotiating "difference": Representing disabled employees in the British workplace. *British Journal of Industrial Relations*, *48*(3), 560–582. https://doi.org/10. 1111/j.1467-8543.2009.00748.x

Foster, D., & Wass, V. (2013). Disability in the labour market: An exploration of concepts of the ideal worker and organisational fit that disadvantage employees with impairments. *Sociology*, *47*(4), 705–721. https://doi.org/10.1177%2F0038038512454245

Friedman, C. (2020). The relationship between disability prejudice and disability employment rates. *Work*, *65*(4). http://dx.doi.org/10.3233/WOR-203113

Gabel, S., & Peters, S. (2004). Presage of a paradigm shift? Beyond the social model of disability toward resistance theories of disability. *Disability & Society*, *19*(6), 585–600. https://doi.org/ 10.1080/0968759042000252515

Goodley, D. (2011). *Disability studies: An interdisciplinary introduction*. Sage.

Goodley, D., Lawthom, R., & Runswick-Cole, K. (2014). Dis/ability and austerity: Beyond work and slow death. *Disability & Society*, *29*(6), 980–984. https://doi.org/10.1080/ 09687599.2014.920125

Grue, J. (2011). Discourse analysis and disability: Some topics and issues. *Discourse & Society*, *22*(5), 532–546. https://doi.org/10.1177%2F0957926511405572

Harlan, S. L., & Robert, P. M. (1998). The social construction of disability in organizations: Why employers resist reasonable accommodation. *Work and Occupations*, *25*(4), 397–435. https://doi.org/10.1177%2F0730888498025004002

Harpur, P., & Blanck, P. (2020). Gig workers with disabilities: Opportunities, challenges, and regulatory response. *Journal of Occupational Rehabilitation*, *30*(4), 511–520. https://doi.org/ 10.1007/s10926-020-09937-4

Holmqvist, M., Maravelias, C., & Skålén, P. (2013). Identity regulation in neo-liberal societies: Constructing the "occupationally disabled" individual. *Organization*, *20*(2), 193–211. https://doi.org/10.1177%2F1350508412438704

Hoque, K., Bacon, N., & Parr, D. (2014). Employer disability practice in Britain: Assessing the impact of the Positive About Disabled People "Two Ticks" symbol. *Work, Employment and Society*, *28*(3), 430–451. https://doi.org/10.1177%2F0950017012472757

Hoque, K., & Noon, M. (2004). Equal opportunities policy and practice in Britain: Evaluating the "empty shell" hypothesis. *Work, Employment and Society*, *18*(3), 481–506. https://doi.org/ 10.1177%2F0950017004045547

Hughes, B., & Paterson, K. (1997). The social model of disability and the disappearing body: Towards a sociology of impairment. *Disability & Society*, *12*(3), 325–340. https://doi.org/ 10.1080/09687599727209

Jammaers, E. (2021a). Embodied reflections of an able-bodied disability scholar. *Gender, Work & Organization*. https://doi.org/10.1111/gwao.12714

Jammaers, E. (2021b). On ableism and anthropocentrism: A canine perspective on the workplace of disabled people. *Human Relations*. https://doi.org/10.1177/00187267211057549

Jammaers, E., & Williams, J. (2021a). Care for the self, overcompensation and bodily crafting: The work–life balance of disabled people. *Gender, Work & Organization*, *28*, 119–137. https://doi. org/10.1111/gwao.12531

Jammaers, E., & Williams, J. (2021b). Turning disability into a business: Disabled entrepreneurs' anomalous bodily capital. *Organization*. https://doi.org/10.1177/13505084211032312

Jammaers, E., & Zanoni, P. (2020). Unexpected entrepreneurs: The identity work of entrepreneurs with disabilities. *Entrepreneurship & Regional Development*, *32*(9–10), 879–898. https://doi.org/10.1080/08985626.2020.1842913

Jammaers, E., & Zanoni, P. (2021). The identity regulation of disabled employees: Unveiling the "varieties of ableism" in employers' socio–ideological control. *Organization Studies*, *42*(3), 429–452. https://doi.org/10.1177%2F0170840619900292

Jammaers, E., Zanoni, P., & Hardonk, S. (2016). Constructing positive identities in ableist workplaces: Disabled employees' discursive practices engaging with the discourse of lower productivity. *Human Relations*, *69*(6), 1365–1386. http://dx.doi.org/10.1177/0018726715612901

Jammaers, E., Zanoni, P., & Williams, J. (2019). Not all fish are equal: A Bourdieuan analysis of ableism in a financial services company. *The International Journal of Human Resource Management*, *32*(11), 2519–2544. https://doi.org/10.1080/09585192.2019.1588348

Janssens, M., & Steyaert, C. (2019). A practice-based theory of diversity: Respecifying (in)quality in organizations. *Academy of Management Review*, *44*(3), 518–537. https://doi.org/10.5465/amr.2017.0062

Janssens, M., & Zanoni, P. (2021). Making diversity research matter for social change: New conversations beyond the firm. *Organization Theory*, *2*(2), 1–21. https://doi.org/10.1177/26317877211004603

Knights, D., & Latham, Y. (2020). Disabled people and digitalization: Disruptive documents in distributing digital devices. *Organization Studies*, *41*(6), 855–872. https://doi.org/10.1177%2F0170840619869744

Kulkarni, M. (2016). Organizational career development initiatives for employees with a disability. *International Journal of Human Resource Management*, *27*(14), 1662–1679. https://doi.org/10.1080/09585192.2015.1137611

Kulkarni, M., & Gopakumar, K. V. (2014). Career management strategies of people with disabilities. *Human Resource Management*, *53*(3), 445–466. https://doi.org/10.1002/hrm.21570

Kulkarni, M., & Lengnick-Hall, M. L. (2011). Socialization of people with disabilities in the workplace. *Human Resource Management*, *50*(4), 521–540. https://doi.org/10.1002/hrm.20436

MacEachen, E., McDonald, E., Neiterman, E., McKnight, E., Malachowski, C., Crouch, M., Varatharajan, S., Dali, N., & Giau, E. (2020). Return to work for mental ill-health: A scoping review exploring the impact and role of return-to-work coordinators. *Journal of Occupational Rehabilitation*, *30*, 455–465. https://doi.org/10.1007/s10926-020-09873-3

Maravelias, C. (2020). Governing impaired jobseekers in neoliberal societies: From sheltered employment to individual placement. *Organization*, 1350508420970476. https://doi.org/10.1177%2F1350508420970476

Meekosha, H., & Shuttleworth, R. (2009). What's so "critical" about critical disability studies? *Australian Journal of Human Rights*, *15*(1), 47–75. https://doi.org/10.1080/1323238X.2009.11910861

Mik-Meyer, N. (2016a). Othering, ableism and disability: A discursive analysis of co-workers' construction of colleagues with visible impairments. *Human Relations*, *69*(6), 1341–1363. http://dx.doi.org/10.1177/0018726715618454

Mik-Meyer, N. (2016b). Disability and "care": Managers, employees and colleagues with impairments negotiating the social order of disability. *Work, Employment and Society*, *30*(6). https://doi.org/10.1177/0950017015617677

Nastasia, I., Coutu, M. F., Rives, R., Dubé, J., Gaspard, S., & Quilicot, A. (2021). Role and responsibilities of supervisors in the sustainable return to work of workers following a work-related musculoskeletal disorder. *Journal of Occupational Rehabilitation 31*(1), 107–118. https://doi.org/10.1007/s10926-020-09896-w

Oakman, J., Kinsman, N., & Briggs, A. M. (2016). Working with persistent pain: An exploration of strategies utilised to stay productive at work. *Journal of Occupational Rehabilitation, 27*(1), 4–14. https://doi.org/10.1007/s10926-016-9626-5

Oliver, M. (1996). Defining impairment and disability: Issues at stake. In C. Barnes & G. Mercer (Eds.), *Exploring the divide: Illness and disability* (pp. 29–54). The Disability Press.

Phillips, L. A., Carroll, L. J., Voaklander, D. C., Gross, D. P., & Beach, J. R. (2012). Pain coping in injured workers with chronic pain: What's unique about workers? *Disability and Rehabilitation, 34*(21), 1774–1782. https://psycnet.apa.org/doi/10.3109/09638288.2012.662261

Randle, K., & Hardy, K. (2017). Macho, mobile and resilient? How workers with impairments are doubly disabled in project-based film and television work. *Work, Employment and Society, 31*(3), 447–464. https://doi.org/10.1177%2F0950017016643482

Ren, L. R., Paetzold, R. L., & Colella, A. (2008). A meta-analysis of experimental studies on the effects of disability on human resource judgments. *Human Resource Management Review, 18*(3), 191–203. https://psycnet.apa.org/doi/10.1016/j.hrmr.2008.07.001

Richards, J., & Sang, K. (2016). Trade unions as employment facilitators for disabled employees. *The International Journal of Human Resource Management, 27*(14), 1642–1661. https://doi.org/10.1080/09585192.2015.1126334

Robert, P. M., & Harlan, S. L. (2006). Mechanisms of disability discrimination in large bureaucratic organizations: Ascriptive inequalities in the workplace. *The Sociological Quarterly, 47*(4), 599–630. https://doi.org/10.1111/j.1533-8525.2006.00060.x

Roulstone, A. (2002). Disabling pasts, enabling futures? How does the changing nature of capitalism impact on the disabled worker and jobseeker? *Disability & Society, 17*(6), 627–642. https://doi.org/10.1080/0968759022000010416

Sang, K. J. C., Richards, J., & Marks, A. (2016). Gender and disability in male-dominated occupations: A social relational model. *Gender, Work and Organization, 23*(6), 566–581. https://doi.org/10.1111/gwao.12143

Santuzzi, A. M., Keating, R. T., Martinez, J. J., Finkelstein, L. M., Rupp, D. E., & Strah, N. (2019). Identity management strategies for workers with concealable disabilities: Antecedents and consequences. *Journal of Social Issues, 75*(3), 847–880. https://psycnet.apa.org/doi/10.1111/josi.12320

Scholz, F., & Ingold, J. (2021). Activating the "ideal jobseeker": Experiences of individuals with mental health conditions on the UK Work Programme. *Human Relations, 74*(10), 1604–1627. https://doi.org/10.1177%2F0018726720934848

Schur, L., Han, K., Kim, A., Ameri, M., Blanck, P., & Kruse, D. (2017). Disability at work: A look back and forward. *Journal of Occupational Rehabilitation, 27*(4), 482–497. https://doi.org/10.1007/s10926-017-9739-5

Schur, L., Nishii, L., Adya, M., Kruse, D., Bruyère, S. M., & Blanck, P. (2014). Accommodating employees with and without disabilities. *Human Resource Management, 53*(4), 593–621. https://psycnet.apa.org/doi/10.1002/hrm.21607

Schur, L. A. (1998). Disability and the psychology of political participation. *Journal of Disability Policy Studies, 9*(2), 3–31. https://psycnet.apa.org/doi/10.1177/104420739800900202

Shakespeare, T. (2006). *Disability rights & wrongs*: Routledge.

Shakespeare, T., & Watson, N. (2001). The social model of disability: An outdated ideology? In Barnartt, S.N. & Altman, B.M. (Eds.) *Exploring Theories and Expanding Methodologies: Where we are and where we need to go (Research in Social Science and Disability, Vol. 2*, pp. 9–28), Emerald Group Publishing Limited, Bingley. https://doi.org/10.1016/S1479-3547(01)80018-X

Shildrick, M. (2009). *Dangerous discourse of disability, subjectivity and sexuality*. Palgrave Macmillan.

Skaczkowski, G., Asahina, A., & Wilson, C. (2021). Returning to work after cancer in Australia: What facilitates a positive return to work experience? *Journal of Occupational Rehabilitation*, *31*, 41–49. https://doi.org/10.1007/s10926-020-09881-3

Stone, E., & Priestley, M. (1996). Parasites, pawns and partners: Disability research and the role of non-disabled researchers. *British Journal of Sociology*, *47*(4), 699–716.

Thomas, C. (1999). *Female forms: Experiencing and understanding disability*. McGraw-Hill Education (UK).

Thomas, C. (2007). *Sociologies of disability and illness: Contested ideas in disability studies and medical sociology*. Palgrave Macmillan.

United Nations General Assembly (December 13th, 2006). Convention on the rights of persons with disabilities. A/RES/61/106, available at: https://www.un.org/development/desa/disabilities/convention-on-the-rights-of-persons-with-disabilities.html [accessed 19 April 2022]

Van Laer, K., Jammaers, E., & Hoeven, W. (2020). Disabling organizational spaces: Exploring the processes through which spatial environments disable employees with impairments. *Organization*. https://doi.org/10.1177/1350508419894698

Villotti, P., Gragnano, A., Larivière, C., Negrini, A., Dionne, C. E., & Corbière, M. (2021). Tools appraisal of organizational factors associated with return-to-work in workers on sick leave due to musculoskeletal and common mental disorders: A systematic search and review. *Journal of Occupational Rehabilitation*, *31*(1), 7–25. https://doi.org/10.1007/s10926-020-09902-1

Vornholt, K., Uitdewilligen, S., & Nijhuis, F. J. (2013). Factors affecting the acceptance of people with disabilities at work: A literature review. *Journal of Occupational Rehabilitation*, *23*(4), 463–475. https://doi.org/10.1007/s10926-013-9426-0

Williams, J., & Mavin, S. (2012). Disability as constructed difference: A literature review and research agenda for management and organization studies. *International Journal of Management Reviews*, *14*, 159–179. https://doi.org/10.1111/j.1468-2370.2012.00329.x

Williams, S. J. (1999). Is anybody there? Critical realism, chronic illness and the disability debate. *Sociology of Health & Illness*, *21*(6), 797–819. https://doi.org/10.1111/1467-9566.00184

Winance, M., & Devlieger, P. (2009). Disability in medicine, culture and society: An introduction. In R. Addlakha, S. Blume, P. J. Devlieger, O. Nagase, & M. Winance (Eds.), *Disability and society: A reader* (pp. 3–6). Orient Blackswan Pvt Ltd.

Wong, J., Kallish, N., Crown, D., Capraro, P., Trierweiler, R., Wafford, Q. E., Tiema-Benson, L., Hassan, S., Engel, E., Tamayo, C., & Heinemann, A. W. (2021). Job accommodations, return to work and job retention of people with physical disabilities: A systematic review. *Journal of Occupational Rehabilitation*, *31*, 474–490. https://doi.org/10.1007/s10926-020-09954-3

Woodhams, C., & Corby, S. (2007). Then and now: Disability legislation and employers' practices in the UK. *British Journal of Industrial Relations*, *45*(3), 556–580. https://doi.org/10.1111/j.1467-8543.2007.00628.x

Woods, M., Macklin, R., Dawkins, S., & Martin, A. (2019). Mental illness, social suffering and structural antagonism in the labour process. *Work, Employment and Society*, *33*(6), 948–965. https://doi.org/10.1177/0950017019866650

Elisa S. M. Fattoracci, Megan R. McSpedon, Mikki Hebl,
Timothy A. Oxendahl, and Elisabeth R. Silver

2 The Future of Disability Research in the Workplace

Abstract: This chapter focuses on the importance of conducting disability research and discusses five particular issues. First, we discuss the diversity and complexity that exists within differing definitions of disability, something that future researchers must address. Second, we suggest future research address the intersection of disability status with other social identities (e.g., race, gender, socioeconomic status [SES]). Third, we draw future research attention to the critical workplace-related transitions in the lives of people with disabilities (PWD), including entry into and progress through the employment cycle. Fourth, we hope future research examines how disability status influences experiences in teams, given that teamwork is becoming a mainstay of organizational practice and effectiveness (Mathieu et al., 2019). Fifth and finally, we address the importance of future research addressing the strategies that organizations should adopt to enable the full inclusion of PWD at work. We hope that attention to the issues we raised in this chapter will maximize the importance and effectiveness of future disability research.

Keywords: disability, intersectionality, employment cycle transitions, teams

Currently, 61 million individuals in the U.S. (26%) have a disability (CDC, 2020). Given that the percentage of adults age 65 and older in the workplace and rates of disability are increasing (Crimmins et al., 2016), researchers must acknowledge the experiences of people with disabilities (PWD) in the workplace, in part by identifying and meaningfully filling gaps in the existing literature. To this end, the current chapter focuses on the U.S. workforce and highlights five areas especially ripe for additional scholarship on disability.

First, we discuss one of the biggest issues that researchers face when they study disability–the enormous diversity that lies within, which we describe before offering suggestions to approach such variability. Second, we focus on the intersection of disability status with social identities such as race and gender. This area of focus is critical because employees' experiences as PWD are inseparable from the impacts of sexism,

Note: All authors contributed equally to this chapter and authorship was decided alphabetically.

**Elisa S. M. Fattoracci, Megan R. McSpedon, Mikki Hebl, Timothy A. Oxendahl,
and Elisabeth R. Silver,** Rice University

https://doi.org/10.1515/9783110743647-003

racism, and classism in the workplace. Third, we draw attention to critical workplace-related transitions in the lives of PWD. All employees experience the challenges of entry into and progress through the employment cycle; but, we argue that particular issues are under-researched when it comes to examining how PWD navigate transitions between education and entering into and progressing up the employment ladder. Fourth, we examine how disability status influences experiences in teams. We focus on this multilevel area of research given that teamwork is becoming a mainstay of organizational effectiveness (Mathieu et al., 2019). Fifth and finally, we review the strategies that organizations should adopt to enable the full inclusion of PWD at work.

The Diversity of Disability

One in four Americans has some type of disability (CDC, 2020). This statistic not only indicates the prevalence of disability in the U.S., but – as the words "*some type*" suggest – it highlights how disability encompasses a host of conditions and experiences. The Americans with Disabilities Act (ADA; Americans with Disabilities Act, 1990) defines disability as a "physical or mental impairment that substantially limits one or more major life activities, a person who has a history or record of such an impairment, or a person who is perceived by others as having such an impairment." Based on this definition, what constitutes an impairment remains open to interpretation. This ambiguity allows a broad array of individuals to claim legal protection. However, it also constitutes a double-edged sword for others, given that not everyone with a disability will identify as disabled, and some who do will face discrimination for disclosing. Moreover, two individuals with the same condition may have disparate experiences, and not all disabilities are visible. Organizationally, these distinctions are crucial: the ADA requires employers to provide "reasonable accommodations," or work-related adjustments that enable PWD to perform their best work (U.S. Equal Employment Opportunity Commission, 2002).

Legal definitions of disability provide little guidance, placing the burden of negotiating what counts as a reasonable accommodation on PWD and their employers. To begin this negotiation, the ADA (1990) requires employees, especially those with invisible or concealable disabilities, to disclose their disability. Disclosure necessitates that PWD identify with and claim a disability identity at work, which is influenced by intra- and inter-individual processes (Santuzzi & Waltz, 2016). People may not embrace a disability identity if the condition is imperceptible to them (Prigatano, 2005), if they assume that it is normal (Reeve, 2004), or if they have internalized disability stigma (Quinn & Earnshaw, 2011). Indeed, PWD do not comprise a homogenous group. For instance, disabilities may be apparent (e.g., quadriplegia) or concealable (e.g., chronic pain) and as a result, individuals will employ different identity management strategies. Those with invisible disabilities may conceal their disability to evade stigmatization (Jones & King, 2014); they may signal their disability without referencing it explicitly; or they may disclose it via integration or de-categorization, which respectively entail emphasizing the positive aspects of a disability identity or downplaying the disability identity (Lyons et al., 2016). In the case of visible disabilities, individuals may downplay (i.e., shift attention away from) or claim (i.e., emphasize positive aspects of) a disability (Lyons et al., 2016).

Perceptions of disability also relate to organizational outcomes. Medically-debated disabilities may lead co-workers, supervisors, and organizations to perceive certain disabilities as spurious, especially when PWD do not "look sick." In some cases, this doubt influences co-worker perceptions of accommodation fairness (Colella, 2001). Further, employment opportunities vary based on disability type. When Boman and colleagues (2015) compared hearing, speech and reading, visual, psychological, medical, and physical disabilities, they found that employees with hearing impairments had the highest employment rates while employees with psychological disabilities were less likely to be employed. Based on these findings, we propose several avenues for future research.

First, we urge researchers to continue researching the complexity and variability of disability. While findings suggest that the experiences of PWD vary greatly, additional insight into these differences and how they affect workplace experiences among PWD is warranted. Second, because social identities are negotiated within interpersonal interactions, we encourage further research on disability within leader-follower dyads, collegial relationships, and teams, a topic we expound in the fourth section of this chapter. Third, given that disability often entails dynamic processes, researchers should consider how a disability label influences career trajectories and appraisals of PWD as conditions worsen or remit. Fourth, we encourage researchers to consider how the legal definition of disability influences workplace policy and outcomes. Finally, we encourage researchers to expand stigma and disability frameworks to create a more holistic paradigm for the study of disability (see Santuzzi & Waltz, 2016).

Disability Community and Intersectionality

In addition to the diversity of disability itself, future research should consider how other social identities intersect with disability identity to influence workplace experiences. Intersectionality describes the unique experiences that arise at the nexus of race, gender, dis/ability, and virtually any other social identity. In Crenshaw's (1990) seminal writing on intersectionality, she stated, "The problem with identity politics is not that it fails to transcend difference, as some critics charge, but rather the opposite-that it frequently conflates or ignores intragroup differences" (p. 1242). Building on this work, Purdie-Vaughns and Eibach (2008) proposed a model of *intersectional invisibility*, which posits that people with multiple marginalized identities, such as Black women, are perceived as non-prototypical of both Black people (i.e., Black men) and women (i.e., white women), creating complex experiences of (dis)advantage compared to "prototypical members of their groups" (p. 381).

The intersectional invisibility framework explains the experiences of PWD who are diverse with respect to race, gender, and social class. Frederick and Shifrer (2019) note that multiple factors contribute to the marginalization and invisibilization of people of color with disabilities. They argue that the "minority model" of disability constructed by early disability rights advocates used racism as an analogy for understanding ableism. Unfortunately, this rhetoric centers the experiences of white, middle-class PWD by invisibilizing the intersection of racism and ableism and assuming that "disability discrimination is a monolithic experience that is divorced from other forms of oppression" (p. 203). Additionally, Frederick and Shifrer (2019) argue discourse surrounding racial justice has relied on disability analogies to catalyze action (e.g., "color-blind racism", "post-race paralysis"). Analogizing ableism and racism ignores the racialized (and classed) nature of diagnoses and labels, police violence against disabled people of color, and the marginalization of people of color with disabilities within the disability community.

Research demonstrates the danger of treating PWD as a homogenous group of disabled white men. The gap in employment rates reflects this: Black people with and without disabilities are employed at respective rates of 27.3% and 72.9%, while white people with and without disabilities are employed at respective rates of 35.9% and 77.9% (Sevak et al., 2015). Social identities also intersect with specific types of disabilities. Coleman et al. (2015) found that participants desired more social distance from a woman with an intellectual disability than with a physical disability but made no such distinction when a man had the different disabilities. Despite these findings, organizational research at the intersection of race, gender, and disability status remains sparse. Nonetheless, insights can be gained from considering research on PWD in the workplace within the context of the broader diversity literature. For instance, managers are more likely to comply with accommodation requests when an employee's past performance is positive (Florey & Harrison, 2000). This finding is troubling given that Black employees receive less favorable performance evaluations than their white counterparts, even when objective productivity is comparable (Elvira & Town, 2001). As a consequence of the intersection of racism and ableism, accommodation requests from Black employees with disabilities may be granted less frequently. Indeed, one study of over 500 employees with disabilities found that white people were more likely to be granted accommodations for mobility impairments than people of color (Balser, 2007). However, the mechanisms underlying this phenomenon remain unclear and warrant further investigation.

Some disabilities and ways of managing them are also associated with gender stereotypes. Perceptions of others' chronic and acute pain exemplify this phenomenon. A study of nurses' heuristics revealed that the perceived "typical" pains for women included headaches; abdominal, back, and musculoskeletal pain; and pain caused by hormonal and reproductive systems (Bernardes et al., 2014). "Typical" pains for men included only back and musculoskeletal pain. Consequently, male employees who present with counter-stereotypical pain (e.g., migraines) might be taken less seriously than women because the latter is perceived as experiencing "normal" pain. Age and life stage can also create invisibility for PWD. The literature on accommodations for those with attention deficit/hyperactivity disorder (ADHD) is extensive for children and young adults in education; however, research investigating workplace accommodations for adults with ADHD remains severely limited. Likewise, workplace experiences associated with life stages surrounding pregnancy and parenting for PWD is an underdeveloped area of study.

The paucity of research at the intersection of disability and other social identities highlights several fruitful avenues for future research. As stipulated by the intersectional invisibility framework, PWD who are members of other stigmatized social groups are rendered invisible by virtue of their perceived deviation from mental models of PWD as white and middle class (Frederick & Shifrer, 2019; Purdie-Vaughns & Eibach, 2008). Recognizing the diversity of identities and experiences of PWD in the workplace can challenge this invisibilization. Specifically, we advocate for future research examining the intersection of racism, sexism, and classism in the workplace as it relates to accommodations, workplace bullying, and turnover. We also call for research investigating how social identities intersect with specific types of disabilities to shape perceptions of normativity and legitimacy. Finally, we recognize the need for further organizational disability research across life stages, a topic that we will explore in the following section. Addressing these gaps in the literature will be critical to answering Frederick and Shifrer's (2019) call to move "from analogy to intersectionality" in workplace disability studies.

Disability and Employment Cycle Transitions

Barriers to accessibility exist across the work cycle for PWD, and we particularly focus on two moments of transition: from school to work, and work to retirement. Each of these transitions act as a filter, reducing the percentage of PWD who continue through the pipeline. Disparities in employment rates and salary persist across educational attainment levels for PWD: among those who have completed high school, only 13.8% of PWD are employed, compared to 58.1% of people without disabilities (U.S. Bureau of Labor Statistics, 2021). Similarly, only 25% of PWD with at least a bachelor's degree were employed in 2020, compared to 71% of bachelor's degree-holders without a disability (U.S. Bureau of Labor Statistics, 2021). Thus, the transition from educational to vocational attainment is an early work cycle barrier for PWD.

For PWD diagnosed in childhood, the transition from secondary and/or post-secondary education to the workforce presents potential challenges, ranging from changes in legal protections, employment discrimination, and inaccessible organizational settings and processes (Bonaccio et al., 2020). Currently, most research connecting the school experiences of PWD with post-school outcomes is correlational (see Haber et al.'s 2016 meta-analysis). These studies suggest that initial post-high school job outcomes for PWD vary depending on the nature and severity of disability/ies; demographic factors such as race, gender, and socioeconomic status; and academic performance in high school (Murray et al., 2021). There is not yet a significant body of research for practitioners on either side of the school-to-work transition to draw from as they seek to improve employment outcomes for PWD. Longitudinal research following PWD through school-to-work transitions, rather than cross-sectional work on either side of this juncture, is needed.

The transition from post-secondary education to the workplace for PWD has received less focus than the transition from high school, possibly due to differences in legal accommodations for minors (Americans with Disabilities Act, 1990; Individuals with Disabilities Education Act, 2004; U.S. Rehabilitation Act, 1973). For K-12 students, public schools are required to identify and support students with disabilities, either through accommodations or individualized education plans (IEPs). IEPs have standardized requirements, including transition planning to capture interests and goals after high school, which can serve as the basis for the K-12-to-work studies discussed above (see Lipscomb et al., 2017). However, once PWD leave the K-12 system for post-secondary education, they become responsible for disclosing disability/ies and requesting accommodations that may not be granted by their college or university. Research agendas exploring factors that contribute to outcomes for PWD both during and after post-secondary education are needed to address these challenges.

Just as disability status can impact the transition from school to work, it can also shape later stages of an employee's work-cycle experiences, including decisions to stop working. Moen et al. (2021) examined the impact of disability status on decisions to leave the workforce among adults aged 50+. Disability paths to retirement varied with age, race, gender, and educational attainment, highlighting the importance of intersectionality in understanding disability throughout the work cycle. Disability also impacts post-retirement outcomes more negatively when retirement is involuntary versus voluntary (Szinovacz & Davey, 2005). Additional research might explore personal and organizational factors that allow for greater alignment and sense of control in retirement choices for PWD. One such organizational mechanism might be idiosyncratic deals (i-deals), or unique work arrangements negotiated for an individual, which have been found to reduce turnover intentions among PWD (Brzykcy et al., 2019). Thus, organizational contexts that are amenable to adaptation are likely key to retaining PWD who want to remain in the workforce. Continued research into individual factors, organizational contexts, and the intersection of the two is warranted.

Disability in Teams

Organizations increasingly rely on teams to accomplish tasks, and teams have been referred to as "the basic building blocks of present-day organizational designs" (Mathieu et al., 2019, p. 18). Despite calls for disability research at the team level, there remains a paucity of research in this area (Bonnaccio et al., 2020). Drawing on workplace disability and group diversity research, this section addresses the potential benefits and barriers PWD face in teams, the group-level factors that influence disability accommodations, the salience of shared perceptions and team-level inclusion, and avenues for future research.

The interdependent nature of teamwork may influence team members' perceptions of PWD and result in the exclusion of PWD from teams. For example, past research shows that, regardless of the extent to which a person's disability is perceived to impact job performance, potential team members with a disability receive lower rankings than non-disabled people when performance evaluations are interdependent (team-based) as opposed to independent (individual-based; Colella et al., 1998). These negative perceptions of PWD may exclude them from teamwork; consequently, PWD in organizations are less likely to be included in teams and may miss out on informal learning.

Ableism in team settings not only creates barriers to joining teams for PWD but may also create unique challenges for team members requiring accommodations. PWD's concerns about the impositions that accommodations place on co-workers and supervisors (Baldridge & Veiga, 2006) may be amplified by the interdependent nature of teamwork, as they may perceive that an accommodation increases other members' workloads. Additionally, even though an accommodation might positively influence collective team outcomes by providing a more accessible environment for PWD, granting accommodations can lead to perceptions of unfairness by team members, even if the ultimate outcome benefits them as well (Paetzold et al., 2008). Qualitative research suggests that team members perceive disability accommodations negatively and often stigmatize those who request them (Vickers, 2012). Although it has been proposed that the length of time a PWD has been on a team influences other members' reactions to accommodations – such that the longer they have worked together and established familiarity, the more likely they are to react positively (Colella, 2001) – the influence of time has yet to be explored empirically.

Conversely, the collective influence of team members may have a positive impact on PWD. Zhu et al. (2019) found that the positive impact of an inclusive workplace was strengthened when PWD were in teams who embraced open dialogue, inquiry, and interactive learning. Communication between PWD and non-disabled team members may also be better when teams are smaller in size (Cramm et al., 2008). Additionally, inclusive team climates have been shown to mitigate the negative relationship between supervisor-subordinate disability dissimilarity and the quality of leader-follower communication, suggesting that group-level support may positively impact dyadic relationships across organizational levels (Dwertmann & Boehm, 2014). However, more research is needed to understand disability within team climates.

The experience of PWD in teams may also hinge on the distribution of disability attributes within a team, or the team's composition (Levine & Moreland, 1990). Although relatively little work focused on team disability composition, past research on group diversity provides insight into its potential links with team interactions and performance. Research on demographic diversity in groups, which has largely ignored disability, shows a double-edged sword effect, such that diversity has the potential to positively or negatively impact performance (Milliken & Martins, 1996). The positive side of group diversity relates to information processing advantages in that multiple perspectives can be used to solve complex problems, while the negative side of group diversity relates to a process of social categorization in which in-groups and out-groups form as a result of demographic differences (Williams & O'Reilly, 1998). One study assessing disability as a team composition variable showed that both the number and proportional representation of disability categories in a team were related to team productivity (Narayanan & Terris, 2020). Teams with moderate numbers of disability categories as well as an even distribution of disability categories were more productive than teams with fewer categories of disabilities represented. Although these findings are encouraging, more research is needed to determine the relationship between team disability composition and performance.

The complexities of disability in teams and the relative lack of research suggest that this area is a timely topic for future research. First, disability research must determine how team disability composition relates to team processes, emergent states, and outcomes. Such processes may include requesting accommodations and team communication; emergent states may include team cohesion and psychological safety; and outcomes may include team performance, satisfaction, and viability. Additionally, research must address how disability in teams manifests over time, exploring how team member perceptions of accommodation requests change based on the level of familiarity with PWD. Furthermore, because the term "disability" subsumes a wide range of conditions, future research should account for differences between people with visible and invisible disabilities as they relate to teamwork. For example, does the double-edged sword of group diversity only occur for visible disabilities, or does it also apply to invisible disabilities? Finally, future research should explore the nature of intersectionality in teams, as PWD not only possess distinct disability identities but also other social identities, which add complexity to team processes. Embracing the complexity of disability in addition to the intricacies of social structures within organizations will enhance our understanding of not only the barriers faced by PWD, but also the ways in which organizations allow PWD to thrive at work.

Organizational Factors to Promote Workplace Inclusion and Equity for Employees with Disabilities

We conclude by considering the role of organizations in promoting fair and optimal workplace experiences for PWD. There is surprisingly little empirical research in this area; however, two recent reviews provide summaries of existing work. In the more recent of the two articles, Bonaccio et al. (2020) outline concerns and myths that managers have about the employability of PWD. One of the biggest concerns is the belief that accommodation costs will be exorbitant; yet, accommodations typically range from $0 to $500 (Solovieva & Walls, 2013), a cost that is likely offset by hiring and retaining qualified, talented incumbents. This common misperception is indicative of a much larger problem: the general lack of disability-related diversity training in many organizations. This lack of training raises many needs for future research – how to frame training, what to deliver as content, how to best serve as an ally, how to ensure trust, and how to foster physically and psychologically safe environments for PWD to request accommodations.

In a second review, Santuzzi and Waltz (2016) summarize four areas of knowledge that disability researchers have begun to understand, including 1) workplace stress and injuries, 2) climate for flexibility and accommodations, 3) organizational culture of inclusion, and 4) job demands and change. First, unsafe or dangerous working conditions within organizations may be responsible for developing a disability (i.e., an accident in the workplace). For instance, organizations might impose unhealthy work demands or be negligent in adhering to safety practices. Second, organizations differ in the extent to which they hold a favorable climate for flexibility and accommodations, which in turn influences workplace experiences of PWD. To this point, inflexible organizational policies create negative attitudes toward and decrease disclosure rates of PWD (e.g., Paetzold et al., 2008). Third, organizations differ in terms of possessing and promoting an inclusive culture. Undoubtedly, employees with disabilities look around to see if there are other co-workers with disabilities. A lack of similar people can signal that an organization does not actually value diversity. Finally, employees with disabilities are particularly vulnerable to economic and employment precarity, given potential fluctuations in health status. Some employees may experience changes from remission to recurrence. Employees are often forced, then, to learn how to manage others' perceptions of their disability status, which involves deciding whether, how, and when to acknowledge and/or disclose a disability (e.g., Lyons et al., 2016).

There are many areas of organizational research on disability identity that have received very little attention. We highlight some particularly fruitful areas for future research by considering three different stages (see Schneider, 1987) of the employment cycle: a) attraction, b) selection, and c) attrition. In the attraction stage, researchers might examine how PWD find or apply for jobs, particularly when these processes are inaccessible with respect to transportation, architecture, or application materials and instructions. Nittrouer et al. (2021a) have addressed this issue by examining how allies can successfully influence employers to improve inclusion by pressuring them to show interest in applicants with disabilities and call applicants with disabilities back for job interviews. Future research should fully examine what particular incentives organizations might need to recruit more PWD. Section 503 of the U.S. Rehabilitation Act (1973) provides at least one answer, as it encourages federal contractors to ensure that at least 7% of their workforce consists of PWD. A recent study examining the organizational implications of this law revealed that organizations are complying by hiring more PWD (Nittrouer et al., 2021b), perhaps signaling a shift in social norms towards disability rights. Another aspect of attracting PWD involves ensuring that organizations embrace universal design by designing buildings, products, and technologies that can be used by everyone, regardless of disability status. Research might address how to motivate organizational leaders to ensure that entryways are ramped, that parking routes to buildings include unblocked curb cuts, that workplace audiences have captions for video messages and text-to-speech-compatible written communication, and that websites are easily navigable.

In the selection stage, researchers should examine how hiring practices influence evaluations of PWD. Some scholars have suggested that measures of personality attributes unfairly discriminate against PWD (Melson-Silimon et al., 2019). Moreover, the COVID-19 pandemic decimated the U.S. job market, although there are signs that the labor force is beginning to recover (see U.S. Bureau of Labor Statistics, 2021). Employees with (versus without) disabilities are particularly likely to face unemployment, but there is potential for PWD to reap benefits due to new norms surrounding telework. Frustratingly, it was not until the pandemic affected the workplace safety of those without disabilities that organizations finally began to allow practices like remote interviewing and flexible telecommuting arrangements.

Turning to the attrition stage, researchers need to consider how organizations can create safe spaces and adapt to the needs of PWD. Indeed, the COVID-19 pandemic has forced organizations to be flexible and adaptable, as evidenced by allowing employees to telecommute (see Schur et al., 2020). Over the past year, video conferencing has become an integral part of work for many employees. This shift has challenged preconceived notions about the quality of remote work, presenting an opportunity for PWD. While working from home is a preference or luxury for some non-essential workers, it is a reasonable accommodation for some PWD. The technological norms that have reshaped the workforce and allowed (economically privileged) employees to telework could continue to benefit millions of individuals for whom work environments are currently inaccessible. Researchers should consider how team members, supervisors, and those in upper management react to working with an increasingly large number of employees who are engaged but not physically present in the workplace. Researchers should also examine the impact of flexible and adaptable work schedules and locations from the perspective of PWD: how can they feel included in the work environment, develop supportive collegial relationships, and meet their instrumental and psychosocial needs while contributing substantially to organizations?

Organizations that better serve PWD may very well benefit themselves from doing so. As the number of PWD increases nationwide (e.g., Crimmins et al., 2016), the perspectives of PWD on accessible product design will become increasingly valuable. Future research has the potential to showcase how inclusive environments can benefit PWD and organizations. Indeed, much investigation is still needed to understand the impacts of a dynamic labor market on people with and without disabilities; it offers an exciting opportunity for organizations and PWD to mutually benefit.

Conclusion

In this chapter, we hoped to stimulate the next generation of scholarship on workplace experiences among PWD by focusing attention on five areas that we see as particularly urgent. To summarize, we believe future research should focus on a) diversity within the disability community with respect to specific disability identities; b) the ways in which disability interacts with other aspects of an individual's identity (e.g., race, gender, age) to influence workplace experiences; c) how PWD navigate transitions between life stages and circumstances; d) how teams adapt to include PWD, paving the way for teams and individuals to be effective, productive, and satisfied in the workplace; and e) organizational contexts that promote workplace inclusion and equity for PWD. These areas offer particularly promising directions for disability scholars. While there are challenges to such research programs, we have no doubt that an expanded study of disability at work will benefit PWD and organizations alike.

References

Americans with Disabilities Act, 42 U.S.C § 12101 (1990). https://www.ada.gov/pubs/
    adastatute08.htm
Baldridge, D. C., & Veiga, J. F. (2006). The impact of anticipated social consequences on recurring
    disability accommodation requests. *Journal of Management, 32*(1), 158–179. https://doi.org/
    10.1177/0149206305277800
Balser, D. B. (2007). Predictors of workplace accommodations for employees with mobility-related
    disabilities. *Administration & Society, 39*(5), 656–683. https://doi.org/10.1177/
    0095399707303639

Bernardes, S. F., Silva, S. A., Carvalho, H., Costa, M., & Pereira, S. (2014). Is it a (fe)male pain? Portuguese nurses' and laypeople's gendered representations of common pains. *European Journal of Pain*, *18*(4), 530–539. https://doi.org/10.1002/j.1532-2149.2013.00387.x

Boman, T., Kjellberg, A., Danermark, B., & Boman, E. (2015). Employment opportunities for persons with different types of disability. *Alter*, *9*(2), 116–129. https://doi.org/10.1016/j.alter.2014.11.003

Bonaccio, S., Connelly, C.E., Gellatly, I.R., Jetha, A., & Martin Ginis, K. A. (2020). The participation of people with disabilities in the workplace across the employment cycle: Employer concerns and research evidence. *Journal of Business and Psychology*, *35*, 135–158. https://doi.org/10.1007/s10869-018-9602-5

Brzykcy, A. Z., Boehm, S. A., & Baldridge, D. C. (2019). Fostering sustainable careers across the lifespan: the role of disability, idiosyncratic deals and perceived work ability. *Journal of Vocational Behavior*, *112*, 185–198. https://doi.org/10.1016/j.jvb.2019.02.001

CDC. (2020, September 16). Disability Impacts All of Us Infographic. Centers for Disease Control and Prevention. https://www.cdc.gov/ncbddd/disabilityandhealth/infographic-disability-impacts-all.html

Colella, A., DeNisi, A. S., & Varma, A. (1998). The impact of ratee's disability on performance judgments and choice as partner: The role of disability-job fit stereotypes and interdependence of rewards. *Journal of Applied Psychology*, *83*(1), 102–111. https://doi.org/10.1037/0021-9010.83.1.102

Colella, A. (2001). Coworker distributive fairness judgments of the workplace accommodation of employees with disabilities. *Academy of Management Review*, *26*(1), 100–116. https://doi.org/10.2307/259397

Coleman, J. M., Brunell, A. B., & Haugen, I. M. (2015). Multiple forms of prejudice: How gender and disability stereotypes influence judgments of disabled women and men. *Current Psychology: A Journal for Diverse Perspectives on Diverse Psychological Issues*, *34*(1), 177–189. https://doi.org/10.1007/s12144-014-9250-5

Cramm, J.-M., Tebra, N., & Finkenflügel, H. (2008). Colleagues' perception of supported employee performance. *Journal of Policy and Practice in Intellectual Disabilities*, *5*(4), 269–275. https://doi.org/10.1111/j.1741-1130.2008.00188.x

Crenshaw, K. (1990). Mapping the margins: Intersectionality, identity politics, and violence against women of color. *Stanford Law Review*, *43*, 1241.

Crimmins, E. M., Zhang, Y., & Saito, Y. (2016). Trends over 4 decades in disability-free life expectancy in the United States. *American Journal of Public Health*, *106*(7), 1287–1293. https://doi.org/10.2105/AJPH.2016.303120

Dwertmann, D. J. G., & Boehm, S. A. (2014). The moderating effect of climate for inclusion on supervisor-subordinate dissimilarity outcomes. *Academy of Management Proceedings*, *2014*(1). https://doi.org/10.5465/ambpp.2014.188

Elvira, M., & Town, R. (2001). The effects of race and worker productivity on performance evaluations. *Industrial Relations: A Journal of Economy and Society*, *40*(4), 571–590. https://doi.org/10.1111/0019-8676.00226

Florey, A. T., & Harrison, D. A. (2000). Responses to informal accommodation requests from employees with disabilities: Multistudy evidence on willingness to comply. *The Academy of Management Journal*, *43*(2), 224–233. https://doi.org/10.2307/1556379

Frederick, A., & Shifrer, D. (2019). Race and disability: From analogy to intersectionality. *Sociology of Race and Ethnicity*, *5*(2), 200–214. https://doi.org/10.1177/2332649218783480

Haber, M. G., Mazzotti, V. L., Mustian, A. L., Rowe, D. A., Bartholomew, A. L., Test, D. W., & Fowler, C. H. (2016). What works, when, for whom, and with whom: A meta-analytic review of predictors of postsecondary success for students with disabilities. *Review of Educational Research*, 86(1), 123–162. https://doi.org/10.3102/0034654315583135

Individuals with Disabilities Education Act, 20 U.S.C. § 1400 (2004).

Jones, K. P., & King, E. B. (2014). Managing concealable stigmas at work: A Review and multilevel model. *Journal of Management*, 40(5), 1466–1494. https://doi.org/10.1177/0149206313515518

Levine, J. M., & Moreland, R. L. (1990). Progress in small group research. *Annual Review of Psychology*, 41(1), 585–634.

Lipscomb, S., Hamison, J., Liu Albert, Y., Burghardt, J., Johnson, D. R., & Thurlow, M. (2017). Preparing for Life after High School: The Characteristics and Experiences of Youth in Special Education. Findings from the National Longitudinal Transition Study 2012. Volume 2: Comparisons across Disability Groups. Full Report. NCEE 2017-4018. *National Center for Education Evaluation and Regional Assistance*.

Lyons, B. J., Martinez, L. R., Ruggs, E. N., Hebl, M. R., Ryan, A. M., O'Brien, K. R., & Roebuck, A. (2016). To say or not to say: Different strategies of acknowledging a visible disability. *Journal of Management*, 44(5), 1980–2007. https://doi.org/10.1177/0149206316638160

Mathieu, J. E., Gallagher, P. T., Domingo, M. A., & Klock, E. A. (2019). Embracing complexity: Reviewing the past decade of team effectiveness research. *Annual Review of Organizational Psychology and Organizational Behavior*, 6(1), 17–46. https://doi.org/10.1146/annurev-orgpsych-012218-015106

Melson-Silimon, A., Harris, A. M., Shoenfelt, E. L., Miller, J. D., & Carter, N. T. (2019). Personality testing and the Americans with Disabilities Act: Cause for concern as normal and abnormal personality models are integrated. *Industrial and Organizational Psychology: Perspectives on Science and Practice*, 12(2), 119–132. https://doi.org/10.1017/iop.2018.156

Milliken, F. J., & Martins, L. L. (1996). Searching for common threads: Understanding the multiple effects of diversity in organizational groups. *Academy of Management Review*, 21(2), 403–433. https://doi.org/10.5465/amr.1996.9605060217

Moen, P., Flood, S. M., & Wang, J. (2021). The uneven later work course: Intersectional gender, age, race, and class disparities. *The Journals of Gerontology: Series B*.

Murray, C., Kosty, D., Doren, B., Gau, J. M., & Seeley, J. R. (2021). Patterns of early adult work and postsecondary participation among individuals with high-incidence disabilities: A longitudinal person-centered analysis. *Developmental Psychology*. https://doi.org/10.1037/dev0001163

Narayanan, S., & Terris, E. (2020). Inclusive manufacturing: The impact of disability diversity on productivity in a work integration social enterprise. *Manufacturing & Service Operations Management*, 22(6), 1112–1130. https://doi.org/10.1287/msom.2020.0940

Nittrouer, C. L., Fa-Kaji, N., Hebl, M., & King, E. (2021a). Allies as intermediaries: Strategies that promote hiring people with intellectual disabilities [Unpublished manuscript].

Nittrouer, C. L., Fa-Kaji, N., & Hebl, M. (2021b). Reducing discrimination against individuals with mental impairments: The influence of Section 503 on social norm perceptions [Under review].

Paetzold, R. L., García, M. F., Colella, A., Ren, L. R., Triana, M. D. C., & Ziebro, M. (2008). Perceptions of people with disabilities: When is accommodation fair? *Basic and Applied Social Psychology*, 30(1), 27–35. https://doi.org/10.1080/01973530701665280

Prigatano, G. P. (2005). Disturbances of self-awareness and rehabilitation of patients with traumatic brain injury: A 20-year perspective. *The Journal of Head Trauma Rehabilitation*, 20(1), 19–29. https://doi.org/10.1097/00001199-200501000-00004

Purdie-Vaughns, V., & Eibach, R. P. (2008). Intersectional invisibility: The distinctive advantages and disadvantages of multiple subordinate-group identities. *Sex Roles*, 59(5–6), 377–391. https://doi.org/10.1007/s11199-008-9424-4

Quinn, D. M., & Earnshaw, V. A. (2011). Understanding concealable stigmatized identities: The role of identity in psychological, physical, and behavioral outcomes. *Social Issues and Policy Review, 5*(1), 160–190. https://doi.org/10.1111/j.1751-2409.2011.01029.x

Reeve, D. (2004). Psycho-emotional dimensions of disability and the social mode. In C. Barnes & G. Mercer (Eds.), Implementing the Social Model of Disability: Theory and Research, Leeds (pp. 83–100). The Disability Press.

Santuzzi, A. M., & Waltz, P. R. (2016). Disability in the workplace: A unique and variable identity. *Journal of Management, 42*(5), 1111–1135. https://doi.org/10.1177/0149206315626269

Schneider, B. (1987). The people make the place. *Personnel Psychology, 40*(3), 437–453. https://doi.org/10.1111/j.1744-6570.1987.tb00609.x

Schur, L. A., Ameri, M., & Kruse, D. (2020). Telework after COVID: A "silver lining" for workers with disabilities? *Journal of Occupational Rehabilitation, 30*(4), 521–536. https://doi.org/10.1007/s10926-020-09936-5

Sevak, P., Houtenville, A. J., Brucker, D. L., & O'Neill, J. (2015). Individual characteristics and the disability employment gap. *Journal of Disability Policy Studies, 26*(2), 80–88. https://doi.org/10.1177/1044207315585823

Solovieva, T. I., & Walls, R. T. (2013). Implications of workplace accommodations for persons with disabilities. *Journal of Workplace Behavioral Health, 28*(3), 192–211.

Szinovacz, M. E., & Davey, A. (2005). Predictors of perceptions of involuntary retirement. *The Gerontologist, 45*(1), 36–47. https://doi.org/10.1093/geront/45.1.36

U.S. Bureau of Labor Statistics (March, 2021). Economic situation summary. https://www.bls.gov/news.release/empsit.nr0.htm

U.S. Equal Employment Opportunity Commission. (2002). Enforcement guidance on reasonable accommodation and undue hardship under the ADA. https://www.eeoc.gov/laws/guidance/enforcement-guidance-reasonable-accommodation-and-undue-hardship-under-ada

U.S. Rehabilitation Act of 1973, 29 U.S.C. § 701 *et seq.* (1973). https://uscode.house.gov/view.xhtml?req=(title:29%20section:701%20edition:prelim)

Vickers, M. H. (2012). "For the Crime of Being Different . . .": Multiple sclerosis, teams, and stigmatisation at work – Lessons from a case study. *Employee Responsibilities and Rights Journal, 24*(3), 177–195. https://doi.org/10.1007/s10672-011-9186-y

Williams, K. Y., & O'Reilly, C. A. (1998). Demography and diversity in organizations: A review of 40 years of research. *Research in Organizational Behavior, 20*, 77–140.

Zhu, X., Law, K. S., Sun, C. T., & Yang, D. (2019). Thriving of employees with disabilities: The roles of job self-efficacy, inclusion, and team-learning climate. *Human Resource Management, 58*(1), 21–34. https://doi.org/10.1002/hrm.21920

Katherine L. Moore

3 The Current and Future Law of Accommodation

Abstract: Innovations in technology can drive law and policy. Employers must make reasonable accommodations for employees with disabilities in the workplace, but what counts as "reasonable" may change over time. Advances in technology, changing norms, and the realities of remote work may contribute to a reimagining of employer obligations. This article explains the history and current status of accommodation under the Americans with Disabilities Act, including guidance from the Equal Employment Opportunity Commission, and then looks to the future of accommodation law by looking at new guidance. Finally, this article explores concepts in universal design that may drive changes to law and policy.

Keywords: accommodation law, reasonable accommodations, universal design

Employers must make reasonable accommodations for employees with disabilities as part of the nondiscrimination requirements of the Americans with Disabilities Act. This chapter explains the current legal requirements and describes some potential future innovations in law, policy, and practice. As technology advances, law and policy should similarly advance.

The Current Legal Landscape

The Basic Nondiscrimination Requirement

Before delving into the relationship between disability and reasonable accommodations in the workplace, it may be helpful to understand some of the statutory protections afforded to people with disabilities.

The employment provisions of the Americans with Disabilities Act of 1990 (ADA) require courts to walk a fine line in determining who is a person with a disability entitled to a reasonable accommodation and what, exactly, is reasonable. The Americans with Disabilities Act Amendments Act of 2008 (ADAAA) sought to remedy some of the most restrictive interpretations of the ADA, such that disability may be broadly construed, but a problem remains that courts must balance determinations of disability against determinations of ability to perform essential job functions, with or without accommodations.

Katherine L. Moore, Independent Researcher

https://doi.org/10.1515/9783110743647-004

The 2008 amendments added a "Note" to the "Findings and Purpose" section of the ADA (this Note having the force of law) explicitly overturning prior Supreme Court cases that had narrowly interpreted the definition of disability, thus indicating an intention that the Court interpret disability more broadly (ADAAA, 2008).

The basic definition of disability, however, remains the same in the ADA and in the ADAAA:

(1) a physical or mental impairment that substantially limits one or more major life activities of such individual;
(2) a record of such an impairment; or
(3) being regarded as having such an impairment (ADAAA, 2008, §12102)

Prong (1) refers to an individual with a disability, inclusive of physical or mental impairments that substantially limit a major life activity. Major life activities can include working, learning, reading, thinking, caring for oneself, hearing, seeing, eating, walking, breathing, concentrating, communicating, and more (ADAAA, 2008, §12102). The ADAAA includes major bodily functions along with activities. Prong (2) is similar to (1) but includes someone who experienced the impairment in the past, whether or not the impairment continues. Prong (3) refers to individuals who are regarded as disabled but whose major life activities or bodily functions are not, in fact, limited. People who qualify under any of the three prongs may experience discrimination on the basis of disability.

When considering the relationship between disability and employment, there are two main relevant provisions of the ADA: Title I and Title II. Title I is titled "Employment" and applies to "covered entities" which employ at least 15 people with a few exceptions (ADAAA, 2008, §12111). Title II, "Public Services," also touches employment because it covers any state or local government employers, though the wording and requirements differ (ADAAA, 2008, §12181).

Even though Titles I and II have differing provisions, the Equal Employment Opportunity Commission promulgates rules and regulations under Title I that are equally applicable to employers covered by Title II.

Finally, one more statute to be aware of is Section 504 of the Rehabilitation Act, which covers all entities receiving federal financial assistance (Rehabilitation Act, 1973). Much of the provisions of Section 504 are duplicated in Title II of the ADA. Furthermore, the Rehabilitation Act covers federal employees.

The general rule prohibiting discrimination in employment from Title I of the ADA states:

No covered entity shall discriminate against a qualified individual on the basis of disability in regard to job application procedures, the hiring, advancement or discharge of employees, employee compensation, job training, and other terms, conditions, and privileges of employment. (ADAAA, 2008, §12112(a))

Qualified Individuals

The definitions of qualified individual and reasonable accommodation are interrelated, but it is worth parsing each individually.

While each title of the ADA defines who is a "qualified individual" entitled to the protections of the ADA, in the employment context, the definition is as follows. A qualified individual under Title I:

> means an individual who, with or without reasonable accommodation, can perform the essential functions of the employment position that such individual holds or desires. For the purposes of this subchapter, consideration shall be given to the employer's judgment as to what functions of a job are essential, and if an employer has prepared a written description before advertising or interviewing applicants for the job, this description shall be considered evidence of the essential functions of the job. (ADAAA, 2008, §12111(8))

To be a qualified individual, performing the essential functions of the employment position with or without reasonable accommodation is a foundational requirement. In *Albertson's, Inc. v. Kirkingburg* (1999), the court gave a level of deference to employers to justify their qualification standards. Title I explicitly refers to the "essential" functions of the employment position, but employers are often given deference to determine what exactly are the essential versus non-essential functions of the job. This deference is a consequence of Title I's indication that courts should give "consideration" to the employer's judgment regarding which functions are essential; exactly what level of consideration should be given to employers is not specified.

Next, the interaction between the ADA and the Social Security Disability Insurance (SSDI) program is also an important component for workers and employers to consider, not least because many individuals who file claims for discrimination under the ADA have also filed claims for compensation under SSDI. In *Cleveland v. Policy Management Systems Corporation* (1999), the Supreme Court determined that even though SSDI and the ADA have quite different statutory schemes, requirements, definitions, and purposes, they are often consistent. Applying for and receiving SSDI benefits does not stop the recipient from pursing an ADA claim, but there is still a key tension here.

As the Court noted, even though a particular plaintiff might be able to overcome it, there will still be a problem in that receipt of SSDI benefits will be contingent on a person having a "severe impairment" that "significantly limits [the applicant's] ability to do basic work activities" (Code of Federal Regulations, Basic Definition of Disability; Social Security Administration, Disability benefits: How you qualify, n.d.). There are two conflicts here for workers. First, SSDI prevents recipients from engaging in substantial gainful activity (SGA). SGA was defined in 2021 as earning more than $1,310 per month (or $2,190 per month if the worker is blind) (Social Security Administration, Substantial gainful activity, n.d.). On the other hand, in order to be a "qualified individual" as discussed above, the worker must be able to "perform the essential functions" of the position. How can a worker be both unable to "do basic work activities" and also able to "perform the essential functions" of a job?

Nevertheless, the Court in *Cleveland v. Policy Management Systems Corporation* (1999) identified "situations in which an SSDI claim and an ADA claim can comfortably exist side by side." The Court found that, for a particular individual, it may be that they qualify for SSDI under the administrative rules and yet, "due to special individual circumstances," can also perform the essential functions of their job (*Cleveland v. Policy Management Systems Corporation*, 1999).

Finally, accommodations, discussed in the next section, may play a key role here. The plaintiff in this case, Carolyn Cleveland, claimed that reasonable workplace accommodations are not accounted for by SSDI, and that she was both disabled for SSDI purposes and able to perform her job with accommodations under the ADA.

Reasonable Accommodations and Undue Hardship

The requirement to provide reasonable accommodations as part of the nondiscrimination provisions of the ADA is one of the most well-known, and misunderstood, pieces of the legislation.

The basic provision is as follows. Section 12112(b) provides that the term "discriminate" includes:

(5) (A) not making reasonable accommodations to the known physical or mental limitations of an otherwise qualified individual with a disability who is an applicant or employee, unless such covered entity can demonstrate that the accommodation would impose an undue hardship on the operation of the business of such covered entity; or

(B) denying employment opportunities to a job applicant or employee who is an otherwise qualified individual with a disability, if such denial is based on the need of such covered entity to make reasonable accommodation to the physical or mental impairments of the employee or applicant . . .

Section 12111(9) further defines reasonable accommodation to include:

(A) making existing facilities used by employees readily accessible to and usable by individuals with disabilities; and

(B) job restructuring, part-time or modified work schedules, reassignment to a vacant position, acquisition or modification of equipment or devices, appropriate adjustment or modifications of examinations, training materials or policies, the provision of qualified readers or interpreters, and other similar accommodations for individuals with disabilities.

As for the definition of undue hardship, Section 12111(d) provides that:

(A) In general

The term "undue hardship" means an action requiring significant difficulty or expense, when considered in light of the factors set forth in subparagraph (B).

(B) Factors to be considered

In determining whether an accommodation would impose an undue hardship on a covered entity, factors to be considered include –

(i)   the nature and cost of the accommodation needed under this chapter;

(ii) the overall financial resources of the facility or facilities involved in the provision of the reasonable accommodation; the number of persons employed at such facility; the effect on expenses and resources, or the impact otherwise of such accommodation upon the operation of the facility;

(iii) the overall financial resources of the covered entity; the overall size of the business of a covered entity with respect to the number of its employees; the number, type, and location of its facilities; and

(iv) the type of operation or operations of the covered entity, including the composition, structure, and functions of the workforce of such entity; the geographic separateness, administrative, or fiscal relationship of the facility or facilities in question to the covered entity.

Finally, there is a provision that:

> Nothing in this chapter shall be construed to require an individual with a disability to accept an accommodation, aid, service, opportunity, or benefit, which such individual chooses not to accept. (Americans with Disabilities Act Amendments Act, §12201(d))

The reasonable accommodation provisions of the ADA are unique in anti-discrimination law in that they require affirmative action on the part of employers to take steps to change something about the way they do business in order to comply. This is distinct from merely failing to discriminate against a job applicant with a disability, for example, as is the requirement in other anti-discrimination contexts such as race, gender, sex, religion, etc. Rather, employers are required to pay particular notice to the barriers set up, intentionally or not, that keep people with disabilities out of the workforce. This requirement is also unique in that it requires a fairly complex understanding of an individual worker's circumstances: what would accommodate their disability and what would not, for example. Finally, the requirement has the potential to create a visual marker that might not otherwise be present – a modified workspace, new equipment – which may make an individual worker's disability "visible" in way it was not visible before (Feldblum, 1993, pp. 35–36).

Consider, for example, a case from the 7th Circuit, *Gratzl v. Office of the Chief Judges* (2010). Jeanne Gratzl experienced incontinence and was able to manage her disability when she was assigned to work as a court reporter in a control room. Then her job responsibilities were changed to require in-courtroom work. She was offered an accommodation that would require her to raise her hand when she needed a break, which she believed would require a large number of people to be notified of her medical information; she wished to remain in the control room, but that request was denied. The 7th Circuit affirmed that her employer had offered a reasonable accommodation, even though it was one that made her previously invisible disability visible in a way that she did not wish (*Gratzl v. Office of the Chief Judges*, 2010).

Subsequent to the amendments in 2008 (the ADAAA), courts have more frequently reached the question of whether a worker was unlawfully denied reasonable accommodation. This is primarily due to the changes in the ADAAA itself, as well as interpretive guidance from the Equal Employment Opportunity Commission (EEOC), which explained that the 2008 amendments were a "signal to both lawyers and courts to spend less time and energy on the minutia of an individual's impairment, and more time and energy on the merits of the case – including whether discrimination occurred because of a disability, whether an individual was qualified for a job or eligible for a service, and whether a reasonable accommodation or modification was called for under the law" (Code of Federal Regulations, Equal Employment Opportunity Commission, Discrimination prohibited). For this reason, there are a number of cases defining and refining what is a reasonable accommodation and what is undue hardship (*EEOC v. UPS Supply Chain*, 2010; *Jakubowski v. The Christ Hospital*, 2010; *Valle-Arce v. Puerto Rico Ports Authority*, 2011).

Another 7th Circuit case, *Vande Zande v. State of Wisconsin Department of Administration* (1995), is often cited for its explanation of the interpretation of the "reasonableness" requirement and how it relates to cost and other considerations. Importantly, this case established that even *de minimus* costs for an accommodation – in this case, $150 – might not be reasonable under the circumstances. As the Court identified, the term "reasonable" is an often-contentious term in all sorts of legal scenarios. Chief Judge Posner wrote that costs enter the calculus not *only* at the undue hardship point – where if an action requires "significant difficulty or expense" it will not be required under the ADA – but also enters into the definition of "reasonable." Furthermore, Judge Posner opined that the reasonableness requirement must carefully take into account what is exactly required in order to perform the functions of the job. He wrote, "we do not think an employer has a duty to expend even modest amounts of money to bring about an absolute identity in working conditions between disabled and nondisabled workers . . . The duty of reasonable accommodation is satisfied when the employer does what is necessary to enable the disabled worker to work in reasonable comfort" (*Vande Zande v. State of Wisconsin Department of Administration*, 1995).

Finally, the *Vande Zande* case was perhaps both prescient and perhaps unimaginative when viewed in the light of the drastic changes to American workplaces that took place 25 years later in 2020. Judge Posner wrote what was the majority view of Circuits in 1995: that "[m]ost jobs in organizations public or private involve team work under supervision rather than solitary unsupervised work, and team work under supervision generally cannot be performed at home without a substantial reduction in the quality of the employee's performance. This will no doubt change as communications technology advances, but is the situation today. Generally, therefore, an employer is not required to accommodate a disability by allowing the disabled worker to work, by himself, without supervision, at home" (*Vande Zande v. State of Wisconsin Department of Administration*, 1995). For the majority view at the time of the Vande Zande decision see *Tyndall v. National Education Centers* (1994) and *Law v. United States Postal Service* (1988). For the minority view see *Langon v. Dept. of Health & Human Services* (1992) and *Carr v. Reno* (1994).

As discussed in the next section, perhaps the advances in communications technology, spurred by the changes experienced in 2020, have created a new situation that will change what accommodations employers are required to offer in the future.

The Future of Accommodation

As technology changes, the law changes . . . often slowly and imperfectly, but nonetheless, it does change. There are two places to look for clues to what the future looks like in the workplace accommodation space, and potentially in the law: EEOC guidance and innovative corporations.

New EEOC Guidance

The Equal Employment Opportunity Commission (EEOC) is charged with enforcing federal laws regarding illegal discrimination against job applicants and employees on the basis of race, color, religion, sex, national origin, age, disability, or genetic information (U.S. Equal Employment Opportunity Commission; Equal Employment Opportunity Act of 1972).

The EEOC takes on a number of tasks to fulfill that responsibility. The EEOC investigates charges of discrimination against covered employers, negotiates settlements, files lawsuits, engages in outreach, education, and technical assistance, and provides leadership and guidance to federal agencies on the equal employment opportunity program.

Previously, the EEOC has issued the following interpretative guidance related to accommodation:

> In general, an accommodation is any change in the work environment or in the way things are customarily done that enables an individual with a disability to enjoy equal employment opportunities. There are three categories of reasonable accommodation. These are (1) accommodations that are required to ensure equal opportunity in the application process; (2) accommodations that enable the employer's employees with disabilities to perform the essential functions of the

position held or desired; and (3) accommodations that enable the employer's employees with disabilities to enjoy equal benefits and privileges of employment as are enjoyed by employees without disabilities. It should be noted that nothing in this part prohibits employers or other covered entities from providing accommodations beyond those required by this part. (Code of Federal Regulations, Interpretive Guidance on Title I of the Americans with Disabilities Act)

The EEOC has also previously issued pandemic-specific guidance. In 2009, in response to the H1N1 virus, the EEOC prepared a policy document to respond to anticipated interaction between a pandemic and the ADA. In Pandemic Preparedness in the Workplace and the Americans with Disabilities Act, the EEOC attempted to provide clarity as to the existing laws as they would apply during a pandemic (U.S. Equal Employment Opportunity Commission, Pandemic Preparedness in the Workplace and the Americans with Disabilities Act).

Ultimately, the COVID-19 pandemic required real-time responsive policy, and the EEOC issued new guidance. Two points here are particularly relevant to workers and employers when considering the interaction of disability, the ADA, and accommodations.

First is that employers may not *bar* someone from the workplace due to their disability.

The EEOC guidance provides:

If the employer is concerned about the employee's health being jeopardized upon returning to the workplace, the ADA does not allow the employer to exclude the employee – or take any other adverse action – *solely* because the employee has a disability that the Centers for Disease Control and Prevention (CDC) identifies as potentially placing him at "higher risk for severe illness" if he gets COVID-19. Under the ADA, such action is not allowed unless the employee's disability poses a "direct threat" to his health that cannot be eliminated or reduced by reasonable accommodation.

The ADA direct threat requirement is a high standard. As an affirmative defense, direct threat requires an employer to show that the individual has a disability that poses a "significant risk of substantial harm" to his own health under 29 C.F.R. section 1630.2(r) (regulation addressing direct threat to health or safety of self or others). A direct threat assessment cannot be based solely on the condition being on the CDC's list; the determination must be an individualized assessment based on a reasonable medical judgment about this employee's disability – not the disability in general – using the most current medical knowledge and/or on the best available objective evidence. The ADA regulation requires an employer to consider the duration of the risk, the nature and severity of the potential harm, the likelihood that the potential harm will occur, and the imminence of the potential harm. Analysis of these factors will likely include considerations based on the severity of the pandemic in a particular area and the employee's own health (for example, is the employee's disability well-controlled?), and his particular job duties. A determination of direct threat also would include the likelihood that an individual will be exposed to the virus at the worksite. Measures that an employer may be taking in general to protect all workers, such as mandatory social distancing, also would be relevant.

Even if an employer determines that an employee's disability poses a direct threat to his own health, the employer still cannot exclude the employee from the workplace – or take any other adverse action – unless there is no way to provide a reasonable accommodation (absent undue hardship). The ADA regulations require an employer to consider whether there are reasonable accommodations that would eliminate or reduce the risk so that it would be safe for the employee to return to the workplace while still permitting performance of essential functions. This can involve an interactive process with the employee. If there are not accommodations that permit this, then an employer must consider accommodations such as telework, leave, or reassignment (perhaps to a different job in a place where it may be safer for the employee to work or that permits telework). An employer may only bar an employee from the workplace if, after going through all these steps, the facts support the conclusion that the employee poses a significant risk of substantial harm to himself that cannot be reduced or eliminated by reasonable accommodation. (U.S. Equal Employment Opportunity Commission, What You Should Know About COVID-19 and the ADA, the Rehabilitation Act, and other EEO Laws, Question G.4)

Second, and highly relevant to this discussion of accommodations, is the question of whether remote work has or will become a standard reasonable accommodation. So far, the EEOC has indicated that it is not currently a requirement, but also implies that it may be advisable.

In answer to the question "Assume that an employer grants telework to employees for the purpose of slowing or stopping the spread of COVID-19. When an employer reopens the workplace and recalls employees to the worksite, does the employer automatically have to grant telework as a reasonable accommodation to every employee with a disability who requests to continue this arrangement as an ADA/Rehabilitation Act accommodation?" the EEOC responded:

No. Any time an employee requests a reasonable accommodation, the employer is entitled to understand the disability-related limitation that necessitates an accommodation. If there is no disability-related limitation that requires teleworking, then the employer does not have to provide telework as an accommodation. Or, if there is a disability-related limitation but the employer can effectively address the need with another form of reasonable accommodation at the workplace, then the employer can choose that alternative to telework.

To the extent that an employer is permitting telework to employees because of COVID-19 and is choosing to excuse an employee from performing one or more essential functions, then a request – after the workplace reopens – to continue telework as a reasonable accommodation does not have to be granted if it requires continuing to excuse the employee from performing an essential function. The ADA never requires an employer to eliminate an essential function as an accommodation for an individual with a disability.

The fact that an employer temporarily excused performance of one or more essential functions when it closed the workplace and enabled employees to telework for the purpose of protecting their safety from COVID-19, or otherwise chose to permit telework, does not mean that the employer permanently changed a job's essential functions, that telework is always a feasible accommodation, or that it does not pose an undue hardship. These are fact-specific determinations. The employer has no obligation under the ADA to refrain from restoring all of an employee's essential duties at such time as it chooses to restore the prior work arrangement, and then evaluating any requests for continued or new accommodations under the usual ADA rules. (U.S. Equal Employment Opportunity Commission, What You Should Know About COVID-19 and the ADA, the Rehabilitation Act, and other EEO Laws, Question D.15)

While not requiring telework as a universal accommodation, the fact-specific inquiry identified in the EEOC guidance may indeed lead courts to require telework in individual cases. Additionally, an employer that previously allowed telework and found it to be successful could have undergone a trial period during which the employee's ability to perform the essential functions of the job was tested (Perez-Yanez, 2020). This may mean that upon court review, the burden will be placed on employers to show that telework, especially continued telework where it was temporarily authorized in the past, would not adequately allow an employee to continue to perform the essential functions of the job. If the employee was performing the essential functions with telework during the pandemic, it will likely be an uphill battle for employers to argue otherwise.

Universal Design

When we think of innovation in the disability and accommodations space, we often think of technology first. Arlene Kanter has recently written about the advances in technology that make remote work more possible than ever in Remote Work and the Future of Disability Accommodations (forthcoming), noting that during the COVID-19 pandemic, more than half of the labor force worked remotely. In the past, Kanter notes, most courts have found that employers have not been required to offer remote work as a reasonable accommodation under the ADA. However, Kanter argues that the time to change that precedent is now.

As she notes, there are currently "increasing opportunities" for remote work for disabled employees furthers the goal of the ADA to promote economic self-sufficiency of disabled people. It is also one way to challenge the ongoing and systemic ableism that exists within society and at many workplaces today (Kanter, forthcoming 2022, p. 1).

Kanter goes on to propose amendments to current regulations with the aim of ultimately increasing the rate of employment for people with disabilities, which is still low even thirty years after the passage of the ADA. Kanter suggests that the EEOC propose an amendment to Title I regulations indicating that remote work is a reasonable accommodation in appropriate cases. This could be accomplished, first, by shifting the burden to employers to prove how remote work would be an undue hardship. Second, Kanter proposes that courts consider not just the employer's view of whether essential functions of the job can be performed remotely, but that they be required to also consider the employee's judgment as to whether that work can be performed with this particular accommodation. Kanter also proposes amending Title I so that the calculus becomes whether an accommodation would "fundamentally alter" the job, a concept from Titles II and III not yet incorporated into Title I. Finally, Kanter suggests that the EEOC take the stance that requirements for physical presence on the job may violate Title I in specific instances. Finally, Kanter argues for more specificity from covered entities when determining which jobs may or may not be performed remotely.

Beyond technology, there is potential for innovation in the entire construction of workplace accommodation. Scholars have written about concepts in universal design that would achieve dual goals of accommodating all workers, disabled and nondisabled, and as a consequence reduce stigma both for disability and for accommodations themselves.

Elizabeth Emens has written about this concept in Integrating Accommodation (2008), where she argues that accommodations are available to benefit all employees and employers as well, if they are viewed broadly and not merely as a means to comply with the law as it protects people with disabilities (Emens, 2008). Emens gives the examples of ramps that are accessible for people who use mobility aides but also parents pushing strollers, or telecommuting initiatives that may be favored among all sorts of employees both disabled and nondisabled. Furthermore, there is a growing group of individuals with impairments who do not qualify for formal protection from the ADA, but for whom universal accommodations might be beneficial and preferable. Emens proposes that designing interventions can be accomplished by utilizing a framework to maximize potential benefits by looking both at attitudinal benefits, that is improvements in attitudes towards people with disabilities or the ADA, and usage benefits, which directly impact disabled and nondisabled users. Similarly to Kanter's article, one design intervention that would maximize both usage and attitudinal benefits would be a broad telework policy available to all employees, regardless of status, but with knowledge that the ADA was the source for the reconception of work space policies. Emens further argues for increased attitudinal benefits via the mechanisms of publicity and disclosure, in certain circumstances.

A group of law and philosophy professors also wrote about these concepts in Accommodating Every Body, 2014. Michael Ashley Stein, Anita Silvers, Bradley A. Areheart and Leslie Pickering Frances argue that reasonable accommodations should be extended to all work-capable people who need accommodation in order to access employment. Stein et al. (2014) argue that rather than status-based accommodations that are predicated on the restrictive ADA definition of disability, accommodations should be predicated on elevating functionality for everyone who needs it. They argue for an "effectiveness standard," which would predicate the provision accommodation on the effectiveness of the accommodation in elevating an individual's functionality, rather than on the status of being disabled. As they argue, "accommodations would benefit all individuals for whom workplace alterations enable the performance of essential job functions or provide opportunity that would otherwise not exist" (Stein et al., 2014, p. 738).

These scholars show that thinking more broadly than the ADA provides about reasonable accommodations can be helpful to disabled and nondisabled people, as well as employers that wish to innovate and offer the most accessible work spaces.

Conclusion

Advancements in technology, understanding, and inclusion can drive change. We will very likely see new court challenges to the current standard of reasonable accommodations arising out of the broad telework norm that took root during the COVID-19 pandemic. Law and policy will often follow practice, and innovative corporations can get ahead of the curve by providing robust workplace options for all employees, regardless of disability or other status.

References

Americans with Disabilities Act Amendments Act. (ADAAA), 42 U.S.C. ch. 126 §12101 et. seq.; §§12101, 12102, 12111, 12112, 12181, 12201 (2008).

Albertson's, Inc. v. Kirkingburg, 527 U.S. 555 (1999).

Carr v. Reno, 23 F.3d 525, 530 (D.C. Cir. 1994).

Cleveland v. Policy Management Systems Corporation, 526 U.S. 795 (1999).

Code of Federal Regulations, Equal Employment Opportunity Commission, Discrimination prohibited, 29 C.F.R. § 1630.4 app.

Code of Federal Regulations, Equal Employment Opportunity Commission, Definitions: Reasonable Accommodation, 29 C.F.R. §1630.2(o).

Code of Federal Regulations, Interpretive Guidance on Title I of the Americans with Disabilities Act, 29 C.F.R. Appendix to Part 1630.

Code of Federal Regulations, Social Security Administration, Basic Definition of Disability, 20 C.F.R. 404.1505.

EEOC v. UPS Supply Chain, 620 F.3d 1103 (9th Cir. 2010); *Valle-Arce v. Puerto Rico Ports Authority*, 651 F.3d 190 (1st Cir. 2011).

Emens, E. (2008). Integrating accommodation. *University of Pennsylvania Law Review, 156*(4), 839–922. https://scholarship.law.upenn.edu/penn_law_review/vol156/iss4/1

Equal Employment Opportunity Act of 1972, 42 U.S.C. §§ 2000e–2000e-8; 5 U.S.C. § 5108.

Feldblum, C. R. (1993). Antidiscrimination requirements of the ADA. In L. O. Gostin & H. A. Beyer (Eds.), *Implementing the Americans with Disabilities Act: Rights and responsibilities of all Americans* (pp. 35–36). Paul H. Brookes Publishing.

Gratzl v. Office of the Chief Judges, 601 F.3d 675 (7th Cir. 2010).

Jakubowski v. The Christ Hospital, 627 F.3d 195 (6th Cir. 2010).

Kanter, A. S. (forthcoming). Remote work and the future of disability accommodations. *Cornell Law Review*, 107. https://ssrn.com/abstract=3895798

Langon v. Dept. of Health & Human Services, 959 F.2d 1053, 1060–61 (D.C. Cir. 1992).

Law v. United States Postal Service, 852 F.2d 1278 (Fed. Cir. 1988).

Perez-Yanez, M. (2020, November 23). Will working from home be a reasonable accommodation post-COVID? *American Bar Association GPSolo EReport*, https://www.americanbar.org/groups/gpsolo/publications/gpsolo_ereport/2020/november2020/will-working-home-be-reasonable-accommodation-post-covid/

Rehabilitation Act, 29 U.S.C. §701 et. seq.; §794 (1973).

Social Security Administration. (n.d.). *Disability benefits: How you qualify*. www.ssa.gov/benefits/disability/qualify.html

Social Security Administration (n.d.). *Substantial gainful activity*. www.ssa.gov/oact/cola/sga.html

Stein, M. A., Silvers, A., Areheart, B. A., & Francis, L. P. (2014). Accommodating Every Body. *University of Chicago Law Review, 81*(2), 689–756.

Tyndall v. National Education Centers, Inc., 31 F.3d 209, 213–14 (4th Cir. 1994).

U.S. Equal Employment Opportunity Commission. www.eeoc.gov

U.S. Equal Employment Opportunity Commission. *Pandemic Preparedness in the Workplace and the Americans with Disabilities Act*. https://www.eeoc.gov/laws/guidance/pandemic-preparedness-workplace-and-americans-disabilities-act

U.S. Equal Employment Opportunity Commission. *What You Should Know About COVID-19 and the ADA, the Rehabilitation Act, and other EEO Laws*. https://www.eeoc.gov/wysk/what-you-should-know-about-covid-19-and-ada-rehabilitation-act-and-other-eeo-laws

Valle-Arce v. Puerto Rico Ports Authority, 651 F.3d 190 (1st Cir. 2011).

Vande Zande v. State of Wisconsin Department of Administration, 44 F.3d 538 (7th Cir. 1995).

Victoria Wass and Melanie Jones

4 Organisational Disability Measurement and Reporting in the UK

Abstract: A new demand-side policy approach to narrowing disability-related employment disadvantage in the UK requires that the government and organisations carefully consider how to enhance organisational workforce data collection on disability. Within organisations, identifying disability inequality, the impact of management practice and employees covered by disability equality legislation are only possible where disability is accurately measured. However, the coverage and quality of existing organisational data is poor, such that it restricts the development and evaluation of policy and practice at both the national and organisational levels. This data deficit, and the need for a lead from government to address it, is insufficiently recognised. Learning from national data collection and monitoring, this chapter provides a set of recommendations to promote organisational data collection on disability based on an approach that is useful, meaningful and manageable for the organisation, and which will have significant benefits for national policy development.

Keywords: disability, measurement, inequality indicators, organisations, reporting

Introduction

Inclusion of disabled people in the workplace has been a long-standing policy concern internationally, including in the UK. The 25th anniversary of the Disability Discrimination Act (DDA), in 1995, prompted reflection on progress on disability employment disadvantage through public inquiries, consultations and policy de-

Acknowledgements: Data from WERS 2011 was collected by NatCen Social Research on behalf of the Department for Business, Innovation and Skills, Economic and Social Research Council, UK Commission for Employment and Skills, Advisory, Conciliation and Arbitration Service and National Institute of Economic and Social Research. These data have been accessed through the UK Data Archive. We are grateful to Nick Bacon and the editors for comments on an earlier draft. None of these people or organisations bear any responsibility for the analysis or interpretation within this chapter.

Victoria Wass, Cardiff Business School, Cardiff University
Melanie Jones, Cardiff Business School, Cardiff University, IZA, Bonn

https://doi.org/10.1515/9783110743647-005

velopments.[1] Employment disadvantage is regarded as an indicator of wider inequalities facing disabled people, including barriers to independent living and economic and social wellbeing (see Barnes & Mercer, 2005). Past and existing polices and approaches based on incentivising disabled people into the labour market through the manipulation of welfare benefits, together with additional and specialised support with job search, are seen to have been unsuccessful in addressing the scale of employment disadvantage. In response, attention is moving to employers, and to the role of labour demand, where organisational barriers can discourage and preclude disabled people from joining, remaining and progressing in the workplace. As explained by the Centre for Social Justice (CSJ) (2021, p. 52),

> Supply-side efforts to support disabled people into work will not prove effective if employers view disabled people as a problem to be managed rather than as a valuable resource, or if they are unwilling to implement the sorts of employment practices that will enable disabled people to thrive.

The enhancement of employer practice and progress on workplace outcomes relies on accurate evidence on disability inequality within organisations. Data in the UK is severely lacking in this regard, with the last nationally representative survey of employers containing information on disability, the Workplace Employment Relations Survey (WERS), undertaken in 2011. Therefore, and as is increasingly recognised in policy proposals, implementing and evaluating this demand-side policy orientation will rely on organisations' own data collection.

Measuring, monitoring and reporting disability are separate but related activities. For organisations, data collection through the careful measurement of disability among the workforce is first and foremost. This is useful on its own account to identify employees for whom the organisation has responsibility under the Equality Act (2010). Importantly though, measurement is a pre-requisite for internal monitoring and external reporting of disability statistics. Internal tracking allows the organisation to uncover and understand patterns and trends in its disability statistics and to identify factors which influence disability inequality at work. Reporting these figures externally provides wider benefits in the form of transparency and scrutiny through comparison across organisations and with national benchmarks. For the government, organisational measures of disability prevalence are pre-requisites for the evaluation of organisational commitments, including those which form part of recent policy enhancements (2021) to the *Public Services (Social Value) Act* (2012), covering public procurement, and state recognition under the *Disability Confident* employer good practice accreditation scheme (2016).[2] The current

---

1 For example, the Centre for Social Justice (2021), House of Commons Work and Pensions Committee (2021) and the Cabinet Office (2021).

2 See https://www.gov.uk/government/publications/social-value-act-information-and-resources/ social-value-act-information-and-resources and https://www.gov.uk/government/collections/dis ability-confident-campaign

'framework' for disability reporting is contained in the *Framework for Voluntary Employer Reporting on Disability, Mental Health and Wellbeing* (2018), hereafter *VRF*, which provides some encouragement to employers to report on their activities in relation to recruitment and retention of disabled people and to measure and report their workforce composition by disability status.[3] Greater ambition is evident in proposed legislation for mandatory organisational reporting on two headline statistics, the disability pay gap and the percentage of disabled employees, contained within the *Workforce Information Bill* (2020).[4]

Relative to the measurement of other protected characteristics, operationalising the concept of disability presents particular methodological difficulties because of its subjective, hidden and dynamic nature and because it has social, cultural, legal as well as functional components. It is well known that different definitions and understandings of disability give rise to different calculations of its prevalence, different compositions in terms of the characteristics of disabled people and different measures of inequality of outcome (for example, see Amilon et al., 2021; Grönvik, 2009). These difficulties affect data collection and analysis at the aggregate and organisational levels and, if not addressed, limit the quantity and quality of monitoring and reporting on disability prevalence and disability-related disadvantage. These issues have proved difficult for both the state and the central statistical office (CSO) and are likely to give rise to additional challenges for organisations. The opportunities and incentives for the mis-measurement of disability by employers and employees in a human resource (HR)-led administrative process are different from (and greater than) for respondents to an anonymous national household survey. If the government is to succeed in encouraging employers to take greater responsibility for disability inclusion in the workplace, it must lead on improving and implementing disability measurement at the organisational level. Learning from best practice in national-level reporting will help support the implementation of an informative, consistent, and manageable framework for measuring and reporting at the organisational level.

The focus of this chapter is disability measurement: the difficulties it presents for data collection and analysis, and some proposed solutions. It is structured around a review of progress on reducing disability-related employment disadvantage based on national statistics which highlight both the scale of disadvantage and the complexities in measuring it. This is followed by an examination of the current state of measurement of disability within organisations in the UK. Evidence of gaps in data collection and weaknesses in existing measures prompt a set of recommendations towards improved practice.

---

3 See https://assets.publishing.service.gov.uk/government/uploads/system/uploads/attachment_data/file/758000/voluntary-reporting-on-disability-mental-health-and-wellbeing.pdf
4 HL Bill 82, 2020.

Measuring Disability in the UK

The treatment of disabled people in the UK is regulated through legislation. The DDA (1995), implemented in 1996, was superseded by the Equality Act (2010). There is nothing in law about organisational monitoring or reporting on disability. However, the law provides a definition of disability, namely, a physical or mental impairment that has a 'substantial' and 'long-term' negative effect on a person's ability to do normal daily activities.[5] Long-term requires that the impact has lasted or will last for 12 months or more. A legal decision in 2013 re-interpreted 'substantial' in relation to activity-limitation to mean anything which is not 'trivial' or 'insubstantial'.[6] Replacement by the Equality Act in 2010 involved relatively minor changes to the DDA but, significantly for measuring disability prevalence, reference to a set of 'defining' functional capacities and thresholds of activity-limitation which distinguish the disabled from the non-disabled was removed. Although intended as guidance, and not to be exhaustive or exclusive, they were removed because they appeared to be overly restrictive leading to the under-reporting of disability, especially that relating to mental impairment.[7]

Disability is a complex and multi-faceted concept with legal, social, cultural and functional components. Whether or not someone is disabled is the outcome of the interaction between the person with a health condition or impairment and environmental factors such as the accessibility of the built environment, the availability of assistive technology and society's attitudes towards impairment and disability. These determine the opportunities for activity and participation that define disability. Disability is not fixed over time and is affected by changing impairment and/or environmental factors. Further, the hidden nature of many impairments, and the stigma which attaches to a disabled identity, can lead to non-disclosure and/or mis-measurement. Definitions used to identify disability differ according to the relative weight given to aspects of functional impairment and to activity-limitation and participation in society. For all these reasons, reporting disability is contingent on terminology, context and purpose and, as such, it is difficult to define and to measure.

The Equality Act definition of disability used in UK National Statistics is collected in the Labour Force Survey (LFS) and comprises two parts: the presence of a long-standing physical or mental health condition or illness; and that this reduces the ability to carry out day-to-day activities, either 'a little' or 'a lot'. Disability is therefore a derived variable defined by a self-reported long-term health condition which causes activity-limitation. Based on questions that do not include the word 'disability', it does not require self-identification as a disabled person. It is self-

---

5 The legal definition is different from (and wider than) administrative definitions used to qualify for disability-related welfare benefits and services.

6 See Langstaff, J. in *Aderemi v London and South Eastern Railway Ltd* (2013) ICR 591.

7 See Jones and Wass (2018) for summary list of capacities and thresholds.

reported and highly subjective. The respondent chooses between 'yes, a little', 'yes, a lot' and 'not at all' based on their own view of a health condition or impairment and where their activity-limitation fits within the three-way classification. The threshold for disability, defined at the junction of 'not at all' and 'yes, a little', sets this at a modest level of activity-limitation, and arguably one which is more modest than prior to 2013 when the LFS questions requested a dichotomous (yes, no) response. This wording change implies a widening of the definition of disability, and it adds to the potential widening effects noted above of removing the DDA (1995) guidance and reference points[8] and the judicial re-interpretation of the meaning of 'substantial'.[9]

Definition widening based on a change in wording, legal interpretation and/or social understanding is both long-term and ongoing. Amilon et al. (2021) note that with the deinstitutionalisation of disability care, and with increased advocacy by disability groups, the medical model of disability dominant in the 1970s and 1980s has given way to the social model. In the UK, we have seen legal definitions become less prescriptive and restrictive and public awareness, cultural interpretation and social acceptance broaden. Disability prevalence under the most recent LFS socio-legal definition expanded from 17% to 20% of the working-age population between 2013 and 2021.[10] The socio-cultural expansion is not the only explanation of the increase in the disability prevalence rate but seems the most likely. Others include an increase in the incidence of underlying functional impairment leading to activity-limitation (unlikely outside war-time or a pandemic) or an increase in activity-limitation arising from a fixed level of impairment because, for example, normal day-to-day activities (including work) are becoming more complex and more demanding (see Foster & Wass, 2013). The latter is countered by assistive technology and home-working which make some tasks more accessible. With the exception of functional deterioration relative to demands, these explanations imply a change in the composition of disabled people towards those with less severe activity-limitation and greater proximity to employment. As we shall see in the following section, a change in the composition of disabled people confounds trends in indicators of disability inequality.

National Reporting: Interpreting Trends on Progress

Having examined some of the difficulties encountered in the measurement of disability at the national level and the 'plasticity' of the socio-legal definition, we

---

8 These were removed from the LFS questionnaire in 2013.

9 Also in 2013. See footnote 6.

10 The increase in reporting of mental health conditions has been particularly pronounced (see Jones & Wass, 2013).

consider one of the consequences for its use as a measure of progress on narrowing disability employment disadvantage. In fact, increasing recognition of poor progress on this national equality indicator was an important prompt for action (and information) at the organisational level. Equally, difficulties encountered in national data collection are relevant to organisations when measuring and monitoring the proportion of the workforce that is disabled and in-work disability-related gaps, such as related to pay, particularly when comparisons are made across organisations and across time where definitions and understandings differ.

The confounding effects of the widening disability definition discussed above are illustrated in the example of the government's targeting of two employment-related disability equality indicators. The first government commitment (or target) for narrowing the disability employment gap (DEG) was set in 2015. It was to halve the DEG over the course of five years. The DEG measures the percentage point difference in the employment rate between non-disabled and disabled people and has been tracked by the UK government from 2010 using data collected in the LFS. Progress on this scale would have been unprecedented and, without a substantial (and unprecedented) investment in policy, it was reckless in its ambition. This soon became clear to ministers and the commitment was changed in 2017 to achieving one million more disabled people in employment over ten years.

Table 4.1 reports progress on these two commitments between 2013 and 2020, the period after which the Equality Act definition of disability was introduced in the LFS. Also reported is a third indicator which controls for the confounding effect of increasing disability prevalence discussed above. The number of disabled people in employment, the absolute measure which has been targeted from 2017, is reported in column (i). The DEG, a relative measure which was targeted between 2015 and 2017, is reported in column (v). The final column (vii) reports the proportion of working-age people who are prevented from working by disability (PWD). It is a composite measure comprising the product of the prevalence rate (vi) and the DEG. This is a measure developed by academics to explore the distorting effects of the expanding disability prevalence rate on the DEG (see Berthoud, 2011; Jones & Wass, 2013; Wass & Jones, 2020).

From the bottom row of Table 4.1, progress looks very different according to the choice of indicator. The number of disabled people in employment (column i) increased by almost 50 per cent. Between 2015 and 2020, this measure increased by 1.06 million of which a 0.68 million increase was from 2017 to 2020. This presents as excellent progress in terms of the one-million commitment. The DEG (column v) measures the difference between the employment rate for non-disabled (column iii) and disabled people (column iv) and narrowed from 33.7 to 29.0 percentage points. Here performance is positive (4.7 percentage points) but falls short of the commitment to halve the DEG, which required a narrowing of 16.7 points. The composite PWD measure (column vii) indicates no progress since 2013. This is because the falling DEG is matched by increasing disability prevalence, consistent with the latter

Table 4.1: Disability and employment 2013–2020.

	Number in employment (million)		Employment rate (%)		DEG percentage point (v)	Disability prevalence rate % (vi)	PWD % (vii)
	Disabled people (i)	Non-disabled people (ii)	Non-disabled (iii)	Disabled (iv)			
2013	2.9	26.0	77.4	43.7	33.7	16.6	5.6
2020	4.3	26.9	81.5	52.5	29.0	19.9	5.8
% change	*47.5*	*3.3*	*5.3*	*20.1*	*−13.9*	*20.2*	*3.5*

Source: ONS Table A08 (August 2021).
Notes: Author-calculated annual averages from the quarterly figures published by ONS from the LFS. The choice of 2013 and 2020 are determined by the availability of consistent disability statistics. Disability-specific impacts of Covid-19 are not evident in employment data for 2020.

arising due to socio-cultural expansion of the definition and being associated with a reduction in the average severity of activity-limitation.

The definition of disability, both within legislation and the LFS, is consistent from 2013 so that an increased propensity to report disability from this date (column vi) arises from changes in public understanding, interpretation, and acceptance rather than a change in question wording. The confounding effects of these changes arise because of the impact on the characteristics of people defined as disabled. A widening of the definition of disability for cultural rather than functional reasons lowers the functional threshold and has the effect of reducing the average severity of activity-limitation among disabled people and, as a result, increases the employment rate.[11] The effect of this is to narrow the DEG, but the employment prospects for the same disabled person reporting at the beginning and end of the period could have remained unchanged.

Three implications for organisational reporting arise from the results in Table 4.1. First, the questioning of progress on disability-related employment inequality has motivated an extension of government policy, including towards the workplace drivers of disability-related disadvantage. Secondly, as measuring disability prevalence is central to concerns over national progress, it also needs to be central to employers in organisational monitoring. Given the complexities in measurement, organisations need clear guidance and support from government in order to collect meaningful and comparable statistics on organisational disability inequality. In short, organisational measurement must be a government-led national project.

---

11 Evidence from the National Audit Office to the HoCWPC (2021, Q28, p. 13) indicates that the increase in disability reporting is a particular feature of those in employment, "it is only people who are in employment where the trend has happened" and "it is a pretty staggering number".

Thirdly, the definition of disability, and the disability prevalence rate and composition of disabled people it generates, underpins disability equality statistics, not just the DEG, but workforce composition, the disability pay gap (DPG) and gaps in recruitment, promotion and job satisfaction. In Table 4.1, changing prevalence confounds the national DEG. For the organisation, growth in workplace prevalence may reflect increasing reporting among existing employees who increasingly self-identify as disabled (see footnote 11) as well as increased recruitment and retention of disabled people. As with trends in national statistics, inter-organisation comparisons will be distorted by differences in reporting propensity across organisations, such as those driven by organisational equality culture and management support.

The DPG is subject to a further complicating factor since it is measured conditional on employment. Where organisations increase the employment of disabled people, it is likely that recruitment will be biased towards less skilled or experienced workers into relatively low pay jobs creating a corresponding compositional shift among disabled workers. The impact of this compositional shift towards entry-level jobs among disabled workers, both nationally and within organisations, is to reduce the average pay of disabled workers and widen the DPG. The potential conflict between the two headline organisational indicators of increasing the proportion of disabled employees and a widening DPG was noted by the Disability Minister as a reason for not recommending DPG reporting for organisations (House of Commons Work and Pensions Committee [HoCWPC], 2021, para. 37). As with tracking progress on the DEG, there is an equivalent prevalence adjustment available for the DPG at national and organisational levels. Where the DPG is reported as a percentage gap, this requires dividing the DPG by the proportion of employees who are disabled nationally or within the organisation.

Organisational Measurement and Analysis of Disability Equality in the UK

Our starting point for information on disability at the organisational level is WERS (2011), the latest in a series of nationally representative periodic matched employer-employee surveys sampled across British workplaces with five or more employees. WERS data has supported virtually all the UK studies on disability and the workplace (for example, Hoque et al., 2018; Jones, 2016; Jones et al., 2021; Jones & Latreille, 2010; Woodhams & Corby, 2007) and is used here to highlight patterns of disability prevalence and disability monitoring. A management questionnaire (MQ) is completed by the person with responsibility for employment relations in 2,680 workplaces and an employee questionnaire (EQ) is sent to a random sample of up to 25 employees in each workplace.

Disability prevalence is measured in the MQ and EQ. Managers are asked to report the percentage of the workforce who are disabled and employees are asked to self-report activity-limiting disability.[12] The data reveal a large discrepancy with employers reporting an average of 1.4% of their workforce as disabled compared to an average of 9.1% from the sample of employees. This provides a first indication of the challenges around accurate data collection on disability at the organisational level (see Jones & Latreille, 2010; Woodhams & Corby, 2007).

The MQ collects data on five workplace-level equality practices across a range of protected characteristics (see Table 4.2 for details). This is supplemented with information on whether accessibility of the workplace for disabled people has been assessed and whether applications from disabled people are encouraged. Two of these practices require that disability is measured among existing employees: monitoring disability in relation to promotions and reviewing the relative pay of disabled employees. Table 4.2 reports the use of these practices across all workplaces and separately for the public and private sectors. In 2011, just less than half of workplaces had assessed their accessibility to disabled people. For the two practices requiring measurement of disability among employees, practice adoption was much lower with 8% monitoring promotion and 3% reviewing relative pay by disability. This also contrasts with the 19% of workplaces monitoring recruitment and selection by disability, which requires measurement of disability among job applicants. Albeit dated, the figures suggest a very low level of disability equality monitoring at British workplaces. To the extent that absence of monitoring reflects the absence of data collection on disability among current employees, these results undermine proposals for the reporting of organisational measures including in relation to existing initiatives such as public sector procurement and *Disability Confident*.

Consistent with previous evidence, and the additional duties required under the Public Sector Equality Duty (PSED) from 2010, the public sector makes greater use of disability equality practices. For example, nearly 55% of public sector workplaces monitor recruitment and selection by disability compared to 11% in the private sector. Again, however, within the public sector, there is much lower use of practices which require organisational measurement of disability, including the review of relative pay at 15%.

Further and more recent exploration of organisational disability data outside of WERS is hampered by its sparse and ad-hoc nature. This has severely restricted academic research on the relationship between organisational practice and disability inequality in the UK. Where collection occurs, it is through a variety of methods,

---

12 Employers are asked to provide the number (or percentage) of employees with a 'long-term disability that affects the amount or type of work they can do'. Employees are asked "Are your day-to-day activities limited because of a health problem or disability that has lasted, or is expected to last, at least 12 months?", with the following response options: "No"; "Yes, limited a little"; or "Yes, limited a lot." The latter two responses are aggregated to form activity-limiting disability.

Table 4.2: Workplace equality practices in relation to disability, 2011.

Workplace practice (%)	All establishments	Public sector	Private sector
Monitor recruitment and selection	19.3	54.7	11.0
Monitor promotions	7.7	26.7	3.4
Review recruitment and selection procedures for indirect discrimination	16.4	45.1	10.1
Review promotion procedures for indirect discrimination	9.4	27.3	5.0
Review relative pay	3.2	14.6	1.4
Assessed accessibility of workplace to disabled people	47.2	78.5	39.8
Procedures to encourage applications from disabled people	7.6	31.0	2.9

Notes: WERS 2011 MQ. Figures are weighted and refer to the percentage of workplaces.

including self-declarations at the recruitment stage, periodic updating of HR records, and via staff attitude surveys, and typically uses different definitions of disability. Even among public sector employers and 'best practice' private sector employers, disability is often not defined according to the Equality Act, nor regularly updated. Within the public sector, where there is an obligation to collect and report on disability in the workforce, data collection is by employee self-declaration via HR records. Analysis of data from the Annual Civil Service Employment Survey (2021) demonstrates the challenge of non-disclosure.[13] Across the Civil Service, 77% of employees declare their disability status with 6% explicitly refusing and 18% failing to respond. While 14% of the workforce with a disability status are disabled, this represents 10% of all employees. However, the variability in response rates across departments (from less than 10% [e.g., Scottish Courts and Tribunals Service] to 100% [e.g., the Met Office]) limits internal comparability. Such difficulties are exacerbated in inter-organisation comparisons where there is a lack of consistency in the definition of disability and methods of data collection. While measurement problems are understandable given the conceptual and practical challenges in defining disability and collecting data discussed earlier, they severely restrict the value of any data collected, limiting comparisons across organisations and time.

Organisational Measurement and Monitoring in Government Disability Policy

The government has sought to harness the efforts of organisations in achieving its commitment to reduce disability employment disadvantage, including through

---

13 See https://www.gov.uk/government/statistics/civil-service-statistics-2021.

enhancements to *Disability Confident*, and the *Public Services Social Value Act*. The *VRF* offered a limited attempt by government to provide guidance to organisations to start collecting and reporting on workforce composition by disability. This has been superseded by a legislative proposal, the *Workforce Information Bill,* which covers statutory reporting on the pay gap and employment proportion for disability. The following considers each initiative from the point of view of disability measurement, monitoring and reporting.

Recognising the low profile of disability within organisational practice, *Disability Confident* (2016) aimed to encourage employers to adopt equality practices towards the better management of disabled job seekers and employees. It re-badged an almost identical scheme called Two Ticks started in 1990. Employers sign up to *Disability Confident* at three levels. At Level 1 (Committed), there are five commitments concerning the treatment of disabled people in relation to access and support at recruitment and in employment. Commitments extend at Level 2 (Employer) and Level 3 (Leader) to include promotion and retention and an explanatory narrative. The emphasis is on process rather than outcome and on encouragement without scrutiny or sanction. There is no external monitoring on whether the five commitments are actively used or whether they are effective in increasing the employment of disabled people. From the inception of Two Ticks, there was no requirement on employers to measure and report on disability within their workforce and no definition of disability was provided which might facilitate this. From 2021, organisations applying or renewing at *Disability Confident* Level 3 are required to use the *VRF* ('where possible') to report on the proportion of disabled employees. However, there is no requirement that organisations employ a single disabled person or make progress on this. It is unsurprising, therefore, that a comparison between organisations with and without Two Ticks within WERS 2011 found no difference in the adoption of six of the seven equality practices analysed in Table 2, or in the proportion of disabled people employed (Bacon & Hoque, 2019).

In the *Public Services Social Value Act* (2012), the government seeks to leverage organisational commitment to employ disabled people through public sector procurement. The Act allows government departments to use a social value model to assess and score suppliers. There is no evidence on whether government contracts have been awarded on the basis of the employment of disabled people as a social benefit or indeed whether any contractors have bid on this basis. Given that organisational reporting and departmental 'consideration' of social value are both voluntary, and that financial cost has traditionally been the overwhelmingly important criterion, it seems unlikely, outside of the Department for Work and Pensions, that they have. An extension to the Act, launched in 2021, requires that all major procurements across all government departments 'explicitly evaluate' social value (where appropriate), rather than 'just consider' it.[14] The extension requires that so-cial value accounts for a minimum of 10% of the bid and suggests a range of objectives and target groups which qualify under social value. The employment of disabled people is an explicit criterion (alongside climate change, Covid-recovery, employee wellbeing and community integration), though no definition of disability or metric for reporting is provided.[15]

Recent implementation (January 2021) precludes evaluation, but it is not clear that there is either the intention or ability to evaluate the effectiveness of the extension. Without a standard for reporting on a common definition of disability which comes with an expectation of scrutiny, the prospect of evaluation and impact are low.

The *VRF*, launched in November 2018, was primarily a response to the Stevenson-Farmer Review (2017) into the prevalence and experience of people with mental ill-health in the workplace.[16] Reporting was later extended to disability more generally in response to findings from the government consultation (2017) on the role of work in promoting health and wellbeing for disabled people, *Improving Lives*.[17] The resulting framework provides little more than encouragement to employers to report on their activities in relation to recruitment and retention of disabled people and to measure and report their workforce composition by disability status. The *VRF* was conceived of and presented as a separate and stand-alone initiative despite its obvious links to both the procurement and accreditation initiatives. Weaknesses in the framework limit its effectiveness in terms of its own objectives and in terms of underpinning other government policies, which rely on organisational measurement and reporting (for a detailed discussion see Bacon et al., 2020). Methods of data collection are left to individual employers, the recommended definition of disability is not mandatory, and there is no requirement to publish the figures.

Importantly, the definition of disability recommended in the framework is not aligned to the Equality Act or National Statistics.[18] This precludes identifying employees covered by legislation and benchmarking against nationally representative statistics. The absence of a mandatory definition also precludes benchmarking across organisations. In any event, the use of different data collection methods (HR

---

14 https://assets.publishing.service.gov.uk/government/uploads/system/uploads/attachment_data/file/921437/PPN-06_20-Taking-Account-of-Social-Value-in-the-Award-of-Central-Government-Contracts.pdf
15 In contrast the US, voluntary self-identification of disability form CC-305 which supports US federal government section 503 of the Rehabilitation Act of 1973 specifies the definition of disability and the reporting metric.
16 https://assets.publishing.service.gov.uk/government/uploads/system/uploads/attachment_data/file/658145/thriving-at-work-stevenson-farmer-review.pdf
17 https://assets.publishing.service.gov.uk/government/uploads/system/uploads/attachment_data/file/663399/improving-lives-the-future-of-work-health-and-disability.PDF
18 'Do you consider yourself to have a disability or long-term health condition (mental health and/or physical health)?'

records or anonymous staff surveys) renders reported statistics non-comparable even where definitions are consistent. The contrast with the US procurement reporting framework on disability where organisations report on a standard metric calculated from a standard question or the UK 2017 Gender Pay Gap (GPG) reporting legislation where, in addition, there is public access to the standardised statistics, could not be greater.

Mandatory reporting in the form of the *Workforce Information Bill (2020)* proposes a further amendment to section 78 of the Equality Act (2010) to extend pay gap reporting to disabled employees. Legislation for GPG reporting provides a model of successful reporting practice. Here reporting is compulsory, in a standard tightly prescribed format with submissions published centrally to facilitate comparisons. Disability status is more difficult to define and, given current workplace representation at around 14%, there are further difficulties with smaller sample sizes. However, the proposal to measure and report on the DPG and percentage of employees who are disabled is feasible and permits the DPG-adjustment for disability prevalence at the workplace as explained above.

Mandatory reporting relies on good measurement where the benefits of transparency and comparison are realised only with standardised data collection and a standardised measure of disability. Standardisation in measurement and reporting is a pre-requisite for other government policy interventions and evaluation, including procurement decisions and *Disability Confident* accreditation. For the government, it would signal which organisations contribute to its DEG target; for the public, it illustrates organisational equality practice and workforce diversity; and, for disabled job applicants, which organisations might be more attractive to work for.

Recommendations for Organisational Disability Measurement

The *VRF* demonstrates government failure to recognise the critical importance of accurate measurement for monitoring and reporting on disability, and thereby undermines its commitment to reducing disability-related employment disadvantage through harnessing the efforts of employers. We build on established CSO national practice to develop a set of recommendations for organisational data collection and measurement as a means of achieving monitoring and reporting which is accurate and meaningful, and data that provide a useful resource for employers, government and future academic research.

(i) *A government-led national level project* Organisational measurement and reporting needs to be co-produced with organisations but ultimately requires government co-ordination to ensure standardised methods of data collection and definitions and the promotion of high organisational and employee response rates. The use of benchmarks either from national statistics or from good practice peers, requires data collection which is comparable across organisations and with national standards.

(ii) *A definition of disability* By adopting the Equality Act definition, and LFS question wording, the information collected by organisations becomes more meaningful and valuable through (i) being comparable across employers, (ii) facilitating comparisons with national/regional and sectoral statistics and (iii) adopting a definition which aligns to employer obligations under UK equality legislation.

(iii) *Data collection method* There are two methods for data collection: disclosure on HR records and via an anonymous response within a staff survey. The advantage of the latter is the higher potential willingness of employees to disclose disability and the ability to link information on disability to a wide range of in-work outcomes collected in the same survey. However, many organisations do not run staff surveys (38% of large organisations; Bacon & Hoque, 2019) and anonymous responses do not identify disabled employees who may be entitled to protection and reasonable adjustments under the Equality Act. The HR disclosure method avoids the burden of extra data collection and it identifies employees covered by the legislation. Through a link to employee pay records, it also enables a straightforward calculation of the DPG. The likely disadvantage is a lower response rate due to employee concerns over disclosure (see below).

(iv) *Enhancing disclosure* Disabled employees are discouraged from disclosing their disability if they fear a negative reaction from their employer and/or co-workers (von Schrader et al., 2014). The extent of reporting may then reflect the equality environment within the organisation itself. Under a national reporting regime, with a focus on organisational disability workforce composition, the organisation has an interest in encouraging disclosure and identifying its barriers. The inclusion of organisational rates of disability disclosure within a final government reporting framework potentially offers another incentive for organisations to support employee disclosure.

(v) *Mandatory or voluntary reporting* Experience of organisational reporting on a voluntary basis in relation to GPGs is that most employers do not engage. Prior to legislation, six organisations reported on a voluntary basis (Milner, 2021). In the first year of statutory GPG reporting (2018–19), there was 100 per cent employer compliance, with 48 per cent publishing action plans (Government Equalities Office, 2018). The publication of a high-profile statistic in a standard format creates a level playing field and enables employers, employees and stakeholders to benchmark the organisation's position and progress against others.

(vi) *Which measures and indicators?* Outcome measures are preferred over softer indicators (for example, the presence of equality policies and practices) as the subject of reporting, as the latter might not be effective or actively used. In fact, it is a focus on outcomes which is likely to promote the effective design and application of supporting policies and practices. Consistent with the national focus on the DEG, there is consensus that the initial outcome indicator should be the percentage of employees who are disabled. This relative measure will facilitate comparisons across organisations.

There is an expectation that GPG reporting will also extend to other protected groups (Milner, 2021) and a measure of disability is pre-requisite to DPG reporting. Monitoring of the DPG (and any other disability equality measure) across organisations and over time will be subject to the confounding effects of a changing prevalence of disability within the workforce. Such confounding effects can be explored at the organisational level using measures adjusted for workforce disability prevalence.

(vii) *Scrutiny* The reliability of reported metrics depends on a process of verification. While verification is likely to be difficult, without some sort of scrutiny, and threat of legal sanction or adverse publicity, there are incentives for organisations to overstate disability prevalence among the workforce and its improvement over time. Reliability might be increased through the reporting of disability metrics in annual company accounts signed off by the insert Chief Executive Officer (CEO).

Conclusion

As in many countries, disability-related employment disadvantage is evident from UK national statistics. It is monitored and targeted by the UK government where experience has shown that disability measurement is difficult and trends in progress require careful interpretation. Lack of progress over a long period of intervention has prompted a shift in focus from a supply- to a demand-side approach and to the role of organisations in reducing the DEG. However, developments in policy and practice, and the academic research necessary to design and assess interventions, is compromised by a lack of high-quality data on disability at the organisational level.

The importance of measurement and reporting was raised in three anniversary reflections:

> the government should require larger employers (those with 250+ employees) to publish data on the proportion of their employees who are disabled. (HoCWPC, 2021, p. 19)

> employers should be required to report their workforce disability prevalence to the government. The government should publish these figures. (CSJ, 2021, p. 98)

> the Cabinet Office will consult on workforce reporting on disability for large employers, exploring voluntary and mandatory workplace transparency. (Cabinet Office, 2021, p. 57)

However, without a government lead, and regulation and sanction, few organisations will measure, collect and analyse data on disability. For those that do, the likelihood is that without strong guidance, their value will be undermined by non-standard, non-aligned definitions and ad-hoc data collection.

By understanding the complex nature of disability and the difficulties in national data collection and reporting, we set out recommendations to enhance and enrich organisational data on disability inequality. At the forefront is the quality of disability measurement and, from the analysis of this chapter, we distil three key principles for organisational measurement. First, **consistency** between organisations, over time and with national statistics. This is achieved through a national framework with standardised methods, definitions and reporting requirements. Secondly, **compliance** with the legal definition of disability so that data collection serves multiple purposes and identifies those covered by legislation and with reporting regulation and standards. Finally, maximum **coverage** across organisations through the introduction of mandatory reporting by government which supports employers to identify and reduce barriers to disability disclosure at work. These lessons, critical as the UK develops its approach to measuring disability within organisations, are likely to have international relevance. They would seem particularly important in countries where disability-related labour market inequality is pronounced, organisational data collection is weak or absent, and demand-side policies are being implemented or strengthened.

References

Amilon, A., Hansen, K., Kjaer, A., & Steffensen, T. (2021). Estimating disability prevalence and disability related inequalities: Does the choice of measure matter? *Social Science & Medicine*, *272*, 113740. https://doi.org/10.1016/j.socscimed.2021.113740

Bacon, N., & Hoque, K. (2019). *Two Ticks or no ticks? An assessment of Two Ticks 'Positive About Disabled People' certification*. Briefing Note, Disability at Work.

Bacon, N., Hoque, K., Jones, M., & Wass, V. (2020). *Recommendations for amendments to the framework for voluntary reporting on disability, mental health and wellbeing*. Briefing Note, Disability at Work.

Barnes, C., & Mercer, G. (2005). Disability, work, and welfare: Challenging the social exclusion of disabled people. *Work Employment & Society*, *19*(3), 527–545. https://doi.org/10.1177%2F0950017005055669

Berthoud, R. (2011, January). *Trends in the employment of disabled people in Britain* (Working Paper No. 2011-3). Institute of Economic and Social Research, University of Essex.

Cabinet Office. (2021, July 28). *National Disability Strategy, Part 1: Practical steps now to improve disabled people's everyday lives*. U.K. Government Command paper no. CP 512. https://www.gov.uk/government/publications/national-disability-strategy/part-1-practical-steps-now-to-improve-disabled-peoples-everyday-lives

Centre for Social Justice (CSI). (2021, March). *Now is the time: A report by the CSJ Disability Commission*.

Foster, D., & Wass, V. (2013). Disability in the labour market: An exploration of concepts of the "ideal worker" and organisational "fit" that disadvantage employees with impairments. *Sociology*, *47*(4), 705–721. https://doi.org/10.1177%2F0038038512454245

Government Equalities Office. (2018). *Gender Pay Gap Information Regulations 2017: Summary of reported data for 2017/18*. GEO-RR-005. https://www.gov.uk/government/publications/gender-pay-gap-information-regulations-summary-of-201718-data

Grönvik, L. (2009). Defining disability: Effects of disability concepts on research outcomes. *International Journal of Social Research Methodology*, *12*(1), 1–18. https://doi.org/10.1080/13645570701621977

Hoque, K., Jones, M., Wass, V., & Bacon, N. (2018). Are high-performance work practices enabling or disabling? Exploring the relationship between HPWPs and work-related disability disadvantage. *Human Resource Management*, *57*(2), 499–513. https://doi.org/10.1002/hrm.21881

House of Commons Work and Pensions Committee (HoCWPC). (2021). *Disability employment gap*, HC189 30 July. https://committees.parliament.uk/work/751/disability-employment-gap/publications/

Jones, M., Hoque, K., Wass, V., & Bacon, N. (2021). Inequality and the economic cycle: Disabled employees' experience of work during the Great Recession in Britain. *British Journal of Industrial Relations*, *59*(3), 788–815. https://doi.org/10.1111/bjir.12577

Jones, M., & Wass, V. (2013). Understanding changing disability-related employment gaps in Britain 1998–2011. *Work Employment and Society*, *27*(6), 982–1003. https://doi.org/10.1177%2F0950017013475372

Jones, M., & Wass, V. (2018). *Defining disability in government surveys*. Briefing Note, Disability at Work.

Jones, M. K. (2016). Disability and perceptions of work and management. *British Journal of Industrial Relations*, *54*(1), 83–113.

Jones, M. K., & Latreille, P. (2010). Disability and earnings: Are employer characteristics important? *Economic Letters*, *106*, 191–194. http://dx.doi.org/10.1016/j.econlet.2009.11.017

Milner, S. (2021, May 24). Ethnicity pay gap: Why the UK needs mandatory reporting. *The Conversation*. https://theconversation.com/ethnicity-pay-gap-why-the-uk-needs-mandatory-reporting-160735

von Schrader, S., Malzer, V., & Bruyère, S. (2014). Perspectives on disability disclosure: The importance of employer practices and workplace climate. *Employee Responsibilities and Rights Journal*, *26*, 237–255. https://doi.org/10.1007/s10672-013-9227-9

Wass, V., & Jones, M. (2020). *Measuring disability and interpreting trends in disability-related disadvantage*. Briefing Note, Disability at Work.

Woodhams C., & Corby, S. (2007). Then and now: Disability legislation and employers' practices in the UK. *British Journal of Industrial Relations*, *45*(3), 556–580. https://doi.org/10.1111/j.1467-8543.2007.00628.x

Part 2: **Intersectionality**

Lisa Schur, Yana van der Meulen Rodgers, and Douglas Kruse

5 COVID-19 and Employment Losses for Workers with Disabilities: An Intersectional Approach

Abstract: This chapter studies the disparate effects of COVID-19 on workers with physical and mental disabilities, paying particular attention to an intersectional analysis by disability, race/ethnicity, and gender. Results indicate that White and Black women with disabilities experienced relatively greater employment losses during the pandemic compared to White men without disabilities. Our decomposition procedures reveal that the disability employment gap increased during the pandemic, and a substantial portion of the increased gap is explained by differential effects of the pandemic across occupations. The unexplained component of the disability gap also rose, which could partly reflect growing discrimination against people with disabilities.

Keywords: COVID-19, disability, race, gender, unemployment, jobs, intersectional

Introduction

The COVID-19 pandemic has caused immense social and economic harm around the globe. In the U.S., tens of millions of workers lost their jobs starting in March 2020, with a prolonged period of high unemployment and persistent hardships well into 2021. Hourly, contingent, and lower-wage employees were more likely to be fired, furloughed, and suffer pandemic-related unemployment and economic harm (Bartik et al., 2020). People with disabilities are almost twice as likely to fall into those employment categories (Schur, 2003). Women and people of color also faced relatively greater

Acknowledgements: We thank Peter Blanck, Thomas Masterson, Corine Joy Tamayo, Sophie Mitra, and participants in the URPE panel on COVID-19 at the 2021 ASSA meetings for their useful comments.

Funding: This line of study was supported in part by grant from the National Institute on Disability, Independent Living, and Rehabilitation Research (NIDILRR) for the Rehabilitation Research and Training (RRTC) on Employment Policy: Center for Disability-Inclusive Employment Policy Research, Grant #90RTEM0006-01-00; and for the RRTC on Employer Practices Leading to Successful Employment Outcomes Among People with Disabilities, Grant #90RTEM0008-01-00. The views provided herein do not necessarily reflect the official policies of NIDILRR nor do they imply endorsement by the Federal Government.

Lisa Schur, Yana van der Meulen Rodgers, and Douglas Kruse, Rutgers University

https://doi.org/10.1515/9783110743647-006

employment losses as they were disproportionately represented in sectors with the most business closures (Alon et al., 2020; Bahn et al., 2020). The effects are were likely to be even greater for women and people of color who have disabilities as well as for other individuals with multiple minority identities (Blanck, 2020; Blanck et al., 2020).

Prior to the pandemic, fewer than one in three (30.9%) working-age people with disabilities were employed, as compared to three-fourths (74.6%) of their nondisabled peers (BLS, 2020). This chasm in employment exists even though people with disabilities have the same motivation for employment and markers of employability as similarly-situated people without disabilities (Ali et al., 2011). While the employment gap between people with and without disabilities generally increased up until 2015 (Kraus et al., 2017; Lauer and Houtenville, 2017), the gap narrowed in the tight labor markets from 2015 to 2019, with a gain of 4.0 points in the employment rate for people with disabilities compared to 2.4 points for people without disabilities (BLS, 2016, 2020).

The COVID-19 pandemic erased many of these gains and exacerbated the employment disparity between people with and without disabilities. To explore this assertion, our chapter uses Current Population Survey (CPS) data to examine the employment status of workers with and without disabilities following the onset of the COVID-19 pandemic relative to previous years. Based on earlier research finding greater job loss rates among workers with disabilities during economic recessions, we expect to find that COVID-19 played a larger role in employment losses for individuals with disabilities compared to individuals without disabilities.

Background: Employment by Disability, Gender, and Race

Why are people with disabilities less likely to be employed? While education gaps and disability income support from the government are important factors, employer attitudes and organizational culture also contribute to their low employment rates. Audit studies show that employers are less likely to express interest in job applicants with disabilities even when their resumes are identical to those of applicants without disabilities, and the disabilities are irrelevant to job performance (Ameri et al., 2018, Baert, 2018). Other studies have shown that, once hired, many workers with disabilities must contend with negative attitudes from supervisors and co-workers that limit career growth and the quality of their work life, as well as with structural barriers in workplace policies (Ren et al., 2008; Schur et al., 2013). They are more likely to work in low-wage, part time, and contingent jobs (Schur et al., 2013) where they receive lower pay and benefits compared to workers without disabilities in similar jobs (Schur, 2002, 2003). Disability accommodations are generally well-received by co-workers, but they sometimes generate resentment (Schur et al., 2014). Employees with disabilities also face a pay gap after accounting for productive characteristics such as education and job experience, and are more likely to be laid off by employers when times are bad (Kruse et al., 2018; Mitra & Kruse, 2016).

Workers with disabilities are underrepresented in white-collar jobs and overrepresented in service and blue-collar jobs (BLS, 2020; Schur et al., 2020). While these types of jobs are less amenable to work from home, pre-pandemic data show that people with disabilities were in fact about 20% more likely to work at home than otherwise-similar workers without disabilities. This differential points to the benefits that work-from-home accommodations can provide to persons with mobility impairments or other conditions that make it difficult or risky to work a regular schedule at the employer's location. During the pandemic, service and blue-collar jobs were especially hard-hit with closures – the sectors in which people with disabilities are disproportionately employed. The restructuring of many jobs during the pandemic, however, may ultimately benefit many people with disabilities by making employers more willing to accommodate the need for home-based work (Schur et al., 2020).

The experience of disability is influenced by other salient characteristics such as gender and race. Women with disabilities, for example, may have different experiences than men with disabilities based on how they are socialized and the different gender roles they are expected to fulfill (Fine & Asch, 1988; Hanna & Rogovsky, 1991). Multiple marginalized identities may combine not simply in an additive way, but may interact to create unique forms of disadvantage (Hanna & Rogovsky, 1991). Women with disabilities, for example, can face extra challenges in becoming employed as a disability may reinforce negative stereotypes about the abilities and job performance of women. Men with disabilities, however, may face extra challenges both economically and psychologically if their disability limits their employment and ability to fulfill the traditional male "breadwinner" role. The effects of gender and disability combine to give women with disabilities especially low employment rates (16.5% compared to 19.7% for men with disabilities in 2019), although the disability employment gap is larger among men than among women (Schur et al., 2013: 161–162; BLS, 2020). Disabled women's especially low employment rate contributes to their higher poverty rate compared to both men with disabilities and women without disabilities (Schur et al., 2013). In the context of the pandemic, women who bear primary childcare responsibility may face extra employment challenges if they must spend time at home supervising children kept from attending school in person. This additional care work can pose particular challenges for women who have to contend with the time and energy demands of a disability.

Similarly, disability may interact with race in affecting employment and human capital outcomes. Bailey and Mobley note that "Much of the Black experience is shaped by an understanding of Black bodies as a productive labor force, leaving little room for an identity-based approach to disability," and that "Ableism and notions of disability are a major component of anti-Black racism" (2019: 25). Native Americans and Blacks have the highest prevalence of disability in the U.S., reflecting lack of access to healthcare and other social disparities (Schur et al., 2013). The disability employment gap is larger among Blacks than among White non-Latinx, resulting in an especially low employment rate among Blacks with disabilities (15.6% in 2019) compared both to Blacks without disabilities (64.9%) and White non-Latinx with disabilities (19.7%)(BLS, 2020). This disparity may partly stem from the extra difficulties faced by both Blacks and Latinx with disabilities in school-to-work transitions (Hasnain & Balcazar, 2009). As among women with disabilities, low employment rates contribute to especially high poverty rates among Blacks and Latinx with disabilities (Schur et al., 2013: 184). The interaction of disability with race and ethnicity also shows up in political and social measures, particularly in insufficient access to services and equipment, reduced social support, and inadequate policies for equitable treatment and accommodations (Gary et al., 2011; Schur et al., 2013).

Disability may combine with both race and gender in ways that create particular disadvantages. Degener (2011:31) writes of the need for greater awareness of multidimensional discrimination: "Discrimination at the intersection of race, gender and disability will rarely be composed of discrete jigsaw pieces corresponding exactly to the three separate grounds. More commonly, it will be based on a mélange of overlapping and undefined prejudices and stigmas." Bailey and Mobley (2019) argue that both Disability Studies and Black Studies should have a comprehensively intersectional approach that takes account of the particular experiences of Black women, who spend relatively more time in caring for disabled family members and keeping them connected with members of the community. Having a disability may especially challenge the social role of Black women who are expected to be strong leaders in their families and communities (Hanna & Rogovsky 1991). While some research has examined the intersection of disability with gender and race separately, very little research has explored the intersections of all three dimensions.

Data and Methodology

In this study, employment measures are constructed using data from the CPS, a monthly survey collected by the Bureau of Labor Statistics (BLS), which has a sample of about 1,800,000 individuals per year. It provides data on various demographic characteristics as well as measures of disability based on a six-question set (asked since 2008). The six disability questions identify hearing, vision, cognitive, and mobility impairments, and difficulty with self-care or going outside alone.[1] Because the BLS does not do a seasonal adjustment on the numbers for employment and unemployment by disability status, we do our own seasonal adjustment and reweight the

---

1 These six categories are based on the following six questions: 1) "Is this person deaf or does he/she have serious difficulty hearing?"; 2) "Is this person blind or does he/she have serious difficulty seeing

data accordingly so that the changes we observe in 2020 do not reflect seasonal patterns. We kept all individuals ages 18–64 without missing observations for the key variables in our analysis, leaving a total sample size of 745,036 individuals (comprised of 686,367 people without disabilities and 58,669 people with disabilities).

These data are first used to construct descriptive statistics on employment rates and number of jobs by disability status. These statistics are then broken down by type of disability, gender, race, ethnicity, education, and age, taking an intersectional approach to explore how disability interacts with these characteristics in affecting employment. We also examine employment patterns by disability status in occupations and industries, focusing on the occupations and industries hardest hit by the pandemic. After a brief review of annual trends, we analyze monthly patterns in 2020 during the COVID-19 pandemic. We focus in particular on changes from January to April when there was a large pandemic-related employment drop, and from January to December (accounting for the combined effect of the April drop and the partial recovery since April).

After examining these basic patterns, we run logit regressions to predict the percent change in the likelihood of disability employment, controlling for demographic characteristics, occupation, and industry. The final part of the analysis uses a decomposition approach to examine the extent to which the differences in employment rates between those with and without a disability are explained by differences in observed characteristics, or remains unexplained. The decomposition, which is based on logit regressions for employment status, follows the precedent set by Fairlie (1999, 2003) and is a variation of the common Oaxaca-Blinder decomposition first developed to explain wage gaps (Oaxaca 1973; Blinder 1973). The explained gap is the portion of the gap attributed to disability differences in demographic, occupation, and industry variables; the residual gap is the portion attributed to disability differences in market returns to those characteristics. To best approximate the baseline structure of employment determinants that would exist in the absence of discrimination or other differential treatment based on disability, we use the coefficients from pooled regressions as suggested by Neumark (1988) and Oaxaca and Ransom (1994). The residual (unexplained) employment gap is simply the difference between actual employment rates and predicted employment rates. Note that the CPS contains questions about previous occupation and industry of employment in the past 12 months, so information on occupation and industry is available for individuals who are not currently employed but were

---

even when wearing glasses?"; 3) "Because of a physical, mental, or emotional condition, does this person have serious difficulty concentrating, remembering, or making decisions?"; 4) "Does this person have serious difficulty walking or climbing stairs?"; 5) "Does this person have difficulty dressing or bathing?"; 6) "Because of a physical, mental, or emotional condition, does this person have difficulty doing errands alone such as visiting a doctor's office or shopping?" Respondents may choose more than one category, so the categories are not mutually exclusive.

employed in the past 12 months. Given the importance of industry and occupation in our analysis, we present models with industry and occupation controls, meaning that our regression and decomposition analyses focus on a sub-sample of individuals with strong connections to the job market who are currently employed or have been employed in the past 12 months. This sub-sample has 568,089 observations (547,319 people without disabilities and 20,770 people with disabilities).

The determinants of whether or not individual i is employed in year t are expressed as follows:

$$Y_{it} = \alpha + \beta_1 \, X_{it} + e_{it} \tag{1}$$

The variables in the X matrix include individual characteristics that influence people's employment status: gender, race/ethnicity, educational attainment, marital status, and age. The term e_{it} is an individual-specific idiosyncratic error term. All regressions are weighted using sample weights provided in the CPS, modified to reflect a seasonal adjustment by disability status.

Sample statistics are found in online data appendices.[2] These appendices show large declines in the absolute number of employed individuals between January and April 2020 for all demographic groups among individuals with and without a disability (broken down by gender, race/ethnicity, education, and age). All groups except Latinx workers with disabilities showed at least a partial rebound by December 2020. Those who were doing even better in December 2020 relative to the beginning of the year in terms of employment gains include disabled workers with a Bachelor's degree, and all workers with a graduate degree. The appendices also point to sizeable declines in the absolute number of people employed in most, but not all, occupations and industries between January and April 2020 for both disabled and non-disabled people, with partial recoveries in most categories (and even full recoveries in a few) by December 2020. Occupations with the largest job losses in absolute terms include food preparation, sales, production, and transportation. Finally, sample means in the appendices for all variables used in the regression analysis indicate that the non-disabled and disabled sub-samples are comparable except in the case of employment status, education, and marital status. Individuals with disabilities are less likely to be employed or to have a Bachelor's or graduate degree, and they are more likely to be separated/divorced or widowed. Consistent with their lower average levels of education, people with disabilities tend to be overrepresented in blue-collar and service occupations, and underrepresented in white-collar occupations— the biggest difference is for managerial jobs, held by 11.9% of non-disabled workers and 9.2% of disabled workers.

---

2 Appendix tables are available by request from the lead author.

Trends in Employment: Descriptive Analysis

In looking at longer-term trends, we see that working-age individuals with disabilities had a declining employment rate following the 2008–09 financial crisis through 2014. This decline was considerably sharper and lasted longer than it did for individuals without a disability, as the disabled population experienced a longer lag time in finding new jobs (Figure 5.1). The relative employment of the disabled population improved strongly, however, from 2015 to 2019. Using 2008 as a base year, Figure 5.1 shows that the relative employment rate in 2019 was similar for people with and without disabilities, and there was a sharp decrease for both groups in the 2020 pandemic.

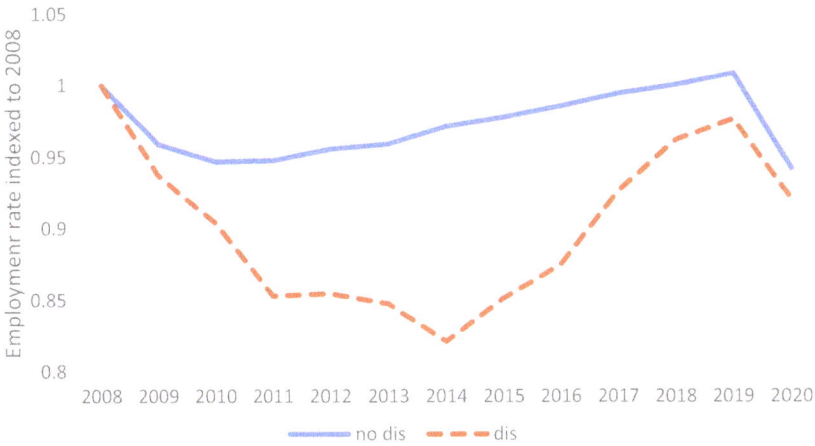

Figure 5.1: Changes in Annual Employment Rates by Disability Status, 2008–2020.

Monthly data for 2020 point to a stronger pandemic-related drop in the number of jobs for workers with disabilities. As shown in Figure 5.2, individuals with disabilities reported a markedly larger decline in the number of jobs in April compared to January (Panel A). Lockdowns, workplace closures, and layoffs, which started in late March 2020 and intensified in April, resulted in enormous job losses across the country. The number of jobs was also slower to bounce back for individuals with disabilities in the summer and fall of 2020. Notably, job losses in 2020 were stratified by disability status, as shown in the figure (Panel B). The most severe employment declines were experienced by people who identified as having trouble with self-care and having trouble with going outside alone. These disability categories are generally considered as indicators of severity, which implies that people with more severe disabilities had the largest employment declines and the most trouble in finding work again as the pandemic wore on. The markedly different employment patterns for people with different types of disabilities supports the point made

Panel A: Overall

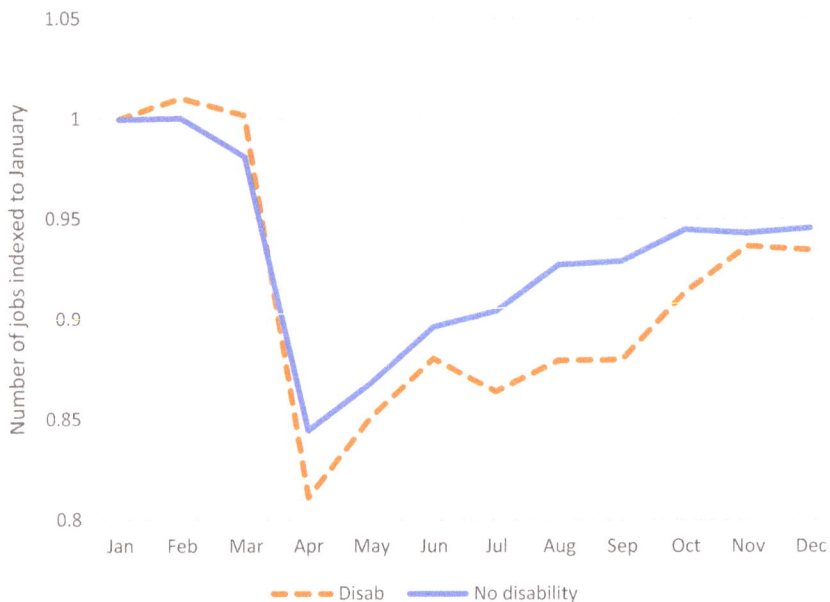

Panel B: By Type of Disability

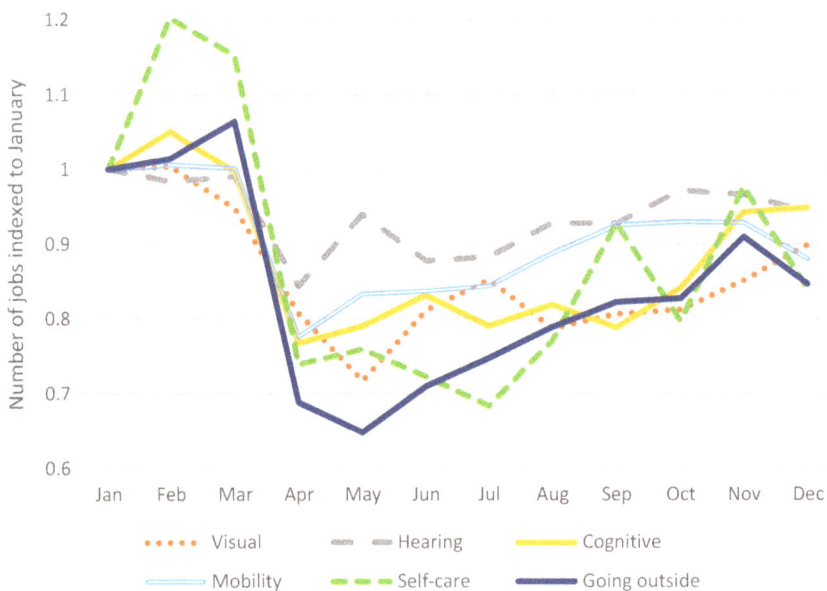

Figure 5.2: Changes in Monthly Employment (Number of Jobs) by Disability Status, 2020.

in Baldwin and Choe (2014) that it is important to examine heterogeneity within the disabled population when examining labor market outcomes.

These patterns are shown in Table 5.1. Overall the employment rate for people with disabilities dropped by 18.9% from January to April in 2020, compared to 15.5% for people without disabilities. Although each drop is statistically significant, the difference between them is not significant (columns 7 and 8). Table 5.1 further shows that individuals with disabilities have considerably lower overall employment rates compared to the non-disabled population, so a drop of about 5 percentage points in the employment rate between January and April (from 31.8% to 26.7%) amounts to a substantial decline given the relatively low starting point. The table also shows that the large employment drops from January to April occurred across types of disabilities, with declines ranging from 15.6% for people with a hearing impediment to 31.1% for people with difficulty going outside. These declines from January to April are both large in magnitude and statistically significant (except for people with self-care limitations, most likely due to a smaller sample size for this type of disability). In contrast, the employment declines for January to December across disability types are smaller in magnitude and mostly not significant.

The employment declines were stratified not only by disability, but also by gender, race/ethnicity, and age, as well as the intersections of these categories. Figure 5.3 shows that the largest employment declines were experienced by female, Black, and middle-aged workers with disabilities. Women and middle-aged workers with disabilities also experienced the slowest recoveries, while Black workers with disabilities showed a surge in employment growth in the fall of 2020 followed by a sharp drop-off at the end of the year. The underlying data are reported in Table 5.2, which shows that the estimated January-April drop was larger among workers with disabilities across almost all demographic categories compared to workers without disabilities in the same categories. For example, among Black workers, total employment dropped 16.4% for people without disabilities and 31.8% for people with disabilities, accounting for a 15.4% disability gap. Only for three out of the 14 demographic groups reported were the employment drops in January to April smaller for people with disabilities: Latinx individuals, people with some college, and those ages 50–64. Note that most of the disability gaps are not statistically significant, largely due to small sample sizes of people with disabilities within the demographic categories (column 3). Also in Table 5.2, the drop for the entire year (January to December) was relatively larger for workers with disabilities compared to workers without disabilities in the majority of demographic categories, but the magnitudes of the drops are not as large as they were in the first quarter. Again the differences between people with and without disabilities are mostly not statistically significant, largely due to the small sample sizes within some of the demographic categories for people with disabilities (e.g., the 11.3% gap among those age 35–49 is significant while the larger 15.4% gap among Black non-Latinx is not significant because the latter sample size is smaller and therefore has a wider margin of error)(column 6).

Table 5.1: Employment by Disability in 2020.

	Total employed (000's)			Employment rate			Percent change in total employed	
	January (1)	April (2)	December (3)	January (4)	April (5)	December (6)	January-April (7)	January-December (8)
No disability	141,586	119,622	133,919	77.6%	65.4%	73.3%	-15.5% **	-5.4% **
Any disability	4,678	3,796	4,373	31.8%	26.7%	29.9%	-18.9% **	-6.5% *
Percent with disability	3.2%	3.1%	3.2%					
Disability type								
Hearing impairment	1,437	1,212	1,354	50.8%	44.7%	47.7%	-15.6% **	-5.8%
Vision impairment	795	643	715	37.1%	33.7%	37.2%	-19.2% **	-10.1%
Cognitive impairment	1,589	1,220	1,507	26.4%	22.2%	25.0%	-23.2% **	-5.1%
Mobility impairment	1,469	1,141	1,293	19.7%	16.4%	17.6%	-22.3% **	-12.0% *
Self-care limitation	248	183	208	10.5%	8.0%	9.5%	-26.1%	-16.1%
Difficulty going outside alone	694	478	588	13.8%	10.1%	12.2%	-31.1% **	-15.4%

Note: *Significantly different from zero at p<.05, **p<.01.

Panel A: By Disability and Gender

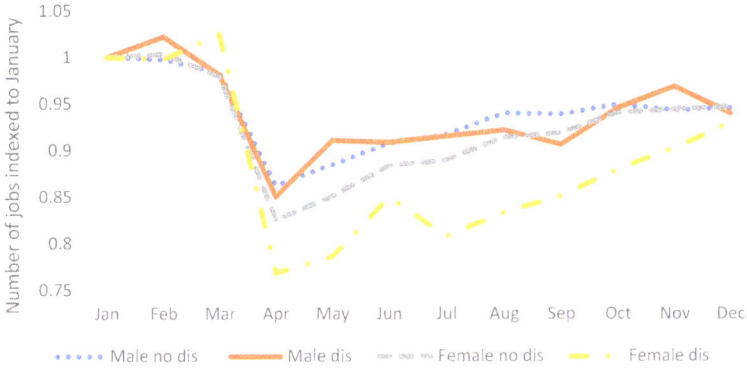

Panel B: By Disability and Race

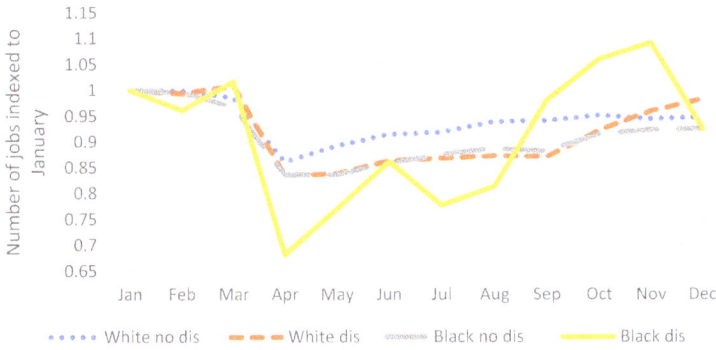

Panel C: By Disability and Age

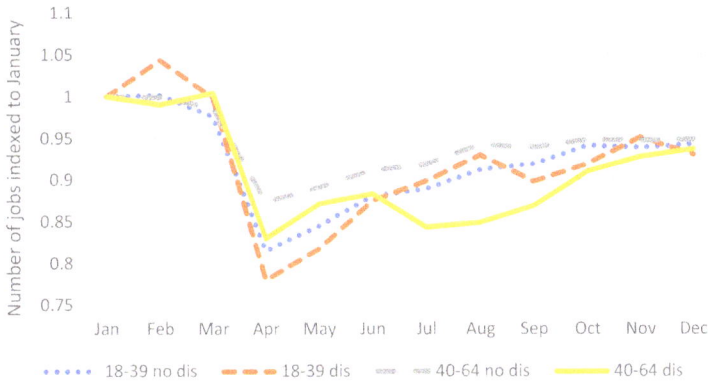

Figure 5.3: Changes in Monthly Employment by Disability and Gender, Race, and Age, 2020.

Table 5.2: Employment Changes by Disability and Demographics in 2020.

	January-April percent change in total employed			January-December percent change in total employed		
	No disability (1)	Disability (2)	Disability gap (3)	No disability (4)	Disability (5)	Disability gap (6)
Overall	−15.5% **	−18.9% **	−3.3%	−5.4% **	−6.5% **	−1.1%
Gender						
Male	−13.8% **	−15.0% **	−1.2%	−5.5% **	−6.0%	−0.6%
Female	−17.5% **	−23.1% **	−5.7%	−5.4% **	−7.0%	−1.7%
Race and ethnicity						
White non-Latinx	−13.9% **	−16.4% **	−2.5%	−5.2% **	−1.7%	3.5%
Black non-Latinx	−16.4% **	−31.8% **	−15.4%	−7.5% **	−7.5%	0.0%
Latinx	−20.1% **	−17.1% *	3.0%	−6.5% **	−20.8% *	−14.3%
Other race/ethnicity	−15.8% **	−25.8% *	−10.1%	−1.9%	−22.0% *	−20.1%
Education						
No HS degree	−24.2% **	−27.3% *	−3.1%	−8.9% **	−21.7%	−12.8%
HS degree	−22.4% **	−24.3% **	−1.9%	−4.9% **	−20.0% **	−15.1% **
Some college/AA	−19.2% **	−13.6% **	5.6%	−9.0% **	0.0%	9.0%
Bachelor's degree	−9.2% **	−16.2% **	−7.0%	−4.2% **	7.0%	11.3%
Grad degree	−3.2% **	−17.1% *	−13.8%	0.2%	3.4%	3.1%
Age						
18–34	−20.5% **	−22.6% **	−2.1%	−5.9% **	−5.8%	0.1%
35–49	−12.0% **	−23.3% **	−11.3% *	−4.7% **	−16.0% **	−11.3% **
50–64	−13.4% **	−13.1% **	0.3%	−5.6% **	0.0%	5.6%

Note: Figures represent percent change in total employed among working-age people (18–64). The notation * is significantly different from zero at $p<.05$, ** $p<.01$. See Table A-1 for employment levels by month and disability status (appendix tables are available by request from the lead author).

Workers with disabilities are more prevalent in the occupations that had larger employment declines, as shown in Table 5.3. Among the top four occupations ranked by prevalence of disability (column 1), the January-April employment drop was clearly larger than average in three of them (building and grounds cleaning, food preparation and serving, and transportation and material moving). As shown in column 4, across the 22 occupations, the employment drop in the first four months of 2020 was larger for workers with disabilities compared to workers without disabilities in 15 occupations. We also analyzed industry and reached a similar conclusion: that is, individuals with disabilities tend to work in the industries that had larger employment declines at the height of the pandemic (results not shown but available). With some variations across particular occupation and industry categories, these overall conclusions also apply to the January-December 2020 data.

Logit Results

We next analyze the employment changes with logit estimations of equation (1) using the sample of individuals employed currently or in the preceding 12 months based on the monthly CPS for January-December 2020. The logit predicts employment using a post-March dummy variable and a post-March trend term. To allow for differential patterns in employment by demographic and job characteristics, both the post-March dummy and the trend terms are interacted with all the independent variables, including three-way interactions among disability, gender, and race/ethnicity. Column 1 reports employment estimations for January-April 2020, and column 2 reports estimations for January-December 2020. In both columns, each row presents the predicted percent change in the likelihood of employment relative to the January-March 2020 period.

In Table 5.4, the first row shows the base change for people without disabilities, which is negative and statistically significant in both periods, and the second row shows the additional effect for people who have disabilities. These estimates indicate that the disability gaps in the employment changes for January-April and January-December are significantly different from zero in both periods.

Does disability intersect with gender and race in affecting employment drops? Results in Table 5.4 for the three-way interactions of disability with gender and race/ethnicity categories. Here we examine the potential additive effect of all three dimensions (disability, gender, and race/ethnicity) by comparing each group to the base group of White men without disabilities. As can be seen in the "without disability" rows in both columns, almost every gender and racial/ethnic category had a significantly larger employment drop than did White men without disabilities, and all of these negative marginal effects are statistically significant. Only White non-Latinx women without disabilities have no additional employment drops during the January-

Table 5.3: Employment Changes by Occupation in 2020.

	% with disability in Jan. (1)	January-April percent change			January-December percent change		
		No disability (2)	Disability (3)	Disability gap (4)	No disability (5)	Disability (6)	Disability gap (7)
Overall	3.2%	−15.5% **	−18.9% **	−3.3%	−5.4% **	−6.5% **	−1.1%
Occupation (ranked by pct. w/disability)							
Building and grounds cleaning and maintenance	5.5%	−18.2% **	−30.8% *	−12.6%	−1.0%	−23.0%	−22.0%
Community and social service	4.3%	−9.0%	−2.1%	6.9%	−1.3%	−29.2%	−28.0%
Food preparation and serving related	4.1%	−48.5% **	−53.8% **	−5.4%	−25.2% **	−27.5% *	−2.4%
Transportation and material moving	3.9%	−20.9% **	−21.3%	−0.4%	−7.6% **	−3.6%	4.0%
Installation, maintenance, and repair	3.9%	−14.3% **	−3.4%	10.9%	−7.0%	−16.0%	−9.0%
Production occupations	3.8%	−24.7% **	−28.2% *	−3.5%	−3.5%	−19.4%	−15.9%
Healthcare support occupations	3.7%	−16.2% **	−15.6%	0.6%	−3.2%	0.7%	3.9%
Farming, fishing, and forestry	3.7%	−0.3%	−25.1%	−24.7%	−6.7%	−37.7%	−31.0%
Sales and related occupations	3.6%	−19.9% **	−35.7% **	−15.8%	−4.0%	−21.2% *	−17.2%
Protective service occupations	3.4%	−10.3% *	−15.3%	−5.0%	−8.2%	−13.1%	−4.9%
Personal care and service occupations	3.2%	−44.5% **	−41.3% *	3.3%	−21.6% **	−39.6% *	−18.0%
Computer and mathematical science	3.1%	1.1%	−6.5%	−7.6%	−0.4%	−22.3%	−21.9%
Office and administrative support	3.0%	−11.9% **	18.3%	30.3%	−1.8%	13.6%	15.4%
Business and financial operations	2.9%	−6.0% *	−20.3%	−14.3%	−5.2%	−17.1%	−11.8%
Arts, design, entertainment, sports	2.8%	−21.9% **	1.5%	23.4%	−15.6% **	66.5%	82.1%
Legal	2.7%	−9.9%	−57.8% **	−47.9% *	−3.0%	−78.5% **	−75.5% **
Life, physical, and social science	2.7%	0.0%	−36.5%	−36.6%	2.1%	−17.9%	−20.0%
Construction and extraction	2.7%	−19.5% **	−20.1%	−0.6%	−6.5% *	0.8%	7.3%
Education, training, and library	2.7%	−13.3% **	−30.1% *	−16.8%	−3.5%	16.5%	20.0%
Management occupations	2.3%	−5.2% **	−3.7%	1.5%	−2.7%	21.4%	24.2%
Healthcare practitioner and technical	2.2%	−8.2% **	−10.8%	−2.7%	−1.4%	18.6%	20.0%
Architecture and engineering	1.8%	−5.8%	−6.2%	−0.4%	−1.6%	−11.4%	−9.8%

Note: The notation * is significantly different from zero at p<.05, ** p<.01.

December period relative to White men without disabilities. Similarly, almost all of the results in the "with disability" rows indicate larger employment drops for workers with disabilities across the gender and racial/ethnic categories. However, only half of these are significantly different from zero in the January-April period, and three out of eight are significantly different from zero in the January-December period. This latter set of results for the entire year indicate a larger and persistent employment drop for Latinx men with disabilities and for White and Black women with disabilities. Given the challenge of obtaining precise estimates in the face of small sample sizes when adding a 3-way interaction term, these results provide compelling evidence that Latinx men with disabilities and White and Black women with disabilities bore a relatively heavy burden of employment losses during the pandemic.

Table 5.4: Employment Changes by Disability Intersected with Gender and Race, 2020.

	Employment drop in April			Employment drop plus recovery through December		
Base change for people without disabilities	−8.9%	(0.001)	**	−2.2%	(0.001)	**
Marginal effect of disability	−2.3%	(0.009)	*	−1.6%	(0.007)	*
Base change for White men without disabilities	−6.0%	(0.002)	**	−1.7%	(0.001)	**
Marginal effects relative to White men without disabilities						
Without disability						
Males						
Black non-Latinx	−4.2%	(0.007)	**	−3.1%	(0.006)	**
Latinx	−5.0%	(0.005)	**	−1.6%	(0.004)	**
Other race/ethnicity	−4.3%	(0.007)	**	−0.8%	(0.004)	*
Females						
White non-Latinx	−3.2%	(0.003)	**	0.0%	(0.002)	
Black non-Latinx	−5.3%	(0.007)	**	−2.2%	(0.005)	**
Latinx	−8.7%	(0.006)	**	−1.5%	(0.004)	**
Other race/ethnicity	−5.8%	(0.007)	**	−1.0%	(0.005)	*
With disability						
Males						
White non-Latinx	−1.7%	(0.013)		0.3%	(0.011)	
Black non-Latinx	−7.2%	(0.067)		7.4%	(0.050)	
Latinx	−10.3%	(0.035)	**	−10.5%	(0.035)	**
Other race/ethnicity	−1.6%	(0.056)		−2.8%	(0.053)	

Table 5.4 (continued)

	Employment drop in April			Employment drop plus recovery through December		
Females						
White non-Latinx	−6.2%	(0.015)	**	−3.4%	(0.011)	**
Black non-Latinx	−11.4%	(0.043)	**	−8.3%	(0.038)	*
Latinx	−10.3%	(0.045)	*	−1.5%	(0.035)	
Other race/ethnicity	−5.4%	(0.050)		−8.3%	(0.048)	
Sample size	568,013					

Note: Figures represent predicted percent change in likelihood of employment relative to the pre-April period, based on logit regression using data for all 12 months of 2020. The notation * is significantly different from zero at p<.05, ** p<.01 (standard errors in parentheses). Both columns are based on coefficients from one logit regression predicting employment using a post-March dummy and post-March linear term. To allow differential drops and recoveries by demographic and job characteristics, both terms were interacted with education (5 categories), age (three categories), marital status (4 categories), occupation (22 categories), industry (13 categories), and full interactions of disability, gender, and race/ethnicity. Sample is limited to those with job currently or in past 12 months, since occupation and industry codes are available only for those workers.

Decomposition Results

The results so far indicate that employment appeared to drop more in the pandemic among workers with disabilities compared to workers without disabilities, and the regression results lend confidence to the assertion that the employment drops were relatively more severe for workers with disabilities, especially Latinx men and White and Black women. Tables 5.5 and 5.6 present the decomposition results using two different comparisons to sort out the role of occupation and industry in explaining the relative effect of the pandemic on employment outcomes of workers with disabilities. Table 5.5 compares the decomposition results between the "pre-lockdown" January-March 2020 period and the "post-lockdown" April-December 2020 period, while Table 5.6 uses a matched sample of individuals from March and April to examine employment transitions in 2020 compared to March-April transitions in earlier years. Note that both analyses are restricted to the sub-sample of workers with strong connections to the job market.

Table 5.5 shows that the disability gap in proportion employed increased from 0.059 in January-March to 0.076 in April-December, and this increase of 0.017 was statistically significant (column 3). Within both periods very little of the disability employment gap is explained by occupation, industry, education, and demographic variables (8.3% in January-March and 15.6% in April-December), indicating that disability is a dominant factor at each point in time. Moving between the periods,

Table 5.5: Decomposition of Employment Levels, 2020.

	Jan-March, 2020 (1)			April-Dec, 2020 (2)			Change (3)		
Employment levels									
No disability	0.960	(0.001)	**	0.899	(0.001)	**	−0.061	(0.001)	**
Disability	0.901	(0.005)	**	0.823	(0.005)	**	−0.078	(0.007)	**
Difference	0.059	(0.005)	**	0.076	(0.005)	**	0.017	(0.007)	*
Explained									
Total	0.005	(0.001)	**	0.012	(0.001)	**	0.007	(0.001)	**
Occupation	0.001	(0.000)	**	0.005	(0.001)	**	0.003	(0.001)	**
Industry	0.000	(0.000)		0.001	(0.000)	**	0.001	(0.001)	
Education	0.002	(0.000)	**	0.003	(0.000)	**	0.002	(0.000)	**
Other demographics	0.001	(0.000)	**	0.002	(0.001)	**	0.001	(0.001)	
Unexplained	0.054	(0.005)	**	0.064	(0.005)	**	0.010	(0.007)	
Percent of difference explained	8.3%			15.6%			40.8%		
Sample size	154,523			413,490					

Note: Figures represent Oaxaca decomposition of likelihood of employment for those of working age (18–64) who have a job currently or in the past 12 months. Occupation and industry are coded only for those with job currently or in past 12 months. The notation * is significantly different from zero at p<.05, ** p<.01 (standard errors in parentheses). Based on Oaxaca decompositions accounting for gender, race/ethnicity (4 categories), education (5 categories), age (three categories), marital status (4 categories), occupation (22 categories) and industry (13 categories).

however, about 41% of the increase in the disability employment gap is explained by these factors, indicating that they play a substantial role in explaining disability employment dynamics over the pandemic. Among the predictors, the occupational distribution accounts for the largest portion of the increase, followed by education.

Taking a different approach that focuses on the large pandemic-related employment drop in April 2020, Table 5.6 analyzes the April employment status of those who were employed in March, and decomposes the disability gap in their April employment. The disability gap in proportion employed in April was 0.031 (representing 3.1 percentage points) in the 2014–2019 period, rising to 0.054 in 2020, reflecting an increase of 0.022 (column 3). While this increase is greater than the Table 5.5 increase in the disability gap, the Table 5.6 increase is not significantly different from zero owing in part to the much smaller sample size. The explained portion of the gap was 3.8% before 2020 and 36.3% in 2020, and the demographic, occupation, and industry factors explained 82.0% of the increase in the disability gap. The occupation and education factors shared a nearly equal amount of the increase in the explained gap.

Table 5.6: Decomposition of Employment Changes for March-April Matched Samples.

	2014–2019 combined (1)			2020 (2)			Change (3)		
Employment in April									
No disability	0.967	(0.000)	**	0.840	(0.003)	**	−0.127	(0.003)	**
Disability	0.936	(0.002)	**	0.787	(0.014)	**	−0.149	(0.015)	**
Difference	0.031	(0.002)	**	0.054	(0.015)	**	0.022	(0.015)	
Explained									
Total	0.001	(0.000)	**	0.019	(0.004)	**	0.018	(0.004)	**
Occupation	0.001	(0.000)	**	0.008	(0.002)	**	0.008	(0.002)	**
Industry	0.000	(0.000)		0.002	(0.002)		0.002	(0.002)	
Education	0.001	(0.000)	**	0.007	(0.001)	**	0.007	(0.001)	**
Other demographics	0.000	(0.000)	**	0.002	(0.002)		0.002	(0.002)	
Unexplained	0.030	(0.002)	**	0.034	(0.014)	*	0.004	(0.014)	
Percent of difference explained	3.8%			36.3%			82.0%		
Sample size	229,934			29,949					

Note: Figures represent probability of employment in April among those employed in March. The notation * is significantly different from zero at $p<.05$, ** $p<.01$ (standard errors in parentheses). Based on logit Oaxaca decompositions accounting for gender, race/ethnicity (4 categories), education (5 categories), age (three categories), marital status (4 categories), occupation (22 categories), and industry (13 categories).

Conclusion

This chapter has explored the intersection of race, gender, and disability status in the impact of the COVID-19 pandemic on employment losses. Findings from the logit regressions testing for intersectional differences indicate that White and Black women with disabilities experienced relatively greater employment losses during the pandemic compared to White men without disabilities. Moreover, the decomposition results tell us that: a) in each period, there remains a substantial disability gap in employment after controlling for demographic, occupation, and industry factors; b) these disability gaps appeared to increase during the pandemic; c) a good portion of the increased disability gap is accounted for by how the pandemic differentially affected occupations and industries; and d) there was still an increase in the unexplained component of the disability employment gap during the pandemic. These results are consistent with pre-pandemic research indicating higher layoff rates among workers with disabilities that are not fully explained by observed characteristics (Kaye et al., 2011; Mitra & Kruse, 2016). Although the unexplained gap is usually attributed to insufficient data on all characteristics that affect employment and earnings, our result could reflect growing discrimination by employers against people with disabilities during the pandemic.

An important question for future research is the extent to which individuals with disabilities have more trouble finding and maintaining new jobs following the relaxation of stay-at-home orders relative to workers without disabilities. These differences could be even larger for women and people of color with disabilities compared to their counterparts without disabilities. Another relevant question is the extent to which the disability earnings gap has changed due to the pandemic and how changes in occupation and industry distributions help to explain the change in the gap. It would also be interesting to see how childcare responsibilities affect employment when parents – primarily mothers – stay home as their children are taught virtually in the pandemic; this additional responsibility may place particular burdens on mothers who have to contend with the time and energy demands of a disability. Finally, it will be interesting to see how the labor shortages and tight labor market coming out of the pandemic may have both a short-term and long-term effect on the employment of people with disabilities.

The results help to inform the direction of employment policies during and after COVID-19 by showing how employment outcomes have changed for people across the spectrum of disabilities and for individuals from underserved/minority backgrounds in the context of the pandemic. Our results also have important implications for employer policies to provide telecommuting accommodations rather than trying to pigeonhole individuals with disabilities into a traditional workspace. Part of the difficulties faced by many people with disabilities in the pandemic is that they are more likely to be in the kinds of jobs that need to be done on-site and cannot be done at home (e.g., buildings and grounds maintenance, food service) (Schur et al., 2020). To the extent that their work can be moved home, however, home-based work may have particular value for people with disabilities in ensuring that their pay levels and raises are determined more by actual job performance and qualifications, rather than by stereotypes and workplace cultural dynamics that have been shown to disadvantage workers with disabilities (Schur et al., 2013). The unprecedented increase in working from home for many professional workers during the pandemic may have lasting effects on employers' acceptance of such arrangements, for instance, as workplace accommodations for persons with disabilities and others. These circumstances may create and reinforce a new norm of workplace accommodation with positive outcomes, as working from home has advantages for many people with disabilities on dimensions of productivity, health, and quality of life. In short, while the pandemic disproportionately hurt the employment of people with disabilities, especially among women and people of color, the overall effects of job restructuring may ultimately benefit many people with disabilities.

References

Ali, M., L. Schur, & P. Blanck (2011). What types of jobs do people with disabilities want? *Journal of Occupational Rehabilitation, 21*(2), 199–210.

Alon, T., Doepke, M., Olmstead-Rumsey, J., & Tertilt, M. (2020). The impact of the coronavirus pandemic on gender equality. *Covid Economics Vetted and Real-Time Papers, 4*, 62–85.

Ameri, M., L. Schur, M. Adya, S. Bentley, P. McKay, & D. Kruse (2018). The disability employment puzzle: A field experiment on employer hiring behavior. *ILR Review, 1*(2), 329–364.

Baert, S. (2018). Hiring discrimination: an overview of (almost) all correspondence experiments since 2005. In S. M. Gaddis (Ed.), *Audit Studies: Behind the Scenes with Theory, Method, and Nuance* (pp. 63–77). Cham: Springer.

Bahn, K., Cohen, J., & Rodgers, Y. (2020). A feminist perspective on COVID-19 and the value of care work globally. *Gender, Work and Organization, 27*(5), 695–699.

Bailey, M., & Mobley, I. A. (2019). Work in the intersections: A black feminist disability framework. *Gender and Society, 33*(1), 19–40.

Baldwin, M. L., & Choe, C. (2014). Wage discrimination against workers with sensory disabilities. *Industrial Relations, 53*(1), 101–124.

Bartik, A. W., Bertrand, M., Lin, F., Rothstein, J., & Unrath, M. (2020). Measuring the labor market at the onset of the COVID-19 crisis. National Bureau of Economic Research Working Paper No. 27613.

BLS (2016). Persons with a disability: Labor force characteristics – 2015. USDL-16-1248. U.S. Bureau of Labor Statistics, June 21.

BLS (2020). Persons with a disability: Labor force characteristics – 2019. USDL-20-0339. U.S. Bureau of Labor Statistics, February 26.

Blanck, P. (2020). *Disability law and policy*. St. Paul, MN: Foundation Press.

Blanck, P., Abdul-Malak, Y., Adya, M., Hyseni, F., Killeen, M., & Altunkol Wise, F. (2020). Diversity and inclusion in the legal profession: Preliminary findings from a national study of lawyers with disabilities. *University of the District of Columbia Law Review, 23*, 23–87.

Blinder, A. (1973). Wage discrimination: Reduced form and structural estimates. *Journal of Human Resources*, 8(4), 436–55.

Degener, T. (2011). Intersections between disability, race, and gender in discrimination law. In D. Schiek, and A. Lawson (Eds.), *European union non-discrimination law and intersectionality* (pp. 29–46). Burlington, VT: Ashgate Publishing.

Fairlie, R. W. (1999). The absence of the African-American owned business: An analysis of the dynamics of self-employment. *Journal of Labor Economics, 17*(1), 80–108.

Fairlie, R. W. (2003). An extension of the Blinder–Oaxaca decomposition technique to logit and probit models. Center Discussion Paper No. 873. CT, USA: Economic Growth Center, Yale University.

Fine, M., & Asch, A. (1988). *Women with disabilities: Essays in psychology, culture, and politics*. Philadelphia, PA: Temple University Press.

Gary, K. W., Nicholls, E., Shamburger, A., Stevens, L. F., & Arango-Lasprilla, J. (2011). Do racial and ethnic minority patients fare worse after SCI?: A critical review of the literature. *NeuroRehabilitation, 29*(3), 275–293.

Hanna, W. J., & Rogovsky, B. (1991). Women with disabilities: Two handicaps plus. *Disability, Handicap and Society, 6*(1), 49–63.

Hasnain, R., & Balcazar, F. (2009). Predicting community-versus facility-based employment for transition-aged young adults with disabilities: The role of race, ethnicity, and support systems. *Journal of Vocational Rehabilitation, 31*(3), 175–188.

Kaye, H. S., Jans, L. H., & Jones, E. C. (2011). Why don't employers hire and retain workers with disabilities? *Journal of Occupational Rehabilitation, 21*(4), 526–536.

Kruse, D., Schur, L., Rogers, S., & Ameri, M. (2018). Why do workers with disabilities earn less? Occupational job requirements and disability discrimination. *British Journal of Industrial Relations, 56*(4), 798–834.

Kraus, L., Lauer, E., Coleman, R., & Houtenville, A. (2017). *Disability statistics annual report.* Durham, NH: University of New Hampshire.

Lauer, E., & Houtenville, A. (2017). *Annual Disability Statistics Compendium: 2016.* Durham, NH: University of New Hampshire, Institute on Disability.

Mitra, Sophie, & Douglas Kruse. (2016). Are workers with disabilities more likely to be displaced? *The International Journal of Human Resource Management, 27*(14), 1550–1579.

Neumark, D. (1988). Employers' discriminatory behavior and the estimation of wage discrimination. *Journal of Human Resources, 23*(3), 279–295.

Oaxaca, R. (1973). Male-female differentials in urban labor markets. *International Economic Review, 14*(3), 693–709.

Oaxaca, R. L., & Ransom, M. R. (1994). On discrimination and the decomposition of wage differentials. *Journal of Econometrics, 61*(1), 5–21.

Ren, L. R., Paetzold, R. L., & Colella, A. (2008). A meta-analysis of experimental studies on the effects of disability on human resource judgments. *Human Resource Management Review, 18*(3), 191–203.

Schur, L. (2003). Barriers or opportunities? The causes of contingent and part-time work among people with disabilities. *Industrial Relations, 42*(4), 589–622.

Schur, L. (2002). Dead-end jobs or a path to economic well-being? The consequences of non-standard work for people with disabilities. *Behavioral Sciences and the Law, 20*, 601–20.

Schur, L., Ameri, M., & Kruse, D. (2020). Telework after COVID: a 'silver lining' for workers with disabilities? *Journal of Occupational Rehabilitation, 30*, 521–536.

Schur, L., Kruse, D., & Blanck, P. (2013). *People with disabilities: Sidelined or mainstreamed?* Cambridge, UK: Cambridge University Press.

Schur, L., Nishii, L., Adya, M., Kruse, D., Bruyère, S. M., & Blanck, P. (2014). Accommodating employees with and without disabilities. *Human Resource Management, 53*(4), 593–621.

Lara Bellotti, Sara Zaniboni, Isabelle Langlois, and Patrizia Villotti

6 Age, Mental Disorders and Work Design Factors

Abstract: The chapter proposes to introduce an intertwined issue related to age and mental disorders at work. Both are timely and important topics that need further understanding in order to identify successful work interventions and strategies. In particular, work accommodations have been studied to help the work integration of people with mental disorders. However, previous research indicates age differences in work-related aspects (e.g., work design characteristics impact younger and older workers differently). This conceptual contribution aims to critically review and summarize the existing literature on age differences in the effect of work-related design factors on mental disorders and employment outcomes. We organized its structure dividing the work-related design factors between physical and psychosocial factors. Additionally, we attempted to identify possible work accommodations and interventions to promote the work integration and work participation of differently aged workers with mental disorders.

Keywords: age at work, mental disorders, mental disability, work design factors, psychosocial work environment, physical work environment

Introduction

In the last 30 years, the population has aged steadily. Data from Organization for Economic Co-operation and Development (OECD) countries analysis showed that in the years 1990–2020, the aged population (i.e., >65 years) grew from 9.30% to 17.46% of the total population, while the working-age population (i.e., aged between 15 and 64 years old) only grew from 61.8% to 64.8%, and has been steadily decreasing since 2011 (when it accounted for 66% of the total population). Moreover, the impact of mental disorders on the working population and organizations in terms of unemployment, sickness absence, and reduced productivity is substantial (Richter et al., 2019). For instance, it is calculated that common mental disorders such as depression and anxiety cost the global economy around 1 trillion US

Lara Bellotti, Department of Psychology, University of Bologna, 47521 Cesena, Italy
Sara Zaniboni, Department of Psychology, University of Bologna, 47521 Cesena, Italy; Department of Management, Technology, and Economics, ETH Zürich, 8092 Zürich, Switzerland
Isabelle Langlois, and Patrizia Villotti, Département d'Éducation et Pédagogie, Université du Québec à Montréal, H2X 3R9 Montréal, PQ, Canada

https://doi.org/10.1515/9783110743647-007

dollars each year (Liu et al., 2020; "Mental health matters," 2020). Therefore, an extremely complex set of issues revolve around the intersection of aging, mental disorders, and work-related factors.

The present contribution will critically review and summarize the existing literature on age-related differences in the effect of work-related design factors on mental disorders and employment outcomes. First, we will provide an overview of the topic of age and aging at work and research on age-related differences in work-related aspects (e.g., work design characteristics impact differently older and younger workers). Second, we will present the topic of mental disability and mental disorders contextualized to the work environment (e.g., challenges associated with stigma oftentimes leading to exclusion from the labor market and/or recurrent sickness absence). Then, we intertwined those issues by presenting research findings on work-related physical and psychosocial design factors differently impacting the mental health and work outcomes of employees of different ages. Lastly, we attempted to identify possible work accommodations and/or interventions that may help the work integration of people of different ages with mental disorders.

Age at Work

As the population is aging, the workforce is becoming increasingly age diverse. More specifically, all industrialized countries have witnessed an increase in life expectancy that came with a concurrent decrease in fertility rates. A 2019 report from the United Nations highlighted that fertility rates decreased from 4.97 births per woman in the 1950–1955 cohort to 2.47 in the 2015–2020 cohort, and is thought to decline further in the future (United Nations, 2019), while OECD (2020) experts projected the share of the population aged 50+ years old to jump from 37% in 2020 to 45% in 2050. Therefore, over the years, chronological age has gained prominence among researchers as a main variable of interest, and it now becomes decisive to address the role of age in work contexts rather than use it as a simple control variable (Bohlmann et al., 2017).

Within the work and organizational research literature, different approaches have been used to understand the mechanisms and work outcomes of age-related differences. In fact, the aging experience itself entails many biological, affective, and cognitive changes. On the one hand, aging is associated with a progressive decline in physical, social, and fluid cognitive capabilities (De Lange et al., 2006; Sterns & Miklos, 1995). For instance, older people are subject to visual and hearing losses and reduced capability to maintain homeostasis, which increase the time needed to recover from stressors. Consequently, older individuals' capability to sustain certain work accommodations such as night shifts is reduced (Truxillo et al., 2015). On the other hand, the progression of age can also comes with functional gains such as increased crystallized cognitive and socioemotional abilities (Grossmann et al., 2010; Kanfer et al., 2013), greater accumulated knowledge, and improved emotional regulation (Truxillo et al., 2015). Therefore, age-related changes across the lifespan encapsulate both age-related losses (e.g., fluid intelligence) and age-related gains (e.g., resources and experiences).

While early studies were based on the gerontology literature and focused on healthy aging for old and very old individuals, later developments drew from the lifespan developmental perspective that tends to pay closer attention to the entire span of life, sometimes comparing individuals of different ages (Zacher & Rudolph, 2017). Moreover, lifespan developmental theories do not address the aging process per se, as in the gerontology perspective, but rather investigate which mechanisms support successful aging and for whom (Zacher & Rudolph, 2017). In fact, all lifespan developmental theories share the idea that successful aging means finding a balance between age-related losses (e.g., reduced capability to maintain homeostasis) and gains (e.g., increased knowledge and experience). Parallel to the increase of research based on the lifespan developmental theories, we witnessed the conceptualization of the *successful aging at work* approach. Aging successfully within the work context means maintaining, developing, or growing favorable work outcomes even with the increasing of age (Kooij, 2015; Zacher, 2015). In contrast with the previous approaches (i.e., the gerontology and lifespan developmental perspectives), whose principles have been applied to the work context a posteriori, the approach of *successful aging at work* is grounded in the interplay between age and different work-related aspects in predicting work outcomes. Therefore, this approach has gained great prominence for both research and organizations.

By now, research has accounted for the role of chronological age and acknowledged the impact of age-related changes on some work and organizational aspects. For instance, older workers have been shown to engage more in organizational citizenship behaviors and less in counterproductive behaviors (O'Driscoll & Roche, 2017). Meta-analytical findings have also shown a positive significant relationship between chronological age and job attitudes (e.g., job satisfaction) (Ng & Feldman, 2010) and intrinsic motives (e.g., achievement), as well as a negative significant relationship with growth-related motives (e.g., training and advancement) (Kooij et al., 2011). Scientific contributions distinguishing and comparing these age-related differences are vital to organizations planning to support the needs and preferences of an age-diverse workforce. Moreover, it is important to distinguish between evidence-based age-related differences and differences that have no empirical support. In fact, biased beliefs and attributions on age and age related differences can have a significant impact on the formation of age stereotypes and discrimination targeting both younger and older workers. For example, common stereotypes towards older workers accuse them of poorer performance and greater resistance to changes such as the implementation of new technologies (Finkelstein et al., 1995; Posthuma et al., 2012). Comparatively, younger workers are often thought to be tech-savvy, ambitious, and unreliable (King et al., 2012). Alas, stereotypes can sometimes turn into workplace discrimination, such as unfair hiring decisions (Truxillo et al., 2017; Zaniboni et al., 2019), different opportunities for training and development (Sterns & Miklos, 1995), and retention (Paullin & Whetzel, 2012).

In conclusion, the growing age diversity of workplaces is pushing organizations to account for the effect of age when designing work processes and practices (Truxillo et al., 2015). In fact, the ability to answer the different age-related needs and preferences of the workforce is crucial to unlock businesses' full potential. At the same time, we must distinguish between what is supported by the literature and what is part of common beliefs instead. The integration of work processes and practices based on age stereotypes and not evidence-based data can hinder the achievement of organizational goals and the successful integration of workers of different ages (e.g., increasing communication barriers and decreasing workers' willingness to work together) (Urick, 2017).

Work Disability and Mental Disorders

Because of the increase of chronic health conditions, the work participation of individuals with a disability is more and more valuable in both the public and private sectors (Vornholt et al., 2018). Over 1 billion of the world's population is living with a disability and it is estimated that everyone, at some point in life, will experience some degree of difficulty in functioning (temporary or permanent), or require some sort of healthcare service (World Health Organization [WHO], 2011). This has important consequences in terms of employment. In fact, individuals acquiring a disability or with reduced functional capacity are potentially affected in their ability to enter, remain in, or return to the workforce (Dewa et al., 2014).

According to the UN Convention on the Rights of Persons with Disabilities (UNCRPD) (2006), an individual with a disability is someone who suffers from a long-term physical, mental, intellectual, or sensory impairment. This impairment must be evaluated in interaction with several barriers that may or may not hinder the individual's full participation in society on an equal basis with others (UNCRPD, 2006). Similarly, the International Classification of Functioning, Disability and Health (ICF) of the World Health Organization (WHO, 2011) defines the term disability as an umbrella concept which covers impairments, activity limitation, and participation restrictions originating from the interaction between an individual and their environment. The emphasis on the interaction of person-environment forces us to go beyond the simple medical impairment by also considering the influence/contribution of the environment (for example, the workplace).

Work is a central theme to a person's identity, social role, community status, and overall wellbeing (Corbière et al., in press). Despite legislation on diversity in the workplace, individuals with disabilities still do not experience the same access to work opportunities as do their counterparts without disabilities. As a result, the employment gap between people with and without disabilities (i.e., disability gap) affects individuals worldwide. For instance, the unemployment rate of disabled people is twice that of people without disabilities in the United States (U.S. Bureau of Labor Statistics, 2016). Similar employment gaps have been observed among working-age Canadians living with a disability (49% vs 79% for those without a disability; Turcotte, 2014) as well as in the European Union (57.3% vs 66.9% respectively; Eurostat, 2017). These employment disparities ultimately entail important consequences on individuals with disabilities' economic wellbeing, social participation, and overall health.

Mental disorders often limit individuals' possibilities for employment by reducing their work ability or forcing them into sick leave (Lidwall, 2015) and are therefore to a large degree associated with disability. Compared to those with other disabilities, people with mental disorders face the greatest barriers to work participation: in fact, there's a considerable amount of social stigma and further pessimistic views which translate into hiring discrimination that makes it difficult for them to enter the workforce (Hipes et al., 2016; Nigatu et al., 2017). Stigma is an underserved label applied to a person diagnosed with a mental disorder. Based on prejudice and misinformation, it prevents people with mental disorders from accessing valuable life opportunities, including employment (Corrigan, 2016). Therefore, despite legislation and societal efforts, stigma against people with mental disorders is still pervasive (Baldwin & Marcus, 2011) and it constitutes one of the main reasons these individuals are prevented from full integration and participation in society. The low employment participation rate among people with mental disorders is problematic, as work is a leading factor in promoting recovery and facilitating social integration. The literature (e.g., Corbière et al., 2013) distinguishes between common mental disorders (e.g., adjustment, mood, anxiety disorders) – usually associated with short-term disability – and severe mental disorders (e.g., schizophrenia, bipolar disorders), linked to long-term disability. Common mental disorders, such as mood disorders and anxiety disorders, are of particular importance as they have been estimated to affect up to 20–30% of employed populations and they represent a prominent cause of sickness absence and work disability worldwide (Dewa et al., 2014). These disorders can lower the general wellbeing and the level of psychosocial and work-related functioning of those affected, leading to a lowered work ability or even an early exit from working life (Lahelma et al., 2015). Common mental disorders are also problematic because there is a high risk (estimated 3-times higher risk; Kivimäki et al., 2004) of recurrent sickness absence after a first successful return to work (Roelen et al., 2015). Furthermore, the risk of permanent exclusion from the labor market increases with the number of sickness absence episodes (Koopmans et al., 2011; Pedersen et al., 2012). The process of successfully returning to work and achieving a sustainable return, therefore, play an essential role in the recovery from a common mental disorder and in the prevention of further negative consequences like job loss or disability retirement (Hiilamo et al., 2019; van Rijn et al., 2014).

In sum, people with mental disorders are particularly at risk of being left out of the workforce because of stigma and discrimination, and because of the absence of adequate work accommodations that satisfy their needs. This has important consequences for their financial wellbeing, social participation, and health, and therefore mental disorders are frequently associated with a condition of disability, and early exit from the workforce. To limit the disruption caused by mental disorders, it is important to work towards a successful and sustainable process of returning to work, followed by practices for maintaining the employment.

Age, Mental Disorders and Work Design Factors

An extremely complex set of issues revolve around the intersection of aging, disability due to mental disorders, and work-related factors. Moreover, multiple are the biases and the stereotypes against both people with a disability and aged individuals. Bjelland and colleagues (2010) used data from the U.S. Equal Employment Opportunity Commission Integrated Mission System to investigate the nature of employment discrimination charges that cite individually or jointly the Americans with Disabilities Act (ADA)[1] and the Age Discrimination in Employment Act (ADEA).[2] Their findings highlighted that 80% of ADEA charges and 72% of ADA/ADEA jointly-filed charges were submitted by those aged 50 and over, while 60% of ADA charges alone were filed by individuals over 40 years old (Bjelland et al., 2010). Moreover, several factors were associated with perceived discrimination for the jointly-filed charges, such as workplace harassment, unfair hiring procedures, lack of promotion, demotion, and wages.

Therefore, whether the mental disorder exists since birth or from a relatively young age, or is acquired later in life, it is important to understand how to help these individuals to gain or maintain employment. In this regard, the process of successfully returning to work can contribute to the recovery from a common mental disorder and to the prevention of further negative consequences, like job loss or disability retirement (Hiilamo et al., 2019; van Rijn et al., 2014). Extended research on people with mental disability has focused on the predictors and aspects of both returning to work and job maintenance and agreed that age is a key personal factor negatively

---

1 i.e., a regulation prohibiting employers to discriminate against qualified individuals with disabilities in hiring and retention phases of employment.
2 i.e., a regulation protecting employees and job applicants who are 40 years of age or older from employment discrimination based on age.

associated with these outcomes (e.g., Blank et al., 2008; Dewa et al., 2014; Lagerveld et al., 2010). For example, studies found that younger age predicts an earlier return to work for both common and severe mental disorders (Bejerholm & Areberg, 2014; Dias et al., 2019), even after temporal disability pension (Laaksonen & Gould, 2015). Moreover, research has shown that the risk of a recurrent episode of work disability due to mental disorders (i.e., a significant mental impairment limiting the individual's work activity) was significantly higher in the older age group compared to the younger one (Mattila-Holappa et al., 2017). Findings from systematic reviews have confirmed these results, providing consistent evidence on the inverse relationship between age and returning to work (i.e., young age helps achieving a return to work) (de Vries et al., 2018; Etuknwa et al., 2019).

The aforementioned evidence underlines the important role that age plays in understanding the work integration of people with common and severe mental disorders. Further findings have shown that some aspects related to the work environment (i.e., work-related physical and psychosocial design factors) may facilitate or hinder this process, and more research is needed in this direction (e.g., Halonen et al., 2020; Huijs et al., 2017). For example, a two-year follow-up cohort study (Huijs et al., 2017), on long-term sick-listed Dutch employees (i.e., at least 13 weeks of leave), found an effect of negative psychosocial work factors in increasing the participants' depressive symptoms. In particular, those employees with depressive symptoms at baseline took longer before returning to work and, in general, were less likely to return to work as compared to those with no depressive symptoms at baseline. Psychosocial work factors such as low decision authority, high psychological demands, and low supervisor support significantly increased the participants' depressive symptoms, which in turn were associated with a longer sick leave duration until returning to work.

Considering the importance of understanding the intersection of aging, disability due to mental disorders, and work-related factors, the present contribution aims to critically review and summarize the existing literature on this topic.

We divided the work-related design aspects into physical and psychosocial factors. On the one hand, the physical aspects of work refer to the biological, physical, or chemical factors of the working environment (Halonen et al., 2020). On the other hand, the work-related psychosocial factors refer to those characteristics of work in terms of design, organization, and management (Corbière et al., 2013). Research findings have shown that all these factors can affect, to a certain degree, workers' mental health (Bonde, 2008; Corbière et al., 2013). For instance, a recent French national survey associated some physical work aspects (i.e., exposure to noise and chemicals) and a wide number of psychosocial work factors (i.e., job demands, role clarity, role conflict, job insecurity, workplace bullying, meaning of work, coworkers and supervisor support) to both major depressive disorder and generalized anxiety disorder in men and women (Bertrais et al., 2021).

Therefore, the scope of the following subsections is to highlight research results on age-related differences in the impact of physical and psychosocial work-related aspects on employees with mental disorders (see Table 6.1). Moreover, we will try to identify possible work accommodations and interventions to promote the work integration and work participation of younger and older workers with mental disorders.

Table 6.1: Summary of the research findings, organized by work-related design factors.

Work-Related Design Factor	Age Target	Key Findings	References
Physical Factors			
Workplace hazards	Younger	Exposure to loud/persistent noise and chemicals is associated with a general mental health decline.	Zeng et al., 2014
Long weekly hours	Younger Middle-Age Older	Associated with depressive symptoms, higher suicidal ideation, and mental health decline.	Kim & Park, 2021; Park et al., 2020; Zeng et al., 2014;
Working overtime	Younger	No relationship with the onset of depression but predictive of mental health decline.	Law et al., 2020; Ogasawara et al., 2011
Working night shifts	Middle-age Older	No effect on middle-aged workers but showed to be associated with older workers' mental health decline.	Olinto et al., 2017; Øyane et al., 2013
Repeated movements; adoption of awkward postures	Middle-age Older	Associated with onset of common mental disorders.	Kouvonen et al., 2016
Decrease in the physical workload	Middle-age Older	Predicted improved mental health (i.e., measured by reduced use of psychotropic medications).	Kouvonen et al., 2017
Psychosocial Factors			
Low skill variety	Younger	Associated with mental health decline.	Law et al., 2020
Lack of rewards	Younger Middle-age	Associated with mental health decline and increase in suicidal ideation.	Kim et al., 2020; Law et al., 2020

Table 6.1 (continued)

Work-Related Design Factor	Age Target	Key Findings	References
High job insecurity	Younger Middle-age Older	Associated with mental health decline for all age groups, increase in anxiety symptoms for younger ones (female only), and increase in suicidal ideation (middle-age and older man only).	Kim et al., 2020; Law et al., 2020; Lee et al., 2015
Job autonomy	Younger Middle-age Older	Predicting mental health decline and onset of common mental disorders when low. Associated with successful return to work and increased work ability (middle-age only) workers when high.	Kouvonen et al., 2016; Kouvonen et al., 2017; Lau et al., 2019; Law et al., 2020; Weber et al., 2021
High job demands	Younger Middle-age Older	Associated with onset of minor psychiatric and common mental disorders, increase in depressive thoughts, and greater suicidal ideation (younger and middle-age only). Predicting increased work ability (middle-age only) workers when high.	Kim et al., 2020; Kouvonen et al., 2016; Kouvonen et al., 2017; Urbanetto et al., 2013; Weber et al., 2021
Opportunities for development	Middle-age	Predicting increased work ability and successful return to work.	Lau et al., 2019; Weber et al., 2021
Social support	Middle-age Older	Associated with improved common mental disorders' conditions, greater work ability, and successful return to work (when high).	Laine et al., 2014; Lau et al., 2019; Weber et al., 2021
Quality of leadership	Middle-age	Predicting increased work ability (when high).	Weber et al., 2021
Organizational injustice	Younger Middle-age Older	Associated with increased suicidal ideation.	Kim et al., 2020
Discomfort in organizational climate	Younger Middle-age Older	Associated with increased suicidal ideation.	Kim et al., 2020

Table 6.1 (continued)

Work-Related Design Factor	Age Target	Key Findings	References
Workplace bullying/conflicts	Younger Middle-age Older	Predicting increased anxiety symptoms (younger only) and deterioration of common mental disorders' conditions (middle-age and older only)	Laine et al., 2014; Lee et al., 2015

Work-Related Physical Design Factors, Age, and Mental Disorders

As we previously described, the physical aspects of work refer to the biological, physical, or chemical factors of the working environment. Research results found that these work-related physical factors may influence aging workers' health, possibly shortening their working life by pushing them into early retirement through disability retirement (Lahelma et al., 2012; Tüchsen et al., 2008). In particular, a recent cohort study explored the joint effect of work-related physical factors (i.e., hazardous exposures, physical workload, computer and shift work) and common mental disorders on disability retirement and found a significant synergistic positive association (i.e., meaning the effect of the two combined variables is greater than the effect of the variables in isolation) (Halonen et al., 2020).

Our review yielded different results for several work-related physical design factors, such as posture and job-related movements, workload, workplace hazards, and work schedule factors (i.e., working hours, shift work). For instance, in a cohort study on Finnish middle-aged and older workers, common mental disorders were associated with the execution of repeated movements and the adoption of awkward postures (Kouvonen et al., 2016). Moreover, in a cross-sectional study on Chinese employees, young workers' general mental health was negatively affected by the exposure to different workplace hazards (e.g., noise and chemicals) (Zeng et al., 2014). If recurrent exposure to adverse physical working conditions is associated with a deterioration of the mental health status, Kouvonen and colleagues (2017) suggested that, otherwise, the improvement of physical working conditions (i.e., the decreased the physical workload) promotes workers' mental health, lowering the risk for mental illnesses (measured by the use of psychotropic medications).

In regard to the impact of work schedule factors, such as the number of working hours, findings are still not fully consistent (Kim & Park, 2021; Ogasawara et al., 2011; Park et al., 2020). For instance, in Kim and Park's (2021) cross-sectional study, middle-aged and older Korean employees who worked long weekly hours (i.e., 40+ hours) had higher depressive symptoms scores. The same result was found by Park and colleagues' (2020) panel study on young Koreans, and by Zeng and colleagues' (2014) cross-sectional study on young Chinese employees. However, in an earlier study on young Japanese office workers no significant association was found between working overtime and depression scores (Ogasawara et al., 2011). Nevertheless, a recent systematic review seemed to clarify these results, identifying working overtime as one of the major causes of poor mental health among young workers (Law et al., 2020). In the attempt to explore further work schedule factors, a cross-sectional study on Brazilian shift workers found that working on night shifts provoked a general mental health decline in older workers (Olinto et al., 2017). However, in a cross-sectional study on the effect of night shifts on middle-aged Norwegians, no effect on depression and anxiety was found (Øyane et al., 2013). Additional evidence on young female Korean workers found no correlation between working on shifts and anxiety scores (Lee et al., 2015).

To summarize, research is starting to show some age-related effects on physical work factors (e.g., repeated movements, workload, workplace hazards, work schedule factors) and workers' mental health and mental disorders. While findings on the adverse effects of factors such as repeated movements, awkward postures, and workplaces' hazards on different age groups are still limited, literature on work schedule aspects is more abundant. For instance, working overtime appears to play an essential role in the mental health deterioration process of young workers. At the same time, shift work yields different results across age groups, seemingly negatively affecting older workers but not middle-aged and younger ones.

Work-Related Psychosocial Design Factors, Age, and Mental Disorders

In this section we explore the literature accounting for the effects of age and psychosocial work factors on mental health outcomes. For what concerns the younger age group, a recent systematic review identified four psychosocial factors mainly responsible for younger workers' decline in mental health: low skill variety, lack of rewards, high job insecurity, and low autonomy (Law et al., 2020). Moreover, findings from multiple studies pointed at a negative impact of several factors (e.g., high job demands, low rewards, and social support) on young workers' mental status (Li et al., 2013; Urbanetto et al., 2013; Zeng et al., 2014). For instance, Urbanetto and colleagues (2013) investigated the onset of minor psychiatric disorders and depressive thoughts on a young group of Brazilian nurses. Based on the Job-Demand-Control model (Karasek, 1979), the authors found that high job demands, rather than the quantity of available resources, triggered a decline in mental health status. Specifically, all conditions of high job demands were associated with minor psychiatric disorders and depressive thoughts, despite the number of available resources. For what concerns the older age groups, similar to the results of Urbanetto and colleagues (2013), a cohort study on middle-aged and older Finnish employees (Kouvonen et al., 2016) found that common mental disorders were significantly associated with high job demands and low job control. A follow-up study confirmed these results, showing that high job demands and low job control negatively affected middle-aged and older workers' general mental health, measured by the use of psychotropic medications (Kouvonen et al., 2017). In a recent cohort study investigating the moderating role of psychosocial work factors in the relationship between depressive symptoms and work ability of German workers, the researchers found that high job demands did not interact with depressive symptoms, but rather directly influenced middle-aged workers' work ability (Weber et al., 2021). Further factors negatively impacting work ability were opportunities for development, job control, social support, and quality of leadership (Weber et al., 2021).

Some researchers accounted for a gender effect as well, while investigating the effect of psychosocial work factors on workers' mental health by age. For instance, Lee and colleagues' (2015) cross-sectional study on young Korean female workers showed that job demands, conflicts within the workplace, job insecurity, and lack of rewards predicted higher anxiety symptoms. Additionally, a cohort study on Korean employees suggested a combined effect of age and gender (Kim et al., 2020) on workers' mental health status. More specifically, the authors considered the role of high job demands, lack of rewards, job insecurity, discomfort in the organizational climate, and organizational injustice on suicidal ideation, stratifying the data by age and gender. Findings showed that organizational injustice and discomfort in the organizational climate significantly predicted suicidal ideation in younger women, middle-aged and older men (for organizational injustice), and men of all age groups (for discomfort in the organizational climate). Interestingly, job insecurity was significant only for middle-aged and older men while high job demands and lack of rewards significantly impacted younger and middle-aged male workers, but no effect for women was found (Kim et al., 2020).

A cohort study on Finnish workers observed not only the effect of adverse psychosocial working conditions on mental health, but also the outcomes of favorable ones (Laine et al., 2014). The authors found that while workplace bullying produced a deterioration of common mental disorders in middle-aged and older workers, a strong social support system (i.e., from colleagues and supervisors) contributed to improving workers' common mental disorder conditions.

We found only one study investigating the intersectional relationship between mental health status, age, and psychosocial work factors in predicting returning to work for people with mental disorders (Lau et al., 2019). Findings showed that three factors substantially promoted return to work for workers of all age groups: decision latitude, colleagues' support, and job promotion opportunities. This is important because the process of successfully returning to work plays an important role in the recovery from a common mental disorder and in the prevention of further negative consequences like job loss or disability retirement (Hiilamo et al., 2019; van Rijn et al., 2014).

To sum up, there is consistent evidence supporting the negative role played by job demands in workers' mental health changes, especially for younger workers. Moreover, some studies highlighted potential gender differences in the impact of job demands on mental health, indicating a greater effect on young and middle-aged men. The quality of social support within the workplace seems to play a key role as well, promoting mental health outcomes in middle-aged and older workers. Moreover, support from colleagues appears to be essential not only for the development of a favorable mental health status, but also for the process of returning to work per se.

Work Design and Work Accommodations Strategies to Support Age-Related Needs of Workers with Mental Disorders

Designing work and work environments to accommodate the needs of individuals with mental disorders across the entire lifespan is imperative. In general, previous studies consistently showed the impact that job or work design has on multiple work and organizational outcomes (e.g., work motivation, wellbeing, performance, job attitudes, and intentions to continue working) (Morgeson & Campion, 2003). Specifically considering age and job characteristics, Truxillo and colleagues (2012) proposed that different work design interventions might be more beneficial for workers of diverse ages (e.g., enhancing job autonomy and social support may be more beneficial for older workers by allowing them to suit the job to their needs). Moreover, there is evidence that job or work design interventions can accommodate the needs of people with mental disorders too. For example, social support has emerged as an important characteristic for people with mental disorders (Villotti et al., 2018). In fact, having a solid network to turn to in times of need can be a conduit to recovery and facilitate effective participation in society (Bjørlykhaug et al., 2021; Etuknwa et al., 2019).

Research findings from our literature review support the importance of designing jobs considering the specific needs of differently aged workers with mental disorders. For example, both the workstation and the job task should be adjusted in order to avoid uncomfortable postures, excessive workload, or high noises. In fact, the presence of one or more mental disorders aggravates the challenges placed by the biological physical decline that comes with aging (De Lange et al., 2006; Sterns & Miklos, 1995).

Furthermore, managers and human resources personnel should be taught about the relevance of these work-related factors to implement work accommodations and interventions that allow employees with mental disorders to continue being part of the workforce during their entire lifespan. For example, work accommodations that enhance flexibility and control over one's work could promote mental health, work ability, and a successful return to work of people of all ages (Kim & Park, 2021; Law et al., 2020; Olinto et al., 2017; Park et al., 2020).

Another important issue is related to the training of managers. Indeed, supervisors should be able to recognize their unconscious biases and taught how to avoid them by setting a virtuous standard for all employees and implementing fair and standardized procedures. This could help decrease stigma and discrimination, whether it is age-based or directed towards people with mental disorders (e.g., WAGES-Business and Google's "re:Work" case studies; McCormick-Huhn et al., 2020), and potentially, prevent workplace bullying and conflicts that seem to provoke a deterioration of common mental disorder symptoms in all age groups (Laine et al., 2014; Lee et al., 2015). Lastly, perceptions of social support could be increased by integrating workers with mental disorders into team-based activities, which could hold particular benefits with increasing age (Laine et al., 2014; Lau et al., 2019; Weber et al., 2021).

Conclusions

Overall, we found research investigating the age-differential effect of work-related design factors on mental health. Some variables stem from a more solid ground and are of particular interest such as psychosocial factors like job demands and social support (Li et al., 2013; Urbanetto et al., 2013; Weber et al., 2021; Zeng et al., 2014) and physical factors like working long weekly hours (Law et al., 2020; Zeng et al., 2014). Others deserve more research attention (e.g., shift work, overtime work, job insecurity) in order to clarify their role in the work integration of different age groups of workers with mental disorders.

At the same time, while we were able to suggest a number of evidence-based job or work design interventions for several factors (i.e., social support, job autonomy, long weekly hours, workplace hazards), there is a call for more research on the effectiveness of the actual implementation of the proposed interventions (Fraccaroli et al., 2017).

Moreover, the combined effect of age and gender on workers' mental health has not been fully investigated and more research is needed to improve our understanding of potential paths of vulnerability emerging from multiple interactions between demographic variables.

To conclude, the population is aging, and chronic health conditions are increasing (OECD, 2020; Vornholt et al., 2018). Therefore, the work participation of individuals of different ages with mental disorders or any kind of disability is even more valuable. Especially in today's work models where employees are the driving forces for organizations' success, overcoming the barriers of stigma and providing work design factors (i.e., favorable physical and psychosocial working conditions) that facilitate the working life of age-diverse people with mental disorders is becoming an important challenge that needs to be faced.

References

Baldwin, M. L., & Marcus, S. C. (2011). Stigma, discrimination, and employment outcomes among persons with mental health disabilities. In I. Z. Schultz & E. S. Rogers (Eds.), *Work accommodation and retention in mental health* (pp. 53–69). Springer. https://doi.org/10.1007/978-1-4419-0428-7_3

Bejerholm, U., & Areberg, C. (2014). Factors related to the return to work potential in persons with severe mental illness. *Scandinavian Journal of Occupational Therapy*, *21*(4), 277–286. https://doi.org/10.3109/11038128.2014.889745

Bertrais, S., Mauroux, A., Chastang, J.-F., & Niedhammer, I. (2021). Associations of multiple occupational exposures with major depressive and generalized anxiety disorders: Findings from the French National Working Conditions Survey. *Depression and Anxiety*, *38*(3), 337–350. https://doi.org/https://doi.org/10.1002/da.23111

Bjelland, M. J., Bruyère, S. M., von Schrader, S., Houtenville, A. J., Ruiz-Quintanilla, A., & Webber, D. A. (2010). Age and disability employment discrimination: Occupational rehabilitation implications. *Journal of Occupational Rehabilitation*, *20*(4), 456–471. https://doi.org/10.1007/s10926-009-9194-z

Bjørlykhaug, K. I., Karlsson, B., Hesook, S. K., & Kleppe, L. C. (2021). Social support and recovery from mental health problems: A scoping review. *Nordic Social Work Research*. https://doi.org/10.1080/2156857X.2020.1868553

Blank, L., Peters, J., Pickvance, S., Wilford, J., & MacDonald, E. (2008). A systematic review of the factors which predict return to work for people suffering episodes of poor mental health. *Journal of Occupational Rehabilitation*, *18*(1), 27–34. https://doi.org/10.1007/s10926-008-9121-8

Bohlmann, C., Rudolph, C. W., & Zacher, H. (2017). Methodological recommendations to move research on work and aging forward. *Work, Aging and Retirement*, *4*(3), 225–237. https://doi.org/10.1093/workar/wax023

Bonde, J. P. (2008). Psychosocial factors at work and risk of depression: A systematic review of the epidemiological evidence. *Occupational and Environmental Medicine*, *65*(7), 438–445. https://doi.org/10.1136/oem.2007.038430

Corbière, M., Negrini, A., & Dewa, C. S. (2013). Mental health problems and mental disorders: Linked determinants to work participation and work functioning. In P. Loisel & J. R. Anema (Eds.), *Handbook of work disability: Prevention and management* (pp. 267–288). Springer. https://doi.org/10.1007/978-1-4614-6214-9_17

Corbière, M., Villotti, P., & Pachoud, B. (in press). Les facteurs du maintien en emploi de personnes aux prises avec un trouble psychique: Une synthèse des écrits. [Factors in job retention for people with mental illness: A synthesis of the literature.] In C. Lagabrielle & S. Croity-Belz (Eds.), *Psychologie et carrière.[Psychology and career.] (titre provisoire).* De Boeck Superieur S.A.

Corrigan, P. W. (2016). Lessons learned from unintended consequences about erasing the stigma of mental illness. *World Psychiatry: Official Journal of the World Psychiatric Association (WPA)*, *15*(1), 67–73. https://doi.org/10.1002/wps.20295

De Lange, A., Taris, T., Jansen, P., Smulders, P., Houtman, I., & Kompier, M. (2006). Age as a factor in the relation between work and mental health: Results of the longitudinal TAS survey. In J. Houdmont & S. McIntyre (Eds.), *Occupational health psychology: European perspectives on research, education and practice Vol. 1* (pp. 21–45). ISMAI Publications.

de Vries, H., Fishta, A., Weikert, B., Rodriguez Sanchez, A., & Wegewitz, U. (2018). Determinants of sickness absence and return to work among employees with common mental disorders: A ccoping review. *Journal of Occupational Rehabilitation*, *28*(3), 393–417. https://doi.org/10.1007/s10926-017-9730-1

Dewa, C. S., Loong, D., Bonato, S., & Hees, H. (2014). Incidence rates of sickness absence related to mental disorders: A systematic literature review. *BMC Public Health*, *14*(1), 205. https://doi.org/10.1186/1471-2458-14-205

Dias, A., Bernardes, J., Coquemala, S., Gómez-Salgado, J., & Ruiz Frutos, C. (2019). Predictors of return to work with and without restrictions in public workers. *PLOS ONE*, *14*, e0210392. https://doi.org/10.1371/journal.pone.0210392

Etuknwa, A., Daniels, K., & Eib, C. (2019). Sustainable return to work: A systematic review focusing on personal and social factors. *Journal of Occupational Rehabilitation*, *29*(4), 679–700. https://doi.org/10.1007/s10926-019-09832-7

Eurostat. (2017). *Disability statistics.* http://ec.europa.eu/eurostat/statistics-explained/index.php?title=Disability_statistics

Finkelstein, L. M., Burke, M. J., & Raju, M. S. (1995). Age discrimination in simulated employment contexts: An integrative analysis. *Journal of Applied Psychology*, *80*(6), 652–663. https://doi.org/10.1037/0021-9010.80.6.652

Fraccaroli, F., Zaniboni, S., & Truxillo, D. (2017). Job design and older workers. In S. Profili, A. Sammarra & L. Innocenti (Eds.), *Advanced series in management: Age diversity in the workplace: An organizational perspective* (Vol. 17, pp. 139–159). Emerald Group Publishing Ltd.

Grossmann, I., Na, J., Varnum, M., Park, D., Kitayama, S., & Nisbett, R. (2010). Reasoning about social conflicts improves into old age. *Proceedings of the National Academy of Sciences of the United States of America*, *107*, 7246–7250. https://doi.org/10.1073/pnas.1001715107

Halonen, J. I., Mänty, M., Pietiläinen, O., Kujanpää, T., Kanerva, N., Lahti, J., Lahelma, E., Rahkonen, O., & Lallukka, T. (2020). Physical working conditions and subsequent disability retirement due to any cause, mental disorders and musculoskeletal diseases: Does the risk vary by common mental disorders? *Social Psychiatry and Psychiatric Epidemiology*, *55*(8), 1021–1029. https://doi.org/10.1007/s00127-019-01823-6

Hiilamo, A., Shiri, R., Kouvonen, A., Mänty, M., Butterworth, P., Pietiläinen, O., Lahelma, E., Rahkonen, O., & Lallukka, T. (2019). Common mental disorders and trajectories of work disability among midlife public sector employees – A 10-year follow-up study. *Journal of Affective Disorders*, *247*, 66–72. https://doi.org/10.1016/j.jad.2018.12.127

Hipes, C., Lucas, J., Phelan, J. C., & White, R. C. (2016). The stigma of mental illness in the labor market. *Social Science Research*, *56*, 16–25. https://doi.org/https://doi.org/10.1016/j.ssresearch.2015.12.001

Huijs, J. J. J. M., Koppes, L. L. J., Taris, T. W., & Blonk, R. W. B. (2017). Work characteristics and return to work in long-term sick-listed employees with depressive symptoms. *Journal of Occupational Rehabilitation*, *27*(4), 612–622. https://doi.org/10.1007/s10926-017-9696-z

Kanfer, R., Beier, M., & Ackerman, P. (2013). Goals and motivation related to work in later adulthood: An organizing framework. *European Journal of Work and Organizational Psychology, 22*, 253–264. https://doi.org/10.1080/1359432X.2012.734298

Karasek, R. A. (1979). Job demands, job decision latitude, and mental strain: Implications for job redesign. *Administrative Science Quarterly, 24*, 285–308. https://doi.org/10.2307/2392498

Kim, J., & Park, E. C. (2021). The impact of work hours on depressive symptoms among Koreans aged 45 and over. *International Journal of Environmental Research and Public Health, 18*(3), 853. https://doi.org/10.3390/ijerph18030853

Kim, S. Y., Shin, Y. C., Oh, K. S., Shin, D. W., Lim, W. J., Cho, S. J., & Jeon, S. W. (2020). Association between work stress and risk of suicidal ideation: A cohort study among Korean employees examining gender and age differences. *Scandinavian Journal of Work, Environment and Health, 46*(2), 198–208. https://doi.org/10.5271/sjweh.3852

King, E., Finkelstein, L., & Ryan, K. (2012). What do the young (old) people think of me? Content and accuracy of age-based metastereotypes. *European Journal of Work and Organizational Psychology, 22*, 633–657. https://doi.org/10.1080/1359432X.2012.673279

Kivimäki, M., Forma, P., Wikström, J., Halmeenmäki, T., Pentti, J., Elovainio, M., & Vahtera, J. (2004). Sickness absence as a risk marker of future disability pension: The 10-town study. *Journal of Epidemiology and Community Health, 58*(8), 710–711. https://doi.org/10.1136/jech.2003.015842

Kooij, D. T. A. M. (2015). Successful aging at work: The active role of employees [Review]. *Work, Aging and Retirement, 1*(4), 309–319. https://doi.org/10.1093/workar/wav018

Kooij, D. T. A. M., De Lange, A. H., Jansen, P. G. W., Kanfer, R., & Dikkers, J. S. E. (2011). Age and work-related motives: Results of a meta-analysis. *Journal of Organizational Behavior, 32*(2), 197–225. https://doi.org/10.1002/job.665

Koopmans, P. C., Bültmann, U., Roelen, C. A., Hoedeman, R., van der Klink, J. J., & Groothoff, J. W. (2011). Recurrence of sickness absence due to common mental disorders. *International Archives of Occupational and Environmental Health, 84*(2), 193–201. https://doi.org/10.1007/s00420-010-0540-4

Kouvonen, A., Mänty, M., Lallukka, T., Lahelma, E., & Rahkonen, O. (2016). Changes in psychosocial and physical working conditions and common mental disorders. *European Journal of Public Health, 26*(3), 458–463. https://doi.org/10.1093/eurpub/ckw019

Kouvonen, A., Mänty, M., Lallukka, T., Pietiläinen, O., Lahelma, E., & Rahkonen, O. (2017). Changes in psychosocial and physical working conditions and psychotropic medication in ageing public sector employees: A record-linkage follow-up study. *BMJ Open, 7*, e015573. https://doi.org/10.1136/bmjopen-2016-015573

Laaksonen, M., & Gould, R. (2015). Return to work after temporary disability pension in Finland. *Journal of Occupational Rehabilitation, 25*(3), 471–480. https://doi.org/10.1007/s10926-014-9554-1

Lagerveld, S. E., Bültmann, U., Franche, R. L., van Dijk, F. J., Vlasveld, M. C., van der Feltz-Cornelis, C. M., Bruinvels, D. J., Huijs, J. J., Blonk, R. W., van der Klink, J. J., & Nieuwenhuijsen, K. (2010). Factors associated with work participation and work functioning in depressed workers: A systematic review. *Journal of Occupational Rehabilitation, 20*(3), 275–292. https://doi.org/10.1007/s10926-009-9224-x

Lahelma, E., Laaksonen, M., Lallukka, T., Martikainen, P., Pietiläinen, O., Saastamoinen, P., Gould, R., & Rahkonen, O. (2012). Working conditions as risk factors for disability retirement: A longitudinal register linkage study. *BMC Public Health, 12*(1), 309. https://doi.org/10.1186/1471-2458-12-309

Lahelma, E., Pietiläinen, O., Rahkonen, O., & Lallukka, T. (2015). Common mental disorders and cause-specific disability retirement. *Occupational and Environmental Medicine*, *72*(3), 181–187. https://doi.org/10.1136/oemed-2014-102432

Laine, H., Saastamoinen, P., Lahti, J., Rahkonen, O., & Lahelma, E. (2014). The associations between psychosocial working conditions and changes in common mental disorders: A follow-up study. *BMC Public Health*, *14*, 588. https://doi.org/10.1186/1471-2458-14-588

Lau, B., Shiryaeva, O., Ruud, T., & Victor, M. (2019). What are they returning to? Psychosocial work environment as a predictor of returning to work among employees in treatment for common mental disorders: A prospective observational pre–post study. *PLOS ONE*, *14*(4), e0215354. https://doi.org/10.1371/journal.pone.0215354

Law, P. C. F., Too, L. S., Butterworth, P., Witt, K., Reavley, N., & Milner, A. J. (2020). A systematic review on the effect of work-related stressors on mental health of young workers. *International Archives of Occupational and Environmental Health*, *93*(5), 611–622. https://doi.org/10.1007/s00420-020-01516-7

Lee, K. H., Ho Chae, C., Ouk Kim, Y., Seok Son, J., Kim, J.-H., Woo Kim, C., Ouk Park, H., Ho Lee, J., & Saeng Jung, Y. (2015). Anxiety symptoms and occupational stress among young Korean female manufacturing workers. *Annals of Occupational and Environmental Medicine*, *27*, 24–24. https://doi.org/10.1186/s40557-015-0075-y

Li, J., Weigl, M., Glaser, J., Petru, R., Siegrist, J., & Angerer, P. (2013). Changes in psychosocial work environment and depressive symptoms: A prospective study in junior physicians. *American Journal of Industrial Medicine*, *56*(12), 1414–1422. https://doi.org/10.1002/ajim.22246

Lidwall, U. (2015). Sick leave diagnoses and return to work: A Swedish register study. *Disability and Rehabilitation*, *37*(5), 396–410. https://doi.org/10.3109/09638288.2014.923521

Liu, Q., He, H., Yang, J., Feng, X., Zhao, F., & Lyu, J. (2020). Changes in the global burden of depression from 1990 to 2017: Findings from the Global Burden of Disease study. *Journal of Psychiatric Research*, *126*, 134–140. https://doi.org/10.1016/j.jpsychires.2019.08.002

Mattila-Holappa, P., Ervasti, J., Joensuu, M., Ahola, K., Pentti, J., Oksanen, T., Vahtera, J., KivimÄki, M., & Virtanen, M. (2017). Do predictors of return to work and recurrence of work disability due to mental disorders vary by age? A cohort study. *Scandinavian Journal of Public Health*, *45*(2), 178–184. https://doi.org/10.1177/1403494816686467

McCormick-Huhn, K., Kim, L. M., & Shields, S. A. (2020). Unconscious bias interventions for business: An initial test of WAGES-Business (workshop activity for gender equity simulation) and Google's "re: Work"trainings. *Analyses of Social Issues and Public Policy*, *20*(1), 26–65. https://doi.org/https://doi.org/10.1111/asap.12191

Mental health matters [Editorial]. (2020, November 1). *The Lancet Global Health*, *8*(11), e1352. https://doi.org/10.1016/S2214-109X(20)30432-0

Morgeson, F. P., & Campion, M. A. (2003). Work design. In W. C. Borman, D. R. Ilgen & R. J. Klimoski (Eds.), *Handbook of psychology: Industrial and organizational psychology* (Vol. 12, pp. 423–452). John Wiley & Sons Inc. http://search.ebscohost.com/login.aspx?direct=true&db=psyh&AN=2003-04689-017&site=ehost-live

Ng, T. W. H., & Feldman, D. C. (2010). The relationships of age with job attitudes: A meta-analysis. *Personnel Psychology*, *63*(3), 677–718. https://doi.org/10.1111/j.1744-6570.2010.01184.x

Nigatu, Y. T., Liu, Y., Uppal, M., McKinney, S., Gillis, K., Rao, S., & Wang, J. (2017). Prognostic factors for return to work of employees with common mental disorders: A meta-analysis of cohort studies. *Social Psychiatry and Psychiatric Epidemiology*, *52*(10), 1205–1215. https://doi.org/10.1007/s00127-017-1402-0

O'Driscoll, M. P., & Roche, M. (2017). Age, organizational citizenship behaviors, and counterproductive work behaviors. In N. A. Pachana (Ed.), *Encyclopedia of geropsychology* (pp. 113–122). Springer Singapore. https://doi.org/10.1007/978-981-287-082-7_196

Ogasawara, K., Nakamura, Y., Aleksic, B., Yoshida, K., Ando, K., Iwata, N., Kayukawa, Y., & Ozaki, N. (2011). Depression associated with alcohol intake and younger age in Japanese office workers: A case-control and a cohort study. *Journal of Affective Disorders*, *128*(1–2), 33–40. https://doi.org/10.1016/j.jad.2010.06.015

Olinto, M. T. A., Garcez, A., Henn, R. L., Macagnan, J. B. A., Paniz, V. M. V., & Pattussi, M. P. (2017). Sleep-related problems and minor psychiatric disorders among Brazilian shift workers. *Psychiatry Research*, *257*, 412–417. https://doi.org/10.1016/j.psychres.2017.08.018

Organization for Economic Co-operation and Development. (2020). *Promoting an age-inclusive workforce*. https://doi.org/10.1787/59752153-en

Øyane, N. M., Pallesen, S., Moen, B. E., Akerstedt, T., & Bjorvatn, B. (2013). Associations between night work and anxiety, depression, insomnia, sleepiness and fatigue in a sample of Norwegian nurses. *PLOS ONE*, *8*(8), e70228. https://doi.org/10.1371/journal.pone.0070228

Park, S., Kook, H., Seok, H., Lee, J. H., Lim, D., Cho, D.-H., & Oh, S.-K. (2020). The negative impact of long working hours on mental health in young Korean workers. *PLOS ONE*, *15*(8), e0236931. https://doi.org/10.1371/journal.pone.0236931

Paullin, C., & Whetzel, D. (2012). Retention strategies and older workers. *The Oxford handbook of work and aging*. https://doi.org/10.1093/oxfordhb/9780195385052.013.0125

Pedersen, J., Bjorner, J. B., Burr, H., & Christensen, K. B. (2012). Transitions between sickness absence, work, unemployment, and disability in Denmark 2004–2008. *Scandinavian Journal of Work, Environment and Health*, *38*(6), 516–526. https://doi.org/10.5271/sjweh.3293

Posthuma, R. A., Wagstaff, M. F., & Campion, M. A. (2012). Age stereotypes and workplace age discrimination. In J. W. Hedge & W. C. Borman (Eds.), *The Oxford handbook of work and aging* (pp. 298–312). Oxford University Press.

Richter, D., Wall, A., Bruen, A., & Whittington, R. (2019). Is the global prevalence rate of adult mental illness increasing? Systematic review and meta-analysis. *Acta Psychiatrica Scandinavica*, *140*(5), 393–407. https://doi.org/10.1111/acps.13083

Roelen, C. A., Heymans, M. W., Twisk, J. W., van Rhenen, W., Pallesen, S., Bjorvatn, B., Moen, B. E., & Magerøy, N. (2015). Updating and prospective validation of a prognostic model for high sickness absence. *International Archivers of Occupational and Environmental Health*, *88*(1), 113–122. https://doi.org/10.1007/s00420-014-0942-9

Sterns, H. L., & Miklos, S. M. (1995). The aging worker in a changing environment: Organizational and individual issues. *Journal of Vocational Behavior*, *47*(3), 248–268. https://doi.org/10.1006/jvbe.1995.0003

Truxillo, D., Fraccaroli, F., Yaldiz, L., & Zaniboni, S. (2017). Age discrimination at work. In E. Parry & J. McCarthy (Eds.), *The Palgrave handbook of age diversity and work* (Vol. 1, pp. 447–472). Palgrave Macmillan. https://doi.org/10.1057/978-1-137-46781-2_18

Truxillo, D. M., Cadiz, D. M., & Hammer, L. B. (2015). Supporting the aging workforce: A review and recommendations for workplace intervention research. *Annual Review of Organizational Psychology and Organizational Behavior*, *2*(1), 351–381. https://doi.org/10.1146/annurev-orgpsych-032414-111435

Truxillo, D. M., Cadiz, D. M., Rineer, J. R., Zaniboni, S., & Fraccaroli, F. (2012). A lifespan perspective on job design: Fitting the worker to the job to promote job satisfaction, engagement, and performance. *Organizational Psychology Review*, *2*(4), 340–360. https://doi.org/10.1177/2041386612454043

Tüchsen, F., Christensen, K. B., Lund, T., & Feveile, H. (2008). A 15-year prospective study of shift work and disability pension. *Occupational and Environmental Medicine*, *65*(4), 283–285. https://doi.org/10.1136/oem.2007.036525

Turcotte, M. (2014). *Persons with disabilities and employment (Statistics Canada Cat. No. 75-006-X)*. Statistics Canada.

United Nations. (2019). *World population prospects 2019*.

United Nations Convention on the Rights of People with Disabilities. (2006). *Convention on the Rights of Persons with Disabilities, 13 December 2006*. https://www.refworld.org/docid/4680cd212.html

Urbanetto, J., Magalhães, M., Maciel, V., Sant'anna, V., Gustavo, A., Poli de Figueiredo, C., & Magnago, T. (2013). *Estrés laboral según el modelo demanda–control y trastornos psiquiátricos menores en trabajadores de enfermería*. [Work-related stress according to the demand–control model and minor psychic disorder in nursing workers.] *Revista da Escola Enfermagem da USP, 47*, 1180–1186. https://doi.org/10.1590/S0080-623420130000500024

Urick, M. (2017). Adapting training to meet the preferred learning styles of different generations. *International Journal of Training and Development, 21*(1), 53–59. https://doi.org/10.1111/ijtd.12093

U.S. Bureau of Labor Statistics. (2016). *Persons with a disability: Labor force characteristics – 2015*. https://www.bls.gov/news.release/archives/disabl_06162015.htm

van Rijn, R. M., Robroek, S. J., Brouwer, S., & Burdorf, A. (2014). Influence of poor health on exit from paid employment: A systematic review. *Occupational and Environmental Medicine, 71*(4), 295–301. https://doi.org/10.1136/oemed-2013-101591

Villotti, P., Zaniboni, S., Corbière, M., & Guay, S. (2018). Reducing perceived stigma: Work integration of people with severe mental disorders in Italian social eEnterprise. *Psychiatric Rehabilitation Journal, 41*(2), 125–134. https://doi.org/10.1037/prj0000299125

Vornholt, K., Villotti, P., Muschalla, B., Bauer, J., Colella, A., Zijlstra, F., Van Ruitenbeek, G., Uitdewilligen, S., & Corbière, M. (2018). Disability and employment – Overview and highlights. *European Journal of Work and Organizational Psychology, 27*(1), 40–55. https://doi.org/10.1080/1359432X.2017.1387536

Weber, J., Hasselhorn, H. M., Borchart, D., Angerer, P., & Müller, A. (2021). The moderating role of psychosocial working conditions on the long-term relationship between depressive symptoms and work ability among employees from the Baby Boom generation. *International Archives of Occupational and Environmental Health, 94*(2), 295–307. https://doi.org/10.1007/s00420-020-01570-1

World Health Organization. (2011). *World report on disability: Summary*.

Zacher, H. (2015). Successful aging at work. *Work, Aging and Retirement, 1*(1), 4–25. https://doi.org/10.1093/workar/wau006

Zacher, H., & Rudolph, C. W. (2017). Successful aging at work and beyond: A review and critical perspective. In S. Profili, A. Sammarra & L. Innocenti (Eds.), *Advanced series in management: Age diversity in the workplace: An organizational perspective* (Vol. 17, pp. 35–64). Emerald Group Publishing Limited. https://doi.org/10.1108/S1877-636120170000017004

Zaniboni, S., Kmicinska, M., Truxillo, D., Kahn, K., Paladino, M., & Fraccaroli, F. (2019). Will you still hire me when I am over 50? The effects of implicit and explicit age stereotyping on resume evaluations. *European Journal of Work and Organizational Psychology, 28*, 1–15. https://doi.org/10.1080/1359432X.2019.1600506

Zeng, Z., Guo, Y., Lu, L., Han, L., Chen, W., & Ling, L. (2014). Mental health status and work environment among workers in small- and medium-sized enterprises in Guangdong, China – A cross-sectional survey. *BMC Public Health, 14*(1), 1162. https://doi.org/10.1186/1471-2458-14-1162

Kayla B. Follmer and Mackenzie J. Miller

7 Workplace Accommodations for Employees with Concealable Identities: An Overview of Theoretical Paradigms and Review of Empirical Research

Abstract: Although millions of employees worldwide live with a concealable disability, organizations remain underprepared to meet the needs of this population. In this chapter, we provide a review of the existing research related to employees with concealable disabilities and, in doing so, highlight the ways these conditions can affect employees' work performance. This chapter presents evidence on the benefits of reasonable accommodations for both employees and employers and identifies reasons why employees who require reasonable accommodations fail to request them at work. We conclude the chapter by providing practical suggestions for providing reasonable accommodations to individuals with concealable identities, as well as highlighting areas for continued research. In doing so, our aim is to draw attention to a group of employees that have traditionally been underrepresented in the extant research so that organizations can more effectively support these individuals throughout their employment.

Keywords: concealable disabilities, reasonable accommodations, disclosure, stigma

Although disability can take many forms, it is often assumed that if a person has a disability, it will be visible through observation. However, there are many physical, psychological, and cognitive conditions that meet the definition of disability but are not readily visible to observers. Disabilities can be distinguished based on many characteristics, including the extent to which the disability is visible to, or concealable from, others. Concealable disabilities include physical or mental conditions that may be difficult to recognize in others such as mental illness, diabetes, chronic pain, multiple sclerosis, and arthritis (Follmer et al., 2020). On average, it is estimated that approximately 15% of the global workforce has a disability, though this number is likely an underestimate since many employees with disabilities choose not to disclose these conditions to their employers (Santuzzi et al., 2014) out of fear of stigmatization and discrimination. Even though concealable identities are not always apparent, they are covered by the same protections that are extended to visible disabilities under the Americans with Disabilities Act (ADA) of 1991 and the Americans with Disabilities Act Amendments Act (ADAAA) of 2008. It is imperative

Kayla B. Follmer and Mackenzie J. Miller, West Virginia University

https://doi.org/10.1515/9783110743647-008

that organizations understand how concealable identities impact employees and that they are prepared to provide reasonable accommodations and support to these individuals. By doing so, organizations are likely to reap many benefits including a more productive, committed employee base.

In this book chapter, we define concealable identities and explain the challenges that these identities may create in the workplace, including the symptomatology and stigma that may be associated with a given disability. Next, we discuss the legal protections afforded to employees with concealable disabilities, namely through the process of requesting reasonable accommodations, and identify barriers to requesting these accommodations. We conclude by offering suggestions for how organizations can accommodate employees with concealable disabilities, and identifying opportunities for continued academic research that are needed to advance the understanding of the work experiences of employees with disabilities.

Defining Concealable Identities

Concealable disabilities encompass physical and psychological conditions that do not have a physical manifestation or have visible features that are not clearly attributable to a disability (Santuzzi et al., 2014). In the extant literature, both "concealable" and "invisible" are used to describe these types of disabilities; however, we opt to use concealable throughout this chapter as our position is that even if a disability is not readily observed by others, it is present in the life of the individual with the disability, who may choose to conceal or reveal the disability. Examples of physical concealable disabilities include HIV/AIDS, arthritis, epilepsy, diabetes, fibromyalgia, while examples of psychological concealable identities include depression, bipolar disorder, attention deficit hyperactivity disorder (ADHD), autism spectrum disorder (ASD), and post-traumatic stress disorder (PTSD).

Each concealable identity is characterized by unique symptoms or side effects, which can vary in severity or frequency of presentation. These symptoms can be physical, emotional, or cognitive in nature. *Physical symptoms* affect an individual's body and associated responses, and can include debilitating pain (e.g., fibromyalgia, lupus, endometriosis), fatigue (e.g., lupus, depression, Lyme disease), digestive upset (e.g., Crohn's diseases, depression, AIDS), and sleep disturbance (e.g., bipolar disorder, PTSD). *Emotional symptoms* are related to emotional regulation dysfunction, or the associated emotions felt in response to maintaining a concealable disability. For instance, many psychological disorders are characterized by extreme mood fluctuations (e.g., depression, bipolar disorder, anxiety, ADHD), in which case the disability itself is not visible but the changes in mood are readily observable by others. Such mood changes can also occur with physical disabilities including diabetes, lupus, and Lyme disease. The diagnosis and management of a concealable disability can also result in emotional symptoms such as guilt, sadness, irritability, and anger. *Cognitive symptoms* are those that interfere with perception, acquisition and comprehension of knowledge (Follmer & Jones, 2018). For example, lupus can impact an individual's attention, memory, and visuospatial processes (Ho et al., 2018); Lyme disease can contribute to difficulty with word retrieval, impair focus and concentration, and result in memory loss; and PTSD has been associated with reduced psychomotor speed and attention and impairments in learning and working memory (Sumner et al., 2017). Lastly, *behavioral symptoms* affect what a person does or does not do as a result of their disability. Individuals with epilepsy, for instance, can experience staring spells and uncontrollable jerking movements of the arms and legs while individuals with ADHD might display fidgeting, excessive talking, or interrupt others' conversation (Wilens et al., 2009).

The symptoms associated with a disability will vary across conditions and individuals, with some conditions and persons manifesting more severe or mild symptoms than others. Additionally, the presentation of symptoms can fluctuate within a person, with some time periods resulting in worsened symptoms or periods when symptoms are not present at all (Beatty & Joffe, 2006). These variations in symptomatology can lead to unpredictable disruptions in work functioning and can influence how others perceive the individual. For instance, someone who manifests symptoms only intermittently may not be perceived as having a legitimate disability or could be perceived as faking. There may also be an expectation that others expect an employee's disability to align with prevailing stereotypes about that condition – and diverging from this stereotypical profile may lead to skepticism about the legitimacy of disability. We underscore the fact that concealable disabilities manifest in many forms, affect employees' work experiences in distinct ways. When a disability interferes with an individual's ability to meet the demands of their daily job functions, they may seek accommodations in their workplace.

Legal Protections for Employees with Concealable Disabilities

Employees with disabilities are offered legal protections in the workplace through the ADA of 1990 and the ADAAA of 2008. These laws prohibit discrimination against individuals with disabilities in all areas of public life, including the workplace, and require organizations to provide employees with reasonable accommodations that may allow them to meet the requirements of their jobs. Importantly, an individual is entitled to the protections of the ADA and ADAAA even if their disability is not readily observable by others.

An employee may request an accommodation from their employer at any time and may do so either verbally or in writing (Job Accommodation Network [JAN],

2020). To request an accommodation, an employee must clearly indicate that they have a medical reason for seeking workplace changes. The amount of information that an employee should provide will vary across organizations: for some individuals simply saying they have a medical need will be sufficient, but in other instances, employers may require medical documentation to show evidence of a disability. Indeed, requests for documentation often occur when the need for an accommodation is not obvious, as is often the case for employees with concealable disabilities (JAN, 2020).

Providing reasonable accommodations may result in changes to the way work has been traditionally completed, which may be perceived as a burden by employers. However, evidence indicates that providing accommodations for employees yields both direct and indirect benefits for the organization (Solovieva et al., 2011). Direct benefits to the organization include increased employee retention and productivity as well as reduced costs with training new employees. Indirect benefits included improved interactions among coworkers and increased company morale. Multiple studies have demonstrated very low direct costs associated with providing accommodations for concealable disabilities (for a review see McDowell & Fossey, 2015), suggesting that these types of accommodations yield little financial hardship for organizations. According to JAN (2020) roughly 56% of workplace accommodations cost nothing and accommodations that do cost the employer money typically do not exceed $500.

Providing accommodations also has a positive impact on employees. For instance, in a study of employees with mental illness, those who received workplace accommodations demonstrated a lower risk of mood/anxiety disorder one year later (Bolo et al., 2013). Findings also indicate that reasonable accommodations can increase employees' attachment to their jobs (Charles, 2004). Similarly, employees who need accommodations but choose not to use them reported worsened work outcomes, including decreased work activity and reduced working hours (Gignac et al., 2015).

On balance, accommodations can help employees to perform their jobs and generally do not create a financial burden for employers. For these reasons, accommodations should be touted as a positive benefit for employees who need them, yet, there are some reasons why employees may not reap these benefits. Requesting accommodations can be especially challenging for employees with concealable disabilities, as they must first disclose their disability to their employer. In other words, an employee must "out" themselves to their organization. Although workplace accommodations can help employees to perform their work responsibilities, they also can make themselves vulnerable to discrimination and mistreatment by others after they disclose (Follmer et al., 2020). For this reason, employees who require accommodations may fail to request them, even if receiving accommodations would improve their overall job performance (Dong & Guerette, 2013). These fears mainly arise due to the stigma associated with having a disability (Follmer & Beatty, 2018).

Stigma of Concealable Identities

Stigma is a negative attitude or belief about a particular group/identity due to the perception that the identify is flawed, deviant, or abhorrent (Goffman, 1963). According to Jones and colleagues (1984) there are six dimensions of stigma that explain when an identity may be subject to stigmatization. These include *concealability* which refers to the extent to which a stigmatizing identity is visible to others; *course* which refers to the pattern of a stigmatized condition overtime; *disruptiveness* concerns the extent to which a stigmatized identity impedes social interaction and communication; *aesthetic qualities* which highlight the extent to which a stigmatized identity makes a person "ugly" or "repellant"; *origin* refers to how the individual acquired the stigmatized identity; and *peril* is the extent to which the stigmatizing identity is dangerous to the individual as well as others.

The variability in the characteristics of a disability means that stigma operates differently across individuals and disabilities, with some conditions subject to more stigmatization than others. The extent to which a disability is considered stigmatizing will depend upon which dimensions of stigma apply to the condition. For instance, bipolar disorder reflects a stigmatized identity because it can be difficult to manage and is a condition that is likely to persist across time (i.e., course); it can significantly impair social functioning (i.e., disruptiveness); and manic episodes are often characterized by impulsive behaviors which can result in potentially harmful outcomes for the individual (i.e., peril). On the other hand, HIV is stigmatizing because it is often believed that the individual acquired the disorder through their own negligence (i.e., origin), can put others' health at risk if exposed (i.e., peril), and is unlikely to be cured over time (i.e., course). Thus, to understand the stigma associated with a given disability, it is necessary to understand how its characteristics and symptoms may be viewed through the lens of the stigma dimensions identified by Jones et al. (1984).

Stigma is especially pernicious because it can also impact the way individuals feel about themselves, which can influence their attitudes and behavior. According to social identity theory, individuals derive portions of their self-concept from their group membership (Tajfel et al., 1979). That is, people's self-evaluations are largely influenced by the social standing of their respective group (Brown, 2000). Meaning, if the group with which they belong to is generally viewed negatively by the public, then their own self-evaluations can be negatively impacted. In this way, stigma can operate as dual processes: public stigma and self-stigma. Public stigma refers to the collective negative attitudes regarding a particular social group, while self-stigma refers to an individual's internalization of those negative attitudes (Corrigan, 2004).

Stigma can have serious, tangible consequences for individuals as it contributes to prejudice and discrimination across multiple life domains, including employment. Research indicates that employees with disabilities often experience both unemployment and underemployment (Bureau of Labor Statistics, 2021) at rates higher than those without disabilities, and may be evaluated more negatively as compared to other employees due to the belief that they are less competent and productive as a result of their disability (von Schrader, Malzer, & Bruyère, 2014). In a workplace setting, stigma can lead to strained work relationships as others may wish to avoid interacting with someone known to have a stigmatized disability. Self-stigma can also contribute to social isolation as individuals may avoid social situations due to fear of stigmatization (Beatty & Kirby, 2006). Given the negative effects associated with stigma, employees may be fearful of alerting others about their disability, which can ultimately impact their decision to request accommodations.

Barriers to Requesting Accommodations

As discussed above, employees with disabilities are legally entitled to workplace accommodations, which can help them to more fully meet the requirements of their job. Yet, research indicates that a vast majority of employees with concealable identities choose not to seek accommodations at work. It is estimated that only 12.2% of individuals with disabilities (both visible and concealable) request workplace accommodations (von Schrader, Xu, & Bruyère, 2014). Although not all employees with a disability with require accommodations, evidence suggests that accommodations are indeed effective for helping employees meet the demands of their jobs (Fabian et al., 1993; JAN, 2020). Thus, employees may be placing themselves at a disadvantage by failing to seek accommodations which they have the right to use. By recognizing the barriers to requesting accommodations, organizations can proactively support employees and the accommodation request process. The barriers to requesting accommodations can be placed into two categories: individual barriers and organizational barriers.

Individual Barriers to Requesting Accommodations

There are several individual factors that might influence an individual's decision to seek accommodations at work. These factors include characteristics of the disability, job position, previous disclosure experiences, and ability to acquire necessary documentation.

Visibility and Severity of Disability

Although concealable disabilities are generally not readily observable by others, manifest symptoms might be difficult to conceal depending on their severity. For this reason, some disabilities are easier to conceal than others. An individual with a less visible identity may feel as though they have more of a choice in deciding whether to disclose their identity relative to someone with a more visible identity. When a disability yields noticeable symptoms, an individual may feel external pressure to disclose their identity to explain their behaviors. Indeed, prior research has demonstrated that those with more severe concealable disabilities were more likely to disclose their identity at work (for a review see Follmer et al., 2020), and this was true across multiple types of disabilities including arthritis, hearing loss, mental illness, and multiple sclerosis. Because an individual must disclose their disability before receiving accommodations, it may be the case that individuals with less severe manifestation of symptoms are less likely to receive accommodations. Importantly, even if symptom manifestation appears mild, an individual could still require accommodations – particularly for disabilities that are related to extreme physical pain (e.g., fibromyalgia, lupus).

Stigma. Fear of stigmatization is one of the most notable barriers to requesting workplace accommodations. Individuals with stigmatized concealable disabilities may choose not to use accommodations (even if they are needed) as a way to avoid negative social judgment from others in the workplace. Since others cannot "see" concealable disabilities they may not understand or be empathetic to the difficulties that accompany certain types of concealable disabilities. For example, an individual with dyslexia may find themselves struggling to read certain work-related material but may be hesitant to disclose their identity due misconceptions about dyslexia that often lead to negative stereotyping (e.g., the misconception that dyslexia is associated with lower intelligence).

Previous Disclosure Experiences. Previous disclosure experiences, particularly first disclosure experiences, play a significant role in an individual's decision to disclose in the future (Jones & King, 2014). For example, Chaudoir and Quinn (2010) found that individuals who reported positive first disclosure experiences had higher self-esteem compared to those who reported negative first disclosure experiences. Given the stress and anxiety that come with the decision to disclose, having a positive first disclosure experience is thought to reduce the fear of disclosure in the future (Chaudoir & Quinn, 2010). With that said, if an individual's first disclosure experience was negative then they may be hesitant to disclose their disability, ultimately preventing them from requesting accommodations. This suggests that individuals at all organizational levels should be prepared in advance to respond to an employee's disclosure so that when disclosures occur, the responses are supportive rather than demeaning.

Job Status and Power. One's position in the organizational hierarchy can also have a significant impact on the decision to disclose. Those who are at higher levels within the organization possess more power and ultimately greater access to resources and outcomes. As such, employees at higher levels within the organization are more likely to reveal their stigmatized identity compared to employees at lower levels within the organization (Jones & King, 2014). One potential reason for this discrepancy is that those with concealable identities who work at higher levels within the organization are less likely to fear the outcomes of disclosure compared to those at lower levels (Jones & King, 2014).

Barriers in Obtaining Documentation. Often, obtaining workplace accommodations involves providing some type of official documentation regarding one's disability; however, not everyone has the means to obtain the proper documentation or even a diagnosis for their concealable disability. This is especially true for individuals with mental health disorders since mental health services are not always covered by insurance or simply may not be available. People of color and individuals in lower socio-economic statuses, for example, are far less likely to have access to adequate mental health services, resulting in decreased likelihood of obtaining a proper diagnosis (Newacheck et al., 2003). Additionally, acquiring proper paperwork might require an individual to take time off from work to visit a medical professional, which could result in reduced pay or punitive outcomes (e.g., being written up) for missing work – all of which further disadvantage those from lower socioeconomic statuses.

Even those with adequate access to healthcare can still face challenges in obtaining proper diagnoses/documentation. Women often have their pain dismissed by medical professionals; this is especially true for women of color (Johnson et al., 2019). So, a woman who is suffering from endometriosis, a condition that is characterized by significant pain and excessive menstrual bleeding, may have her pain ignored preventing her from obtaining a proper diagnosis and ultimately hindering her ability to obtain workplace accommodations.

Intersectionality of Invisible Disabilities

While many individuals with invisible disabilities can experience the aforementioned barriers, individuals with multiple stigmatized identities, may experience "double jeopardy" in which they are disadvantaged for both their disability and additional identity characteristics. Racial minorities as well as those without a college degree, for example, are less likely to receive accommodations (Blanck et al., 2020). Additionally, while women with disabilities are more likely to request accommodations compared to their male counterparts, they are more likely to have their accommodation requests denied (Harlan & Robert, 1998). This is particularly concerning given that 32% of employed women have some type of disability (Sherbin et al., 2017). Understanding how individuals with multiple identities differentially approach and experience accommodation requests can be useful for addressing barriers and increasing comfort with making such requests.

Organizational Barriers to Requesting Accommodations

In addition to the individual barriers discussed above, there are organizational barriers that also play a role in an individual's decision or ability to request accommodations.

Workplace Culture. Even if an individual has already disclosed their stigmatized identity, they still may be hesitant to seek accommodations due to fear of being perceived as incompetent or of seeking special treatment (Dong et al., 2017). This can be further exacerbated by employer attitudes and workplace culture surrounding disability and diversity broadly (Dong et al., 2017). It is necessary for organizations to evaluate their formal policies and procedures surrounding disability accommodations as well as the informal messaging that is conveyed when someone seeks accommodations. Although employees are legally entitled to accommodations, a threatening work environment may preclude them from actually taking action to receive accommodations. On the other hand, supportive organizational policies and perceived support from peers/superiors can not only lessen the fear associated with disclosure but can actually promote disclosure of stigmatized identities (Jones & King, 2014). Organizations should openly discuss reasonable accommodations so that employees know their rights in the workplace. Furthermore, promoting an inclusive culture among all employees is necessary to lessen prejudice toward those who seek and use accommodations.

Procedural Barriers. Even if employees are aware of their rights under the ADA, obtaining and even requesting workplace accommodations can still prove difficult. Procedural issues in the request process can create barriers to obtaining accommodations (Dong et al., 2017). For instance, if there are numerous hoops that one must go through in order to officially request accommodations or if the departments responsible for handling these requests are understaffed and/or underfunded, this can prolong the request process. Although the Equal Employment Opportunity Commission (EEOC) (2002) states that employers should respond as quickly as possible to accommodation requests, there is no set time frame for which employers must respond to or implement requests. Since employees are still expected to work while accommodation requests are pending, lengthy request procedures can deter individuals from requesting accommodations all together.

Knowledge of Accommodations. Not all accommodations are created equal and some accommodations that are deemed reasonable by the employer may not be all that useful to the individual needing the accommodations. According to the EEOC (2002) employers are not required to provide the requested reasonable accommodation. Rather, they can choose among other alternative accommodations as long as they are effective. The issue here, however, is that what is deemed to be an effective reasonable accommodation for one person may not be effective for another person with the same disability. Moreover, if the accommodations that are offered by the employer do not meet the unique needs of the employee, then the employee may forgo requesting accommodations all together. One reason that employees may not receive adequate accommodations is due to the fact that many managers lack knowledge of appropriate accommodations for those with concealable identities. In one research study involving HR professionals and managers, requests for accommodations for psychological disabilities were perceived as less reasonable and were less likely to be granted as compared to accommodations for physical disabilities (Telwatte et al., 2017). Because the work impairments associated with concealable disabilities are not clearly visible to others, managers may struggle with providing or identifying accommodations for these conditions due to a lack of personal knowledge. Moreover, employees themselves may not be certain of what they are allowed to request, meaning they may desire accommodations but do not know exactly what can be provided. Ensuring that HR professionals and managers have proper knowledge of accommodations can reduce these knowledge gaps and improve the reasonable accommodation process for employees.

Providing Accommodations for Concealable Disabilities

There continues to be a dearth of research focused on the experiences of employees with concealable disabilities. Perhaps for this reason, HR professionals and managers often lack the understanding of how to support these employees (Dong et al., 2017), particularly when it comes to providing workplace accommodations. Most accommodations, however, are easy to implement and are cost effective. Rather than manipulations of physical spaces and structures, these employees often require manipulation of schedules, job duties, and environmental factors. Given that disabilities exist on a spectrum, the accommodations needed for various concealable disabilities can vary from person to person such that what works for one person may not be sufficient for someone else with same disability. In this final section, we provide an overview of accommodations that could be offered for employees with concealable disabilities to aid professionals in better supporting their employees. We note the list is not exhaustive but provides a good foundation upon which organizations can build.

Schedule-based Accommodations

Concealable disabilities can affect employees' day-to-day functioning, with symptomatology fluctuating throughout the day or in certain environments. In these situations, the employee's schedule can be altered to better enable them to manage their disability while also meeting the requirements of their work. Changes to one's work schedule can include structuring work hours around an employee's medical appointments, allowing employees to complete work outside of traditionally scheduled shifts, and providing time for structured breaks throughout the work day. Concealable disabilities may require employees to attend doctor's appointments or to seek professional care, which can create schedule conflicts as these types of appointments often coincide with traditional working hours. Allowing an employee to craft their work schedule around their medical appointments can enable them to seek care for their disability condition while also still accomplishing their job responsibilities.

Alterations to one's work schedule can also assist employees with managing the symptoms associated with their disability. For instance, an employee with ADHD may struggle to work during peak office hours due to excess environmental noise or social distractions. In these instances, allowing the employee to work during "off" hours when there are fewer people and ultimately less distractions can aid in accomplishing their work tasks. Employees with bipolar disorder, early-onset Alzheimer's, or sleep disorders often require consistency in routine and can be negatively impacted by unstable or non-standard work schedules. For these individuals, maintaining a routinized schedule – as compared to switching shifts – can help in managing both their disability and work requirements.

During times when a disability is particularly disruptive for an employee, it may also be necessary to reduce their work hours or allow the employee to work part-time. These changes can be especially helpful for individuals with episodic disabilities, such as employees with Lupus, depression, or Crohn's disease. Flexibility in scheduling during these flare-ups can enable an employee to maintain their employment while also attending to their health.

Lastly, organizations can offer flexibility throughout the work day by providing employees with extra breaks or combining multiple mini breaks into one larger break (Prince, 2017). Allowing employees to take additional breaks can be helpful for individuals with disabilities that require increased access to the restroom (e.g., Crohn's disease, irritable bowel syndrome, endometriosis); disabilities that result in attentional deficits (e.g., depression, obsessive-compulsive disorder [OCD], anxiety); and physical disabilities that are improved with movement (epilepsy, fibromyalgia).

Job Task Accommodations

Reasonable accommodations for concealable disabilities can also involve changes to the way work tasks are distributed or to the tasks themselves. For instance, employees who have cognitive disruptions as a result of their disability may benefit from receiving written to-do lists or written feedback from their managers. A written list of responsibilities can help ensure the employee actively completes new projects or tasks and can be a helpful reminder for employees who experience problems related to memory loss or attentional focus (e.g., ADHD, Lyme disease, OCD, PTSD). Similarly, receiving written feedback can help employees to process comments from their managers, which can aid in improving their overall work performance – an accommodation that might be especially helpful for employees with ASD.

Employees with concealable disabilities might also benefit from regularly scheduled meetings with their supervisors. These meetings can be used to address any challenges the employee is experiencing, to provide suggestions for continued performance improvement, and to just generally check in on how the employee is doing – all of which can increase employees' self-confidence and provide routine opportunities for open dialogue with their supervisors.

Based on the specific disability, there may be some tasks that employees find difficult to complete and for which accommodations may be difficult to provide. In these instances, organizations can reasonably accommodate these employees through task-switching. Employees with disabilities may either switch out tasks during times when they are experiencing more severe symptomatology or engage in more permanent switching between employees. For instance, an employee undergoing fertility treatments may need to stop performing physically demanding job tasks during certain stages in their treatment cycle, in which case other employees could be assigned these tasks intermittently. On the other hand, an employee with a back injury should refrain from engaging in physically demanding job tasks at any time, in which case these responsibilities could be assigned indefinitely to other employees.

Environmental Accommodations

Altering the work environment can also represent a form of reasonable accommodations. In these situations, organizations make changes to the ambient work setting such as through noise reduction, lighting changes, and management of triggering smells (Prince, 2017). For instance, employees who experience concentration difficulties (e.g.., early-onset Alzheimer's, Lyme disease, OCD, ADHD) might find their work productivity improved when allowed to work in a quiet, distraction-free zone. When separate work spaces are unavailable, organizations could reduce noise by allowing employees to wear noise-cancelling headphones or to play music of their choosing.

Changes to lighting can be helpful for employees who may be sensitive to brightness (e.g., employees with migraines) or for those who require increased light to aid in remaining alert and focused (e.g., seasonal affective disorder, sleep disorders). In these instances, organizations may opt to reduce bright lights, purchase specific lighting sources, or allow employees access to natural light – all depending on their unique needs.

Additionally, organizations can make changes to the physical workspace through specialized equipment or furniture that alleviate discomfort caused by a disability. For instance, some employees may require alterations to how they perform work, either standing or sitting. In these cases, an employee who typically is required to stand may be given a chair or other equipment on which they can rest while doing their work, while some employees who routinely sit may be provided an opportunity to use a standing desk or other arrangement. Employees may also require use of text-to-speech software which can help in reducing cognitive disruptions caused by writing (e.g., ASD, ADHD, and dyslexia). Other ergonomic changes can be useful for accommodating employees with disabilities that are associated with physical pain, for instance, using ergonomic floor mats, keyboards, and chairs. These changes alter the work setting by ultimately making it more comfortable for employees to perform the work.

Lastly, organizations can make changes to location where work is performed by allowing employees to work from home. These changes could be permanent or allowed during times when the symptoms of a disability are especially severe. For instance, an employee with Crohn's disease may feel more comfortable working from home so they could frequently use the bathroom in a private space. Employees with depression or bipolar disorder may find that they require time away from other people or that working from home allows them to better regulate their emotions during the work day. By and large, work-from-home arrangements provide employees flexibility and privacy so that they can appropriately attend to their disabilities while also completing their assigned work tasks. Indeed, recent changes in the global work environment have demonstrated that telecommuting is more feasible than ever.

Future Research of Employees with Concealable Disabilities

Although employees with disabilities comprise a significant portion of the working population, on the whole, there is a lack of research related to their workplace experiences. Of the available empirical research, much has been focused on highlighting the mistreatment these individuals experience through stigma and discrimination (Beatty et al., 2019). Much less research, however, has focused on ways to improve these employees' work experiences.

Related to providing accommodations to employees with concealable disabilities, most research studies have been descriptive in nature, providing information on the types and number of accommodations that employees have requested and received in the workplace (Fabian et al., 1993; JAN, 2020; von Schrader, Xu, & Bruyère, 2014). Though this information is helpful for knowing the global landscape of accommodation, the research can be advanced by using theoretical paradigms to better understand when and why employees request accommodations and the impact those accommodations have on their workplace outcomes. There are ample opportunities for organizational scholars to apply management theories to the study of employees with concealable disabilities, and we present some of the most compelling below.

The study of employees with disabilities has been guided, to a large extent, by attempts to understand how others in the workplace treat those with disabilities (see Beatty et al., 2019, for a review). Yet, little research has been focused on the ways in which individuals with disabilities uniquely experience the workplace. Adopting a person-centered approach to research (Meyer et al., 2013) can advance the field by examining the perceptions, attitudes, and behaviors of individuals with concealable disabilities. Further, prior research has demonstrated that because concealable identities vary in their characteristics, a "one-size-fits-all approach" to studying this population is not appropriate (Follmer et al., 2020). Rather, researchers should consider the specific nature of the disability and use this to guide research questions, as different disabilities are expected to have unique impacts on employees' work attitudes and behaviors. Additionally, the study of employees with disabilities can be advanced by adopting an intersectional lens to more fully understand how multiple intersecting identities shapes an employee's likelihood to request and use accommodations at work.

There are several models of concealable identity management which explain when and why an employee might choose to conceal or reveal their identity at work. Much less empirical work has fully tested these models. Using advanced research methods, we encourage researchers to study the process of identity management to better understand the daily and weekly decisions that employees with disabilities make related to their identity management. Disclosure and concealment are not one-time decisions, but rather decisions that employees make repeatedly throughout their careers. Continued investigation of the organizational factors that contribute to disclosure and accommodation requests would be useful in creating more inclusive workplaces. For instance, how do leadership styles, power dynamics, and organizational policies influence disclosure and accommodation decisions?

Related to disclosure, there are several opportunities to use existing theories of motivation to understand why an employee chooses to seek accommodations. For instance, how might accommodations be used to fulfill basic psychological needs of competence, autonomy, and relatedness? How does equity sensitivity influence employees' beliefs regarding their rights to seek accommodations? What role do goal orientation and self-regulation play in the decision to request accommodations at work? By understanding *why* individuals actively seek out accommodations, scholars can provide more nuanced recommendations to both employees and employers to better facilitate these processes.

Existing research outside of organizational studies has indicated that accommodations can yield positive benefits for employees and organizations. However, more work is needed to demonstrate the unique ways in which accommodations impact employee outcomes, such as holistic job performance (e.g., organizational citizenship behaviors, counterproductive work behaviors), organizational commitment, and engagement.

Adopting a positive psychology lens to the study of employees with concealable disabilities would be useful to highlight the ways in which a disability enriches employees' work experiences and could be used to minimize the stigma that is so often associated with these conditions. For instance, prior research has shown that there are positive benefits of having a mental illness at work (Hennekam et al., 2021) which better equip employees to meet the demands of their job. We encourage researchers to continue to explore the ways that employees can leverage their disability at work and how their unique approaches to work can be used to improve overall organizational effectiveness (Ely & Thomas, 2001).

Altogether, there are ample opportunities to expand the understanding of the work experiences of employees with disabilities. Drawing upon existing theoretical paradigms to explore these experiences can lead to theory expansion (as existing theoretical mechanisms are tested in unique populations) and refinement (as boundary conditions and mediating mechanisms are identified).

Conclusion

It has previously been estimated that 15% of the global workplace meets the criteria for having a concealable disability. Unfortunately, many of these disabilities are subject to stigmatization in the broader public, which can discourage employees from openly disclosing their disability to others in the workplace. Because disclosure is a necessary condition for receiving workplace accommodations, the consequence is that a significant number of employees who are legally entitled to accommodations may fail to request them. Reasonable workplace accommodations not only help employees to fulfill their job responsibilities but also provide benefits to the organization, through increased worker morale and attachment. In this chapter, we defined concealable disabilities and explained the ways in which these disabilities may uniquely manifest across disorders and individuals. We also provided an overview of the legal protections afforded to employees with concealable disabilities and discussed both individual and organizational barriers to requesting accommodations. Finally, we discussed ways in which organizations can provide reasonable accommodations through schedule adjustments, alterations to task assignments, and environmental changes. In doing so, we hope to draw awareness to a group of employees that remains underrepresented in organizational research as well as provide insight into how organizations can better support these individuals in the workplace.

References

Beatty, J. E., Baldridge, D. C., Boehm, S. A., Kulkarni, M., & Colella, A. J. (2019). On the treatment of persons with disabilities in organizations: A review and research agenda. *Human Resource Management*, *58*(2), 119–137. https://psycnet.apa.org/doi/10.1002/hrm.21940

Beatty, J. E., & Kirby, S. L. (2006). Beyond the legal environment: How stigma influences invisible identity groups in the workplace. *Employee Responsibilities and Rights Journal*, *18*(1), 29–44. https://doi.org/10.1007/s10672-005-9003-6

Beatty, J. E., & Joffe, R. (2006). An overlooked dimension of diversity: The career effects of chronic illness. *Organizational Dynamics*, *35*(2), 182–195. https://psycnet.apa.org/doi/10.1016/j.org dyn.2006.03.006

Blanck, P., Hyseni, F., & Altunkol Wise, F. (2020). Diversity and inclusion in the American legal profession: Workplace accommodations for lawyers with disabilities and lawyers who identify as LGBTQ+. *Journal of Occupational Rehabilitation*, *30*(4), 537–564. https://doi.org/10.1007/s10926-020-09938-3

Bolo, C., Sareen, J., Patten, S., Schmitz, N., Currie, S., & Wang, J. (2013). Receiving workplace mental health accommodations and the outcome of mental disorders in employees with a depressive and/or anxiety disorder. *Journal of Occupational and Environmental Medicine*, *55*(11), 1293–1299. https://www.jstor.org/stable/48500557

Brown, R. (2000). *Group processes* (2nd ed.). Blackwell Publishing.

Bureau of Labor Statistics. (2021). *Persons with a disability: Labor force characteristics – 2020*. U.S. Department of Labor. https://www.bls.gov/news.release/pdf/disabl.pdf

Charles, K. K. (2004). The extent and effect of employer compliance with the accommodations mandates of the Americans with Disabilities Act. *Journal of Disability Policy Studies*, *15*(2), 86–96. https://doi.org/10.1177%2F10442073040150020301

Chaudoir, S. R., & Quinn, D. M. (2010). Revealing concealable stigmatized identities: The impact of disclosure motivations and positive first-disclosure experiences on fear of disclosure and well-being: Revealing concealable stigmatized identities. *Journal of Social Issues*, *66*(3), 570–584. https://dx.doi.org/10.1111%2Fj.1540-4560.2010.01663.x

Corrigan, P. (2004). How stigma interferes with mental health care. *American Psychologist*, *59*(7), 614–625. https://doi.org/10.1037/0003-066X.59.7.614

Dong, S., & Guerette, A. R. (2013). Workplace accommodations, job performance and job satisfaction among individuals with sensory disabilities. *The Australian Journal of Rehabilitation Counselling*, *19*(1), 1–20. https://doi.org/10.1017/jrc.2013.1

Dong, S., Warner, A., Mamboleo, G., Guerette, A., & Zalles, M. Z. (2017). Barriers in accommodation process among individuals with visual impairments. *Journal of Rehabilitation*, *83*(2), 27–35. https://www.researchgate.net/publication/319008458_Barriers_in_accommodation_pro cess_among_individuals_with_visual_impairments

Fabian, E. S., Waterworth, A., & Ripke, B. (1993). Reasonable accommodations for workers with serious mental illness: Type, frequency, and associated outcomes. *Psychosocial Rehabilitation Journal*, *17*(2), 163–172. https://psycnet.apa.org/doi/10.1037/h0095591

Follmer, K. B., & Beatty, J. E. (2018, August). The roles of perceived need and stigma in the decision to request accommodations at work. In D. C. Baldridge (Chair), *New directions in disability research: Work contexts, inclusivity, and wellbeing interactions*. Symposium conducted at the annual Academy of Management Conference, Chicago, IL.

Follmer, K. B., & Jones, K. S. (2018). Mental illness in the workplace: An interdisciplinary review and organizational research agenda. *Journal of Management*, *44*(1), 325–351. https://doi.org/10.1177%2F0149206317741194

Follmer, K. B., Sabat, I. E., & Siuta, R. L. (2020). Disclosure of stigmatized identities at work: An interdisciplinary review and agenda for future research. *Journal of Organizational Behavior*, *41*(2), 169–184. https://doi.org/10.1002/job.2402

Gignac, M. A., Cao, X., & McAlpine, J. (2015). Availability, need for, and use of work accommodations and benefits: Are they related to employment outcomes in people with arthritis? *Arthritis Care & Research*, *67*(6), 855–864. https://doi.org/10.1002/acr.22508

Goffman, E. (1963). *Stigma: Notes on the management of spoiled identity*. Prentice-Hall.

Harlan, S. L., & Robert, P. M. (1998). The social construction of disability in organizations: Why employers resist reasonable accommodation. *Work and Occupations*, *25*(4), 397–435. https://doi.org/10.1177%2F0730888498025004002

Hennekam, S., Follmer, K., & Beatty, J. E. (2021). The paradox of mental illness and employment: A person-job fit lens. *The International Journal of Human Resource Management*, *32*(15), 3244–3271. https://doi.org/10.1080/09585192.2020.1867618

Ho, R. C., Husain, S. F., & Ho, C. S. (2018). Cognitive dysfunction in patients with systemic lupus erythematosus: The challenge in diagnosis and management. *Rheumatology Practice and Research*, *3*, 1–12. https://doi.org/10.1177%2F2059902118792434

Job Accommodation Network. (2020, October 21). *Benefits and costs of accommodation*. https://askjan.org/topics/costs.cfm

Johnson, J. D., Asiodu, I. V., McKenzie, C. P., Tucker, C., Tully, K. P., Bryant, K., Verbiest, S., & Stuebe, A. M. (2019). Racial and ethnic inequities in postpartum pain evaluation and management. *Obstetrics & Gynecology*, *134*(6), 1155–1162. https://doi.org/10.1097/aog.0000000000003505

Jones, E. E., Farina, A., Hastorf, A., Markus, H., Miller, D., & Scott, R. (1984). *Social stigma: The psychology of marked relationships*. Freeman.

Jones, K. P., & King, E. B. (2014). Managing concealable stigmas at work: A review and multilevel model. *Journal of Management*, *40*(5), 1466–1494. https://doi.org/10.1177%2F0149206313515518

McDowell, C., & Fossey, E. (2015). Workplace accommodations for people with mental illness: A scoping review. *Journal of Occupational Rehabilitation*, *25*(1), 197–206. https://doi.org/10.1007/s10926-014-9512-y

Meyer, J. P., Stanley, L. J., & Vandenberg, R. J. (2013). A person-centered approach to the study of commitment. *Human Resource Management Review*, *23*(2), 190–202. https://psycnet.apa.org/doi/10.1016/j.hrmr.2012.07.007

Newacheck, P. W., Hung, Y. Y., Jane Park, M., Brindis, C. D., & Irwin, C. E. (2003). Disparities in adolescent health and health care: Does socioeconomic status matter? *Health Services Research*, *38*(5), 1235–1252. https://dx.doi.org/10.1111%2F1475-6773.00174

Prince, M. J. (2017). Persons with invisible disabilities and workplace accommodation: Findings from a scoping literature review. *Journal of Vocational Rehabilitation*, *46*(1), 75–86. https://psycnet.apa.org/doi/10.3233/JVR-160844

Santuzzi, A. M., Waltz, P. R., Finkelstein, L. M., & Rupp, D. E. (2014). Invisible disabilities: Unique challenges for employees and organizations. *Industrial and Organizational Psychology*, *7*(2), 204–219. https://doi.org/10.1111/iops.12134

Sherbin, L., Kennedy, J. T., Jain-Link, P., & Ihezie, K. (2017). *Disability and inclusion*. Center for Talent Innovation. https://www.talentinnovation.org/_private/assets/Disabilities Inclusion_KeyFindings-CTI.pdf

Solovieva, T. I., Dowler, D. L., & Walls, R. T. (2011). Employer benefits from making workplace accommodations. *Disability and Health Journal*, *4*(1), 39–45. https://doi.org/10.1016/j.dhjo.2010.03.001

Sumner, J. A., Hagan, K., Grodstein, F., Roberts, A. L., Harel, B., & Koenen, K. C. (2017). Posttraumatic stress disorder symptoms and cognitive function in a large cohort of middle-aged women. *Depression and Anxiety, 34*(4), 356–366. https://doi.org/10.1002/da.22600

Tajfel, H., Turner, J. C., Austin, W. G., & Worchel, S. (1979). An integrative theory of intergroup conflict. *Organizational Identity: A Reader, 56*(65), 9780203505984–16.

Telwatte, A., Anglim, J., Wynton, S. K., & Moulding, R. (2017). Workplace accommodations for employees with disabilities: A multilevel model of employer decision-making. *Rehabilitation Psychology, 62*(1), 7–19. https://psycnet.apa.org/doi/10.1037/rep0000120

Ely, R. J., & Thomas, D. A. (2001). Cultural diversity at work: The effects of diversity perspectives on work group processes and outcomes. *Administrative Science Quarterly, 46*(2), 229–273. https://doi.org/10.2307%2F2667087

U.S. Equal Employment Opportunity Commission. (2002). *Enforcement guidance on reasonable accommodation and undue hardship under the ADA.* https://www.eeoc.gov/laws/guidance/enforcement-guidance-reasonable-accommodation-and-undue-hardship-under-ada

von Schrader, S., Malzer, V., & Bruyère, S. (2014). Perspectives on disability disclosure: The importance of employer practices and workplace climate. *Employee Responsibilities and Rights Journal, 26*(4), 237–255. https://doi.org/10.1007/s10672-013-9227-9

von Schrader, S., Xu, X., & Bruyère, S. M. (2014). Accommodation requests: Who is asking for what? *Rehabilitation Research, Policy, and Education, 28*(4), 329–344.

Wilens, T. E., Biederman, J., Faraone, S. V., Martelon, M., Westerberg, D., & Spencer, T. J. (2009). Presenting ADHD symptoms, subtypes, and comorbid disorders in clinically referred adults with ADHD. *The Journal of Clinical Psychiatry, 70*(11), 1557–1562. https://doi.org/10.4088/jcp.08m04785pur

Part 3: **Social Reactions to Disability**

Alecia M. Santuzzi, Robert T. Keating, Jesus J. Martinez, and Courtney L. Baker

8 Understanding the Complexity of Disability Stigma and its Consequences for Workers and Organizations

Abstract: This chapter describes the complexity of factors that contribute to social disadvantages experienced by workers with disabilities and divergent abilities in the workplace. We highlight patterns of general stereotypes and reactions to disability, as well as perceptions that are specific to categories of differences including invisible disabilities, mental illness, and neurodivergence. We identify social, psychological, and performance-related impacts that these reactions might create for workers with disabilities. We also argue that these experiences must be considered in a larger context of factors, both within the individual (e.g., intersecting identities) and organization (e.g., climate), to better understand the variability in experiences among workers with disabilities. Finally, we offer insights from research on inclusion practices and experiences to recommend evidence-based strategies to reduce disability stigma and alleviate its negative consequences in organizations.

Keywords: disability stigma, disability stereotype, disability inclusion, disability type, stigma consequences

Introduction

Working adults with disabilities and divergent abilities (differences that may qualify for disability protections even if the individual does not identify with the label "disability") face persistent employment inequities, as demonstrated in employment statistics and research conclusions. Globally, workers with physical, mental, or cognitive limitations that may qualify as disabilities are more likely unemployed, underemployed, and receive lower wages (Beatty et al., 2019; Bureau of Labor Statistics, 2021; United Nations Enable, 2011; also see Schur et al., 2023, from this volume). Although these trends extend across disability types, recent evidence of discrimination appears to highlight workers with divergent cognitive abilities, or neurodivergence (e.g., autism; Krzeminska et al., 2019) and psychological conditions classified as mental illness (Colella & Santuzzi, forthcoming; Follmer & Jones, 2018). The impact of employment

Alecia M. Santuzzi, and Jesus J. Martinez, Northern Illinois University
Robert T. Keating, Northern Illinois University/Illinois Institute of Technology
Courtney L. Baker, East Carolina University

https://doi.org/10.1515/9783110743647-009

inequities for workers with disabilities and divergent abilities also may extend beyond the employment context as discrimination has been shown to yield anxiety, depression, and other symptoms of poor individual well-being (Schmitt et al., 2014).

The root of the observed discrimination in employment statistics is assumed to be the social disadvantages that workers with disabilities and divergent abilities experience when applying for and while maintaining employment. Workers with disabilities are often the target of negative attitudes, beliefs, and/or behaviors. Such treatment can have direct negative consequences for workers' employment status and compensation, as well as provide indirect routes to those inequities through negative effects on interpersonal relationships, psychological well-being, and work-related attitudes and behavior. This chapter will outline the complexity of factors that contribute to social disadvantages experienced by workers with disabilities and divergent abilities in the workplace. We highlight patterns of general stereotypes and reactions to disability, as well as perceptions that are specific to categories of differences including invisible disabilities, mental illness, and neurodivergence. We identify social, psychological, and performance-related impacts that these reactions might create for workers with disabilities. We further argue that these experiences must be considered in a larger context of factors, both within the individual (e.g., intersecting identities) and organization (e.g., climate), to better understand the variability in experiences among workers with disabilities.

The Dimensions of Disability Stigma

Although the aggregate patterns of employment inequities for workers with disabilities are observable and persist across time (despite legislation such as the Americans with Disabilities Act in the U.S.), the underlying mechanisms that contribute to those employment disadvantages may be less obvious and complex. Research and theory point to social stigma – a negative label ascribed to a person based on a devalued characteristic (Crocker et al., 1998) – as the primary cause of the employment and experience gaps observed for workers with disabilities (Stuart, 2004). A general negative evaluation of disability may be associated with a complex array of emotional reactions and underlying assumptions about disability.

Complex Emotional Reactions to Disability

Observers react to disabilities with a variety of emotions including disgust, sympathy, discomfort, and fear (Fiske et al., 2002; Stone & Colella, 1996). However, negative evaluations of individuals with disabilities are difficult to identify as observers may be reluctant to report them or may mask the negative emotion behind a feeling of inspiration or value for equality. As such, disability is commonly associated with attitudes that are *positive but really negative* (Chan et al., 2009; Findler et al., 2007). Although seemingly driven by positive regard, overtly positive reactions are potentially paternalistic (Colella & Stone, 2005) and may generate reactions of pity (Fiske et al., 2002). Pity can be especially damaging in the workplace as such reactions reinforce stereotypic perceptions of low ability and competence among workers with disabilities (Santuzzi & Cook, 2020). Moreover, the reported positive regard toward persons with disabilities may be diluted in the workplace when a co-worker with a disability is perceived as a burden (Colella & Stone, 2005) or accommodations for a co-worker are perceived as unfair (Colella, 2001).

Although difficult to assess directly, negative emotional reactions may be detected in observable behavior toward workers with disabilities, such as displays of discomfort (Fichten et al., 1989; Hebl & Kleck, 2000; Kleck et al., 1966) and physical distancing or avoidance (Snyder et al., 1979). This puts workers with disabilities at risk of fewer interpersonal connections in the workplace, which can be quite damaging given the strong situational demand for creating a positive professional workplace identity (Roberts, 2005). For example, workers with disabilities might be excluded from informal social connections that serve as bridges to more formal professional networks and advancement opportunities.

Beyond restricted social networks and important work relationships, actively managing a disability to reduce the likelihood of being stigmatized at work comes with costs to individual health and well-being. This may be especially problematic for workers who are effortfully concealing the disability or avoiding situations to downplay it (DeJordy, 2008). Adults with disabilities and health conditions perceived as stigmatized (according to Jones et al., 1984) have reported more social isolation and challenges with developing social support systems, more impairments to health and well-being, and more emotional regulation difficulties (Pachankis et al., 2017). Moreover, if the disability-related stigma is internalized, it can be detrimental to worker job performance and career decision-making as it impacts their beliefs that they can do the job, perceived competence, and motivation (Corrigan et al., 2009).

Complex Assumptions About Disability

Although negative evaluation in itself can be damaging to the social network and individual well-being of workers with disabilities, the underlying beliefs that drive those evaluations may be especially problematic in a performance domain such as the workplace.

General disability stereotypes. Observers may hold assumptions and stereotypes about individuals with disabilities that fuel inferences about those workers' traits, including performance-related traits such as ability and motivation. For instance, general stereotypes about individuals with disabilities suggest that they are less competent (Cuddy et al., 2007) and unqualified to perform in jobs, despite evidence to the contrary (Olkin, 1999; Stone & Colella, 1996; see Santuzzi & Cook, 2020 for a review). Additionally, those with disabilities are often viewed as being unable to interact well with others, especially when the disability is psychological or cognitive (Follmer & Jones, 2018). Such beliefs would lead observers to infer that workers with disabilities may be less qualified for customer-facing and other roles that rely on social and communication skills. Broadly, disability stereotypes can be detrimental to several personnel outcomes for workers with disabilities, including hiring, performance evaluation, and advancement decisions.

It is important to note that much of the past research on general disability stereotypes and assumptions has been conducted on visible, physical disabilities (Stone & Colella, 1996). Although a visible physical disability is often the image that comes to mind when cued by the term "disability," there is a wide variety of limitations that are not physical or visible to others that may qualify as disabilities in the workplace. Recent research has expanded beyond physical impairments to highlight other types of disabilities and ability differences, revealing some similarities as well as unique features of the disability stigma across disability types.

Stigma differences among disability types. Disabilities vary widely in the features that are associated with them. Several typologies in the literature highlight the way stigma may vary due to specific attributes of the stigmatized characteristic. For example, Jones and colleagues (1984) indicate that reactions may vary based on the characteristic's concealability, course, disruptiveness, aesthetics, origin, and peril. Likewise, observers may hold different assumptions and beliefs about specific disabilities, such as for concealable disabilities, mental illness, or neurodivergence, which may provide different stigma experiences and routes to inequities.

Concealable disabilities. One of the key dimensions from the Jones et al. (1984) typology – concealability – has been examined as particularly important to the experiences of disability in the workplace. Concealable disabilities are those that do not have visible signs of disability or observable differences are not clearly connected to disability (Santuzzi & Keating, 2020). Examples of concealable disabilities range from chronic illnesses to autoimmune disorders to psychological disorders. When an employee has a concealable stigmatized identity, they are faced with the additional task of determining whether to disclose this status. While it may seem like the obvious solution to disclose as this allows employees to get access to legal protections and accommodations they may need, they are often met with suspicion and uncertainty due to the invisible features of these disabilities. Because of this potential stigma, workers with disabilities often choose not to disclose and forfeit needed accommodations so they are not met with the social cost of doing so.

Although perhaps avoiding the immediate negative evaluation from others' knowing about a disability, concealing a disability at work may come with its own costs to health, well-being, and workplace relationships (Santuzzi et al., 2019). Concealing an identity at work leads to lower self-esteem and job satisfaction compared to those who reveal their identities (Newhesier et al., 2017). Concealing may also require effortful self-regulation, which may interfere with individual well-being and task performance (DeJordy, 2008). These challenges may create secondary impairments that indirectly affect performance, others' evaluations of motivation and ability, and personnel decisions in the workplace.

Mental illness. The stigma attached to mental illness has been described as especially severe as it includes components of unpredictability and dangerousness that are not ascribed to physical disabilities. Very common psychological disorders such as major depression and anxiety might cue uncertainty and fear in others due to concerns about unpredictable behavior. Other disorders like drug addiction may signal a level of personal accountability (e.g., Corrigan et al., 2007). Krupa et al. (2009) identified four major assumptions about mental illness in the workplace that contribute to inequities among workers. These assumptions suggest workers with mental illness do not have the competence to meet task and social demands, are dangerous and unpredictable, do not have a legitimate illness, and are employed due to charity. Such beliefs impact personnel decisions including hiring and job placement. For instance, workers with mental illness are more likely to be assigned to jobs with lower difficulty, at lower levels of the organization, and that involve less social interaction (Garske & Stewart, 1999; see Colella & Santuzzi, forthcoming, for a review). The stigmatizing judgment faced by workers with mental illness in the workplace have been associated with poor health and well-being (Follmer & Jones, 2018), as workers with mental illness tend to engage in effortful identity management strategies to conceal the illness at least partially at work (Follmer & Jones, 2021) and react to threats of stigma by overworking, incur more stress at work, and managing demands with fewer coping resources (Hennekam et al., 2021).

Neurodivergence. Although previously discussed in the literature as a subcategory of mental illness, neurodivergent features such as attention deficit/hyperactivity disorder (ADHD) and autism spectrum disorder are now considered a separate category of ability divergence with unique stigma experiences (Boysen, Chicosky, & Delmore, 2020; Boysen, Isaacs, et al., 2020; Cage et al., 2019). Neurodiversity marks a change towards acknowledging that the cognitive differences that are features of certain types of mental illnesses are a part of the greater human variation in cognitive functioning, and not a sign of an impairment (Krzeminska et al., 2019). Attitudes toward neurodivergence have been evolving in recent years and adds additional complexity to the already complicated situation of disclosure in the workplace (Santuzzi & Keating, in press). Neurodivergent workers are still met with the inaccurate assessment of their abilities and treated in stereotypic ways associated with disabilities (Santuzzi &

Cook, 2020). Particularly, people who are labeled as neurodivergent may face assumptions of incompetence, depleted general abilities, and a lack of independence (Colella & Stone, 2005). This can be especially detrimental as workers with neurodivergent features are often within average human variation on cognitive functioning, yet they experience mistreatment on a stigmatized identity despite their high potential for contributions to the workplace (Austin & Pisano, 2017). Yet, current statistics show that neurodivergent workers have high unemployment rates and low wages compared to the general population of workers in the U.S. (Butterworth et al., 2015; Roux et al., 2017; Santuzzi & Keating, in press), and are at higher risk of poor well-being at work due to concerns about stigma (Johnson & Joshi, 2016).

Intersecting Identities: Complex Associations with Other Meaningful Identities

Workers with disabilities and divergent abilities may vary greatly in the degree to which they hold such differences as central to their self-definitions (Kapp et al., 2013; Santuzzi & Waltz, 2016). Workers with disabilities integrate their disability with their other important roles and identities in the workplace, including occupation, gender, race, and ethnicity. Despite the range of individual differences and identities that comprise one's self-definition, researchers have viewed disability as the prominent social identity that shapes an individual's work experience (Bell, 2006; Miles et al., 2017). Indeed, the current literature on disability issues largely treats disability as a singular issue, downplaying the differences among types and failing to acknowledge the experience of disability in the context of other social identities and roles (Santuzzi & Cook, 2020). Unfortunately, this results in an inaccurate and incomplete image of the experiences of workers with disabilities. A shift to an intersectional perspective would encourage researchers and practitioners to broaden their perspectives on how disability affects workers with disabilities and their organizations.

Broadly, the culture that informs an intersecting identity or role may contribute to a worker's internal experience and others' evaluations of disability. For example, the development, expression, treatment, and understanding of mental illness are known to be influenced by culture (Mizock & Russinova, 2013). According to that work, the emphasis on the warrior role and history of substance abuse contributes to the Native American culture being less accepting of schizoaffective disorder. Furthermore, the researchers suggested cultures that do not place blame on an individual for their condition were more likely to be accepting of mental illness. Thus, the extent to which culture encourages individual blame for disability might predict the degree of stigma and its consequences for members of those cultures who also have disabilities.

Gender also might influence the extent to which workers with disabilities are willing to integrate disability into their identity as expressed to others. Based on gender role expectations, men might be less likely to disclose a disability than women. Santuzzi and Cook (2020) suggest that women (and older people) appear to be more willing to accept a disability identity. Men's resistance to disclosure could stem from wanting to maintain a masculine image. Strength and energy are connected with the masculine male prototype, unlike the disability prototype, which is associated with weakness (Stone & Colella, 1996). Women might not experience the same image conflict given that the stereotypic traits (e.g., dependent, weak) linked to the female prototype better align with those of the disability prototype.

Although women with disabilities generally may be more likely to disclose them, they could experience distinct challenges when disclosing compared to men with disabilities. For instance, women with disabilities might face more skepticism than men about their disability. This could stem from differences in expectations for specific types of disabilities. For instance, given the higher diagnosis rates, men should be seen as the ADHD prototype. Additionally, earlier in the lifespan, girls tend to display more subtle symptoms (e.g., inattention) than boys (American Psychiatric Association, 2013). This would make it more difficult to detect ADHD in girls and, thus, reinforce the image of ADHD as a disability more likely to affect men. Thus, a woman disclosing ADHD might be more surprising and yield more reactions of skepticism at work.

The limited research available on the intersection of disabilities with other identities (e.g., gender) focus on employment and pay inequities (Doren & Benz, 2001; O'Hara, 2004). Although continued research on intersectionality with disability is much needed, the literature implies that focusing only on disability in isolation of other relevant identities and roles would yield a deficient understanding of the stigma experience for workers with disabilities. Similarly, any organizational efforts to reduce stigma aimed only at disability as a singular identity might not be as effective as desired if the complexity of disability stigma is not fully considered.

The Role of Employing Organizations in Reducing Disability Stigma

Although many of the direct consequences of managing a disability in the workplace are experienced at the individual level, organizations are in a position to reduce the disadvantage experienced by workers with disabilities (Beatty et al., 2019; Stone & Colella, 1996). While guidance on specific strategies for doing so are currently lacking in the literature, emerging research has identified several organizational practices and interventions that show promise in reducing complex disability-related stigma and increasing the visibility and inclusion of workers with disabilities into the organizational culture and work processes.

Given the stated role of stigma in facilitating disadvantage among persons with disabilities, it seems logical that organizations should prioritize reducing stigma as an initial step in their inclusion efforts. This has been accomplished to some degree by anti-discrimination policies mandated by legislation at national and local government levels. However, even when instances of overt discrimination are prevented, subtle forms of bias are likely to persist (Jones et al., 2016). Furthermore, individuals may carry internalizations of this stigma into the work context and anticipate negative reactions regardless of whether discrimination was directly experienced (Quinn et al., 2015). Thus, it becomes important for organizations to prioritize policies and practices that not only directly target overt behavioral manifestations of disability stigma but also at creating work environments in which the threat of stigma is minimized among workers with different types of disabilities and individual differences.

Organizations may be able to overcome the complexity of disability stigma and increase their competitive advantage (Kalargyrou, 2014) by promoting inclusive workplace policies and practices. Workplace inclusion is a broad concept that involves increasing participation from all employees in formal and informal (social) work processes (Ferdman, 2014; Mor-Barak & Cherin, 1998; Shore et al., 2018). Organizational practices that are considered "inclusive" vary extensively and have robust applicability and effectiveness – they are generally associated with positive psychological and behavioral outcomes in the workplace regardless of the content of the practice or employee social identity. Their broad applicability may make inclusion practices especially valuable to the complexity of disability stigma and intersecting identities.

Ideally, disability inclusion practices start at the recruitment stage of the employee life cycle and continue through hiring and retention (Kulkarni et al., 2016; Suresh & Dayaram, 2020). However, most studies have examined antecedents and outcomes of workplace disability inclusion on incumbent employees. Several of these studies focused on associating indicators of organizational support and interpersonal support with perceptions of disability inclusion and disability disclosure (a key marker of inclusiveness toward workers with disabilities; von Schrader et al., 2014). In a survey of workers with disabilities, von Schrader et al. (2014) reported that a supportive supervisor relationship, knowledge that one's employer made efforts to create a disability-friendly workplace and recruit workers with disabilities, and inclusion of disability in the company diversity statement and promotional materials contributed to more disability disclosure.

More recently, Heera and Maini (2019) surveyed workers with disabilities in India and found positive associations between several organizational factors (workplace treatment, HR practices, and disability initiatives) and interpersonal factors (supportive co-workers and supervisors) and perceptions of disability inclusion, which, in turn, had positive associations with job satisfaction, organizational commitment, and intentions to stay. Building on this work and related studies from India, Suresh and Dayaram (2020) indicated that practices such as targeted recruitment drives, interviewer sensitivity training, mentorship programs, accessible workplaces, and job mapping may be effective in increasing disability inclusion. At the interpersonal level, practices centered on respectful and unbiased treatment, helping behaviors, and communication from co-workers and supervisors without disabilities, as well as facilitating social connections and mentorships with other workers with disabilities might be especially effective.

Organizational support for workers with disabilities also might be manifested in organizational practices demonstrating flexibility. For example, organizational flexibility, defined as diffusion of decision-making power, moderated the relationship between having a disability (vs. not having a disability) and job satisfaction, such that when decision-making power is more distributed (low centralization) workers with disabilities experience more job satisfaction than workers without disabilities (Baumgärtner et al., 2014). Thus, it appears that providing workers with disabilities with a stake in organizational decisions may be an effective disability inclusion strategy that has implications for job attitudes and performance.

Another indicator of workplace inclusion specific to workers with disabilities is an employer's openness to work accommodations. Accommodations facilitate work accessibility and equitable performance conditions for workers whose limitations interfere with essential functions of the job. However, many workers with disabilities are reluctant to request accommodations due to fear of discrimination, perceived unfairness from co-workers, and noncompliance by the employer (Baldridge & Veiga, 2001). When accommodation requests are granted, they could be met with a wide range of very positive or very negative interpersonal experiences with co-workers and degrees of effectiveness of accommodations (Kensbock et al., 2017). An organization's accommodation climate is likely a qualifying factor in the direction of the accommodation experience for workers with disabilities (Baldridge & Veiga, 2001). Employers that are welcoming to accommodation requests, give requests fair consideration, and comply with relevant requests communicate a climate of inclusion toward workers with disabilities (Baldridge & Swift, 2016; Gates & Akabas, 2011). Taken together, research suggests that organizations can play a role in the work-related and social integration of workers with disabilities through increasing work accessibility through accommodations and/or flexible job design.

More recently, researchers have extended the conceptualization of inclusion as an organizational practice to inclusion as an individual psychological experience of belongingness and authenticity (Jansen et al., 2014; Shore et al., 2011). The shift to an intrapersonal perspective of inclusion was due in large part to the proliferation of definitions of inclusion practices and, thus, the utility of identifying a common underlying inclusion process. Moreover, a focus on generating *felt* inclusion experiences when developing interventions may have broader applicability compared to the inclusion practices in research that often target specific types of disabilities or identities. In a recent study with a sample of employed adults who reported a physical or psychological disability, Keating and Santuzzi (2019) found that those who were exposed to an inclusive organizational statement were more likely to reveal and less likely to conceal their disability, and this occurred indirectly through decreased anticipated stigma, compared to those who viewed non-inclusive statements. Inclusive organizations that provide employees with a sense that they belong and are valued for their authentic selves may be effective in creating work climates for a variety of disabilities and other identities.

Conclusion

As research continues to unfold, the characteristics of the disability experience among workers has become more complex. Others' reactions, as well as the internal experience, may vary greatly by the nature of the disability, associated beliefs and stereotypes, and the other identities expressed by the workers with disabilities. Organizations must better understand how workers vary in their experiences with disabilities in the context of their other individual differences, and then capitalize on that knowledge to develop inclusive policies and practices. A broad approach to disability inclusion may be better suited to the complexity of disability stigma, wide variety of disability types, and intersecting identities than a specific target to reduce disability stigma based on a narrow definition.

References

American Psychiatric Association. (2013). *Diagnostic and statistical manual of mental disorders* (5th ed.).

Austin, R. D., & Pisano, G. P. (2017). Neurodiversity as a competitive advantage. *Harvard Business Review, 95*(3), 96–103. https://hbr.org/2017/05/neurodiversity-as-a-competitive-advantage

Baldridge, D. C., & Swift, M. L. (2016). Age and assessments of disability accommodation request normative appropriateness. *Human Resource Management, 55*(3), 385–400.

Baldridge, D. C., & Veiga, J. F. (2001). Toward a greater understanding of the willingness to request an accommodation: Can requesters' beliefs disable the Americans with Disabilities Act? *Academy of Management Review, 26*(1), 85–99.

Baumgärtner, M. K., Dwertmann, D. J. G., Boehm, S. A., & Bruch, H. (2014). Job satisfaction of employees with disabilities: The role of perceived structural flexibility. *Human Resource Management, 54*(2), 323–343. https://doi.org/10.1002/hrm.21673

Beatty, J. E., Baldridge, D. C., Boehm, S. A., Kulkarni, M., & Colella, A. J. (2019). On the treatment of persons with disabilities in organizations: A review and research agenda. *Human Resource Management, 58*(2), 119–137. https://doi.org/10.1002/hrm.21940

Bell, C. (2006). Introducing white disability studies: A modest proposal. In L. Davis (Ed.), *The disability studies reader* (pp. 275–282). Routledge.

Boysen, G. A., Chicosky, R. L., & Delmore, E. E. (2020). Dehumanization of mental illness and the stereotype content model. *Stigma and Health*. https://psycnet.apa.org/doi/10.1037/sah0000256

Boysen, G. A., Isaacs, R. A., Tretter, L., & Markowski, S. (2020). Evidence for blatant dehumanization of mental illness and its relation to stigma. *The Journal of Social Psychology*, *160*(3), 346–356. https://psycnet.apa.org/doi/10.1080/00224545.2019.1671301

Bureau of Labor Statistics. (2021). Persons with a disability: Labor force characteristics – 2020. https://www.bls.gov/news.release/pdf/disabl.pdf

Butterworth, J., Hiersteiner, D., Engler, J., Bershadsky, J., & Bradley, V. (2015). National Core Indicators ©: Data on the current state of employment of adults with IDD and suggestions for policy development. *Journal of Vocational Rehabilitation*, *42*(3), 209–220. https://doi.org/10.3233/jvr-150741

Cage, E., Di Monaco, J., & Newell, V. (2019). Understanding, attitudes and dehumanization towards autistic people. *Autism: The International Journal of Research and Practice*, *23*(6), 1373–1383. https://doi.org/10.1177/1362361318811290

Chan, F., Livneh, H., Pruett, S. R., Wang, C.-C., & Zheng, L. X. (2009). Societal attitudes toward disability: Concepts, measurements, and interventions. In F. Chan, E. Da Silva Cardoso & J. A. Chronister (Eds.), *Understanding psychosocial adjustment to chronic illness and disability: A handbook for evidence-based practitioners in rehabilitation* (pp. 333–367). Springer.

Colella, A. (2001). Coworker distributive fairness judgments of the workplace accommodation of employees with disabilities. *Academy of Management Review*, *26*, 100–116. https://doi.org/10.2307/259397

Colella, A., & Santuzzi, A. M. (forthcoming). Known and unknown mental illness: Uncovering the hidden routes to workplace inequities. *Journal of Management*.

Colella, A., & Stone, D. L. (2005). Workplace discrimination toward persons with disabilities: A call for some new research directions. In R. Dipboye & A. Colella (Eds.), *Discrimination at work: The psychological and organizational bases* (pp. 227–253). Lawrence Erlbaum.

Corrigan, P. W., Larson, J. E., & Kuwabara, S. A. (2007). Mental illness stigma and the fundamental components of supported employment. *Rehabilitation Psychology*, *52*(4), 451–457. https://psycnet.apa.org/doi/10.1037/0090-5550.52.4.451

Corrigan, P. W., Larson, J. E., & Rusch, N. (2009). Self-stigma and the "why try" effect: Impact on life goals and evidence-based practices. *World Psychiatry*, *8*, 75–81. https://dx.doi.org/10.1002%2Fj.2051-5545.2009.tb00218.x

Crocker, J., Major, B., & Steele, C. M. (1998). Social stigma. In D. T. Gilbert, S. T. Fiske & G. Lindzey (Eds.), *The handbook of social psychology* (Vol. 2, pp. 504–553). Oxford University Press.

Cuddy, A. J., Fiske, S. T., & Glick, P. (2007). The BIAS map: Behaviors from intergroup affect and stereotypes. *Journal of Personality and Social Psychology*, *92*(4), 631–648. https://psycnet.apa.org/doi/10.1037/0022-3514.92.4.631

DeJordy, R. (2008). Just passing through: Stigma, passing, and identity decoupling in the work place. *Group & Organization Management*, *33*, 504–531. https://doi.org/10.1177%2F1059601108324879

Doren, B., & Benz, M. (2001). Gender equity issues in the vocational and transition services and employment outcomes experienced by young women with disabilities. In H. Roussom & M. L. Wehmeyer (Eds.), *Double jeopardy: Addressing gender equity in special education* (pp. 289–312). SUNY Press.

Ferdman, B. M. (2014). The practice of inclusion in diverse organizations: Toward a systematic and inclusive framework. In B. M. Ferdman & B. R. Deane (Eds.), *Diversity at work: The practice of inclusion* (pp. 3–54). Jossey-Bass.

Fichten, C. S., Robillard, K., Judd, D., & Amsel, R. (1989). College students with physical disabilities: Myths and realities. *Rehabilitation Psychology*, *34*(4), 243–257. https://psycnet.apa.org/doi/10.1037/h0091729

Findler, L., Vilchinsky, N., & Werner, S. (2007). The multidimensional attitudes scale toward persons with disabilities (MAS) construction and validation. *Rehabilitation Counseling Bulletin*, *50*(3), 166–176. https://psycnet.apa.org/doi/10.1177/00343552070500030401

Fiske, S. T., Cuddy, A. J. C., Glick, P., & Xu, J. (2002). A model of (often mixed) stereotype content: Competence and warmth respectively follow from perceived status and competition. *Journal of Personality and Social Psychology*, *42*(6), 878–902. https://psycnet.apa.org/doi/10.1037/0022-3514.82.6.878

Follmer, K. B., & Jones, K. S. (2021). Navigating depression at work: Identity management strategies along the disclosure continuum. *Group & Organization Management*, https://doi.org/10.1177/10596011211002010

Follmer, K. B., & Jones, K. S. (2018). Mental illness in the workplace: An interdisciplinary review and organizational research agenda. *Journal of Management*, *44*(1), 325–351. https://doi.org/10.1177%2F0149206317741194

Garske, G. G., & Stewart, J. R. (1999). Stigmatic and mythical thinking: Barriers to vocational rehabilitation services for persons with severe mental illness. *Journal of Rehabilitation*, *65*(4), 4–8. https://link.gale.com/apps/doc/A58575805/AONE?u=anon~cb857259&sid=googleScholar&xid=1bf65e40

Gates, L. B., & Akabas, S. H. (2011). Inclusion of people with mental health disabilities into the workplace: Accommodation as a social process. In I. A. Schultz & E. S. Rogers (Eds.), *Work accommodation and retention in mental health* (pp. 375–391). Springer.

Hebl, M. R., & Kleck, R. E. (2000). The social consequences of physical disability. In T. F. Heatherton, R. E. Kleck, M. R. Hebl & J. G. Hull (Eds.), *The social psychology of stigma* (pp. 419–439). Guilford Press.

Heera, S., & Maini, A. (2019). Examining the antecedents and consequences of disability inclusion at the workplace: A study of persons with disabilities (PWDs) in the union territory (UT) of Jammu and Kashmir, India. *South Asian Journal of Management*, *26*(4), 109–132.

Hennekam, S., Follmer, K., & Beatty, J. (2021). Exploring mental illness in the workplace: The role of HR professionals and processes. *The International Journal of Human Resource Management*, *32*(15), 3135–3156. https://doi.org/10.1080/09585192.2021.1960751

Jansen, W. S., Otten, S., van der Zee, K. I., & Jans, L. (2014). Inclusion: Conceptualization and measurement. *European Journal of Social Psychology*, *44*, 370–385. https://doi.org/10.1002/ejsp.2011

Johnson, T. D., & Joshi, A. (2016). Dark clouds or silver linings? A stigma threat perspective on the implications of an autism diagnosis for workplace well-being. *Journal of Applied Psychology*, *101*(3), 430–449. https://doi.org/10.1037/apl0000058

Jones, E. E., Farina, A., Hastorf, A. H., & Markus, H., Miller, D. T., & Scott, R. A. (1984). *Social stigma: The psychology of marked relationships*. Freeman.

Jones, K. P., King, E. B., Gilrane, V. L., McCausland, T. C., Cortina, J. M., & Grimm, K. J. (2016). The baby bump: Managing a dynamic stigma over time. *Journal of Management*, *42*(6), 1530–1556. https://doi.org/10.1177%2F0149206313503012

Kalargyrou, V. (2014). Gaining a competitive advantage with disability inclusion initiatives. *Journal of Human Resources in Hospitality & Tourism*, *13*(2), 120–145. https://doi.org/10.1080/15332845.2014.847300

Kapp, S. K., Gillespie-Lynch, K., Sherman, L. E., & Hutman, T. (2013). Deficit, difference, or both? Autism and neurodiversity. *Developmental Psychology*, *49*(1), 59–71. https://doi.org/10.1037/a0028353

Keating, R. T., & Santuzzi, A. M. (2019, August). The role of inclusive work environments in disclosure of concealable disabilities. In D. C. Baldridge & M. Kulkarni (Chairs), *Advances in disability research: Toward greater understanding of inclusive organizations*. Symposium conducted at the 79th Annual Meeting of the Academy of Management, Boston, MA.

Kensbock, J. M., Boehm, S. A., & Bourovoi, K. (2017). Is there a downside of job accommodations? An employee perspective on individual change processes. *Frontiers in Psychology, 8,* 1536–1536. https://doi.org/10.3389/fpsyg.2017.01536

Kleck, R., Ono, H., & Hastorf, A. H. (1966). The effects of physical deviance upon face-to-face interaction. *Human Relations, 19*(4), 425–436. https://doi.org/10.1177/001872676601900406

Krupa, T., Kirsh, B., Cockburn, L., & Gewurtz, R. (2009). Understanding the stigma of mental illness in employment. *Work, 33*(4), 413–425. https://doi.org/10.3233/WOR-2009-0890

Krzeminska, A., Austin, R. D., Bruyère, S. M., & Hedley, D. (2019). The advantages and challenges of neurodiversity employment in organizations. *Journal of Management & Organization, 25*(4), 453–463. https://doi.org/10.1017/jmo.2019.58

Kulkarni, M., Boehm, S. A., & Basu, S. (2016). Workplace inclusion of persons with a disability: Comparison of Indian and German multinationals. *Equality, Diversity and Inclusion: An International Journal, 35*(7/8), 397–414. http://dx.doi.org/10.1108/EDI-08-2016-0066

Miles, A. L., Nishida, A., & Forber-Pratt, A. J. (2017). An open letter to white disability studies and ableist institutions of higher education. *Disability Studies Quarterly, 37*(3). https://doi.org/10.18061/dsq.v37i3.5997

Mor-Barak, M. E., & Cherin, D. A. (1998). A tool to expand organizational understanding of workforce diversity: Exploring a measure of inclusion-exclusion. *Administration in Social Work, 22*(1), 47–64. https://doi.org/10.1300/J147v22n01_04

Newheiser, A.-K., Barreto, M., & Tiemersma, J. (2017). People like me don't belong here: Identity concealment is associated with negative workplace experiences. *Journal of Social Issues, 73,* 341–358. https://doi.org/10.1111/josi.12220

Mizock, L., & Russinova, Z. (2013). Racial and ethnic cultural factors in the process of acceptance of mental illness. *Rehabilitation Counseling Bulletin, 56*(4), 229–239. https://psycnet.apa.org/doi/10.1177/0034355213475823

O'Hara, B. (2004). Twice penalized: Employment discrimination against women with disabilities. *Journal of Disability Policy Studies, 15*(1), 27–34. https://doi.org/10.1177%2F10442073040150010501

Olkin, R. (1999). The personal, professional and political when clients have disabilities. *Women & Therapy, 22*(2), 87–103. https://doi.org/10.1300/J015v22n02_07

Pachankis, J. E., Hatzenbuehler, M. L., Wang, K., Burton, C. L., Crawford, F. W., Phelan, J. C., & Link, B. G. (2017). The burden of stigma on health and well-being: A taxonomy of concealment, course, disruptiveness, aesthetics, origin, and peril across 93 stigmas. *Personality and Social Psychology Bulletin, 44*(4), 451–474. https://doi.org/10.1177%2F0146167217741313

Quinn, D. M., Williams, M. K., & Weisz, B. M. (2015). From discrimination to internalized mental illness stigma: The mediating roles of anticipated discrimination and anticipated stigma. *Psychiatric Rehabilitation Journal, 38*(2), 103–108. https://doi.org/10.1037/prj0000136

Roberts, L. M. (2005). Changing faces: Professional image construction in diverse organizational settings. *Academy of Management Review, 30*(4), 685–711. https://doi.org/10.2307/20159163

Roux, A. M., Shattuck, P. T., Rast, J. E., & Anderson, K. A. (2017). *National autism indicators report: Developmental disability services and outcomes in adulthood*. Life Course Outcomes Research Program, A. J. Drexel Autism Institute, Drexel University. https://drexel.edu/autismoutcomes/publications-and-reports/publications/National-Autism-Indicators-Report-Developmental-Disability-Services-and-Outcomes-in-Adulthood/

Santuzzi, A. M., & Cook, L. (2020). Stereotypes about people with disabilities. In J. Nadler & E. Voyles (Eds.), *Stereotypes: The incidence and impacts of bias* (pp. 243–263). Praeger Publishing.

Santuzzi, A. M., & Keating, R. (in press). Neurodiversity disclosure. Invited chapter to appear in S. Bruyere & A. Colella (Eds.), *Neurodiversity in the workplace*. SIOP Organizational Frontiers Series.

Santuzzi, A. M., Keating, R., Martinez, J., Finkelstein, L., Rupp, D., & Strah, N. (2019). Uncovering antecedents and consequences of identity management strategies for workers with concealable disabilities. *Journal of Social Issues, 75*(3), 847–880. https://doi.org/10.1111/josi.12320

Santuzzi, A. M., & Keating, R. T. (2020). Managing invisible disabilities in the workplace: Identification and disclosure dilemmas for workers with hidden impairments. In S. L. Fielden, M. E. Moore & G. L. Bend (Eds.), *The Palgrave handbook of disability at work* (pp. 331–349). Palgrave Macmillan.

Santuzzi, A. M., & Waltz, P. R. (2016). Disability in the workplace: A unique and variable identity. *Journal of Management, 42*(5), 1111–1135. https://doi.org/10.1177%2F0149206315626269

Schmitt, M. T., Branscombe, N. R., Postmes, T., & Garcia, A. (2014). The consequences of perceived discrimination for psychological well-being: A meta-analytic review. *Psychological Bulletin, 140*(4), 921–948. https://doi.org/10.1037/a0035754

Shore, L. M., Cleveland, J. N., & Sanchez, D. (2018). Inclusive workplaces: A review and model. *Human Resource Management Review, 28*(2), 176–189. https://doi.org/10.1016/j.hrmr.2017.07.003

Shore, L. M., Randel, A. E., Chung, B. G., Dean, M. A., Holcombe Ehrhart, K., & Singh, G. (2011). Inclusion and diversity in work groups: A review and model for future research. *Journal of Management, 37*(4), 1262–1289. https://doi.org/10.1177/0149206310385943

Snyder, M. L., Kleck, R. E., Strenta, A., & Mentzer, S. J. (1979). Avoidance of the handicapped: An attributional ambiguity analysis. *Journal of Personality and Social Psychology, 37*(12), 2297–2306. https://doi.org/10.1037/0022-3514.37.12.2297

Stone, D. L., & Colella, A. (1996). A model of factors affecting the treatment of disabled individuals in organizations. *Academy of Management Review, 21*(2), 352–401. https://doi.org/10.2307/258666

Stuart, H. (2004). Stigma and work. *Healthcare Papers, 5*(2), 100–111. https://doi.org/10.12927/hcpap.16829

Suresh, V., & Dayaram, L. (2020). Workplace disability inclusion in India: Review and directions. *Management Research Review, 43*(12). https://doi.org/10.1108/MRR-11-2019-0479

United Nations Enable. (2011, April). Convention on the Rights of Persons with Disabilities Enable newsletter. http://www.un.org/disabilities/latest.asp?id=169

von Schrader, S., Malzer, V., & Bruyère, S. (2014). Perspectives on disability disclosure: The importance of employer practices and workplace climate. *Employee Responsibilities and Rights Journal, 26*, 237–255. https://doi.org/10.1007/s10672-013-9227-9

Alexandra Lefcoe, Silvia Bonaccio, and Catherine E. Connelly

9 Managers' Reactions to Job Applicants and Employees with Disabilities

Abstract: Employers frequently hold misconceptions and negative attitudes towards job applicants and employees with disabilities. In this chapter, we review the literature on manager reactions to individuals with disabilities during three key stages of the employment cycle of individuals with disabilities: recruitment and selection, the provision of accommodations, and performance management. We consider the organizational context, in particular organizational size and climate, diversity policies and support from senior leadership as important contextual factors that may shape managers' behaviors and attitudes towards individuals with disabilities. We end the chapter by presenting future research opportunities to guide further study in this important area of inquiry.

Keywords: applicants with disabilities, discrimination, employees with disabilities, employer misconceptions, stigma

Individuals with disabilities are significantly less likely to be employed in comparison to those without disabilities (International Labour Organization, 2020), regardless of their age or educational attainment (Bureau of Labor Statistics, 2021), and despite their desire to participate in the labor force (Ali, Schur & Blanck, 2011; Prince, 2016). This disparity is often a result of managers' misconceptions about employees with disabilities, such as the myth that employees with disabilities are less competent (Lyubykh et al., 2020), a misplaced belief that accommodations are expensive (Fisher & Connelly, 2020), or that employees with disabilities are difficult to manage or discipline (Kaye, Jans & Jones, 2011). Prejudicial attitudes such as these influence whether individuals with disabilities are hired or accommodated in the workplace (Burke et al., 2013), and can significantly harm their opportunities for promotion and development (Jans et al., 2012).

These findings are surprising when evaluated in the context of disability legislation, such as the *Canadian Human Rights Act* or the *Equality Act* in the U.K., which prohibits discrimination on the basis of disability during all (human resources) HR processes. While critical, this type of legislation has been criticized because it often

Note: The second and third authors would like to acknowledge the support of a Social Sciences and Humanities Research Council of Canada Grant (grant number 435-2020-0270).

Alexandra Lefcoe, and Catherine E. Connelly, DeGroote School of Business, McMaster University, Ontario, Canada
Silvia Bonaccio, Telfer School of Management, University of Ottawa, Ontario, Canada

https://doi.org/10.1515/9783110743647-010

results in managers adopting a compliance mindset (Kuznetsova & Yalcin, 2017). Furthermore, there is substantial evidence that legislation alone is insufficient to provide workplace conditions that allow workers with disabilities to flourish to the same extent as those without disabilities, and key to those conditions are managers' attitudes and behaviors. Indeed, managers who hold negative attitudes towards individuals with disabilities may hire these applicants due to fear of legal consequences rather than because they recognize the value they would bring to the organization (Kuznetsova & Yalcin, 2017), may provide minimal accommodations leading to unmet needs (Haynes & Linden, 2012), or may discriminate against employees with disabilities when evaluating their performance (Dwertmann & Böhm, 2016). In this chapter, we review and integrate the literature on managers' misconceptions about workers with disabilities at three critical points in the employment cycle: recruitment and selection, the provision of accommodations, and performance management. We further consider the importance of the organizational context on managers' attitudes, and we end the chapter with avenues for future research.

Managers' Perspectives on Recruitment and Selection of Applicants with Disabilities

Hiring managers typically underestimate the number of qualified applicants with disabilities in the labor pool (Bonaccio et al., 2020), and may report that individuals with disabilities rarely apply for jobs at their organization (Kaye et al., 2011). This lack of understanding may be because several disabilities are invisible (e.g., diabetes, dyslexia, bipolar disorder), and applicants may choose not to disclose a disability during the recruitment and selection process (Von Schrader, Malzer & Bruyère, 2014). The decision to disclose a hidden stigmatized identity may depend on the perceived likelihood of mistreatment and discrimination by the recipient of the disclosed information (Follmer, Sabat & Siuta, 2020).

For individuals with visible disabilities, the question may be about whether and how to address one's disability (Lyons et al., 2018). Some experts argue for preparing a script highlighting the positive aspects of one's abilities (SEEC, 2020), speaking in simple, non-medical terms (Jans et al., 2012), and making attempts to assuage any doubts about one's ability to perform the job effectively (The Careers Service, 2009). However, managers may form misconceptions, especially about individuals with visible disabilities, before these candidates have even begun their interview (Schumer, 2019).

Reluctance to disclose a disability is understandable because applicants who do disclose may be less likely to advance in the recruitment process in comparison to non-disabled applicants with similar levels and types of experience (Pearson et al., 2003). Furthermore, rather than modifying existing roles to support the employment of individuals with disabilities, some organizations may not actively recruit these individuals unless they feel there is a "suitable" role available (Moore, McDonald & Bartlett, 2018). However, suitability can often be applied in ways that suggest managers are forming misconceptions about the capabilities of employees with disabilities. Managers may even react with apprehension after the disclosure of a disability (Johnson, Joshi & Hogan, 2020). Disclosure alerts managers to an aspect of an employee's identity that had been previously hidden, which may create discomfort and anxiety (Johnson et al., 2020). Managers may respond to this anxiety by trying to avoid the stigmatizing trait, such as acting in ways that invalidate the experiences of the stigmatized individual. Therefore, many legal experts and disability advocates recommend that applicants disclose a disability only after they have been hired (Jans et al., 2012; Johnson, 2016). However, in some cases, managers may react negatively no matter when an individual discloses a disability (Von Schrader et al., 2014).

A study by Lyons et al. (2018) offers some guidance on how applicants with disabilities can effectively discuss their disabilities during a job interview. It seems that claiming (i.e., highlighting positive aspects of the disability) is more effective than not acknowledging or downplaying (i.e., shifting others' focus away from the disability), especially in jobs that require high interpersonal demands. This finding can be understood through application of the Stereotype Content Model (SCM: Cuddy, Fiske & Glick, 2008), whereby individuals with disabilities are stereotypically categorized as low competence-high warmth (i.e., they are seen as friendly but unintelligent). When making judgments about job applicants with disabilities, managers may wrongly perceive these individuals as incompetent, helpless and inferior, and may feel sorry for them (Lyons et al., 2018). However, when applicants claim a disability, this encourages evaluators to focus on the applicant's ability to perform the job and may lead to increased competence ratings (Lyons et al., 2018).

Reactions to Accommodation Requests of Employees with Disabilities

Despite legislation such as the *Equality Act* in the U.K., which requires employers to make reasonable accommodations, one of the most common allegations against employers by employees with disabilities involves failure to provide these accommodations (Graham et al., 2019). This finding is surprising given the low cost of most accommodations; many accommodations may not cost the employer anything (e.g., flexible work schedule) or at most a one-time fee, of which the median expense reported by employers is $500 USD (Job Accommodation Network, 2020). Furthermore, not only do employees without disabilities also ask for accommodations (Schur et al, 2014), but the costs associated with not accommodating an employee may actually be higher (e.g., costs for hiring a replacement; Fisher & Connelly, 2020). Furthermore, when accommodations are granted, there are positive outcomes for employees, including higher levels of commitment and job satisfaction (Schur et al., 2014), and for the organization in the form of increased productivity and morale (Solovieva & Walls, 2013). Unfortunately, managers may be more concerned with the potential cost of accommodations rather than the benefits (Gaunt & Lengnick-Hall, 2014), or may instead focus on the perceived negative impact on work processes and workload associated with having to accommodate the individual (Johnson et al., 2020).

Manager misconceptions and stigma surrounding disability influence whether employees request accommodation in the first place (Jans et al., 2012). Choosing to disclose may result in potential stigmatization and alienation, social consequences which may be even more pronounced for those who request a recurring accommodation (Baldridge & Veiga, 2006). In contrast, choosing not to request accommodation means that employees with disabilities may possibly risk poor performance and potential termination. Employees with disabilities may not request accommodation due to fears that they will be perceived as less competent, or that they are burdening others with their needs (e.g., requiring people to talk slowly or repeat themselves during meetings; Baldridge & Veiga, 2006). These fears are not unfounded. In fact, when managers assess accommodation requests, they make judgments based on the perceived fairness of the request (Dong et al. 2013) and the impact this may have on the larger work unit (Florey & Harrison, 2000).

Managers' reactions to accommodation requests may be further complicated in the instance of invisible disabilities. For example, individuals with psychological disabilities such as schizophrenia may receive less empathy from managers, their accommodation request may be seen as less legitimate, less necessary, and less reasonable than accommodation requests related to physical disabilities (Telwatte et al., 2017). This disparity may exist because psychological disabilities are the most stigmatized form of disability (Baldridge et al., 2018). Indeed, managers may expect individuals with psychological disabilities to behave according to stereotypes, that is, in volatile or dangerous manners (Lyubykh et al., 2020). Therefore, accommodation requests may be met with skepticism, especially if workers do not exhibit these stereotypical behaviors that managers come to expect from such disabilities (Markel & Barclay, 2009). Some managers may even have the impression that employees with disabilities have "attitudes of entitlement" (Kaye et al., 2011, p.531), in that they are undeservingly requesting special treatment. In these cases, managers may be much less likely to grant accommodations.

Legislation regulating accommodations has been described as having a "positive impact" (Clayton et al., 2012, p.438), such as a positive economic impact for individuals with disabilities (Wu et al., 2021), yet managers may not always provide accommodations. Managers may not have experience providing accommodations (Wong et al., 2021), they may have minimal understanding of disabilities in general (Dong et al., 2013), or they may not be familiar with the legislation or their specific duties (Clayton et al., 2012; Telwatte et al., 2017). Inexperienced managers may find the accommodation process challenging (Bonaccio et al., 2020). Indeed, managers, especially those who do not benefit from dedicated human resources departments or professionals, may be unaware of the particulars of their regulatory environment (e.g., the *Americans with Disabilities Act [ADA]*) or the many and often free resources and assistance available to employers (e.g., the Job Accommodation Network, a free consulting service on accommodations funded by the U.S. Department of Labor, Office of Disability Employment Policy).

Manager Misconceptions about the Performance of Employees with Disabilities

Many employment-related outcomes are contingent upon successful performance appraisals (e.g., promotions, pay); therefore, manager misconceptions around performance can have a significant impact on the careers of employees with disabilities. For example, employees with disabilities may be pigeonholed into particular jobs based on manager expectations of their capabilities (Moore et al., 2018). Furthermore, employees with disabilities are more likely to work in lower-paying, lower-status jobs in comparison to employees without disabilities (Day & Taylor, 2019), and only 20% of individuals with disabilities work in full-time jobs, in comparison to 50% of individuals without disabilities (Kulkarni & Gopakumar, 2014). While some managers report positive attitudes regarding the performance of employees with disabilities (see Burke et al., 2013), there are several studies that demonstrate negative manager attitudes (e.g., Amir, Strauser & Chan, 2009; Khayatzadeh-Mahani et al., 2020; Lyubykh et al., 2020).

Managers tend to think employees with disabilities are lower performers than their counterparts without disabilities (Vornholt et al., 2018), do not have the same capabilities or capacity to do a job (Khayatzadeh-Mahani et al., 2020) and have trouble meeting the standards of the organization (Amir et al., 2009). Managers may also assume that employees with disabilities have minimal flexibility and can only perform one task at a time (Kaye et al., 2011). There is also additional stigma surrounding on-the-job behavior of employees with certain types of disabilities (Baldridge et al., 2018). For example, employees with developmental disabilities are sometimes seen as safety risks and liabilities to organizations (Khayatzadeh-Mahani et al., 2020). In reality, research indicates that employees with disabilities may actually have fewer incidents on the job than employees without disabilities and may be more concerned about safety (Kaletta, Binks & Robinson, 2012). Furthermore, employees with disabilities may actually perform at average or above average levels than those without disabilities, and the net financial value of their performance can be estimated at approximately $15,000 CAD greater than that of employees without disabilities (Fisher & Connelly, 2020).

In some cases, managers may evaluate the performance of employees with disabilities more positively than warranted (Kulkarni & Gopakumar, 2014; Ren, Paetzold & Colella, 2008). Meta-analytic evidence suggests that while disability status has a negative effect on performance expectations and hiring decisions, it has a positive effect on performance evaluations of employees with disabilities (Ren et al., 2008). Ren et al. (2008) argue that this could be a result of negative perceptions that employees with disabilities are not able to perform a job. At the same time, some employees with disabilities have indicated that managers may use "default ratings" to evaluate their performance, rather than giving honest feedback (Kulkarni & Gopakumar, 2014, p.457). This can be a source of frustration for employees with disabilities who consider these ratings as "charity," or the manager being "nice" without truly considering their performance (Kulkarni & Gopakumar, 2014). The result is a leniency bias, where individuals with disabilities may be rated more favorably than equally qualified individuals without disabilities (Brecher, Bragger & Kutcher, 2006), limiting the opportunity for employees with disabilities to develop their skills and progress in their careers (Kulkarni & Gopakumar, 2014).

Of note, managers without disabilities may not understand the "experience of work" for employees with disabilities (Lyubykh et al., 2020, p.771). Instead, they may focus on apparent differences between themselves and subordinates with disabilities, leading to stereotypical expectations of these workers (Dwertmann & Böhm, 2016). The theory of leader member exchange (LMX; Liden, Sparrowe & Wayne, 1997) illustrates the influence of this incongruence in disability status on important employee outcomes, such as supervisor ratings of employee performance (Zhang, Wang & Shi, 2012). This theory proposes that similarities between a supervisor and subordinate may make the employee more appealing, while differences, such as disability status, may lead to a lower quality exchange relationship (Liden et al., 1997). Indeed, in dyads where the subordinate has a disability and the supervisor does not, performance ratings for the employee may be lower (Dwertmann & Böhm, 2016). These findings further illustrate the far -reaching consequences of inaccurate performance evaluations and negative performance expectations on the careers of employees with disabilities (Kulkarni & Lengnick-Hall, 2014).

It is important to note that just like employees without disabilities, performance issues for employees with disabilities can be a result of several underlying factors, such as managers possessing limited knowledge regarding accommodations (Wong et al., 2021), or a lack of social support in the workplace (Baumgärtner, Böhm & Dwertmann, 2014). If an employee with a disability does exhibit performance issues, managers are often unsure of how to handle this concern, especially if the matter requires disciplinary action (Bonaccio et al., 2020). This in part is due to fear of potential legal consequences associated with poor performance management and accommodation practices. Legislation such as the *ADA* may impose penalties on employers for dismissing an employee with a disability (Baldridge et al., 2018). However, courts often interpret the *ADA* narrowly and generally favor the employers' side (Atkins, 2006). Moreover, fear of litigation might increase managers' reluctance to hire individuals with disabilities (Baldridge et al., 2018). Therefore, while the legislation discourages wrongful dismissals, it may also have an unanticipated, longer-term, negative impact on the employment of individuals with disabilities.

Organizational Context

The organizational context plays an important role in shaping managers' attitudes and behaviors towards job applicants and employees with disabilities. First, the trends we review in this chapter may be particularly acute in smaller organizations with fewer resources (Fraser et al., 2011). In these organizations, hiring managers may not be inclined to hire individuals with disabilities at all, unless they are persuaded of the productivity and financial benefits of doing so (Domzal, Houtenville & Sharma, 2008). Larger organizations tend to possess important resources such as human resources and legal departments to support this process (Bonaccio et al., 2020). HR staff that are knowledgeable about disabilities and familiar with disability legislation serve as a significant resource for managers, especially when existing employees disclose a disability (Martin & Fisher, 2014).

Organizational climate also influences managers' attitudes and behaviors towards employees with disabilities (Martin & Fisher, 2014). A positive diversity climate, where social norms are centered around inclusion of all employees regardless of disability status, may encourage managers to be more open and accepting of disability (Böhm & Dwertmann, 2015), and may reduce discrimination towards employees with disabilities (Triana et al., 2021). In contrast, in organizations with no clear disability strategy and a climate that does not support the disclosure of a disability, managers' attitudes may be even more stigmatizing towards employees with disabilities (e.g., seeing the disability as a weakness or as the employee's fault) (Martin, 2010). Importantly, managers at all levels, but especially those in senior leadership roles, play a critical role helping realize the potential of inclusive organizational climates by modeling attitudes and behaviors that allow people with disabilities to thrive in the workplace.

Inclusive organizational climates are also signaled by diversity policies and practices. Indeed, managers may be more inclined to hire individuals with disabilities when disability is incorporated into their organizations' diversity policies (Araten-Bergman, 2016). However, a recent national survey in the U.S. indicates that, while 57% of supervisors report that their organizations have *diversity* hiring goals, only 28% had *disability*-specific hiring goals (Kessler Foundation, 2017). Furthermore, a recent survey of over 5,000 employees with disabilities indicates that only 20% of these individuals feel that their organization is committed to helping them succeed in the workplace (Henneborn, 2021). Thus, the existence of inclusive hiring practices or programs, such as using employment agencies to source qualified applicants with disabilities, are important, but do not guarantee, by themselves, to result in actual hiring or support the ongoing employment of individuals with disabilities (Moore et al. 2018).

Research Opportunities

Despite the findings presented in earlier sections, there has been a greater emphasis in the literature on the perspective of employees with disabilities. However, managers have a significant influence on the careers of subordinates, and their attitudes and behaviors can limit or facilitate opportunities for employees with disabilities. This may be especially true during the hiring stage when applicants disclose a disability, following accommodation requests, and when managers evaluate the performance of employees with disabilities. There are several avenues for future research within these key areas of inquiry.

First, while the legal and social environment, as well as organization-level and person-level factors shape managers' attitudes and behaviors towards individuals with disabilities, additional research is needed to achieve a greater understanding of the interplay of factors at these various levels of analysis. For example, research suggests that female and minority individuals may be less judgmental and more accommodating towards individuals with disabilities (McLaughlin, Bell & Stringer, 2004). The authors suggest that this finding may be a reflection of larger social and political contexts and the historical discrimination against females and minorities, which contributes to their empathy towards individuals with disabilities. Further research on the role of the broader social context in shaping managers' attitudes and perceptions may help organizations to create more targeted practices and programs to support the hiring and advancement of workers with disabilities.

Second, future research should consider what programs or resources may be most effective in reducing manager misconceptions and negative attitudes towards individuals with disabilities, particularly during the hiring stage, accommodations, and performance management. Prior to the hiring stage, internships provide valuable opportunities for individuals with disabilities to showcase their abilities and challenge misconceptions about their performance, making organizations more likely to hire these individuals (Erickson et al., 2014). Are there particular programs that are most effective in diminishing manager reluctance to accommodate employees with disabilities, or to ensure managers are evaluating the performance of employees with disabilities more accurately? Are certain programs more effective in reducing manager misconceptions towards particular types of disabilities? For example, many psychological and mental health conditions are often invisible disabilities (e.g., bipolar disorder), which carry greater stigma (Baldridge et al., 2018). Thus, programs like internships that seek to bridge education and employment may be an important, but not sufficient, first step to creating long-term conditions for employment success. Here, additional programs may be needed. For example, training programs which not only focus on educating managers on the signs and symptoms of psychological conditions, but also increase managers' awareness of their unconscious biases, may be the most efficacious when aiming to create organizational contexts inclusive of employees with invisible disabilities.

In addition, when considering intersectionality of other identities with disability, how effective are interventions such as equity, diversity, and inclusion (EDI) training at improving the full participation of people with disabilities in the workplace? Research suggests that enhancing the disability confidence of managers, such as through disability awareness training and by challenging stereotypes, is critical to supporting the inclusion of employees with disabilities in the workplace (Lindsay et al., 2019). However, little is known about how increased disability confidence influences employment-related decisions such as a manager's approach to accommodations or the performance evaluation of employees with disabilities. Furthermore, managers have been considered "conduits" between organizational diversity practices and the actual implementation of these practices (Johnson et al., 2020). Therefore, it is important to consider how and why managers' attitudes and behaviors may support or impede the translation of organization-level practices down to the unit level.

Finally, little is known about how managers' attitudes towards employees with disabilities change over time (Breen, 2018; Palad et al., 2016). Research tends to rely on attitudinal assessments at single points in time (Breen, 2018). However, attitudes towards individuals with disabilities may become particularly apparent at a few critical points, such as when an applicant with disabilities is hired, after an employee discloses a disability, or when an employee requests accommodation. For example, managers may be concerned with how existing workers will respond to the hiring of an applicant with a disability (Kaye et al., 2011), or if the disclosure of a disability may disrupt the performance of a work team (Johnson et al., 2020). Do managers' attitudes change over time, such as following the successful or unsuccessful accommodation of an employee with a disability? Do managers' attitudes toward visible and invisible disabilities change over time in different ways? It may be that managers react more negatively to an employee's visible disability initially, but their attitudes become more positive over time, as a working relationship is established. For example, managers may no longer "notice" a mobility aid once they get to know their employee as a person. On the other hand, how do managers' attitudes change as they begin intuiting that an employee may possibly live with an invisible disability, such as when they slowly realize that their employee uses lip reading to support their hearing? Future research should employ longitudinal designs to assess these changes.

Conclusion

Organizational blindness, when "organizations and their members fail to see the potential of people with disabilities" (Bend & Fielden, 2020, p.485), can have a detrimental impact on the experiences of individuals with disabilities in the workplace. In this chapter, we discuss manager misconceptions about employees with disabilities, focusing in particular on reactions during hiring, accommodations, and performance management. Managers tend to make overly negative assumptions about applicants with disabilities which serve as a major barrier to their participation in the labor market (Vornholt et al., 2018). Furthermore, the stigma of disability not only influences whether a manager will provide accommodations to employees who request them, but also impacts manager expectations around the performance capabilities of employees with disabilities and their opportunities for promotion (e.g., Kaye et al., 2011; Kulkarni & Lengnick-Hall, 2014). Research suggests that greater exposure to, and awareness of, individuals with disabilities may reduce this stigma and allow for greater integration of employees with disabilities into workplaces (Telwatte et al., 2017). While the legal environment and disability legislation, for example hiring quotas in some countries such as Germany, and a duty to accommodate present in most countries, play a role in deterring employee discrimination, research suggests that some managers may not willingly hire individuals with disabilities and may find ways to avoid doing so (such as paying fines) (Baldridge et al., 2018; Vornholt et al., 2018).

Some managers may hire individuals with disabilities for token positions rather than truly considering their value, leaving these individuals in a segregated labor market of low-skilled, low-paying jobs (Clayton et al., 2012). Disability advocates argue for organizations to hire applicants with disabilities, not as a reaction to legal requirements, or for face value, but as an active strategy which recognizes the true value of these individuals (Markel & Barclay, 2009). Not only has the changing social and legal climate made diversity an important component of organization strategy and success (Bleasdale, 2021), organizations also benefit from the inclusion of individuals with disabilities in the workplace (see Lindsay et al., 2018).

Education and training which provide managers with a more accurate and realistic picture of individuals with disabilities needs to be disseminated on a larger scale. One way to facilitate this is for organizations to make use of available resources, such as disability training and placement agencies (Kulkarni & Kote, 2014). Diversity is not "simply checking a box or filling a quota"; organizations need to recognize the value of diversity and how to cultivate a diverse workforce, which includes employees with disabilities.

References

Ali, M., Schur, L. & Blanck, P. (2011). What types of jobs do people with disabilities want? *Journal of Occupational Rehabilitation*, *21*(2), 199–210.

Amir, Z., Strauser, D. R., & Chan, F. (2009). Employers' and survivors' perspectives. In *Work and cancer survivors* (pp. 73–89). Springer, New York, NY.

Araten-Bergman, T. (2016). Managers' hiring intentions and the actual hiring of qualified workers with disabilities. *The International Journal of Human Resource Management*, *27*(14), 1510–1530.

Atkins, C. G. K. (2006). Cripple at a Rich Man's Gate: A Comparison of Disability, Employment and Anti-Discrimination Law in the United States and Canada, A. *Can. JL & Soc.*, *21*, 87.

Baldridge, D. C., Beatty, J. E., Böhm, S. A., Kulkarni, M., & Moore, M. E. (2018). Persons with (dis) abilities. In *The Oxford handbook of diversity in organizations* (pp. 469–498). Oxford University Press, Oxford.

Baldridge, D. C., & Veiga, J. F. (2006). The impact of anticipated social consequences on recurring disability accommodation requests. *Journal of Management*, *32*(1), 158–179.

Baumgärtner, M. K., Böhm, S. A., & Dwertmann, D. J. (2014). Job performance of employees with disabilities: Interpersonal and intrapersonal resources matter. *Equality, Diversity and Inclusion: 33*(4), 347–360.

Bend, G. L., & Fielden, S. L. (2020). Organizational Blindness: Why People with Disabilities Do Not 'Fit'. In *The Palgrave Handbook of Disability at Work* (pp. 485–504). Palgrave Macmillan, Cham.

Bleasdale, M. (2021, April 2). 'IT hiring targets the talent of the neurodiverse community'. *CIO*. https://www.cio.com/article/3613909/it-hiring-targets-the-talent-of-the-neurodiverse-community.html

Böhm, S. A., & Dwertmann, D. J. (2015). Forging a single-edged sword: Facilitating positive age and disability diversity effects in the workplace through leadership, positive climates, and HR practices. *Work, Aging and Retirement*, *1*(1), 41–63.

Bonaccio, S., Connelly, C. E., Gellatly, I. R., Jetha, A., & Ginis, K. A. M. (2020). The participation of people with disabilities in the workplace across the employment cycle: employer concerns and research evidence. *Journal of Business and Psychology*, *35*, 135–158.

Brecher, E., Bragger, J., & Kutcher, E. (2006). The structured interview: Reducing biases toward job applicants with physical disabilities. *Employee Responsibilities and Rights Journal*, *18*(3), 155–170.

Breen, J. S. (2018). Attitudes toward employees with disabilities: A systematic review of self-report measures. *The Australian Journal of Rehabilitation Counselling*, *24*(2), 67.

Bureau of Labor Statistics. (2021, February 21). Persons with a disability: Labor Force Characteristics 2020. https://www.bls.gov/news.release/pdf/disabl.pdf

Burke, J., Bezyak, J., Fraser, R. T., Pete, J., Ditchman, N., & Chan, F. (2013). Employers' attitudes towards hiring and retaining people with disabilities: A review of the literature. *The Australian Journal of Rehabilitation Counselling*, *19*(1), 21–38.

Clayton, S., Barr, B., Nylen, L., Burström, B., Thielen, K., Diderichsen, F., . . . & Whitehead, M. (2012). Effectiveness of return-to-work interventions for disabled people: a systematic review of government initiatives focused on changing the behaviour of employers. *The European Journal of Public Health*, *22*(3), 434–439.

Cuddy, A. J., Fiske, S. T., & Glick, P. (2008). Warmth and competence as universal dimensions of social perception: The stereotype content model and the BIAS map. *Advances in experimental social psychology*, *40*, 61–149.

Day, J.C., & Taylor, D. (2019, March 21). In Most Occupations, Workers With or Without Disabilities Earn About the Same. *United Status Census Bureau*. https://www.census.gov/library/stories/2019/03/do-people-with-disabilities-earn-equal-pay.html

Domzal, C., Houtenville, A., & Sharma, R. (2008). Survey of employer perspectives on the employment of people with disabilities: Technical report. (Prepared under contract to the Office of Disability and Employment Policy, U.S. Department of Labor). McLean, VA: CESSI.

Dong, S., Oire, S. N., MacDonald-Wilson, K. L., & Fabian, E. S. (2013). A comparison of perceptions of factors in the job accommodation process among employees with disabilities, employers, and service providers. *Rehabilitation Counseling Bulletin*, *56*(3), 182–189.

Dwertmann, D. J., & Böhm, S. A. (2016). Status matters: The asymmetric effects of supervisor–subordinate disability incongruence and climate for inclusion. *Academy of Management Journal*, *59*(1), 44–64.

Erickson, W. A., von Schrader, S., Bruyère, S. M., VanLooy, S. A., & Matteson, D. S. (2014). Disability-inclusive employer practices and hiring of individuals with disabilities. *Rehabilitation Research, Policy, and Education*, *28*(4), 309–328.

Fisher, S. L., & Connelly, C. E. (2020). Building the "Business Case" for Hiring People with Disabilities. *Canadian Journal of Disability Studies*, *9*(4), 71–88.

Florey, A. T., & Harrison, D. A. (2000). Responses to informal accommodation requests from employees with disabilites: Multistudy evidence on willingness to comply. *Academy of Management Journal*, *43*(2), 224–233.

Follmer, K. B., Sabat, I. E., & Siuta, R. L. (2020). Disclosure of stigmatized identities at work: An interdisciplinary review and agenda for future research. *Journal of Organizational Behavior*, *41*(2), 169–184.

Fraser, R., Ajzen, I., Johnson, K., Hebert, J., & Chan, F. (2011). Understanding employers' hiring intention in relation to qualified workers with disabilities. *Journal of Vocational Rehabilitation*, *35*(1), 1–11.

Gaunt, P. M., & Lengnick-Hall, M. L. (2014). Overcoming misperceptions about hiring people with disabilities. *CPRF*. https://www.cprf.org/studies/overcoming-misperceptions-about-hiringpeople-with-disabilities/

Graham, K. M., McMahon, B. T., Kim, J. H., Simpson, P., & McMahon, M. C. (2019). Patterns of workplace discrimination across broad categories of disability. *Rehabilitation psychology*, *64*(2), 194.

Haynes, S., & Linden, M. (2012). Workplace accommodations and unmet needs specific to individuals who are deaf or hard of hearing. *Disability and Rehabilitation: Assistive Technology*, *7*(5), 408–415.

Henneborn, L. (2021, June 28). Make It Safe for Employees to Disclose Their Disabilities. *Harvard Business Review*. https://hbr.org/2021/06/make-it-safe-for-employees-to-disclose-their-disabilities

International Labour Organization. (2020, December 3). *International day of persons with disabilities: How disability affects labour market outcomes*. International Labour Organization. https://ilostat.ilo.org/international-day-of-persons-with-disabilities-how-disability-affects-labour-market-outcomes/

Jans, L. H., Kaye, H. S., & Jones, E. C. (2012). Getting hired: Successfully employed people with disabilities offer advice on disclosure, interviewing, and job search. *Journal of occupational rehabilitation*, *22*(2), 155–165.

Job Accommodation Network (Updated 2020, October 19). Workplace accommodations: Low cost, high impact. *Job Accommodation Network*. https://askjan.org/topics/costs.cfm

Johnson, R.B. (2016, March 30). Your Legal Rights and Responsibilities Around Disclosure. *DABC's Transition Magazine Spring 2016*, pp.12–13. https://issuu.com/disabilityalliancebc/docs/transspring16-web/12

Johnson, T. D., Joshi, A., & Hogan, T. (2020). On the front lines of disclosure: A conceptual framework of disclosure events. *Organizational Psychology Review*, *10*(3–4), 201–222.

Kaletta, J. P., Binks, D. J., & Robinson, R. (2012). Creating an inclusive workplace: Integrating employees with disabilities into a distribution center environment. Professional Safety: *Journal of the American Society of Safety Engineers*, *57*(6), 62–71.

Kaye, H. S., Jans, L. H., & Jones, E. C. (2011). Why don't employers hire and retain workers with disabilities? *Journal of occupational rehabilitation*, *21*(4), 526–536.

Kessler Foundation. (2017, October 10). *National Employment & Disability Survey Supervisor Perspectives*. [PowerPoint slides]. Kessler Foundation. https://kesslerfoundation.org/research center-employment-and-disability-researchemployment-and-disability-survey-2017/ presentation

Khayatzadeh-Mahani, A., Wittevrongel, K., Nicholas, D. B., & Zwicker, J. D. (2020). Prioritizing barriers and solutions to improve employment for persons with developmental disabilities. *Disability and rehabilitation*, *42*(19), 2696–2706.

Kulkarni, M., & Gopakumar, K. V. (2014). Career management strategies of people with disabilities. *Human Resource Management*, *53*(3), 445–466.

Kulkarni, M., & Kote, J. (2014). Increasing employment of people with disabilities: The role and views of disability training and placement agencies. *Employee Responsibilities and Rights Journal*, *26*(3), 177–193.

Kulkarni, M., & Lengnick-Hall, M. L. (2014). Obstacles to success in the workplace for people with disabilities: A review and research agenda. *Human Resource Development Review*, *13*(2), 158–180.

Kuznetsova, Y., & Yalcin, B. (2017). Inclusion of persons with disabilities in mainstream employment: is it really all about the money? A case study of four large companies in Norway and Sweden. *Disability & Society*, *32*(2), 233–253.

Liden, R. C., Sparrowe, R. T., & Wayne, S. J. (1997). Leader-member exchange theory: The past and potential for the future. In G. R. Ferris (Ed.), *Research in personnel and human resources management, 15,* 47–119. Elsevier Science/JAI Press.

Lindsay, S., Cagliostro, E., Albarico, M., Mortaji, N., & Karon, L. (2018). A systematic review of the benefits of hiring people with disabilities. *Journal of occupational rehabilitation*, *28*(4), 634–655.

Lindsay, S., Leck, J., Shen, W., Cagliostro, E., & Stinson, J. (2019). A framework for developing employer's disability confidence. *Equality, Diversity and Inclusion*, *38*(1), 40–55.

Lyons, B. J., Martinez, L. R., Ruggs, E. N., Hebl, M. R., Ryan, A. M., O'Brien, K. R., & Roebuck, A. (2018). To say or not to say: Different strategies of acknowledging a visible disability. *Journal of Management*, *44*(5), 1980–2007.

Lyubykh, Z., Turner, N., Barling, J., Reich, T. C., & Batten, S. (2020). Employee disability disclosure and managerial prejudices in the return-to-work context. *Personnel Review*, *50*(2), 770–788.

Markel, K. S., & Barclay, L. A. (2009). Addressing the underemployment of persons with disabilities: Recommendations for expanding organizational social responsibility. *Employee Responsibilities and Rights Journal*, *21*(4), 305–318.

Martin, A. (2010). Individual and contextual correlates of managers' attitudes toward depressed employees. *Human Resource Management*, *49*(4), 647–668.

Martin, A., & Fisher, C. D. (2014). Understanding and improving managers' responses to employee depression. *Industrial and Organizational Psychology*, *7*(2), 270–274.

McLaughlin, M. E., Bell, M. P., & Stringer, D. Y. (2004). Stigma and acceptance of persons with disabilities: Understudied aspects of workforce diversity. *Group & Organization Management*, *29*(3), 302–333.

Moore, K., McDonald, P., & Bartlett, J. (2018). Emerging trends affecting future employment opportunities for people with intellectual disability: The case of a large retail organisation. *Journal of Intellectual & Developmental Disability*, *43*(3), 328–338.

Palad, Y. Y., Barquia, R. B., Domingo, H. C., Flores, C. K., Padilla, L. I., & Ramel, J. M. D. (2016). Scoping review of instruments measuring attitudes toward disability. *Disability and Health Journal*, *9*(3), 354–374.

Pearson, V., Ip, F., Hui, H., & Yip, N. (2003). To tell or not to tell? Disability disclosure and job application outcomes. *Journal of Rehabilitation*, *69*, 35–38.

Prince, M.J. (2016). *Canadians with disabilities need real work, real pay, real leadership*. Institute for Research on Public Policy. https://irpp.org/op-ed/canadians-with-disabilities-need-real-work-real-pay-real-leadership/

Ren, L. R., Paetzold, R. L., & Colella, A. (2008). A meta-analysis of experimental studies on the effects of disability on human resource judgments. *Human Resource Management Review*, *18*(3), 191–203.

Schumer, L. (2019, July 10). How to Disclose a Disability to Your Employer (and Whether You Should). *The New York Times*. https://www.nytimes.com/2019/07/10/smarter-living/disclose-disability-work-employer-rights.html

Schur, L., Nishii, L., Adya, M., Kruse, D., Bruyère, S. M., & Blanck, P. (2014). Accommodating employees with and without disabilities. *Human Resource Management*, *53*(4), 593–621.

SEEC. (2020). Career disability disclosure for individuals with disabilities. *SEEC Online*. https://www.seeconline.org/wp-content/uploads/2020/03/Career-Disability-Disclosure-for-Individuals-with-Disabilities.pdf

Solovieva, T. I., & Walls, R. T. (2013). Implications of workplace accommodations for persons with disabilities. *Journal of Workplace Behavioral Health*, *28*(3), 192–211.

Telwatte, A., Anglim, J., Wynton, S. K., & Moulding, R. (2017). Workplace accommodations for employees with disabilities: A multilevel model of employer decision-making. *Rehabilitation psychology*, *62*(1), 7.

The Careers Service. (2009, August). *Should I Disclose a Disability to a Potential Employer?* Cardiff University. https://www.chs.ca/sites/default/files/uploads/should_i_disclose_a_disability_to_a_potential_employer_updat.pdf

Triana, M. D. C., Gu, P., Chapa, O., Richard, O., & Colella, A. (2021). Sixty years of discrimination and diversity research in human resource management: A review with suggestions for future research directions. *Human Resource Management*, *60*(1), 145–204.

Von Schrader, S., Malzer, V., & Bruyère, S. (2014). Perspectives on disability disclosure: the importance of employer practices and workplace climate. *Employee Responsibilities and Rights Journal*, *26*(4), 237–255.

Vornholt, K., Villotti, P., Muschalla, B., Bauer, J., Colella, A., Zijlstra, F., . . . & Corbiere, M. (2018). Disability and employment–overview and highlights. *European journal of work and organizational psychology*, *27*(1), 40–55.

Wong, J., Kallish, N., Crown, D., Capraro, P., Trierweiler, R., Wafford, Q. E., . . . & Heinemann, A. W. (2021). Job accommodations, return to work and job retention of people with physical disabilities: A systematic review. *Journal of Occupational Rehabilitation*, 1–17.

Wu, F. Y., Nittrouer, C., Nguyen, V., Hebl, M., Oswald, F. L., & Frieden, L. (2021). Now protected or still stigmatized? A 25-year outlook on the impact of the Americans with Disabilities Act. *Equality, Diversity and Inclusion*, *41*(3), 383–403.

Zhang, Z., Wang, M. O., & Shi, J. (2012). Leader-follower congruence in proactive personality and work outcomes: The mediating role of leader-member exchange. *Academy of Management Journal*, *55*(1), 111–130.

Dianna L. Stone, Kimberly M. Lukaszewski, Melissa Feigelson, and Kevin Williams

10 The Influence of a "Best Employer Award" on Hiring Managers' Beliefs and Intentions to Hire People with Disabilities

Abstract: The present study examined the relation between a "Best Employer Award for Hiring People with Disabilities" and non-winning managers' beliefs and intentions to hire people with disabilities (hereinafter PWDs.) We based our predictions on social learning theory that suggested hiring managers would emulate the winning company's behaviors if they perceived it would lead to future rewards or recognition. Our results revealed that several of the hiring managers' beliefs were more positive after the award than prior to it. For example, hiring managers reported that PWDs had higher levels of skills and abilities after the award was presented than prior to it. Further, the data indicated that hiring managers reported that they would be more comfortable working with PWDs, and indicated that the costs of accommodations would be lower after the award was granted than prior to it. These results have important implications for enhancing managers' beliefs about PWDs, and increasing their employment rates. The chapter considers the implications of our findings for future research and practice.

Keywords: Best Employer Award, hiring, people with disabilities, comfort

Despite the passage of the Americans with Disabilities Act (ADA) (1990) and similar legislation passed around the world (e.g., The European Accessibility Act), PWDs still have difficulties gaining and maintaining employment. For example, 17.9% of PWDs in the U. S. were employed in 2020, compared to 61.8% of those without a disability (Bureau of Labor Statistics [BLS], 2021.) It merits noting that all of the statistics reported in this chapter refer to PWDs in the U. S. Further, the median earnings rates for full-time workers with disabilities ($40,360) were $8,046 lower than those without disabilities ($48,406) (BLS, 2021.) As a result, PWDs were less likely to be employed in 2021, and had lower income levels than their counterparts.

Further, unemployment has a negative impact on those with disabilities in a variety of ways. For example, it means that they will live in poverty, experience social isolation, and face higher levels of psychological problems (e.g., depression,

Dianna L. Stone, Universities of New Mexico, Albany, and Virginia Tech
Kimberly M. Lukaszewski, Wright State University
Melissa Feigelson, Verisk Analytics
Kevin Williams, University at Albany

https://doi.org/10.1515/9783110743647-011

stress) than those who are employed (Hernandez, 2020.) Although there are a number of reasons for the employment problems of PWDs, one of the most important reasons is that employers continue to have negative attitudes toward hiring them (Gasper et al., 2020.) For example, a recent survey by Gasper et al. (2020) revealed that 87% of employers were concerned that those with disabilities will have lower performance levels (55.5%), higher rates of absenteeism (52.7%) and turnover (42.2%), higher costs associated with accommodating them (45.0%), and will create difficulties for supervisors (e.g., managing, disciplining). Other research has shown that these concerns are unfounded, and PWDs have performance rates as high, if not higher, than those without disabilities and higher retention rates than workers without disabilities (Hernandez & McDonald, 2010.) Further, the median costs of accommodations are relatively low ($1,850) so employers' concerns about the high costs of accommodations are not substantiated by the data. Despite these findings, results of other research showed that employers with high levels of concerns about job performance were less likely to actively recruit or employ PWDs (e.g., Kulkarni & Lengnick-Hall, 2014.)

Although PWDs may perform as well, if not better, than those without disabilities, it is clear that employers' negative attitudes about hiring them may still have a detrimental impact on recruiting and hiring PWDs. Further, the use of legislation, like the ADA, may not always be an effective means of motivating employers to hire PWDs. One reason for this is that legislation often produces compliance among people or organizations rather than commitment to the purpose of the law (Etzioni, 2000.) For instance, despite posted speed limits people continue to speed. As a result, sociologists (Etzioni, 1996) have argued that unless people are committed to the underlying values of laws, they will be set aside and rarely heeded. Another reason that legislation may not be effective is that organizations often adopt an economic philosophy that stresses financial self-interest rather than the "greatest good for the society" (Steiner & Steiner, 1991.) Thus, we need to explore other strategies that might be used to motivate employers to hire PWDs (e.g., tax incentives, positive feedback). Although there may be a number of potential strategies, we believe that recognition and reward systems for employers who hire PWDs may be an especially effective means of enhancing positive attitudes and motivating them to employ PWDs. Quite simply, we maintain that recognition systems may encourage more employers to hire PWDs than compliance with disability laws.

Given that employers still have negative attitudes toward hiring PWDs, and these attitudes often have a detrimental effect on hiring rates, we believe that company recognition and rewards systems may have a positive influence on employers' attitudes and increase the employment of PWDs. Thus, the primary purpose of the present chapter is to present the results of a study that assessed the relations between the use of a community-based "Best Company Award" for hiring PWDs on employers' attitudes and intentions toward hiring PWDs. As a result, in the sections that follow we (a) provide a theoretical basis for the effects of company award systems on employers' intentions to hire PWDs, (b) review the existing literature on the issues, (c) present testable hypotheses and relay the results of the study, and (d) consider the implications for future research and practice.

Theoretical Rationale

It has long been known that people do what they are rewarded for, but one theory suggests that people do not have to directly receive rewards or reinforcements to engage in a behavior (Bandura, 1989.) They may experience vicarious reinforcement when they observe others receive rewards. This theory is known as social learning theory (Bandura, 1989), and we believe that it helps explain the reasons that "Best Company Awards for Hiring PWDs" may positively affect non-winning managers' intentions to hire PWDs. Quite simply, social learning theory predicts that new behaviors and attitudes can be acquired by observing the behavior of others and imitating their behavior. This theory also argues that learning is a cognitive process that takes place through direct instruction and/or observation. It also predicts that the learning process does not always require direct reinforcement, but people can learn through vicarious reinforcement where social models are rewarded for the behavior. Thus, when hiring managers observe that other companies are given an award for hiring PWDs, then they should also be motivated to hire those with disabilities in order to gain valued company awards.

Social learning theory also predicts that the influence of social models on observers' behaviors may be framed into several categories. Two of those categories are response facilitating effects and observational learning effects. For instance, when observers are exposed to the actions of others these actions may facilitate the performance of behaviors that are similar to the original behavior of others. This process is known as response facilitating effects, and research has shown that this process facilitates a variety of behaviors including volunteering one's services to help others, and aiding individuals in distress. When observers are exposed to the behavior of social models an observational learning effect may also occur. In this context, observers may acquire entirely new forms of behavior by observing social models without imitating the behavior in the model's presence. It merits emphasis that response facilitating effects and observational learning may also serve to decrease or inhibit unwanted behaviors when social models are punished for a behavior.

Social learning theory argues that there are four stages in the observational learning process: attention, retention, production/initiation and motivation. Attention refers to an observer paying attention to another person's behavior, and retention means that the observers store the behavior in memory. Production or initiation refers to the fact that observers must acquire the skills needed to reproduce the behavior, and motivation implies that the observer must find a reason to reproduce the behavior. For instance, in order for an agent of an organization to imitate "the company that does the best job of hiring PWDs," they must pay attention to the behavior and outcomes, then acquire the skills needed to hire PWDs (e.g., learn how to recruit PWDs). Further, the model suggests that they must be motivated to hire PWDs, and hiring behaviors will only be activated when the observer anticipates some form of reward for the actions. As a result, managers in a company will only increase their hiring of PWDs when they perceive that they are likely to receive an award or be recognized for the behavior. There has been considerable support for this process, and research has shown that observational learning may facilitate a wide array of behaviors in organizations including teamwork, leadership, creativity, and training.

Thus, based on the model of social learning, we predict that when communities give an award to the "Best Company that Hires PWDs" then managers in non-winning companies are likely to imitate the hiring behaviors of the award-winning company. These imitative behaviors should be especially likely when the managers believe that they might win an award or be publicly recognized for their actions. Thus, we predict that the use of "Best Company Disability Awards" should have a spillover or ripple effect on non-winning companies and motivate them to hire more PWDs.

Review of the Literature

There has been relatively little research on the relation between best company awards and the behaviors of non-winning organizations. However, the research that exists indicates that "Best Company Awards" have an impact on (a) employees' behaviors and attitudes, (b) job applicants' attraction to organizations, (c) corporate social responsibility, and (d) company stock prices. We review this literature below.

Impact on Employee Behavior

Research has shown that a "Best Company Award" has a favorable effect on a company's reputation and brand which enhances employees' pride and increases their desire to be part of the company's winning team (Finkelstein, 2016). Studies have also shown that best company awards increase employees' perceptions that the company values people and puts them first, which has a positive impact on employee engagement, motivation, retention rates, and performance (Li et al., 2020; Neckermann et al., 2014). For example, research by Neckermann et al. (2014) found that a company award increased the performance of underperforming call center employees, but the effect was short lived. Other researchers have argued that a company award is likely to capture a deep-seated competitive drive among employees which increases their risk taking, willingness to take on new challenges, and innovation in organizations (Ammann et al., 2016). Taken together, these studies suggest that a best company award has an important impact on employees' motivation, job attitudes and attitudes, and performance.

Impact on Job Applicants

Research has also shown that "Best Company Awards" positively influence job applicants' attraction to organizations (Baum & Überschaer, 2018.) There are several reasons for this. First, company awards signal that an organization is a high-quality employer, and gives applicants information on what it would be like to work for the company (Turban & Cable, 2003.) Second, awards differentiate the company from competitors, set it apart from the crowd, and makes applicants feel that the company has a people-oriented culture (Baum & Überschaer, 2019.) Third, when a company receives a "Best Company Award" it increases organizational prestige, and individuals' identification with the company which also enhances members' self-esteem and social status (Baum & Überschaer, 2018.) Thus, many applicants are motivated to work for highly prestigious organizations because these companies confer prestige to their members (Smidts et al., 2001.) Fourth, best company awards also affect an organization's brand identity which can be viewed as an image of the company experienced by those who come into contact with it. For example, some companies have a brand image that emphasizes corporate social responsibility which means that they operate in ways to enhance society and the environment (e.g., Toms, Bombas.) Taken together, the research just noted indicates that best company awards provide signals to job applicants that the organization has high levels of prestige, has superior quality, and cares about people. As a result, applicants are more attracted to an organization and more likely to apply for jobs when a company wins an award than when it does not.

There have been a few empirical studies on the effects of best company awards on job applicants' pursuit intentions. One study by Baum and Überschaer (2018) found that best company awards have a positive effect on applicants' job pursuit intentions, but this effect is moderated by (a) the corporate brand, and (b) the degree to which the award is well known. The results of this study revealed that best company awards have more of an impact on applicants' pursuit intentions when (a) (a) the companies are not well known, and (b) when the award is well known. Further, the results indicated that best company awards send a strong signal that the company is high quality, and they have more of an impact on small than large companies.

Baum and Überschaer (2018) also found that best company awards increase the number of applicants who apply for jobs with the company, but may not enhance the quality of those applicants. For example, this research found that applicants pay less attention to job information (e.g., policies, mission, benefits) when the company has won an award than when they have not. Further, companies that have won best company awards attract applicants who have less of a person-organization fit than those who have not won an award. As a result, job applicants do not self-select themselves out of the applicant pool when they do not fit with the organization's values, and this may have a negative impact on productivity, commitment, and retention rates (Baum & Überschaer, 2018.) These authors argue that applicants tend to self-select themselves out of the applicant pool when they do not perceive that there is a fit between their skills and values and the organization's goals. This is helpful to organizations because they do not hire those individuals who are not a good fit with the organization. Thus, best company awards may have both positive and negative effects on attraction and retention in organizations.

Impact of Awards on Winning and Non-Winning Companies

Most companies operate in a highly competitive environment, and when one company wins an award, the non-winners are often motivated to emulate the behaviors of the winning company (Gallus & Frey, 2016.) One reason for this is that company awards often increase a company's public reputation, and enhance their prestige in the marketplace (Gallus & Frey, 2016.) Another reason is that awards often inspire non-winning companies to improve their performance, and have a spillover or ripple effect on the actions of non-winning companies so that they can gain recognition (Shi et al., 2017.) For example, results of some recent research revealed that when a company won an award for corporate social responsibility (CSR) the non-winning companies in the industry increased their emphasis on CSR (Li et al., 2022.) However, the study indicated that the motivational effects for non-winners depends on the visibility or amount of press coverage given the CSR award, and the performance gap between the winning company and non-winners. The companies that were already pursing CSR were more likely to emulate the winning company's CSR than those that were not pursuing CSR.

In support of the spillover effects of best company awards, other research found that CEO awards have an intraindustry spillover effect on non-winner's company performance, innovation, and investment in research and development in China (Wu & Hu, 2021.) However, the findings of this study also indicated that the size of the spillover effects depends on the similarity between winning and non-winning CEOs, and industry competitive pressures (Wu & Hu, 2021.) Similarly, a study by Shi et al. (2017) found that when CEOs win an award the nonwinning CEOs are motivated to pursue visible acquisitions and actually obtain more acquisitions to enhance their own reputation and visibility. Finally, some research has shown that a U.S. Department of Labor award for exemplary affirmative action enhances a company's stock prices, but the effects of damage awards from civil rights lawsuits had a negative impact on these prices (Wright et al., 1995.)

Taken together, our literature review indicated that best company or CEO awards have a positive influence on (a) employee motivation and performance, (b) job applicants' attraction to organization and job pursuit intentions, and (c) non-winning company's motivation to emulate the behavior of the winning company. The research also shows that best company awards may have a positive effect on the stock prices of winning companies. These results provide support for our prediction that "Best Employer Awards for Hiring PWDs" will motivate non-winning companies to emulate the actions of the winning company, and increase their hiring of PWDs. We are not aware of any empirical research on this prediction, so we offer the following hypotheses to guide research.

H1: When an award is given for the best employer for those with disabilities, non-winning employers' beliefs about PWDs will be more positive in terms of (a) the costs of accommodation, (b) ratings of the skills and abilities of those with disabilities, (c) feelings of comfort associated with working with people with disabilities, and (d) perceptions of their dependability after the award is given than prior to the award.

H2: When an award is given to the best employer for those with disabilities, the non-winning companies will report that they intend to hire more PWDs after the award is presented than prior to the presentation of the award.

Presentation of the Best Employer Award

Prior to conducting the study, a human service agency, the local Rotary club, and a university in the northeastern U. S. formed a partnership to present an award to the company in the area that was the best employer for those with disabilities. Nominations were solicited via press releases, email, and professional organizations from all of the public and private sector companies operating and providing services in the standard metropolitan statistical area (SMSA) (approximately 2,300 companies.) Judges were selected from disability experts and leaders in other areas of the state so that they were not associated with the individuals in the original partnership or the organizations in the area. One best employer award was presented by a prominent state senator at a luncheon, but two other companies received honorable mention plaques for their outstanding employment practices related to PWDs. The best employer award was promoted widely in local and state newspapers, TV stations, websites, and professional organizations.

Method

Overview

A pretest-posttest design was used to examine the extent to which employers' beliefs and intentions to hire PWDs were more positive after the presentation of a best company award than prior to the presentation of the award. The beliefs measured in the study included perceptions about the (a) cost of accommodations, (b) skills and abilities, (c) comfort levels, and (d) dependability of those with disabilities. Employers' intentions to hire PWDs in the future were also measured.

Procedure

Data were collected in two phases. Phase 1 was conducted approximately one month before the best company award was presented. A sample of 200 companies in the standard metropolitan statistical association (SMSA) were mailed a consent form, questionnaire number 1, and a demographic form. We also asked employment managers who attended the award luncheon to complete the questionnaire prior to the presentation of the award. Sixty-four employers completed and returned the questionnaires. The response rate was 32%.

Eight weeks after the award was presented at the luncheon, the 64 employers were mailed and asked to complete a second set of questionnaires. The second questionnaires were the same as the ones used in phase 1. Self-addressed stamped envelopes were used to facilitate survey responses. The response rate for phase 2 was approximately 44%. All participants noted that they were aware of the award.

Participants

Data Collection Time 1

Participants were representatives of 64 organizations in a large SMSA in the northeastern U. S that had responsibility for hiring employees. Questionnaires for phase 1 were mailed to representatives of 200 companies in the SMSA. Sixty-four questionnaires were returned by employers in phase 1. Participants included 19 men and 45 women. Their average age was 42.32, and on average, they had 19.16 years of work experience. Five participants were African American, 57 were European-American, and 3 were Asian. They were employed in the following job types: human resource managers, executive directors, hiring managers, and others who made hiring decisions. Companies were in a variety of industries including services, retail, health care, state government, human services, and manufacturing.

Data Collection Time 2

The 64 participants who completed the questionnaires at time 1 were mailed the second set of questionnaires. Twenty-eight company representatives returned the second questionnaires. Six of these participants were men, and 22 were women, and their average age was 41.43. They had an average of 17.25 years of work experience. There were 24 European-Americans in the sample and 3 Asians. They were employed in the same types of jobs and organizations as the participants at time 1.

Measures

The questionnaires were designed to assess several beliefs about employing PWDs (e.g., cost of accommodation, skill levels of PWDs, comfort levels of working with PWDs, their dependability, and hiring intentions). It used a 26-item scale having a 6-point "strongly disagree" to "strongly agree" response format. Items in subscales were summed to form overall beliefs. The subscales are described below.

- *Beliefs About the Costs of Accommodating PWDs*
  These beliefs were measured with a 6-item scale, and one example of an item is "Organizations have to make expensive accommodations to hire more PWDs." The coefficient alpha reliability estimate at time 1 was .65 and at time 2 it was .67.
- *Beliefs About the Skills and Abilities of PWDs*
  The level of skills and abilities associated with PWDs were measured with a 3-item scale, and a sample item was "People with disabilities often have unique talents and skills." The coefficient alpha reliability estimate was .68 for this subscale at time 1 and .68 for it at time 2.
- *Beliefs About Degree of Comfort Associated with Working with PWDs*
  These beliefs were measured with a 5-item scale, and a sample item was "I would feel uncomfortable working with someone with a disability." The coefficient alpha reliability estimate for this scale at time 1 was .70, and at time 2 it was .66.
- *Beliefs About the Dependability of PWDs*
  Beliefs about the dependability of PWDs was measured with a 2-item scale. An example item is "I believe that people with disabilities make dependable employees."
- *Intentions to Hire PWDs in the Future*
  Intentions to hire PWDs in the future were measured with a 1-item scale that read "It is feasible for my company to hire more PWDs."

Analyses

The data were analyzed using *paired t tests* so that employers' beliefs and intentions to hire PWDs were measured prior to and after the presentation of the award.

Results

Means, standard deviations, and sample sizes for each of the pretest and posttest beliefs and intentions are reported in Table 10.1. The overall results of the present study provided support for 3 out of the 5 hypotheses tested by it. The results revealed that employers indicated that they would be more comfortable working with PWDs, felt that those with disabilities had higher skill levels, and believed that the costs of accommodation were low after the award was presented than prior to it. However, the data revealed that employers did not perceive that PWDs were more dependable, and did not intend to hire more PWDs after the award than prior to it.

Table 10.1: Descriptive Statistics for Managers' Beliefs and Intentions Before and After the Award.

	Data Collection Before and After Award					
Hiring Managers' Beliefs and Intentions	Before the Award			After the Award		
	M	*s*	*n*	*M*	*s*	*n*
Skills and Abilities	9.84	2.06	26	11.88	2.57	25
Comfort level	33.27	3.00	26	37.00	3.00	26
Low Cost of Accommodation	27.08	3.79	21	32.58	4.07	21
Dependability	10.62	1.50	27	10.48	1.19	27
Hiring Intentions	5.33	1.23	24	4.83	1.01	24

Hypotheses Tests

Hypothesis 1a

This hypothesis argued that employers would perceive that the cost of accommodation was lower after the best company award was presented than prior to its presentation. High scores represented lower costs of accommodation. The results showed support for H1a. Employers believed that there were lower costs associated with accommodating PWDs after the presentation of the award than prior to it ($M1 = 27.08$, $M2 = 32.58$, $t = -7.906$, $p = .000$).

Hypothesis 1b

This hypothesis predicted that employers would perceive that PWDs had higher levels of skills after the best company award than prior to it. The data from the present study provided support for this hypothesis. Mean levels of rated skills and abilities of PWDs were higher after the award was presented than before it was given (*M time 1* = 9.84, *M time 2* = 11.88, *t* = 4.88, *p* = .00).

Hypothesis 1c

Hypothesis 1c maintained that employers' feelings about the comfort level of working with PWDs would be more positive after the best company award than prior to it. The results from the present study provided support for this hypothesis. Mean levels of rated comfort were higher after the award was given than prior to the award (*M time 1* = 33.27, *M time 2* = 37.00, *t* = −6.051, *p* =.000).

Hypothesis 1d

This hypothesis argued that employers would believe that PWDs would be more dependable after the best company award was presented than prior to its presentation. The data did not provide support for this hypothesis. The mean levels of dependability were not different at time 2 than time 1 (*M time 1* = 10.62, *M time 2* = 10.48, *t* = .642, *p* > .05).

Hypothesis 2

Hypothesis 2 maintained that employers would intend to hire more PWDs after the best company award was presented than before its presentation. The findings did not provide support for this hypothesis. The mean intentions to hire PWDs were not different after the award than prior to it (*M time 1* = 5.33, *M time 2* = 4.83, *t* = 3.564, *p* > .05).

Supplemental Analyses

Although no specific hypotheses were presented, we examined the relations between participants' demographic variables and their beliefs and intentions to hire PWDs at time 2. The results of the supplemental analyses revealed that participants' age was related to beliefs about cost of accommodations at time 1 ($r = -.235$, $p <.05$), skill level at time 2 ($r = .462$, $p <.05$), dependability at time 2 ($r = .462$, $p <.05$), and intentions to hire at time 2 ($r = .428$, $p < .05$). In addition, participants' level of work experience was related to skill level at time 2 ($r = .464$, $p <.05$), and dependability at time 2 ($r.=438$, $p <.05$). These findings suggest that company awards may have more of an effect on older managers and those with more experience. However, additional research is needed to determine if these and other individual differences play a major role in managers' beliefs about PWDs.

Potential Limitations of the Study

There are several potential limitations of the study that deserve mention. One potential limitation is that the study used a pretest posttest design, and a primary limitation of this design is that the pre-testing may have influenced the study's results. For instance, when participants completed the questionnaires prior to the "Best Employer Award" they may have guessed the study's hypotheses, and responded to the questionnaires in ways that would support the study's hypotheses. There is no way to assess this potential problem because we did not include a control group. Second, we did not use an experimental design and random assignment to test the study's hypotheses so we cannot make causal inferences from our results. Thus, we cannot infer that the "Best Employer Award" enhanced hiring managers' beliefs about PWDs and their hiring intentions. Third, even though we used a sample of hiring managers in the northeastern U. S., the sample may not be representative of all hiring managers in the U. S. Given these potential limitations, we want to emphasize that additional experimental research is needed to determine if "Best Employer Awards" have a positive effect on managers' beliefs and intentions to hire PWDs. Future research should also include managers from all parts of the U.S. and around the world.

Discussion

In the present study, we argued that a best employer award for a company that successfully hired and integrated PWDs would have a positive influence on non-winning managers' beliefs and intentions to hire them. We predicted that hiring managers would have more positive beliefs (e.g., ratings of skills) after a best employer award was presented than prior to its presentation. Our results supported several of the hypotheses tested by the study. The data revealed that after a best employer award was presented, hiring managers were more likely to perceive that PWDs (a) had the skills and abilities to perform many jobs, (b) felt comfortable working with them, and (c) believed that the costs of accommodations were lower than prior to the presentation of the award. We did not find that hiring managers intentions to hire PWDs and their ratings of dependability were greater after the award than before it was given. We believe that these findings have important implications for theory, research, and practice on enhancing the employment for PWDs. These issues are considered below.

Implications for Theory

We used social learning theory (Bandura, 1989) to understand and explain why hiring managers would emulate the behaviors of a company that won a best employer award. In particular, the theory predicted that hiring managers would imitate the actions of the company that won an award and motivate them to hire more PWDs. The primary reason for this was that the non-winning companies would imitate the winning company if they perceived that they might receive a reward or recognition for their hiring practices in the future. The data from the present study provided support for many of these theoretical predictions, and suggested that providing positive rewards for companies may be more likely to increase the hiring rate for PWDs than legal requirements (ADA, 1990.)

Although we did not measure competitive feelings, our results and previous research (e.g., Wu & Hu, 2021) suggest that employer awards may evoke competitive feelings among non-winning managers, and these feelings would motivate them to emulate the winning company's behavior. Given these arguments, future research should examine the extent to which competitive feelings motivate managers to imitate the behaviors of award-winning companies.

Implications for Research and Practice

In order to motivate employers to hire people with disabilities, approximately 126 countries (e.g., Argentina, India, European Union, China, U. S.) have adopted legislation that precludes unfair discrimination against qualified people with disabilities (United Nations, 2021). However, legislation is often viewed as punitive by employers, and evokes reactance among them (Brehm, 1966.) Brehm (1966) defines reactance as an unpleasant motivational arousal that occurs when a person feels that someone is threatening or taking away their freedom. One example of this reactance is that an employer told the U.S. Equal Employment Opportunity Commission (EEOC) that he would rather go out of business than be required to hire PWDs (R. King, personal communication, October 2006.)

Many countries also (e.g., U.S., India, Germany) offer various forms of tax incentives for employers who hire people with disabilities. For example, India offers to pay some of the payroll taxes of employers that hire persons with disabilities for three years (Government of India, 2020.) Further, Germany offers to pay 70% of the salary of people with disabilities for 96 months (Kremp, 2020), but Germany also has a quota system that requires public and private sector employees to hire a minimum of 20 PWDs. If they do not meet this quota they must pay a penalty of 320 Euros each month for positions not occupied by people with disabilities. The U.S. also offers tax credits to employers that hire those with disabilities including the Disabled Access Credit of up to $5,000 for small businesses that incur expenditures for providing access to PWDs.

Even though tax incentives can be considered positive outcomes, we do not believe that they are actually strong enough to motivate most employers to hire PWDs. Thus, we argued that award and recognition systems may be much stronger motivators than tax incentives, and they are less likely to create resistance to hiring PWDs among employers than legislation. For instance, our results revealed that a "Best Employer Award" was positively related to managers' beliefs about the skills of PWDs, and the comfort level associated with working with them. The award also affected employers' beliefs about the costs of accommodations, but it was not related to employers' intentions to hire more people with disabilities. Given these findings, we believe that reward and recognition systems may be a much more effective means of changing employers' negative beliefs about PWDs than legislation or tax incentives. However, a best employer award may not always increase the number of people with disabilities hired in the short term because the hiring rate depends on other factors (e.g., profits, status of economy.)

Given these arguments, our study assessed awards at the company level, but we believe that the treatment and inclusion of people with disabilities often occurs at the employee and team level too. Thus, we maintain that individual or team level awards may also be a key way to motivate employees, and managers to increase the inclusion of PWDs. For example, organizations could use (a) various forms of individual or group recognition systems, (b) successful role models, (c) supportive feedback, or (d) corporate gifts to enhance the inclusion of PWDs. Companies might also publicly recognize employees, managers, or teams that make special efforts to attract and retain PWDs. As an example, companies may publicly show their appreciation to people who take special steps to include PWDs. For example, companies may (a) provide employees, managers, or teams with awards for taking steps to include PWDs in their units, (b) create a virtual wall of fame for them, or (c) ask local TV or radio stations to highlight the special behaviors of these individuals.

Conclusion

Our study found that managers felt that PWDs had higher skill levels, reported that they were more comfortable working with them, and believed the costs of accommodations were lower after a best employer award was presented than prior to it. These results suggest that recognition systems may help dispel many of the unfounded beliefs about PWDs more than other strategies (e.g., tax incentives, legislation.) Thus, we hope that our findings will help increase the employment opportunities for PWDs, and ensure that organizations can utilize their many talents and skills. We also hope that it will enable PWDs to enjoy a more satisfying and lucrative work life.

References

Americans with Disabilities Act, U.S. Congress. (1990). https://www.ada.gov/ada_intro.htm

Ammann, M., Horsch, P., & Oesch, D. (2016). Competing with superstars. *Management Science*, *62*(10), 2842–2858. https://econpapers.repec.org/scripts/redir.pf?u=http%3A%2F%2Fdx.doi.org%2F10.1287%2Fmnsc.2015.2266;h=repec:inm:ormnsc:v:62:y:2016:i:10:p:2842–2858

Bandura, A. (1989). Human agency in social cognitive theory. *American Psychologist*, *44*(9), 1175–1184. https://psycnet.apa.org/doi/10.1037/0003-066X.44.9.1175

Baum, M., & Überschaer, A. (2018). When do employer awards pay off and when do they not? The impact of award familiarity on applicants' job pursuit intentions and the moderating role of corporate brand awareness. *The International Journal of Human Resource Management*, *29*(21), 3093–3117. https://doi.org/10.1080/09585192.2016.1254101

Brehm, J. W. (1966). *A theory of psychological reactance*. Academic Press.

Bureau of Labor Statistics. (2021). *Persons with a disability: Labor force characteristics summary*. https://www.bls.gov/news.release/disabl.nr0.htm

Etzioni, A. (1996). *The new golden rule*. HarperCollins Publishers.

Etzioni, A. (2000). Social norms: Internalization, persuasion, and history. *Law and Society Review*, *34*(1), 157–178. https://ssrn.com/abstract=1438172

Finkelstein, R. (2016, October 29–November 2). *Age smart employer awards: A strategy to encourage businesses to hire, engage, and retain older workers* [Paper presentation]. American Public Health Association (APHA) Annual Meeting & Expo, Denver, CO, United States.

Gallus, J., & Frey, B. S. (2016). Awards: A strategic management perspective. *Strategic Management Journal*, *37*(8), 1699–1714. https://doi.org/10.1002/smj.2415

Gasper, J., Palan, M., & Muz, B. (2020). *Survey of employer policies on the employment of people with disabilities*. https://www.dol.gov/sites/dolgov/files/OASP/evaluation/pdf/ODEP_SurveyofEmployerPolicies_FinalReport_June2020.pdf

Government of India (2020, November 12). *Incentive scheme for providing employment to persons with disabilities (PwDs) in the private sector under SIPDA scheme*. https://disabilityaffairs.gov.in/content/page/incentive-to-private-employer.phpo

Hernandez, B., & McDonald, K. (2010). Exploring the costs and benefits of workers with disabilities. *Journal of Rehabilitation*, *76*(3), 15–23.

Hernandez, K. (2020, March 3). *People with disabilities are still struggling to find employment – here are the obstacles they face*. https://www.cnbc.com/2020/03/02/unemployment-rate-among-people-with-disabilities-is-still-high.html

Kremp, P. R. (2020). *Employment and employee benefits in Germany: Overview.* https://uk.practical law.thomsonreuters.com/3-503-3433?transitionType=Default&contextData=(sc.Default)

Kulkarni, M., & Lengnick-Hall, M. L. (2014). Obstacles to success in the workplace for people with disabilities: A review and research agenda. *Human Resource Development Review, 13*(2), 158–180. http://dx.doi.org/10.1177/1534484313485229

Li, J., Yin, J., Shi, W., & Yi, X. (2020). Keeping up with the Joneses: Role of CSR awards in incentivizing non-winners' CSR. *Business & Society, 61*(3), 649–689. https://doi.org/10.1177/ 0007650320982271

Neckermann, S., Cueni, R., & Frey, B. S. (2014). Awards at work. *Labour Economics, 31,* 205–217. https://econpapers.repec.org/scripts/redir.pf?u=http%3A%2F%2Fwww.sciencedirect.com% 2Fscience%2Farticle%2Fpii%2FS0927537114000438;h=repec:eee:labeco:v:31:y:2014:i:c: p:205–217

Shi, W., Zhang, Y., & Hoskisson, R. E. (2017). Ripple effects of CEO awards: Investigating the acquisition activities of superstar CEOs' competitors. *Strategic Management Journal, 38*(10), 2080–2102. https://doi.org/10.1002/smj.2638

Smidts, A., Pruyn, A. T. H., & Van Riel, C. B. (2001). The impact of employee communication and perceived external prestige on organizational identification. *Academy of Management Journal, 44*(5), 1051–1062. https://doi.org/10.5465/3069448

Steiner, G. A., & Steiner, J. F. (1991). *Business, government, and society* (6th ed.). New York.

Turban, D. B., & Cable, D. M. (2003). Firm reputation and applicant pool characteristics. *Journal of Organizational Behavior: The International Journal of Industrial, Occupational and Organizational Psychology and Behavior, 24*(6), 733–751. http://www.jstor.org/stable/ 4093739

United Nations. (2021). *Disability laws and acts by country/area.* https://www.un.org/develop ment/desa/disabilities/disability-laws-and-acts-by-country-area.html

Wright, P., Ferris, S. P., Hiller, J. S., & Kroll, M. (1995). Competitiveness through management of diversity: Effects on stock price valuation. *Academy of Management Journal, 38*(1), 272–287. https://doi.org/10.2307/256736

Wu, Y., & Hu, Y. (2021). Chinese-style incentives: The intraindustry ripple effects of CEO awards. *PLoS ONE, 16*(6), e0252860. https://doi.org/10.1371/journal.pone.0252860

Mustafa F. Özbilgin, Cihat Erbil, and Esra Odabaşı

11 Leaders with Disabilities: A Boardroom Challenge

Abstract: In this chapter, we investigate the emergence of leaders with disabilities (LWD). We provide analyses based on structural and narrative reviews of literature. The structural review identified only a few papers that examine leaders and disabilities together. Through the narrative review, we discuss the emergence of LWD and assess their standing in the boardroom. Reflecting on the polarizing consequences of the neoliberal context in regulated and unregulated countries, we provide two short cases on the inclusion of individuals with disabilities (IWD). In the last part of the chapter, we present an intervention model for the emergence of LWD.

Keywords: leaders with disabilities, disability, leadership, boardroom, diversity, neoliberalism, inclusion model

Introduction

The World Economic Forum (2021) states that the number of individuals with disabilities (IWD) in the world is 1.3 billion. Yet, according to The Valuable 500 report (2020), a global initiative for IWD, 57 percent of organizational leaders state that disability is not on their agenda. Additionally, the report reveals that the representation of IWD in positions of power is deficient. For example, only 37 of the FTSE 100 companies collect data on their employees with disabilities, none of whom hold senior management roles. Furthermore, there has been a dearth of studies focusing on disability with regard to access to senior management, leadership, and boardroom positions. Drawing on a structured and narrative review of the extant literature on disability and leadership, we problematize the absence of IWD in senior management and leadership roles and in the boardroom.

We first explain the methods that we drew on in order to inform our findings in this chapter. Then we provide the results of our structured literature review. The subsequent section focuses on why it is essential to consider disability as a category for boardroom diversity. Then we unpack the concept of leaders with disabilities (LWD) and how disability emergence could occur in the boardroom. Next, we provide two contrasting cases of diversity and leadership. The first case study presents a set of

Mustafa F. Özbilgin, Brunel University London, UK
Cihat Erbil, Ankara HBV University, Turkey
Esra Odabaşı, Es Career Employment Consultancy for Disabled Persons, Turkey

https://doi.org/10.1515/9783110743647-012

examples from countries with regulated neoliberal contexts for disability. The second case study is from a country with an unregulated context of neoliberalism in relation to disability. Through these examples, we identify two contrasting models: the potentiality model (in regulated settings) versus the deficit model (in unregulated settings) for managing disability. Finally, the chapter provides a framework for promoting IWD to leadership and boardroom positions.

Methods

This chapter draws on two research methods. First, we conducted a structured literature review (Armitage & Keeble-Allen, 2008) based on searches of the Web of Science index to understand what has been published on LWD. Our review sought to reveal the extent to which leaders and disabilities are studied together. We used alternative terms to search for leaders (i.e., leader, leadership, boardroom, C-suite, C-level) and disabilities (i.e., disability, physical disability, mental disability, intellectual disability, sensory disability, neurodiversity). The structured review covered papers that were published until September, 2021. Initially, we searched leaders and disabilities separately in the topic, title, and abstract of the papers in the database. This generated 86,869 papers with disability in their titles. The number of papers that included leaders and disabilities in the title was 84. We narrowed down our search to the discipline of business and management in the Web of Science. This search generated eight papers that had leaders and disabilities in their titles in the field of business and management (i.e., Boehm & Dwertmann, 2015; Kazarian et al., 2019; Kensbock & Stephan, 2016; Luria et al., 2014; Luu, 2019; Moore & Huberty, 2018; Rosenbaum &More, 2021; Samosh, 2021). However, two of these articles (i.e., Boehm & Dwertmann, 2015; Moore & Huberty, 2018) deal with non-disabled leaders and their employees with disabilities. Among the disability papers, there was only one paper, which included boardroom in the topic, title, or abstract (i.e., Stowe et al., 2006). There are no papers among the disability related papers that covered either C-suite or C-level as the main focus.

We also included disability subgroups, such as physical, mental, intellectual, sensory, and neurodiversity. Relatively more research has been done on physical disability than on other subgroups in the general database. Intellectual disability has come to the fore in recent years in leadership studies. At the same time, the number of papers that included leaders and intellectual disability in their titles was 18 in the general database. There were fewer papers on mental disability when compared with papers on physical and intellectual disability. Sensory disability and neurodiversity related papers were even fewer in number.

Second, we built a narrative review (Wiles et al., 2011) based on a select number of significant and relevant papers, reports, and other published works on disability and leadership from different social science disciplines. Using both methods, we analyzed why LWD lack visibility in the field of business and management and what organizations could do to promote the emergence and inclusion of LWD.

Findings based on the Review of Literature on Leaders and Disability

Our structured literature review revealed that publications on disability at work focus more on physical impairments. Sensory, intellectual, and mental disabilities and neurodiversity have gained visibility in the literature over the past few years. However, most of these studies did not explore disability in relation to leaders and senior management. Procknow and Rocco (2021) state that leadership studies have long focused on non-disabled leaders. Our findings support their assertion that disability is studied mainly on basic access to social, economic, and political life. The literature study on leaders and disabilities reveals that IWD experience a general state of exclusion from the labor market, devaluation of knowledge, skills, and abilities, and suffer resultant absence from positions of power, authority, and leadership.

Why is it Imperative to Consider Disability as a Category of Leadership Diversity?

Drawing on a narrative review, we answer this question. Disability is defined differently across different economic, social, political, and healthcare fields. In fact, there are different legal and medical definitions of disability across different national systems (Banks et al., 2017). The United Nations (UN) definition of disability is "a long-term physical, mental, intellectual or sensory impairment that may hinder individuals from participating fully and effectively in society on an equal basis with others" (UN, 2006, p. 3). At the global level, disability is protected with a convention. The rights of IWD are protected by the Universal Declaration of Protection of People with Disabilities. To date, 164 countries have signed up for this declaration. Therefore, disability appears to be the third category of diversity that has received global protection. The other two categories are gender and ethnicity. As a result, disability discrimination is widely endorsed internationally. However, as we explore below, the content, substance, and impact of disability discrimination legislation have been hugely varied across national borders and socio-economic systems.

Disability is not a monolithic and unified diversity category. There are many subgroups under the banner of disability. For example, physical disability is a considerable and enduring condition that affects individuals' bodies and limits their actions. Sensory disability includes all kinds of impairments that hinder or prevent individuals' senses, such as sight, hearing, tasting, touching, and smelling. The inability of individuals to perform major life activities due to mental disorders such as anxiety, bipolar, and depression is a mental disability (Kruse & Oswal, 2018). Intellectual disability refers to a limitation in cognitive functions and restricted communication capacity, weak social skills, and difficulty performing personal care (Schalock et al., 2010). In addition, individuals with intellectual disabilities may suffer from behavioral and mental problems, such as the low capacity to cope with personnel problems and limited social skills (Rapley, 2004). Across these subcategories of disability, what IWD demand for workplace accommodation could be highly varied. For example, what visually impaired individuals need for access could conflict with what individuals with hearing impairment may need. Thus organizational efforts for accommodation and access for IWD need to be sensitive to the varied needs of the full range of disabilities.

Despite international recognition of their general socio-economic exclusion, IWD suffer from extensive labor market discrimination. As a result, they are severely under-represented in economic activity and positions of power and privilege. In addition, they face lower wage offers for the same position and have fewer career advancement opportunities (Brouwers, 2020). The dire neglect of IWD in terms of access to work and employment partly explains their overall omission from leadership positions.

Better representation of IWD in the boardroom could challenge the able-bodied and able-minded leadership stereotypes (Bebbington & Özbilgin, 2013). In addition, fair representation of IWD in the boardroom would signal pathways for the emergence of LWD. It is common for mentally and physically fragile individuals to remain silent in the face of stigmatization (Elraz, 2018) and personally take on the burden of responsibility to be included and accepted at work (Görgen & Ziervogel, 2019). The lowly representation of IWD in the boardroom shows the limited will of organizations to overcome discrimination, stigma and prejudice against disabilities. Organizations that recognize and accommodate IWD in leadership positions improve the resilience of IWD and create a more inclusive working environment for all.

Reforms in education, advances in social mores, the emergence of social movements and progress in legal regulation drive organizations to recognize the untapped potential of historically disadvantaged communities (Özbilgin & Erbil, 2021) such as IWD in advanced democratic countries. There are many ways to redress the systemic inequalities that IWD experience in the labor market. Reforms in the education system have opened up routeways for IWD, such as those with neurodiversity and other forms of psychological and physical disabilities, to seek education and acquire skills and knowledge across many fields of study. Yet, the labor markets have consistently failed to capture the talent of IWD, relegating them to lowly positions and keeping them from accessing opportunities for work and employment. We posit that recognizing the untapped talent of IWD with the requisite knowledge, skills, and experience will allow them to progress into leadership positions and help organizations benefit from their untapped potential.

What does it mean to have LWD in the Boardroom and how do LWD Emerge in the Boardroom?

Not all disabilities are resent at birth. Of all IWD, only 17 percent had a congenital disability. The majority of disabilities are acquired through the life course of an individual. Chronic diseases such as diabetes or stroke, which can lead to functional disability, usually occur with aging (Boehm & Dwertmann, 2015). In particular, for leadership positions, certain forms of disability could be acquired due to old age. The fact that disabilities are acquired by age makes leaders more susceptible to disability as their average age tends to be higher than those of other staff. However, reports on leaders and disabilities show that very few leaders disclose any disability, possibly fearing stigmatization. Leaders also have access to a broad range of financial, social, and cultural resources to have their disabilities accommodated, should they acquire disabilities with age. For example, Hiroki Takeuchi, the cofounder of GoCardless, an account-to-account payment system, was paralyzed after a bike accident. However, the impairment he acquired later did not stop his career as one of the UK's most inspiring technology leaders (Hamilton et al., 2019). Takeuchi emphasized his company's supportive policy. Takeuchi remained on the board of GoCardless during and after his recovery (O'Hear, 2017).

Leaders may also have developmental disabilities and may realize it later. One of these leaders is Caroline Casey, social entrepreneur and co-founder of The Valuable (Casey, 2010). Casey was born with ocular albinism, which causes visual impairment and is considered a disability by law. Casey stated that the inclusion of IWD paves the way for different thinking and accelerates innovation. She also declared that gathering untapped talent provides expected benefits through weakening social barriers that exclude IWD (Di Sibio, 2021).

Not all disabilities are visible. Some forms of disability are invisible. Individuals have the choice to disclose or not to disclose their disabilities. Studies on disability show that individuals often refrain from revealing their disabilities with the fear of reprisal, stereotyping, and prejudice that they may experience. Thus the emergence of more IWD may indicate that such prejudices no longer present impediments for individuals to self-identify as IWD in the context of work. The inclusion of IWD at work and positions of power encourages their visibility and facilitates their representation in senior management. The visibility of high-status positions, along with their disabilities, can encourage employees with disabilities to participate and encourage other leaders who hide their disability to become visible (Ghin, 2019). Luria et al. (2014)

state that visibility allows IWD to demonstrate their leadership skills and enhances positive frames for the leadership potential of IWD.

Whether an individual has a visible or invisible disability, their pursuit of leadership will be shaped by the model by which disability is framed in their particular context. There are two different models for the inclusion of IWD in leadership positions. One is the potentiality model, which recognizes the potential contribution of IWD. The potentiality model is based on the social and economic empowerment approaches. The social empowerment approach to disability focuses on the social construction of disability and suggests that disabilities are social choices. Therefore, a disability arises from social systems' stigmatizing and exclusionary mechanisms, and empowerment would come from constructive social decisions about the inclusion of IWD (Oliver, 2013). In the same way, critical disability theory argues that disability results from normative assumptions that are embedded in interpersonal relations (Roberson et al., 2021). Thus, the empowerment of the IWD rests on transforming those normative assumptions. The economic empowerment approaches to disability focus on the inability of individuals to participate in paid work (Jongbloed, 2003). The economic empowerment approaches focus on disability on the return-cost axis. They compare the contribution of IWD participation in the economy with the costs associated with disability welfare arrangements (Cullinan et al., 2013). The social and economic empowerment approaches emphasize crafting mechanisms that enable IWD to overcome systemic inequalities and reach their full potential (Barton, 2017). Thus, Sprague and Hayes (2000) point out that empowerment is one of the potential features of mutual social relations, enabling diverse contributions and minimizing inequalities.

The second model is the deficit model for the inclusion of IWD. The disability model is based on the medical-welfare approach to disability, which suggests that IWD lack certain abilities. The medical-welfare approach to disability assesses whether IWD are fit to work in certain occupations or to perform their life functions. While this approach accepts ableism as the norm, it considers disability as pathological (Williams & Mavin, 2012). Therefore, in this model, the inability of individuals to perform what is deemed normal for others is often used as an excuse for their exclusion from social and economic life (Van Aswegen, 2020). The deficit model is the older and more dominant model for the inclusion of IWD and it lacks the impetus to drive for the emergence of LWD.

Leaders and Disabilities in Two Contrasting Neoliberal Settings

Stiglitz (2012) argues that neoliberalism has dire consequences for human rights, as neoliberalism could entrench gender, ethnic and disability discrimination. However, he also shows that if neoliberalism is regulated well, those negative consequences of neoliberalism on human rights could be mitigated. Yet, if neoliberalism is left unregulated, unchecked market forces would violate human rights and civil liberties. We provide two contrasting examples. The first case study is from countries with regulated neoliberal systems. The second case study is from a country with an unregulated neoliberal approach to disability in the labor market. We offer the case of New Zealand, Canada, and the UK for the potentiality model of disability based on the social and economic empowerment of IWD. At the same time, the Turkish case is presented as the deficit model, which draws on the medical-welfare approach as an excuse for demarcation and limited inclusion of IWD based on an outdated quota system.

The Context of Disability and Leadership in Regulated Neoliberal Systems

According to the UN (2018) report, only 22 member states offer some provisions in their constitutions to protect the right to work and combat barriers to participation in the workplace for IWD. The report also declares that many governments do not adequately guide employers and other stakeholders or follow up provisions on IWD in the workplace. However, there are also progressive practices in incorporating IWD into the workplace. New Zealand's Disability Strategy, published in 2001 and revised in 2016, is regarded as one of the most progressive strategies on the inclusion of IWD. New Zealand reportedly includes IWD in the design of the system which seeks to promote their inclusion (UN, 2018). New Zealand aims to make leaders of all organizations, including the public, private and not-for-profit sectors, part of the disability community, providing guidance and data that can assess the circumstances of IWD in their decisions (Office for Disability Issues, 2021). Canada is also a progressive country in creating inclusive workplaces for IWD. It has comprehensive and broad disability management approaches (Wagner et al., 2017). The National Institute of Disability Management Research (NIDMAR) and the Workplace Disability Management Program (WDMP) are leading institutions in Canada. NIDMAR focuses on training disability management professionals in order to strengthen the well-being of IWD at work. To this end, NIDMAR provides disability training to professionals and supports cross-sectional work skills to enable them to act together with stakeholders, such as unions and care providers (Quaigrain & Issa, 2018). Employers are responsible for designing an inclusive workplace and collaborating with stakeholders (Conference Board of Canada, 2013). The UK also has a policy for the inclusion of IWD at work (Quaigrain et al., 2014). The National Leadership Center, a governmental organization, released a new program in 2021, the Catalyst Programme, to develop and support LWD in public administration. The program aims to develop IWD in public administration to reach the CEO level. One of the important initiatives is the Business Disability Forum (BDF), formerly known as the Employer Disability Forum, which has 400 members and represents twenty percent of the British workforce (Business Disability Forum [BDF], 2021), and supervises leaders in recruiting and integrating people with a disability (Demougin et al., 2021).

Overall, New Zealand, Canada, and the UK appear as countries with initiatives that seek to support the inclusion of IWD through the potentiality model. In the UK case, one of the caveats is the interplay between welfare regimes that offer disability benefits and the role of industry in supporting IWD. In the UK, the responsibility has shifted from the welfare state to the corporations with the instruction of the disability discrimination act, which brought about additional responsibilities to workplaces to make reasonable adjustments (Goodley & Lawthom, 2019). Besides this cynical shift of responsibility, these three countries regulate the inclusion of IWD using the potentiality model.

The Context of Disability and Leadership in a Country with an Unregulated Neoliberal Context

Studies on Turkey show that the country suffers from an unregulated form of neoliberalism which means that human rights issues are relegated to secondary status in relation to the demands of the market economy, macro-financial concerns, and competitive rationales. Küskü et al. (2021) define Turkey as having an adversarial context for diversity. The situation of IWD is in parallel with this assessment. As of 2019, the population of IWD in Turkey is 15.3 percent (Türkiye İstatistik Kurumu [TÜİK], 2020a). The employment rate among adults with disabilities stands at only 19.9 percent (TÜİK, 2020b). This community cannot realize their full potential to receive the proper education and the right set of jobs yet due to the deficit model that the country adopts. The deficit model manifests with the absence of progressive legislation, lack of responsibilization of the industry, and general disinterest in the inclusion of IWD. Turkey has the lowest rates of employment for disadvantaged groups among all Organization for Economic Co-operation and Development (OECD) countries (OECD, 2018). There are rampant prejudices towards IWD in social and economic life in the country (Koca-Atabey, 2021). When IWD are mentioned, the first thing that often comes to mind is people who have no mobility and are unable to work (Oncel & Karaoglan, 2020). There is no recognition of the potentiality of IWD. The law in Turkey also remains ceremonial and bears similarity to the outdated quota system in the UK; it imposes a quota of three percent disabled staff and a fine for non-compliant organizations. Considering that 15.3 percent of working-age adults have disabilities in Turkey, the three percent quota presents an unambitious target for employers. In response, some companies recruit and pay disabled people, who are signed up to payroll but are not invited to work. These workers with disabilities are typically called "Automated Teller Machine (ATM) workers" (Tezcan, 2013). Although they draw wages from workplaces, they are not allowed to work. Besides the ATM workers, there is no recognition of the managerial and leadership potential of workers with disabilities.

In the absence of supportive leadership discourses, and progressive legislation, most of the work here falls on the goodwill of more enlightened human resources executives and social innovation (Palalar Alkan et al., 2021). As an entrepreneur with a congenital disability, Esra Odabaşı's social enterprise, ES Career, is the sole HR consultancy in Turkey that mediates the inclusion of IWD into the workforce. However, the agency's effort remains limited at the entry-level for IWD. In the future, moving away from the deficit model towards developing a potentiality model would help Turkish workplaces to manage IWD more effectively. Currently, the unregulated nature of the neoliberal context remains taxing for IWD and other communities of disadvantage in Turkey.

A Framework for Promoting Leaders with Disabilities in the Boardroom

Atypical leaders are those individuals who emerge as leaders from under-represented, disenfranchised, and disadvantaged backgrounds (Alter, 2018). What constituted atypicality in the past in terms of leadership potential has shifted significantly over the years thanks to the diversification of talent pools by gender, ethnicity, disability, sexuality, and other factors. Despite the diversification of pools of leadership candidates, the profile of leaders has not significantly transformed. Samdanis and Özbilgin (2020) explain that atypical leaders are innovators from the margins. When, for example, LWD emerge and if accommodations are made in the process, such emergence offers the possibility of transforming how leadership is framed and practiced, as individuals from traditionally disenfranchised backgrounds offer to bring new perspectives and repertoires of being and acting at work. Despite its vast potential and promise, the emergence of LWD is still out of kilter with the growing supply of talented IWD. The numbers of LWD remain negligible, and most disabilities that leaders may acquire in their life course remain invisible due to the strength of the able-bodiedness and mental health ethos of leadership prototypes. Yet, as we outlined in this chapter, times are ripe for change. The leadership potential of IWD and the moral landscape that support the emergence of LWD have been well acknowledged. In the following, we provide a three-step guide to overcoming barriers to the emergence of LWD (see Figure 11.1).

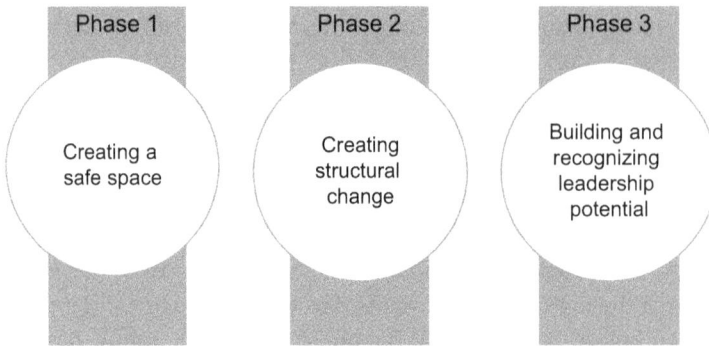

Figure 11.1: Process of supporting the emergence of LWD.

Phase 1: Creating a safe space where IWD may demand accommodation of their unique needs to fulfill their potential at work and address the trust deficit that IWD face in workplaces and positions of power. This phase requires interventions to combat prejudice, biases, and discriminatory statements from policies, practices, and cultures of work and foster proactive behaviors that help IWD overcome barriers (Kensbock & Boehm, 2016; Samosh, 2021). The International Labour Organization (ILO) (2016) mentions formal leadership policy including IWD as interventions in its report on best practices. A formal policy declares the endorsement of top management to IWD. It may prevent the leadership potential of IWD from being tarnished by personal misconceptions and prejudices. However, this preliminary phase is insufficient to combat systemic inequalities that hold IWD back at work.

Phase 2: The second phase involves creating structural changes at work to accommodate the needs of IWD in order to help them reach their full potential at work. This phase consists in identifying progressive approaches (social and economic empowerment) to disability. This phase would also involve proofing leadership succession and career policies and practices to eliminate bias, discrimination, exclusion, and inequality inherent in ongoing systems and structures. This phase involves changes in temporal, spatial, systemic, and cultural, and even technological regulation and designs at work to ensure the full inclusion of IWD (ILO, 2019). This second phase challenges the ableism inherent in current systems and structures, seeking to achieve their longer-term transformation.

Phase 3: As we are focusing on leadership and disability, the third phase of the change model involves building and recognizing the untapped leadership potential of IWD across institutions of importance. Institutions of significance include education, employment, healthcare, and law at the macro-societal level, disability networks, leadership recruitment teams, external headhunter firms at the meso-institutional level and champions, allies, and IWD at the micro-level as agents of change (Boehm & Dwertmann, 2015; Moore & Huberty, 2019). Regulating these actors and agents of change could help transform leadership to become an inclusive domain by contesting ableist discourses, practices, and cultures of leadership emergence (Kazarian et al., 2019). The final phase requires progress in the first two phases before disability could become a leadership priority.

Conclusions

Based on a structured and narrative review, we examined the emergence of LWD. The structured review shows that disability and leadership are not often studied together. The narrative review revealed three significant themes. We first examined the drivers of the emergence of LWD. Second, we discussed the emergence of LWD in the boardroom. We explained that LWD can only emerge when they have exceptional talents even in the most progressive contexts. Leadership emergence for IWD is paved with a trust deficit. We define trust deficit, in this context, as a process by which the talents, leadership potential, credentials, experiences, and achievements of IWD are denigrated, demarcated, and devalued in the labor market. Third, we explored how the neoliberal context impacts the integration of IWD. Providing examples from countries with regulated neoliberal systems, we demonstrated how the integration of IWD could be framed in progressive ways that reveal and utilize the untapped potential of IWD. Drawing on the example of a country with an unregulated neoliberal context, we explained how the deficit model, which undermines the potentiality of IWD, is adopted. These two contrasting neoliberal models show the significance of the interplay between macro-economic systems and their effective regulation through responsibilization of the state, institutions of relevance in the inclusion of IWD. Based on these three themes, we provided a multiphase intervention model for the emergence of LWD.

References

Alter, N. (2018). *The strength of difference: Itineraries of atypical bosses.* Emerald Group Publishing. https://doi.org/10.1108/S2051-2333201805

Armitage, A., & Keeble-Allen, D. (2008). Undertaking a structured literature review or structuring a literature review: Tales from the field. *Proceedings of the 7th European Conference on Research Methodology for Business and Management Studies: ECRM2008, Regent's College, London* (p. 35).

Banks, L. M., Mearkle, R., Mactaggart, I., Walsham, M., Kuper, H., & Blanchet, K. (2017). Disability and social protection programmes in low- and middle-income countries: A systematic review. *Oxford Development Studies*, *45*(3), 223–239. https://doi.org/10.1080/13600818.2016.1142960

Barton, L. (2017). Disability, empowerment and physical education. In J. Evans (Ed.), *Equality, equity and physical education* (pp. 43–54). Routledge.

Bebbington, D., & Özbilgin, M. (2013). The paradox of diversity in leadership and leadership for diversity. *Management international/International Management/Gestiòn Internacional*, *17*, 14–24. https://doi.org/10.7202/1015808ar

Boehm, S. A., & Dwertmann, D. J. (2015). Forging a single-edged sword: Facilitating positive age and disability diversity effects in the workplace through leadership, positive climates, and HR practices. *Work, Aging and Retirement*, *1*(1), 41–63. https://doi.org/10.1093/workar/wau008

Brouwers, E. P. (2020). Social stigma is an underestimated contributing factor to unemployment in people with mental illness or mental health issues: Position paper and future directions. *BMC Psychology*, *8*(1), 1–7. https://doi.org/10.1186/s40359-020-00399-0

Business Disability Forum. (2021). *About us*. https://businessdisabilityforum.org.uk/about-us/

Casey, C. (2010). *Looking past limits*. TED. https://www.ted.com/talks/caroline_casey_looking_past_limits

Conference Board of Canada. (2013). *Creating an effective workplace disability management program*. http://www.re-integrate.eu/resources/001_rtwbook_e.pdf

Cullinan, J., Gannon, B., & O'Shea, E. (2013). The welfare implications of disability for older people in Ireland. *The European Journal of Health Economics*, *14*(2), 171–183. https://doi.org/10.1007/s10198-011-0357-4

Demougin, P., Gooberman, L., Hauptmeier, M., & Heery, E. (2021). Revisiting voluntarism: Private voluntary regulation by Employer Forums in the United Kingdom. *Journal of Industrial Relations*, *63*(5), 684–705. https://doi.org/10.1177/00221856211038308

Di Sibio, C. (2021). *How can we be inclusive if we don't include everyone*? EY. https://www.ey.com/en_gl/diversity-inclusiveness/how-can-we-be-inclusive-if-we-dont-include-everyone

Elraz, H. (2018). Identity, mental health and work: How employees with mental health conditions recount stigma and the pejorative discourse of mental illness. *Human Relations*, *71*(5), 722–741. https://doi.org/10.1177/0018726717716752

Ghin, P. P. (2019). The sick body: Conceptualizing the experience of illness in senior leadership. In M. Fotaki & A. Pullen (Eds.), *Diversity, affect and embodiment in organizing* (pp. 91–110). Palgrave Macmillan. https://doi.org/10.1007/978-3-319-98917-4_5

Goodley, D., & Lawthom, R. (2019). Critical disability studies, Brexit and Trump: A time of neoliberal-ableism. *Rethinking History*, *23*(2), 233–251. https://doi.org/10.1080/13642529.2019.1607476

Görgens, T., & Ziervogel, G. (2019). From "No One Left Behind" to putting the last first: centring the voices of disabled people in resilience work. In Watermeyer, B., McKenzie, J. & Swartz, L. (Eds.), *The Palgrave handbook of disability and citizenship in the Global South* (pp. 85–102). Palgrave Macmillan.

Hamilton, I. A., Hanbury, M., & Wood, C. (2019). *UK Tech 100: The 100 most influential people shaping British technology in 2019*. https://www.businessinsider.com/uk-tech-100-2019-most-important-interesting-and-impactful-people-uk-tech-2019-9

International Labour Organization. (2016). *Disability in the workplace: Employers' organizations and business networks*, *2016*. http://www.businessanddisability.org/wp-content/uploads/2018/07/Disability_business_networks.pdf

International Labour Organization. (2019). *Making the future of work inclusive of persons with disabilities*. http://www.businessanddisability.org/wp-content/uploads/2020/03/ GBDN_Conference_Report_Making_the_Future_of_Work_Inclusive_of_persons_with_disabilities.pdf

Jongbloed, L. (2003). Disability policy in Canada: An overview. *Journal of Disability Policy Studies*, *13*(4), 203–209. https://doi.org/10.1177/104420730301300402

Kazarian, G., Gryshova, R., & Durglishvili, N. (2019). Regulatory environment for the formation of leadership positions for the persons with disabilities. In W. Strielkowski (Ed.), *Sustainable leadership for entrepreneurs and academics* (pp. 171–179). Springer. https://doi.org/10.1007/978-3-030-15495-0_18

Kensbock, J. M., & Boehm, S. A. (2016). The role of transformational leadership in the mental health and job performance of employees with disabilities. *The International Journal of Human Resource Management, 27*(14), 1580–1609. https://doi.org/10.1080/09585192.2015.1079231

Koca-Atabey, M. (2021). Disability and old age: The COVID-19 pandemic in Turkey. *Disability & Society, 36*(5), 834–839. https://doi.org/10.1080/09687599.2021.1907550

Kruse, A. K., & Oswal, S. K. (2018). Barriers to higher education for students with bipolar disorder: A critical social model perspective. *Social Inclusion, 6*(4), 194–206. https://doi.org/10.17645/si.v6i4.1682

Küskü, F., Aracı, Ö., & Özbilgin, M. F. (2021). What happens to diversity at work in the context of a toxic triangle? Accounting for the gap between discourses and practices of diversity management. *Human Resource Management Journal,* 31(2),553–574.

Luria, G., Kalish, Y., & Weinstein, M. (2014). Learning disability and leadership: Becoming an effective leader. *Journal of Organizational Behavior, 35*(6), 747–761. https://doi.org/10.1002/job.1896

Luu, T. (2019). Relationship between benevolent leadership and the well-being among employees with disabilities. *Journal of Business Research, 99*, 282–294. https://doi.org/10.1016/j.jbusres.2019.03.004

Moore, M. E., & Huberty, L. L. (2018). Diversity orientation and disability in organizational leadership. In A. M. Broadbridge & S. L. Fielden (Eds.), *Research handbook of diversity and careers* (pp. 147–160). Edward Elgar Publishing.

Office for Disability Issues. (2021). *New Zealand Disability Strategy.* https://www.odi.govt.nz/nz-disability-strategy/

O'Hear, S. (2017, September 18). *GoCardless CEO: "I still feel like I'm the same person."* TechCrunch. https://techcrunch.com/2017/09/18/hiroki-interview/

Oliver, M. (2013). The social model of disability: Thirty years on. *Disability & Society, 28*(7), 1024–1026. https://doi.org/10.1080/09687599.2013.818773

Oncel, B. D., & Karaoglan, D. (2020). Disability and labour force participation in a developing country: Evidence from Turkish males. *Global Business and Economics Review, 22*(3), 270–288. https://doi.org/10.1504/GBER.2020.106245

Organization for Economic Co-operation and Development. (2018). *The new OECD Jobs Strategy: Good jobs for all in a changing world of work.* https://www.oecd.org/iceland/jobs-strategy-ICELAND-EN.pdf

Özbilgin, M., & Erbil, C. (2021). Social movements and wellbeing in organizations from multilevel and intersectional perspectives: The case of the #BlackLivesMatter movement. In T. Wall, S. C. Cooper & P. Brough (Eds.), *The SAGE handbook of organisational wellbeing* (pp. 119–138). SAGE Reference. https://doi.org/10.4135/9781529757187.n9

Palar Alkan, D., Ozbilgin, M., & Kamasak, R. (2021). Social innovation in managing diversity: Covid-19 as a catalyst for change. *Equality, Diversity and Inclusion: An International Journal.* https://doi.org/10.1108/EDI-07-2021-0171

Procknow, G., & Rocco, T. S. (2021). Contesting "authenticity" in authentic leadership through a Mad Studies lens. *Human Resource Development Review, 20*(3), 345–373. https://doi.org/10.1177/15344843211020571

Quaigrain, R. A., & Issa, M. H. (2018). Development and validation of disability management indicators for the construction industry. *Journal of Engineering, Design and Technology, 36*, 6–30. https://doi.org/10.1108/JEDT-04-2017-0032

Quaigrain, R. A., Winter, J., & Issa, M. H. (2014). A critical review of the literature on disability management in the construction industry. In A. Raiden, S. Reid & M. Loosemore (Eds.), *Motivations and barriers to social procurement in the Australian construction industry. Proceedings of the 33rd Annual ARCOM Conference, 4–6 September 2017* (pp. 643–651). Association of Researchers in Construction Management.

Rapley, M. (2004). *The social construction of intellectual disability*. Cambridge University Press. https://doi.org/10.1017/CBO9780511489884

Roberson, Q., Quigley, N. R., Vickers, K., & Bruck, I. (2021). Reconceptualizing leadership from a neurodiverse perspective. *Group & Organization Management, 46*(2), 399–423. https://doi.org/10.1177/1059601120987293

Rosenbaum, D., & More, E. (2021). Risk and opportunity – The leadership challenge in a world of uncertainty – Learnings from research into the implementation of the Australian National Disability Insurance Scheme. *Journal of Risk and Financial Management, 14*(8), 383. https://doi.org/10.3390/jrfm14080383

Samdanis, M., & Özbilgin, M. (2020). The duality of an atypical leader in diversity management: The legitimization and delegitimization of diversity beliefs in organizations. *International Journal of Management Reviews, 22*(2), 101–119. https://doi.org/10.1111/ijmr.12217

Samosh, D. (2021). The three-legged stool: Synthesizing and extending our understanding of the career advancement facilitators of persons with disabilities in leadership positions. *Business & Society, 60*(7), 1773–1810 https://doi.org/10.1177/0007650320907134

Schalock, R. L., Borthwick-Duffy, S. A., Bradley, V. J., Buntinx, W. H. E., Coulter, D. L., Craig, E. M., Gomez, S. C., Lachapelle, Y., Luckasson, R., Reeve, A., Shogren, K. A., Snell, M. E., Spreat, S., Tasse, M. J., Thompson, J. R., Verdugo-Alonso, M. A., Wehmeyer, M. L., & Yeager, M. H. (2010). *Intellectual disability: Definition, classification, and systems of supports*. American Association on Intellectual and Developmental Disabilities.

Sprague, J., & Hayes, J. (2000). Self-determination and empowerment: A feminist standpoint analysis of talk about disability. *American Journal of Community Psychology, 28*(5), 671–695. https://doi.org/10.1023/A: 1005197704441

Stiglitz, J. E. (2012). *The price of inequality: How today's divided society endangers our future*. WW Norton & Company.

Stowe, M. J., Turnbull III, H. R., & Sublet, C. (2006). The Supreme Court, "our town," and disability policy: Boardrooms and bedrooms, courtrooms and cloakrooms. *Mental Retardation, 44*(2), 83–99. https://doi.org/10.1352/0047-6765(2006)44[83:TSCOTA]2.0.CO;2

Tezcan, T. (2013). *Discrimination experienced by disabled employees in the public sector as an "institutional discrimination area"* [Master's thesis, Middle East Technical University].

Türkiye İstatistik Kurumu. (2020a). *Engelli bireylerin yaş grubu ve cinsiyete göre dağılımı.* [Distribution of disabled people by age, group, and gender.] https://data.tuik.gov.tr/Kate gori/GetKategori?p=Nufus-ve-Demografi-109

Türkiye İstatistik Kurumu. (2020b). *Engelli bireylerin işteki durumu, çalışma durumu ve cinsiyete göre dağılımı.* [Distribution of disabled people by their status at work, working status, and gender.] https://data.tuik.gov.tr/Kategori/GetKategori?p=Nufus-ve-Demografi-109

United Nations. (2006). *United Nations Convention on the Rights of Persons with Disabilities*. https://www.un.org/disabilities/documents/convention/convention_accessible_pdf.pdf

United Nations. (2018). *Disability and development report*. https://www.un.org/development/ desa/disabilities/wp-content/uploads/sites/15/2019/07/disability-report-chapter2.pdf

The Valuable 500. (2020). *The leaders of the inclusion revolution*. https://www.thevaluable500. com/wp-content/uploads/2020/01/The-Leaders-of-the-Inclusion-Revolution-2019-Summary-Report.pdf

Van Aswegen, J. (2020). Disabling discourses and charitable model of disability: Labour market activation for people with disabilities, Ireland – a critical policy analysis. *Disability & Society*, *35*(3), 435–459. https://doi.org/10.1080/09687599.2019.1634519

Wagner, S., Harder, H., Scott, L., Buys, N., Yu, I., Geisen, T., Randall, C., Lo, K., Tang, D., Fraess-Phillips, A., Hassler, B., & Howe, C. (2017). Canadian employee perspectives on disability management. *International Journal of Disability Management*, *12*(3), 1–9. https://doi.org/10.1017/idm.2017.3

Wiles, R., Crow, G., & Pain, H. (2011). Innovation in qualitative research methods: A narrative review. *Qualitative Research*, *11*(5), 587–604. https://doi.org/10.1177/1468794111413227

Williams, J., & Mavin, S. (2012). Disability as constructed difference: A literature review and research agenda for management and organization studies. *International Journal of Management Reviews*, *14*(2), 159–179. https://doi.org/10.1111/j.1468-2370.2012.00329.x

World Economic Forum. (2021). *Closing the disability inclusion gap with business leadership*. https://www.weforum.org/our-impact/closing-the-disability-inclusion-gap-through-the-power-of-business-leadership/

World Health Organization and World Bank. (2011). *World report on disability 2011*. https://apps.who.int/iris/handle/10665/44575

Part 4: **The Role of Context**

David J. G. Dwertmann and Kristie L. McAlpine

12 A Disability Contingency Framework for the Workplace

Abstract: In this chapter, we introduce a Disability Contingency Framework that draws from the person-job fit literature. It is centered on the idea of actual fit between the functional abilities of a person with a disability and the job demands or requirements of a specific job – disability-job fit. With this focus, our framework shares similarities with workplace accommodations (i.e., a focus on actual abilities and demands; acknowledgement of varying levels of fit between disabilities and jobs) and the disability-job fit stereotype literature (i.e., an emphasis on the importance of the job in question; a focus on the idea of fit). Yet, our framework also extends and integrates these ideas by focusing on the abilities of people with disabilities and highlighting that functional limitations in some areas can come with functional advantages in other areas and, if these advantages align with the demands of the job, performance advantages can result.

Keywords: Disability-Contingency Framework, person-job fit, disability-job fit, people with disabilities, inclusion

Introduction

The term disability implies an inability to perform certain tasks of daily life and, when defining disability, the two prevalent models are the medical model of disability and the social model of disability (Dwertmann, 2016). The former is based on the idea that people with disabilities deviate from the norm – the "healthy" population – and do not meet its medical standards (Albrecht, 2006). The latter model focuses on the environment and the interaction between individuals and the environment. An individual impairment only becomes a disability if the environment does not allow the person to fully function within it (Schoeni et al., 2008). In contrast to the focus on impairments and disabilities, disability advocates and scholars have instead emphasized the abilities that individuals have. For example, Baldridge et al. (2018, p. 111) write that their chapter "is about ability. The skills, knowledge, and abilities of over a billion people worldwide who have one or more (dis)abilities."

In the employment context, a focus on the abilities of people with disabilities implies that most individuals can be productive members of the labor market, a

David J. G. Dwertmann and Kristie L. McAlpine, Rutgers University

https://doi.org/10.1515/9783110743647-013

perspective that holds a lot of potential and value. What is underrepresented in the literature, however, is a clear focus on the job and the fit between the abilities of people with disabilities and the demands of the job in question. A Google Scholar search of the term "disability-job fit" within publications in the English language resulted in 174 hits.[1] However, when focusing only on the idea of disability-job fit and excluding publications that speak about "disability-job fit stereotypes" (Colella et al., 1998; Colella & Varma, 1999), the number of hits dropped to 10, with only 5 of them being articles in peer-reviewed journals. With this chapter, we aim to bring the idea of disability-job fit into greater focus for disability researchers through the development of a Disability Contingency Framework.

In the next sections of this chapter, we will introduce the concept of person-job fit and the two areas of the disability literature that most closely relate to it: workplace accommodations and disability-job fit stereotypes. This will serve as a foundation for the introduction of our integrative Disability Contingency Framework. We will conclude the chapter with a discussion of the implications of our ideas for the disability literature and practice.

Person-job fit

A job involves a set of work activities that individuals are expected to perform in exchange for compensation. To perform these activities, individuals must have the necessary set of knowledge, skills, abilities, and other characteristics (KSAOs) (Sanchez & Levine, 2012). Person-job fit is a specific form of person-environment fit, which concerns the compatibility between individuals and their environments (van Vianen, 2018). Person-job fit refers to the fit between a person's abilities and the demands of the job (demands-abilities fit) or a person's desires and the attributes of a job (needs-supplies fit) (Edwards, 1991). In this chapter, we focus on demands-abilities fit as the foundation for our Disability Contingency Framework because we argue that predicting the performance outcomes of persons with disabilities requires a fundamental understanding of the nature of the job demands in question.

Fit theories posit that the fit between an individual and his or her environment is a better predictor of individual outcomes than the attributes of the individual or environment alone (Edwards, 2008; Schneider, 1978; van Vianen, 2018). In other words, it is not the degree to which an individual has a particular set of abilities but rather the congruence between these abilities and the requirements of the job that drives performance. The importance of person-job fit for individual workplace outcomes was supported by a 2005 meta-analysis on person-job fit, which found that fit was a positive predictor of job attitudes (e.g., job satisfaction and organizational commitment) and of overall individual

---

1 The search was conducted on 9/2/2021.

performance (Kristof-Brown et al., 2005). A recent review of the person-job fit literature found that, whereas needs-supplies fit is a better predictor of individual job attitudes, demands-abilities fit is a better predictor of performance outcomes (van Vianen, 2018). Person-job fit has been examined across a range of individual performance outcomes, including in-role performance (e.g., task performance) and extra-role performance (e.g., organizational citizenship behaviors). Our framework is centered on individual in-role job performance, specifically on performance of the essential functions of the job.

Given the empirical support for the general importance of person-job fit and its connection between abilities and demands in the workplace, it is surprising that these ideas have not received more attention in the disability literature. The area of the literature that is arguably most closely related to the idea of a fit between the abilities of a person with a disability and the requirements of a job is the workplace accommodations literature.

Workplace Accommodations

Workplace accommodations are defined as "modifications in the job, work environment, work process, or conditions of work that reduce physical and social barriers so that people with disabilities experience equal opportunity in a competitive work environment" (Colella & Bruyère, 2011, p. 478) and the importance of accommodations for people with disabilities has been shown in numerous studies (e.g., Baldridge & Veiga, 2006; Colella et al., 2004; Paetzold et al., 2008). The idea is that accommodations enable people with disabilities to perform certain tasks at a level that is comparable to people without disabilities or, as the Department of Labor puts it: "These modifications (*accommodations*) enable an individual with a disability to have an equal opportunity not only to get a job, but successfully perform their job to the same extent as people without disabilities" (U.S. Department of Labor, 2021). This is one reason why, for example, in the U.S., the Americans with Disabilities Act of 1990 (ADA) mandates that organizations provide reasonable workplace accommodation to employees and potential employees with disabilities who can perform essential job functions (U.S. Equal Employment Opportunity Commission, 2002).

Essential job functions refer to the "basic job duties that an employee must be able to perform, with or without reasonable accommodation" (U.S. Equal Employment Opportunity Commission, 1991). In effect, essential functions are the core demands of a job. In this sense, the idea of workplace accommodations for essential functions of a job represents the creation of a match or fit between the core demands of a job and the abilities of a person. One key point here is that not all workplaces or jobs can be accommodated for all types or severities of disabilities. Under the ADA, a person is not qualified for a position if they do not have the required KSAOs and the ability to perform the essential functions of that position, with or without accommodation (U.S. Equal Employment Opportunity Commission, 2002). As a result, there can be varying levels of pre- and still post-accommodation person-job fit (i.e., demands-abilities fit). We will revisit this idea later.

While we argue that there is an actual fit between disabilities and jobs, whether there is a fit between certain disabilities and jobs is also a perception. In fact, this perception, and the extent to which it is driven by stereotypes of people with disabilities, has previously received substantial attention in disability literature. We will introduce this idea of disability-job fit stereotypes next.

Disability-job fit Stereotypes

Stereotypes have been a central research topic within in the disability literature (Colella, 1996; Fichten & Amsel, 1986). They are generally defined as socially shared sets of beliefs about positive and negative traits and behaviors of members of a social group (Greenwald & Banaji, 1995). People with disabilities are ascribed certain positive traits, such as gentle-hearted and saintly (Colella, 1996), but mostly negative traits such as helpless and low performing (Bruyère et al., 2004; Fichten & Amsel, 1986; Ren et al., 2008; Unger, 2002). Competence stereotypes for people with disabilities are particularly negative in the work context (Rohmer & Louvet, 2018) and such negative stereotypes are a central barrier for their workplace integration (Kulkarni & Lengnick-Hall, 2014). They prevent decision-makers from hiring people with disabilities and can lead to negative performance evaluations.

The disability literature has also acknowledged that stereotypes vary among types of disabilities (Dwertmann, 2016; Vornholt et al., 2013) and, importantly for this chapter, it has highlighted the importance of fit between certain disabilities and jobs for the formation of fit stereotypes (Colella et al., 1998; Colella & Varma, 1999). Evaluators hold differing stereotypes based on the type of disability, which may or may not align well with the perceived nature of the job. These disability-job fit stereotypes concern "raters' stereotypes about the extent to which a specific disability might affect performance on a particular job" (Colella & Varma, 1999, pp. 79–80). This literature has been critical in understanding the role of gatekeepers in employment contexts, whose biased perceptions often function to limit the opportunities of people with disabilities. Colella and Varma (1999) also note that evaluators' stereotypes are often mistaken, which can additionally contribute to suboptimal organizational outcomes.

Rather than focus on raters' stereotypes, we argue that disabilities and health conditions can engender a range of functional differences that have varying implications for performance in a range of jobs. This is because an existing health condition is a precondition for having and being diagnosed with a disability (Dwertmann, 2016). In the following section, we integrate some of the outlined idea and develop our Disability Contingency Framework.

Disability Contingency Framework

The idea that we are advancing in this chapter with our Disability Contingency Framework shares commonalities with – but also differs from – the ideas of workplace accommodations and disability-job fit stereotypes in nontrivial ways; it is the idea of disability-job fit: the fit between the functional abilities of the person with a disability and the job demands or requirements. As such, our idea focuses on actual abilities, rather than stereotypes, just like workplace accommodations. Yet, contrary to the core idea of workplace accommodations, we focus on the abilities (not lack of abilities) of people with disabilities and emphasize that certain disabilities can lead to a better fit with certain jobs and, thus, yield potential performance advantages for people with disabilities over people without disabilities. This means that people with disabilities may not just be able to perform comparably to people without disabilities after receiving accommodations, but that they may perform better even before receiving an accommodation. Our idea also shares a key insight with disability-job fit stereotypes in that we emphasize the importance of the job in question and a fit between disabilities and jobs. Yet, our idea differs from disability-job fit stereotypes (Colella et al., 1998; Colella & Varma, 1999) because we consider actual performance and fit instead of perceived fit based on potentially wrong and negatively biased stereotypes. As such, our Disability Contingency Framework integrates the accommodations and disability-job fit stereotypes ideas (Dwertmann & van Knippenberg, 2021). For an overview of these similarities and differences, see Figure 12.1.

	Similarities	Differences
Workplace accommodations	Emphasis on actual job fit with abilities (not lack thereof) and functional limitations; acknowledgement that there are varying levels of pre-accommodation fit	Emphasis on abilities and recognition that people with disabilities may have performance advantages over people without disabilities, both pre- and post-accommodation
Disability-job fit stereotypes	Emphasis on the importance of the job in question and the fit between the job and the disability	Emphasis on actual abilities and fit instead of stereotypical abilities and fit

Figure 12.1: Overview of the similarities and differences in the core ideas of the Disability Contingency Framework and the workplace accommodations and disability-job fit stereotypes.

One area in which our idea overlaps with the core tenets of workplace accommodations is the understanding that not all workplaces or jobs can be accommodated for all types or severities of disabilities and that the effort needed to accommodate certain jobs for certain disabilities can vary greatly. This is one reason why the ADA emphasizes *reasonable* accommodations (U.S. Equal Employment Opportunity Commission, 2002). Accommodations are considered reasonable if they do not create undue hardship for employers or create a direct threat (ADA National Network, 2021). While the determination of whether an accommodation constitutes undue hardship is made on a case-by-case basis, undue hardship is defined as "significant difficulty or expense and focuses on the resources and circumstances of the particular employer in relationship to the cost or difficulty of providing a specific accommodation. Undue hardship refers not only to financial difficulty, but to reasonable accommodations that are unduly extensive, substantial, or disruptive, or those that would fundamentally alter the nature or operation of the business" (U.S. Equal Employment Opportunity Commission, 2002). Thus, both workplace accommodations and our Disability Contingency Framework acknowledge that there are varying levels of pre- and post-accommodation person-job fit (i.e., demands-abilities). This means that performance levels of people with disabilities before and after accommodations will vary (see right side of Figure 12.2).

In Figure 12.2, we depict the idea of varying levels of pre- and post-accommodation disability-job fit. The expected performance level of an average person without a disability is represented as the baseline average. With workplace accommodations, the

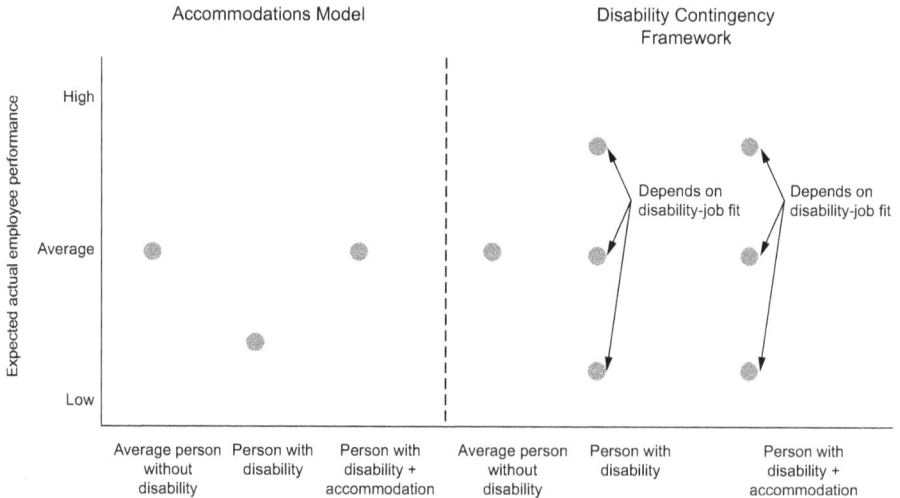

Figure 12.2: Overview of the pre- and post-accommodations performance for people with disabilities and people without disabilities in the workplace accommodations versus Disability Contingency Framework.

implicit idea is that the performance level of a person with a disability before receiving a reasonable accommodation is often low. Yet, after receiving an accommodation, the performance level of a person with a disability should be comparable to the average person without a disability. Thus, workplace accommodations imply a deficit of people with disabilities and assume that accommodations level the playing field and provide equal employment opportunities. In this view, accommodations allow people with disabilities to "successfully perform their job to the same extent as people without disabilities" (U.S. Department of Labor, 2021).

The Disability Contingency Framework that we suggest here diverges from this fundamental assumption and posits that the expected performance of a person with a disability will vary depending on the disability-job fit (see Figure 12.2). This means that a person with a disability can perform at similar or *higher* levels than an average person without a disability. This is because functional limitations in certain areas can come with functional advantages in other areas and, if these advantages align with the demands of the job, performance advantages can result.

Examples of Varying disability-job fit

Increasing the fit between a specific disability and a job through accommodations may be easier or harder depending on the pre-accommodation fit between the functional abilities and functional limitations that are associated with certain disabilities and the essential functions of the job. For example, without changing the nature and tasks of the job, it may be more challenging to create a good fit between a job that requires a lot of personal interaction (e.g., a job as a therapist) and disabilities that relate to difficulties in personal interactions (e.g., social anxiety, more severe forms of autism spectrum disorder). For some combinations of jobs and disabilities, creating a sufficient or good fit may be impossible.

We acknowledge that there is variation in the expression, severity, and resulting functional abilities and restrictions associated with disabilities that would influence the level of fit (Dwertmann, 2016). With this in mind, there are combinations of jobs and disabilities that may result in below average disability-job fit with respect to demands and abilities. For example, many physical disabilities can make it challenging to work on construction sites that are typically not accessible (e.g., availability of wheelchair ramps) or require heavy lifting. Even if workarounds could be identified, the employee may be slowed down, which would lower their job performance. Similarly, while many visual impairments can easily be accommodated through the usage of glasses, persons with more severe visual impairments that cannot be fully accommodated would fit less well in commercial driving jobs such as bus driver or semi-truck driver. Yet, even there, debate exists (Federal Motor Carrier Safety Administration, 2021).

There are also many combinations of jobs and disabilities that should result in average disability-job fit with respect to demands and abilities. Call centers, for example, can provide jobs that are suited for people with many disabilities such as visual impairments (Baumgärtner et al., 2014). In addition, most knowledge jobs that are performed at a desk in an office do not present major hurdles to persons with limb (leg) loss. While these are examples in which the disability-job fit does not pose particular challenges, they do also not suggest a better fit between the abilities of person with a disability and the job over a person without a disability.

Finally, there are several combinations of jobs and disabilities that may result in above average disability-job fit with respect to demands and abilities. The example that has probably garnered the most recent attention is persons on the autism spectrum (autism spectrum disorder) in IT jobs, more specifically as software testers (Austin & Pisano, 2017). The idea here is that an increased attention to detail and the ability to focus can result in a better demands-abilities fit for employees on the autism spectrum. Similarly, there is some evidence that people who are blind and trained in braille may have an enhanced tactile sense. This could give them an above average demands-abilities fit if they work as breast cancer screeners because they are able to detect smaller abnormalities in the breast (D'Arcy, 2015; Universität Erlangen, 2015). In more rural areas or regions with fewer financial resources, in which additional technological equipment to detect breast cancer is unavailable, this ability can provide important advantages. This form of detection might also be very helpful for initial screening to decide whether additional examinations are indicated.

In sum, there are combinations of jobs and disabilities that result in varying degrees of disability-job fit. While functional limitations that result from having a disability can lead to below average disability-job fit in terms of demands and abilities, there are also examples of disabilities that result in functional advantages for people with disabilities. Our Disability Contingency Framework logic suggests that when paired with jobs that demand these abilities, people with disabilities can benefit from above-average disability-job fit that can result in higher task performance.

Contributions and Future Research

In this chapter, we develop a Disability Contingency Framework that acknowledges differing levels of fit between the abilities of a person with disabilities with the demands of a job in question. With this, we aim to bring the idea of disability-job fit into the focus of disability researchers. Doing so gives rise to several important implications for disability researchers and practitioners.

First, one aspect that our Disability Contingency Framework shares with recent disability research (Baldridge et al., 2018) is a focus on the abilities of people with disabilities. Unfortunately, this idea is currently underrepresented in the literature, despite having important consequences for researchers and practitioners alike. From a research standpoint, a focus on abilities – rather than limitations – prompts new questions. For example, does a focus on abilities result in the recruitment and selection of people with disabilities into a wider range of jobs? Does above-average performance of people with disabilities in certain jobs give rise to a new set of positive stereotypes that generate expectations that all individuals with a particular disability will perform at similarly high levels? If yes, does that create problems for individuals who do not meet these expectations (e.g., is every person on the autism spectrum a mathematics savant, a stereotype that was also perpetuated by the movie *Rain Man*; Knights, 2018)? Also, rather than investigating which factors lead to the acceptance of workplace accommodations for people with disabilities (Colella, 2001; Florey & Harrison, 2000; García et al., 2005), researchers could investigate whether potential functional advantages of people with disabilities over people without disabilities are seen as unfair by coworkers if they are attributed to the disability (e.g., my colleague only performs better at finding errors in software code because they have autism which gives them an unfair advantage). For practitioners, the key question of workplace integration of people with disabilities would center not on which job can be accommodated for a person with a disability but, primarily, on which job is the right fit for a person with a disability to effectively leverage their abilities. This shift in thinking situates disability within an organization's regular strategic staffing processes and not within a separate set of diversity, equity, and inclusion initiatives. In this respect, it is important to find a balance and not to restrict choices for people with disabilities (e.g., not every individual on the autism spectrum wants to work in IT). Further, it underscores the need for systematic, up-to-date job analysis, as the foundation of our framework centers on an accurate understanding of the essential functions of the job in question. Job analysis, despite being fundamental to nearly all of an organization's talent management activities, is often neglected by practitioners and has received a concomitant decrease in scholarly attention over time (Sanchez & Levine, 2012). Yet, it is critical to understanding which KSAOs are most relevant for a particular job, a starting point for practitioners looking to select and deploy people – with and without disabilities – in the best-fitting jobs within the organization. In line with our arguments in this Disability Contingency Framework, a focus on abilities that would help individuals perform particularly well may offer important insights into the qualities of a successful candidate that may perform better than average.

Second, our Disability Contingency Framework adds more nuance to the idea of a business case for disability (Gould et al., 2020; Hernandez, 2018). The idea of a business case for the inclusion of individuals from historically underrepresented groups was initially put forth to refer to a range of dimensions of diversity; in the most basic sense, it refers to the idea that more diverse teams and organizations automatically perform better than less diverse teams and organizations and, therefore, that organizations should seek to diversify their workforces in an effort to boost performance Yet, the extant scientific evidence does not support this perspective

(Ely & Thomas, 2020; van Knippenberg et al., 2020) and it is unlikely that the results generated from studies on gender, race, and age would differ substantively for disability. This chapter outlines some of the problems with such a broad statement, as it does not acknowledge the boundary conditions, or contingencies, that are likely necessary for achieving positive performance outcomes. In the disability literature, for example, Dwertmann and Boehm (2016) found that a positive climate for inclusion allowed persons with disabilities to form higher-quality relationships with their employees and that this, in turn, had a positive effect on the employees' performance. In line with this general idea, as we depict in Figure 2, a focus on ensuring fit between the demands of a job and the abilities of a person with a disability does not imply that their abilities – pre- or post-accommodation – are above average; rather, it implies that, as is the case for people without disabilities, an individual's ability to perform in a particular job will vary. Thus, just as we join other researchers in a shift away from a focus on limitations and towards a more balanced view of abilities, we also urge caution in assuming that "different" abilities necessarily implies better abilities. People with disabilities can certainly be valuable additions to a range of organizations; however, hiring them without attention to good disability-job fit, and in the absence of support structures – such as onboarding, coaching, and training opportunities – is often unlikely to lead to positive performance outcomes on its own.

Third, in drawing on the person-job fit literature and advancing the idea that fit is critical to understanding the outcomes of individuals with disabilities in the workplace, we intend to provide a more nuanced and balanced perspective of the outcomes of disability. While we focus on the link between demands-abilities fit and in-role job performance in our Disability Contingency Framework, we urge researchers to explore the effects of person-job fit on a range of individual and organizational outcomes. For example, in one of the rare examples investigating person-job fit in the context of disabilities in the workplace, Hennekam et al. (2021) find evidence that needs-supplies fit may be particularly important for driving employees' individual job attitudes and mental health outcomes in a qualitative investigation of individuals with mental illness. Further, we emphasize the role of objective disability-job fit in our framework, which can differ from perceptual, or subjective, person-job fit, perhaps especially for individuals with disabilities. As Hennekam et al. (2021) note in their findings from two studies based on self-reports, internalized negative stereotypes may lead employees with disabilities to underemphasize the nature of their abilities and the extent to which they fit with their jobs. We join the authors in calling for managers and organizations to assist individuals with disabilities to identify their strengths and facilitate the match between their abilities and relevant jobs within the organization.

Finally, ensuring good disability-job fit is also crucial because it can help alleviate negative stereotypes that people without disabilities hold about people with disabilities. Stereotypes can change through contact with members of the stereotyped group (Hilton & von Hippel, 1996). Importantly, though, the quality of contact plays a role in facilitating positive change (Dovidio et al., 2017). Whereas positive contact that provides stereotype-disconfirming information can reduce negative stereotypes, negative contact can worsen stereotypes (Hayward et al., 2017). Dwertmann et al. (2021), for example, find in a mixed-methods, multi-study investigation that positive contact between cashiers with hearing disabilities and customers in a supermarket has beneficial effects for the competence and disability-job fit stereotypes that customers hold about people with hearing disabilities in cashier jobs and even more broadly. Customers with stereotype-disconfirming experiences seemed to reflect on their negative stereotypes toward people with disabilities when they had a positive interaction, meaning that the cashier with a disability performed well. In line with our idea, this finding highlights the need for companies to ensure a good fit between the abilities and skills of employees with disabilities and their jobs (in addition to providing sufficient support and resources such as onboarding and training). This is particularly important since perceptions of low competence and negative disability-job fit stereotypes, in turn, have been seen as a central obstacle to employment for people with disabilities (Lengnick-Hall et al., 2008; Louvet, 2007).

In sum, we introduce a Disability Contingency Framework that calls attention to the fit between the functional abilities of a person with a disability and the job demands or requirements of a specific job. We differentiate our framework from key concepts in the workplace accommodations and the disability-job fit stereotype literatures by focusing on the actual abilities (rather than stereotypes or limitations) of people with disabilities and highlighting that disabilities, in the right job context, have the potential to generate performance advantages. We call for more research that takes the idea of disability-job fit into account and urge both researchers and practitioners to pay close attention to the job in question when selecting and deploying people with disabilities within an organization.

References

ADA National Network. (2021). *Reasonable accommodations in the workplace.* https://adata.org/factsheet/reasonable-accommodations-workplace

Albrecht, G. L. (Ed.) (2006). *Encyclopedia of disability.* Sage Publications, Inc. https://doi.org/10.4135/9781412950510

Austin, R. D., & Pisano, G. P. (2017). Neurodiversity as a competitive advantage. *Harvard Business Review, 95*(3), 96–103.

Baldridge, D. C., Beatty, J. E., Boehm, S. A., Kulkarni, M., & Moore, M. E. (2018). Persons with (dis) abilities. In A. Colella & E. B. King (Eds.), *The Oxford handbook of workplace discrimination* (pp. 111–127). Oxford University Press.

Baldridge, D. C., & Veiga, J. F. (2006). The impact of anticipated social consequences on recurring disability accommodation requests. *Journal of Management, 32*(1), 158–179. https://doi.org/10.1177/0149206305277800

Baumgärtner, M. K., Böhm, S. A., & Dwertmann, D. J. G. (2014). Job performance of employees with disabilities: Interpersonal and intrapersonal resources matter. *Equality, Diversity and Inclusion: An International Journal, 33*(4), 347–360. https://doi.org/10.1108/EDI-05-2013-0032

Bruyère, S. M., Erickson, W. A., & VanLooy, S. (2004). Comparative study of workplace policy and practices contributing to disability nondiscrimination. *Rehabilitation Psychology, 49*(1), 28–38. https://doi.org/10.1037/0090-5550.49.1.28

Colella, A. (1996). Organizational socialization of new-comers with disabilities: A framework for future research. In G. R. Ferris (Ed.), *Research in personnel and human resources management* (Vol. 14, pp. 351–417). JAI Press.

Colella, A. (2001). Coworker distributive fairness judgments of the workplace accommodation of employees with disabilities. *Academy of Management Review, 26*(1), 100–116. https://doi.org/10.2307/259397

Colella, A., & Bruyère, S. M. (2011). Disability and employment: New directions for industrial and organizational psychology. In S. Zedeck (Ed.), *Handbook of industrial and organizational psychology* (Vol. 1, pp. 473–503). American Psychological Association Press. https://doi.org/10.1037/12169-015

Colella, A., DeNisi, A. S., & Varma, A. (1998). The impact of ratee's disability on performance judgments and choice as partner: The role of disability–job fit stereotypes and interdependence of rewards. *Journal of Applied Psychology, 83*(1), 102–111. https://doi.org/10.1037/0021-9010.83.1.102

Colella, A., Paetzold, R. L., & Belliveau, M. A. (2004). Factors affecting coworkers' procedural justice inferences of the workplace accommodations of employees with disabilities. *Personnel Psychology, 57*(1), 1–23. https://doi.org/10.1111/j.1744-6570.2004.tb02482.x

Colella, A., & Varma, A. (1999). Disability–job fit stereotypes and the evaluation of persons with disabilities at work. *Journal of Occupational Rehabilitation, 9*(2), 79–95. https://doi.org/10.1023/A: 1021362019948

D'Arcy, A. (2015). The blind breast cancer detectors. *BBC News Magazine*, 23. https://www.bbc.com/news/magazine-31552562

Dovidio, J. F., Love, A., Schellhaas, F. M. H., & Hewstone, M. (2017). Reducing intergroup bias through intergroup contact: Twenty years of progress and future directions. *Group Processes & Intergroup Relations, 20*(5), 606–620. https://doi.org/10.1177/1368430217712052

Dwertmann, D. J. G. (2016). Management research on disabilities: Examining methodological challenges and possible solutions. *The International Journal of Human Resource Management, 27*(14), 1477–1509. https://doi.org/10.1080/09585192.2015.1137614

Dwertmann, D. J. G., & Boehm, S. A. (2016). Status matters: The asymmetric effects of supervisor–subordinate disability incongruence and climate for inclusion. *Academy of Management Journal, 59*(1), 44–64. https://doi.org/10.5465/amj.2014.0093

Dwertmann, D. J. G., Goštautaitė, B., Bučiūnienė, I., & Kazlauskaitė, R. (2021). Receiving service from a person with a disability: Perceptions of corporate social responsibility and the opportunity for increased corporate reputation. *Academy of Management Journal.* https://doi.org/10.5465/amj.2020.0084

Dwertmann, D. J. G., & van Knippenberg, D. (2021). Capturing the state of the science to change the state of the science: A categorization approach to integrative reviews. *Journal of Organizational Behavior, 42*(2), 104–117. https://doi.org/10.1002/job.2474

Edwards, J. R. (1991). Person–job fit: A conceptual integration, literature review, and methodological critique. In C. L. Cooper & I. T Robertson (Eds.), *International review of industrial and organizational psychology* (Vol. 6, pp. 283–357). John Wiley & Sons.

Edwards, J. R. (2008). Person–environment fit in organizations: An assessment of theoretical progress. *The Academy of Management Annals, 2*(1), 167–230. https://doi.org/10.1080/19416520802211503

Ely, R. J., & Thomas, D. A. (2020). Getting serious about diversity: Enough already with the business case. *Harvard Business Review, 98*(6), 114–122.

Federal Motor Carrier Safety Administration. (2021). Qualifications of Drivers; Vision Standard. https://www.federalregister.gov/documents/2021/01/12/2020-28848/qualifications-of-drivers-vision-standard#footnote-8-p2349

Fichten, C. S., & Amsel, R. (1986). Trait attributions about college students with a physical disability: Circumplex analyses and methodological issues. *Journal of Applied Social Psychology, 16*(5), 410–427. https://doi.org/10.1111/j.1559-1816.1986.tb01149.x

Florey, A. T., & Harrison, D. A. (2000). Responses to informal accommodation requests from employees with disabilities: Multistudy evidence on willingness to comply. *Academy of Management Journal, 43*(2), 224–233. https://doi.org/10.2307/1556379

García, M. F., Paetzoldd, R. L., & Colella, A. (2005). The relationship between personality and peers' judgments of the appropriateness of accommodations for individuals with disabilities. *Journal of Applied Social Psychology, 35*(7), 1418–1439. https://doi.org/10.1111/j.1559-1816.2005.tb02177.x

Gould, R., Harris, S. P., Mullin, C., & Jones, R. (2020). Disability, diversity, and corporate social responsibility: Learning from recognized leaders in inclusion. *Journal of Vocational Rehabilitation, 52*(1), 29–42. https://doi.org/10.3233/jvr-191058

Greenwald, A. G., & Banaji, M. R. (1995). Implicit social cognition: Attitudes, self-esteem, and stereotypes. *Psychological Review, 102*(1), 4–27. https://doi.org/10.1037/0033-295X.102.1.4

Hayward, L. E., Tropp, L. R., Hornsey, M. J., & Barlow, F. K. (2017). Toward a comprehensive understanding of intergroup contact: Descriptions and mediators of positive and negative contact among majority and minority groups. *Personality and Social Psychology Bulletin, 43*(3), 347–364. https://doi.org/10.1177/0146167216685291

Hennekam, S., Follmer, K., & Beatty, J. E. (2021). The paradox of mental illness and employment: A person–job fit lens. *International Journal of Human Resource Management, 32*(15), 3244–3271. https://doi.org/10.1080/09585192.2020.1867618

Hernandez, C. A. (2018). Market reactions to the inclusion of people with disabilities. Evidence for the business case. *Academy of Management Proceedings* (p. 18277). Academy of Management. https://doi.org/10.5465/AMBPP.2018.18277abstract

Hilton, J. L., & von Hippel, W. (1996). Stereotypes. *Annual Review of Psychology, 47*, 237–271. https://doi.org/10.1146/annurev.psych.47.1.237

Knights, K. (2018, December 17). Rain Man made autistic people visible. But it also entrenched a myth. *The Guardian.* https://www.theguardian.com/commentisfree/2018/dec/17/rain-man-myth-autistic-people-dustin-hoffman-savant

Kristof-Brown, A. L., Zimmerman, R., & Johnson, E. C. (2005). Consequences of individuals' fit at work: A meta-analysis of person–job, person–organization, person–group, and person–supervisor fit. *Personnel Psychology, 58*, 281–342. https://doi.org/10.1111/j.1744-6570.2005.00672.x

Kulkarni, M., & Lengnick-Hall, M. L. (2014). Obstacles to success in the workplace for people with disabilities: A review and research agenda. *Human Resource Development Review, 13*(2), 158–180. https://doi.org/10.1177/1534484313485229

Lengnick-Hall, M. L., Gaunt, P. M., & Kulkarni, M. (2008). Overlooked and underutilized: People with disabilities are an untapped human resource. *Human Resource Management, 47*(2), 255–273. https://doi.org/10.1002/hrm.20211

Louvet, E. (2007). Social judgment toward job applicants with disabilities: Perception of personal qualities and competences. *Rehabilitation Psychology, 52*(3), 297–303. https://doi.org/10.1037/0090-5550.52.3.297

Paetzold, R. L., García, M. F., Colella, A., Ren, L. R., Triana, M. D. C., & Ziebro, M. (2008). Perceptions of people with disabilities: When is accommodation fair? *Basic and Applied Social Psychology, 30*(1), 27–35. https://doi.org/10.1080/01973530701665280

Ren, L. R., Paetzold, R. L., & Colella, A. (2008). A meta-analysis of experimental studies on the effects of disability on human resource judgments. *Human Resource Management Review, 18*(3), 191–203. https://doi.org/10.1016/j.hrmr.2008.07.001

Rohmer, O., & Louvet, E. (2018). Implicit stereotyping against people with disability. *Group Processes and Intergroup Relations, 21*(1), 127–140. https://doi.org/10.1177/1368430216638536

Sanchez, J. I., & Levine, E. L. (2012). The rise and fall of job analysis and the future of work analysis. *Annual Review of Psychology, 63*, 397–425. https://doi.org/10.1146/annurev-psych-120710-100401

Schneider, B. (1978). Person–situation selection: A review of some ability–situation research. *Personnel Psychology, 31*(2), 281–297. https://doi.org/10.1111/j.1744-6570.1978.tb00447.x

Schoeni, R. F., Freedman, V. A., & Martin, L. G. (2008). Why is late-life disability declining? *The Milbank Quarterly, 86*(1), 47–89. https://doi.org/10.1111/j.1468-0009.2007.00513.x

U.S. Department of Labor. (2021). *Accommodations.* https://www.dol.gov/agencies/odep/program-areas/employers/accommodations

U.S. Equal Employment Opportunity Commission. (1991). *The ADA: Your responsibilities as an employer.* https://www.eeoc.gov/laws/guidance/ada-your-responsibilities-employer#~:text=Essential functions are the basic,tasks are essential to performance

U.S. Equal Employment Opportunity Commission. (2002). *Enforcement guidance on reasonable accommodation and undue hardship under the ADA.* https://www.eeoc.gov/laws/guidance/enforcement-guidance-reasonable-accommodation-and-undue-hardship-under-ada

Unger, D. D. (2002). Employers' attitudes toward persons with disabilities in the workforce – Myths or realities? *Focus on Autism and Other Developmental Disabilities, 17*(1), 2–10. https://doi.org/10.1177/108835760201700101

Universität Erlangen. (2015). Kurzbericht zur Studie der Universität Erlangen – Optimierung der klinischen Brustuntersuchung durch den Einsatz von Medizinisch-Taktilen Untersucherinnen (MTU). [Short report for the study by the University of Erlangen–Optimization of clinical breast examinations by utilizing medical-tactile examiners] https://www.discovering-hands.de/fileadmin/content/images/publikationen/Prax_6_dh_Kurzbericht_Studie_Erlangen.pdf

van Knippenberg, D., Nishii, L. H., & Dwertmann, D. J. G. (2020). Synergy from diversity: Managing team diversity to enhance performance. *Behavioral Science and Policy, 6*(1), 75–92. https://doi.org/10.1353/bsp.2020.0007

van Vianen, A. E. M. (2018). Person–environment fit: A review of its basic tenets. *Annual Review of Organizational Psychology and Organizational Behavior, 5*, 75–101. https://doi.org/https://doi.org/10.1146/annurev-orgpsych-032117-104702

Vornholt, K., Uitdewilligen, S., & Nijhuis, F. J. N. (2013). Factors affecting the acceptance of people with disabilities at work: A literature review. *Journal of Occupational Rehabilitation, 23*(4), 463–475. https://doi.org/10.1007/s10926-013-9426-0

Emily H. Rosado-Solomon, Sasha Bolivar Trouwborst,
Lisa Schur, and Douglas Kruse

13 Temporal Challenges at the Intersection of Mental Illness and Work

Abstract: Time-based tensions at the intersection of mental illness and work are a pervasive yet understudied challenge for employees with mental illness. In this chapter, we review the temporal features of mental illness and explain how such features challenge the time-related assumptions and structure of organizations. In particular, we explicate the fact that many mental illnesses can create episodic changes to employees' productivity and unforeseeable variability in performance where such fluctuations are not normative in traditional workplaces. The chapter concludes with suggestions for ways that organizations can address these tensions and remove time-related barriers to successful employment for those with mental illness.

Keywords: mental illness, time, temporal focus, temporal fit

Golda Meir, a former Prime Minister of Israel, famously noted that a key strategy of her work was that she "must govern the clock, not be governed by it" (Fallaci, 1972). As this quote illustrates, many accomplished people recognize the importance of time in their success. Yet, working in modern organizations requires the fundamental compromise of giving up some control over one's time. Self-proclaimed night owls get out of bed early and prop themselves up with caffeine to attend morning meetings, and busy chefs are driven to keep moving by an unrelenting dinner rush when they might rather stop and rest (Fine, 1990). These temporal compromises are a fact of life for everyone who works in an organization, yet they are especially salient – and often challenging – for people living with mental illness. Mental illnesses are health conditions that impact one's emotion, thinking, behavior, or a combination of these (American Psychiatric Association [APA], 2013). Although symptoms differ across conditions, temporal fluctuations are a hallmark of many forms of mental illness. Indeed, while most paid employment requires employees to follow a predictable temporal structure, such as 9 a.m. to 5 p.m., most mental illness defies planning and structure. Persons with anxiety or depression may have no symptoms for days, weeks, or months, then unpredictably develop severe symptoms that change their ability to perform expected work tasks (APA, 2013). Understandably, this can cause

Emily H. Rosado-Solomon, Babson College, MA
Sasha Bolivar Trouwborst, Independent researcher
Lisa Schur, and Douglas Kruse, Rutgers University, NJ

https://doi.org/10.1515/9783110743647-014

frustration that has tangible consequences for both individuals with mental illness and for the organizations that employ them (Follmer & Jones, 2018).

The prevalence of this challenge cannot be overstated. In the United States one in five adults are affected by mental illness, with depression and anxiety being the most common conditions (National Alliance on Mental Illness [NAMI], 2022), while in the United Kingdom it is estimated that one in six employees has some form of mental illness (Taylor & Hampson, 2017). In other words, any organization with more than a handful of employees is likely to employ someone with a mental illness, although employees may conceal their diagnoses for a variety of reasons (Greenwood et al., 2019). Beyond the human cost, there is a business case for organizations properly addressing mental illness. Research suggests that over 200 million workdays are lost due to mental health conditions, which costs an estimated $16.8 billion in employee productivity each year through absenteeism, presenteeism (being physically present but not psychologically engaged), and other barriers to optimal contribution (Evans-Lacko & Knapp, 2016; Follmer & Jones, 2021). There may, however, be performance-related benefits to mental illness, as employees with certain conditions have unique skills that can lead to better performance in certain circumstances compared to neurotypical colleagues (Hennekam et al., 2021). Nevertheless, mental illness is still heavily stigmatized, and discussion of mental illness is widely seen as a taboo at work (Follmer & Jones, 2021; Rüsch et al., 2005). This has led up to 60% of employees to hide their mental illness from managers (Greenwood et al., 2019), which can further complicate an organization's ability to support employees who try to balance work and mental illness.

In this chapter, we explore the often overlooked time-based tensions at the intersection of mental illness and work. We specifically frame this tension through the lens of the social model of disability (Oliver, 1983), which suggests the disadvantages associated with a given condition are not inherent in the condition itself but result from societal factors that disadvantage people with disabilities (Oliver, 2013). For instance, the social model of disability suggests that people with mobility limitations are often hindered by the lack of ramps that would enable them to move efficiently, not by the inherent nature of their physical differences. The implication for this issue is that challenges for employees with mental illness can be improved by re-thinking the way business is conducted, not sidelining employees because they accomplish their work differently from neurotypical peers.

To be clear, we acknowledge that organizations must obviously influence the timing of employees' work to achieve their broader goals (Shipp & Jansen, 2021). Congruent with this fact of organizational life, this chapter illuminates ways that organizations might consider alternatives to taken-for-granted processes when realizing their unintended impact on those with mental illness. Returning to the example of persons with limited mobility, just as organizations have recognized that ramps and elevators can effectively move employees from a lower floor to a higher floor while including those with mobility challenges, we propose that recalibrating the temporal structures of work might increase accessibility for employees with mental illness while still promoting effective work in organizations. Furthermore, just as elevators can benefit people without physical disabilities, increased temporal flexibility could also benefit employees without mental illness.

The remainder of this chapter reviews the importance of time in organizational studies and describes some of time's most relevant features within organizations. We then review the ways that mental illness influences employees' experience of time and causes fluctuations in behaviors, and explore how this fundamental incompatibility between the temporal constraints of work and mental illness creates a barrier for those with mental illness. The chapter concludes with suggestions for ways organizations might mitigate barriers for employees with mental illness. By exploring this under-articulated tension at the intersection of mental illness and work, we hope to begin a conversation that spurs action to support employees with this pervasive challenge.

Time and Work

The development of clocks was a key condition for the industrial revolution, enabling employers to coordinate and control the pace of work (Landes, 1984). The timing of employees' work is an important but often overlooked element of professional success; indeed, time is an essential concept for understanding how individuals, teams, and organizations evolve, grow, learn, and change (Shipp & Jansen, 2021). Common time-related features in organizations include elements such as deadlines, regular meetings, and routines (Leroy et al., 2015). When employees synchronize their efforts in a way that supports a common time structure (e.g., adhering to the same set of deadlines, regularly attending required meetings), this can enable an organization's success by coordinating employees' efforts (Shipp & Richardson, 2019). Therefore, it is often critical for organizations to temporally coordinate their employees to achieve common goals (Kouchaki et al., 2012). This is accomplished in many ways, including socializing newcomers to understand temporal norms (e.g., expectations around adherence to deadlines; Leroy et al., 2015), hiring project managers to explicitly coordinate work sequences (Turner & Müller, 2005) and using targeted communications and integrated calendar systems to schedule meetings and deadlines (Landy et al., 1991). Within an organization, an employee's work success is driven, in part, by the degree to which their time-related attributes fit the organization's temporal needs. For example, in an environment where time urgency is needed, individuals who adjust quickly to change will be more successful than those who take longer to pivot their focus (Leroy et al., 2015).

Despite its importance, temporal synchronization is complicated and often difficult to achieve. Employees have a range of temporal needs (e.g., requiring more or less time to complete a given task; Gevers et al., 2006), preferences (e.g., not being a "morning person"; Shipp & Richardson, 2019), and constraints (e.g., scheduling limitations due to childcare responsibilities; Michel et al., 2011) and employers should account for these varied factors when delegating tasks and responsibilities (Leroy et al., 2015). These differences are further complicated by the fact that time is partially subjective (Shipp & Jansen, 2021), such that individuals experience movement through time differently from one another. Temporal focus, defined as "the degree individuals think about past, present, and/or future" (Shipp & Aeon, 2019, p. 1), is one concept that exemplifies how individuals differentially experience time in their personal and professional lives (Shipp & Aeon, 2019). In other words, some individuals regularly focus more on the past, whereas others direct their energies toward consideration of the future.

These individual differences make it difficult to solely rely on objective time structures such as deadlines, especially when working in a team or doing other coordinated work (Shipp & Richardson, 2019). For example, some employees work on their tasks immediately while others prefer to procrastinate. Coordinating these disparate styles requires managers to acknowledge the type of task, time of execution, and know how and when to utilize the strategies that work for each employee (Leroy et al., 2015). When teams are large, work is highly interdependent, and there is significant diversity in employees' temporal focus, even the best organizations may struggle to achieve temporal coordination. Organizations that are able to achieve temporal coordination have a distinct advantage over competitors, and employees who are able to entrain themselves to their colleagues' pace of work are well positioned to succeed in their jobs (Shipp & Richardson, 2019).

Temporal Features of Mental Illness

There are a variety of well-established temporal implications of mental illness, and a full accounting of them is beyond the scope of this chapter. However, common temporal fluctuations include those of mood disorders, or psychological disorders characterized by the elevation or lowering of a person's mood, such as depression or bipolar disorder (Anderson et al., 2012). To varied extents, these conditions involve temporal fluctuations by definition, as people's moods change at different times and for varied durations. An especially relevant condition, bipolar disorder (a type of mood disorder) is defined by alternating periods of depressive and manic symptoms, the latter of which are characterized by increased energy and arousal (McIntyre et al., 2015). These fluctuations can occur at different and often unpredictable intervals, and episodes of depression or mania can last as long as a few weeks or change as quickly as multiple times per day (McIntyre et al., 2015). Such conditions affect an employee's ability to perform their work consistently, possibly causing lower than normal productivity during periods of depression and higher than normal productivity during periods of mania (Simon et al., 2008). While bipolar disorder is characterized by dramatic mood swings, many other conditions – ranging from schizophrenia to common conditions such as attention deficit hyperactivity disorder (ADHD) – can cause mood swings as one of several symptoms (Carlson, 1998). Such changes in affect may, in turn, subsequently influence their behavior (Carlson, 1998). For instance, persons who are experiencing extreme low mood, as is characteristic of mental illness with depressive symptoms, may not be able to think as clearly or perform their work as quickly during periods of intense symptoms (Follmer & Jones, 2018).

Other mental illness symptoms are also characterized by their inconsistency. For example, anxiety disorders, or a group of related conditions involving "persistent, excessive fear or worry in situations that are not threatening" (APA, 2013), may involve general fluctuations in levels of arousal or reactions to a given stimuli (e.g., a phobia is triggered by the presence of certain stimuli; APA, 2013). As with mood disorders, symptoms of anxiety disorders often involve aversive feelings that subsequently impact behaviors. Additionally, anxiety disorders are often attended by aversive physical sensations, such as nausea, headaches, and difficulty breathing that may make it difficult for employees to work effectively during periods of intense symptoms (Kehoe, 2017). As these examples suggest, mental illness can strongly influence people's capacity to work.

Beyond these fluctuations, there are other symptoms of mental illness that can impact the way employees experience time. Some symptoms can directly impact how employees with mental illness shift their temporal focus; for instance, rumination, a repetitive self-focused state involving thoughts about one's negative feelings and past events (Morrow & Nolen-Hoeksema, 1990), inherently involves a temporal focus on the past and present, and thereby precludes a future-oriented focus. Rumination can be a symptom of common mental illnesses, including major depressive disorder, anxiety disorders, obsessive compulsive disorder, and post-traumatic stress disorder (PTSD) (APA, 2013; Michael et al., 2007; Yook et al., 2010). Related symptoms include intolerance of uncertainty, or "a cognitive bias that affects how a person perceives, interprets, and responds to uncertain situations" (Yook et al., 2010, p. 623), which is a future-oriented cognitive style that is frequently symptomatic of major depressive disorder and anxiety disorders. These are merely two examples of symptoms that directly influence the temporal focus of employees above and beyond their inherent personality traits, and may cause difficulty for temporal coordination within the workplace (Leroy et al., 2015).

Additionally, the realities of having a mental illness may impact employees' timing at work beyond the effects of the condition itself. For instance, people with mental illness often benefit from therapy or support groups, but these resources are frequently scheduled at times that conflict with traditional work hours (Dilgul et al., 2018) Many people with mental illness also benefit from medication, yet it is a non-trivial matter to find the correct medication (Schön et al., 2009). This challenge is compounded by notoriously long periods between initial onset of symptoms and receiving a correct mental illness diagnosis; the current average in the United States is eleven years between the onset of mental illness symptoms and receiving an accurate diagnosis (Wang et al., 2004). Moreover, people with mental illness may try several medications before finding the best one to ameliorate their symptoms (Knopf, 2014). Meanwhile, the process of changing prescriptions or dosages may affect an individual's ability to work for several weeks until the right combination of medications is identified (Schultz & Joish, 2009). During this time, individuals with mental illness may be less productive as they experience both ongoing symptoms and side effects of new medication, and may either have diminished performance at work or need to take a leave from their jobs altogether.

Explicating the Temporal Incompatibility of Modern Work and Mental Illness

Linear versus episodic productivity. Some jobs require linear productivity, which may be hard for people with mental illness to achieve. Implicitly or explicitly, many managers and organizational scholars expect that employees will be relatively consistent in their productivity regardless of their personal circumstances (Gilboa et al., 2008). Although researchers acknowledge intra-individual differences in performance at work, the assumption of most managers is that employees will work at a consistent pace (Dalal et al., 2014). In other words, they expect linear productivity, or the idea that employees' output will remain constant until they learn new efficiencies and develop new skills through training (Black & Lynch, 1996).

Contrastingly, as we have explained above, mental illness is not linear. While many physical disabilities have consistent symptoms – for instance, someone without the ability to hear will typically have consistent symptoms across time – symptoms of mental illness can be expected to change drastically. In particular, common mental illnesses (e.g., mood and anxiety disorders) are episodic (APA, 2013). Tensions arise for persons with mental illness when fluctuations of their symptoms are juxtaposed with expectations of linear productivity at work. When these influences overlap, employees with mental illness may experience tension in ways that require modifying their work to accommodate both the temporal demands of the organization and the constraints of their fluctuating symptoms (Zuckerman, 1993). While some employees request a formal accommodation such as intermittent leave to overcome this tension, such accommodations are not always requested or granted for a variety of reasons (Schur et al., 2014). Because research on mental illness at work remains underdeveloped (Follmer & Jones, 2018), it is not yet known exactly how employees without accommodations manage the tension of competing temporal expectations during periods of elevated symptoms.

Foreseeable versus unforeseeable changes. The other way mental illness complicates organizations' temporal norms is in the degree of predictability. While there are many phenomena that impact the timing of work, these are often predictable fluctuations that can be planned for and accommodated accordingly. For instance, work itself may cause fluctuations, either in the short term (e.g., busy weekends at a retail establishment) or over the course of the year (e.g., increased work for retail employees during the holiday season). Yet these tend to be cyclical and predictable, and therefore employees can plan accordingly for changes in their work. Organizations also have the opportunity to plan and hire more workers as necessary to cover gaps in employees' ability to produce the requisite output. Employees may also drive fluctuations in productivity, such as drops in productivity surrounding the birth of a child (Krapf et al., 2017) or training that gives them new skills (Black & Lynch, 1996). While these fluctuations may all complicate the performance of work, their foreseeable nature makes them generally manageable.

In contrast, a defining feature of mental illness-driven temporal fluctuations is that they are often unpredictable. This is especially true for certain conditions; for example, the changes associated with bipolar disorder are often impossible to recognize until the changes in affect and behavior are already underway (Dunner, 2003). Moreover, employees with mental illnesses may have varied ability to foresee the onset of their symptoms, thereby rendering the changes effectively unpredictable (Dunner, 2003). This may be especially true for employees who do not receive robust psychological care, which would help them identify potential triggers of their symptoms. In contrast, persons who have received good psychiatric care for a long time might recognize their triggers and may be able to predict fluctuations in their affect and behavior (Hirschfeld et al., 1997), thereby potentially working to avoid those triggers.

Potential Solutions

Often organizations become aware of mental illnesses only when they investigate why an employee is performing poorly (Dewa et al., 2011). This occurs because many employees do not feel comfortable disclosing a mental health problem due to potential stigma, and thus work to hide their conditions while making idiosyncratic attempts to overcome tensions between their symptoms and work (Hastuti & Timming, 2021). Therefore, since almost all organizations have (or will have) employees with mental illness, it is critical that companies develop comprehensive strategies to help employees with mental illness balance the temporally-relevant elements of their experience with the needs of the organization. The suggestions below involve both behavioral change on the part of individual supervisors and managers – who are often interpreted by employees as representative of the organization's caring toward their workers (Sluss & Ashforth, 2008) – and organizational policy and practice change, such as training and job restructuring. Below we suggest several solutions in the areas of flexibility, culture change, job design, and benefits.

Flexibility

Short-term flexibility. Among the most important workplace responses is providing a flexible schedule for all employees, which enables temporal agility for employees with mental illness regardless of whether they choose to disclose their condition or seek a formal accommodation (Zuckerman, 1993). Research has found that employees who have a mental illness can benefit from a flexible schedule as it increases productivity, commitment to the organization, and retention (Schermuly & Meyer, 2016). This suggests that enhanced flexibility is both an investment in employees' mental well-being and a prudent business decision. Flexible work schedules can include allowing employees to work from home part- or full-time, allowing different work hours rather than 9 to 5, and allowing breaks when needed (McGuire & Liro, 1986). Employees with disabilities were more likely to work from home before the pandemic, and the pandemic plus ongoing technological developments are likely to increase this option (Schur et al., 2020).

While it is important for all employees to have breaks during a work day (Sianoja et al., 2016), people with mental illness may particularly benefit from more frequent breaks. Because it is common for individuals with mental illness to struggle with falling asleep (Dopke et al., 2004), they may experience fatigue differently throughout the day and therefore require different breaks than their neurotypical colleagues. Additionally, some mental illnesses are associated with varied cognitive capacity; for instance, some persons with mental illness may have periodic difficulty concentrating on certain tasks or have trouble making decisions and remembering important details (Ipsos, 2014). Given these different experiences, it is not prudent for managers to micromanage the pacing of employees' work because strict temporal expectations are unlikely to align with the temporal fluctuations associated with common mental illnesses.

While research is scarce on coping strategies of employees with mental illness, it is likely that many engage in job crafting to manage temporal tensions. Job crafting refers to "the physical and cognitive changes individuals make in the task or relation boundaries of their work" (Wrzesniewski & Dutton, 2001, p. 26). For example, individuals can align their roles with individual strengths, preferences, and resources to improve job satisfaction by eliminating or altering undesirable aspects of their job (Wrzesniewski & Dutton, 2001). Job crafting is associated with both job performance and self-efficacy (Tims et al., 2014; Tims & Bakker, 2010) as employees change their work in ways that best leverage unique talents and abilities. Importantly, organizations and managers should be explicit about the limits of job flexibility in a given role, as individual job crafting can lead to detrimental outcomes if the job crafter does not coordinate with management and colleagues to ensure all essential tasks are completed (Tims et al., 2014, 2015).

Long-term flexibility. In the long term, major depressive episodes and other conditions may require taking a medical leave from work (Blackmore et al., 2007). Among individuals who are off work for six months or more, only 50% return to work (Blank et al., 2008). While many influences on employees' return to work are not within an organization's control, such as family support and cognitive functioning (Tsang et al., 2000), there is much that supervisors and organizations can do to influence whether an employee is able to return to work. Indeed, research suggests that supervisors have a substantial impact on return to work by offering accommodations as well as frequent communication with the employee. Specifically, Nieuwenhuijsen and colleagues (2004) found that employees were more likely to return to work when supervisors contacted the employee at least once every two weeks during their leave of absence. In addition to showing support, such communication should discuss the potential for flexibility in the employee's schedule (e.g., a gradual re-entry period) and job content (e.g., offering less stressful tasks) to facilitate their return to work (Nieuwenhuijsen et al., 2004).

Culture Change

In a recent review of mental illness disclosure and work, Hastuti and Timming (2021) identified the critical importance of having a workplace culture that supports mental health. Such a culture can help employees feel more comfortable in disclosing mental illness and asking for accommodations, and improve relations with co-workers. An important step in establishing such a culture is the provision of guidelines and resources to support individuals with mental illness (Follmer & Jones, 2018). This education helps destigmatize mental illness and shows that the employer cares about employees with these conditions, which is an important element of creating organizational culture change (Denison & Spreitzer, 1991). Educating employees about mental illnesses enables colleagues, human resources (HR) personnel, and supervisors to discuss and understand the implications of temporally-related symptoms associated with a mental illness. This may allow the earlier detection of symptoms and make it easier to provide needed accommodations (Szeto & Dobson, 2010). It may also help promote mental health literacy among the entire workforce, which will enable employees to be more empathetic toward their colleagues with mental illness (Moll et al., 2017). Finally, managers can act as role models, such as by encouraging use of available benefits and openly discussing the ways they themselves require temporal changes such as taking time for therapy or "mental health days" (Dimoff & Kelloway, 2019). This demonstrates to subordinates the importance of providing support and flexibility to promote inclusion of colleagues with mental illness, and creates a workplace in which individuals with mental illness can feel comfortable requesting accommodations to manage time-based challenges.

Job Design

There are ways that employers should consider designing jobs and work policies to better enable those with mental illness to manage the temporal expectations of work. One such change would be basing performance evaluations on results instead of a requirement to expend effort during a set time period, thereby enabling employees to choose when and how they work best. The benefits of autonomy in work are well established (cf. Hackman & Oldham, 1974), and time scholars have recognized that scheduling around energy, instead of a temporally fixed schedule, has benefits for all employees because it enables them to work when they are naturally most productive (Shipp, 2021). This is even more important for those with mental illness who may have more extreme fluctuations in productivity, or who may benefit from rearranging their work to accommodate treatments such as mid-day therapy appointments or support groups.

Research has also found that certain job attributes are well-suited to facilitate success for employees with mental illness. For example, Michie and Williams (2003) found that jobs with more modest workloads and clearer tasks were associated with fewer symptoms of mental ill-health. Managers might rearrange the workload of employees with mental illness by redistributing tasks to prevent employees from taking on more tasks than they can complete. In the case of time-based challenges of mental illness, this would enable employees to complete their work while having time to manage temporal fluctuations and unexpected conflicts that might arise between work and self-care. Additionally, managers might offer employees clearer and more detailed job descriptions or provide more explicit information about expectations for performance and available support. Such information can be useful to help employees understand what tasks must be completed in order to fulfill the organization's requirements (Zuckerman, 1993).

Benefits

Finally, organizations can offer benefits to assist employees with mental illness. Employee Assistance Programs (EAPs), or programs that offer a range of benefits to employees through a third-party provider, can help by providing access to therapy and referrals to other professionals who might be of assistance (e.g., substance abuse programs; Richmond et al., 2016). Additionally, organizations should consider offering high-quality medical insurance that provides a wide choice of convenient mental health care. Finally, a new benefit that offers promise for addressing the temporal tensions between mental illness and work is the advent of third-party mental health support apps. These applications offer access to teletherapy through video chat or text capabilities with licensed counselors, and some apps also offer complimentary access to self-help techniques, such as guided meditation and mindfulness exercises (Mascaro et al., 2020). These apps may be especially helpful in solving employees' time-based challenges, as they could enable employees to access support during breaks without having to take additional time to drive to the therapist's office and disrupt a regularly scheduled work day. Such apps might also help employees address symptoms that could otherwise cause fluctuations in performance, such as using the mindfulness component of an app to mitigate an anxiety attack. Importantly, these apps may not only benefit employees with diagnosed mental illness, but could also offer support to those who have sub-clinical levels of poor mental health, such as stress or burnout that might benefit from therapeutic intervention.

Conclusion

This chapter explores the pervasive but often invisible time-based tensions at the intersection of mental illness and work. We hope that by articulating these barriers, researchers and practitioners alike will begin to re-think the temporal expectations that are inherent in many organizational structures. Such advances would not only benefit employees with mental illness, but can also benefit those with other disabilities such as physical conditions that create fatigue or unpredictable medical problems, as well as employees in general whose work and lives can improve with greater flexibility. In addition, these advances can benefit companies and the economy, given the extraordinary costs associated with poorly attending to employees' mental health. Taken together, increased attention to time is a critical addition to the study of disability and work, and progress in this field can help promote inclusion for people with mental illness.

References

American Psychiatric Association. (2013). *Diagnostic and statistical manual of mental disorders* (5th ed.). https://doi.org/10.1176/appi.books.9780890425596
Anderson, I. M., Haddad, P. M., & Scott, J. (2012). Bipolar disorder. *BMJ, 345*, e8508. https://doi.org/10.1136/bmj.e8508
Black, S. E., & Lynch, L. M. (1996). Human-capital investments and productivity. *American Economic Review, 86*(2), 263–267.
Blackmore, E. R., Stansfeld, S. A., Weller, I., Munce, S., Zagorski, B. M., & Stewart, D. E. (2007). Major depressive episodes and work stress: Results from a national population survey. *American Journal of Public Health, 97*(11), 2088–2093. https://doi.org/10.2105/AJPH.2006.104406
Blank, L., Peters, J., Pickvance, S., Wilford, J., & Macdonald, E. (2008). A systematic review of the factors which predict return to work for people suffering episodes of poor mental health. *Journal of Occupational Rehabilitation, 18*(1), 27–34. https://doi.org/10.1007/s10926-008-9121-8
Carlson, G. A. (1998). Mania and ADHD: Comorbidity or confusion. *Journal of Affective Disorders, 51*(2), 177–187. https://doi.org/1016/S0165-0327(98)00179-7
Dalal, R. S., Bhave, D. P., & Fiset, J. (2014). Within-person variability in job performance: A theoretical review and research agenda. *Journal of Management, 40*(5), 1396–1436. https://doi.org/10.1177/0149206314532691
Denison, D. R., & Spreitzer, G. M. (1991). Organizational culture and organizational development: A competing values approach. *Research in Organizational Change and Development, 5*(1), 1–21.
Dewa, C. S., Thompson, A. H., & Jacobs, P. (2011). The association of treatment of depressive episodes and work productivity. *Canadian Journal of Psychiatry, 56*(12), 743–750. https://doi.org/10.1177/070674371105601206
Dilgul, M., McNamee, P., Orfanos, S., Carr, C. E., & Priebe, S. (2018). Why do psychiatric patients attend or not attend treatment groups in the community: A qualitative study. *PLoS ONE, 13*(12): e0208448. https://doi.org/10.1371/journal.pone.0208448
Dimoff, J. K., & Kelloway, E. K. (2019). With a little help from my boss: The impact of workplace mental health training on leader behaviors and employee resource utilization. *Journal of Occupational Health Psychology, 24*(1), 4–19. https://doi.org/10.1037/ocp0000126
Dopke, C. A., Lehner, R. K., & Wells, A. M. (2004). Cognitive–behavioral group therapy for insomnia in individuals with serious mental illnesses: A preliminary evaluation. *Psychiatric Rehabilitation Journal, 27*(3), 235–242. https://doi.org/10.2975/27.2004.235.242
Dunner, D. L. (2003). Clinical consequences of under-recognized bipolar spectrum disorder. *Bipolar Disorders, 5*(6), 456–463. https://doi.org/10.1046/j.1399-5618.2003.00073.x
Evans-Lacko, S., & Knapp, M. (2016). Global patterns of workplace productivity for people with depression: Absenteeism and presenteeism costs across eight diverse countries. *Social Psychiatry and Psychiatric Epidemiology, 51*(11), 1525–1537. https://doi.org/10.1007/s00127-016-1278-4
Fine, G. A. (1990). Organizational time: Temporal demands and the experience of work in restaurant kitchens. *Social Forces, 69*(1), 95–114.
Follmer, K. B., & Jones, K. S. (2018). Mental illness in the workplace: An interdisciplinary review and organizational research agenda. *Journal of Management, 44*(1), 325–351. https://doi.org/10.1177/0149206317741194
Follmer, K. B., & Jones, K. S. (2021). Navigating depression at work: Identity management strategies along the disclosure continuum. *Group & Organization Management*, https://doi.org/10.5960/11211002010

Gevers, J. M. P., Rutte, C. G., & Van Eerde, W. (2006). Meeting deadlines in work groups: Implicit and explicit mechanisms. *Applied Psychology: An International Review*, *55*(1), 52–72. https://doi.org/10.1111/j.1464-0597.2006.00228.x

Gilboa, S., Shirom, A., Fried, Y., & Cooper, C. (2008). A meta-analysis of work demand stressors and job performance: Examining main and moderating effects. *Personnel Psychology*, *61*(2), 227–271. https://doi.org/10.1111/j.1744-6570.2008.00113.x

Greenwood, K., Bapat, V., & Maughan, M. (2019, October 7). People want their employers to talk about mental health. *Harvard Business Review*.

Hackman, J. R., & Oldham, G. R. (1974). *The job diagnostic survey: An instrument for the diagnosis of jobs and the evaluation of job redesign projects*. Yale University Department of Administrative Sciences.

Hastuti, R., & Timming, A. R. (2021). An inter-disciplinary review of the literature on mental illness disclosure in the workplace: Implications for human resource management. *International Journal of Human Resource Management*, *32*(15), 3302–3338. https://doi.org/10.1080/09585192.2021.1875494

Hennekam, S., Follmer, K., & Beatty, J. (2021). The paradox of mental illness and employment: A person–job fit lens. *International Journal of Human Resource Management*, *32*(15), 3244–3271. https://doi.org/10.1080/09585192.2020.1867618

Hirschfeld, R. M. A., Keller, M. B., Panico, S., Arons, B. S., Barlow, D., Davidoff, F., Endicott, J., Froom, J., Goldstein, M., Gorman, J. M., Guthrie, D., Marek, R., Maurer, T. A., Meyer, R., Phillips, K., Ross, J., Schwenk, T. L., Sharfstein, S. S., Thase, M. E., & Wyatt, R. J. (1997). The national depressive and manic-depressive association consensus statement on the undertreatment of depression. *JAMA*, *277*(4), 333–340. https://doi.org/10.1001/jama.1997.03540280071036

Fallaci, O. (1972, November). I must govern the clock, not be governed by it. Interview with Golda Meir, *Ms. Magazine*, Vol. 1.

Ipsos. (2014, July). *Executive summary, IDEA Survey, Impact of depression at work: U.S. report*.

Kehoe, W. A. (2017). Generalized anxiety disorder. In B. J. Dong & D. P. Elliott (Eds.), *ACSAP 2017 Book 2 Neurologic/psychiatric care* (pp. 2–27). ACCP.

Knopf, A. (2014). Implement precision medicine right now: The trial-and-error method of selecting psychiatric medications is gradually being replaced by the precision of personalized medicine. *Behavioral Healthcare*, *34*(4), 26–29.

Kouchaki, M., Okhuysen, G. A., Waller, M. J., & Tajeddin, G. (2012). The treatment of the relationship between groups and their environments: A review and critical examination of common assumptions in research. *Group & Organization Management*, *37*(2), 171–203. https://doi.org/10.1177/1059601112443850

Krapf, M., Ursprung, H. W., & Zimmermann, C. (2017). Parenthood and productivity of highly skilled labor: Evidence from the groves of academe. *Journal of Economic Behavior & Organization*, *140*, 147–175. https://doi.org/10.1016/j.jebo.2017.05.010

Landes, D. S. (1984). *Revolution in time: Clocks and the making of the modern world*. Harvard University Press.

Landy, F. J., Rastegary, H., Thayer, J., & Colvin, C. (1991). Time urgency: The construct and its measurement. *Journal of Applied Psychology*, *76*(5), 644–657. https://doi.org/10.1037/0021-9010.76.5.644

Leroy, S., Shipp, A. J., Blount, S., & Licht, J. (2015). Synchrony preference: Why some people go with the flow and some don't. *Personnel Psychology*, *68*(4), 759–809. https://doi.org/10.1111/peps.12093

Mascaro, J. S., Wehrmeyer, K., Mahathre, V., & Darcher, A. (2020). A longitudinal, randomized and controlled study of app-delivered mindfulness in the workplace. *Journal of Wellness*, *2*(1), 4–9. https://doi.org/10.18297/jwellness/vol2/iss1/4

McGuire, J. B., & Liro, J. R. (1986). Flexible work schedules, work attitudes, and perceptions of productivity. *Public Personnel Management*, *15*(1), 65–73. https://doi.org/10.1177/009102608601500106

McIntyre, R. S., Soczynska, J. K., Cha, D. S., Woldeyohannes, H. O., Dale, R. S., Alsuwaidan, M. T., Gallaugher, L. A., Mansur, R. B., Muzina, D. J., Carvalho, A., & Kennedy, S. H. (2015). The prevalence and illness characteristics of DSM-5-defined "mixed feature specifier" in adults with major depressive disorder and bipolar disorder: Results from the International Mood Disorders Collaborative Project. *Journal of Affective Disorders*, *172*, 259–264. https://doi.org/10.1016/j.jad.2014.09.026

Michael, T., Halligan, S. L., Clark, D. M., & Ehlers, A. (2007). Rumination in posttraumatic stress disorder. *Depression and Anxiety*, *24*(5), 307–317. https://doi.org/10.1002/da.20228

Michel, J. S., Kotrba, L. M., Mitchelson, J. K., Clark, M. A., & Baltes, B. B. (2011). Antecedents of work–family conflict: A meta-analytic review. *Journal of Organizational Behavior*, *32*(5), 689–725. https://doi.org/10.1002/job.695

Michie, S., & Williams, S. (2003). Reducing work related psychological ill health and sickness absence: A systematic literature review. *Occupational and Environmental Medicine*, *60*(1), 3–9. https://doi.org/10.1136/oem.60.1.3

Moll, S., Zanhour, M., Patten, S. B., Stuart, H., & MacDermid, J. (2017). Evaluating mental health literacy in the workplace: Development and psychometric properties of a vignette-based tool. *Journal of Occupational Rehabilitation*, *27*(4), 601–611. https://doi.org/10.1007/s10926-017-9695-0

Morrow, J., & Nolen-Hoeksema, S. (1990). Effects of responses to depression on the remediation of depressive affect. *Journal of Personality and Social Psychology*, *58*(3), 519–527. https://doi.org/10.1037/0022-3514.58.3.519

National Alliance on Mental Illness (2022). Mental health by the numbers. *About mental illness*. https://www.nami.org/mhstats

Nieuwenhuijsen, K., Verbeek, J. H. A. M., de Boer, A. G. E. M., Blonk, R. W. B., & van Dijk, F. J. H. (2004). Supervisory behaviour as a predictor of return to work in employees absent from work due to mental health problems. *Occupational and Environmental Medicine*, *61*(10), 817–823. https://doi.org/10.1136/oem.2003.009688

Oliver, M. J. (1983). *Social work with disabled people*. MacMillan Publishers.

Oliver, M. J. (2013). The social model of disability: Thirty years on. *Disability & Society*, *28*(7), 1024–1026. https://doi.org/10.1080/09687599.2013.818773

Richmond, M. K., Pampel, F. C., Wood, R. C., & Nunes, A. P. (2016). Impact of employee assistance services on depression, anxiety, and risky alcohol use. *Journal of Occupational and Environmental Medicine*, *58*(7), 641–650. https://www.jstor.org/stable/48501473

Rüsch, N., Angermeyer, M. C., & Corrigan, P. W. (2005). Mental illness stigma: Concepts, consequences, and initiatives to reduce stigma. *European Psychiatry*, *20*(8), 529–539. https://doi.org/10.1016/j.eurpsy.2005.04.004

Schermuly, C. C., & Meyer, B. (2016). Good relationships at work: The effects of leader–member exchange and team–member exchange on psychological empowerment, emotional exhaustion, and depression. *Journal of Organizational Behavior*, *37*(5), 673–691. https://doi.org/10.1002/job.2060

Schön, U. K., Denhov, A., & Topor, A. (2009). Social relationships as a decisive factor in recovering from severe mental illness. *International Journal of Social Psychiatry*, *55*(4), 336–347. https://doi.org/10.1177/0020764008093686

Schultz, J., & Joish, V. (2009). Costs associated with changes in antidepressant treatment in a managed care population with major depressive disorder. *Psychiatric Services*, *60*(12), 1604–1611. https://doi.org/10.1176/ps.2009.60.12.1604

Schur, L., Nishii, L., Adya, M., Kruse, D., Bruyère, S. M., & Blanck, P. (2014). Accommodating employees with and without disabilities. *Human Resource Management*, *53*, 593–621. https://doi.org/10.1002/hrm.21607

Schur, L. A., Ameri, M., & Kruse, D. (2020). Telework after COVID: A "silver lining" for workers with disabilities? *Journal of Occupational Rehabilitation*, *30*(4), 521–536. https://doi.org/10.1007/s10926-020-09936-5

Shipp, A. J. (2021, June 6). My fixation on time management almost broke me. *Harvard Business Review*, "Managing yourself".

Shipp, A. J., & Aeon, B. (2019). Temporal focus: Thinking about the past, present, and future. *Current Opinion in Psychology*, *26*, 37–43. https://doi.org/10.1016/j.copsyc.2018.04.005

Shipp, A. J., & Jansen, K. J. (2021). The "other" time: A review of the subjective experience of time in organizations. *Academy of Management Annals*, *15*(1). https://doi.org/10.5465/annals.2018.0142

Shipp, A. J., & Richardson, H. (2019). The impact of temporal schemata: Understanding when individuals entrain versus resist or create temporal structure. *Academy of Management Review*, *46*(2). https://doi.org/10.5465/amr.2017.0384

Sianoja, M., Kinnunen, U., de Bloom, J., Korpela, K., & Geurts, S. (2016). Recovery during lunch breaks: Testing long-term relations with energy levels at work. *Scandinavian Journal of Work and Organizational Psychology*, *1* (1),7, 1–12. https://doi.org/10.16993/sjwop.13

Simon, G. E., Ludman, E. J., Unützer, J., Operskalski, B. H., & Bauer, M. S. (2008). Severity of mood symptoms and work productivity in people treated for bipolar disorder. *Bipolar Disorders*, *10*, 718–725. https://doi.org/10.1111/j.1399-5618.2008.00581.x

Sluss, D., & Ashforth, B. (2008). How relational and organizational identification converge: Processes and conditions. *Organization Science*, *19*(6), 807–823. https://doi.org/10.1287/orsc.1070.0349

Szeto, A. C., & Dobson, K. S. (2010). Reducing the stigma of mental disorders at work: A review of current workplace anti-stigma intervention programs. *Applied and Preventive Psychology*, *14*(1–4), 41–56. https://doi.org/10.1016/j.appsy.2011.11.002

Taylor, K., & Hampson, E. (2017). *At a tipping point? Workplace mental health and wellbeing*. The Deloitte Centre for Health Solutions.

Tims, M., & Bakker, A. B. (2010). Job crafting: Towards a new model of individual job redesign. *SA Journal of Industrial Psychology*, *36*(2), 1–9. https://hdl.handle.net/10520/EJC89228

Tims, M., Bakker, A. B., & Derks, D. (2014). Daily job crafting and the self-efficacy–performance relationship. *Journal of Managerial Psychology*, *29*(5), 490–507. https://doi.org/10.1108/JMP-05-2012-0148

Tims, M., Bakker, A. B., & Derks, D. (2015). Examining job crafting from an interpersonal perspective: Is employee job crafting related to the well-being of colleagues? *Applied Psychology: An International Review*, *64*(4), 727–753. https://doi.org/10.1111/apps.12043

Tsang, H., Lam, P., Bacon, N., & Leung, O. (2000). Predictors of employment outcome for people with psychiatric disabilities: A review of the literature since the mid '80s. *Journal of Rehabilitation*, *66*(2), 19–31. https://link.gale.com/apps/doc/A62980225/HRCA?u=anon~cbee61a3&sid=googleScholar&xid=38c7c560

Turner, J. R., & Müller, R. (2005). The project manager's leadership style as a success factor on projects: A literature review. *Project Management Journal*, *36*(2), 49–61. https://doi.org/10.1177/875697280503600206

Wang, P. S., Berglund, P. A., Olfson, M., & Kessler, R. C. (2004). Delays in initial treatment contact after first onset of a mental disorder. *Health Services Research*, *39*(2), 393–415. https://doi.org/10.1111/j.1475-6773.2004.00234.x

Wrzesniewski, A., & Dutton, J. E. (2001). Crafting a job: Revisioning employees as active crafters of their work. *Academy of Management Review*, *26*, 179–201. https://doi.org/10.2307/259118

Yook, K., Kim, K. H., Suh, S. Y., & Lee, K. S. (2010). Intolerance of uncertainty, worry, and rumination in major depressive disorder and generalized anxiety disorder. *Journal of Anxiety Disorders*, *24*(6), 623–628. https://doi.org/10.1016/j.janxdis.2010.04.003

Zuckerman, D. (1993). Reasonable accommodations for people with mental illness under the ADA. *Mental and Physical Disability Law Reporter*, *17*, 311–320.

Mark E. Moore and Lana L. Huberty

14 Organizational Culture's Influence on Employing People with Disabilities

Abstract: Equity, diversity, and inclusion strategies have become a top priority for organizations and their leaders. This chapter specifically examines the role that workplace culture can have on the effectiveness of these EDI strategies. As we conduct this thorough examination of the impact culture has on diversity, we include a specific focus on people with disabilities. Although this population offers a unique human resource for employers, they are often overlooked when it comes to including disabled people in diversity and inclusion strategies. This chapter will assist leaders with examining their workplace culture and formulating EDI attributes into their cultural platform.

Keywords: disability, culture, workplace, EDI, employment

Overview of Organizational Culture and Disability Management

Despite the passage of disability employment laws across the international spectrum over the past thirty years, the disabled population remains inadequately represented in the labor force. U.S. data from 2019 revealed that labor force participation of those with disabilities was 21.5% versus 68.5% of their peers without disabilities (Office of Disability Employment Policy, 2019). To increase the degree of disability diversity among their workforce, employers' use of innovation is vital but requires flexibility and empowerment, as well as control and efficiency. Studies have stressed the role organizational culture can have when it comes to innovation within the workplace. For example, Khazanchi et al. (2007) explored the implementation of advanced manufacturing technology (AMT). This examination featured the following three dimensions of organizational values: value profits, value profiles, and value practice interactions. These dimensions each focused on strategies utilizing various technologies that allowed employers to effectively hire and engage people with disabilities. With the inclusion of all three dimensions in their values, organizations balanced the employee needs with the employers. Therefore, the purpose of this chapter is to explore what it is that we know about culture and what it is that we do not know, and

Mark E. Moore, Eastern Carolina University
Lana L. Huberty, Concordia University – St. Paul

https://doi.org/10.1515/9783110743647-015

therefore need to know more about regarding cultural forces. Finally, we will offer insights as to where we go from here regarding the cultural impact on the disability diversity, equality, and inclusion.

How Culture Shapes Diversity Inclusion

Culture is the foundation that establishes norms and values for an organization and its leadership. In essence, cultural forces set the priorities for the workforce (Beyer & Trice, 1987). The cultural mechanism is continuously involved in moving leaders and workers toward the accomplishment of equality, diversity, and inclusion (EDI) directives, as well as their strategic focuses (Tavakoli, 2015). Pellet (2010) described culture as a road map on how to get things done. Further observations in EDI regarding the employment of people with disabilities suggested that culture has not been optimally utilized to advance this cause (Boyle, 1997; Moore et al., 2010). Moore et al. (2010) found that top management support, a key aspect of organizational culture, was linked to the representation of workers with disabilities in the sport industry. When this level of support was present, there is a better opportunity to create a robust culture for disability inclusion. However, as previously cited in the introduction section, labor force participation continues to be lower for people with disabilities than their peers without disabilities (Office of Disability Employment Policy, 2019).

Organizational culture, when properly structured, can allay employment discrimination in work organizations (Kartolo & Kwantes, 2019). Human resource management (HRM) structures can help reinforce work norms and value structures as well as other cultural forces by hiring individuals with similar tenets and principles (Ang, 2014; Cabrera & Bonache, 1999; Gewurtz et al., 2016). As such, HRM structures are relevant to EDI efforts in the work sector (Twaronite & Henry, 2019) and can foster an inclusive culture.

The cultural mechanism governs staff diversity through a contemporary work organization and is essential in communicating an organizational commitment to staff diversity. This governance is relevant to creating efficacy in the formulation of the organizational mission. In the strategic planning process, the mission statement underscores the organizational purpose, thus enabling priorities to be emphasized. Sezerel and Tonus (2016) described organizational culture as being directly related to the mission in the developmental process.

Cultural forces configure the degree to which employee type inclusion is valued and prioritized in the work structure. These types may include gender, race, ethnicity, or for the purpose of this chapter, disability inclusion (Harris, 2020). Overall, employee inclusion has an array of organizational benefits, including augmented productivity, raised employee morale, and an expanded bottom line (Bozek, 2021).

When focusing on disabled employee types, similar benefits from inclusion have been shown. A 2021 report from the Bureau of Labor Statistics (as listed on their bls. gov website) indicated that disabled workers were more likely than average-abled employees to contribute ideas that added value to their company (75% versus 66%). Despite these cited utilities, concerns remain regarding the employability of individuals with disabilities. To calm these worries, organizational leaders need to amalgamate disability inclusion into the EDI framework. This approach enables organizations to formulate initiatives to define and progress disability aspects within the broader diversity framework that can broaden practices to enhance EDI opportunities ("The neglected class of diversity," 2021).

The process of establishing an effective disability inclusion function begins with cultural aspects, especially those values that are consistent and can provide a supportive underpinning for disability causes (Suresh & Dyaram, 2020). These values are generally underscored through the mission statement as well as underlining norms that control employee treatment (Buys et al., 2017). Norms that are designed to create positive employment treatment can result in a disability-friendly culture that supports work accommodations and gives workers with disabilities the respect and dignity they deserve (Jasper & Waldhart, 2013). Although cultural forces have potential to result in positive outcomes for those with differing abilities, top leadership must be catalyst in making sure that these energies are appropriately utilized to foster disability inclusion. So, how do those at the top rung become catalysts for disability inclusion in their workplace? An astute leader will begin by integrating HRM practices in a way that aligns with the organizational culture. These proactive practices involve recruiting, selection, hiring, training, development, and job promotion (Ang, 2014; Bruyère, 2016; Harris, 2020). As more people with disabilities become members of the organization, workplace accommodations are likely to receive attention as a simple or complex consideration depending on the level of disability orientation. A disability-friendly organization commonly receives requests for simple accommodations like desk adjustments and work breaks to satisfy special needs of disabled workers (Nelson, 2020).

Forber-Pratt (2019) offered a unique recommendation of including employees' personal goals as part of the culture. This author suggested that organizational culture be orchestrated so that employees with disabilities are properly managed to accomplish both organizational and personal goals. This suggests that organizational culture blend core values of the employer that, from a disability-orientation perspective, often lead to values based on independence, social justice, growth, and development to create and advance employment opportunities for individuals with disabilities as members of the workforce (Forber-Pratt, 2019).

Although our analysis, to this point, has highlighted the facilitated effect of organizational culture on diversity and disability inclusion, we know that cultural forces can have an inhibitive effect on inclusive related mechanisms. One notable inhibitor is an organizational culture that does not have the capacity to assess and utilize people with disabilities as stakeholders. As such, these restricted cultures do not foster leadership competencies among those with differing abilities or the necessary support for these workers to succeed as skillful followers. Second, organizational cultures can inhibit the understanding of the utility served by a disability inclusive work climate. Therefore, leaders and organizational members will need an education on establishing a diverse workforce culture. Education conversations should include respectful dialogue, as well as an opportunity to ask questions as to how to best work alongside someone with different abilities. Another inhibitive impact of a restricted culture is not offering assistive technology to individuals with such needs for accommodation. Therefore, having a management team that is proactive in the strategic planning and preparedness processes is a must in the effectiveness of an inclusive organizational culture (Nelson, 2020).

In this section, the focus was on what is known about culture and its influences on diversity and disability inclusion. This section clearly showed that organizational culture has the capability to create positive outcomes for people with disabilities in work setting. The forthcoming will investigate organizational culture dynamics for the purpose of discussing what is not known about organizational culture and workforce inclusion with a particular emphasis on disability diversity.

What is it that We Need to Know more about Regarding the Cultural Forces?

When exploring the unknowns about organizational culture, it is unclear how leadership negativity affects the configuration of cultural indices. Within organizational culture, negative factors have been linked to perceptions about inclusive hiring practices (Heera, 2016). Since the extant findings have been discovered and investigated specifically at the supervisory level, it is uncertain whether top management has similar or varied level risk. Top management support has been shown to support the development of inclusive hiring practices for individuals with disabilities (Moore et al., 2010). We have learned that culture shapes the broader context for how managers and people with disabilities build relationships. Yet, we are unclear as to whether culture gives managers an opportunity to strengthen their personal experiences and exposure to employees with disabilities. If the culture is aligned to managerial and organizational expectations, then greater exposure and interactions with the disabled employee can result in a better comprehension of the potential productivity gained by the organization along with possible related travails it could face due to the diverse hiring (Annett, 2017).

Another topic regarding cultural forces is whether cultural structures have been designed to subject persons with disabilities to occupational distributions. This practice may result in people with disabilities encountering low levels of remunerations and a glaring lack of job mobility. Historically, job patterns for the disabled population have shown low representation in positions of job mobility while being overrepresented in positions with limited career advancement potential (Kaye, 2009). It is also unclear whether the cultural dynamics enable those with mental or physical conditions to acquire the capability to foster gainful job skills. According to Kaye (2009), job skill deficiencies can frequently result in underemployment as well as unemployment.

In addition, it is unclear whether a weakly devised culture facilitates employment discrimination in contemporary organizations (Lyubykh et al., 2021). Overall, employment discrimination can be a salient risk for multinational employers (Posthuma et al., 2011). As such, there is still uncertainty on the linkage between organizational culture and employment discrimination. This is an important issue that requires further exploration (Hunt et al., 2015). Without additional inquiry on the potential effects of cultural mechanisms on employment discrimination, it will remain nebulous whether organizational culture can facilitate inclusion for people with disabilities in work organizations. Moreover, if the culture is prone to discriminative tendencies, then employers will encounter a high level of risk due to the costs of potential legal conflicts. There remains a salient legal risk in recruitment and employment practices that require employers to implement training and development to curb the risks of lawsuits ("Growing HR legal risk: Training discrimination," 2009). If the culture is designed to create a diverse workforce, then an equal opportunity stance can be implemented to mitigate employment discrimination in the workplace.

Another area that needs further comprehension is how organizational culture can facilitate the formulation of disability work policy. Advocates emphasized the importance of having workers with disabilities shape inclusionary policy ("Disability inclusion matters," 2021). By engaging these individuals in the process, organizations can structure policy to alleviate challenges and broaden opportunities for disability diversity to become reality. An additional area that continues to be explored is whether the workplace culture supports and advances effective training to foster diversity inclusion ("Disability inclusion matters," 2021). The focus of this area is to outline what it is to have a disability-friendly culture and how training and development impacts this state. In other words, how a cultural foundation can be orchestrated to address issues on sensitivity, stereotyping, and social etiquette through proper job training ("Disability inclusion matters," 2021). These and other topics can provide insight on the alignment between culture and employee training, development, and inclusion.

There has only been a paucity of information on how cultural components influence the granting of work accommodations by employers. According to advocates ("Disability inclusion matters," 2021), employees should not have to plead for special accommodations to maintain or enhance their job performance. Often, a disability-unfriendly environment is created through ambiguity about disability accommodations. This can cause organizational leadership to miscomprehend the legality of offering integral work-related support. Employers tend to get confused about the costs of accommodations and commonly consider them as expensive investments. However, costs can often be minimal ranging from zero to $50.00 ("Disability inclusion matters," 2021). Cost is an area that frequently underscores the cultural myopic existing about providing disability accommodations in the workplace.

The connection between organizational culture and HRM practices is an additional area that needs further inquiry relating to the representation of workers with disabilities (Bruyère, 2016). One salient issue is how organizational culture shapes how identity-conscious and identity-blind HRM practices relate to the disability orientation of a work organization. Identity-conscious HRM structures have been found to expand employment opportunities for underrepresented population segments (Konrad & Linneham, 1995). Richard et al. (2021) further outlined how identity-conscious and identity-blind HRM practices influence the treatment of individuals with mental health afflictions in work settings. However, HRM practices have been viewed by employees as discriminatory and restrictive of diversity inclusion (Balser, 2002). There is a large degree of attention being given as to how organizational culture evokes these employee perceptions and sentiments. Practices can be inclusive rather than restricted when top management shapes the organizational culture with a proactive vision to include workers with disabilities (Moore et al., 2010). Specifically, leaders at the top level must project a vision so that the culture is seen as legitimate and well orchestrated for inclusion to occur.

As we close out this section, the final issue that must be allocated additional examination is how the building blocks of organizational culture are constructed to enhance disability inclusion (Islam, 2013). This development can begin by integrating the core value with the organizational culture. When this is done effectively, employing and professionally developing people with disabilities can become one of the strategies of carrying forward the organizational mission (Kerns, 2020).

Where do we go from here Regarding Cultural Impact on the Disability Diversity, Equality, and Inclusion?

In this chapter, an analysis was first prepared on what is it that we know about culture then discourse transitioned to what is it that we do not know, with a specific focus on what we need to know about the cultural forces. This section will examine where we go from here regarding cultural impact on the disability diversity, equality, and inclusion.

To fully comprehend the utility of disability-inclusive and -friendly culture within our workplaces, we must continue thorough investigation in this area. This is important as our organizational leaders seek assistance with creating this culture, training and educating employees on the EDI strategies, and supporting those with disabilities. Embracing practices that enable us to have a diverse workforce offers benefits to these leaders and their employees, as well as the organization as a whole, both financially and socially (Andersen & Moynihan, 2016).

When moving forward, the effects of a disability-friendly culture on organizational productivity is an area in need of additional comprehensive review. Goldberg et al. (2019) posited that disability inclusion can lead to a rally effect where it can have positive increases in organizational productivity for all employees. Despite these reported outcomes, the job outlook continues to be bleak for the disability population. In term of productivity, research should be accelerated to investigate if disability-oriented organizations outperformed disability-unfriendly enterprises ("Importance of culture to the success of product development", 2014). Moreover, there should be more knowledge on whether a disability-friendly culture fosters a commitment to talent instead of embodying stigmas, stereotypes, and negative perceptions (International Labour Organization, 2020).

Scholars and practitioners must progress forward to see if cultural interventions can be applied to decrease and ultimately eradicate the employment discrepancies and discrimination currently facing people with disabilities (Tiliuta & Diaconu, 2020). Regarding these foci, there need to be progressed assessments on how organizational culture influences the processes relating to the management of a disabled workforce. To better gauge the cultural implications in the managerial sphere, we must continue to study and comprehend the employment experiences of those with mental and physical afflictions, specifically those who are a part of the disabled population (Desai et al., 2021). To have a robust examination of the employment experience, new technology is available and can be efficiently utilized in this investigation. There are a multitude of workplace analytics and collaboration tools (Rudderham, 2019) that are often conducted to gauge employee experiences.

There will continue to be a thirst for understanding about staff diversity. In many instances, these diversity actions across the globe include those with disabilities (Anca & Sloka, 2020). Since these movements are designed to demonstrate the utility provided by disabled populations (Anca & Sloka, 2020), there must be ascertained effort to investigate and expand the knowledge base about the cultural building blocks and their relationships to workplace diversity, including how to leverage a compelling diversity orientation in alignment with the organization's strategic intent. Social entrepreneurship is the process where individuals, organizations, and entrepreneurs apply their human capital to address pressing social issues. The unemployment and underemployment of disabled people remains formable with social travails across much of the world. As such, social entrepreneurship is likely to have more of a stakeholder presence in gaining future intelligence on diversity, disability, and the cultural building blocks that foster their existence (Anca & Sloka, 2020).

Organizational culture trends offer insights on important dynamics of the ongoing efforts to enable better representation in the labor market for individuals with disabilities. One growing development in this regard is strategic vision (Karapancheva, 2020). Moore and colleagues (2010) identified vision as an important means for creating an accepting climate for leaders with disabilities. Top leaders with strategic visions offer us a rich outlook on how an organization's cultural base influences EDI in the workplace.

Future Implications

In the future, people with disabilities have an opportunity for a stronger presence in the labor force. For this to happen, a receptive environment must by structured within our work organizations (ILO, 2016). This process must begin with the cultural dynamics that shape the commitment toward equality, diversity, and inclusion, especially inclusion of disability populations (Moore et al., 2020). Culture can be the driving force for EDI infusion since it blends the values, norms, and symbols into the work climate that can facilitate or impede employment opportunities for unrepresentative groups. To better understand the role of this cultural element in diversifying the organization, practitioners and scholars must provide a closer inspection of the cultural realm. Such analyses should be performed with applied and basic investigative designs that develop creative ethnographic, case method, and observational techniques. If these investigative tasks are correctly done, findings can be translated to robust action to increase disability diversity in the work sector, thus enabling employees with disabilities and their respective employers to obtain professional success.

To install a clear commitment to diversity and disability, organizational leadership must formulate these attributes into its mission, core values, and organizational identity. If these components are to be part of shared aspirations and vision, they must be incorporated into the cultural platform (Karapancheva, 2020). A culture oriented toward employment advancements must foster practical and marketable training opportunities for individuals with mental and physical afflictions (Desai et al., 2021). Moreover, disability-friendly employers must indicate a willingness to consider job accommodations during the pre-employment and employment stages. The commitment to job accommodations should be emphasized in job announcements and job descriptions.

Conclusion

The pursuit to enhance EDI employment prospects must be predicated on a mutually beneficial relationship. This chapter focused on employers' contributions through cultural mechanisms that, when properly structured, can prioritize staff diversity.

Culture can create a receptive work climate where individuals with disabilities are proactively recruited, hired, and promoted to fill crucial workforce needs (Accenture, 2018). This is congruent with the sentiments of top leaders who understand their role as facilitators for disability diversity in work settings. In this role, employers must devise and implement strategies to increase human capital of the disability populations. Not only should these skill development quests be developed through emphasizing job accommodations blended with the legal paraments, but there must also be training and development interventions to enable those with mental and physical afflictions to be marketable commodities. If employees are to be true stakeholders, culture must be at the forefront of efforts to devise receptive climates and formulate innovative training and development opportunities. If these tactics are optimally built through a cultural focus, then prospects and employment fabrics will enable lasting changes for the employee and employer.

References

Accenture. (2018). *Getting to equal: The Disability Inclusion advantage.* American Association of People with Disabilities (AAPD) and Disability: IN. https://www.accenture.com/_acnmedia/PDF-89/Accenture-DisabilityInclusion-Research-Report.pdf

Anca, E., & Sloka, B. (2020). Social entrepreneurship and employment challenges of persons with mental disabilities. *New challenges of economics & business development – 2020: Economic inequality and well-being: Proceedings* (12th International Scientific Conference, October 2, 2020) (pp. 9–16). University of Latvia. https://doi.org/10.22364/ncebd.2020.01

Andersen, S. C., & Moynihan, D. P. (2016). How leaders respond to diversity: The moderating role of organizational culture on performance information use. *Journal of Public Administration Research & Theory, 26*(3), 448–460. https://doi.org/10.1093/jopart/muv038

Ang, M. C. H. (2014). Do persons with disabilities actions and organizational culture influence managerial intention to hire persons with disabilities? The Malaysian Perspective. *Journal Pengurusan, 41,* 81–89. https://doi-org.mutex.gmu.edu/10.17576/pengurusan2014-41-07

Annett, M. (2017). Categorizing supervisor reflections on risks of hiring persons with disabilities. *Journal of Organizational Psychology, 17*(4), 29–35. http://mutex.gmu.edu/login?url=https://www-proquest-com.mutex.gmu.edu/scholarlyjournals/categorizing-supervisor-reflections-on-risks/docview/1967312447/se2?accountid=14541

Balser, D. B. (2002). Agency in organizational inequality: Organizational behavior and individual perceptions of discrimination. *Work & Occupations, 29*(2), 137–165. https://doi.org/10.1177/0730888402029002002

Beyer, J. M., & Trice, H. M. (1987). How an organization's rites reveal its culture. *Organizational Dynamics, 15*(4), 5–24. https://doi.org/10.1016/0090-2616(87)90041-6

Boyle, M. A. (1997). Social barriers to successful reentry into mainstream organizational culture: Perceptions of people with disabilities. *Human Resource Development Quarterly, 8*(3), 259–268. https://doi.org/10.1002/hrdq.3920080308

Bozek, R. (2021). The hidden value of disability inclusion: 5 benefits that can help your company, *Understood.org.* https://www.understood.org/en/articles/hidden-value-of-disability-inclusion-5-benefits-that-can-help-company

Bruyère, S. M. (2016). *Disability and employer practices: Research across the disciplines*. Cornell University Press. https://doi.org/10.7591/cornell/9781501700583.001.0001

Buys, N., Wagner, S., Randall, C., Harder, H., Geisen, T., Yu, I., Hassler, B., Howe, C., & Fraess-Phillips, A. (2017). Disability management and organizational culture in Australia and Canada. *Work, 57*(3), 409–419. https://doi.org/10.3233/WOR-172568

Cabrera, E. F., & Bonache, J. (1999). An expert HR system for aligning organizational culture and strategy. *Human Resource Planning, 22*(1), 51–60.

Desai, M. U., Paranamana, N., Restrepo-Toro, M., O'Connell, M. M., Davidson, L., & Stanhope, V. (2021). Implicit organizational bias: Mental health treatment culture and norms as barriers to engaging with diversity. *American Psychologist, 76*(1), 78–90. https://doi.org/10.1037/amp0000621

Disability inclusion matters. (2021). *Ask EARN*. https://askearn.org/disability-inclusion-matters/

Forber-Pratt, A. J. (2019). (Re)defining disability culture: Perspectives from the Americans with Disabilities Act generation. *Culture & Psychology, 25*(2), 241–256. https://doi.org/10.1177/1354067X18799714

Gewurtz, R. E., Langan, S., & Shand, D. (2016). Hiring people with disabilities: A scoping review. *Work, 54*(1), 135–148. https://doi.org/10.3233/WOR-162265

Goldberg, S. R., Kessler, L. L., & Govern, M. (2019). Fostering diversity and inclusion in the accounting workplace: Certified Public Accountant. *The CPA Journal, 89*(12), 50–57. http://mutex.gmu.edu/login?url=https://www-proquest-com.mutex.gmu.edu/scholarly-journals/fostering-diversity-inclusion-accounting/docview/2398186908/se-2?accountid=14541

Growing HR legal risk: Training discrimination. (2009). *Human Resource Specialist: Employment Law, 39*(9), 1.

Harris, R. (2020). Managing the big five: Culture–change–diversity–well-being–experience. *Supervision, 81*(12), 7–9.

Heera, S. (2016). Employers' perceptive towards people with disabilities: A review of the literature. *The South East Asian Journal of Management, 10*(1), 54–74. https://doi.org/10.21002/seam.v10i1.5960

Hunt, V., Layton, D., & Prince, S. (2015, January 1). Why diversity matters. *McKinsey*. https://www.mckinsey.com/business-functions/people-and-organizational-performance/our-insights/why-diversity-matters

Importance of culture to the success of product development. (2014, June 15). AIPMM Webinar Series. https://www.slideshare.net/aipmm/importance-of-culture-to-thesuccess-of-product-development

Islam, G. (2013). Recognizing employees: Reification, dignity and promoting care in management. *Cross Cultural Management, 20*(2), 235–250. https://doi.org/10.1108/13527601311313490

Jasper, C. R., & Waldhart, P. (2013). Employer attitudes on hiring employees with disabilities in the leisure and hospitality industry. *International Journal of Contemporary Hospitality Management, 25*(4), 577–594. https://doi.org/10.1108/09596111311322934

Karapancheva, M. (2020). The future of organizational culture. *Journal of Sustainable Development, 10*(25), 42–52.

Kartolo, A. B., & Kwantes, C. T. (2019). Organizational culture, perceived societal and organizational discrimination. *Equality, Diversity & Inclusion, 38*(6), 602–618. https://doi.org/10.1108/EDI-10-2018-0191

Kaye, H. S. (2009). Stuck at the bottom rung: Occupational characteristics of workers with disabilities. *Journal of Occupational Rehabilitation, 19*(2), 115–128. https://doi.org/10.1007/s10926-009-9175-2

Kerns, C. D. (2020). Managing organizational culture: A practice-oriented framework. *International Leadership Journal*, *12*(1), 77–101.

Khazanchi, S., Lewis, M. W., & Boyer, K. K. (2007). Innovation-supportive culture: The impact of organizational values on process innovation. *Journal of Operations Management*, *25*(4), 871–884. https://doi.org/10.1016/j.jom.2006.08.003

Konrad, A. M., & Linnehan, F. (1995). Formalized HRM structures: Coordinating equal employment opportunity or concealing organizational practices? *Academy of Management Journal*, *38*, 787–820. https://doi.org/10.5465/256746

Lyubykh, Z., Turner, N., Barling, J., Reich, T. C., & Batten, S. (2021). Employee disability disclosure and managerial prejudices in the return-to-work context. *Personnel Review*, *50*(2), 770–788. https://doi.org/10.1108/PR-11-2019-0654

Moore, J. R., Hanson, W. R., & Maxey, E. C. (2020). Disability inclusion: Catalyst to adaptive organizations. *Organization Development Journal*, *38*(1), 89–105.

Moore, M. E., Konrad, A. M., & Hunt, J. (2010). Creating a vision boosts the impact of top management support on the employment of managers with disabilities: The case of sport organizations in the USA. *Equality, Diversity, and Inclusion: An International Journal*, *29*(6), 609–626. https://doi.org/10.1108/02610151011067531

Nelson, J. (2020). *What is organizational culture?* Society for Human Resource Management. https://www.shrm.org/resourcesandtools/tools-and samples/toolkits/pages/understandinganddevelopingorganizationalculture.aspx

Office of Disability Employment Policy. (2019). *Monthly labor force participation rate and unemployment rate.* https://www.dol.gov/odep/

Pellet, L. (2010). *The culture fit factor: Creating an employment brand that attracts, retains, and repels the right employees.* Society for Human Resource Management.

Posthuma, R. A., Roehling, M. V., & Campion, M. A. (2011). Employment discrimination law exposures for international employers. *International Journal of Law & Management*, *53*(4), 281–298. https://doi.org/10.1108/17542431111147792

Richard, S., Lemaire, C., & Church-Morel, A. (2021). Beyond identity consciousness: Human resource management practices and mental health conditions in sheltered workshops. *International Journal of Human Resource Management*, 32(15), 3218–3243. https://doi.org/10.1080/09585192.2021.1893787

Rudderham, R. (2019, Spring). Creating a compelling workplace experience. *People & Strategy Journal, 42* (2). https://www.shrm.org/executive/resources/people-strategy-journal/Spring2019/Pages/perspectives.aspx

Sezerel, H., & Tonus, H. Z. (2016). The effects of the organizational culture on diversity management perceptions in hotel industry. *Journal of Human Resource Management*, *19*(2), 1–17.

Suresh, V., & Dyaram, L. (2020). Workplace disability inclusion in India: Review and directions. *Management Research Review*, *43*(12), 1–23. https://doi.org/10.1108/MRR-11-2019-0479

Tavakoli, M. (2015). Creating a culture of inclusion to attain organizational success. *Employment Relations Today (Wiley)*, *42*(2), 37–42. https://doi.org/10.1002/ert.21497

The neglected class of diversity: How firms can increase disability inclusion. (2021). *Strategic Direction*, *37*(6), 1–4. https://doi.org/10.1108/SD-04-2021-0047

Tiliuta, B. A., & Diaconu, I. R. (2020). Gender influences on organizational culture. *Cross Cultural Management Journal*, *22*(1), 17–20.

Twaronite, K., & Henry, T. (2019). *From inclusive recruitment tools to accessible websites, learn how to better harness – and retain – the talents of people with disabilities.* EY. https://www.ey.com/en_us/diversity-inclusiveness/six-ways-to-advance-disability-inclusion-in-your-organization

Sarah Richard and Célia Lemaire

15 Tensions in the Management of Disabled Individuals: The Case of the Sheltered Sector in France

Abstract: Individuals with disabilities remain an untapped labor force in mainstream employment (Lengnick-Hall et al., 2008). The unsuitable workplace environment partially explains this situation (Böhm et al., 2011). In this chapter, we consider alternative forms of employment that exist in France and that were implemented to improve the integration of individuals with disabilities in the workforce (Jagorel et al., 2019). We specifically focus on the sheltered sector. We study the specificities and tensions faced by sheltered workshops and consider how they shape managerial practices toward disabled individuals. Three tensions are highlighted: how sheltered workshops deal with specific disability types, how managers play with different organizational logics and, finally, how sheltered workshop professionals deal with confidentiality issues. This chapter contributes to the reflection on managerial practices toward disabled individuals and highlights the creativity and ingenuity that professionals in sheltered workshops have to develop to deal with the multiple tensions they face.

Keywords: sheltered workshop, managerial tensions, adapted working environment, performance practices, confidentiality

Introduction

Individuals with disabilities remain an untapped labor force in mainstream employment (Lengnick-Hall et al., 2008), despite the evolution of disability discrimination legislation (Corby et al., 2019) and their valuable contribution to organizational performance (Kulkarni and Scullion, 2015). The unsuitable workplace environment partially explains this situation (Böhm et al., 2011). In this chapter, we consider alternative forms of employment that exist in France and that were implemented to improve the integration of individuals with disabilities in the workforce (Jagorel et al., 2019). We specifically focus on the sheltered sector.

Sheltered organizations are segregated organizational spaces for disabled workers and tend to specialize in manufacturing or general services (Cimera, 2017; Bend & Priola, 2021). The sheltered sector constitutes a parallel employment system in which disabled individuals work and benefit from medical, social, and educational

Sarah Richard and Célia Lemaire, EM Strasbourg Business School, France

https://doi.org/10.1515/9783110743647-016

support in an adapted environment (Richard, 2020). Work is used as a therapeutic and development tool (Demeule, 2016; Combes-Joret, 2020). In sheltered employment, individuals with disabilities are users and not employees and the organization receives funding from the state to support their employment.

We studied the specificities and tensions faced by sheltered workshops and considered how they shape managerial practices toward disabled individuals. While the term "tension" refers to a physical phenomenon that includes "forces that act to separate the constituent parts of a body" (*Robert Dictionary*), we refer to the organizational dimension for which the tensions lead people to deal with competing demands (Smith & Lewis, 2011).

This topic is important, as sheltered organizations make space for disabled individuals. They try to compensate for the lack of adaptation of mainstream employment while being financially viable (Arena, 2015). They are always torn between their mission of inclusion and their parallel duty to serve as transitional spaces and develop the employability of individuals with disabilities (Bodon et al., 2016; Jagorel et al., 2019). Therefore, sheltered organizations face many tensions due to their ambiguous positions (providing jobs and support, pursuing both financial and social goals) in the labor market.

The empirical data used in this chapter come from three articles related to how the sheltered sector functions in terms of disability management.

The first study, entitled *How the sheltered sector adapts or not its managerial practices to specific forms of disabilities*, shows how professionals simultaneously adapt human resource management (HRM) practices to all disabilities and to specific forms of disabilities (here, individuals with mental health conditions) (Richard et al., 2021).

The second study, *Managers playing with different logics in a hybrid sheltered workshop*, underlines how managers cope with the challenge of balancing opposed logics of performance (social and economic) and transform this constraint into a (hard) game (Lemaire, 2020).

Lastly, the study *Tensions in dealing with confidential information* describes how sheltered organizations face the dilemma associated with confidential information management. It highlights paradoxes surrounding confidentiality management (Richard, 2020) and elaborates strategies adopted by professionals to face unbalanced situations.

From a methodological standpoint, these studies are all qualitative. They leveraged non-participant observations, semi-structured interviews and focus groups. Their data were collected from four sheltered workshops.

In this chapter, we examine two populations: managers, referring to employees managing a team of disabled individuals, and professionals, who, contrary to managers, include people working in the support team (social, developmental, and educational support). We also adopt a multi-level approach that considers (1) interpersonal challenges faced by sheltered workshop professionals (confidentiality issue), (2) the interaction between organizational logics and the individuals in charge of managing people with disabilities, and (3) the organizational level, investigating the implementation of HRM practices within an organization. By adopting a diversity of approaches, we highlight the multiple and diverse tensions (seen from various angles) faced by the sheltered sector.

This chapter contributes to the reflection on managerial practices toward disabled individuals. Although the literature regularly points out the limits of dedicating specific employment spaces for disabled individuals (Cimera, 2011) and the inability of those spaces to include disabled individuals in society (Hemphrill & Kulik, 2017), this chapter highlights the creativity and ingenuity of professionals in sheltered workshops to deal with the multiple tensions they face. Therefore, we propose a nuanced approach when considering the effects of specific employment spaces, focusing on the practices developed in those spaces.

Mainstream *versus* Sheltered Employments

In France, legal incentives exist to favor the employment of disabled individuals. The main incentive is the implementation of a quota system in mainstream employment, in both private and public companies (Corby et al., 2019). Private sector companies and public authorities with 20 employees or more are obliged to include 6% of disabled people in their total workforce. The workers included in the quota are those who have obtained official recognition of their disability, known as "reconnaissance de la qualité de travailleur handicapé" (RQTH). Therefore, disclosing a disability at work allows individuals to obtain accommodations and benefits to compensate for their disability (Richard & Hennekam, 2020).

Apart from mainstream employment, which provides accommodations for individuals who have declared their disability, the sheltered sector was specifically created to employ individuals with disabilities (Jagorel et al., 2019). This sector provides work for a large panel of different disabilities, and disabled individuals constitute a major part of their workforce. Work in the sheltered sector is systematically organized to favor adequacy between one's job, one's disability, and one's productivity rhythm.

The Sheltered Sector: General Characteristics

Sheltered companies are segregated and protective organizational spaces (Bend & Priola, 2021). In France, sheltered organizations are named "Etablissement et service d'aide par le travail" (ESAT). In those organizations, production activity is used as a therapeutic and development tool for people with disabilities (Vidal-Gomel et al., 2012; Demeule, 2016; Combes-Joret, 2020). ESATs are partially financed by public authorities (annual global public funding and subsidies to ensure remuneration for disabled workers) and by their own product and/or production sales. In ESATs, all workers are disabled, except for the managerial and the social support teams, whose responsibility is to ensure adequacy between the activity and the personal development of the disabled workers. Disabled individuals who work in ESATs benefit from a special status: they do not have a working contract but an individualized support plan (www.travail-emploi.gouv.fr). ESATs integrate people with disabilities who do not have enough autonomy to work in mainstream employment (Baret, 2012). To integrate the sheltered sector, disabled individuals are oriented by the Commission des Droits et de l'Autonomie des Personnes Handicapées (CDAPH) after advice from a multidisciplinary team. This commission certifies that their working capacity does not allow them to work in the mainstream or the adapted sector (Article R146-31-1 du Code de l'action sociale et des familles).

The French context is of particular interest because of the importance of the sheltered sector. In 2014, there were 1,429 sheltered workshops (Jagorel et al., 2019), employing 122,600 individuals with disabilities.

Tensions and Management in the Sheltered Sector

Given that the sheltered sector consistently tries to align adaptation to disabilities and objectives (Baret, 2012), managerial practices are continuously torn between opposing forces (Arena et al., 2015). Through three different studies, we present several tensions that exist in the sheltered sector and that influence managerial practices.

Tension 1: How the Sheltered Sector Adapts its Managerial Practices to Specific forms of Disabilities

Although sheltered organizations were initially created to support individuals with developmental disabilities (Richard et al., 2021), today they support a large panel of different conditions. In particular, individuals with mental health conditions constitute a growing population in this sector (Jagorel et al., 2019). A mental health condition is defined as a diagnosable psychological disorder and is "characterized by dysregulation of mood, thought, and/or behavior" (Centers for Disease Control and Prevention, 2016). Sheltered organizations live with the continuous dilemma of choosing between two adaptation approaches: adapting their managerial practices to disability in general, or adapting those practices to each group of disability (i.e., mental health conditions, motor disability, sensory disability). Each approach has its own advantages and drawbacks (van der Torre & Fenger, 2014; Böhm et al., 2011).

We conducted a qualitative study that examined how individuals with mental health conditions (MHCs) were supported and managed in sheltered workshops in France. We relied on data from four sheltered organizations, including non-participant observations (approximately 180 hours), semi-structured interviews (36), and focus groups (2) with a sheltered workshop social support team. This combination of methods was used to approach the studied phenomenon from multiple perspectives. In the studied sheltered workshops, between 10% and 29% of the attendees of each workshop had a mental illness, primarily schizophrenia, bipolar disorder, anxiety disorder, paranoia, or severe depression. All four workshops had comprehensive social support services consisting of a psychologist, a special educational needs coordinator, and professionals specifically trained to organize social support. Workshop managers and monitors managed the production and teams of workers.

Based on the data, we identified and described HRM practices related to individuals with MHCs in sheltered companies and how these practices were established.

To favor the inclusion of disabled individuals, sheltered workshops adapt their HRM practices (Siperstein et al., 2014) and allow disabled individuals to work at their own rhythm (Broderick & Ferri, 2019). The adaptation of the practices can be analyzed through the framework proposed by Konrad and Linnehan (1995), who distinguish identity-blind and identity-conscious diversity practices. This distinction refers to the willingness, or lack thereof, of organizations to adapt to the specific attributes of certain social identities (Tajfel, 1981). Identity-blind practices do not take social identity into account. Employee differences are deliberately ignored to eliminate biased treatments from managers.

Others have argued that these differences cannot be ignored. From this perspective, people are treated differently to arrive at fair outcomes (Konrad & Linnehan, 1995). Practices that respect these principles recognize gender, race, national origin, disability, or other protected or disadvantaged identities as parameters that need to be taken into account in the workplace (Leslie, 2019). Through the objective of providing an adapted work environment (Hemphill & Kulik, 2017), sheltered organizations are identity-conscious entities. In this study, we sought to know whether practices were conscious of disability in general, and whether they were conscious of the specificities of individuals with MHCs.

We identified three types of practices in sheltered organizations: subgroup identity-blind, subgroup identity-conscious, and individual conscious. Subgroup identity-blind practices refer to the absence of adaptation to individuals with MHCs. Such practices are adapted to individuals with disabilities in general but not specifically to individuals with MHCs. The sheltered workshops included in the study were initially designed for individuals with developmental disabilities; therefore, the characteristics of individuals with MHCs were deemed incompatible with the structural constraints of sheltered workshops, and the need to adapt was not systematically considered. Non-differentiated practices were also implemented to maintain equity between workers. In the sheltered workshops, the recruitment system was not competitive, and the compensation policy, team management practices, and motivation practices were the same for everyone and did not depend on disability type. Non-individualized practices had adverse effects, as they hindered motivation and created difficulties for individuals with MHCs in finding an adequate place in the sheltered workshop system.

In parallel, sub-group identity-conscious practices consist of adapting HRM tools to the prototypic functional specificities of individuals with MHCs. Prototypic specificities included individuals' intellectual capacities, the fluctuation of their symptoms, and difficulties regarding how they socialized or dealt with emotions. Examples of practices included how professionals selected accommodations for disabled individuals. MHCs had specific accommodations, such as working-time arrangements and the possibility to isolate. Professionals also adapted disciplinary actions, as it is sometimes not productive to sanction individuals with MHCs when not respecting certain rules is part of their disease. Lastly, monitors also implemented specific talent management practices in an attempt to valorize specific skills of individuals with MHCs, as contrary to developmental disabilities, intellectual capacities are preserved in the case of mental illness.

Individual-conscious practices are adapted to an individual at specific moments in time and go beyond the category of MHCs. Professionals adapted practices to how the person reacted to the specific manifestations of their symptoms. The diversity of mental illnesses and the potential panel of consequences make each individual's reaction to their condition unique. These practices were inconsistent, as they depended entirely on the number of individuals with MHCs and the degree of professional involvement. Examples of practices included an idiosyncratic managerial posture, as some professionals specifically adapted their managerial approaches to each individual with a mental illness. Because the sheltered system is disabled individuals' last option for employment, monitors also adopted idiosyncratic crisis management practices, using all necessary actions to keep the person in the sheltered workshop system. Lastly, dealing with mental illness often implied the necessity of crossing private–professional boundaries to know more about the context of the person before making managerial decisions.

Our findings showed that drivers favored or hindered the implementation of those practices. Subgroup identity-blind practices were favored in the absence of organizational resources and when structural constraints impeded the flexibility to adapt practices. Therefore, in accordance with the initial mission of the sheltered workshops, these practices were adapted to deal with disabilities in general. In parallel, subgroup identity-conscious practices were implemented when organizational members shared the perception of the need for adaptation and when the intention and organizational framework allowed for flexibility. Practices were adapted to consider the prototypic characteristics of individuals with MHCs. Lastly, when individuals with MHCs challenged the functional limits of sheltered organizations but the inadequate organizational framework remained inflexible, professionals took over and circumvented these limits. In such cases, they went beyond the disability category and developed practices adapted to the specific worker and his/her condition, which we call individual-conscious practices.

Therefore, our findings showed that sheltered companies were identity-conscious as they adapted their HRM practices toward disability in general. To integrate individuals with MHCS, they also had to develop sub-group identity-conscious practices to deal with specific aspects of MHC. Nevertheless, subgroup identity-conscious practices were not enough, and sometimes the professionals had to go beyond the rules of the sheltered organizations and adopt an individualized approach to properly perform their jobs and respect the objectives of the organization.

Tension 2: Managers Playing with Different Logics in Hybrid Sheltered Workshops

Social enterprises, such as sheltered workshops, are hybrid organizations that must find a balance between the institutional logics of the market (also called economic or financial) and social services (also called social logic) (Battilana et al., 2015; Garrow & Hasenfeld, 2014). The co-existence of logics conforms to the complexity of performance-measurement systems. Hybridity complicates venues for understanding, quantifying, valuing, and demonstrating results (Hyndman & McConville, 2018); hence, what should be measured is not clear – that is, effectiveness, efficiency, or performance (Grossi et al., 2019).

Drawing on work that analyzes individual responses to institutional logics co-existing in hybrids (e.g., Pache & Santos, 2013), we investigated the strategies managers implement to respond to the logics through their Performance Measurement and Management Practices (PMMP). PMMP are defined as "socially constructed phenomena [and] which [are] deeply implicated in the shaping of organizational objectives and the meanings associated with the very concept of performance" (Modell, 2019, p. 429).

To this end, we developed an interpretive qualitative study in a sheltered workshop that provided support through work to 176 people. For six years, one of the authors was in charge of the regional-level implementation of a dashboard designed by national authorities for health and social care facilities and services. This project enabled the selection of the sheltered workshop to develop an ethnographic investigation work (Golden-Biddle & Locke, 1993) by multiplying access to workers, direct managers, and supervisory staff. We conducted direct observations (50 hours) of the two sheltered workshop activities (catering and packaging). To complement these observations, we interviewed 15 professionals undertaking various duties and from varied backgrounds (the financial officer, director, head of educative mentoring, psychologist, department head of the two activities, customers, managers, and workers).

Our findings showed that the complexity of the environment and the co-existence of logics challenged managers in their daily work. They coped with this by adopting strategies that reveal the various ways in which they incorporate co-existing logics (Modell, 2019). Since the strategies studied are necessarily embodied by individuals, we use the terms tightrope walker, magician, and team juggler to underline the personification of these strategies. The tightrope walker's strategy consists of finding a balance between two logics. The magician's strategy combines the two logics by separating what is assumed in the eyes of all (onstage) from what is produced in a more discreet way (backstage). The strategy of a team juggler consists of participation in a team game, which allows the responsibilities to be distributed within the sheltered workshop. In the image of jugglers who handle balls, managers at different levels had to handle different responsibilities.

The image of a tightrope walker is useful for illustrating that the search for a balance between the logics implemented by managers at different hierarchical levels through their PMMP is an unpredictable and risky process that is part of the performance of the hybrid organization. Rather than seeing balance as a goal to be achieved, it seems to us that it is the process of seeking balance that constitutes the performance of the organization.

The magician metaphor enables us to underline how managers play with the degree to which PMMPs are formalized. Formalized practices enable managers to make the issues they wish to show to the various stakeholders visible. Informal practices help to keep certain dynamics carried out backstage invisible to maintain a balance between logics.

While the tightrope walker's pendulum shows the different logics and their importance, the magician's hat and wand make it possible to keep invisible what must be invisible for the illusion to be complete.

Lastly, the strategy of the team juggler is adequate to show that management in sheltered workshops is a collaborative game in which each person assumes a role – a responsibility concretized by practices – in the pursuit of a common goal, the support of the user, and by adopting a playful attitude oriented toward games, fun, positivity, and flexibility. By developing lightheartedness, creativity, and spontaneity in their relations with users, as well as in the way they approach the social and economic dimensions of their work, managers play by the rules of the game.

Thus, managers who are subject to the practical consequences of the tensions between economic and financial logics showed differentiated modalities of play between the logics. The daily difficulty of managing these tensions between logics was found at every hierarchical level (top manager, head of services, direct managers), and the term "game" chosen here did not mean that the process was easy. On the contrary, it was a permanent challenge, and if managers played, it is also to avoid becoming discouraged.

Tension 3: Dealing with Confidential Information

Contrary to the mainstream sector, in the sheltered sector professionals need to deal with a lot of confidential information. That information is, for example, the disability type, what is happening in one's private life, and what happened to the person before their integration into the ESAT (Richard, 2020; Richard et al., 2021). Even if, according to the law (loi n° 2016-41 du 26 janvier 2016), information may be shared among professionals, the reality remains ambiguous, as respecting privacy means respecting the worker (Richard, 2020). Professionals are sometimes torn between being able to do their job properly and respecting the worker's privacy.

In the literature, finding such an equilibrium is supposed to follow a need-to-know basis (Grey & Costas, 2016). The need to know supposedly allows the selection of information useful to guarantee the functioning of an organization (Grey & Costas, 2016). Nevertheless, the "need to know" is an ambiguous concept, since it is difficult to determine the necessity to know something before knowing it (Grey & Costas, 2016). In this research, we first explain the advantages and drawbacks of knowing and ignoring. We then show how the professionals deal with breach of knowing versus ignoring equilibrium.

To study confidentiality phenomena, we conducted two case studies (Yin, 1994) of two sheltered workshops. The aim of this method was to favor a contextual approach (Flyvberg, 2006) while allowing the creation of relevant data from a managerial point of view (Leonard-Barton, 1990). The first sheltered workshop was composed of 50 social support professionals and 130 workers, while the second one was composed of 30 social support professionals and 120 workers. To collect the data, we used a non-participating observation approach (80 hours), achieved by conducting 15 interviews with several social support professionals from each sheltered workshop, including psychologists, special educational needs coordinators, a social support manager, workshops monitors, and a head workshop manager. Professionals had to define when to know and when to ignore. Knowing was important, as it allowed workers to remain safe while working. Indeed, professionals must establish compatibility between the disability and the type of professional activity. "Knowing" also allowed the worker to be protected in relation to other workers. Sheltered organizations are places where different types of disabilities interact with each other in common work spaces. Specific attitudes are favored when dealing with certain types of disabilities in social interactions. Further, information was necessary when it protected the professional him- or herself and prevented the quality of the support from deteriorating. Professionals had sometimes to deal with aggressive situations when a worker's treatment was stopped without the knowledge of the management team.

Ignoring information also had advantages. Respect for privacy allowed the worker to be considered as a worker and not as a user of the sheltered workshop system. By recognizing their rights in terms of confidential information, professionals treated workers as equals. Not knowing information about one's disability and about previous behaviors (how the person behaved in another establishment) avoided categorizing the worker, thus creating a Pygmalion effect. Ignorance could then be a vector for a better quality of support.

Nevertheless, professionals also managed imbalances in information management. When information ended up in the wrong zone – that is, when information that was supposed to be given was kept and *vice versa* – professionals implemented techniques to access or ignore it. We identified three parallel strategies of access to information favored by the professionals. The first strategy was "inference learning": the professional used his or her own cognitive mechanisms to obtain information. He used his own experience as a technique to access knowledge. The second strategy implemented was the "relational contracting" strategy. This strategy consisted of obtaining the desired information by establishing relationships of trust with the workers. The third strategy, "derogatory franchising," was a technique that consisted of putting pressure on those who know to obtain an exemption to the principle of confidentiality. However, to counter a situation of non-respect of confidentiality, not taking into account the disclosed information in managerial decisions remained the only strategy available to deal with information leakage.

Therefore, in the sheltered sector, finding an equilibrium to correctly deal with confidentiality management is not an easy task. Professionals define areas of knowledge and ignorance that remain ambiguous to define and regularly face breaches in information management that they try to correct using different strategies.

Contributions

With these three studies, we provide insight into tensions and related managerial practices that are specific to the sheltered sector in France. First, we show how the tensions resulting from the co-existence of different forms of disability are handled with originality by the sheltered workshop professionals. We then underline how managers of the sheltered workshops respond to the tensions generated by the simultaneous pursuit of financial and social aims. We also show how professionals maintained the adequate functioning of the organization while respecting the workers' privacy. Lastly, we demonstrate that managers in adapted enterprises also have to manage tensions linked to the different relational needs of disabled workers.

Existing research has mainly focused on the poor economic viability of sheltered organizations and the subsequent low employment success rate of the individuals who attend them (Cimera, 2011). Scholars highlight that sheltered workshops do not challenge the mainstream organization of work but rather segregate "less able" workers (Bend & Priola, 2021). The inclusion mission of these organizations is so criticized that, even in France, the transition role of sheltered workshops has been amplified by the creation of a specific form of ESATs for transition to the competitive sector (Pierrefeu, 2019). Further, research on adapted enterprises is embryonic as this form of employment, specific to the French system, is in between the sheltered and competitive sectors (Bodon et al., 2016).

Nevertheless, in this chapter, we do not focus on the transitional role of those organizations; we specifically consider that practices developed inside those organizations are worth studying for what they are. Practices in sheltered employment have been emphasized in the literature. Sheltered organizations allow professional skill development (Hsu et al., 2009) according to individuals' capacities. Work is, in itself, a tool of social participation (Hemphill & Kulik, 2017). Workers in these organizations also express feelings of contentment and empowerment (Soeker et al., 2018). By identifying types of HRM practices (Richard et al., 2021), strategies to deal with hybridity (Lemaire, 2020), and strategies to deal with the breach of equilibrium in managing confidential information (Richard, 2020), our findings allow for more conceptualization of practices.

If the managerial practices outlined are interesting, it is nevertheless appropriate to recall the responsibility organizations have toward the people who handle those practices. Notably, these practices emerge because organizations do not respond to the challenges that they could (should) take into consideration. The creativity of managers is certainly exemplary, but it emerges because of excessive constraints on them to deal effectively with tensions. In other words, it is because organizations are not ideal that managers become creative. Since organizational support is limited, organizations function largely due to the dedication of professionals and managers. The latter sometimes go beyond their managerial functions (by taking care of the personal issues of the workers); they push the boundaries of the organization (by integrating external stakeholders) and thus play with the pre-established limits to pursue their mission of integrating disability and accompanying the singularity of the person throughout his or her professional life. This dedication seems virtuous at first sight, but it may also lead individuals to burn out.

In terms of practical implications, to prevent the system from relying solely on individuals, the heads of these organizations must therefore capitalize, share, and learn collectively from these practices and propose adequate and relevant support systems.

Indeed, organizations should capitalize on isolated practices to avoid disparities in treatment between disabled individuals. Organizations should create an internal information feedback system and exchange practices with the outside world. Mentoring, tutoring, and workshops where practices are shared need to be further developed.

Regarding HRM practices, it would be useful to implement training sessions for production managers, the social support team, and other workers to improve the working climate, understanding and specifically address crisis management. Training sessions could take the form of role plays, which could include a crisis simulation.

Concerning the balance between organizational logics, managers are constantly making compromises and thus managing tensions. Within the sheltered workshops, managers should share their difficulties with colleagues to find common solutions, make them known, and thus learn collectively. Organizations can foster this process by proposing free discussion supports around the concrete difficulties to be managed to avoid taboos, to encourage employees to talk about them to solve them together, and to establish sustainable solutions. Sheltered workshops can also offer exchanges with the external environment to provide advice and support to managers.

Finally, regarding confidentiality management, sheltered workshops need, as far as possible, to include workers in decisions that necessitate sharing confidential information. In doing so, they also need to consider the vulnerability of the disabled individual, as disabled workers in those workshops do not always have the capacity to give informed consent. From this perspective, sheltered workshop professionals could raise workers' awareness of the risks of confidential information sharing. They could organize workshops, including playful training tools, to train workers to adopt the right and safe attitude regarding confidential information sharing.

Research Perspectives

While we studied tensions in sheltered workshops from various angles, including diverse theoretical perspectives, research on the sheltered workshop system and internal practices need to be reinforced.

Future studies could complement our work by examining the tensions from the disabled individual perspective. One limitation of our work is that it assessed only the managerial and organizational perspectives, as access to disabled individuals was only realized through non-participant observations. Having a better view of how disabled individuals themselves perceive the tensions and paradoxes that we mentioned would, in accordance with emancipatory disability research (Barnes & Mertens, 2005), bring a deeper comprehension of the phenomena we studied. It would also better highlight how disabled individuals respond to those tensions, emphasizing disabled individuals' agency capacities, as indicated by recent disability research (Richard & Hennekam, 2020). Reactions to tensions could, for example, create an empowering effect.

In parallel, disability researchers call for more research using cross-country comparisons (Beatty et al., 2019). Such a suggestion is particularly relevant when studying the sheltered workshop system. As the European Parliament (2015) pointed out, the development of sheltered workshops is influenced by the legal and cultural environment of each European member state, and different understandings of sheltered workshops co-exist in Europe (European Parliament, 2015). Studying sheltered workshops and their inherent tensions from a cross-country perspective could therefore contribute to a better understanding of existing alternative forms of employment for disabled individuals. Tensions are likely to differ depending on the type of disabilities included in the workshops and the percentage of disabled individuals among the global workforce.

References

Arena, M., Azzone, G., & Bengo, I. (2015). Performance measurement for social enterprises. VOLUNTAS: *International Journal of Voluntary and Nonprofit Organizations*, *26*(2), 649–672. https://doi.org/10.1007/s11266-013-9436-8

Baret, C. (2012). Les établissements et services d'aide par le travail (ESAT) parviennent-ils à concilier objectifs économiques et missions médico-sociales? Une proposition de matrice stratégique [Are the establishments and services for people with disabilities (ESAT) able to reconcile economic and medico-social objectives? A proposed strategic matrix]. *RIMHE: Revue Interdisciplinaire Management, Homme (s) and Entreprise*, *2*(2), 66–82. https://doi-org/10.3917/rimhe.002.0066

Barnes, C., & Mercer, G. (2005). Disability, work, and welfare: Challenging the social exclusion of disabled people. *Work, employment and society*, *19*(3), 527–545. https://doi.org/10.1177/0950017005055669

Battilana, J., Sengul, M., Pache, A.-C., & Model, J. (2015). Harnessing productive tensions in hybrid organizations: The case of work integration social enterprises. *Academy of Management Journal*, *58*(6), 1658–1685. https://doi.org/10.5465/amj.2013.0903

Beatty, J. E., Baldridge, D. C., Boehm, S. A., Kulkarni, M., & Colella, A. J. (s. d.). On the treatment of persons with disabilities in organizations: A review and research agenda. *Human Resource Management*, *0*(0). https://doi.org/10.1002/hrm.21940

Bend, G. L., & Priola, V. (2021). 'There Is nothing wrong with me': The materialisation of disability in sheltered employment. *Work, Employment and Society*, 09500170211034762. https://doi.org/10.1177/09500170211034762

Bodon, Alain, Palach, Jean-Marie, Bazin, Paul et al. 2016. "Les entreprises adaptées, Rapport de l'Inspection des finances et de l'inspection des affaires sociales." Inspection générale des finances et des affaires sociales.

Böhm, S. A., Dwertmann, D. J. G., & Baumgärtner, M. K. (2011). How to deal with disability-related diversity: Opportunities and pitfalls. In T. Geisen & H. G. Harder, *Disability management and workplace integration: international research findings* (pp. 85–98). Gower Publishing, Ltd.

Broderick, A., & Ferri, D. (2019). *International and European disability law and policy*. Cambridge University Press.

Centers for Disease Control and Prevention. (2016). *Mental illness*. https://www.cdc.gov/mental health/basics/mental-illness.htm

Cimera, R. E. (2011). Does being in sheltered workshops improve the employment outcomes of supported employees with intellectual disabilities? *Journal of Vocational Rehabilitation*, *35*(1), 21–27. https://doi.org/10.3233/JVR-2011-0550

Cimera, R. E. (2017). The percentage of supported employees with significant disabilities who would earn more in sheltered workshops. *Research and Practice for Persons with Severe Disabilities*, *42*(2), 108–120. https://doi.org/10.1177/1540796917697448

Combes-Joret, M. (2020). Inclusion des personnes en situation de handicap: Quand le travail n'est pas le problème mais la solution. Les enseignements de 10 ESAT pionniers. @ *GRH*, *4*, 87–113. https://doi-org/10.3917/grh1.204.0087

Corby, S., William, L., & Richard, S. (2019). Combatting disability discrimination: A comparison of France and Great Britain. *European Journal of Industrial Relations*, *25*(1), 41–56. https://doi.org/10.1177/0959680118759169

Costas, J., & Grey, C. (2014). Bringing secrecy into the open: Toward a theorization of the social processes of organizational secrecy. *Organization Studies*, *35*(10), 1423–1447. https://doi.org/10.1177%2F0170840613515470

Demeule, C. (2016). Handicap et coconstruction de l'identité professionnelle: L'entrée en esat [Disability and co-construction of a professional identity: Entering an ESAT}. In: R. Scelles éd. , *Naître, grandir, vieillir avec un handicap: Transitions et remaniements psychiques* [Being born, growing up and growing old with a disability: Transitions and psychological changes] (pp. 219–237). Toulouse: Érès. https://doi-org./10.3917/eres.scell.2016.01.0219

European Parliament. (2015). Reasonable accommodation and sheltered workshops for people with disabilities: Costs and returns of investments. *Study for the EMPL Committee*, January 2015. https://www.europarl.europa.eu/RegData/etudes/STUD/2015/536295/IPOL_STU(2015) 536295_EN.pdf

Flyvbjerg, B. (2006). Five misunderstandings about case-study research. *Qualitative inquiry*, *12*(2), 219–245. http://dx.doi.org/10.1177/1077800405284363

Garrow, E. E., & Hasenfeld, Y. (2014). Social enterprises as an embodiment of a neoliberal welfare logic. *American Behavioral Scientist*, *58*(11), 1475–1493. https://doi.org/10.1177/0002764214534674

Golden-Biddle, K., & Locke, K. (1993). Appealing work: An investigation of how ethnographic texts convince. *Organization Science*, *4*(4), 595–616. https://doi.org/10.1287/orsc.4.4.595

Grey, C., & Costas, J. (2016). *Secrecy at work: The hidden architecture of organizational life.* Stanford University Press.

Grossi, G., Kallio, K.-M., Sargiacomo, M., & Skoog, M. (2019). Accounting, performance management systems and accountability changes in knowledge-intensive public organizations. *Accounting, Auditing and Accountability Journal*. https://doi.org/10.1108/AAAJ-02-2019-3869

Hemphill, E., & Kulik, C. T. (2017). The tyranny of fit: Yet another barrier to mainstream employment for disabled people in sheltered employment. *Social Policy & Administration*, *51*(7), 1119–1134. https://doi.org/10.1111/spol.12220

Hsu, T.-H., Ososkie, J., & Huang, Y.-T. (2009). Challenges in Transition from Sheltered Workshop to Competitive Employment: Perspectives of Taiwan Social Enterprise Transition Specialists. *Journal of Rehabilitation*, *75*(4), 19–26.

Hyndman, N., & McConville, D. (2018). Trust and accountability in UK charities: Exploring the virtuous circle. *The British Accounting Review*, *50*(2), 227–237. https://doi.org/10.1016/j.bar. 2017.09.004

Jagorel, Q., Jacquey, B., & Laurent, A. (2019). *Les établissements et services d'aides par le travail (ESAT), Rapport de l'Inspection des finances et de l'inspection des affaires sociales* [The work-related establishments and support service (ESAT), Report of the Audit of Finance and Social Affairs]. Inspection générale des finances et des affaires sociales.

Konrad, A. M., & Linnehan, F. (1995). Formalized HRM structures: Coordinating equal employment opportunity or concealing organizational practices? *Academy of Management Journal*, *38*(3), 787–820.

Kulkarni, M., & Scullion, H. (2015). Talent management activities of disability training and placement agencies in India. *International Journal of Human Resource Management*, *26*(9), 1169–1181. https://doi.org/10.1080/09585192.2014.934896

Lemaire, C. (2020) Coping with conflictual logics in hybrid organizations, let's play with performance measurement and management systems in a sheltered workshop. *American Accounting Association Annual Meeting (AAA)* (Atlanta, August 2020).

Lengnick-Hall, M. L., Gaunt, P. M., & Kulkarni, M. (2008). Overlooked and underutilized: People with disabilities are an untapped human resource. *Human Resource Management*, *47*(2), 255–273. https://doi.org/10.1002/hrm.20211

Leonard-Barton, D. (1990). A dual methodology for case studies : Synergistic use of a longitudinal single site with replicated multiple sites. *Organization science*, *1*(3), 248–266. https://doi.org/10.1287/orsc.1.3.248

Leslie, L. M. (2019). Diversity Initiative Effectiveness: A Typological Theory of Unintended Consequences. *Academy of Management Review*, *44*(3), 538–563. https://doi.org/10.5465/amr.2017.0087

Modell, S. (2019). Constructing institutional performance: A multi-level framing perspective on performance measurement and management. *Accounting and Business Research*, *49*(4), 428–453. https://doi.org/10.1080/00014788.2018.1507811

Pache, A.-C., & Santos, F. (2013). Embedded in hybrid contexts: How individuals in organizations respond to competing institutional logics. In M. Lounsbury & E. Boxenbaum (Eds.), *Institutional logics in action, Part B* (Vol. 39, pp. 3–35). Emerald Group Publishing Limited. https://doi.org/10.1108/S0733-558X(2013)0039AB014

de Pierrefeu, I. (2019). Les ESAT de transition Messidor: Une activité professionnelle en milieu protégé pour accéder au milieu ordinaire pour les personnes en situation de handicap psychique [The Messidor transitional ESAT: A professional activity in a protected environment to access the mainstream sector for people with mental disabilities.]. *Pratiques en Santé Mentale*, *65*(3), 6–13. https://doi.org/10.3917/psm.193.0006

Richard, S. (2020). Entre contrainte managériale et opportunité de développement du travailleur: l'application du "besoin de savoir" dans le secteur protégé [Between managerial constraints and opportunities for worker development: the application of the "need to know" in the protected sector]. *Annales des Mines – Gérer et Comprendre*, *140*(2), 30–40. https://doi-org/10.3917/geco1.140.0030

Richard, S., & Hennekam, S. (2020). When can a disability quota system empower disabled individuals in the workplace? The case of France. *Work, Employment and Society*. https://doi-org.scd-rproxy.u-strasbg.fr/10.1177/0950017020946672

Richard, S., Lemaire, C., & Church-Morel, A. (2021). Beyond identity consciousness: Human resource management practices and mental health conditions in sheltered workshops. *The International Journal of Human Resource Management*, *32*(15), 3218–3243. https://doi.org/10.1080/09585192.2021.1893787

Robert Dico en ligne. https://dictionnaire.lerobert.com/definition/tension

Siperstein, G. N., Heyman, M., & Stokes, J. E. (2014). Pathways to employment: A national survey of adults with intellectual disabilities. *Journal of Vocational Rehabilitation*, *41*(3), 165–178. https://doi.org/10.3233/JVR-140711

Smith, W. K., & Lewis, M. W. (2011). Toward a theory of paradox: A dynamic equilibrium model of organizing. *Academy of management Review*, *36*(2), 381–403. https://doi.org/10.5465/amr.2009.0223

Soeker, M. S., De Jongh, J. C., Diedericks, A., Matthys, K., Swart, N., & van der Pol, P. (2018). The experiences and perceptions of persons with disabilities regarding work skills development in sheltered and protective workshops. *Work*, *59*(2), 303–314. https://doi.org/10.3233/WOR-172674

Tajfel, H. (1981). *Human groups and social categories: Studies in social psychology*. Cambridge University Press.

van der Torre, L., & Fenger, M. (2014). Policy innovations for including disabled people in the labour market: A study of innovative practices of Dutch sheltered work companies. *International Social Security Review, 67*(2), 67–84. https://doi.org/10.1111/issr.12038

Vidal-Gomel, C., Rachedi, Y., Bonnemain, A., & Gébaï, D. (2012). *Concevoir des environnements capacitants en atelier de travail protégé*. [Designing Enabling Environments in a Protected Workshop.] *67*(1), 122–146. https://doi.org/10.7202/1008198ar

Yin, R. K. (1994). Case Study Research Design and Methods: Applied Social Research and Methods Series. Second edn. Thousand Oaks, CA: Sage Publications Inc.

Part 5: **Expanding Disability Definitions**

Maria H. Khan, Muhammad Ali, Mirit K. Grabarski,
and Katherine Moore

16 Reframing Management of Organisational Neurodiversity in Australia: A Contextual Approach

Abstract: Neurodiversity is an umbrella term, encompassing a broad and non-exhaustive range of neurological conditions including behavioral and intellectual conditions such as autism and attention-deficit/hyperactivity disorder. Neurodiversity at work is an emerging field; little is known about how to effectively manage organisational neurodiversity for sustainable employment of neurodiverse individuals. This knowledge is especially important in the wake of widespread stereotypes and perceived challenges of working with neurodiverse workers, such as communication difficulties and costs of workplace accommodations. This chapter presents a contextual human resource management of neurodiversity to transform the associated challenges into opportunities. A review of existing empirical research and lived experiences of neurodiverse workers have identified stigma and discrimination resulting from disclosure and requests for workplace accommodations as key impediments to their sustainable employment, exacerbated by workplace communication challenges. HR-driven practices in organisations can address the challenges experienced by neurodiverse employees and reframe them as opportunities. These proposed HR solutions encompass reducing bias and discrimination in organisational practices, extending the benefits of workplace accommodations to all employees, creating safe communication spaces, and improving communication practices. The resultant inclusive workplaces will help achieve positive employee and organisational outcomes.

Keywords: neurodiversity, organisational context, barriers to employment, sustainable employment, organisational management

Introduction

Neurodiversity is an evolving umbrella term, encompassing a broad and non-exhaustive range of neurological conditions that have historically been viewed as atypical (Armstrong, 2015; Krezminska et al., 2019). Neurodiversity has commonly

Maria H. Khan, Muhammad Ali, and Katherine Moore, Queensland University of Technology,
Australia
Mirit K. Grabarski, Lakehead University, Canada

https://doi.org/10.1515/9783110743647-017

been associated with variations in neurocognitive processes among individuals who reflect characteristics of developmental conditions, such as autism spectrum disorder (ASD) or attention-deficit/hyperactivity disorder (ADHD), and learning/applied conditions, such as dyslexia, and developmental coordination disorder (DCD) or dyspraxia (Sumner & Brown, 2015). Globally, 15–20% of the world's population is speculated to be neurodiverse (Moeller, Ott, & Russo, 2021), yet the employment participation rate for neurodiverse adults of working age remains low. In Australia, neurodiverse individuals comprise about a quarter of those reported with disability conditions (23.3%), but experience unemployment at a rate up to 3 times more than people with physical/other disabilities, and almost six times the rate of people without disability (Australian Bureau of Statistics, 2019). Emerging literature is beginning to focus on the strengths of neurodiversity related to higher order cognitive functioning, such as creativity and comprehension, that can be beneficial to organisations (Armstrong, 2015; Hurley-Hanson, Giannantonio & Griffiths, 2020; Kirby & Smith, 2021). However, prior research has traditionally focused on how neurodiversity in individuals, particularly in the areas of communication, executive functioning, attention regulation, working memory, and time management, *impede* their ability to gain and sustain employment (Waisman-Nitzan, Gal, & Schreuer, 2019). In fact, Richards (2012) suggests that critical human resources (HR) practices, such as recruitment and selection, are designed with neurotypical employees in mind and are likely to exclude neurodiverse individuals from employment.

Moreover, as neurodiversity usually encompasses invisible conditions, neurodiverse workers report a reluctance to disclose their conditions to management and co-workers due to the fear that disclosure may lead to stereotyping (Hurley-Hanson et al., 2020; Priscott & Allen, 2021) and affect their health and wellbeing, social relationships, and work performance (Santuzzi, Waltz, Finkelstein, & Rupp, 2014). This also impacts the decision to ask for reasonable work accommodations, a mechanism that can be effective in managing neurodiverse employees and reducing intentions to leave (Johnson, Ennis-Cole, & Bonhamgregory, 2020, Waisman-Nitzan et al., 2019). Research on neurodiversity in organisations suggests that perceptions of challenges of working with neurodiverse workers center around expectations of high costs, perceived fairness of workplace accommodations, communication difficulties, and low productivity, and can impede long-term employment for neurodiverse individuals (Colella, 2001; Patton, 2019; Waisman-Nitzan et al., 2019). Organisational contextual factors, such as level of understanding of neurodiversity, organisational practices, workplace culture, knowledge and awareness about neurological conditions, nature of work, access to experts, and training on neurodiversity and leadership, impact effective management of organisational neurodiversity.

This chapter highlights a contextual understanding of management of neurodiversity to transform the associated challenges into opportunities for sustainable employment. We begin with a general understanding of neurodiversity, followed by an overview of a context-specific understanding of neurodiversity in organisations and the key structural and systemic challenges faced by neurodiverse workers. We then discuss how HR practices can be employed to reframe these challenges as opportunities for sustainable employment, providing actionable solutions to create socially just and sustainable opportunities for neurodiverse workers. Finally, we suggest directions for future research.

Neurodiversity

Neurodiversity is an umbrella term coined by the Australian sociologist Judy Singer. It refers to a range of neurological conditions people are born with which are connected to the functioning of the brain. Neurodiversity acknowledges that the brain structure and functioning can be different across individuals, with no person superior or inferior to others (Armstrong, 2015; Dalton, 2013). These neurological conditions reflect various biological and genetic variations (Kirby & Smith, 2021) and include behavioral conditions (e.g., autistic spectrum disorder, attention-deficit/hyperactivity disorder, and Tourette's Syndrome) and learning/applied conditions (e.g., dyslexia, dyspraxia, dyscalculia, and dysgraphia) (Bewley & George, 2016). People with one or more of these conditions can be termed neurodivergent or neurodiverse, while others are generally referred to as neurotypical (Kirby & Smith, 2021).

It is important to understand how the literature distinguishes mental illness from neurodiverse conditions. Mental illness includes several psychological conditions, such as anxiety, depression, and obsessive-compulsive disorder, that can originate from genes or social/psychological incidents or experiences, and that can be medically treated at least to some extent (McManus, 2011). On the other hand, neurodiversity is about how the brain is wired differently for each individual who require adjustments to become effective participants in neurotypical settings (Dalton, 2013). Mental illnesses are often described as symptoms, while neurodiversity forms are described as traits and characteristics (McManus, 2011). There is a growing understanding that unlike mental illnesses which negatively affect social lives and overall wellbeing and therefore require medical and/or behavioral treatments, neurodiversity refers to "differences" that can be managed through social and workplace accommodations. Moreover, social scientists and practitioners have started advocating positive characteristics of neurological conditions, such creativity and attention to details (Armstrong, 2015; Kirby & Smith, 2021). Next, we provide a brief description of the commonly known forms of neurodiversity.

Autistic Spectrum Disorder (ASD). ASD is an umbrella term used for conditions including autism, Asperger syndrome, and pervasive developmental disorder. It is a set of complex conditions pertaining to challenges associated with social communication, repetitive behaviors, and restrictive movements. The signs include a lack of eye contact, limited facial expressions, repetition of words, obsessive interests, and a lack of time management. People with ASD are often creative, pay attention to details, focus on their task, and prefer visual aids (Armstrong, 2015; Barnhart, 2015).

Attention-Deficit/Hyperactivity Disorder (ADHD). This neurodiversity form pertains to the executive function of the brain. People with ADHD may struggle with focusing on one task and the organising function of their brain. They exhibit excessive movements known as hyperactivity and hasty movements known as impulsivity. People with ADHD do not pay attention to details; however, they can excel in problem-solving, creative thinking, and multi-tasking (Dalton, 2013).

Tourette's Syndrome. The French neurologist Georges Gilles de la Tourette described this form of neurodiversity in 1885. It refers to spontaneous, repetitive movements and sounds displayed by individuals (Martino & Leckman, 2013). These movements can be classified as simple motor tics (e.g., repeatedly blinking the eyes or twitching the nose) or complex motor tics (e.g., jumping or throwing). Similarly, simple phonic tics include clearing throat or sniffing and complex phonic tics include echoing others or repeating oneself. People with Tourette's Syndrome often exhibit high energy levels, good verbal skills, and creative quick thinking (Averns et al., 2012).

Dyslexia. Originating from the English word *dys* (meaning difficult) and Greek word *lexia* (meaning speech), it refers to struggling with speaking, reading, and/or writing (Reid, 2011). Dyslexic people can have difficulty with certain letters, words, and forming sentences, but may have exceptional abilities in visual processing and creative thinking (Armstrong, 2015).

Dyspraxia. Originating from the Greek word *duspraxis* which means difficulty in doing (Grant & French, 2017). Dyspraxia is also known as developmental coordination disorder, and relates to motor skills, coordination of movement, and balance and sense of direction. The motor skills include gross motor skills (e.g., jumping and running) and fine motor skills (e.g., writing and cutting out shapes) as well as coordination skills that can affect tasks such as driving that require hand-eye coordination. People with dyspraxia can also struggle with planning and organising thoughts and tasks, however, the condition is not related to intelligence or higher cognitive functioning.

Dyscalculia and Dysgraphia. Dyscalculia's literally means "not so good at counting". People with this form of neurodiversity struggle with numbers and learning mathematics (Grant & French, 2017). Dysgraphia relates to challenge of written expression. It can affect the writing speed due to difficulty in forming letters (McBride, 2019). People with dysgraphia face difficulties with spellings (e.g., omit vowels and consonants sounds) and written expressions (e.g., grammar and punctuation errors, lack of clarity), but it does not relate to intelligence or higher cognitive functioning.

Neurodiverse individuals often report more than one neurodiverse condition such as dyslexia and dyspraxia or ADHD and dyslexia.

Context-Specific Understanding of Neurodiversity in the Workplace

Neurodiversity as a concept aligns with the social model of disability, which was proposed as an instrument to examine the disabling tendencies of society and to inform the adoption of inclusionary practices for people with disabilities (Barnes, 2000; Galvin, 2004). This holistic model counters the mindset that disability in itself is an impediment (medical model) and attends to the interrelationship between the barriers to social and economic inclusion across all areas of life, created by disabling attitudes and environments (Terzi, 2004). The underlying premise of the social model is the socially constructed attitudes and meanings attached to disability within a given context that creates barriers for inclusion rather than the actual impairment (Galvin, 2004; Gannon & Nolan, 2007). Simply put, individuals with differences are confronted with barriers within their environments, limiting their social and economic inclusion within a society (Barnes, 2000). This view has influenced legislation to eradicate physical and infrastructural barriers in society, which extends to organisational environments to make workplaces more inclusive for employees with disabilities. Neurological conditions, however, are often invisible, difficult to detect, and seldom understood by neurotypical individuals (Santuzzi et al., 2014). Therefore, it is important to understand how the characteristics of neurodiversity interact with contextual and structural elements of employing organisations. Context-specific organisational aspects include factors such as organisational practices, workplace culture, knowledge and awareness about neurological conditions, nature of work, access to experts, and training on neurodiversity and leadership.

A number of context-specific barriers have been identified in the existing literature by considering the experience of neurodiverse workers, their specific neurological conditions, and the organisations that seek to hire them. We provide an overview of the most commonly cited challenges impeding employment of neurodiverse workers that encompass a broad range of neurological conditions but may vary in how they operate within diverse organisational contexts. These are discussed in the next section.

Challenges for Neurodiverse Employees

Neurodiversity in the workplace is a nascent topic, with very limited empirical evidence available on managing organisational neurodiversity. A review of existing empirical research and lived experiences of neurodiverse workers has identified stigma and discrimination resulting from disclosure and requests for and provision of workplace accommodations as key impediments to sustainable employment for neurodiverse workers. The most unique challenge for the sustainability of a neurodiverse workforce within the organisational context is workplace communication which amplifies and exacerbates other factors (Annabi & Locke, 2019; Macdonald & Cosgrove, 2019; Morris, Begel & Wiedermann, 2015; Patton, 2019).

Disclosure by Neurodiverse Workers

The decision to disclose one's disability is a dilemma for many individuals, especially those with invisible neurodiverse conditions. Disclosure, which is crucial at an early stage for neurodiverse job seekers in order to demonstrate their full potential, often leads to their exclusion, discrimination, and feeling stigmatised (Khayatazadeh-Mahani et al., 2020). Empirical studies on employment experiences of workers with a range of neurological conditions indicate that they are reluctant to disclose their neurodiversity at the outset and often do so after starting a job (Hurley-Hanson et al., 2020; Romualdez et al., 2021). Sanderson (2011) highlights the plight of dyslexic workers who conceal their conditions due to a general lack of understanding exhibited by managers and colleagues. However, some neurological conditions, such as autism or Tourette's Syndrome, are characterised by specific reactions or behaviours. Thus, workers often feel the need to disclose to explain adverse events or lack of socially-accepted behaviours (Tomczak, 2021). In Australia, there is no legal obligation for employees to disclose disability unless it restricts them from performing the inherent requirements of the job (Ricci, 2007). Most often, the extent to which neurodiverse workers are comfortable and willing to disclose their conditions and seek accommodations depends on the organisational culture, attitude of managers and co-workers, and availability or accessibility of support (Sanderson, 2011).

From an organisational standpoint, early disclosure of neurodiversity is important. Managers and supervisors of neurodiverse workers indicate that prior knowledge of their needs could enable them to better understand their requirements for accommodations and even mitigate any discriminatory practices (Annabi & Locke, 2019; Carrero, Krzeminska, & Härtel, 2019). According to the *Disability Discrimination Act 1992,* in Australia, employers cannot discriminate against disabled employees, and upon disclosure, employers may only seek further information for legitimate purposes related to the performance of the job. Employers are further obligated to respect and protect sensitive information relating to their employees (Australian Network on Disability, 2014; Ricci, 2007). Moreover, while disclosure provides critical knowledge, organisational leadership needs to provide complementary support and create a positive organisational culture including improved employment experiences for neurodiverse workers, without which disclosure alone will not be effective (Meacham et al., 2019; 2017; Meltzer et al., 2020; Parr, Hunter, & Ligon, 2013).

Requesting Accommodations

In addition to the implications arising from disclosure, a prominent challenge faced by neurodiverse workers is the lack of mechanisms and structural support in organisations to request accommodations. Accommodations include a range of individualised considerations, reasonable adjustments or support activities that can facilitate neurodiverse workers' job performance (Carrero et al., 2019; Richards et al., 2019), such as modifications to job roles and/or physical environment and providing assistive technologies (Schreuer & Dorot, 2017; Waisman-Nitzan et al., 2019). For example, providing headphones to autistic employees can help address auditory overstimulation, and dyslexic workers can benefit from modifying font size and colour in documents and slides (Austin & Pisano, 2017; Bewley & George, 2016). Workers with sensory sensitivity will benefit from having a dedicated workspace instead of open plan offices; workers with ADHD may perform better if meetings are audio-recorded and having a treadmill or a standing desk (Morris et al., 2015). Modifications to job roles may include additional and flexible time to complete tasks for workers with learning disabilities, or co-workers providing additional clarifications regarding work requirements, support and mentorship (Wille & Sajous-Brady, 2018).

While the accommodations are often easily implemented for neurodiverse workers, the challenges associated with requesting them go hand-in-hand with the hesitation to disclose neurodiversity due to fear of being stigmatised and perceived negatively. This is further exacerbated by the organisational context, as most organisations lack policies on disability and specific procedures to request accommodations (Sanderson, 2011). Although legislative obligations and anti-discrimination laws require organisations to support and facilitate disabled workers, these often result in surface-level efforts (Sanderson, 2011). For example, in Australia, the *Disability Discrimination Act 1992* makes it obligatory for employers to prevent indirect discrimination against disabled workers but does not include the term "reasonable adjustments" that could help specify the requirements (Australian Network on Disability, 2021; Mason, 2007). In order to gain access to accommodations, neurodiverse workers may have to undergo long and tedious processes seeking permissions from multiple supervisory levels and HR (Romualdez et al., 2021; Williams & Koenig, 2014). A lack of understanding of the importance of accommodations for neurodiverse workers and misconceptions of high costs of the requested changes (Wille & Sajous-Brady, 2018) have a spillover effect on colleagues and co-workers who perceive accommodations as unfair or preferential treatment (Colella, 2001; Kirby & Gibbon, 2018). Altogether, systemic challenges such as a lack of procedures, resistance from co-workers and team members, and perceptions of negative attitudes of managers and supervisors (Annabi & Locke, 2019; Meacham et al., 2017) affect the extent to which neurodiverse workers feel comfortable disclosing neurodiversity and requesting accommodations (Remington & Pellicano, 2019; Sumner & Brown, 2015).

Workplace Communication

While disclosure and accommodations create barriers to different types of diverse employees, a unique factor in managing organisational neurodiversity is communication. Communication in general is a complex organisational process (Fulk & Boyd, 1991) which is already ridden with innate challenges and barriers. The classic communication model (Shannon & Weaver, 1949) describes this process as based on sending and receiving encoded information between two or more entities. During the exchange, information needs to be coded, sent, received and decoded, where each of these steps does not always lead to intended consequences. For example, there may be difficulties with encoding information by the sender, choosing an ineffective channel for communications, losing or distorting information, difficulties with receiving the information and/or decoding it, and more (Carlson & Zmud, 1999). Furthermore, the communication process happens in different sub-systems, including formal and informal networks (Fulk & Boyd, 1991). While these complexities are challenging for all employees, they can be amplified when managing neurodiverse workers whose condition affects their ability to participate in different stages of the process as they experience differences in information processing, sensory perceptions, and social interactions (Ortiz, 2020).

In particular, neurological conditions such as autism, Tourette's Syndrome or ADHD make it difficult for workers to comprehend ambiguous instructions and engage with team meeting dynamics (Wille & Sajous-Brady, 2018; Johnson & Joshi, 2016). In addition, while neurodiverse workers are often high functioning in many cognitive areas and creative, they struggle to articulate their ideas and work outcomes in oral and formal presentations, leading to them being dismissed or undervalued by peers and supervisors (Meltzer et al., 2020; Tomczak, 2021). While dyslexia and/or dysgraphia by definition can inhibit encoding (writing) and decoding (reading) information, the most difficult aspect of workplace communication for employees with autism is social or interpersonal (McKnight-Lizotte, 2018). Because their condition is directly related to social communication, they often misinterpret and misunderstand the nuances in emotions in conversations which limits their ability to accurately decode messages (Morris et al., 2015). Neurodiverse workers often do not conform to social interaction norms, such as not making eye contact or preferring isolation (Morris et al., 2015), and they may have difficulties controlling their temper (Richards, 2012). Difficulties with social interactions can be misunderstood by colleagues and perceived as rude or deliberately unpleasant, particularly where they are unaware of or unfamiliar with neurological conditions (Ortiz, 2020; Richards, 2012; Romualdez et al., 2021). All of the above inhibits the development of trust and understanding between neurodiverse workers and their colleagues (Richards et al. 2019), such that neurodiverse workers experience even more difficulties in terms of inclusion and socialisation. Finally, while neurodiverse employees may experience workplace bullying (Beardon & Edmonds, 2007), they may not recognise it as such and therefore not report it (McKnight-Lizotte, 2018). It is therefore important to address these issues in organisations.

Communication in organisations is a key mechanism for coordination and organisational functioning. It is managed using formal elements such as written policies and procedures as well as informal practices through daily supervision, conversations, and leadership (Schreuer & Dorot, 2017; Waisman-Nitzan et al., 2019, Parr et al., 2013). For example, in Australia, the *Disability Discriminiation Act 1992* created legislative obligations to comply, making it unlawful to discriminate against people with disabilities and promoting equal access and equal employment opportunities (Australian Network on Disability, 2021; Ricci, 2007). In practice, these general policies only lead to surface-level compliance, whereas the extent to which they are indeed inclusive is determined by informal communication structures and practices (Sanderson, 2011; Schreuer & Dorot 2017). In the case of neurodiversity, a lack of knowledge of the conditions and time constraints limit the ability to communicate and increase awareness about neurodiverse workers (Kirby & Gibbon, 2018; Macdonald & Cosgrove, 2019). While allowing and encouraging formal and informal communication between neurodiverse employees and their colleagues can improve their integration in the workplace (Riches & Green, 2003), this is rarely done in practice. This lack of knowledge about neurodiversity leads to different negative reactions from discomfort and avoidance (Pouliot et al., 2017) to resistant behaviours and negative attitudes, which in turn further undermine the integration and inclusion of the neurodiverse workers (Meacham et al., 2019; Richards, 2012).

Figure 16.1 summarises the key challenges experienced in employment by neurodiverse workers that can become barriers to sustainable employment depending on the organisational context.

Figure 16.1: Challenges for Neurodiverse Workers.

The next section explores how HR management and practices can reframe these challenges to become opportunities for successful integration of neurodiverse workers and mechanisms for sustainable employment outcomes.

HR Solutions to Challenges Faced by Neurodiverse Employees

The extent to which these identified challenges become barriers to sustainable employment for neurodiverse workers is influenced by how these challenges are perceived and managed within the organisational context. HR-driven practices in organisations can be mobilised to provide solutions to the challenges experienced by neurodiverse employees and reframe them as opportunities for sustainable employment (Bhattacharya, Gibson, & Doty, 2005). The HR solutions encompass reducing bias and discrimination in HR practices, extending the benefits of workplace accommodations to all employees, creating safe and accessible communication spaces, and improving organisational communication practices. These solutions require introducing mechanisms for inclusivity in traditional HR functional practices such as recruitment and selection, performance management, and training and development (see Table 16.1).

Reducing Bias and Discrimination in HR Practices

In order to transform disclosure-related challenges into opportunities for sustainable employment for neurodiverse workers, HR-driven solutions need to proactively reduce bias and discrimination embedded within organisational practices.

Austin and Pisano (2017) highlight that characteristics of neurodiverse employees are screened out of organisations as they do not conform to normative perceptions of an *ideal employee*. For example, neurodiverse employees may exhibit difficulties with interpersonal and communication skills, the ability to work in teams and the need for reasonable adjustments to perform work (Krezminska et al., 2019). Moreover, stereotyping and a lack of knowledge and understanding of neurological conditions drive interactions, decisions and management of neurodiverse employees (Kirby & Gibbon 2018; Annabi & Locke, 2019). Developing awareness and sensitivity towards neurological conditions can help address unconscious bias and misconceptions about competence, skills and behaviours of neurodiverse workers (Morris et al., 2015; Khan et al., 2021). For example, bias and indirect discrimination against neurodiverse workers can manifest in performance evaluations, where generic indicators such as social skills and interpersonal relationships are assessed rather than actual performance of work (Metlzer et al., 2020). Rao and Polepeddi (2019) suggest that unconscious bias and discriminatory practices can only be reduced when neurodiversity-specific inclusivity becomes a strategic objective, communicated by organisational leadership. HR-driven solutions to drive inclusivity include:

– Engaging specialists and experts on neurodiversity to develop organisational education and awareness programmes.
– Proactively promoting culture of respect, compassion and collaboration for all workers. Improving recognition of contribution from neurodiverse workers.
– Management leading diversity initiatives, including mentorship, coaching, and developing team-based support circles to foster authentic social relationships. Organisational leadership should exhibit inclusive behaviours towards neurodiverse workers to set the tone of workplace culture.

Extending the Benefits of Workplace Accommodations to All Employees

Workplace accommodations can be reframed as opportunities for sustainable employment for neurodiverse workers by addressing the misconceptions of high costs and expenses associated with accommodations as well as mitigating negative attitudes and perceptions of preferential treatment among co-workers (Meacham et al., 2017; Annabi & Locke, 2019).

Awareness training on the need for reasonable adjustments and for understanding how they facilitate the performance of work for neurodiverse employees can help foster understanding, empathy, and respect among co-workers (Remington & Pellicano, 2019; Wille & Sajous-Brady, 2018). HR-driven practices can promote broader benefits of workplace accommodations and reasonable adjustments for all diverse groups, including neurotypical employees. For example, assistive functionality in mainstream technologies, such as grammar and spell-checking software, diverse fonts and readability options, may facilitate dyslexic workers (Sanderson, 2011), but can also benefit employees from other diverse groups, such as employees from non-English-speaking backgrounds and employees with vision impairments. Similarly, diverse methods of content delivery in training sessions, in-person meetings to discuss performance, mentoring and flexible work practices (Australian Network on Disability, 2021; Khan et al., 2021) can also positively impact workers from diverse age groups and educational backgrounds and those with caring responsibilities. The following HR-driven initiatives for accommodations being offered to all employees without the need for disclosure can mitigate any associated stigma and help create an inclusive environment:

– Offering flexibility in working hours, work tasks and location to all employees.
– Considering all types of learning and communication preferences in formal organisational communications and developing training content. Proactive inclusion of options to assist dyslexic and autistic workers.

- Leveraging availability of reasonable adjustments to encompass broader diverse groups and improve productivity.

Creating Safe and Accessible Communication Spaces

Ineffective workplace communication practices exacerbate the challenges associated with disclosure and workplace accommodations and are arguably at the heart of impeding sustainable employment for neurodiverse workers. HR-driven solutions to address ineffective workplace communication should focus on modifying formal policies to signal inclusivity, transforming communication structures to be more accessible, and developing informal practices that encourage collaboration and authentic relationships among employees (Bewley & George, 2016). When neurodiverse workers feel respected as individuals and are able to openly and directly address concerns with supervisors and co-workers without fear of being perceived as incompetent, they will likely experience less workplace stress and achieve positive performance reviews (Brinzea, 2019). Moreover, co-workers and other employees can benefit from HR practices to create safe communication spaces, particularly where they feel overwhelmed or under pressure to provide additional support to their colleagues such as through mentoring, coaching or buddy systems (Bewley & George, 2016; Austin & Pisano, 2017). This can be achieved through offering the following HR-driven practices:
- Physical spaces to help manage stress, such as quiet rooms and yoga activities, to address the needs of neurodiverse workers with auditory or sensory sensitivities. These can also be utilised by neurotypical workers to manage stress.
- Cognitive behavioural therapy to signal open and stigma free access to resources.
- Flexible working practices to meet the individualised needs of workers.
- Reasonable adjustments to the requirements of the work where the nature of work is not adversely affected.

Improving Organistional Communication Practices

Organisational policies, formal instructions, and processes should be revised to convey inclusivity, for example instead of requiring certain workers to disclose conditions, offering an opportunity to all employees to share information to facilitate the performance of work (Bewley & George, 2016; Morris et al., 2015). Similarly, organisational practices, such as performance reviews, can be adjusted to mitigate communication challenges such as through ongoing monitoring and frequent private meetings rather than formal complicated processes (Kirby & Gibbon, 2018; Khan et al., 2021). Carrero et al.'s (2019) case study of recruitment and selection of autistic workers by DXC Technology in Australia illustrates the role of informal communication practices of hiring managers. They included attending to the body language and behaviours of applicants and then making real-time modifications in their interactions with applicants to be more empathic and responsive and having flexible options to deliver and obtain content.

Some specific HR-driven initiatives to improve formal and informal communication practices, with a specific focus on neurodiverse workers include:

– Discussing and addressing work related concerns and individualised considerations for neurodiverse workers as well as co-workers
– Providing awareness and training for all employees about neurodiversity and types of reasonable adjustments including associated benefits and outcomes
– Adopting clear, unambiguous, and inclusive language in formal and informal communication

Table 16.1 provides illustrative examples of how organisational HR practices can be reframed as inclusive and accessible mechanisms for sustainable employment.

Table 16.1: Reframing Management of Organisational Neurodiversity.

HR Practice	Reducing Bias and Discrimination	Extending Benefits of Workplace Accommodations	Improving Communication Practices
Recruitment and Selection	*Removing psychometric testing, open-ended hypothetical questions in application and interviews*	*Allowing reasonable adjustments that do not disadvantage other applicants such as extra time or translation services*	*Embedding requests for adjustments and support in application process, enabling opportunities to discuss requirements*
	Impact on Managing Neurodiversity: *Improve recruitment outcomes for applicants with autism, ADHD or Tourette's Syndrome*	**Impact on Managing Neurodiversity:** *Assist neurodiverse applicants with dyslexia or other conditions in being considered fairly*	**Impact on Managing Neurodiversity:** *Improve recruitment and selection experience by making reasonable adjustments to process to address individualised needs, e.g., altering lighting and sound in physical environment for autistic applicants*

Table 16.1 (continued)

HR Practice	Reducing Bias and Discrimination	Extending Benefits of Workplace Accommodations	Improving Communication Practices
Performance Management	*Promoting frequent check-ins, frequent monitoring of work performance by direct supervisors*	*Offering flexible working practices to foster compassion, empathy and trust and facilitate performance of work*	*Leadership commitment to creating a supportive work environment, recognising and adapting to individualised needs*
	Impact on Managing Neurodiversity: *Opportunities for recognition of individual performance of neurodiverse workers and appropriate medium to discuss improvement, e.g., autistic workers could benefit from real-time feedback on tasks*	**Impact on Managing Neurodiversity:** *Improve contribution from neurodiverse workers by addressing individualised needs, e.g., workers with ADHD who do not excel in regimented work routines*	**Impact on Managing Neurodiversity:** *Signal inclusivity by implementing initiatives to attract a neurodiverse workforce, working with specialists and experts to tailor HR practices to be more neurodiversity friendly, e.g., recruitment drives to attract neurodiverse workers or crafting jobs to benefit both the organisation and neurodiverse worker*
Training and Development	*Catering to diverse range of learning and communication preferences*	*Facilitate access to trainings and skills development sessions*	*Providing clear information and instructions in advance, utilising assistive technologies and appropriate visual aids*
	Impact on Managing Neurodiversity: *Proactive efforts to embed easy readability, accessibility software, clear language, e.g., to facilitate dyslexic or autistic workers*	**Impact on Managing Neurodiversity:** *Work with neurodiversity experts and specialists develop performance improvement plans, e.g., skills development of neurodiverse workers*	**Impact on Managing Neurodiversity:** *Work with neurodiversity experts and specialists to make modifications to existing training sessions and develop new sessions, e.g., impact of group or team workshops on autistic workers*

Directions for Future Research

While in line with the movement toward diversity and inclusion, companies demonstrate interest in employing neurodiverse individuals, academic research lags behind. What we currently know about attracting and integrating neurodiverse workers is published mostly in disability and rehabilitation journals, or in practitioner-oriented literature. In order to improve our understanding of the organisational aspects of working with neurodiverse employees, there is a need to adopt a holistic and social approach (Macdonald & Cosgrove, 2019) in undertaking future research, particularly in management studies. Although it is important to investigate the neurodiverse employees' and their supervisors' perspectives on barriers and ways to overcome them, a broader perspective should include co-workers and other organisational stakeholders (Bewley & George, 2016; Krzeminska et al., 2019; Richards, 2012). Within the organisation, it is especially important to consider the HR professionals who are in charge of recruitment and selection but also training managers and supervisors (Hagner & Kooney, 2005; Johnson et al., 2020). Outside of the organisation it would be of value to understand the customers' and even the competitors' reactions to neurodiversity initiatives (Tomczak, 2021). Most importantly, because the barriers to integration of neurodiverse employees are deeply linked with organisational culture, studying the overall organisational context and leadership is of key importance (Meacham et al., 2017; Patton, 2019). Therefore, a multilevel approach that considers both the high-level contextual variables and immediate circles of contact is needed to see a full picture of employing neurodiverse workers and to help organisations achieve their full potential. The insights gained from this line of inquiry will inform future work on inclusion of neurodiverse workers.

Chapter Summary

The purpose of this chapter was to provide an understanding of the contextual factors that may influence the extent to which neurodiverse workers experience sustainable employment. Drawing insights from existing studies on neurodiversity in the workplace, three key challenges experienced by neurodiverse workers were identified as disclosure, request for accommodations and workplace communication. Contextual factors within organisations, such as the understanding of neurodiversity, organisational practices, workplace culture, knowledge and awareness about neurological conditions, nature of work, access to experts, and training on neurodiversity and leadership, can emerge as barriers to sustainable employment for neurodiverse workers. We highlight how reframing HR practices to incorporate inclusive and accessible mechanisms reduce bias and discrimination, extend benefits associated with workplace accommodations, and create safe and accessible communication spaces. This reframing of HR practices can not only help transform these challenges into opportunities for managing organisational neurodiversity, it can also create an inclusive workplace that will foster high performance and satisfaction leading to sustainable employment outcomes.

References

Annabi, H., & Locke, J. (2019). A theoretical framework for investigating the context for creating employment success in information technology for individuals with autism. *Journal of Management and Organization*, 25(4),499–515. doi:http://dx.doi.org/10.1017/jmo.2018.79

Armstrong, T. (2015). The myth of the normal brain: Embracing neurodiversity. *AMA journal of ethics*, *17*(4), 348–352.

Austin, R.D & Pisano, G.P. (2017). Neurodiversity as a competitive advantage. *Harvard Business Review*, *95*, 96–103.

Australian Bureau of Statistics (2019). *Disability, ageing and carers, Australia: Summary of findings*. Retrieved from https://www.abs.gov.au/statistics/health/disability/disability-ageing-and-carers-australia-summary-findings/latest-release (accessed 02 Jan 2022)

Australian Network on Disability (2014) *Disclosure of disability – Join the discussion*. Retrieved from https://www.and.org.au/news.php/231/disclosure-of-disability-join-the-discussion

Australian Network on Disability (2021) *Workplace adjustments*. Retrieved from https://www.and.org.au/pages/workplace-adjustments.html

Averns, D., Jakubec, S. L., Thomas, R., & Link, A. (2012). Working with uniqueness: optimizing vocational strengths for people with Tourette syndrome and co-morbidities. *Procedia-Social and Behavioral Sciences*, *47*, 1426–1435.

Barnes, C. (2000). A working social model? Disability, work and disability politics in the 21st century. *Critical Social Policy*, *20*(4), 441–457. doi: 10.1177/026101830002000402

Barnhart, G. (2015). Neurodiversity: Celebrating the unique abilities of persons with autism. *Journal of Intellectual Disability Research*, 59–73.

Beardon, L. and Edmonds, G. (2007), *Aspect consultancy report: a national report on the needs of adults with Asperger syndrome*, Sheffield: The Autism Centre, Sheffield Hallam University.

Bewley, H., & George, A. (2016). *Neurodiversity at work*. National Institute of Social and Economic Research.

Bhattacharya, M., Gibson, D. E., & Doty, D. H. (2005). The effects of flexibility in employee skills, employee behaviors, and human resource practices on firm performance. *Journal of Management*, *31*(4), 622–640. https://doi.org/10.1177/0149206304272347

Brinzea, V.M. (2019) Encouraging Neurodiversity in the evolving workforce – The next frontier to a diverse workplace, *Scientific Bulletin – Economic Sciences, 18*.

Carlson, J. R., & Zmud, R. W. (1999). Channel expansion theory and the experiential nature of media richness perceptions. *Academy of Management Journal*, *42*(2), 153–170.

Carrero, J., Krzeminska, A., & Härtel, C.,E.J. (2019). The DXC technology work experience program: Disability-inclusive recruitment and selection in action. *Journal of Management and Organization*, 25(4), 535–542. doi:http://dx.doi.org/10.1017/jmo.2019.23

Colella, A. (2001). Coworker distributive fairness judgments of the workplace accommodation of employees with disabilities. *Academy of Management Review*, *26*(1), 100–116.

Dalton, N. S. (2013). Neurodiversity & HCI. In CHI'13 Extended Abstracts on Human Factors in Computing Systems (pp. 2295–2304).

Fulk, J., & Boyd, B. (1991). Emerging theories of communication in organizations. *Journal of Management*, *17*(2), 407–446.

Galvin, R. (2004). Can welfare reform make disability disappear? *Australian Journal of Social Issues*, *39*(3), 343–355.

Gannon, B., & Nolan, B. (2007). The impact of disability transitions on social inclusion. *Social Science & Medicine*, *64*(7), 1425–1437. Doi: http://dx.doi.org/10.1016/j.socscimed.2006.11.021

Grant, D. & French, H. E. (2017). *That's the way I think : dyslexia, dyspraxia, ADHD and dyscalculia explained* (Third edition.). Routledge. https://doi.org/10.4324/9781315647005

Hagner, D., & Cooney, B.F. (2005). "I do that for everybody": Supervising employees with autism. *Focus on Autism and Other Developmental Disabilities*, *20*(2), 91–97.

Hurley-Hanson A.E., Giannantonio C.M., & Griffiths A.J. (2020). *The benefits of employing individuals with autism*. In: Autism in the Workplace: Creating Positive Employment and Career Outcomes for Generation A. Palgrave Macmillan, Cham. https://doi.org/10.1007/978-3-030-29049-8_12

Johnson, K. R., Ennis-Cole, D., & Bonhamgregory, M. (2020). Workplace success strategies for employees with autism spectrum disorder: A new frontier for human resource development. *Human Resource Development Review*, *19*(2), 122–151. https://doi.org/10.1177/1534484320905910

Johnson, T. D., & Joshi, A. (2016). Dark clouds or silver linings? A stigma threat perspective on the implications of an autism diagnosis for workplace well-being. *Journal of Applied Psychology*, *101*(3), 430–449. 20p. DOI: 10.1037/apl0000058.

Kirby, A., & Gibbon, H. (2018). Dyslexia and employment. *Perspectives on Language and Literacy*, *44*(1), 27–31.

Kirby, A. and Smith, T. (2021). Neurodiversity at work: drive innovation, performance and productivity with a neurodiverse workforce, Kogan Page, Limited, 2021.

Khan, M., Grabarski, M., Buckmaster, S. & Ali, M. (2021). Neurodiversity: An HR framework to create an inclusive workplace. *In Proceedings of 58ᵗʰ Annual Meeting of the Eastern Academy of Management (EAM) (in press)*.

Khayatzadeh-Mahani, A., Wittevrongel, K., Nicholas, D. B., & Zwicker, J. D. (2020). Prioritizing barriers and solutions to improve employment for persons with developmental disabilities. *Disability and Rehabilitation*, *42*(19), 2696–2706.

Krzeminska, A., Austin, R.D., Bruyere, S.M. & Hedley, D. (2019) The advantages and challenges of neurodiversity employment in organizations, *Journal of Management and Organization 25*, 453–463 doi:10.1017/jmo.2019.58

Macdonald, S. J., & Cosgrove, F. (2019). Dyslexia and policing. Equality, *Diversity and Inclusion: An International Journal*, *38*(6), 634–651. doi:http://dx.doi.org/10.1108/EDI-11-2018-0218

Martino, & Leckman, J. F. (2013). *Tourette syndrome*. Oxford University Press, USA.

Mason, D. (2007) Reasonable adjustment. Employers Network on Disability Seminar, Sydney.

McBride, C. (2019). *Coping with dyslexia, dysgraphia and ADHD : a global perspective*. New York, NY: Routledge https://doi.org/10.4324/9781315115566

McKnight-Lizotte, M. (2018). Work-related communication barriers for individuals with autism: a pilot qualitative study. *The Australian Journal of Rehabilitation Counselling*, *24*(1), 12–26.

McManus, S. (2011). Mental illness =/= neurodiversity: the differences between psychological and neurological conditions. Retrieved from https://medium.com/artfullyautistic/mental-illness-neurodiversity-the-differences-between-psychological-and-neurological-22a1653682a7 (access 03 Jan 2022)

Meacham, H., Cavanagh, J., Bartram, T., & Laing, J. (2019). Ethical management in the hotel sector: Creating an authentic work experience for workers with intellectual disabilities. *Journal of Business Ethics*, *155*, 823–835.

Meacham, H., Cavanagh, J., Shaw, A., & Bartram, T. (2017). HRM practices that support the employment and social inclusion of workers with an intellectual disability. *Personnel Review*, *46*(8), 1475–1492.

Meltzer, A., Robinson, S., & Fisher, K. R. (2020). Barriers to finding and maintaining open employment for people with intellectual disability in Australia. *Social Policy & Administration*, *54*(1),88–101.

Moeller, M., Ott, D.L., & Russo, E. (2021). *Neurodiversity can be a workplace strength, if we make room for it* [online], The Conversation. Available at: < https://theconversation.com/neurodiversity-can-be-a-workplace-strength-if-we-make-room-for-it-164859> [Accessed 05 August 2022]:

Morris, M. R., Begel, A., & Wiedermann, B. (2015). Understanding the challenges faced by neurodiverse software engineering employees: Towards a more inclusive and productive technical workforce. *In Proceedings of the 17th International ACM SIGACCESS Conference on Computers & Accessibility* (pp. 173–184).

Ortiz, L. A. (2020). Reframing neurodiversity as competitive advantage: opportunities, challenges, and resources for business and professional communication educators. *Business and Professional Communication Quarterly*, *83*(3), 261–284.

Parr, A. D., Hunter, S. T., & Ligon, G. S. (2013). Questioning universal applicability of transformational leadership: Examining employees with autism spectrum disorder. *Leadership Quarterly*, *24*(4), 608.

Patton, E. (2019). Autism, attributions and accommodations: Overcoming barriers and integrating a neurodiverse workforce. *Personnel Review*, *48*(4), 915–934. https://doi.org/10.1108/PR-04-2018-0116

Priscott, T., & Allen, R. A. (2021). Human capital neurodiversity: an examination of stereotype threat anticipation. *Employee Relations*, (ahead of print). https://doi.org/10.1108/ER-06-2020-0304

Pouliot, D. M., Müller, E., Frasché, N. F., Kern, A. S., & Resti, I. H. (2017). A tool for supporting communication in the workplace for individuals with intellectual disabilities and/or autism. *Career Development and Transition for Exceptional Individuals*, *40*(4), 244–249.

Rao, B., & Polepeddi, J. (2019) Neurodiverse workforce: inclusive employment as an HR strategy, *Strategic HR Review*, *18*(5), 204–209.

Reid, G. (2011). *Dyslexia*. (3. ed.). Bloomsbury Publishing: London.

Remington A and Pellicano E (2019) 'Sometimes you just need someone to take a chance on you': an internship programme for autistic graduates at Deutsche Bank, UK, *Journal of Management and Organization 25*(4): 516–534.

Ricci, C. (2007) *Disclosure of disability in the workplace: Rights and responsibilities of employers and actual or potential employees with disability: Suggestions for best practice*, Human Rights and Equal Opportunity Commission.

Richards, J. (2012). Examining the exclusion of employees with Asperger syndrome from the workplace. *Personnel Review*, *41*(5), 630–646. https://doi.org/10.1108/00483481211249148

Richards, J., Sang, K., Marks, A., & Gill, S. (2019). "I've found it extremely draining" Emotional labour and the lived experience of line managing neurodiversity. *Personnel Review*, *48*(7), 1903–1923.

Riches, V., Green, V. (2003). Social integration in the workplace for people with disabilities: An Australian perspective. *Journal of Vocational Rehabilitation*, *19*, 127–142.

Romualdez, A. M., Heasman, B., Walker, Z., Davies, J., & Remington, A. (2021). "People Might Understand Me Better": Diagnostic disclosure experiences of autistic Individuals in the workplace. *Autism in Adulthood*, doi10.1089/aut.2020.0063.

Sanderson, A. (2011). Shedding light on a "hidden" disability. *Human Resource Management International Digest*, *19*(1), 36–38. doi:http://dx.doi.org/10.1108/09670731111101615

Santuzzi, A. M., Waltz, P. R., Finkelstein, L. M., & Rupp, D. E. (2014). Invisible disabilities: unique challenges for employees and organizations. *Industrial and Organizational Psychology*, *7*(2), 204–219. https://doi.org/10.1111/iops.12134

Schreuer, N. & Dorot, R. (2017). Experiences of employed women with attention deficit hyperactive disorder: A phenomenological study. *Work*, *56*(3), 429–441.

Shannon, C. E., & Weaver, W. (1949). *The mathematical theory of communication*. Urbana: University of Illinois Press.

Sumner, K. & Brown, T. (2015). Neurodiversity and human resource management: employer challenges for applicants and employees with learning disabilities. *The Psychologist-Manager Journal*, *18*(2), 77–85.

Terzi, L. (2004). The social model of disability: A philosophical critique. *Journal of Applied Philosophy*, *21*(2), 141–157. doi: 10.1111/j.0264-3758.2004.00269.x

Tomczak, M. T. (2021). Employees with autism spectrum disorders in the digitized work environment: Perspectives for the future. *Journal of Disability Policy Studies*, *31*(4), 195–205. doi:http://dx.doi.org/10.1177/1044207320919945

Waisman-Nitzan, M., Gal, E., & Schreuer, N. (2019). Employers' perspectives regarding reasonable accommodations for employees with autism spectrum disorder. *Journal of Management & Organization*, *25*(4), 481–498. https://doi.org/10.1017/jmo.2018.59

Wille, S., & Sajous-Brady, D. (2018). The inclusive and accessible workplace. *Communications of the ACM*, *61*(2), 24–26.

Williams, L. H., & Koenig, K. (2014). Autism in the workplace: How occupational therapy practitioners can support the neurodiverse workforce. *OT Practice*, *19*(2), 14–16.

Brent J. Lyons, Camellia Bryan, and Sabrina D. Volpone

17 Neuroqueerness and Management Research

Abstract: We explore how management researchers interested in disability and neuro-diversity at work can benefit from taking a neuroqueerness perspective. A neuroqueerness perspective highlights the ways in which neurodivergent people can subvert and disrupt culturally dominant notions of neurotypicality and neurodivergence, that are largely informed by neurotypical perspectives, to reveal able-bodied assumptions and the exclusionary effects of neurotypical perspectives (Walker, 2015; Yergeau, 2018). We suggest that introducing the perspective of neuroqueerness into management research can further help organizations formulate alternative perspectives in their quest to de-pathologize neurodivergence and the identities of neurodivergent people within their work environments. In this chapter, we define neuroqueerness, and we describe how autistic employees can neuroqueer organizational life. With the aim of spurring further research on the topic of neuroqueerness, we also describe how management researchers can aim to better understand neuroqueerness through researching the topics of organizational support, disclosure and identity management, and leadership.

Keywords: neurodiversity, neuroqueer, medical model of disability, organizational support, identity management, disclosure, leadership

> I know what I need, far better than doctors, diagnostic manuals, and social stories. I've got myself here [. . .] via a sensory story that very few people could comprehend. I am beyond the definition of most people, even beyond myself using language, despite instinctively feeling like I'm figuring out the edges. Contributor (Jackson-Perry et al., 2020; p. 134)

Neurodiversity, an umbrella term that can take numerous forms (e.g., autism, attention deficit hyperactivity disorder [ADHD], bipolar disorder, dementia, Down's syndrome, dyslexia, Tourette's), is defined as the natural variation between people in social, cognitive, and emotional processing and bodily motions (Singer, 1999). Historically, society's broad knowledge of neurodiversity and the experiences of people with different types of neurodiversity typically has come from medical, psychological, and legal perspectives that rely on the prevailing "medical model of disability" to describe individuals who vary from "neurotypical" as deviant (Rosqvist et al., 2020). Recent research, following movements within the neurodiversity community, has moved away from describing neurodivergent experiences only from the perspective of the medical model of disability.

Brent J. Lyons, Camellia Bryan, Schulich School of Business, York University, Canada
Sabrina D. Volpone, Leeds School of Business, University of Colorado, Boulder

https://doi.org/10.1515/9783110743647-018

The shift away from the medical model of disability is needed when understanding the lived experiences of neurodivergent employees because the medical model of disability describes neurodivergence in a negative and limited way – as defects and characteristics of individuals (Rosqvist et al., 2020; Shakespeare, 2006). Indeed, according to the medical model, society should rectify the difficulties and improve the "functioning" of neurodivergent people, so that neurodivergent people live a life that is as close to neurotypical ideals and norms as possible; and these ideals include independence, economic productivity, and sociability, for example (Rosqvist et al., 2020). To date, the medical model has (a) been used in medical, psychological, and legal disciplines that is overwhelmingly informed by perspectives of neurotypical perspectives, and has (b) pathologized neurodivergent people as deviant, with disadvantages in social, cognitive, and emotional processing (Rosqvist et al., 2020). The purpose of the current chapter is to further work that has been done to *counter* neurotypical perspectives, that are based on the medical model of disability, to inform our knowledge of neurodiversity and neurodivergent people that are employed in organizations.

To demonstrate the refreshing insights that can be gleamed from incorporating the voices of neurodivergent employees in understanding their lived experiences inside and outside the workplace, we note that the contributor of the opening quote, describes how their experiences as an autistic person[1] are often in contrast to perspectives held in the field of medicine, psychology literature, and commonplace "allistic" (i.e., non-autistic people; Yergeau, 2018) accounts of neurodivergent people (Jackson-Perry et al., 2020). This example speaks to how the pathologization of neurodivergence is troublesome because it subjects neurodivergent people to disadvantage throughout work and life domains, including social exclusion and inferior employment outcomes (Doyle & McDowall, 2021; Oliver, 1996; Shakespeare, 2006). In this chapter, we aim to contribute to conversations about neurodiversity in organizations by drawing on alternative perspectives to the medical model of disability, perspectives that disability advocates and academics have been providing about neurodiversity for decades (Singer, 1999). To do so, we focus on one form of neurodivergence: autism. We seek to highlight how centering the voices of autistic people can create a fruitful foundation for furthering the re-definition and re-imagining of the experiences of neurodivergent employees in the workplace.

---

[1] There is ongoing debate regarding the use of person-first and identity-first language in disability scholarship (Dunn & Andrews, 2015). In this chapter, we follow disability advocates and disability scholars and adopt identity-first language (e.g., autistic individuals) to center understandings of disability as a social, rather than individual, phenomenon and to also center disability as an integral part of peoples' identities (Titchosky, 2001).

Within emerging conversations on neurodiversity (and its related work) that serve to counter the medical model of disability, two common themes are often noted: (a) the need to de-pathologize neurodiversity and (b) the need to increase recognition that neurodivergence is a natural component of human variation (Rosqvist et al., 2020). In building on the movement to counter the medical model of disability, especially as it relates to scholars' understanding of de-pathologizing neurodiverse employees and harnessing neurodivergence as a natural phenomenon, we find interest in *neuroqueerness* as a central topic of this chapter. Neuroqueerness is a perspective that reflects an interest in understanding how neurodivergent people can, through embodying neurodivergence, subvert, disrupt, and reposition prevailing understandings of neurotypicality and neurodivergence (Walker & Raymaker, 2021). Through introducing the concept of neuroqueerness to management research, we aim to help organizations formulate alternative perspectives in their quest to de-pathologize neurodivergence and the identities of neurodivergent people within their work environments.

In the opening quote, the contributor provides an excellent example of neuro-queering (the actions associated with applying a neuroqueer perspective), showing how their autistic sensory experiences and nonverbal communication are comprehensible and legitimate in the workplace, thereby challenging prevailing assumptions about how communication can happen at work and "who" is capable of being social (Jackson-Perry et al., 2020). In other words, they "queer" by pushing back against the prevailing understanding of themselves as autistic. Just as heteronormativity can be queered by people re-thinking heteronormative gender roles (Butler, 2004), neuroqueering challenges underlying assumptions of differences between neurotypicality and neurodivergence, and prevailing assumptions in what the dominant culture (e.g., often found in workplaces) considers a "normal" person (Yergeau, 2018), or a "typical" employee. Neuroqueerness enables neurodivergent employees to move toward a future at work that is free of harmful perspectives on neurodivergence and that is instead made up of their own ideals and desires (Walker, 2015).

In the remainder of this chapter, we explore the potential for management researchers in studying neuroqueerness. Drawing on critical disability scholarship, we first define neuroqueerness and explore the benefits of taking a neuroqueerness perspective for management researchers interested in disability and neurodiversity at work. After doing so, we then describe instances of autistic employees neuroqueering organizational life. We conclude by considering how management researchers can better understand neuroqueerness through researching the management topics of organizational support, disclosure and identity management, and leadership.

Literature Review

Neurodiversity and Neuroqueerness

Autism is one form of neurodiversity, and the perspectives and experiences of autistic people have played a large role in driving understanding of neuroqueerness. In the book *Authoring Autism*, Melanie Yergeau (2018) describes the perils of the medical model of disability and autism diagnosis for autistic people. According to Yergeau, an autism diagnosis provides a lens through which allistic people (e.g., non-autistic doctors, parents, researchers, therapists) *author* or story autistic peoples' lives. Through a neurotypical lens, autistic individuals are understood through the criteria of neurodevelopmental disability, which authors autistic people as "victim-captives of a faulty neurology" (p. 3). The clinical literature on autism (see Assessment of Autism Spectrum Disorders; American Psychiatric Association, 2013) characterizes autistic people as contrasting neurotypicality, and describes autism as a disorder that prevents individuals from exercising intentionality, free will, control over themselves and precluding them from self-knowledge, empathy, knowledge about others, and as asocial. In other words, according to Yergeau, autistic people are authored by culturally normative ("medical") perspectives on autism as passive subjects who are captive to an impaired brain and body.[2] When autistic people are authored in this way, autistic bodyminds (i.e., social, cognitive, and emotional processing and bodily motions; Yergeau, 2018) are not understood as human but as problematic symptoms of a "disorder of social communication" that should be fixed. For example, Yergeau describes how repetitive hand gestures are commonly understood through a neurotypical medical lens as "autistic stereotypy," a symptom of faulty neurology. Viewing hand gestures as a symptom erases any possible communicative, social, and human meaning that can be associated with the hand gestures. Yergeau challenges this medical interpretation of hand gestures, and describes how hand gestures can be diverse and expressive with lots of communicative meaning. That is, medical perspectives on disability limit understanding of diverse social potential that is an inherent part of neurodiversity.

In reaction to medical models of disability, the social model of disability moves the analytical lens from the individual to the social environment and is concerned with "all the things that impose restrictions on disabled people; ranging from individual prejudice to institutional discrimination, from inaccessible public buildings to unusable transport systems, from segregated education to excluding work arrangements, and so on" (Oliver, 1996, p. 33). The social model of disability aims to understand how society can remove barriers, which are social and cultural responses to impairment that restrict life choices for disabled people (Rosqvist et al., 2020). From the perspective

---

2 Even media depictions of autistic savants highlight autistic people as critically impaired (Yergeau, 2018).

of the social model of disability, neurodivergence is not "deviant" or in need of being fixed, but reflects a wide variety of differences between people, some of which are good and not so good, and society should understand how to remove barriers for neurodivergent people.

In recognizing that commonplace and normative perspectives on neurodivergence continue to largely be driven by the medical, rather than the social, model of disability, scholars are starting to explore how stories (perspectives and experiences) authored by neurodivergent individuals themselves challenge prevailing medical perspectives (Jackson-Perry et al., 2020). In centering the perspectives and experiences of neurodivergent people, neurodivergent individuals draw attention to acknowledge and re-think the contours and edges of contemporary understanding of neurotypicality and neurodivergence (Yergeau, 2018). Stories authored by neurodivergent people broaden a sense of what it means to be social (Mullaney, 2020), toward an understanding of sociality (i.e., qualities of being social) that projects the desires and ideals of neurodivergent people. As Yergeau notes, stories by autistic people resist the "pathologization of difference" (p. 24).

Through this chapter, we hope to discuss how critical disability scholars have long noted the pathologization of neurodivergence through the medical model of disability, and we do so to complement burgeoning research on neurodiversity in organizations. Indeed, management research has recently started to integrate ideas from the neurodiversity movement (that push back against the once prevailing medical model of disability) in work about neurodiversity in the workplace and the cultures/climates of organizations that support this new lens of doing a better job of including neurodiverse employees (Doyle & McDowall, 2021; Volpone et al., in press). We discuss neuroqueerness as a useful perspective to consider how organizations can further their interest in neurodiverse employees in a way that amplifies their voices and experiences.

Neuroqueerness. *Neuroqueer(ness)* is a term coined by disability activists and scholars (Walker, 2015; Yergeau, 2018) and overlaps conceptually with the notion of queering gender and sexuality. Academic queer theory originated in radical gay politics in the 1990s to embrace the position that gender and sexual identities cannot be understood as fixed male/female and homosexual/heterosexual binaries, but as diverse gender representations (e.g., cis-woman, cis-man, trans-woman, trans-man, gender non-conforming, gender fluid) and sexual desires, behaviors, and identities (e.g., lesbian, gay, bisexual, pansexual, fluid; Miller, Taylor, & Rupp, 2016). For example, in the field of queer theory gender is understood as an embodied performance in which the dominant culture socializes people to perform certain narrow and specific (man and woman) gender roles (Butler, 2004). Queering gender refers to actively subverting, disrupting, and deviating from these gender roles to reveal how the gender roles are not inclusive of diverse gender and sexual representations (Walker & Raymaker, 2021). In similar ways, the dominant culture socializes people into embodied performances of neurotypicality, or what the dominant culture considers a "normal" bodymind. Queering neurotypicality (or neuroqueering) thus refers to subverting, disrupting and deviating from culturally dominant notions of neurotypicality and neurodivergence that are largely informed by neurotypical perspectives (Walker & Raymaker, 2021). More specifically, neuroqueering involves actively choosing to embody one's neurodivergence and revealing able-bodied assumptions and exclusionary effects of dominant cultural perspectives on neurotypicality and neurodivergence (Roscigno, 2019; Walker, 2015). According to Yergeau (2018), neuroqueering is a verb, a motion of rejecting things as they are and moving toward a potential future that constitutes neurodivergent peoples' ideals and desires.

Yergeau (2018) describes how autistic people can neuroqueer. The perspectives and experiences of autistic people can queer notions of sociality that are largely informed by neurotypical perspectives. Rather than authoring autistic people as lacking intentionality and free will in communication and as being asocial, Yergeau points to the ways in which autism is inherently relational and in doing so defies and enriches understanding of what it means to be social, and thereby neurotypical and neurodivergent. Through their stories, autistic people can insist on the communicative potential of their ticks, stims, echoed words and phrases, avoiding eye contact, relations with shiny objects, and repeated hand gestures. In detailing an example of neuroqueering in popular media, Mullaney (2020) interprets the 2007 viral video "In My Language" by Mel Baggs, a nonspeaking autistic person. In the video, Baggs showcases *hir*[3] modes of communication. Ze rubs hir hand over the keyboard, twists hir fingers around a doorknob, and dangles a necklace in front of a window, all while recording hir humming. To allistic people, language may seem absent from the video. But, in the translation, Baggs explains how hir language is not about using words or visual symbols that can be interpreted by others, but rather hir language is about being in conversation with hir environment. Although neurotypical perspectives on sociality would pathologize Baggs as asocial, Baggs' embodiment of autistic communication neuroqueers neurotypical perspectives by redefining prevailing perspectives on communication and sociality to include autistic bodyminds (Mullaney, 2020).

The Mel Baggs example highlights how neurodivergent people can neuroqueer normative perspectives on neurotypicality and neurodivergence that are largely informed through a neurotypical (and medical) lens. Through embodying neurodivergence as social, neurodivergent people occupy space between socially constructed categories of neurotypicality and neurodivergence, categories that position neurodivergent people as asocial and in contrast to neurotypical people. Through occupying space in between the categories of neurotypicality and neurodivergence,

---

3 Hir and ze are gender-neutral pronouns.

neurodivergent people challenge assumptions of commonplace perspectives on the neurotypical-neurodivergent dichotomy and create potential for understanding sociality in ways that incorporate neurodivergent bodyminds and stories, and that reflect the ideals and desires of neurodivergent people (Yergeau, 2018).

Next, we consider five ways neuroqueering can manifest in organizational life.

Neuroqueering in Organizational Life

According to disability advocates and scholars, neurodivergent employees can neuroqueer neurotypical perspectives on sociality, neurotypicality, and neurodivergence in organizations. Though we focus on actions that neurodivergent employees can take, we do not mean to imply that the onus for creating supportive cultures and climates within workspaces is the responsibility of neurodivergent employees; rather, we believe that responsibility should fall to the organization. As is evidenced in the opening quote of this chapter, autistic employees can re-define and re-imagine their experiences and the contours and edges of themselves as neurodivergent and in doing so create potential for new ways of understanding themselves and sociality in their organizations. For example, as we have noted, medical perspectives represent autistic vocalizations, stims, and complex bodily movements as involuntary and pathological symptoms of faulty neurology and thus autistic employees are seen as asocial and incapable of effective communication in organizations. However, autistic employees (and those with other types of neurodiversity) can neuroqueer the dichotomy between social and asocial acts in organizations. Stories by autistic individuals describe how autistic vocalizations, stims, and complex bodily movements have social potential (Mullaney, 2020). Neuroqueering thus creates potential for understanding sociality in organizations in new ways.

To detail examples of how neuroqueering can manifest in organizational life, we draw on stories authored by autistic individuals. Jackson-Perry and colleagues (2020) report on a qualitative study of autistic individuals, some of whom worked as academics and others as authors. The authors aimed to unearth how autistic individuals navigate commonplace neurotypical perspectives on sociality in organizational life that pathologize neurodivergence as deficient in communication and as asocial. Many of the study participants described an awareness that commonplace perspectives about autism at their workplaces are insufficient to describe the sociality and communicative potential of autistic individuals (Jackson-Perry et al., 2020). In response to this awareness, participants described how they subverted, disrupted, and deviated from prevailing pathologizing stories to alternative perspectives of autistic people. Indeed, one participant noted how prevailing stories about autism and the language used to describe effective communication in their organization generally failed to capture how autistic individuals can be social:

> Autistic people with learning difficulties . . . may have a wealth of sensoreality experiences that just cannot be approached through language, [. . .], because the senses are something we don't usually talk about to a great extent and so we are very limited discursively. (p. 129)

Thus, the first way in which autistic individuals can neuroqueer organizational life is by crafting narratives that re-define what it means to be neurodivergent. In reaction to exclusionary stories about sociality in their organizations, participants sought out alternatives, crafting their own stories to re-imagine and re-define the limits and possibilities of autistic people. However, importantly, in crafting their own stories, participants incorporated medical stories of autism. They mainly did so by claiming the disabled or autistic diagnosis, but rejecting notions of deficiency. For example, one participant described claiming the identity as a disabled person, without having to conceive of it as missing something that needs to be fixed and instead highlighting its emancipatory potential (Jackson-Perry et al., 2020). That is, the "diagnosis of autism is a recognition of a way of being in the world that, while it may well carry greater or lesser degrees of disadvantage, also holds emancipatory and explanatory value for individuals" by adopting the use of the words, phrases, and language that these employees use to describe themselves (p. 132).

Second, in addition to re-defining what is means to be neurodivergent, neuro-queering can also involve using community with other neurodivergent people to center their own, rather than neurotypical, perspectives on what it means to be a neurodivergent employee. Jackson-Perry and colleagues (2020) describe how the autistic participants engage with other members of autistic communities, such as through online communities or through disability affinity networks at their organizations, to become exposed to stories and language used by other autistic individuals. The move from "being talked about" to being involved in actively crafting their own stories through engagement with other autistic individuals, helped them re-think their work and life as an employee on their own terms. For example, one participant noted:

> Figuring out little by little not only what my relationship with myself was, but also contextualizing my relationships with others, the ways in which others storied me (e.g., as someone who is 'talented' in their work with autistic students). It became a powerful source of agency in my personal life, whether I felt able or empowered to exercise it or not. [It became] an epistemological and discursive location that gave me the freedom to approach my life phenomenologically from the events, rather than theoretically from abstract, and very flawed, theoretical frameworks I was familiar with. Ultimately [it empowered] me in the process of owning the words that describe my own experiences. (p. 132)

That is, autistic individuals used community with other autistic individuals, and the stories and language that derive from those interactions, to neuroqueer perspectives of themselves as autistic employees.

Third, another example of neuroqueering in organizational life is how communication of autistic individuals can neuroqueer neurotypical perspectives on sociality and communication in the organization. Yergeau (2018) describes how echophenomenology, or the echoing of bodily movements, sounds, facial expressions, and written words, etc., neuroqueers neurotypical perspectives that position autistic individuals as asocial. Neurotypical perspectives on echoing suggest that echoing is simply mimicry with autistic individuals attempting to assimilate into "normal" bodyminds and pass like allistic people. Inherent in this neurotypical perspective on echoing is that allistic people's modes of communication are the natural sociality, effectively othering autistic modes of communication. For example, when echolalia (verbal echoing) is interpreted through a neurotypical lens as involuntary, rather than voluntary, any possible communicative or social meaning connected to the echolalia is obscured. Yergeau notes that echolalia may be involuntary sometimes but that does not mean it is devoid of social meaning. For example, echolalia can reflect an employee processing the information they have been given by another employee, including anxiety and emotional connections to that information. The meanings of echolalia lie more in affect and anxiety than neurotypical syntax. That is, echolalia can convey an autistic employee's emotional connection to the information they are processing (Yergeau, 2018).

Fourth, neuroqueering can also involve invention. According to Yergeau (2018), in the space between socially constructed categories of social and asocial or neurotypical and neurodivergent, as understood through a neurotypical lens, the communication of autistic people can be inventive. Invention is defined as the "process of making connections, rearranging materials (words, images, concepts) in unexpected ways" (p. 181). Yergeau notes that for autistic people, embodied communication forms (e.g., echo, tic, stim, rocking body, twirl) represent acts that create potential for re-inventing what organizations and employees know about communication. Autistic individuals, through echoing, participate in the construction of new forms of communication (Yergeau, 2018). For example, imitating a coworker's facial expression while also vocalizing something else that is seemingly unrelated can in fact invent an entirely different or novel meaning that is conveyed in the interaction, such as conveying distrust between the employee and their coworker, or creating mutual anxiety between them. That is, through embodying autistic communication, such as echoing, autistic individuals neuroqueer (subvert, disrupt, deviate from) prevailing perspectives on sociality in the organization, including how members of the organization story who is and is not capable of being social.

Finally, neuroqueering can also involve active resistance to intervention and control from the organization. Roscigno (2019) describes how autistic individuals can resist socialization attempts from authority figures by challenging assumptions about what is considered a good employee. Templates for employee behavior can often stress compliance and homogeneity, framing forms of difference as something that must be corrected. Through embodying autistic bodyminds, autistic employees can queer neurotypical perspectives on order and structure in the organization, thereby challenging assumptions about how appropriate ways of being are policed in the organization, particularly who and who is not considered appropriate for the organization.

Now that we understand how neuroqueering can manifest in organizational life, we turn to unpacking how management researchers can aim to better understand neuroqueerness through researching the topics of organizational support, disclosure and identity management, and leadership.

Neuroqueerness and Management Research

Recently, management scholars have begun exploring how organizations can be supportive of neurodivergent employees by embracing neurodiversity. We build on this research to understand how organizations can support neuroqueering.

Organizational Support

First, Volpone, Avery, and Wayne (in press) describe how organizations can develop diversity climates, inclusion climates, and ethical climates that provide a foundation for supporting and leveraging the strengths of neurodivergent individuals. Organizations focusing on equality of treatment for all employees through fair policies and absence of discrimination can build strong diversity climates. Following human resources practices that heed regulations put forth by the Americans with Disabilities Act (ADA) and the Equal Employment Opportunities Commission (EEOC) in the United States, and explicitly addressing discrimination and unequal treatment faced by neurodivergent individuals can also help organizations develop strong diversity climates. Moreover, inclusion climates refer to individuals from all backgrounds being treated fairly, valued for who they are, and included in decision-making (Nishii, 2013), and they in turn help individuals feel a sense of belonging at work (Shore et al., 2018). According to Volpone and colleagues, organizations can build strong inclusion climates that are supportive of neurodivergent individuals by carefully considering accommodations, such as quiet workplaces and use of noise-canceling headphones. Furthermore, ethical climates involve establishing and maintaining an ethical code through organizational communication and policies that clarify ethical standards in the organization (Martin & Cullen, 2006). Ethical standards regarding neurodivergent employees can involve addressing social justice issues faced by neurodivergent individuals, such as unequal distribution of wealth, opportunities, and privileges that are barriers to neurodivergent individuals' participation and inclusion at work (Volpone et al., in press).

Building on this previous research that has considered ways organizations can support inclusion and leverage the strengths of neurodivergent individuals, we suggest that there are additional issues to consider for organizations to support neuroqueering in organizations. For neurodivergent individuals' stories and embodiment of neuroqueering to be centered in organizational life, neurodivergent individuals' coworkers need to be open to alternative perspectives that fall outside neurotypical perspectives on neurotypicality, neurodivergence, and sociality. This will require coworkers engaging with stories authored by neurodivergent individuals that open them to alternative possibilities than the pathologization of neurodivergence. That is, coworkers need to recognize neurodivergent individuals' perspectives as valid (Jackson-Perry et al., 2020). Indeed, Walker and Raymaker (2021) note that organizations in societies that embrace neurodiversity would support neuroqueerness, and in particular, in such organizations there would be no such thing as "neurotypicality, no such thing as a 'normal mind.' It would be commonplace for people to regard their own minds and embodiments as fluid and customizable, as canvases for ongoing creative experimentation" (p. 9). That is, organizations that support neuroqueering would support the fluidity and customizability of employees' understandings of the categories of neurotypicality and neurodivergence, including who is capable of being social.

Organizational research on diversity ideologies may offer insight into how organizations can support neuroqueering through being supportive of the fluidity and customizability of categories of neurotypicality and neurodivergence (Clair et al., 2019). Organizational diversity ideologies are defined as "individuals' beliefs regarding how to think about, approach, and manage demographic differences" (Leslie et al., 2020; p. 3). Clair and colleagues suggest that organizations that adopt a polyculturalist ideology are most likely to be supportive of category fluidity. Polyculturalist ideologies recognize "individuals as culturally complex, dynamic, and malleable" (Morris et al., 2015; p. 651). When adopting a polycultural ideology, employees view demographic categories as evolving, unclear, and oftentimes complex (Morris et al., 2015). In organizations that adopt a polycultural ideology, employees are more likely to have a mindset that involves self-questioning, hybridity, and cultural malleability (Clair et al., 2019). Thus, it could be that organizations that adopt polyculturalist ideologies are more likely to support neurodivergent individuals' as they neuroqueer prevailing understandings of neurodivergence and neurotypicality in their organization, and their coworkers' support of such alternative perspectives.

Disclosure and Identity Management

We now consider how the perspective of neuroqueerness helps management research to think about disclosure and identity management in new ways. Management scholars have long been interested in understanding why disabled individuals do or do not disclose a disability at work, and the implications of such disclosure decisions for disabled individuals career opportunities and well-being (Lyons et al., 2017b; Santuzzi et al.,

2019). Disclosure falls under the umbrella term of identity management, or the strategic choices individuals make to manage others' impressions of their association with a social identity group (Lyons et al., 2017a). Identity management research suggests that disabled individuals disclose to secure necessary accommodations and support from coworkers, but the risk of disclosure is that they are also susceptible mistreatment and discrimination from others (Ragins, 2008). As such, disabled individuals often make the decision not to disclose. Contemporary management research on identity management largely frames disclosure or concealment as an intentional decision, suggesting that individuals weigh the pros and cons of disclosure before making the decision to disclose or conceal (Clair et al., 2005; Lyons et al., 2017c).

Very few studies have examined the identity management experiences of neurodivergent individuals. Though, studies that have explored the identity management experiences of neurodivergent individuals highlight how neurodivergent individuals neuroqueer contemporary understanding of disclosure and identity management in organizations. For example, Johnson and Joshi (2016), who conceptualized disclosure as a direct expression of one's diagnosis, found that autistic employees are very careful regarding when and who they disclose their diagnosis to as they are concerned about stigmatizing reactions from others. They also found that disclosure is not always intentional or controllable, as autistic bodyminds can be episodically visible through unintended bodily motions of tics, stims, and twirling that give indications to others about one's diagnosis. Autistic employees' experiences of episodic visibility mean that they sometimes feel pressure to disclose, which leads them at times to feel overexposed at work (Johnson & Joshi, 2016). Therefore, departing from previous management theory that generally conceptualizes disclosure as volitional (i.e., weighing the pros and cons of disclosure), neurodivergent individuals neuroqueer distinctions between visible and non-visible disabilities and intentional and unintentional disclosure (Yergeau, 2018).

In addition to neuroqueering how we understand the dynamics of why neurodivergent individuals (and individuals and stigmatized employees more generally) disclose, we suggest that the perspective of neuroqueerness also requires us to reconsider the consequences of disclosure for disclosure recipients, such as allistic coworkers and supervisors who are recipients of disclosure from autistic employees. As neuroqueering subverts, disrupts, and repositions commonplace and neurotypical perspectives on neurotypical-neurodivergent and social-asocial dichotomies, recipients of disclosure can find themselves re-evaluating and questioning their own assumptions about "normal" bodyminds and who is capable of being social. According to Yergeau (2018), neuroqueering "disorients and unorients" stakeholders involved in disclosure. That is, disclosure recipients may come to see that neurotypical-neurodivergent and social-asocial dichotomies are not fixed categories, but are instead fluid.

To elaborate, as we have noted, neuroqueering is a verb, a motion of rejecting things as they are and involves moving toward a potential future that constitutes neurodivergent peoples' ideals and desires. Disclosure can thus encourage disclosure recipients to re-imagine the edges and contours of neurotypicality and neurodivergence beyond dichotomies that pathologize neurodivergent individuals as asocial, and move closer to gaining perspective that aligns closer with the ideals and desires of the neurotypical individuals with whom they work (through recognizing relational potential). For example, when an autistic individual who discloses (either intentionally or unintentionally) that their bodily motions are sometimes voluntary and sometimes involuntary and sometimes relational, their doing so outlines how neurotypical/social-neurodivergent/asocial dichotomies are muddled, transient, non-binary, and fluid. Therefore, to understand neuroqueering and neurodivergent individuals' experiences of disclosure and identity management at work, management researchers must consider how disclosure changes how recipients think about the socially constructed categories to which they and neurodivergent individuals belong.

Leadership

The perspective of neuroqueerness can also help managers think in new ways about neurodivergent leaders. Management research has begun to explore how neurodiversity can serve as a strength beneficial for leadership. Roberson, Quigley, Vickers, and Bruck (2021) recently developed a conceptual model articulating how cognitive characteristics associated with neurodiversity lead to task-based leadership behavior and follower outcomes. Drawing on research suggesting that characteristics of neurodivergence can be impediments to sociality and the development of effective social relationships through which leadership occurs, Roberson and colleagues suggest that task-oriented leadership behaviors (e.g., information search, information use in problem-solving, novel thinking, stewardship) rather than relationship-oriented behaviors (e.g., consideration) draw on the cognitive strengths of neurodivergent leaders. Through heightened attention to detail, the ability to recognize patterns in stimuli, propensity for visual and spatial thinking, and a need for structure and predictability, they suggest that neurodivergent leaders are more likely to engage in task-oriented behaviors that will help them influence followers. They note that although the vast majority of leadership research has focused on interpersonal and relational behaviors, "more task-focused approaches to leadership may provide conceptual space for neurodiversity" (p. 404).

Although this theory highlights the strengths of neurodivergence for leadership, we suggest that management research on neurodivergent leaders can go even further in rethinking leadership processes to realize the full potential of neuroqueering for leadership. Indeed, approaches to understanding leadership that suggest that neurodivergent leaders are better suited for different kinds of leadership than neurotypical leaders may not fully consider the social potential of neurodivergent leaders. Neurodivergence reflects broad variation in bodyminds with varying implications for communication.

The neurotypical-neurodivergent dichotomy does not capture broad variation among neurodivergent leaders. In taking a neuroqueerness perspective, we advocate for approaches to leadership that also interrogate the neurotypical assumptions underlying perspectives on leadership, sociality, and communication in organizations that are exclusionary to neurodivergent people (Roscigno, 2019; Yergeau, 2018).

As we have noted throughout this chapter, in authoring their own stories, neurodivergent people neuroqueer perspectives that position them as asocial by insisting on the social potential of neurodivergent bodyminds (Jackson-Perry et al., 2020; Mullaney, 2020; Yergeau, 2018). For example, we described how echolalia can convey an autistic employee's emotional connection to the information they are processing. Therefore, we suggest that neurodivergent leaders can excel at both the social and task aspects of leadership.

In line with the social model of disability (Shakespeare, 2006), organizations can support neurodivergent leaders by removing environmental barriers to them, building capacity for success. As we have discussed, removing environmental barriers can involve providing necessary accommodations for leaders and strongly regulating against discrimination (Volpone et al., in press). This can also involve educational interventions for employees through which employees learn about how they can support neurodivergent leaders' success. For example, educational opportunities can address the topic of neurodivergent bodyminds, such as how autistic bodily motions are sometimes social. Such education can help build understanding about the relational, social, and leadership potential of neurodivergent leaders. Additionally, recent leadership research suggests a path through which neurodivergent leaders can build mutually supportive relations with employees that enable both leaders and subordinates to be successful. By embracing identity-conscious approaches to diversity, and communicating openly about identity differences (e.g., disability), rather than avoiding such differences (i.e., identity-blind approaches), Dang, Volpone, and Umphress (under review) find that employees will perceive their leader as more ethical and respond more positively to them. Thus, although we do not suggest that the responsibility for removing barriers should fall on the shoulders of neurodivergent leaders, this research suggests that neurodivergent leaders can benefit from being open about their own and their employees' differences if they feel comfortable doing so.

Conclusion

In this chapter, we draw on critical disability scholarship to explore how management researchers interested in disability and neurodiversity at work can benefit from taking a neuroqueerness perspective as scholars move past the medical model of disability to understand how to better support and harness the talents of neurodivergent employees. A neuroqueerness perspective underscores the idea that neurodivergence confers ways of being that are not lesser, and at times can be advantageous. Through embodying neurodivergent bodyminds, neurodivergent individuals neuroqueer (subvert, disrupt, deviate from) ableist and neurotypical assumptions that underlie prevailing perspectives of neurotypicality, neurodivergence, and sociality (i.e., qualities of being social) in organizations. Neuroqueering creates potential for neurodivergent individuals to move toward a future where they are free of being seen as deviant or in need of being fixed, and instead their unique perspectives, experiences, desires, and ideals are validated. We reveal how the perspective of neuroqueerness allows management researchers to think differently about research topics of organizational support, disclosure and identity management, and leadership for neurodivergent employees in hopes of spurring further management research on the topic of neuroqueerness.

References

American Psychiatric Association. (2013). *Diagnostic and statistical manual of mental disorders* (5th ed.).

Butler, J. (2004). *Undoing gender*. New York: Routledge.

Clair, J. A., Beatty, J. E., & Maclean, T. L. (2005). Out of sight but not out of mind: Managing invisible social identities in the workplace. *Academy of Management Review*, *30*(1), 78–95. https://doi.org/10.2307/20159096

Clair, J. A., Humberd, B. K., Rouse, E. D., & Jones, E. B. (2019). Loosening categorical thinking: Extending the terrain of theory and research on demographic identities in organizations. *Academy of Management Review*, *44*(3), 592–617. https://doi.org/10.5465/amr.2017.0054

Dang, C., Volpone, S. D., & Umphress, E. E. The ethics of diversity ideology: Consequences of leader diversity ideology on ethical leadership perception and organizational citizenship behaviour [under review]. *Journal of Applied Psychology*.

Doyle, N. & McDowall, A. (2021). Diamond in the rough? An "empty review" of research into "neurodiversity" and a road map for developing the inclusion agenda. *Equality, Diversity, and Inclusion: An International Journal*. https://doi.org/10.1108/EDI-06-2020-0172

Dunn, D. S. & Andrews, E. E. (2015). Person-first and identity-first language: Developing psychologists' cultural competence using disability language. *American Psychologist*, *70*, 255–264. https://doi.org/10.1037/a0038636

Jackson-Perry, D., Rosqvist, H. B., Annable, J. L., & Kourti, M. (2020). Sensory strangers: Travels in normate sensory worlds. In H. B. Rosqvist, N. Chown, & A. Stenning (Eds.), *Neurodiversity studies: A new critical paradigm* (pp. 125–140). Routledge.

Johnson, T. D. & Joshi, A. (2016). Dark clouds or silver linings? A stigma threat perspective on the implications of an autism diagnosis for workplace well-being. *Journal of Applied Psychology*, *101*, 430–449. https://doi.org/10.1037/apl0000058

Leslie, L. M., Bono, J. E., Kim, Y., & Beaver, G. (2020). On melting pots and salad bowls: A meta-analysis of the effects of identity-blind and identity-conscious diversity ideologies. *Journal of Applied Psychology*, *105*, 453–471. https://doi.org/10.1037/apl0000446

Lyons, B. J., Pek, S., & Wessel, J. L. (2017a). Toward a "sunlit path": Stigma identity management as a source of localized social change through interaction. *Academy of Management Review*, *42*(4), 618–636. https://doi.org/10.5465/amr.2015.0189

Lyons, B. J., Volpone, S. D., Wessel, J. L., & Alonso, N. (2017b). Disclosing a disability: Do strategy type and onset controllability make a difference? *Journal of Applied Psychology*, *102*, 1375–1383. https://doi.org/10.1037/apl0000230

Lyons, B. J., Zatzick, C., Thompson, T., & Bushe, G. (2017c). Stigma identity concealment in hybrid organizational cultures. *Journal of Social Issues*, *73*, 255–272. https://doi.org/10.1111/josi.12215

Martin, K. D., & Cullen, J. B. (2006). Continuities and extensions of ethical climate theory: A meta-analytic review. *Journal of Business Ethics*, *69*, 175–194. https://doi.org/10.1007/s10551-006-9084-7

Miller, S. D., Taylor, V., & Rupp, L. J. (2016). Social movements and the construction of queer identity. In J. E. Stets, J & R. Serpe, *Advances in identity theory and research* (pp. 443–470). Oxford University Press.

Morris, M. W., Chiu, C., & Liu, Z. (2015). Polycultural psychology. *Annual Review of Psychology*, *66*, 631–659. https://doi.org/10.1146/annurev-psych-010814-015001

Mullaney, C. (2020). Fucking with rhetoric: Antisociality and neuroqueerness. *A Journal of Lesbian and Gay Studies*, *26*, 355–357. https://doi.org/10.1215/10642684-8141942

Nishii, L. H. (2013). The benefits of climate for inclusion for gender diverse groups. *Academy of Management Journal*, *56*, 1754–1774. https://doi.org/10.5465/amj.2009.0823

Oliver, M. (1996). *Understanding disability: From theory to practice*. Macmillan.

Ragins, B. R. (2008). Disclosure disconnects: Antecedents and consequences of disclosing invisible stigmas across life domains. *Academy of Management Review*, *33*(1), 194–215. https://doi.org/10.5465/amr.2008.27752724

Roberson, Q., Quigley, N.R., Vickers, K., & Bruck, I. (2021). Reconceptualizing leadership from a neurodiverse perspective. *Group & Organization Management*, *46*, 399–423. https://doi.org/10.1177/1059601120987293

Roscigno, R. (2019). Neuroqueerness as fugitive practice: Reading against the grain of applied behavioral analysis scholarship. *Educational Studies*, *55*, 405–419. https://doi.org/10.1080/00131946.2019.1629929

Rosqvist, H. B., Stenning, A., & Chown, N. (2020). Introduction. In H.B. Rosqvist, N. Chown, & A. Stenning (Eds.), *Neurodiversity studies: A new critical paradigm* (pp. 1–12). Routledge.

Santuzzi, A. M., Keating, R., Martinez, J., Finkelstein, L., Rupp, D., & Strah, N. (2019). Uncovering antecedents and consequences of identity management strategies for workers with concealable disabilities. *Journal of Social Issues*, *75*, 847–880. https://doi.org/10.1111/josi.12320

Shakespeare, T. (2006). The social model of disability. In L. J. Davis (Ed.), *The disability studies reader* (pp. 197–204). Routledge.

Shore, L. M., Cleveland, J. N., & Sanchez, D. (2018). Inclusive workplaces: A review and model. *Human Resource Management Review*, *28*, 176–189. https://doi.org/10.1016/j.hrmr.2017.07.003

Singer, J. (1999). Why can't you be normal for once in your life? From a 'problem with no name' to the emergence of a new category of difference. In M. Corker & S. French (Eds.), *Disability discourse* (pp. 59–67). Open UP.

Titchosky, T. (2001). Disability: A rose by any other name? "People-first" language in Canadian society. *Canadian Review of Sociology*, *38*, 125–140. https://doi.org/10.1111/j.1755-618X.2001.tb00967.x

Volpone, S. D., Avery, D. R., & Wayne, J. (in press). Using organizational cultures and climates to leverage workforce neurodiversity. In A. J. Collela & S. M. Bruyere (Eds.), *Neurodiversity*. SIOP Organizational Frontiers Series.

Walker, N. & Raymaker, D. M. (2021). Toward a neuroqueer future: An interview with Nick Walker. *Autism in Adulthood*, *3*, 5–10. https://doi.org/10.1089/aut.2020.29014.njw

Walker, N. (2015). *Neuroqueer heresies: Notes on the neurodiversity paradigm, autistic empowerment, and postnormal possibilities*. Autonomous Press.

Yergeau, M. (2018). *Authoring autism: On rhetoric and neurological queerness*. Duke University Press.

Frederike Scholz and Koen Van Laer

18 Burnout From an Extended Social Model Perspective: Lived Experiences of Burnout, Lasting Burnout Effects and Returning to Work

Abstract: Even before the COVID-19 pandemic, workplaces were already creating a pandemic leading to the burnout of its workers. Depending on the severity, burnout can result in extended periods of inability to work, after which individuals potentially return to work. However, the effects of burnout are often not over when individuals return to their workplace, not only as it can impact their future careers, but also as individuals can experience lasting burnout effects. Despite recognizing the role of organizational causes, research on burnout and interventions adopts a largely individualized, medical and psychological lens. Adopting a disability studies lens, this chapter aims to go beyond this individualized view of burnout and draws on 13 interviews with individuals who had a burnout to explore their experiences with burnout, lasting burnout effects and their return to work. We show how the predominant ways of thinking about burnout result in it being largely approached as an individual failure rather than an organizational problem. This leads to organizational sources of burnout being unaddressed and forces individuals returning to work to conform again to the norms of the economic system that led to their burnout in the first place.

Keywords: ableism, burnout, burnout effects, return to work, extended social model of disability

Introduction

Even before the COVID-19 pandemic, a pandemic was already plaguing workers, as workplaces were creating a burnout pandemic. Burnout is commonly characterized by combinations of exhaustion, cynicism and reduced professional efficacy that are the result of prolonged exposure to work-related stress. Burnout is linked to various psychological (e.g., depressive symptoms and mental health problems) and physical (e.g., fatigue, pain and headaches) consequences and to long-term health issues (e.g., heart disease, diabetes, and premature death). Depending on the severity, burnout

Frederike Scholz, Tilburg University
Koen Van Laer, Hasselt University

https://doi.org/10.1515/9783110743647-019

can result in extended periods of inability to work, after which individuals potentially return to work (Ahola & Hakanen, 2014; Halbesleben & Buckley, 2004; Mäkikangas & Kinnunen, 2016; Perski et al., 2017; Schaufeli & Buunk, 2003). However, the effects of burnout are often not simply over when individuals return to work. Not only might individuals not yet be fully recovered and continue to experience effects of their burnout, but it can also have a long-term impact on their future careers (Golembiewski & Munzenrider, 1988; van Dam, 2021).

While it remains a point of contention in both academic and policy debates whether (severe) burnout should be considered an impairment or not (Bianchi et al., 2021; Eurofound, 2018; Koutsimani et al., 2019), we do believe that debates on burnout, lasting burnout effects and returning to work could be enriched by approaching it through the lens of disability studies. Moreover, this can give us broader insights into the specific challenges and experiences of individuals with invisible and potentially reversible or fluctuating impairments in the labor market. Drawing on 13 interviews with individuals who had a burnout, the aim of this chapter is to explore their experiences of burnout and of returning to work.

The Concept of Burnout

With a growing number of employees being vulnerable to and suffering from burnout, the academic literature on the topic has, especially in the field of psychology, increased steadily over time. Core topics in this mainly quantitative literature are the nature, psychological and medical consequences, and origins of burnout (Rooman et al., 2021; Salminen et al., 2017). Burnout is generally characterized as resulting from prolonged work-related stress comprising of three dimensions: exhaustion, cynicism or mental distance from work, and reduced personal accomplishment or professional efficacy (Ahola & Hakanen, 2014; Bakker & de Vries, 2021; Mäkikangas & Kinnunen, 2016). Depending on the severity of these symptoms, diverse types of burnouts have been identified. On the one end, there are milder forms of burnout, which can be a short-lived problem and might affect employees' professional functioning, but do not completely prevent them from working (Perski et al., 2017). On the other end are severe forms of burnout, sometimes called clinical burnouts (Schaufeli et al., 2001) or 'burnout mental disabilities' (Paine, 1982). These result in significant effects on individuals' careers and professional functioning, in often lengthy absences from work, and in the need for professional help. In these cases, recovery might be a lengthy process and some individuals might still not be fully recovered after several years (Schaufeli et al., 2001; van Dam, 2021).

While there is quite some consensus on its typical characteristics, important debates exist on the official classification of burnout (Bianchi et al., 2021; Halbesleben & Buckley, 2004; Koutsimani et al., 2019). In its International Classification of Diseases

(2019), the WHO explicitly states that burnout is not a medical condition, but rather an occupational phenomenon affecting individuals' health. Common health consequences related to burnout are, among others, heart disease, diabetes, musculoskeletal pain, and premature death (Ahola & Hakanen, 2014). Nevertheless, some countries officially classify burnout as a disease or a disorder, and those suffering from it often end up accessing disability benefits (Ahola & Hakanen, 2014; Eurofound, 2018). Moreover, there is an intense debate on the distinction between burnout and depression; some scholars argue that the two constructs are related but differ, while others conclude that burnout could be seen as job-induced depression (Bianchi et al., 2017; Koutsimani et al., 2019).

Some have particularly contended that the origin in the sphere of work is what makes burnout different from other conditions such as depression (Maslach & Leiter, 2016). High job demands, such as role ambiguity, role conflict, workload, and mental and emotional demands, have been identified as important organizational causes for burnout (Bakker & de Vries, 2021; Halbesleben & Buckley, 2004; Maslach & Leiter, 2016). However, psychological research has also tied burnout to individual characteristics, such as neuroticism, perfectionism, and emotional instability (Korhonen & Komulainen, 2021; Rooman et al., 2021). Despite the recognition that working conditions are crucial in causing burnout, most interventions to prevent and alleviate burnout symptoms focus on ensuring that individuals are better equipped to deal with the demands of work by teaching them to control and manage their minds and bodies, rather than on changing those job demands. For example, common burnout interventions include stress management training, relaxation or mindfulness programs or physical activity (Bakker & de Vries, 2021; Korhonen & Komulainen, 2021; Leiter & Maslach, 2014; Perski et al., 2017).

Interventions to enable recovery from burnout and return to work also focus heavily on the development of individual strategies to better deal with workplace demands. Treatment of burnout traditionally starts with the recognition that one suffers from it, followed by a period of recovery through detachment from stress-inducing activities (such as work) and relaxation, and an exploration of the reasons for one's burnout to avoid relapse (van Dam, 2021). While most interventions focus on the individual, a successful return to work also depends to a large degree on other organizational actors, such as employers, supervisors, occupational health physicians, or return-to-work coordinators. They are not only important to provide social and emotional support, but also to allow a gradual return and implement (potentially temporary) modifications to work demands. For example, return to work might begin with reduced working hours or tasks to progressively reintegrate the individual and to avoid a relapse (Perski et al., 2017; Rooman et al., 2021; Salminen et al., 2017; van Dam, 2021).

While this literature has provided us with a lot of insights into burnout, it has predominately relied on quantitative research strategies or on the perspective of occupational health physicians and return-to-work coordinators. As a result, we have less in-depth insight into the lived experiences of individuals with burnout

(Kärkkäinen et al., 2018; Salminen et al., 2017; Schaufeli et al., 2018). Moreover, research on burnout and interventions to deal with burnout take a largely individualized, medical and psychological lens, thereby paying much less attention to the organizational and societal structures in which individual experiences of burnout occur (Korhonen & Komulainen, 2021; Leiter & Maslach, 2014). While it is not the aim of this chapter to make a final determination on whether burnout needs to be officially considered as an impairment, we do believe burnout and its potentially lasting burnout effects are a relevant topic to study through the lens of disability studies.

Burnout through the Lens of Disability Studies

In this chapter, we first draw inspiration from materialist disability studies, which have long recognized the role of capitalist modes of organizing in impairments through accidents, dangerous working conditions, or the exposure to specific products or machines (Abberley, 1987; Armer, 2004; Oliver, 1999). Furthermore, such a perspective considers disability to be socially produced through the way individuals with impairments become seen as inferior in relation to ableist economic structures and organizations of work, but also approaches impairment to be socially produced as certain conditions become recognized as impairments, which occurs in the context of economic structures that attempt to reject responsibility for the illnesses and impairments it causes (Abberley, 1987; Armer, 2004; Oliver, 1999).

The current economic context is strongly shaped by neoliberalism, in which individuals' worth and contribution to society is judged based on their involvement in paid employment, thereby serving as a marker of being an 'ideal citizen.' This requires adherence to taken for granted ableist norms of 'ideal qualities and behavior' (Goodley, 2014; Scholz, 2020; Scholz & Ingold, 2020), such as entrepreneurship, self-management, individualism, and resilience. By approaching burnout through this theoretical lens, question labor market norms and offer a counterweight to the largely individualized interpretations of burnout that tie it to individuals' inability to cope with the 'normal' stress of the workplace.

Drawing on a social relational perspective of disability (Reeve, 2004; Thomas, 1999) further allows us to explore the connection between individuals' well-being and their social context. Specifically, (the materialist version of) the social model of disability has traditionally focused on the way social barriers disable individuals with impairments by restricting their activities. An extended social model of disability highlights the personal experiences of disability and impairment effects and acknowledges that the oppression experienced by disabled people also affects their psycho-emotional well-being (Reeve, 2004; Scholz, 2020). This occurs as individuals are made to feel of 'lesser value' in their relations with those around them and in the way society is organized 'against' them, resulting in, for example, emotional pain, self-doubt, blame and fear to face further disabling experiences and practices (Reeve, 2004, 2014; Scholz, 2020; Scholz & Ingold, 2020; Thomas, 1999; Van Laer et al., 2022). Rather than individualizing these experiences, this view locates the causes of psycho-emotional disablism in relation to social barriers external to the individual (Reeve, 2014; Thomas, 1999).

By studying burnout through this lens, this chapter not only aims to contribute to our understanding of the lived experiences of individuals with burnout, but also adds to our knowledge of experiences with invisible and potentially reversible or fluctuating impairments in the labor market, with gaining an impairment at work and with returning to work.

Methods

This qualitative study was undertaken in Flanders, Belgium during 2019 and 2021, with the aim of providing insights about burnout and reintegration at work from the perspective of individuals who had experienced a burnout. In 2016, 12.3% of Flemish employees suffered from acute psychological fatigue problems due to excessive work pressure, emotional burden, and lack of autonomy, which means that they have an elevated risk of dropping out due to burnout (Bourdeaud'hui et al., 2018). Over the past 4 years, the number of people experiencing severe burnout and depression has seen an increase of 39.23% in Belgium (RIZIV, 2021). The non-probability sample of respondents was obtained through snowball sampling. In total, 13 semi-structured interviews were undertaken with employees who had experienced a burnout. The sample consisted of 8 women and 5 men between the ages of 32 and 65 (see Table 18.1).

Table 18.1: Interviews with individuals with a burnout.

Interview undertaken	Participants (Pseudonyms)	Gender	Age	Hierarchical Position	Year of Burnout
2019	Alina	Female	48	Manager	2012/2017
2019	Britt	Female	51	Employee	2014
2019	Carolien	Female	32	Employee	2017
2019	Dorien	Female	50	Manager	2014
2019	Eric	Male	42	Supervisor	2007
2021	Femke	Female	45	Supervisor	2018
2021	Geert	Male	40	Employee	2019
2021	Hilda	Female	38	Employee	2016/2018
2021	Jaap	Male	65	Employee	Twice in 2020
2021	Lars	Male	48	Manager	2019
2021	Marieke	Female	37	Employee	2020
2021	Nadine	Female	48	Employee	2019
2021	Ruben	Male	39	Supervisor	2019

Before the interviews, participants were informed about their rights and asked to sign an informed consent form stating their voluntary participation in this study. Interviews took place in person or, because of the COVID-pandemic, online by using Microsoft Teams or Google Meet. After the interviews were pseudonymized, a thematic analysis (Terry et al., 2017) focusing on the personal experiences of becoming burned out and of returning to work was undertaken. After two rounds of analysis, common themes emerged from the data. In terms of the experiences of having a burnout, the main themes included the importance of work-related causes of burnout as well as of interviewees individualizing their experience of burnout and downplaying organizational factors. In terms of return to work, the main themes were the lack of sufficient organizational support, as well as the stigma of having gone through a burnout.

Findings

Experiences of becoming burned out

First focusing on individuals' experiences of burnout, we found that the causes of burnout were clearly related to organizational factors exploiting interviewees' minds and bodies through norms that prioritize performance and productivity. Nevertheless, interviewees often internalized an individual understanding of burnout as being a personal failure, leading them to look for individual solutions, or to ignore or hide the way their minds and bodies were being drained by work. This often continued until they were ultimately forced to stop working as they were diagnosed with burnout by a medical professional.

Specifically, while some interviewees pointed to their managers as being the source of their burnout, many highlighted the role of intensified work pressure and workload. However, as they experienced burnout as a taboo and a personal failure, individuals often looked for individual solutions to this organizational problem. Dorien made this evident:

> My situation at work about 4 to 5 years ago was so stressful, so busy, so confusing, so unclear and chaotic that I personally couldn't stand it anymore . . . I then started to feel like 'Don Quixote' in the sense that I did not feel that I still had any grip on the situation, and I wanted to keep it anyway. I just started working harder and harder and started thinking more and more. And then you get into overdrive, you get overloaded, and you fall out. I fell silent overnight. (Dorien, 50, Manager)

To deal with increasing work-related pressures, uncertainties and stress, Dorien felt forced to personally deal with this situation affecting her well-being by working even harder and complying even more strongly with the demands of work, until finally her body shut down. Many interviewees discussed this view that their burnout was linked to their work context, yet that they felt individually responsible for dealing with the work pressures they were under. In doing so, they took part of the burden on themselves, treating burnout as a personal failure. This was evident in Nadine's account, an administrator who initially had difficulties accepting that she needed sick leave to deal with her burnout:

> I had already been to a physiotherapist because I thought there was something more going on with my head and had a scan. She [the doctor] said to me: 'Nadine, you're stuck with a burnout.' And every time she said that to me, I was crying. She said: 'I'll have to put you on sick leave, and for a long time.' I said: 'No, I will continue. Soon I will have time off and then I can rest well.' But even on leave, I couldn't turn off my WhatsApp, and there were people who continued to work [and send work-related messages]. (Nadine, 48, Employee)

Other individuals also tried to keep working, or even work more as they feared they would no longer be seen (and see themselves) as adhering to professional norms on the qualities and behavior an 'ideal worker' should displays, which impacted on their psycho-emotional well-being. For example, Alina said:

> You don't want to admit it to yourself because you are afraid about the judgment of others. That you are no longer seen as professional, that your professionalism is questioned, and that my internal customers will no longer consider me professional. While I do my best until the last minute to deliver quality. It's like you're failing, a kind of failure. You really don't want that because you just want to be strong and do your best and give the best of yourself. And when that doesn't work anymore, that's so frustrating, it almost gives a feeling of personal shame. (Alina, 48, Manager)

Alina explained how she felt obligated to comply with the professional norms of her job to the point where she felt slowly drained by her work, which exacerbated her burnout. She was not only concerned about other people's opinions, but also felt that acknowledging a burnout would entail recognizing herself as a failure. This feeling of having to work until completely 'burning out' and being put on sick leave by a doctor was also evident in Marieke's account. She explained that the feeling of burdening her colleagues with extra work due to her being absent led her to continue to work until she crashed:

> You know that your workload ends up on the shoulders of your colleagues. That's also why I kept going for so long, of course. 'I can't drop out,' I have so many clients, what's going to happen next . . . That's kind of in my personality, I think I'm kind of focused on the other and don't sufficiently indicate my own limits. (Marieke, 37, Employee)

These narratives not only show that organizational factors caused individuals to burn out, but also that individuals responded to this experience by internalizing the negative view of burnout that exists in society. This impacted on their psycho-emotional well-being as they tried to sustain their level of professional functioning as long as they could before eventually being forced to stop working.

Return to Work after Burnout

Focusing on the experiences of returning to work, the interviewees had a variety of positive and negative experiences when they re-entered their workplace after their sick leave. The duration of their sick leaves ranged from 2 months up to 2 years, depending on the severity of their burnout. Many interviewees often felt compelled to go back to work too early, which meant that they did not feel ready yet and still experienced lasting burnout effects. While some received to some degree the support they needed, the stories showed a general lack of adequate organizational interventions to facilitate a successful return to work. In this way, these responses demonstrated a lack of recognition of the organizational causes of burnout, and implicitly reproduced an individualized view of burnout. As a result, three out of the thirteen individuals also shared that they had a second burnout and had to go through this process again in the same or a different organization.

The moment of return to work was often one that was not voluntary, but for example mandated by therapists or doctors. This was evident Carolien's case:

> I spent 3 months at home. After that, I didn't feel like I was ready to go back to work, but in that therapy, they said: '3 months and then you have to go back to work because otherwise it's much harder to get back into that rhythm and go back to work.' So, I started part-time for a month. (Carolien, 32, Employee)

Pushed to return to work while she was still suffering from lasting burnout effects, she was accommodated for a brief period by being allowed to work part-time. However, this organizational support was only temporary, as her workload quickly increased again, leading to intensified burnout effects. Realizing that her organization would not fundamentally address the causes of her burnout, she left this position after 9 months to avoid a second burnout. Carolien explained:

> That went well for the first 3–4 months and then it started again. They said: 'We are going to re-examine that job description because actually, you should take on a number of things.' . . . At that moment I realized: 'This is going in the wrong direction here. I'm just going to look for other work.' I worked full-time for 9 months before I really said it was enough. Because I had another day on which I was completely overwhelmed when I came home. I again felt that I had a lot of muscle pain and that I couldn't bear anything.

Other individuals shared related stories of amplifying burnout effects and of lacking organizational interventions. Lars discussed experiencing lasting burnout effects and how it is impossible to find individual solutions to excessive organizational pressures:

> You have a 'before' and you have an 'after.' And in this 'after,' that [burnout] always remains dormant . . . So, you have to be attentive for the rest of your career so that you do not relapse into being burned out. And also, when you return to work if you feel 100% good, that's not enough. You have to feel 180%. Because when you start working again, you go back and

experience those frustrations, those stressors, get back into that routine, that flow. And then it kicks back in . . . And don't just say overnight: 'I've recovered, and I pick up back where I was.' (Lars, 48, Manager)

While some were helped by a medical diagnosis to get a reduction in working hours, many companies did not provide any further support to change the work situation causing the burnout in the first place. For instance, Dorien said that an occupational physician decided that she was fit to return to work part-time:

> He confirmed: 'Dorien cannot work full-time. Dorien has to start part-time and build that up.' That's how it happened, but there was nothing from a prevention consultant, or psychological support, or any in-house support. No, nothing . . . The only caveat I have about that is that in fact, one should also be given adapted work. Because it's difficult for some jobs to be done on a part-time basis. Then you're really going to have to limit things for that person. (Dorien, 50, Manager)

Even though some respondents were offered temporary adjustments such as reduced working hours, they did not feel that real changes were made to the content of their job and the workload attached to it. This was evident in Britt's account:

> I was allowed to work 4 days per week, but I didn't do that . . . Because you have to do the same in 4 days as someone else in 5 days, and you are paid less for it. So, I just chose to work full-time. I think that way, you have less stress than if you try to do it all in 4 days. (Britt, 51, Employee)

Britt felt that it was her individual responsibility to cope with the same pressures that caused her burnout. Accepting the accommodation of her burnout effects through reduced hours would not only mean earning less money, but also increasing her stress levels as the workload would remain the same. Another problem experienced by interviewees when returning to work was that their burnout became seen as a sign that they were no longer able to do the job. For example, Eric discussed the following:

> Let's just say that my career opportunities or my future prospects in management were burned . . . There were a lot of people saying: 'Eric, we're not going to use him for that anymore.' So, in that respect, there was some damage. But in terms of the performance of my job . . . there was no problem at all. Somehow, it was normal, I think. It's kind of separating the wheat from the chaff. (Eric, 42, Supervisor)

While Eric explained that he was able to perform, relations with others had changed, as they doubted his abilities and no longer saw him as able to take on more responsibilities. This had an impact on his psycho-emotional well-being, as he felt being treated 'differently' and 'of less value.' Interviewees mentioned that a successful reintegration would require a broader re-distribution of workload and the stress levels attached to it. Eric talked about the stress of having to be solely responsible for certain decisions:

> Perhaps create a kind of assessment system in which the manager can make an estimate of the workload or the work or stress level of his employees . . . The decision tree comes to one level

and full responsibility [for a decision] is carried there. That automatically creates stress. Whereas if the decision is supported by an entire team, then that stress is distributed, and it all becomes much more humane and bearable. You quickly know which projects or products, or situations or services create stress. As long as that is a temporary peak it is not so bad, but if that is long-term, that is problematic. I think an employer can predict that very well.

However, addressing the organizational problem of stress requires a mind shift of employers to acknowledge that burnout is an organizational problem and not created by individuals themselves. As the stories shared by the respondents clearly show, this view rarely exists. This causes reintegration after burnout to come with many obstacles, as it sometimes forces the person to accept the same pressures and to find individual ways to deal with them.

Discussion

This study contributes to the literature on burnout and return to work in two ways. First, reflecting arguments in materialist disability studies (Abberley, 1987; Armer, 2004; Oliver, 1999), it argues that burnout is produced by capitalist economic structures that privilege productivity and performance over individuals' well-being and health. Moreover, it shows how the individualization of burnout (Korhonen & Komulainen, 2021) obscures the economic exploitation causing it, thereby normalizing job-related stress, and problematizing the individual dealing with it. Specifically, the prevention and recognition of burnout are made more difficult because of the taken-for-granted ableist norms on entrepreneurship, self-management, individualism, and resilience (Goodley, 2014; Scholz, 2020; Scholz & Ingold, 2020) that normalize and reproduce the exploitative economic structures that cause it. It is in relation to these norms that burnout, while connected to job demands, becomes labelled and experienced as a personal failure or a burden on other potentially overworked colleagues. The research shows how burnout is connected to psycho-emotional consequences (Reeve, 2014; Thomas, 1999), involving feelings of shame and guilt. These experiences, however, would not exist without society's stigma of burnout as a sign of individual fragility, which in turn contributes to the reproduction of the very demands undermining individuals' minds and bodies. Thus, discourses on burnout need to move away from individualizing burnout towards recognizing burnout as a social problem and acknowledging that individuals are exploited and burned out because of the way work is organized. More broadly, this alerts us to how individuals gaining an invisible impairment at work might undergo a long struggle to recognize themselves as impaired and to accept that they should blame the organization rather than themselves for their impairment.

Second, the research shows that when returning to work, burnout remains largely approached as an individual problem, which causes the organizational sources of burnout to remain unaddressed and forces individuals to again conform to the norms of the economic system that led to their burnout in the first place. Meanwhile, they not only have to navigate the stigma resulting from having deviated from this 'ideal worker' norm (Goodley, 2014; Scholz, 2020; Scholz & Ingold, 2020), but also face the constant fear of relapsing. Moreover, return to work is not necessarily a voluntary process, but often mandated by medical professionals, which again reflects neoliberal discourses promoting the responsibility of all individuals to contribute, and comply, to the economic system (Goodley, 2014). However, when returning to work, many individuals still experienced lasting burnout effects, such as being more susceptible to stress, which was not always, or only temporarily or superficially, accommodated. This general assumption by the employer that once people return to work, they can be exposed to the same job demands not only shows a lack of attention for lasting burnout effects, but also a lack of recognition for the organizational causes of burnout. In general, this highlights how individuals with other fluctuating impairments might be faced with serious access challenges to gain accommodations or with pressures to 'give up' accommodations as they become perceived as no longer needing them.

Implications for Research

First, we hope this exploratory study inspires more qualitative research that captures the lived experiences of workers with a burnout rather than reproducing the views of medical experts or reintegration specialists. Bringing the voice of those experiencing burnout into the debate seems vital to fully understand its causes and consequences, as well as the interventions that are needed to prevent burnout. Given the processual, evolving and potentially lasting nature of burnout (van Dam, 2021), it might be especially useful to adopt longitudinal approaches involving multiple interviews with the same respondents over a longer period. Second, adopting a disability studies perspective, or other perspectives that draw attention to problematic elements from the organizational context, can enable research to move beyond the focus on finding an individual cure for burnout towards a focus on identifying and addressing the organizational factors and social power structures underlying burnout. Third, we support the call (Rooman et al., 2021) for more empirical evidence on successful return-to-work practices and policies that help the reintegration of burned-out workers.

Implications for Practice

Lastly, this study also makes several practical contributions. First, it shows that organizations need policies to ensure that early signs of burnout are identified, that individuals experiencing them feel safe disclosing these experiences, and that relevant prevention interventions are implemented. While these can include interventions focused on the individual, such as mindfulness programs (Bakker & de Vries, 2021), they also should involve policies to address individuals' workload and job demands. Second, organizations need to acknowledge potential lasting burnout effects experienced by employees returning to work. As these can vary depending on the individual and their job demands, they require personalized interventions at work. Third, to deal with burnout, employers should not merely focus on making employees more mindful, but also on creating a more mindful organization. This would involve adopting a combination of interventions aimed at continuously monitoring stress levels, reviewing job tasks, workloads, and removing work-related stressors to prevent burnout and facilitate successful reintegration at work. Fourth, this study points to the need for societal debates on burnout to move away from largely discussing it in individual psychological terms. Rather, we need to approach burnout as what it is: a pandemic caused by economic structures. Doing so might enable those suffering from it to see it not as a failing of themselves but as a failing of their workplace. This might contribute to the acknowledgement that there is a need to fundamentally rethink the role of work in individuals' lives, reassess its effects on these lives, and review the amount of stress and strain we deem 'normal.' If we do not do this, the economic system will continue to produce burnouts, which come at an individual and societal cost.

References

Abberley, P. (1987). The concept of oppression and the development of a social theory of disability. *Disability, Handicap & Society*, *2*(1), 5–19. https://doi.org/10.1080/02674648766780021

Ahola, K., & Hakanen, J. (2014). Burnout and health. In M. P. Leiter, A. B. Bakker & C. Maslach (Eds.), *Burnout at work: A psychological perspective* (pp. 10–31). Psychology Press.

Armer, B. (2004). In search of a social model of disability: Marxism, normality and culture. In C. Barnes & G. Mercer (Eds.), *Implementing the social model of disability: Theory and research* (pp. 48–64). The Disability Press.

Bakker, A. B., & de Vries, J. D. (2021). Job demands–Resources theory and self-regulation: New explanations and remedies for job burnout. *Anxiety, Stress, & Coping*, *34*(1), 1–21. https://doi.org/10.1080/10615806.2020.1797695

Bianchi, R., Schonfeld, I. S., Vandel, P., & Laurent, E. (2017). On the depressive nature of the "burnout syndrome": A clarification. *European Psychiatry*, *41*(1), 109–110. https://doi.org/10.1016/j.eurpsy.2016.10.008

Bianchi, R., Verkuilen, J., Schonfeld, I. S., Hakanen, J. J., Jansson-Fröjmark, M., Manzano-García, G., Laurent, E., & Meier, L. L. (2021). Is burnout a depressive condition? A 14-sample meta-analytic and bifactor analytic study. *Clinical Psychological Science*, *9*(4), 579–597. https://doi.org/10.1177%2F2167702620979597

Bourdeaud'hui R., Janssens F., & Vanderhaeghe S. (2018, March 15). *Acute psychische vermoeidheidsproblemen bij werknemers en zelfstandigen* [Acute psychological fatigue problems among employees and the self-employed]. SERV-Stichting Innovatie & Arbeid.

Eurofound. (2018). *Burnout in the workplace: A review of data and policy responses in the EU.* Publications Office of the European Union.

Golembiewski, R. T., & Munzenrider, R. F. (1988). *Phases of burnout: Developments in concepts and applications.* Praeger Publishers.

Goodley, D. (2014). *Dis/ability studies: Theorising disablism and ableism.* Routledge.

Halbesleben, J. R. B., & Buckley, M. R (2004). Burnout in organizational life. *Journal of Management, 30*(6), 859–879. https://doi.org/10.1016%2Fj.jm.2004.06.004

Kärkkäinen, R., Kinni, R. L., Saaranen, T., & Räsänen, K. (2018). Supervisors managing sickness absence and supporting return to work of employees with burnout: A membership categorization analysis. *Cogent Psychology, 5*(1). https://doi.org/10.1080/23311908.2018.1551472

Korhonen, M., & Komulainen, K. (2021). Individualizing the burnout problem: Health professionals' discourses of burnout and recovery in the context of rehabilitation. *Health (London).* https://doi.org/10.1177/13634593211063053

Koutsimani, P., Montgomery, A., & Georganta, K. (2019). The relationship between burnout, depression, and anxiety: A systematic review and meta-analysis. *Frontiers in Psychology, 10*, 284. https://www.frontiersin.org/article/10.3389/fpsyg.2019.00284

Leiter, M. P., & Maslach, C. (2014). Interventions to prevent and alleviate burnout. In M. P. Leiter, A. B. Bakker & C. Maslach (Eds.), *Burnout at work: A psychological perspective* (pp. 145–167). Psychology Press.

Mäkikangas, A., & Kinnunen, U. (2016). The person-oriented approach to burnout: A systematic review. *Burnout Research, 3*(1), 11–23. https://doi.org/10.1016/j.burn.2015.12.002

Maslach, C., & Leiter, M. P. (2016). Understanding the burnout experience: Recent research and its implications for psychiatry. *World Psychiatry, 15*(2), 103–111. https://doi.org/10.1002/wps.20311

Oliver, M. J. (1999). Capitalism, disability and ideology: A materialist critique of the normalization principle. In R. J. Flynn & R. A. Lemay (Eds.), *A quarter-century of normalization and social role valorization: Evolution and impact* (pp. 163–174). University of Ottawa Press.

Paine, W. S. (1982). The burnout syndrome in context. In J. W. Jones (Ed.), *The burnout syndrome: Current research, theory, interventions* (pp. 1–29). London House Press.

Perski, O., Grossi, G., Perski, A., & Niemi, M. (2017). A systematic review and meta-analysis of tertiary interventions in clinical burnout. *Scandinavian Journal of Psychology, 58*(6), 551–561. https://doi.org/10.1111/sjop.12398

Reeve, D. (2004). Psycho-emotional dimensions of disability and the social model. In C. Barnes & G. Mercer (Eds.), *Implementing the social model of disability: Theory and research* (pp. 83–100). The Disability Press.

Reeve, D. (2014). Psycho-emotional disablism and internalised oppression. In J. Swain, S. French, C. Barnes & C. Thomas (Eds.), *Disabling barriers – Enabling environments* (3rd ed.). Sage.

RIZIV. (2021). *Langdurige arbeidsongeschiktheid: Hoeveel langdurige burn-outs en depressies? Hoeveel kost dat aan uitkeringen?*[Long-term disability: how many long-term burnouts and depressions? How much does that cost in benefits?] https://www.riziv.fgov.be/nl/statistieken/uitkeringen/Paginas/langdurige-arbeidsongeschiktheid-burnout-depressie.aspx

Rooman, C., Sterkens, P., Schelfhout, S., Van Royen, A., Baert, S., & Derous, E. (2021). Successful return to work after burnout: An evaluation of job, person- and private-related burnout determinants as determinants of return-to-work quality after sick leave for burnout. *Disability and Rehabilitation.* https://doi.org/10.1080/09638288.2021.1982025

Salminen, S., Andreou, E., Holma, J., Pekkonen, M., & Mäkikangas, A. (2017). Narratives of burnout and recovery from an agency perspective: A two-year longitudinal study. *Burnout Research, 7*, 1–9. https://doi.org/10.1016/j.burn.2017.08.001

Schaufeli, W. B., Bakker, A. B., Hoogduin, K., Schaap, C., & Kladler, A. (2001). On the clinical validity of the Maslach Burnout Inventory and the burnout measure. *Psychology & Health*, *16*(5), 565–582. https://doi.org/10.1080/08870440108405527

Schaufeli, W. B., & Buunk, B. P. (2003). Burnout: An overview of 25 years of research and theorizing. In M. J. Schabracq, J. A. M. Winnubst & C. L. Cooper (Eds.), *Handbook of work and health psychology* (pp. 383–425). Wiley.

Schaufeli, W. B., Enzmann, D., & Girault, N. (2018). Measurement of burnout: A review. In W. B. Schaufeli, C. Maslach & T. Marek (Eds.), *Professional burnout: Recent developments in theory and research* (pp. 199–215). Taylor & Francis.

Scholz, F. (2020). Taken for granted: Ableist norms embedded in the design of online recruitment practices. In S. L. Fielden, M. E. Moore & G. L. Bend (Eds.), *The Palgrave handbook of disability at work* (pp. 451–469). Palgrave Macmillan.

Scholz, F., & Ingold, J. (2021). Activating the "ideal jobseeker": Experiences of individuals with mental health conditions on the UK Work Programme. *Human Relations*, *74*(10), 1604–1627. https://doi.org/10.1177/0018726720934848

Terry, G., Hayfield, N., Clarke, V., & Braun, V. (2017). Thematic analysis. In C. Willig & W. Stainton-Rogers (2nd ed.), *The Sage handbook of qualitative research in psychology* (pp. 17–37). Sage.

Thomas, C. (1999). *Female forms: Experiencing and understanding disability*. Open University Press.

van Dam, A. (2021). A clinical perspective on burnout: Diagnosis, classification, and treatment of clinical burnout. *European Journal of Work and Organizational Psychology*, *30*(5), 732–741. https://doi.org/10.1080/1359432X.2021.1948400

Van Laer, K., Jammaers, E., & Hoeven, W. (2022). Disabling organizational spaces: Exploring the processes through which spatial environments disable employees with impairments. *Organization*, *29*(6), 1018–1035. https://doi.org/10.1177/1350508419894698

World Health Organization. (2019). *Burn-out an "occupational phenomenon": International Classification of Diseases*. https://www.who.int/news/item/28-05-2019-burn-out-an-occupational-phenomenon-international-classification-of-diseases

Ramona L. Paetzold and Joy E. Beatty

19 Sanism: An Inquiry into and Critique of the Workplace Exclusion of People with Serious Mental Illness

Abstract: Severe mental illnesses (SMIs) such as bipolar disorder, major depression, and schizophrenia are often assumed to be incompatible with employment. The characteristics of people with SMIs are not aligned with the ideal worker myth. Individuals with these conditions tend to be unemployed or marginalized in low level jobs. We argue that this situation is due to sanism, a particular kind of ableism regarding psychological functions. HR policies do not exist for this population because they are assumed incommensurate with regular HR functions. In this chapter we review sanism discrimination, discuss three SMIs and three academics who have them, and provide evidence that people with SMIs can be effective employees in some contexts. We offer recommendations for workplace policies to support these employees. We advocate for greater awareness and inclusion of this potential employee population in all workplaces.

Keywords: severe mental illness, sanism, ableism, discrimination

Imagine leading a routine class discussion. You expect this to be like any other day. Suddenly, about 15 minutes into the class, you feel "wrong" – heart pounding, stomach queasy, chest constricted. You can't breathe. You begin to shake, feeling cold. Instead of seeing discrete students, you see an ocean of colors that will not come into focus. You can't concentrate. You must escape from the room. You panic. With a sense of urgency, no idea of what you are doing, you grab your keys, find your car, and drive yourself home.

Two hours later your husband comes home and finds you curled up on the bed, terrified, unsure of what has happened and what you are doing. You can't recall how you drove home. He gets you to a psychiatrist, who recognizes that at the very least you have had a panic attack. You have dissociated. Additionally, you are psychotic – you do not know what year it is or who the president is. He prescribes medication and sends you home. This begins a journey to find a diagnosis, something to fit a host of symptoms you have dismissed for at least twenty years. Ramona L. Paetzold, one of the authors of this chapter, experienced exactly this. She wondered if she would ever feel "normal," be able to return to work, be accepted by her colleagues. Her fears were rooted in *sanism.*

Ramona L. Paetzold, Texas A&M University
Joy E. Beatty, College of Business, Eastern Michigan University

https://doi.org/10.1515/9783110743647-020

Sanism and Ableism

Sanism is directed at people with a severe mental illness (SMI). Sanism is the irrational, systemic subjugation of people who have received mental health diagnoses/treatment (Perlin & Dorfman, 1993; Poole et al., 2012). It especially sees people with SMIs as incompetent, irrational, unpredictable, violent, and in constant need of supervision (Piuva & Brodin, 2020), and is a form of oppression that values rational thinking and socially acceptable forms of behavior, ostracizing or punishing those who cannot conform (Morrow & Weisser, 2013). Sanism stems from ableism – ideas, practices, institutions, and social relations that presume ablebodiedness (Williams & Mavin, 2012). It constructs people with certain disabilities as "Other." Ableist norms are embedded in organizational structures and job designs standardized for able bodies, shaping job descriptions and content, methods of performance, and remuneration (Foster & Wass, 2013). For example, jobs may require multitasking, interchangeability, and teamwork that are difficult for persons with disabilities, leading them to be seen as inherently less productive or reliable (Foster, 2007). The problematic structure of the social environment that causes people to appear that way is not questioned (Williams & Mavin, 2012, 2015). Ableism is a form of systematic discrimination that limits the full participation of people with disabilities.

According to the DSM-5 (American Psychiatric Association [APA], 2013), there are 157 mental disorders that vary in severity and responsiveness to treatment (Wiklund et al., 2018). SMI is defined as "a mental, behavioral, or emotional disorder resulting in serious functional impairment, which substantially interferes with or limits one or more major life activities" (https://www.nimn.nih.gov/health/statistics/mental-illness.shtml). We focus on two of the most severe examples: schizophrenia-spectrum disorders and bipolar disorder I. Statistics from 2017 estimate that 4.5% of all U.S. adults have SMIs; thus sanism is a potentially relevant problem for a large segment of society.

Most people with SMIs report that they want to work (McAlpine & Warner, 2015), particularly to create a source of meaning (Eklund et al., 2012). However, U.S. unemployment among those with SMI ranges from 60%-90%, which is often attributed to lower educational levels, career interruptions, and employer stigma (Dolce & Bates, 2019). For those with SMIs who are employed, the work may be lower-level, low-wage, and/or part-time (Krupa, 2010). Killeen and O'Day (2004) and Wästberg et al. (2018) found that low expectations about work capacity were embedded in policies and programs, propagated from medical and psychiatric personnel, vocational counselors, family members, friends, and the media. Major concerns included the possibility of relapse due to challenging, stressful work. Low work expectations imply that SMIs will have a limited chance of recovery, but more damage may result from the lack of work to assist in recovery, as well as poverty, low self-esteem, and stigma.

SMIs often occur early in life, disrupting vocational planning and training. Some people with SMIs experience symptoms later in life, affecting their careers. SMIs are sometimes linked with periodic episodes of enhanced productivity, which can mask the need to seek treatment. People with SMIs may experience employment gaps, which are inconsistent with traditional norms of steady paid employment (Krupa, 2010).

Stigma from employers and society may be the biggest workplace barrier (Corrigan, 2005). SMIs have more significant negative effects on hiring decisions and performance expectations than physical disabilities (Ren et al., 2008; Dalgin & Bellini, 2008). Employer concerns include socio-emotional skills (e.g., handling stress), conflict resolution (Hand & Tryssenaar, 2006), and concerns about safety, job attendance, and performance (Dolce & Bates, 2019). Coworkers may have negative attitudes toward SMIs, seeing them as socially undesirable and even self-caused. This produces negative reactions to accommodations for people with SMIs (Colella et al., 2004). People with SMIs therefore experience workplace discrimination, limited advancement opportunities, and patronizing, insensitive language (Russinova et al., 2011). They may try to hide their conditions to avoid stigma, but legislation in many countries requires disclosure to receive accommodations and work adjustments. Brouwers et al. (2020) found that five different focus groups (people with SMIs, employers, human resource [HR] managers, mental health advocates, and reintegration professionals) agreed that there were two major disadvantages to disclosure: it can lead to 1) discrimination in salary, hiring, etc. and 2) stigma, social distancing, disrespect, workplace gossip, lowered performance expectations, and less support at work. The person who disclosed would need to perform better to be seen as "equal," because mistakes would tend to be attributed to SMIs. Disclosure increases the chance that coworkers will learn about a worker's SMI, even if legislation mandates privacy and only "need to know" disclosure to others (Paetzold, 2005). Dolce and Bates (2019) found that employers saw disclosure of SMI as a major concern, acknowledging that preconceived biases and stigma would affect hiring decisions. They recommended that SMIs not be disclosed before being hired, if possible.

People with the most severe cases of SMIs may not be able to work, but many can be successful in demanding professional careers with the right set of accommodations. We argue that people with SMIs can perform virtually any job with better understanding, accommodation, job design, and employer flexibility. Organizations should be aware of the characteristics of sanism and develop policies to support employment for those with SMIs who want to work.

We challenge sanism by examining its evolution and demonstrating how people with SMIs can be successful in the workplace. To do this, we focus on three people in academia – a unique work context that should afford higher flexibility – to illustrate how SMI symptoms and accommodations shape careers. We conclude with recommendations for organizations to better accommodate employees with SMIs.

Sanism and the Evolution of SMIs

From the eighteenth century to the present, SMIs have evolved as problematic. Early focus saw them as defects to be eliminated by removing genetically inferior "stock" (i.e., the eugenics movement) (Paetzold, 2010). People with SMIs were warehoused in various ways and subjected to a variety of "treatments" (e.g., Reaume, 2002). As psychiatric drugs became available, a medical view of SMI as a treatable disease emerged. Increased medicalization of SMIs coincided with psychiatric hospitals reducing their patient populations, and today's medical system focuses on medication management to a greater extent than counseling and social support (Morrow & Weisser, 2013).

The DSM-5 (APA, 2013) aids with medicalization. It recognizes a high degree of comorbidity – shared symptoms – among people with SMIs (Plana-Ripoll et al., 2019). It emphasizes a neurobiological view of SMIs by incorporating cognitive neuroscience and brain imaging (e.g., Kaczkurkin et al., 2020). It also emphasizes a "spectrum" perspective, so that people with SMIs can be seen as having milder or more severe cases (APA, 2013).

SMIs are also biopsychosocial, seen as a combination of the individual's biological makeup, psychological patterns, and social environment and experiences. Treatments focused on "curing" SMIs may overlook the social and environmental factors that interact with biology. Can Öz et al. (2019) indicate that recovery cannot be achieved by simply reducing the severity of SMI symptoms. Improvements are needed to promote independent living, social functionality, interpersonal relationships, and enhanced education and employment to yield well-being for people with SMIs – all to assist them in approaching the ideal worker norm of an able-bodied and able-minded male (Scholz & Ingold, 2020).

We next examine the lived experiences of academics who have worked effectively with SMIs.

Sanism, SMIs, and Cases of Academic Scholars

We first consider Elyn Saks, who has schizophrenia. According to the DSM-5, schizophrenia is a spectrum disorder involving dysfunction in one or more of five domains of psychosis: hallucinations, delusions, disorganized thinking, abnormal motor behavior, and negative symptoms (e.g., reduction in expression, diminished speech, reduced ability to experience pleasure). The spectrum is broad, so we review the major considerations underlying a diagnosis of schizophrenia. Elyn has experienced all of these.

Hallucinations are perceptions of occurrences where no external event or stimulus exists. They are uncontrollable and vivid sensory experiences – e.g., auditory hallucinations are experienced as voices distinct from the individual's own thoughts. Delusions are beliefs that cannot be changed despite evidence to the contrary. For example, grandiose delusions suggest one has exceptional abilities. Disorganized thinking refers to disorganized speech patterns – at the extreme, "word salad." Abnormal motor behavior may manifest as extreme agitation on one extreme or catatonia on the other. Finally, negative symptoms occur in schizophrenia but do not tend to appear in other forms of psychosis (such as psychosis with bipolar disorder I).

Schizophrenia must last for at least 6 months and have one month where symptoms are clearly active. Like other SMIs, people with schizophrenia are often unaware of their disorder. Although aggression can be associated with schizophrenia, it is rare for people with schizophrenia to assault others or engage in violence. Like other SMIs, there are no diagnostic tests for the disorder, although brain regions may vary via neuroimaging. In the U.S., the lifetime prevalence of schizophrenia is approximately .3%-.7%. Onset typically occurs in the late teens until the mid-30s, with peak onset age for the first psychotic episode being early- to late-20s. Symptoms evolve slowly with a difficult prognosis. Approximately 20% of people recover functionality, but most require support for daily living (i.e., daily therapy in addition to medications). Remissions are possible between problematic periods, antipsychotic medications and psychotherapy can often control schizophrenia.

Elyn Saks, despite having schizophrenia for most of her adult life, is a chaired professor of law, psychology, and psychiatry at the University of Southern California Gould School of Law and an adjunct professor of psychiatry at the University of California San Diego School of Medicine. She received her degrees from Vanderbilt (B.A), Oxford (M.Litt), Yale (J.D.) and the New Center for Psychoanalysis (Ph.D.). She published the story of her struggles, *the center cannot hold* (Saks, 2007), and received the John D. and Catherine T. MacArthur Fellowship (the "genius grant") the following year. Elyn has published numerous articles, primarily focusing on the rights of people with SMIs (e.g., issues concerning forced treatment). She has made numerous presentations related to SMIs and mental health, and is high-functioning. She first resisted medical intervention but eventually realized that a combination of medication and therapy (in her case, daily psychoanalysis) was the best way to manage her schizophrenia. While holding her academic position, she earned her Ph.D. in psychoanalysis. Although she is not highly sociable (by her own admission), she is married and can interact in small groups of people.

Because teaching exacerbates her condition, her dean has designed a special arrangement for her: Elyn serves as the Director of the Saks Institute for Mental Health Law, Policy, and Ethics. Each year, the Institute selects a topic for study, and students apply to participate. Elyn selects approximately 8–10 students with whom to work. Her teaching commitment is to work one-on-one with each of those students for the entire academic year, hoping to produce publishable papers at the end of the year. This arrangement is time-consuming, but allows her to satisfy the teaching obligation without worsening her symptoms.

The law school also assists Elyn (and all law students) by beginning the academic year with a mental health orientation program, where Elyn is a featured speaker. She discloses her condition and models how people with SMIs can be successful in challenging environments.

The other two academics we describe are James T.R. Jones and Ramona L. Paetzold, both of whom have experienced bipolar disorder I with psychotic symptoms for years. This form of bipolar disorder is the most severe form, because bipolar disorder II does not involve psychosis and tends to have smaller and less frequent mood swings. Bipolar disorder I leads to more disruptive functioning and is more difficult to control.

Bipolar I disorder requires a period of clear, extreme manic mood for at least a week (and possibly months). During this period, mood is elevated or irritable and accompanied by persistent goal-directed energy virtually every day. Mood disturbance must be severe enough so that it markedly impairs functioning (work, social, etc.) or even requires hospitalization. Impulsive behavior is a significant problem. Suicide is possible during mania, as are psychotic episodes. Periods of major depression are also possible, but not required for a diagnosis of bipolar disorder I. The 12-month prevalence of bipolar disorder I in the U.S. is approximately .6%, with an average age of onset of 18 years. Many people with bipolar disorder receive delayed diagnosis and treatment because of lack of awareness of mania.

It is common for people with bipolar disorder I to change appearance, become more flamboyant, engage in activities such as antisocial or risky behaviors, and become delusional or paranoid. Diagnosis can take years. Full ("normal") functioning can occur between manic and depressive episodes, but people with bipolar disorder I tend to perform lower on cognitive tests than other people, which may contribute to work-related and interpersonal difficulties over the lifespan. Many types of medications, along with psychotherapy, can be used to manage bipolar disorder I.

James (Jim) Jones was a Professor of Law at the Louis D. Brandeis School of Law at the University of Louisville. He had bipolar disorder I with psychotic tendencies, something he did not disclose for 25 years. He managed to navigate teaching and research activities, even with periods of hospitalization. Eventually, when he disclosed his illness, he became an advocate for those with SMIs by writing about his experiences in an article entitled *Walking the Tightrope of Bipolar Disorder: The Secret Life of a Law Professor* (Jones, 2007). He later published his memoir, *A Hidden Madness* (Jones, 2011). To the sorrow of all who knew him, his bipolar disorder was responsible for his suicide in 2018.

Jim had many of the difficulties of people with bipolar disorder I – he needed structure in his life, could not easily adapt to change, and worked to maintain some level of physical fitness to handle stress. Although academia allowed him some of these things, he found personal interactions anxiety-producing and difficult and often had problems with colleagues (e.g., he did not take advice well; he experienced anger easily). He also had paranoia, a common psychotic feature associated with mania. His widow revealed that he also struggled with depression.

Jim hid his condition due to fear of stigma. His eventual disclosure was important, because it illustrated how a law professor could succeed within his profession while having an SMI. Jim was Phi Beta Kappa from the University of Virginia and received his J.D. with honors from Duke University School of Law (selected for Order of the Coif). He served in private practice before joining academia. After his SMI disclosure, he gave numerous talks as an advocate.

Jim received important accommodations. He did not teach before noon – something that was useful due to the side effects of medication. If teaching a course would be too difficult, the course was sometimes cancelled and offered at another time. He found research and publication difficult, and frequently worked from home to be more comfortable. He was not punished for his lower research output – the law school appeared to understand that he was producing at his highest possible level.

Jim had multiple surgeries during 2017, necessitated from years of taking his psychotropic medications. He received a teaching release in 2018. Because he feared a cognitive decline that might interfere with him keeping his job (apparent paranoia), he took his life. His identity was strongly built around his academic career and losing his position would have been devastating.

Ramona, whose story began this chapter, had a path that was different from Jim's, even though they had the same diagnosis. She did not return to her academic position for one and a half years, the time it took to obtain an accurate diagnosis and successful medical treatment. Because of this, she was forced to disclose her medical condition, which was not kept confidential. Returning to teaching and research was difficult after an extended leave, and it took a few years before she was able to publish. When she did, her first publication involved a disclosure to the employment law community, as well as a legal critique of the Americans with Disabilities Act (ADA) (Paetzold, 2005). This article introduced its readership to the characteristics of bipolar disorder, how it was seldom considered a disability under the original ADA, and how difficult it was to receive accommodations even if it was considered a disability. It also signaled a change in her research direction – one that would focus more on disability research, whether it be empirical or advocacy.

Ramona recognized that her earlier years reflected the characteristics of bipolar disorder I – e.g., earning 4 degrees in 8 years from Indiana University. She had taken 18 course hours a semester as an undergraduate while working in a psychology lab for 30+ hours per week. Heightened energy and little need for sleep (about 3 hours per night) were symptoms of mania. Graduate school involved taking and teaching extra courses, as well as symptoms such as hypersexuality, spending sprees, little need for sleep, and excessive energy. As an assistant professor, her goal-directed behavior allowed her to form entire research manuscripts in her head, so that she could write them start to finish and have them accepted for publication. She later attended law school, graduating at the top of her class and receiving the Order of the Coif award.

After returning to work at Texas A&M, Ramona's remission eventually gave way to mania again, and she was forced to take another year and a half of leave. By this time, she had also developed severe generalized anxiety (often comorbid with bipolar disorder I), so that she suffered regular panic attacks. Upon returning to work, her department head assisted her by rolling two sections of a course into one (i.e., job restructuring), so that her actual annual class presentation time involved three presentations per year. This helped to reduce both mania and anxiety.

During the most recent academic year (2020–21) she was not offered this type of accommodation and therefore used sick leave to avoid teaching one of her classes. The change in accommodation was distressing because it upset the stability she had had for years. She will once again have job restructuring during 2021–2022. Like Jim, she does not teach too early in the day due to issues with her psychotropic medications. Additionally, Ramona has weekly two-hour sessions with a psychotherapist to help her manage her bipolar disorder I.

Ramona faces the difficulty of conducting research that is not aligned with her department's goals, even though her work is well-regarded in other fields. Her research also progresses slowly, as did Jim's. Her salary suffers as a result, even though she is consistently rated as one of the top professors by her students and has won numerous teaching awards.

Discussion of Cases in Academia

Across these three cases, the faculty members have (or had) some level of difficulty fitting into their departments or fields. Their field of research may have changed towards advocacy, which may be unacceptable in departments or programs that value basic research and publication in top-tier journals. Faculty with SMIs may publish at a slower rate than others in their departments. Perhaps they are unable to assume administrative positions due to the inherent stress of such roles or because they are not viewed by others as suitable candidates. All of this means that faculty with SMIs may lag in salary and may not receive perks such as chairs or professorships. This is true even though the faculty members may be producing high-quality, imaginative, creative, and important research. For the faculty, this can create the sense that their work does not "count" and they are not valuable members of their departments or universities.

It seems clear that faculty with SMIs will have different needs for balancing the "Holy Trinity" (Baruch, 2013) of their work – research, teaching, and service. More flexible careers could benefit faculty with SMIs. The highest status has traditionally been afforded to those who can produce a steady stream of high-quality research in top-ranked journals, while maintaining adequacy in teaching and service. Higher education institutions have been unbundling and rebundling the tasks and services provided by their institutions, often in ad hoc ways to respond to divergent contextual demands (ACE, 2012). Scholars note that there is a need for more strategic design of faculty roles to give a more diversified configuration of career paths and models for faculty who are in different career stages. Academic career scripts need to be flexible to accommodate a range of personal and contextual factors (Dany et al., 2011). These may provide the ability to regularly rebalance job tasks to meet the employee's SMI needs – for example, decreasing lecture-format teaching with more customized, small format teaching, making changes to service requirements, or increasing/decreasing emphasis on collaborative research. These changes would require that reward structures be based on these flexible arrangements and be made available more broadly – not just for "star" performers.

Implications for Organizations and Research Directions

The faculty members described in the cases above agree (or did agree, while living) that people with SMIs can be functional if given proper support. That support comes initially from psychiatrists and psychotherapists, who help to manage the SMI. Typical employment support for people with mental illnesses includes medication, therapy, case management, and vocational services. Although some people with SMIs may require supported employment to help them maintain appropriate work (NAMI, 2019), people with SMIs can develop treatment plans with their medical team. Instead, what is needed is a reframing of the broader work structures and expectations of the ideal worker.

Functionality depends on personal support – social networks, family, friendships, etc. Because employment is important to individuals with SMIs, support must ultimately come from organizations. Organizations must believe that workers with SMIs can work at a high level, if only they are provided the means to do so. Although we have focused on academia, it should be clear that people with SMIs may have difficulty fitting into traditional organizational models, even when those models tend to be somewhat flexible or autonomous. Managers are often not aware of disability management practices or effective recruitment and retention practices for persons with disabilities and may not know how to respond to workers with mental health conditions (Cavanagh et al., 2017). They may struggle to determine how to intervene, showing care while maintaining professional boundaries.

We suggest some research topics that are needed to improve management and HR practices for employees with SMIs:
- SMI-specific studies. Researchers tend to combine different mental illnesses into a single group. Disaggregation of SMIs could give a better understanding of coping strategies used by people with specific SMIs, and which people are

more likely (or not) to disclose. Disaggregation could also help managers to be more aware of performance issues associated with specific SMIs.
- Studies of accommodations for employees with SMIs. To date, flexible scheduling, modified training, and modified job duties have been the most common accommodations (McDowell & Fossey, 2015). Effectiveness of a broader range of accommodations for SMIs should be investigated (e.g., white noise, space enclosures, working from home, being assigned smaller tasks) (Krupa, 2007).
- Research on effective training for all employees to reduce stigmatization and the promotion of inclusion and acceptance. Corbière et al. (2019) examined factors within organizational cultures that were essential for employees with psychiatric disabilities: supportive colleagues, peer support networks, and increased communication, particularly during periods of sick leave. Disability management and accommodation processes need to be distinct from disciplinary procedures. Research regarding the best ways to handle these policies is needed. Mental health awareness should involve all stakeholders.
- Cross-cultural research on SMIs. There needs to be greater awareness that what is considered mental illness in one culture or society may be viewed as eccentricity, neurodivergence, or merely a slight variation of "normal" behavior in other cultures. Such differences have consequences for discrimination and/or inclusion, stigmatization, and treatment.
- Intersectionality and SMI. Women have traditionally been associated with SMIs (e.g., the notion of "hysteria" stems from the word for "womb," American Heritage Dictionary, 2nd ed., 1991), and early commitment to asylums and hospitals often occurred because males (doctors or husbands) found it an appropriate way to handle women who did not follow gender norms (Smith & Hutchison, 2004). Religion is also an important consideration. For example, how can we know whether people who hear a religious icon speaking to them are hallucinating or adhering to religious norms?
- Community and clinical samples, such as undiagnosed and diagnosed workers, should be compared. Understanding differences in these two populations, both of which may be employed, could help to create a better understanding of coping strategies, how people who are diagnosed develop identities, whether diagnosed people will disclose, and ideas for improved accommodation.
- Sophisticated quantitative studies on SMIs in the workplace. Although autobiographical and qualitative research is valuable, it would be useful to have an enhanced view of the numbers of people in SMIs in organizations, with quantitative information about their experiences. Advanced statistical procedures could be used to examine causal models of how policies and procedures affect identity formation, disclosure, and other workplace behaviors by people with SMIs.
- Expanding samples. A major criticism of research on SMIs is that it tends to study only those people who are working. A close examination of people who do not or cannot work would be beneficial to examine underlying factors that

interfere with their ability to be in the workplace. Although we have made a case that people with SMIs (for the most part) *can* work, a study of nonworking people could help to verify the skills and abilities they could bring to workplaces.

In conclusion, we have argued a moral case that better accommodations for employees with mental illness is the right thing to do, but there is also a strong business case to be made. Mental illness drives nearly 70% of all disability costs in organizations, so preventing mental health problems and promoting employee mental health is important (Dimoff & Kelloway, 2019). Early intervention can stave off more significant performance problems and avoid more disruptive and costlier interventions if symptoms worsen. As Foster (2007, p. 718) notes, people with disabilities "are different and require different treatment, something that continues to confuse managers brought up on liberal concepts of equality." Smart job design entails crafting jobs that are designed for employees with disabilities, instead of trying to fit them into jobs designed for the generic able-bodied employee (Williams-Whitt & Taras, 2010). In the case of SMI, recovery may not mean a full cure, but rather the opportunity to live meaningful and satisfying lives that are not defined by their SMIs (Krupa, 2010). Our proposed research could bring this goal to fruition.

References

ACE. (American Council on Education). (2012). *Unbundling versus designing faculty roles*. Presidential Innovation Lab. https://www.acenet.edu/Documents/Unbundling-Versus-Designing-Faculty-Roles.pdf

American Heritage Dictionary, 2nd College Edition. (1991). Boston: Houghton Mifflin.

American Psychiatric Association. (2013). *Diagnostic and statistical manual of mental disorders* (5th ed.).

Baruch, Y. (2013). Careers in academe: The academic labour market as an eco-system. *Career Development International*, *18*(2), 196–210. https://doi.org/10.1108/CDI-09-2012-0092

Brouwers, E. P. M., Joosen, M. C. W., van Zelst, C., & van Weeghel, J. (2020). To disclose or not to disclose: A multi-stakeholder focus group study on mental health issues in the work environment. *Journal of Occupational Rehabilitation*, *30*, 84–92.

Can Öz, Y., Ünsal Barlas, G., & Yildiz, M. (2019). Opinions and Expectations Related to Job Placement of Individuals with Schizophrenia: A Qualitative Study Including Both Patients and Employers. *Community Mental Health Journal*, *55*(5), 865–872. https://doi.org/10.1007/s10597-019-00374-z

Cavanagh, J., Bartram, T., Meacham, H., Bigby, C., Oakman, J., & Fossey, E. (2017). Supporting workers with disabilities: A scoping review of the role of human resource management in contemporary organisations. *Asia Pacific Journal of Human Resources*, *55*(1), 6–43. https://doi.org/10.1111/1744-7941.12111

Colella, A., Paetzold, R. L., & Belliveau, M. A. (2004). Factors affecting coworkers' procedural justice inferences of the workplace accommodations of employees with disabilities. *Personnel Psychology*, *57*(1), 1–23.

Corbière, M., Zaniboni, S. Dewa, C.S., Villotti, P., Lecomte, T. Sultan-Taïeb, H., Hupé, J., & Fraccaroli, F. (2019). Work productivity of people with a psychiatric disability owrking in social firms. *Work*, *62*, 151–160. https://doi.org/10.3233/WOR-182850

Corrigan, P. W. (Ed.) (2005). *On the stigma of mental illness: Practical strategies for research and social change*. American Psychological Association.

Dalgin, R. S., & Bellini, J. (2008). Invisible disability disclosure in an employment interview: Impact on employers' hiring decisions and views of employability. *Rehabilitation Counseling Bulletin*, *52*(1), 6–15. https://doi.org/10.1177/0034355207311311

Dany, F., Louvel, S., & Valette, A. (2011). Academic careers: The limits of the "boundaryless approach" and the power of promotion scripts. *Human Relations*, *64*(7), 971–996. https://doi.org/10.1177/0018726710393537

Dimoff, J. K., & Kelloway, E. K. (2019). With a little help from my boss: The impact of workplace mental health training on leader behaviors and employee resource utilization. *Journal of Occupational Health Psychology*, *24*(1), 4–19.

Dolce, J. N., & Bates, F. M. (2019). Hiring and employing individuals with psychiatric disabilities: Focus groups with human resource professionals. *Journal of Vocational Rehabilitation*, *50*(1), 85–93. https://doi.org/10.3233/JVR-180990

Eklund, M., Hermansson, A., & Håkansson, C. (2012). Meaning in life for people with schizophrenia: Does it include occupation? *Journal of Occupational Science*, *19*, 93–105.

Foster, D. (2007). Legal obligation or personal lottery?: Employee experiences of disability and the negotiation of adjustments in the public sector workplace. *Work, Employment and Society*, *21*(1), 67–84. https://doi.org/10.1177/0950017007073616

Foster, D., & Wass, V. (2013). Disability in the labour market: An exploration of concepts of the ideal worker and organisational fit that disadvantage employees with impairments. *Sociology*, *47*(4), 705–721. http://search.ebscohost.com/login.aspx?direct=true&db=psyh&AN=2013-29122-007&site=ehost-live

Hand, C., & Tryssenaar, J. (2006). Small business employers' views on hiring individuals with mental illness. *Psychiatric Rehabilitation Journal*, *29*(3), 166–173. https://doi.org/10.2975/29.2006.166.173

Jones, J.T.R. (2011). *A hidden madness*. Self-published.

Jones, J.T.R. (2007). Walking the tightrope of bipolar disorder: The secret life of a law professor. *Journal of Legal Education*, *57*(3), 349–374.

Kaczkurkin, A. N., Sotiras, A., Baller, E. B., Calkins, M. E., Chand, G. B., Cui, Z., Erus, G., Fan, Y., Gur, R. E., Gur, R. C., Moore, T. M., Roalf, D. R., Rosen, A. F. G., Ruparel, K., Shinohara, R. T., Varol, E., Wolf, D. H., Davatzikos, C., & Satterthwaite, T. D. (2020). Neurostructural heterogeneity in youth with internalizing symptoms. *Biological Psychiatry*, *87*, 473–482. https://doi.org/10.1101/614438

Killeen, M. B., & O'Day, B. L. (2004). Challenging expectations: How individuals with psychiatric disabilities find and keep work. *Psychiatric Rehabilitation Journal*, *28*(2), 157–163. 10.2975/28.2004.157.163

Krupa, T. (2007). Interventions to improve employment outcomes for workers who experience mental illness. *Canadian Journal of Psychiatry*, *52*(6), 339–345.

Krupa, T. (2010). Employment and serious mental health disabilities. In I. Z. Schultz & E. S. Rogers (Eds.), *Work Accommodations and Retention in Mental Health* (pp. 91–101). Springer.

McAlpine, D.D., & Warner, L. (2015). *Barriers to employment among persons with mental illness: A review of the literature* (Vol.6, pp. 1–49). Institute for Health, Health Care Policy, and Aging Research. https://doi.org/10.1017/CBO97811074153224.004

McDowell, C., & Fossey, E. (2015). Workplace accommodations for people with mental Illness: A scoping review. *Journal of Occupational Rehabilitation*, *25*(1), 197–206. https://doi.org/10.1007/s10926-014-9512-y

Morrow, M., & Weisser, J. (2013). Towards a social justice framework of mental health recovery. *Studies in Social Justice*, *6*(1), 27–43. https://doi.org/10.26522/ssj.v6i1.1067

NAMI (National Alliance on Mental Illness). (2019, October 2). People with mental illness can Work. www.nami.org/Blogs/NAMI-Blog/October-2019/People-with-Mental-Illness-Can-Work

Paetzold, R. (2005). How courts, employers, and the ADA disable persons with bipolar disorder. *Employee Rights & Employment Policy Journal*, *9*, 293–382.

Paetzold, R.L. (2010). Why incorporate disability studies into teaching discrimination law? *Journal of Legal Studies Education*, *27*, 61–80. https://doi.org/10.1111/j.1744-1722.2010.01068.x

Perlin, M. L., & Dorfman, D. A. (1993). Sanism, social science, and the development of mental disability law jurisprudence. *Behavioral Sciences & the Law*, *11*(1), 47–66. https://doi.org/10.1002/bsl.2370110105

Piuva, K., & Brodin, H. (2020). Just like any other family? Everyday life experiences of mothers of adults with severe mental illness in Sweden. *Community Mental Health Journal*, *56*(6), 1023–1032. https://doi.org/10.1007/s10597-020-00549-z

Plana-Ripoll, O., Pedersen, C., Holtz, Y., Benros, M., Dalsgaard, S., de Jonge, P., Fan, C., Degenhardt, L., Ganna, A., Greve, A., Gunn, J., Iburg, K., Kessing, L., Lee, B., Lim, C., Mors, O., Nordentoft, M., Prior, A., Roest, A., . . . McGrath, J. (2019). Exploring comorbidity within mental disorders among a Danish national population. *JAMA Psychiatry*, *76*(3), 259–270.

Poole, J. M., Jivraj, T., Arslanian, A., Bellows, K., Chiasson, S., Hakimy, H., Pasini, J., & Reid, J. (2012). Sanism, mental health, and social work/education: A review and call to action. *Intersectionalities: A Global Journal of Social Work Analysis, Research, Polity, and Practice*, *1*(0), 20–36.

Reaume, G. (2002). Lunatic to patient to person: Nomenclature in psychiatric history and the influence of patients' activism in North America. *International Journal of Law and Psychiatry*, *25*(4), 405–426. https://doi.org/10.1016/S0160-2527(02)00130-9

Ren, L. R., Paetzold, R. L., & Colella, A. (2008). A meta-analysis of experimental studies on the effects of disability on human resource judgments. *Human Resource Management Review*, *18*(3), 191–203. https://doi.org/10.1016/j.hrmr.2008.07.001

Russinova, Z., Griffin, S., Bloch, P., Wewiorski, N. J., & Rosoklija, I. (2011). Workplace prejudice and discrimination toward individuals with mental illnesses. *Journal of Vocational Rehabilitation*, *35*(3), 227–241. https://doi.org/10.3233/JVR-2011-0574

Saks, E. R. (2007). *The center cannot hold*. Hyperion.

Scholz, F., & Ingold, J. (2020). Activating the 'ideal jobseeker': Experiences of individuals with mental health conditions on the UK Work Programme. *Human Relations*. https://doi.org/10.1177/0018726720934848

Smith, B.G., & Hutchison, B. (Eds.) (2004). *Gendering disability*. New Brunswick, NJ: Rutgers.

Wästberg, B. A., Sandström, B., & Gunnarsson, A. B. (2018). New way of working: Professionals' expectations and experiences of the Culture and Health Project for clients with psychiatric disabilities: A focus group study. *International Journal of Mental Health Nursing*, *27*(1), 329–340. https://doi.org/10.1111/inm.12324

Wiklund, J., Hatak, I., Patzelt, H., & Shepherd, D. (2018). Mental disorders in the entrepreneurship context: When being different can be an advantage. *Academy of Management Perspectives*, *32*(2), 182–206. https://doi.org/10.5465/amp.2017.0063

Williams-Whitt, K., & Taras, D. (2010). Disability and the performance paradox: Can social capital bridge the divide? *British Journal of Industrial Relations*, *48*(3), 534–559. https://doi.org/10.1111/j.1467-8543.2009.00738.x

Williams, J., & Mavin, S. (2012). Disability as constructed difference : A literature review and research agenda for management and organization studies. *International Journal of Management Reviews*, *14*, 159–179. https://doi.org/10.1111/j.1468-2370.2012.00329.x

Williams, J., & Mavin, S. (2015). Impairment effects as a career boundary : A case study of disabled academics. *Studies in Higher Education*, *40*(1), 123–141. https://doi.org/10.1080/03075079.2013.818637

Part 6: **Research and Practice**

Matthew C. Saleh, Valerie B. Malzer, William E. Erickson,
Sarah von Schrader, and Susanne M. Bruyère

20 Disability-Inclusive Online Outreach and Recruitment for Employers

Abstract: For employers, online outreach and recruitment plays a vital role in attracting qualified candidates with disabilities. For jobseekers with disabilities, initial interactions with employer recruitment practices can influence decisions to explore, apply to, or accept a job. While online recruitment takes many forms, certain promising practices exist for tailoring such efforts to attract diverse candidates with disabilities and for modifying existing practices that tend to exclude qualified jobseekers with disabilities. This chapter provides both a description from the literature on promising practices in disability-inclusive online outreach and recruitment, and results from three sequential studies undertaken by the authors to: (1) identify disability-related messaging and content that exists on employer career websites; (2) understand employer perspectives on effective online recruitment practices and barriers; and (3) ascertain the experiences of jobseekers with disabilities in online outreach and recruitment by employers. The implications of these findings for employers are discussed.

Keywords: online recruitment, eRecruiting, disability, inclusive hiring, diverse talent pools

Introduction

For employers, online outreach and recruitment plays a vital role in attracting qualified candidates with disabilities. As the recent COVID-19 pandemic has demonstrated, online recruitment methods are likely to become even more ubiquitous and integral to employer talent-pool development. Additionally, for jobseekers with disabilities, initial interactions with employer recruitment practices can influence decisions to explore, apply to, or accept a job (Chen et al., 2012). While online recruitment takes many forms, certain promising practices exist for tailoring such efforts to attract diverse candidates with disabilities and for modifying existing practices that may exclude qualified jobseekers with disabilities.

Strategies discussed in this chapter include effective messaging on career websites and social media, carefully-worded and disseminated job postings, accessible

Matthew C. Saleh, Valerie B. Malzer, William E. Erickson, Sarah von Schrader, and Susanne M.
Bruyère, Cornell University, ILR School, Yang-Tan Institute on Employment and Disability, Ithaca,
New York USA

https://doi.org/10.1515/9783110743647-021

and inclusive online application components, and partnerships with community organizations. After providing background on promising practices in disability-inclusive online outreach and recruitment, we describe three sequential studies undertaken by the authors to: (1) identify disability-related messaging and content that exists on employer career websites; (2) understand employer perspectives on effective online recruitment practices and barriers; and (3) ascertain the experiences of jobseekers with disabilities in online outreach and recruitment by employers.

In Study 1, we developed a checklist, based on the literature, to assess outreach and messaging components for recruiting people with disabilities. The checklist was used to review forty randomly-selected, U.S.-headquartered Fortune 500 company career websites to assess the frequency and content of evidence-based disability-inclusion messaging elements. In Study 2, we conducted focus groups with employers to better understand the online approaches used to attract candidates with disabilities, the degree to which these are or are not effective, and to identify the most pressing information needs among employers related to online recruitment of candidates with disabilities. In Study 3, we conducted further focus groups with jobseekers with disabilities, to assess online job search strategies, and the impact of specific messaging and online recruitment approaches utilized by employers.

Background

Online recruitment is a broad terminology that includes active processes undertaken by employers – such as targeted outreach on social media or job boards – and more passive processes, such as career websites and online application portals. While many employers conceptualize and implement online recruitment strategies differently – and different sectors will embrace technological options with disparate uptake and enthusiasm – for most employers online recruitment broadly includes efforts to: (a) identify a pool of potential candidates; (b) attract applicants from that pool; (c) efficiently filter, sort, and select top applicants; (d) evaluate and interview those applicants; and (e) ultimately select, hire, and onboard new personnel (Partnership on Employment and Accessible Technology [PEAT], 2015).

Online recruitment can encompass many practices for outreaching to candidates through technological applications and web-based resources, and the proliferation of new technologies offer opportunities for converting traditional recruitment processes to virtual mediums. Examples on the cutting edge of this trend include algorithmic tools for efficiently identifying candidates on social media (Hmoud & Laszlo, 2019), and software platforms for assigning "employability scores" in virtual interviews (Meena, 2016). A more mainstream example is *applicant-tracking software*, which help employers sort applicants with keyword scans; highlight top candidates; coordinate interviews, pre-employment tests, and background checks; and document follow-up and reporting (PEAT, 2015).

Online recruitment can also entail more straightforward – and less automated – practices like having recruiters manually sourcing candidates on professional social media or portfolio websites, partnering with job-placement provider agencies, updating career website content, writing and posting online job advertisements, participating in online career fairs, and more. Taking a holistic view of online recruiting and messaging, we begin with a discussion of the "early online touchpoints" that jobseekers encounter with an employer.

Early Online Touchpoints

There is growing awareness of the extent to which initial impressions of workplace cultural fit affect jobseeker decisions to identify, apply for, and accept jobs (Gallup, 2021). One threshold consideration involves the overall messaging that a company makes available online about their inclusive hiring, workplace culture, and overall mission. Therefore, employers might begin by asking: where are jobseekers with disabilities most likely to first interact with my company's online messaging? Research also shows that early-stage jobseekers' experiences with recruitment, corporate advertising, and firm reputation all have direct effects on applicant pool quantity and quality (Collins & Han, 2004). Employers can begin by taking steps to audit and review their existing online materials to ensure consistent messaging around diversity and inclusion efforts, and to ensure that existing online "real estate" demonstrates that the organization prioritizes disability-inclusive hiring.

Below, we describe some potential early touchpoints that employers should consider, including: (1) career websites; (2) job advertisements; and (3) social media.

Career Websites

Employer career websites are one cost-effective means of messaging to jobseekers with disabilities, as they are a potential early point of contact for interested applicants looking for job openings, or pursuing a job posting found elsewhere online (Lambert et al., 2019). Career websites offer natural opportunities for organizations to highlight initiatives and practices they are undertaking to improve inclusivity, accommodations, flexible work, work-life balance, talent development, and more. Despite the frequency with which candidates access career pages to review job openings, many opportunities to leverage career websites are underutilized (Lambert et al., 2019).

Common weaknesses in employer online messaging around disability hiring practices include: message inconsistency; lack of disability awareness; difficult-to-navigate and inaccessible websites; and inadequately-locatable accommodations information and diversity statements (Couture & Johnson, 2017). When thinking about online content, employers are encouraged to work with their web developers to incorporate both *instrumental* and *symbolic* content and design that attracts diverse talent pools. "Instrumental" online content includes factual and objective job and employer attributes. Examples of instrumental content include realistic job previews (e.g., blog posts) that help jobseekers understand what to expect, including specific organizational practices and policies (e.g., benefits, work-life balance, performance expectations; Banerjee, 2016).

"Symbolic" content entails subjective features of web design that jobseekers use to make inferences about company personality and values (Lambert et al., 2019). Examples of symbolic content can include having diverse, integrated, and non-stereotypical images of people with disabilities, or highlighting awards the organization has won for disability-inclusion, diversity and inclusion, work-life balance or workplace culture (e.g., "best places to work"), to name a few examples. In some cases, content can serve both instrumental and symbolic functions, such as using employee testimonials that convey diversity and inclusion but also cover factual features of working for the company.

Some companies have disability-specific career websites, while others highlight disability-focused hiring priorities on their main career website (Kaye et al., 2011). Career websites can be one venue for publicizing existing targeted hiring and recruitment plans (e.g., neurodiversity or disability hiring plans; Gould et al., 2020), as well as existing disability-focused internship programs or opportunities, which are a known predictor of employer success in hiring people with disabilities (Erickson et al., 2014).

Several employer studies have found that visible top-management commitment to diversity is a key component of successful disability recruiting, and this is another strategy that can be integrated into online reputation-building efforts (Erickson et al., 2014). One study of online messaging by employers nationally recognized for their disability-inclusion efforts found that these companies commonly included robust, visible diversity and inclusion statements that specifically highlight disability, and provided information on disability-related employee resource groups and supplier-diversity initiatives to demonstrate corporate mission around diversity and inclusion (Gould et al., 2020).

Job Advertisements

The wording and dissemination of online job advertisements is another important way through which employers can ensure that public-facing recruitment materials are disability-inclusive (Leary, 2019). While the role of disability-inclusive language in job advertisements has been underexplored empirically, research has shown that word choice in job advertisements can contribute to jobseekers' decisions to apply for the job, especially for underrepresented groups (Born & Taris, 2010).

For example, one study found that including fewer masculine tropes and more feminine word choice in job descriptions helped attract more female applicants to science, technology and medicine (STEM) jobs (Krome, 2016). Other research found that using words with less lexical ambiguity can better support neurodiverse applicants to process and understand job requirements and qualifications (Dow et al., 2020).

The thoughtful selection of accessible and unbiased language in job advertisements may be helpful in ensuring that candidates with disabilities do not select themselves out of a job for which they might be a good fit. Going back to the discussion above about *symbolic* content, it might also be important that human resources (HR) professionals review job advertisements for metaphorical statements that might be interpreted as exclusionary. Simple hypothetical examples of what to avoid might include using disability as a metaphor (e.g., "going in blind") or using sports metaphors that equate athletic or physical ability with job aptitude (e.g., "quarterbacking skills").

Another objective might focus on ensuring that job advertisements aren't overly focused on non-essential job features that might filter out otherwise-qualified candidates with disabilities. Examples of language to avoid might include wording that unnecessarily accentuates social skills, provides unclear expectations like being a "self-starter," accentuates marginal job functions rather than needed technical skills, or engages in the rote inclusion of education or experience levels that don't necessarily translate to successful job performance.

Beyond the words that are used, the places an advertisement is posted can have an important impact. Employers with disability-inclusive online recruitment strategies often utilize disability-specific online job boards and resources (e.g., www.AbilityLinks.org or www.AbilityJobs.com; Employer Assistance and Resource Network on Disability Inclusion [EARN], n.d.), and tailor other online strategies (e.g., social media recruitment) to cast a wider, more inclusive talent pool "net."

Social Media

Social platforms have become an increasingly popular tool that recruiters and companies use to advertise job openings and recruit candidates (Morgan, 2016). The rapid ascension of online visibility through social networks (e.g., professional social media like LinkedIn) offers another avenue for employers to evaluate job candidates during the personnel selection process, but also another source of career capital that may be differentially available to people with disabilities (Berkelaar & Buzzanell, 2015). Research indicates that employers do not always take steps to ensure that diversity-hiring initiatives are properly represented and integrated within social media recruitment strategies, which are often developed separately (Madia, 2011).

For employers, one consideration is that overreliance on social media strategies that are not intentionally disability inclusive might result in *unintentional* filters being placed on applicant pools (Berkelaar & Buzzanell, 2015). For example, digital divides and disparities in "digital career capital" among candidates with disabilities can result in lower representation of people with disabilities in social media recruitment campaigns. Digital career capital refers to jobseekers using social and professional websites to demonstrate skills and competencies and leverage networks to find work (Berkelaar & Buzzanell, 2015). Put simply, groups who experience more barriers to work are likely to have less digital career capital to present on professional social networking sites (Jaeger, 2011).

There is evidence that people with disabilities overall have less access to technology than people without disabilities, including access to and use of social media (Jaeger, 2011; Martin, 2021). The use of social media and online networking platforms is also lower among people with certain types of disabilities – specifically neurodiverse individuals and/or people with intellectual or developmental disabilities – even where equivalent access to technology exists (Raghavendra et al., 2018). One study of jobseekers with disabilities found that 50% of respondents reported using social media as part of their job search process, but of those 40% experienced usability issues, such as features they could not access or that were not user-friendly (PEAT, 2015).

The advertising insights available on increasingly-popular social media advertising platforms (e.g., Facebook advertising) typically don't have disability-specific demographic data; therefore, carefully choosing jobseeker networks within social media platforms (e.g., LinkedIn and Facebook groups) that specifically target diverse populations may be necessary to expand talent pools reached through such campaigns (Harver, 2018). Employers should consider supplemental strategies to counteract potential "invisible" filters that social media platforms might perpetuate.

One strategy involves collaborations with national and local disability organizations and community organizations (PEAT, 2015). Research suggests that partnerships that utilize disability organizations' talent pipelines (e.g., community job-placement providers) and broader online networks (e.g., email listservs, social media pages, online career fairs) are effective but underutilized by employers (Phillips et al., 2019). In working with job-placement providers, one important objective is establishing direct communication between the provider and HR/hiring professionals to discuss specific available positions and establish general familiarity about an agency and its candidates (Erickson et al., 2014).

Getting in the Front Door

Now let's assume that an employer has successfully outreached to a diverse talent pool, and attracted attention from qualified jobseekers with and without disabilities. The process of disability-inclusive online recruitment cannot end there. Increasingly, virtual or online interactions continue as interested job seekers become interested job *applicants*. Clearly, applying for a position entails multiple steps, from applying, to making it through any pre-screening mechanisms, to having one's résumé and application selected, to navigating and succeeding in the assessment and job interview processes. Here we discuss some of these disability-inclusion considerations in the successful job application process for applicants with disabilities, including: accessibility across online applications and applicant tracking software.

Accessibility Across Online Applications

Research shows that job applicants with disabilities tend to find that employers underestimate the need for accessible online platforms and tools, and when these considerations are made they are often only focused on compliance (e.g., Section 508 guidelines) rather on incorporating a usability mindset that considers how people with different impairments might interact with "off-the-shelf" technology platforms from third-party vendors (PEAT, 2015).

In one assessment of the experiences of jobseekers with disabilities using online recruitment tools (n = 427), 46% of respondents rated their last experience applying for a job online as "difficult to impossible" (PEAT, 2015). Common challenges included complex navigation features, timeout restrictions, confusing or inconsistent instructions, and other general accessibility issues (e.g., reliance on text embedded within graphics to convey directions; no alt text; applications requiring mouse input; no closed captioning; inaccessible CAPTCHAs; inaccessible upload features; PEAT, 2015).

Applicant-Tracking Software

Commercial applicant-tracking software used to screen résumés offers a range of opportunities to reduce cost to employers (Chapman & Webster, 2003), however, it may also introduce bias antithetical to disability-inclusion efforts (Trewin, 2018).

Employers might consider reviewing applicant-tracking systems to better understand what disposition codes are used, the filters applied, and to review of hires/non-hires (e.g., recruiter "report cards") to ensure that disability-inclusion efforts are not lost in translation. Employers can carefully vet their third-party systems and vendors to reduce bias (EARN/PEAT, 2020).

To build off this review of the literature, we now turn to a discussion of three sequential research studies conducted by the authors on online disability outreach and inclusion.

Study 1: Assessment of Disability-Inclusive Career Website Content

Methods

From the literature discussed above, it was evident that there are some evidence-based approaches for making organizations more attractive to potential employees with disabilities; however, there was limited research examining how these practices are implemented by organizations in early touchpoints for jobseekers. Therefore, in Study 1 we assessed the extent to which employer career websites contained these promising elements for effectively messaging to jobseekers with disabilities.

We developed an *Employer Career Pages Assessment Checklist* that compiled evidence-based items from the literature (twenty in total) that employers might include on their career websites to demonstrate disability-inclusive hiring. The checklist focuses on positive recruitment and outreach elements, as digital accessibility elements and legal requirements had been covered in existing publications (PEAT, 2015).

The checklist organized the practices into six broad categories: (1) general disability-inclusion components; (2) targeted-hiring and recruitment programs; (3) accommodations, supports, and flexibility-in-work arrangements; (4) partnerships with disability organizations (5) top-leadership commitment to disability-inclusion; and (6) symbolic content and credible media. In summer 2020, researchers used the checklist to review forty randomly-selected, U.S.-headquartered Fortune 500 companies to assess the frequency and manner of inclusion of disability recruitment and messaging components on their career websites. Researchers began from the company's main career website, systematically reviewing it and all content that was within three clicks and not behind a login page. Research has found that a typical web user often "gives up" when information navigation exceeds three clicks (Scaria et al., 2014). Links in the navigation menus at the top, side, or footer of the main career page were also reviewed, as career websites often linked to diversity and inclusion pages that contained relevant disability information. Imagery and media content, such as testimonials, videos, etc., were reviewed for representation or inclusion of disability.

Findings

General Disability-Inclusion Components

Only about one-quarter of the forty organization's career websites contained specific, easily-locatable information about the importance of disability-inclusion in their organization. For instance, 25% (10/40) of companies included a diversity and inclusion statement that mentioned people with disabilities and went beyond a boilerplate Equal Employment Opportunity (EEO) statement. Companies that included such statements tended to incorporate language that aligned inclusive hiring practices with a corporate mission, or a business case for hiring people with disabilities and/or appealing to customers with disabilities. Fewer websites – 20% (8/40) – had a section specifically focused on hiring people with disabilities, while 15% (6/40) had a dedicated careers website for jobseekers with disabilities.

Among those websites with robust disability-inclusion elements, some met nearly all of the checklist elements, and demonstrated a wide array of informative instrumental content (i.e., disability-focused employer resource groups [ERGs], disability-focused hiring and supplier-diversity initiatives) combined with innovative *symbolic* content demonstrating the importance of disability-inclusion within the company (e.g., prominent statements from leadership, inclusive images and design, multimedia examples of the experience of disability within the company, and disability-focused awards). Some of these examples are discussed below.

Targeted-Hiring and Recruitment Programs

Among employers with an overt commitment to disability-inclusive hiring, one of the most common elements included specific reference to their disability-hiring initiative(s), such as a target hiring percentage or alternate application process for applicants with disabilities. In total, 20% of websites (8/40) contained information on existing targeted-hiring and recruitment programs, or initiatives such as neurodiversity, autism-at-work, or disability hiring plans, and 15% (6/40) publicized a disability-focused internship program.

Accommodations, Supports, and Flexibility-in-Work Arrangements

Most – but not all – websites had at least basic information about seeking disability accommodations. Seventy-five percent (30/40) provided specific information about requesting accommodations during the recruitment, application, and interview phases. However, only 23% (9/40) had language demonstrating a commitment to accommodating employees that went beyond basic boilerplate compliance language and contact information. Flexible-work arrangements, which can be both a formal or "informal" accommodation, were highlighted on 35% of websites (13/40), while 48% (19/40) contained information about work-life balance and related benefits (e.g., parental leave, employee education, counseling, wellness opportunities). In terms of on-the-job supports, 58% of websites (22/40), involved highlighting employee resource groups for employees with disabilities or their family members.

Partnerships with Disability Organizations

Finally, 18% of websites (7/40) highlighted specific partnerships with either national or local disability-focused employment organizations including partnerships with national and local job-placement organizations and other nonprofits. Additionally, 23% of websites (9/40) mentioned participation in disability-focused recruitment resources such as disability job posting, job boards, and/or disability-specific job fairs.

Top-Leadership Commitment to Disability-Inclusion

While most websites contained statements from executives about diversity and inclusion broadly, only 15% (6/40) specifically mentioned disability in leadership statements. Examples of content exhibiting top-leadership commitment included quotes from a C-level executive, videos of an executive describing the company's commitment to inclusive hiring, and visual representations of awards won for disability-inclusion. Forty percent of websites (16/40) highlighted awards that the company had received for their disability-inclusion efforts, making it one of the most common ways employers illustrated a commitment to disability-inclusion and hiring.

Symbolic Content and Credible Media

Some of the more innovative elements of the career websites reviewed occurred on those examples with robust diversity and inclusion and disability-inclusion content. A third (13/40) included employee testimonials or blogs by employees with disabilities describing their experience working for the company, pursuing accommodations, disclosing their disability, and/or feeling a sense of belonging. Some contained extensive videos interviewing and/or following employees as they performed their job. Others provided testimonials from different employees in a variety of positions and diverse disabilities including visible disabilities (e.g., mobility impairments) and invisible disabilities (e.g., mental health, learning, or intellectual impairments). Some videos focused on job- or military-service acquired disabilities and return-to-work, while others highlighted disability-focused hiring initiatives.

Building off this, 45% of websites (18/40) included videos or images of employees with disabilities. Some websites included a single stock or "staged" image of a person in a wheelchair or with a cane, while others had images that more directly connected to the experience of working in the company, often integrated into a larger story, article, or video. These were often associated with an employee testimonial, and/or an article that highlighted the company's efforts and commitment towards the inclusion of persons with disabilities, and provision of a supportive environment.

Study 2: Employer Online Approaches to Attract Candidates with Disabilities

Methods

Building off our analysis of career websites, Study 2 sought to better understand how employers conduct online outreach and recruitment of people with disabilities, successful practices, and areas for additional support. In July 2020, we conducted two online focus groups (n = 7 total participants) with employers across a range of sectors (e.g., finance, aerospace, healthcare, engineering, pharma). Participants were recruited through DirectEmployers, a nonprofit, member-owned-and-managed association that supports online recruiting solutions and other member benefits.

Findings

Online Outreach Approaches and Perceived Effectiveness

Participants discussed using a wide range of online outreach and recruitment approaches. One of the most salient approaches involved engaging with partner organizations with a disability focus. This included national organizations with a focus on disability-inclusion (e.g., DirectEmployers, Disability:IN, AbilityJobs), state and local agencies and community-based providers (e.g., vocational rehabilitation agencies, job placement and matching providers), and working with external recruiters. Common strategies included engaging these partners to post jobs or share information about open opportunities. Some employers participated in partners' virtual career fairs or virtual meetings to outreach to potential jobseekers; other employers' HR teams organized similar events.

Participants noted success with hosting their own virtual career fairs to interface with active jobseekers with disabilities. Connected to this, they discussed how having strong connections to colleges allows access to graduating students with disabilities. They also noted sharing the positive stories of employees with disabilities both internally and externally was important to outreach and recruitment efforts, often working with disability ERGs.

When discussing information needs related to online outreach, many of the issues that were raised were well known, including: concern about employee/applicant willingness to self-identify as having a disability, ability to track candidates with disabilities in the outreach and recruitment process, educating hiring managers to ensure applicants with disabilities are not overlooked or screened-out for relevant opportunities, and ensuring digital accessibility for career and other company websites and online applications.

While there are resources to support employers on many of these topics, one area of interest was that employers in the focus groups expressed a need to better understand the perspectives of applicants with disabilities. Specifically, as related to online outreach, there was an interest in how people with disabilities perceive their organization, what potential applicants see as barriers or turn-offs as they review an organization's career website or other messaging, and what would help organizations make themselves more attractive to candidates with disabilities.

Study 3: Jobseeker Perceptions of Online Recruitment Strategies and Messaging

Methods

Based on the findings from Studies 1 and 2, a protocol was developed for focus groups with current or recent jobseekers with disabilities. In winter 2020, we conducted five virtual focus groups (n = 9 total participants, recruited through word-of-mouth using partner organizations and contacts). All participants were individuals with a disability who were currently job searching, or had been within the last year.

The goal was to gather information on: (1) job-search strategies used by jobseekers with disabilities, and (2) types of content and messaging that participants considered most impactful in assessing a company's disability inclusiveness. During the second half of the interviews, participants were offered the opportunity to review and reflect on 1–2 specific career websites that had been reviewed in Study 1.

Findings

Job Search Tools and Strategies

Most participants reported doing the majority of their job searching online. This included using both general job search and social networking websites (e.g., LinkedIn, Indeed, ZipRecruiter, Monster, CareerBuilder) and disability-focused websites (e.g., AbilityJobs). LinkedIn and Indeed were the most frequently mentioned. Participants noted features of these two sites that were particularly appealing, such as LinkedIn's unique networking features, and Indeed's "one-click apply" feature. Participants also noted several other strategies they use when job searching, including: networking with friends, prior colleagues, and other connections; utilizing recruiters/headhunters, college advisors, job coaches, and vocational rehabilitation services.

All participants reported engaging a mix of both broad and highly-targeted job searching. All participants reported searching broadly at first to find a high volume of positions that were a fit for their skills and interests, as well as searching very specifically for positions at organizations in which they were especially interested. Specific to career websites, participants indicated that they were more likely to carefully review these sites for employers in whom they were particularly interested, but that for other employers they often would not navigate to the career page at all and would sometimes apply for a position after seeing only the job advertisement.

In describing their job search, the job features that the participants considered included *position features* (i.e., qualifications, job duties, travel requirements, office location, remote work options, pay and benefits, part- vs. full-time work, their personal "fit" for the position and company, the alignment of job responsibilities with their with disability) and *company features*, such as the organization's financial strength (e.g., recent layoffs, financial issues), reputation around disability considerations, trustworthiness, treatment of employees, and corporate mission. One theme was that the participants tended to focus on job characteristics earlier in their search, but would later consider organizational culture and disability inclusiveness, especially for employers in whom they had the most interest.

Perception of Employer Online Outreach and Messaging

Participants noted a variety of organizational characteristics and online content that signaled the degree of disability-inclusion within an organization. Participants identified a range of organizational polices, practices, and behaviors that communicated a sense of inclusion. Often these characteristics had little to do directly with disability, but broadly signaled that the workplace was one that was flexible, open and likely to be disability-inclusive. These included having a culture/mission aligned with their own personal values (e.g., supporting volunteer/charity work; having statements around valuing inclusion, diversity); having options for flexible work (e.g., remote/virtual work, flexible hours); and providing a competitive benefits package. Participants also noted that it was a plus if an organization gave priority to individuals with disabilities, expressed a willingness to do job trials/probationary periods to allow both sides to assess job fit, and identified that they were open to individuals with gaps in their résumé.

In terms of specific website content, participants were asked to reflect on their experiences in viewing organizations' websites, and were then asked to review real examples of company career websites. Participants identified a variety of content that they found compelling or important. This ranged from content that primarily communicated a message of inclusion (e.g., images), to content that supported inclusion (e.g., website accessibility).

Many participants noted that images and videos that included representations of disability stood out to them, and were an important factor in communicating disability inclusiveness. Some participants observed that diversity and inclusion statements and content that went beyond boilerplate EEO language and specifically mentioned disability demonstrated a genuine commitment to inclusion. Many participants remarked that digital accessibility was significant for practical reasons related to applying, but also as a more symbolic gesture that the organization valued and considered the needs of applicants with disabilities. Two additional salient themes included the importance of providing multiple modes for communicating with recruiters (e.g., instant chat, email, etc.), and clear, straightforward access information on accommodations.

Participants highlighted the value of external perspectives on the organizational culture, in general, and disability inclusiveness, specifically. They reported reviewing testimonials on sites like Glassdoor to locate authentic input from knowledgeable current and former employees; and searching for information on awards, recognitions, or reviews from disability-focused organizations like Disability:IN.

Regarding self-identifying as a person with a disability during the application process, those participants who were generally comfortable with self-identifying indicated that the decision to do so could depend on the employer, and on how inclusive their organization appeared. Among participants willing to self-identify at least sometimes, there was agreement that inclusive website content could be helpful in making that choice. For participants who stated they would never self-identify, there seemed to be near-universal experience with a direct negative consequence of self-identifying (e.g., being dropped as a candidate). For those individuals, inclusive website content was not enough to overcome their worries about the potential negative consequences of self-identifying.

Conclusion

People with disabilities are approximately 10% of the working age population in America, yet less than half of this population is in the workforce – compared to over 80% of their non-disabled peers (Erickson et al., 2021). Each step in the employment process presents potential barriers to disability-inclusion, and employer outreach and recruitment is a critical first step in attracting potential applicants. The literature identifies several promising online outreach practices, which might improve the likelihood of employers attracting potential applicants with disabilities. The purpose of this research was to examine the use of online outreach approaches by employers and to better understand employer and jobseeker perceptions of these efforts.

Our examination of 40 Fortune 500 employers career sites found that many had implemented some of the 20 practices identified in the literature. However, a sizable minority had only implemented a few of them despite the ease of implementation of some of them (e.g., including images of employees with disabilities on their webpage; having clear statements about requesting accommodations, etc.). In conversations with employers, many reported that they believed the online outreach efforts they used were effective in attracting candidates with disabilities, but they noted that challenges in tracking applicants with disabilities (e.g., through the self-identification process) made it difficult to connect their outreach efforts with application or employment outcomes. Similarly, individuals with disabilities reported that employers' online outreach approaches did inform their opinion of the employers' likely level of disability-inclusiveness in ways that would influence their decisions about whether to apply or ultimately accept a job offer. Jobseekers reflected the concerns expressed by employers about self-identification. While some jobseekers felt that online outreach approaches could increase their likelihood of self-identifying, others reported that there was no impact, as there were never circumstances where they would disclose disability to an employer at the application stage.

While this work identifies some promising practices in employers' online outreach to potential candidates with disabilities, there is still a great deal of work to be done to gain a better understanding of which approaches are most impactful. Future work should consider the impact of specific online outreach approaches to the likelihood of candidates with disabilities applying for and accepting positions, including the likelihood they self-identify as a part of this process. This work could examine the precise messaging, images, and types of online and social media content that heighten the likelihood of application, and self-disclosure of disability in the application process. This additional work could help employers better target their online outreach approaches to ensure they have the greatest impact, increasing the number of individuals with disabilities who apply and are hired.

References

Banerjee, P. (2016). Attracting job-seekers through online job advertisements: Application of RJPs, blogs, and video podcasts. *International Journal of Technology and Human Interaction*, *12*(3). https://doi.org/10.4018/IJTHI.2016070101

Berkelaar, B. L., & Buzzanell, P. M. (2015). Online employment screening and digital career capital: Exploring employers' use of online information for personnel selection. *Management Communication Quarterly*, *29*(1), 84–113. https://doi.org/10.1177/0893318914554657 (accessed September 28, 2021).

Born, M. P., & Taris, T. W. (2010). The impact of the wording of employment advertisements on students' inclination to apply for a job. *The Journal of Social Psychology*, *150*(5), 485–502.

Chapman, D. S., & Webster, J. (2003). The use of technologies in the recruiting, screening, and selection processes for job candidates. *International Journal of Selection and Assessment*, *11* (2/3), 113–120. https://doi.org/10.1111/1468-2389.00234 (accessed September 28, 2021).

Chen, C-C, Lin, M-M, & Chen, C-M. (2012). Exploring the mechanisms of the relationship between website characteristics and organizational attraction. *The International Journal of Human Resource Management*, *23*(4), 867–885.

Collins, C. J., & Han, J. (2004). Exploring applicant pool quantity and quality: The effects of early recruitment practice strategies, corporate advertising, and firm reputation. *Personnel Psychology*, *57*(3), 685–717. https://doi.org/10.1111/j.1744-6570.2004.00004.x (accessed September 28, 2021).

Couture, K. A., & Johnson, K. R. (2017). Website barriers to employment for people with disabilities. *The Journal of Business Diversity*, *17*(1), 110–121. https://search.proquest.com/docview/1926954889?accountid=10267 (accessed September 28, 2021).

Dow, M. J., Lund, B. D., & Douthit, W. K. (2020). Investigating the link between unemployment and disability. *The International Journal of Information, Diversity, and Inclusion (IJIDI)*, *4*(1).

Employer Assistance and Resource Network on Disability-Inclusion. (n.d.). Finding candidates with disabilities. Ithaca, N.Y.: Cornell University. https://askearn.org/topics/recruitment-hiring/finding-candidates-with-disabilities/ (accessed September 28, 2021).

EARN/PEAT. (2020). Checklist for employers: Facilitating the hiring of people with disabilities through the use of eRecruiting screening systems, including AI. https://bit.ly/2X3Y1SH (accessed September 28, 2021).

Erickson, W. A., Lee, C., & von Schrader, S. (2021). Disability Statistics from the 2018 American Community Survey (ACS). Ithaca, NY: Cornell University Yang-Tan Institute (YTI). Retrieved from Cornell University Disability Statistics website https://disabilitystatistics.org/ (accessed September 28, 2021).

Erickson, W. A., von Schrader, S., Bruyère, S. M., VanLooy, S. A., & Matteson, D. S. (2014). Disability-inclusive employer practices and hiring of individuals with disabilities. *Rehabilitation Research, Policy, and Education*, *28*(4), 309–328. https://doi.org/10.1891/2168-6653.28.4.309 (accessed September 28, 2021).

Gallup. (2021). Designing the employee experience to improve workplace culture and drive performance. https://www.gallup.com/workplace/323573/employee-experience-and-workplace-culture.aspx (accessed September 28, 2021).

Gould, R., Harris, S. P., Mullin, C., & Jones, R. (2020). Disability, diversity, and corporate social responsibility: Learning from recognized leaders in inclusion. *Journal of Vocational Rehabilitation*, *52*(1), 29–42. https://doi.org/10.3233/JVR-191058 (accessed September 28, 2021).

Harver. (2018, Oct. 9). 9 tips on social media recruiting strategies. https://harver.com/blog/social-media-recruiting-strategies/ (accessed September 28, 2021).

Hmoud, B., & Laszlo, V. (2019). Will artificial intelligence take over human resources recruitment and selection? *Network Intelligence Studies*, *7*(13), 21–30.

Jaeger, P. (2011). Disability and the internet: Confronting a digital divide. Boulder, CO: Lynne Rienner Publishers.

Kaye, H. S., Jans, L. H., & Jones, E. C. (2011). Why don't employers hire and retain workers with disabilities? *Journal of Occupational Rehabilitation*, *21*(4), 526–536. https://doi.org/10.1007/s10926-011-9302-8 (accessed September 28, 2021).

Krome, L. R. (2016). Attracting women to STEM programs: the influence of goal-orientations and the use of gendered wording in recruitment materials [Doctoral dissertation, Kansas State University].

Lambert, R., Nicholson, K., Palmer, K., & Damron, T. (2019). Employer branding on career websites. *Institute for Global Business Research Conference Proceedings*, *3*(1). 178–183. https://www.igbr.org/wp-content/uploads/2019/05/2019-Conference-Proceedings-Vol-3-No-1.pdf#page=179 (accessed September 28, 2021).

Leary, A. (2019, Mar. 12). To be more inclusive to people with disabilities, employers should start with their job descriptions. *Quartz*. https://qz.com/1569134/how-to-write-inclusive-job-descriptions-for-people-with-disabilities/ (accessed September 28, 2021).

Madia, S. A. (2011). Best practices for using social media as a recruitment strategy. *Strategic HR Review*, *10*(6), 19–24. https://doi.org/10.1108/14754391111172788 (accessed September 28, 2021).

Martin, M. (2021, April). *Computer and internet use in the United States: 2018* (American Community Survey Report: ACS-49). https://www.census.gov/content/dam/Census/library/publications/2021/acs/acs-49.pdf (accessed September 28, 2021).

Meena, K. (2016). Blind recruitment: The new hiring buzz for diversity inclusion. *International Journal of Business and General Management*, *5*(5), 25–28.

Morgan, H. (2016). How Social Recruiting Impacts Job Search. *Career Planning and Adult Development Journal*, *32*(2), 33.

Partnership on Employment and Accessible Technology (PEAT). (2015). eRecruiting and accessibility: Is HR technology hurting your bottom line? Report on PEAT's 2015 research findings. https://www.peatworks.org/content/erecruiting-accessibility-report (accessed September 28, 2021).

Phillips, K. G., Houtenville, A. J., O'Neill, J., & Katz, E. (2019). The effectiveness of employer practices to recruit, hire, and retain employees with disabilities: Supervisor perspectives. *Journal of Vocational Rehabilitation*, *51*(3), 339–353.

Raghavendra, P., Hutchinson, C., Grace, E., Wood, D., & Newman, L. (2018). "I like talking to people on the computer:" Outcomes of a home-based intervention to develop social media skills in youth with disabilities living in rural communities. *Research in Developmental Disabilities*, *76*(1), 110–123. https://doi.org/10.1016/j.ridd.2018.02.012 (accessed September 28, 2021).

Scaria, A. T., Philip, R. M., West, R., & Leskovec, J. (2014). The last click: Why users give up information network navigation. *Proceedings of the 7th ACM International Conference on Web Search and Data Mining* (pp. 213–222). https://doi.org/10.1145/2556195.2556232 (accessed September 28, 2021).

Trewin, S. (2018). AI fairness for people with disabilities: Point of view. https://arxiv.org/abs/1811.10670v1 (accessed September 28, 2021).

Jana F. Bauer*, Veronika Chakraverty, Anja Greifenberg,
and Mathilde Niehaus

21 To Tell or Not to Tell? Co-Developing an Interactive Online Tool That Supports Employees with Invisible Disabilities to Make a High-Quality Disclosure Decision

Abstract: For employees with invisible disabilities, the decision of whether or not to disclose their condition to colleagues or supervisors is both far-reaching and hard to make. Support services for making these decisions are available but often insufficiently accessed due to lack of knowledge or hesitancy in approaching them. Therefore, we developed a science-based interactive online tool that provides easily accessible decision support complementing existing support structures for employees with disabilities and fostering the use of those structures. The online tool combines a *self-test* providing individualized feedback on the pros and contras of disclosure with information and additional resources on decision-making, (non-)disclosure, legal matters, further support options, and implementing the decision. We used an iterative participatory co-development process to develop the online tool, integrating theory and empirical findings with input from end-users and other relevant stakeholders. The interactivity of the self-test makes this online tool unique.

Keywords: decision aid, invisible disabilities, e-health, workplace accommodations, stigma

In the course of demographic and societal developments, the number of people that live and work with chronic illnesses or disabilities is increasing and many of these conditions are not immediately visible to others (Charmaz, 2010; Lingsom, 2008; Prince, 2017; Ward, 2015). "Invisible disabilities refer to a range of mental and physical disabilities that, like visible impairments, vary in their origins, degree of severity and in whether they are episodic or permanent" (Prince, 2017, p. 75). Employees with invisible disabilities are in the unique situation that they can decide whether, when, and how to

Note: The development of the online tool has been funded by the German Federal Ministry of Labor and Social Affairs and AbbVie Deutschland GmbH & Co. KG.
   We have no known conflict of interest to disclose.

*Corresponding author: Jana F. Bauer, University of Cologne, Herbert-Lewin-Str. 2, 50931 Cologne, Germany, e-mail: jana.bauer@uni-koeln.de
Veronika Chakraverty, Anja Greifenberg, Research Associates at the Chair of Labor and Vocational Rehabilitation, University of Cologne
Mathilde Niehaus, Chair of Labor and Vocational Rehabilitation, University of Cologne

https://doi.org/10.1515/9783110743647-022

disclose their condition or aspects of it to others (Lingsom, 2008; Norstedt, 2019). While being able to decide about disclosure might sound desirable, it is actually a dilemma. Although employees with invisible disabilities may "pass as normal" (Goffman, 1963) in the sense that they are not categorized as "disabled" by colleagues or supervisors, invisibility does not imply less severe impairments or fewer limitations (Davis, 2005; Lingsom, 2008). When dealing with these impairments and limitations at work, employees with invisible disabilities who do not disclose will have to self-accommodate or perform their work without the needed accommodations. Disclosing, however, puts them at risk of being stigmatized or disbelieved by their social work environment (Davis, 2005; Prince, 2017; Santuzzi et al., 2014).

The decision of whether or not to disclose an invisible disability at work implies that employees weigh up the possible positive and negative consequences of disclosure and non-disclosure. Disclosure may lead to receiving workplace adjustments and social support, benefitting from disability-related rights, or being more authentic (Beatty & Kirby, 2006; Chaudoir & Fisher, 2010; Jones & King, 2014; Munir et al., 2005; Santuzzi et al., 2014; Vickers, 1997). However, it may also have negative consequences such as social exclusion, underestimation, withholding of opportunities, harassment, or even contract termination (Beatty, 2018; Camacho et al., 2020; Graham et al., 2019; Pérez-Garín et al., 2018). Non-disclosure comes on the one hand with the advantage of passing as normal, and it also allows private and professional life to be kept separate (Smith & Brunner, 2017). On the other hand, possible negative consequences of non-disclosure are insufficient management of the health condition, the stress of having to hide parts of one's identity, or others misunderstanding one's behavior or symptoms, which can also lead to social exclusion (Jones & King, 2014; Lindsay et al., 2013; Pachankis, 2007; Santuzzi et al., 2019; Santuzzi et al., 2014). Thus, both disclosure and non-disclosure can lead to consequences that impact the health, well-being, and workability of affected employees (Camacho et al., 2020; Follmer et al., 2019; Pachankis, 2007; Prince, 2017; Santuzzi et al., 2014).

(Non-)disclosure of a stigmatized identity at work is also a predictor of outcomes relevant to management such as job satisfaction, commitment, performance, and withdrawal intentions (Follmer et al., 2019; Santuzzi et al., 2014). Because of (non-)disclosure's varied far-reaching implications, it is pivotal that people with disabilities decide carefully about it at work. But (non-)disclosure "is not a 'one-size-fits-all' process" (Follmer et al., 2019, p. 181). The occurrence of possible positive and negative consequences depends on multiple contextual factors, such as characteristics of the health condition, organizational culture, or relationships with colleagues and supervisors (Beatty & Kirby, 2006; Munir et al., 2005; von Schrader et al., 2014). Consequently, employees with invisible disabilities may feel overwhelmed and unable to make a decision (Santuzzi et al., 2014).

While several stakeholders offer support inside and outside the workplace (e.g., company doctors, employee representatives, or self-help organizations), seeking in-person counseling already requires some form of disclosure, which may be a barrier for some. Therefore, we created an easily accessible, anonymous, and free online tool that supports people with invisible disabilities in making a high-quality (non-)disclosure decision in line with their personal situation and values. It further encourages them to seek in-person counseling from relevant stakeholders to discuss the next steps. This chapter presents the theoretical and empirical underpinnings and the co-development process of that online tool and discusses implications for practice.[1]

The Disclosure Decision in Light of Theory and Research

Expectancy-value theories (e.g., Ajzen, 1985) propose that, when deciding on an action, decision-makers consider possible positive and negative consequences of their decision options. Based on their perception of various contextual factors, individuals try to assess the likelihood with which these consequences may occur (Jones & King, 2014; Ragins, 2008) and evaluate the implications of possible outcomes for their values and goals in life (Feather, 1995). They also anticipate whether they can perform the behaviors necessary to implement a decision option (perceived behavioral control). If their perceived behavioral control is low, they will either not decide on an option or not implement it after the decision (Ajzen, 1985). The complexity of decision-making processes increases with the number of involved variables, with conflicts between possible consequences, and with growing uncertainty about their occurrence because of intransparency, interconnectedness, and the dynamics of the situation (Dörner & Funke, 2017). Against this background, the decision of whether to disclose an invisible disability at work can be classified as highly complex. Both decision options (disclosure and non-disclosure) can have many different, conflicting consequences, depending on various interconnected and changing personal and vocational characteristics. Disclosure is also an emotionally charged decision due to high uncertainty and because some of the consequences may have far-reaching, irreversible, and long-term impacts on a decision-maker's life (Betsch & Kunz, 2008; Loewenstein et al., 2001).

Complex, uncertain, and emotionally charged decisions are susceptible to various types of biases (Kahneman, 2012). The so-called *loss aversion bias* (Tversky & Kahneman, 1991) implies that decision-makers' aversions to losses are stronger than their aspiration for gains. The anticipation of negative consequences that evoke fear and anxiety fosters cautious and low-risk decision-making (Loewenstein et al., 2001). Consequently, the potential positive implications of decision options might be undervalued during the decision-making process. For instance, the risk of

---

1 To date, the online tool is only available in German; an English translation is planned.

stigmatization and discrimination after disclosure is threatening for many (Chaudoir & Fisher, 2010; Ragins, 2008; Santuzzi et al., 2014) and might cause decision-makers to neglect possible positive outcomes such as receiving workplace accommodations. Another form of bias concerns the preference to omit rather than initiate actions (*omission bias*, Ritov & Baron, 1992). Decision-makers perceive their status-quo (in our case, non-disclosure) not as a separate decision option but as a reference point for their decision. They feel more responsible for the negative consequences of action than for those of omission. Thus, disadvantages or risks of maintaining non-disclosure are only evaluated as missed gains while risks of disclosure are perceived as losses. In combination with the tendency to avoid losses, this effect often results in a preference for non-disclosure and a potentially suboptimal decision.

In principle, non-disclosure and disclosure are equally legitimate decision options, and both can represent the individually right decision for a given person. Decisions with no criteria to determine the objectively "right" decision option are called *preference-based* (Braun & Benz, 2015). But how can, for example, someone's non-disclosure decision be evaluated as a "good" decision or a suboptimal one? In the medical field, criteria to evaluate the quality of preference-based decisions have been developed because many treatment decisions are preference-based. Although (non-)disclosure is not a medical decision in the narrower sense, these quality criteria are still applicable. According to O'Connor et al. (2007), "*decision quality* refers to the extent to which patients arrive at choices that are informed and preference-based" (p. 721). In that definition, "informed" refers to the necessity for decision-makers to be aware of the different decision options, their potential positive and negative consequences, and the probabilities of those consequences. "Preference-based" implies that personal preferences and values have to be clarified and connected to potential positive and negative consequences (O'Connor et al., 2007). Being aware of one's values facilitates decision-making in that the values may serve as an "inner compass" (e.g., Harris, 2019).

Another focus within theory and research about "good" decisions concerns the process of decision-making. A controversy exists about whether rational decision-making is always the best way to go. Dijksterhuis and Strick (2016) state that unconscious thought processes may improve the quality of complex and far-reaching decisions that entail integrating large amounts of information. For the practice of decision-making, a sequence of conscious information processing followed by phases of unconscious processing (e.g., sleeping on things) seems to be optimal (Nordgren et al., 2011). Research suggests that individuals also have stable preferences for either unconscious (intuitive) or conscious (deliberative) decision-making. In addition, decision-makers are more satisfied with their choice if the decision-making process is consistent with their preference (Betsch & Kunz, 2008). A further stable preference concerns the goal orientation of decision-makers. People differ in being either *approach motivated* (moving towards a desired end-state) or *avoidance motivated* (moving away from possible negative end-states; e.g., Higgins, 1998). According to Chaudoir and Fisher (2010), avoidance motivation can prove problematic for the disclosure decision. The focus on avoiding rejection by others reduces the chances of disclosure even under favorable circumstances and may result in an attentional focus on potential negative responses from others during and after disclosing, which can become a self-fulfilling prophecy (Chaudoir & Fisher, 2010).

These insights from theory and research have several implications for our goal of supporting people with invisible disabilities in making a high-quality disclosure decision. It is important to establish non-disclosure as a separate decision option and clarify the possible positive and negative consequences of both disclosure and non-disclosure. To give decision-makers a realistic impression of the probabilities of these different consequences, their vocational, personal, and legal circumstances need considering. In addition, decision-makers have to be made aware of their values and decision-related preferences and guided to make their decision accordingly. The decision-making process can be depressurized if ambitions to achieve an objectively perfect decision are put into perspective. Finally, it is crucial to strengthen decision-makers' self-efficacy for implementing the decision and constructively dealing with possible negative consequences.

Co-development of an Interactive Online Tool to Support a High-Quality Decision

This knowledge about important aspects of supporting a good disclosure decision guided the development of our online tool. But, besides our aspiration to provide content based on scientific evidence and theory, another important aim was to ensure acceptance by future end-users and a good fit with their needs. Thus, we chose an iterative participatory co-development approach (Dack et al., 2019; Kushniruk & Nohr, 2016). During all steps of the development process, we integrated insights gained from analyzing theoretical models and empirical studies with input and feedback from future end-users and other important stakeholders. For the design and technical implementation of the online tool, we collaborated closely with a user experience designer and a web developer who were committed to the iterative development process. To secure online accessibility and data protection, we followed the Web Content Accessibility Guidelines and the EU's General Data Protection Regulation. The quality criteria of the HONcode for health information on the internet guided the creation of the tool's content (Health On the Net, 2019). In the following sections, we give an overview of the concept and content of the online tool and illustrate the iterative participatory co-development process.

Concept and Content of the Online Tool

To reach a broad target group, the online tool is applicable across disabilities and health conditions. It is a browser-based web application (https://sag-ichs.de/) with a responsive design, allowing smooth usage on all kinds of devices. It is free of charge and can be used anonymously with no registration needed. The tool provides:

a) an interactive "self-test" with automated individualized feedback on possible positive and negative consequences of (non-)disclosure,

b) the section "good to know" with information relevant to (non-)disclosure decision-making and its implementation,

c) and the section "about this website" with information on the online tool and its development.

The self-test is the core element of the online tool. It facilitates the most complex part of the decision-making process – evaluating the likelihood of possible consequences and weighing them according to personal needs and values. Users are presented with questions helping them to reflect on factors that may influence possible consequences after (non-)disclosure and on individual needs and values that guide how they personally evaluate those consequences. We drew on theory, research, legal requirements, and input from the participatory co-development process to decide what topics to include in the self-test. Whenever possible, we based the self-test items on previous research and existing scales, but we also developed several "new" ones. Table 21.1 gives an overview of the topics included in the self-test and presents example items.[2]

After finishing, users receive automated individualized feedback[3] on how the factors assessed in the self-test influence the likelihood of positive or negative consequences (e.g., job accommodations, supportive or devaluing reactions of others) and what that means for (non-)disclosure. The feedback starts with an overview of all topics included in the self-test. Each topic is tagged with a feedback icon (plus = pro disclosure, minus = contra disclosure, question mark = inconclusive, x = not enough information submitted). The icons facilitate users in getting a general idea of which aspects support disclosure in their specific situation and which do not. To benefit optimally from the extensive amount of feedback information, users can sort the feedback by *pro/contra disclosure* and weigh the different aspects of the feedback in terms of personal relevance. They can also save or print the feedback for later use. By tapping on a specific topic, users receive more detailed information about it. Figure 21.1 shows an example of detailed feedback on perceived *emotional support by the supervisor.*

---

2 For more information on measurement and the rationale for including topics in the self-test, see Chakraverty et al. (2022).

3 For more information on the logic behind the automated feedback, see Chakraverty et al. (2022).

Table 21.1: Topics and example items of the self-test (slightly modified from Greifenberg et al., 2022).

#	Topic	Type (# of items/ answers)	Example items
Organizational factors			
1	Emotional support by the supervisor	M (5)	*My supervisor . . .* *. . . praises me for effort I'm putting in.*
2	Team atmosphere	M (4)	*It is difficult to ask other members of my team for help.*
3–4	Organizational support	M (3) SC (3)	*My employer is open to the needs of employees with health impairments.*
Personal factors			
5	Legal disability status	SC (5)	*Do you have a legal status as "severely disabled"?*
6	Contract	SC (4)	*What kind of contract do you currently have?*
7–8	Accommodation needs/ Workplace fit	MC (16)	*To work efficiently with my health impairment, I need . . .* *. . . accessible buildings*
9	Health development	SC (4)	*In the future, my health will most likely . . .* *. . . not change much.*
10	Endangerment to self or others	SC (4)	*Does your impairment entail symptoms that might put yourself or others at work in danger?*
11	Illness acceptance	M (4)	*I can accept my health impairment well.*
12	Stigmatization	M (4)	*In general, other people probably think my health impairment . . .* *. . . is repulsive.*
Values and needs			
13–16	Personal values	M (2)	*How similar is this person to you?* *. . . This person thinks it's important that every person should have equal chances in life.*
17–18	Personal goals	M (4)	*I like trying out new things.*
19	Need for privacy	M (4)	*I find it difficult to talk about myself.*
20	Need for authenticity	M (5)	*It is important to me to show how I really am.*

Table 21.1 (continued)

#	Topic	Type (# of items/ answers)	Example items
	Experience and current situation		
21–22	Previous disclosure experiences	MC (7) O	*Disclosing my health impairment in the past . . . . . . has led to receiving support.*
23–25	Reflection on the current work-life situation	O	*Where do you see yourself in terms of your career? What does this mean for your disclosure decision?*

Note: Question types: M = Matrix; SC = Single Choice; MC = Multiple Choice; O = Open-ended. All Matrix questions were asked on a scale of 1 (I don't agree at all) – 5 (I agree completely), except question 11 (1 (Others don't think this at all) – 5 (Others think this a lot)) and 12–15 (1 (very similar) – 5 (not similar at all)).

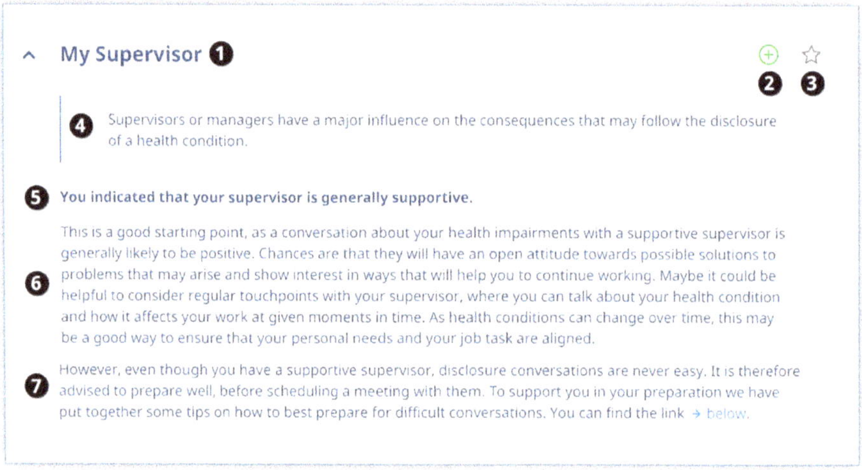

Figure 21.1: Example of a detailed individualized self-test feedback (translated into English; Chakraverty et al., 2022).

Each feedback has a similar structure, starting with the title (1), the feedback icon (2), and a star icon (3), which are displayed in the overview. The star icon allows users to mark a topic as *important*. The more detailed feedback starts with a brief explanation of why the given aspect is relevant for the disclosure decision (4), followed by the personal result (5). In the example, the user perceives their supervisor as supportive, which is a favorable condition for disclosure (as indicated by the green plus icon). The following section (6) explains what this could mean for the (non-)disclosure decision and its consequences. Finally, the feedback refers users to additional resources in the tool's section "good to know" (7), such as worksheets (e.g., how to prepare for a difficult conversation) or an overview of the different stakeholders that provide further (in-person) counseling.

The content of the section "good to know" complements the content of the self-test. The self-test and "good to know" also refer to each other. Table 21.2 gives an overview of the topics covered in this section. The aims are to:

a) illustrate that disclosure and non-disclosure are separate and equivalent decision options, and clarify their potential positive and negative consequences,

b) reduce the risk of biases and facilitate an informed decision,

c) clarify that there is no "perfect" disclosure decision and that good decision-making is an individual process that entails consideration of one's needs, values, and individual decision-making preferences,

d) provide information on important legal aspects,

e) guide users to seek further counseling and support, if needed,

f) and support implementing the decision by addressing potential obstacles and strengthening the focus on users' self-efficacy, positive goals, and coping strategies, thus fostering behavioral control.

Table 21.2: Subpages and content of the section "good to know" (slightly modified from Chakraverty et al., 2022).

Subpage title	Content
Information on (good) decision-making	
The right decision – just for me	*The individuality of decision-making, the impossibility of perfect decisions, strategies to prevent regret*
Head or heart – which decision type am I?	*Advantages of conscious and unconscious thought processes in decision-making, individual preference for intuitive vs. deliberative decision-making*
Creating a good life for myself	*Fear of negative consequences, individual values as compasses for decision-making, exploring individual values.*
Information on (non-)disclosure	
I'll tell!!	*Disclosure and non-disclosure as ends of a continuum, positive and negative consequences of disclosure*
I won't tell!	*Possible reasons for non-disclosure, positive and negative consequences of non-disclosure, strategies to maintain non-disclosure*

Table 21.2 (continued)

Subpage title	Content
Information on legal aspects	
Disability, severe disability, or equivalent	*Different legal statuses, advice on how to apply for legal disability status in Germany*
Duty to disclose	*Exceptional constellations that entail the duty to disclose*
Claims and rights	*Legal entitlements for employees with health impairments in Germany*
A matter of trust	*Personal counseling and support on legal and health-related topics at work*
Can I get fired?	*Protection against dismissal due to health impairments*
Information on further counseling and support	
Counseling and support	*Information on stakeholders offering (in-person) counseling and support in- and outside the work context*
Information to support implementing the decision	
The direction is set: Your next steps	*Developing a plan to implement the decision, accepting obstacles and dealing with them, confidence in one's hopes and desires.*
Having difficult conversations	*Preparing for a difficult conversation*
Using the power of thought	*Risk of an attentional focus on negative situational cues, focus on positive aspects, negative thoughts are part of life*
Risks and side effects	*Preparing for and dealing with negative consequences after implementing the decision*

The section "about this webpage" aims at creating transparency about the online tool, facilitating its use, and offering contact options. The pages in this section present information on the authors of the online tool, the funding, structure, and objectives of the tool, the applied quality criteria, scientific references used in developing the tool, data protection and accessibility and contact information, scientific publications and media coverage related to the tool.

Iterative Participatory Co-development Process

As mentioned earlier, involving end-users and other relevant stakeholders was a key element when developing the online tool. For the participatory development of health-related IT systems, Kushniruk and Nohr (2016) propose two main rationales that were both important to us. First, end-user participation enhances functionalities and service quality of the final product, and second – more political – it empowers users and gives their voices space. Our preparation for the project proposal for the online tool included collaborating with our project partners that represented the perspectives of employees with disabilities (*Federal Association for Self-help of People with Disabilities and Chronic Health Conditions and their Families*) and employers (*German Association of Company Doctors* and *AbbVie Germany*). We also conducted several expert interviews with different stakeholders, including employees with invisible disabilities, and presented our project idea at practice-oriented conferences to verify the identified need and get feedback on our first concept for the tool. With the official start of the project, we assembled an "expert panel" and an advisory board who – together with the project partners – supported the development of the online tool.

Expert Panel

The expert panel is a group of employees with invisible disabilities that serve as experts on their own behalf and represent the end-users. We chose a purposeful sampling strategy to assemble a heterogeneous panel representing the intended broad target group of the online tool regarding relevant disclosure-, person-, and job-related characteristics.[4] Twelve people were recruited for the expert panel. Although we successfully assembled an overall heterogeneous group, some important aspects were not represented (e.g., low educational level) or underrepresented (e.g., non-disclosed). The experts gave their informed consent to participating in the panel and received a small allowance.

The expert panel was involved at four points during the development process (T1 – T4) to provide input and feedback on different aspects of layout, content, comprehensibility, and user guidance of the online tool. At T1 and T2, focus group meetings were held jointly with all experts. At T3 and T4, the experts provided individual feedback on different prototype stages of the online tool (usability tests) via an online survey from home. Table 21.3 provides an overview of the expert panel involvement and gives information on focus topics, duration, and the number of participants involved at each of the four points during the development process.

---

4 An overview of the considered characteristics can be requested from the authors.

Table 21.3: Overview of the expert panel involvement.

T	Format	Focus topics	Duration	Participants
T1	Focus group	Aspects to consider when making the (non-)disclosure decision Overall concept of the online tool	150 min	$n = 8$
T2	Focus group	Concept for self-test feedback Tone of voice and key terms	*150 min*	$n = 4$
T3	Usability test	Overall design of the online tool Structure and user guidance Amount of text on informational pages	$M = 43$ min	$n = 7$
T4	Usability test	Self-test and feedback	$M = 45$ min	$n = 7$

For the focus groups, we prepared short inputs on the given focus topics and used different brainstorming and visualization methods to collect the experts' ideas and feedback. The focus groups were also audiotaped and transcribed verbatim. From the brainstorming, visualizations, and transcripts, we identified key issues that we included in the further development. For the usability tests, an online questionnaire guided the experts to look at several prototype sample pages of the online tool and answer open- and closed-ended questions regarding their experiences with those sample pages. The data from the closed-ended questions were analyzed using descriptive statistics, while additional key issues were identified by clustering the answers from the open-ended questions. This information was used to adapt the online tool. The experts received summaries of the results after each focus group and usability test, allowing them to point out missing aspects or shortcomings.

Examples for additions and alterations to the online tool resulting from the expert panel involvement are:

- the topics *endangerment to self or others, illness acceptance, previous disclosure experiences*, and *reflection on the current work-life situation* were added to the self-test,
- the term "self-test" was used (instead of e.g., decision aid),
- a resource-oriented and empowering tone of voice was used,
- the amount of information on individual pages was kept as limited as possible,
- a sortable feedback overview with icons visualizing disclosure pros and contras was provided,
- and instructions on how to use the self-test feedback were added.

Advisory Board and Project Partners

The advisory board consists of 15 members, including representatives of larger organizations or associations (e.g., health insurances, vocational rehabilitation institutions, self-help organizations) and people with specialized expertise relevant to the project (e.g., patient data-protection or development of evidence-based digital health interventions). In contrast to the experts from our expert panel who were supposed to bring in their lived experiences, the role of the project partners and the advisory board was to provide professional expertise. We held three advisory board meetings – one every year during the development process. In each meeting, we presented information on the current development of the online tool and discussed focus topics. Discussed topics were, for example, dissemination strategies, data protection, user-friendliness, and evaluation. Some of the discussed aspects also led to the online tool being altered. For instance, we discarded the idea that users had to create a login for the self-test. And we added a button allowing users to easily delete their personal data from the self-test. The project partners and advisory board have also been playing a crucial role in disseminating the online tool since its launch.

Conclusion and Outlook

The decision of whether or not to inform others at work about one's invisible disability is complex and challenging. At the same time, the decision must be made carefully because of its far-reaching consequences for employee health, job satisfaction, performance, and workability. Therefore, we created an easily accessible science-based online tool to support employees with invisible disabilities in making a high-quality disclosure decision. The core element of that online tool is an interactive self-test that provides individualized feedback on the pros and contras of disclosure, thus facilitating the most complex part of the decision-making process. The interactive nature of the self-test makes it easier for users to apply the given information to their personal situation, and it also distinguishes our online tool from other similar resources (van Eerd et al., 2021). Still, users have to make the final decision about (non-)disclosure themselves. Therefore, the online tool also offers information on how to use the self-test feedback to make a decision that fits a user's individual situation. Moreover, it encourages users to seek further (in-person) counseling if needed and gives information on where to find appropriate support.

Thus, the online tool aims to complement existing support structures for employees with disabilities and to foster the use of those structures. Users can save the self-test feedback or print it and discuss it with a rehabilitation counselor, company doctor, representative body for disabled employees, or another trusted party. Although employees with disabilities are the primary target group of the online tool, other stake-holders can also benefit from it. For example, the general information on (non-)disclosure, decision-making, and legal matters is a helpful resource for anyone wishing to support employees with invisible disabilities in their disclosure decision. Additionally, by referring employees to the online tool, employers can signalize that they are aware of the disclosure conflict and want to support employees in that regard. They can, thus, contribute to a trusting, supportive, and inclusive corporate culture, representing one of the strongest work-related predictors of disclosure and positive disclosure outcomes.

The next important step is to evaluate the online tool. A follow-up survey will provide data on the (non-)disclosure decision, (non-)disclosure strategies, conse-quences of (non-)disclosure, and different measures of decision quality as estab-lished in medical decision-making. Self-tests and follow-up data can be linked anonymously and used for research purposes and for improving the online tool.

References

Ajzen, I. (1985). From intentions to actions: A theory of planned behavior. In J. Kuhl & J. Beckmann (Eds.), *Action control* (pp. 11–39). Springer.

Beatty, J. E. (2018). Chronic illness stigma and its relevance in the workplace. In S. B. Thomson & G. Grandy (Eds.), *Stigmas, work and organizations* (pp. 35–54). Palgrave Macmillan.

Beatty, J. E., & Kirby, S. L. (2006). Beyond the legal environment: How stigma influences invisible identity groups in the workplace. *Employee Responsibilities and Rights Journal, 18*(1), 29–44. https://doi.org/10.1007/s10672-005-9003-6

Betsch, C., & Kunz, J. J. (2008). Individual strategy preferences and decisional fit. *Journal of Behavioral Decision Making, 21*(5), 532–555. https://doi.org/10.1002/bdm.600

Braun, F., & Benz, P. (2015). *Genese natürlicher Entscheidungsprozesse und Determinanten kluger Entscheidungen: Theoretische und empirische Reflexionen im Spannungsfeld zwischen analytisch-bewusstem und intuitivem Entscheiden.* [Genesis of natural decision processes and determinants of wise decisions: Theoretical and empirical reflections on the tension between analytic-conscious and intuitive decision-making.] Springer. https://doi.org/10.1007/978-3-658-08471-4

Camacho, G., Reinka, M. A., & Quinn, D. M. (2020). Disclosure and concealment of stigmatized identities. *Current Opinion in Psychology, 31*, 28–32. https://doi.org/10.1016/j.copsyc.2019.07.031

Chakraverty, V., Bauer, J. F., Greifenberg, A., & Niehaus, M. (2022). *To tell or not to tell? An interactive online tool to support employees with chronic health impairments.* Manuscript in preparation. Universität zu Köln.

Charmaz, K. (2010). Disclosing illness and disability in the workplace. *Journal of International Education in Business, 3*(1/2), 6–19. https://doi.org/10.1108/18363261011106858

Chaudoir, S. R., & Fisher, J. D. (2010). The disclosure processes model: Understanding disclosure decision-making and post-disclosure outcomes among people living with a concealable stigmatized identity. *Psychological Bulletin, 136*(2), 236–256. https://doi.org/10.1037/a0018193

Dack, C., Ross, J., Stevenson, F., Pal, K., Gubert, E., Michie, S., Yardley, L., Barnard, M., May, C., Farmer, A., Wood, B., & Murray, E. (2019). A digital self-management intervention for adults with type 2 diabetes: Combining theory, data and participatory design to develop HeLP-Diabetes. *Internet Interventions*, *17*, 100241. https://doi.org/10.1016/j.invent.2019.100241

Davis, N. A. (2005). Invisible disability. *Ethics*, *116*(1), 153–213. https://doi.org/10.1086/453151

Dijksterhuis, A., & Strick, M. (2016). A case for thinking without consciousness. *Perspectives on Psychological Science*, *11*(1), 117–132. https://doi.org/10.1177/1745691615615317

Dörner, D., & Funke, J. (2017). Complex problem solving: What it is and what it is not. *Frontiers in Psychology*, *8* (Article 1153), 1–11. https://doi.org/10.3389/fpsyg.2017.01153

Feather, N. T. (1995). Values, valences, and choice: The influences of values on the perceived attractiveness and choice of alternatives. *Journal of Personality and Social Psychology*, *68*(6), 1135–1151. https://doi.org/10.1037/0022-3514.68.6.1135

Follmer, K. B., Sabat, I. E., & Siuta, R. L. (2019). Disclosure of stigmatized identities at work: An interdisciplinary review and agenda for future research. *Journal of Organizational Behavior*, *41*(2), 169–184. https://doi.org/10.1002/job.2402

Goffman, E. (1963). *Stigma: Notes on the management of spoiled identity*. Simon & Schuster, Inc.

Graham, K. M., McMahon, B. T., Kim, J. H., Simpson, P., & McMahon, M. C. (2019). Patterns of workplace discrimination across broad categories of disability. *Rehabilitation Psychology*, *64*(2), 194–202. https://doi.org/10.1037/rep0000227

Greifenberg, A., Bauer, J. F., Chakraverty, V. & Niehaus, M. (2022). Working with chronic health conditions and the disclosure decision-conflict: development of a web-based interactive self-test to support an informed decision – a brief report. *Journal of Vocational Rehabilitation*, *56*, 203–207. https://doi.org/10.3233/JVR-221183

Harris, R. (2019). *ACT made simple*. New Harbinger.

Health On the Net. (2019). *Discover the 8 principles of the HONcode in 35 languages*. https://www.hon.ch/cgi-bin/HONcode/principles.pl?English

Higgins, E. T. (1998). Beyond pleasure and pain. *American Psychologist*, *52*(12), 1280–1300. https://doi.org/10.1037/0003-066X.52.12.1280

Jones, K. P., & King, E. B. (2014). Managing concealable stigmas at work: A review and multilevel model. *Journal of Management*, *40*(5), 1466–1494. https://doi.org/10.1177/0149206313515518

Kahneman, D. (2012). *Thinking, fast and slow*. Penguin.

Kushniruk, A., & Nohr, C. (2016). Participatory design, user involvement and health IT evaluation. In E. Ammenwerth & M. Rigby (Eds.), *Studies in health technology and informatics. Evidence-based health informatics: Promoting safety and efficiency through scientific methods and ethical policy* (pp. 139–151). IOS Press Incorporated.

Lindsay, S., McDougall, C., & Sanford, R. (2013). Disclosure, accommodations and self-care at work among adolescents with disabilities. *Disability and Rehabilitation*, *35*(26), 2227–2236. https://doi.org/10.3109/09638288.2013.775356

Lingsom, S. (2008). Invisible impairments: Dilemmas of concealment and disclosure. *Scandinavian Journal of Disability Research*, *10*(1), 2–16. https://doi.org/10.1080/15017410701391567

Loewenstein, G. F., Weber, E. U., Hsee, C. K., & Welch, N. (2001). Risk as feelings. *Psychological Bulletin*, *127*(2), 267–286. https://doi.org/10.1037/0033-2909.127.2.267

Munir, F., Leka, S., & Griffiths, A. (2005). Dealing with self-management of chronic illness at work: Predictors for self-disclosure. *Social Science and Medicine*, *60*(6), 1397–1407. https://doi.org/10.1016/j.socscimed.2004.07.012

Nordgren, L. F., Bos, M. W., & Dijksterhuis, A. (2011). The best of both worlds: Integrating conscious and unconscious thought best solves complex decisions. *Journal of Experimental Social Psychology*, *47*(2), 509–511. https://doi.org/10.1016/j.jesp.2010.12.007

Norstedt, M. (2019). Work and invisible disabilities: Practices, experiences and understandings of (non)disclosure. *Scandinavian Journal of Disability Research, 21*(1), 14–24. https://doi.org/10.16993/sjdr.550

O'Connor, A., Wennberg, J. E., Legare, F., Llewellyn-Thomas, H. A., Moulton, B. W., Sepucha, K. R., Sodano, A. G., & King, J. S. (2007). Toward the 'tipping point': Decision aids and informed patient choice. *Health Affairs, 26*(3), 716–725. https://doi.org/10.1377/hlthaff.26.3.716

Pachankis, J. E. (2007). The psychological implications of concealing a stigma: A cognitive–affective–behavioral model. *Psychological Bulletin, 133*(2), 328–345. https://doi.org/10.1037/0033-2909.133.2.328

Pérez-Garín, D., Recio, P., Magallares, A., Molero, F., & García-Ael, C. (2018). Perceived discrimination and emotional reactions in people with different types of disabilities: A qualitative approach. *The Spanish Journal of Psychology, 21*, E12. https://doi.org/10.1017/sjp.2018.13

Prince, M. J. (2017). Persons with invisible disabilities and workplace accommodation: Findings from a scoping literature review. *Journal of Vocational Rehabilitation, 46*(1), 75–86. https://doi.org/10.3233/JVR-160844

Ragins, B. R. (2008). Disclosure disconnects: Antecedents and consequences of disclosing invisible stigmas across life domains. *Academy of Management Review, 33*(1), 194–215. https://doi.org/10.5465/AMR.2008.27752724

Ritov, I., & Baron, J. (1992). Status-quo and omission biases. *Journal of Risk and Uncertainty, 5*(1), 49–61. https://doi.org/10.1007/BF00208786

Santuzzi, A. M., Keating, R. T., Martinez, J. J., Finkelstein, L. M., Rupp, D. E., & Strah, N. (2019). Identity management strategies for workers with concealable disabilities: Antecedents and consequences. *Journal of Social Issues, 75*(3), 847–880. https://doi.org/10.1111/josi.12320

Santuzzi, A. M., Waltz, P. R., Rupp, D. E., & Finkelstein, L. M. (2014). Invisible disabilities: Unique challenges for employees and organizations. *Industrial and Organizational Psychology, 7*(2), 204–219. https://doi.org/10.1111/iops.12134

Smith, S. A., & Brunner, S. R. (2017). To reveal or conceal: Using communication privacy management theory to understand disclosures in the workplace. *Management Communication Quarterly, 31*(3), 429–446. https://doi.org/10.1177/0893318917692896

Tversky, A., & Kahneman, D. (1991). Loss aversion in riskless choice: A reference-dependent model. *The Quarterly Journal of Economics, 106*(4), 1039–1061. https://doi.org/10.2307/2937956

van Eerd, D., Bowring, J., Jetha, A., Breslin, F. C., & Gignac, M. A. (2021). Online resources supporting workers with chronic episodic disabilities: An environmental scan. *International Journal of Workplace Health Management, 14*(2), 129–148. https://doi.org/10.1108/IJWHM-08-2020-0137

Vickers, M. H. (1997). Life at work with "invisible" chronic illness (ICI): The "unseen", unspoken, unrecognized dilemma of disclosure. *Journal of Workplace Learning, 9*(7), 240–252. https://doi.org/10.1108/13665629710190040

von Schrader, S., Malzer, V., & Bruyère, S. (2014). Perspectives on disability disclosure: The importance of employer practices and workplace climate. *Employee Responsibilities and Rights Journal, 26*(4), 237–255. https://doi.org/10.1007/s10672-013-9227-9

Ward, B. W. (2015). Multiple chronic conditions and labor force outcomes: A population study of U.S. adults. *American Journal of Industrial Medicine, 58*(9), 943–954. https://doi.org/10.1002/ajim.22439

Frederike Scholz

22 Challenging Disability Inequality Embedded Within the Online Recruitment Process

Abstract: In the last two decades traditional recruitment practices have moved onto the Internet, which has not only changed the way that jobseekers engage with job searches, but has also created additional barriers for disabled jobseekers due to unequal access to the Internet and a lack of IT skills, compounded by inaccessible online recruitment processes. Within the existing literature on recruitment, these voices have been sparse. Using a UK-based sample of 22 jobseekers with visual impairments and/or learning difficulties, and 3 'committed' employers that work for or with disabled people, this study shows that disability inequality practices currently embedded within online recruitment processes can be successfully challenged.

Keywords: online recruitment, disability inequality, change strategies, committed employers

Introduction

In the last two decades, traditional recruitment practices have moved onto the Internet, which has not only changed the way that jobseekers engage with their job searches, but likewise opened new possibilities for employers to find their 'best talent' (Cappelli, 2001). Previous studies have widely advocated that online recruitment tools have advantages for prospective employees and hiring organizations (Ehrhart et al., 2012; Parry & Tyson, 2008), namely, easier access to job opportunities, shortened hiring cycles, and a reduction in recruitment costs and/or standardized selection systems. However, these studies have focused on understanding the way practices can be successfully adopted in organizations to achieve a better person-organization fit, rather than examining whether relocating these practices might have unintended consequences for certain groups of jobseekers who already face unequal access to the Internet (Hogler et al., 1998; Searle, 2006). Until now, there has been little recruitment research that examines the reactions or emotional experiences that disabled jobseekers face with online recruitment practices and how these additional barriers could be challenged from a disability perspective. This perspective, however, is important to consider when the Internet becomes the only channel to apply for jobs, as is increasingly the norm.

Frederike Scholz, Tilburg University

https://doi.org/10.1515/9783110743647-023

This study adds to the scant literature within the field by arguing that online recruitment processes can lead to additional structural barriers for disabled applicants, alongside ongoing attitudinal barriers still persistent in the current labor market (Kulkarni & Gopakumar, 2014; Lengnick-Hall et al., 2008), primarily due to the inaccessibility and automatization of these virtual practices (Lazar et al., 2012; Trewin et al., 2019). Even though recruitment processes can be made more accessible for disabled jobseekers with the help of reasonable adjustments or by complying to web accessibility guidelines (Abascal et al., 2016; Lewthwaite, 2014), and organizations see disabled people as untapped human resources (Lengnick-Hall et al., 2008) or acknowledge that disability inclusion can enhance their social legitimacy (Moore et al., 2017), evidence suggests that disabled people continue to experience these processes as a disabling practice that can impact on an individual's access to paid employment and their psycho-emotional wellbeing (Hoque et al., 2014; Scholz & Ingold, 2021). Despite the UK government's efforts to reduce disability discrimination by making it unlawful, recent anti-discrimination measures to protect individuals from discrimination based on their protected characteristics have failed to proactively address the still existing employment gap of 28.8 per cent between disabled and non-disabled people in the UK, as well as many other countries worldwide (Lawson, 2011; Powell, 2021).

The aim of this chapter is to expose the unintended consequences of online recruitment practices from an 'extended social model of disability' perspective, by sharing change strategies advocated by 22 disabled jobseekers who have visual impairments or learning difficulties, alongside 3 'committed' employers that work for or with disabled people as their core business on how disability inequality embedded in the online recruitment process can be challenged. Thus, the findings of this study do not only contribute to ongoing theoretical debates by acknowledging experiences of disability due to exclusionary recruitment processes and social relations at the workplace, but also provide an empirical contribution through practically demonstrating how employers can re-design online recruitment practices to make them more inclusive for disabled jobseekers.

Conceptual Framework

Drawing upon the 'extended social model of disability' (Reeve, 2004, p. 83), and incorporating the production of disability inequality in organizations within Acker's (2006) conceptual tools of inequality regimes, this study demonstrates how disability inequality, embedded in existing online recruitment processes, can be challenged. By doing so, it makes an original contribution to organization and management research by acknowledging that disabled jobseekers might not only face exclusion because of formal recruitment practices and processes, but also due to informal patterns of everyday social relations with employers or colleagues, which can both equally impact upon a disabled person's psycho-emotional wellbeing by feeling 'hurt' in the form of emotional pain that make individuals feel 'worthless' or of lesser value (Reeve, 2013; Thomas, 2004) as a worker. These experiences can lead to some individuals either giving up applying for jobs entirely or to them concealing their impairment even though they have the right to request reasonable adjustments aimed at preventing these disabling experiences, as a mechanism to protect themselves from further exclusion.

By adding disability as a dimension to Acker's conceptual tool of inequality regimes, recently absent in research (Scholz & Ingold, 2021), this study demonstrates that the social practices which form disability (structural and psycho-emotional disablism) within society are also evident within organizations, and in particular, exist within several practices that are part of the online recruitment process, producing disability inequality. Disability inequality in this chapter is defined as a socially constructed difference based on psychological and physical characteristics, culture and historical domination and oppression between people with and without impairments. Although Acker acknowledges that organizational change is difficult, and change efforts to challenge these inequality dimensions might fail, she maintains that they *can* be challenged regardless. A prerequisite for successful change projects, however, is a combined effort from outside organizations, such as social movements or legislative support, as well as active support efforts within organizations (Acker, 2006).

Empirical Study

Despite the popularity of online recruitment processes and a proliferation of studies, many have ignored the voices and concerns of disabled people and 'committed' employers who work for or with disabled people. This UK-based study adopts a critical and emancipatory research approach widely advocated by the disabled people's movement and scholars (Oliver, 1992) that builds upon the interpretive understanding of social phenomena, in that it acknowledges the knowledge and experiences of disabled people as experts. It gives voice to individuals with visual impairments and individuals with learning difficulties who have only been minimally represented (Chappell et al., 2001; Duckett & Pratt, 2007) in research to date, although this group faces the most difficulties in accessing the Internet (Scholz et al., 2017), which is nowadays increasingly a perquisite for undertaking job searches. Hence, this study was led by disabled people and the disability studies literature rather than the organization and management literature, because mainstream debates on recruitment provide an inadequate account of the agenda of disabled people and their organizations.

Within the UK context, disabled people are protected from employment discrimination by the Equality Act 2010 that merged pre-existing anti-discrimination provisions (such as the Disability Discrimination Act 1995) into one overarching piece of legislation (Easton, 2011). In line with this act, the Equality and Human Rights Commission (EHRC) was formed, which is a non-governmental public body that is mandated by the UK Parliament to challenge discrimination and to protect and promote human rights. While this Act now protects from indirect discrimination based on protected characteristics by employers (Section 39), it has been criticized for maintaining a medicalized definition in that disability is caused by illness or impairment that leads to pain and some social disadvantage, rather than it being primarily organized by oppression, inequality and exclusion (as in the social model of disability) (Thomas, 2004).

Moreover, it entails a 'reactive' duty to provide reasonable adjustments (s.20), where private sector employers only need to provide any reasonable adjustments when a disabled person is put at a substantial disadvantage, compared to a person who is not disabled in regard to first a provision, criterion, and practice (s.20[3]); second, a physical feature (s.20[4]); and third, the absence of auxiliary aid (s.20[5]). Thus, the applicant must notify the employer of any disabling recruitment practices before any adjustments are necessary. At present, only public service providers must monitor their services and functions to anticipate any disadvantage that might have been caused due to their practices, provisions criteria, physical feature or absence of an auxiliary aid or service provision (EHRC, 2014; Lawson, 2011). Scholars (Easton, 2011) claim that the Act has failed to state that websites are also covered by the duty to provide information in an accessible format under Section 20(6). However, with the rise of Information and Communication Technologies (ICTs) over the years, the 'neutral' language of the provision can be used to apply to both current and future uses of ICTs to communicate information (Easton, 2011), and therefore recruitment processes.

The qualitative research presented here is part of a lager study undertaken in 2014–2015 in the UK. The voices shared in this chapter include: (a) 22 disabled jobseekers with learning difficulties and visual impairments (nine women and 12 men between the ages of 20 and 65) interviewed with their employment advisors (EAs), and (b) four managers from 'committed' employers (three women and one man), whose core business focuses on challenging disability inequality in society. Ethical approval for this study was given by the institution; recruitment flyers, information sheets and informed consents were provided in an accessible and easy-to-read format. Gatekeepers were able to direct potential interviewees and the study relied on a self-selection sampling strategy and voluntary participation, which could be the reason for the small sample size. Semi-structured interviews were employed to give voice to participants by representing their stories, experiences, and opinions, which lasted between 30 minutes to 70 minutes, and took place at familiar and accessible places for each interviewee. Questions were directly addressed to jobseekers and employers by use of an interview guide. All interviews were recorded with permission and then transcribed.

The sample of disabled jobseekers was comprised of 13 interviewees who were born with learning difficulties, such as Asperger or dyslexia and/or visual impairments, and nine who acquired their visual impairments during their adult life, while working. The variety of work experience differed: six had a part-time position, nine carried out volunteer work, and seven had undertaken job searches. All but four individuals were actively searching for a job at the time of the fieldwork. In 14 of the 22 interviews with disabled jobseekers, EAs working for Disabled People's Organizations (DPOs) were present, who themselves were disabled except for one. Feedback loops were used to encourage interviewees to provide constructive feedback during the research process, to both assure that any misinterpretations were corrected and to share experiences beyond the set interview questions (Kitchin, 2000). The presence of an employment advisor may have changed the power balance within the interview setting and the types of experiences individuals were willing to share (Low, 2012). Compared to services by Job-centre Plus (public employment support), jobseekers took on the employment support of these DPOs voluntarily, and were neither forced or sanctioned into any jobs and were able to withdraw from these support services or leave any jobs found with help of their EAs if they felt these were not the right fit for them. In each of the eight individual interviews, none of the participants mentioned any negative experiences with their employment advisors or the support services received.

The sample of employers consisted of 3 'committed' employers that demonstrated positive attitudes and positive behavior to challenge the persistence of disability inequality in organizations, and to overcome biases towards hiring and retaining disabled workers (Bredgaard & Salado-Rasmussen, 2020). For instance, Employer A and Employer B, both DPOs, have embedded the social model of disability in their organizational policies and practices, whereas Employer C (a consultancy) provides 'best-practice' services for organizations to make them more inclusive for disabled workers and other groups.

For this study, it was significant that the data analyzed clearly represented the voices of participants themselves. By conducting a thematic analysis, this study was able to bring light to the meaning, richness, and magnitude of their subjective experiences (Atheide & Johnson, 1994). Themes emerged through an iterative process that focused on the importance of raising disability awareness in organizations, making the online recruitment process more inclusive and highlighting the need for more open recruitment processes to challenge disability inequality.

Raising Disability Awareness in Organizations

When disabled participants were asked about their principal change strategy to challenge disabling recruitment processes, all (irrespective of impairment type) recommended that employers should raise disability awareness within organizations to remove stigmatized perceptions of disabled people as workers by way of providing training courses for their entire workforce. It was argued that these training courses could encourage co-workers to be more aware of their own discriminatory behavior, and highlight both organizational practices that are exclusionary and which reasonable adjustments might be required to make the workplace more inclusive for disabled individuals. For instance, Unwin, who is in his 30s, has a visual impairment and is looking for a job as a support worker for disabled children, commented:

> Some form of training courses . . . that basically say, if you have a visually impaired employee, they need this . . . if you have an employee that has Asperger's, you need to be aware of that. I don't think there is enough of that. And therefore, you get these negative attitudes towards disabled people when they try to get a job. Because people don't know, they are not aware and are afraid of it. (Unwin, Jobseeker)

Unwin argues that wider training would help to combat the negative attitudes that disabled people face during their job searches, and move the responsibility of educating about disability awareness and reasonable adjustments from the employee or jobseeker to the employer. This view was echoed by 'committed' employers taking part in this study. One of these employers, Adam, explained why mandatory training courses for all new recruits in his organization are essential:

> Obviously, it covers legal duties, the Equality Act, however the approach is more from a good practice perspective . . . and very much from a social model perspective in terms of looking at the barriers that organizations or employers may have created, which is usually and inadvertently through ignorance. And also, really to get people to change their attitudes and to understand that it is not people's impairment or conditions that limit their ability, but it is actually the lack of understanding or lack of awareness or preparedness on the part of the employer to make adjustments. (Adam, Employer A)

Even though he explains that legal requirements are important, the major focus of their training course is placing the social model at the center, with the aim to not only remove formal social practices, such as recruitment practices, but also to address informal patterns of everyday social relations that disable individuals with impairments. Adam advocated that this understanding is vital in that it has helped to create an inclusive and open organizational culture at Employer A, where individuals feel empowered to disclose an impairment:

> We have a very open attitude towards recruitment of disabled people and promotion of good employment practice that people feel it is a big part of the culture and it is part of what we are about. They have the confidence to actually disclose conditions . . . we hope and believe that people are more confident to do that and therefore if people do need support or adjustments, they ask for them and they get them.

Therefore, he argues that training must be combined with other practices, such as creating a barrier-free working environment, or challenging the stereotype of lower productivity of disabled workers, to foster an inclusive organizational culture. This would encourage the much needed 'open' conversation between jobseekers or employee and employer about reasonable adjustments, because individuals will then feel accepted as workers.

Moreover, DPOs also adopted more proactive measures to challenge disability inequality outside their organizations as advocates of the disabled people's movement by providing training courses, such as disability awareness training to external employers. Yet, reaching less committed employers was difficult, as Beth working for Employer B mentioned:

> The number of people that come have already an interest, so they are halfway there, which is great. But actually, what you want to do is reach people who have no interest. They are not coming, because they have no interest. Those people are really hard to educate and change their attitudes . . . I think people are changing, but it is slow. (Beth, Employer B)

Her story implies that advocacy organizations try to challenge ableist mindsets by demonstrating to other employers the ways in which organizational practices create disability inequality. However, there is still resistance to change and adopting disability awareness training is still seen as a voluntary measure for organizations, and therefore much needed change efforts outside organizations that push employers to adopt these practices are still lacking.

Making the Online Recruitment Process More Inclusive

A recurrent theme in the interviews was that individual experiences with the online recruitment process differed for each interviewee. Not only did individuals encounter structural barriers during their job searches and applications due to unequal access to the Internet, lack of ICT skills (one third of respondents), or the inaccessibility of recruitment processes, but they also expressed issues with the unavailability of accessible technological infrastructure at public places, including the library or Jobcentre Plus. This led to experiences of psycho-emotional disablism, by feeling frustrated or hurt due to barriers faced during job searches, and resulted in them discontinuing their job searches to ease these experiences of exclusion.

A dominant view has been that there is an obvious need for interventions at the organizational and state level. Jobseekers suggested the use of accessibility guidelines, but also the acknowledgement that accessibility changes only benefit those individuals who already have access to the Internet and can use it in the first place. In this study, most individuals with learning difficulties and a handful of individuals with visual impairments were reliant on the job search support by their EA or their relatives. Some mentioned that while they undertook computer courses in the past, they did not learn the IT skills required to undertake independent job searches online. Thus, interviewees advocated that the government should offer more tailored training courses for disabled people to improve their skill set. For example, Radcliffe, who is in his 40s, has a visual impairment and had been out of work for over five years, explained:

> I have been twice on computer courses now. I don't think they are long enough for me. I think my lad [son] can pick it up [easily]. But I think if you [have] got a disability, you need more time [on a computer course], especially if you are blind . . . You need to learn computers, don't you? It is just the new world . . . . Computer courses are not long enough for people with disabilities. I think if I was a government, they need to start offering more computer courses. (Radcliffe, Jobseeker)

Radcliffe felt that using a computer was now essential for successful job searches and was keen to improve his skills. However, he said that access to a good IT course was limited. For other jobseekers such as Ethan, who is in his 40s, has a hearing impairment and a learning difficulty mentioned, their IT training courses were cancelled due to the lack of funding. These experiences not only raise the question about the availability of computer courses, but they also demonstrate that government cuts impact on those individuals who might be furthest away from the labor market because they face digital exclusion.

Simplifying the Design of Online Application Processes

There was a sense among those interviewees who had Internet access or were able to undertake their job searches independently that much needed changes to the design and accessibility of online application processes are required. For individuals with learning difficulties the biggest issue faced the use of exclusionary terminology, whereas individuals with visual impairments struggled with the incompatibility of the website or application forms. Talking about this issue, jobseekers recommended drastic changes to online application forms and recruitment websites. This is evident in Kevin's account. Kevin is in this 40s, has learning difficulties and has been unemployed for over 20 years:

> For the online stuff, making sure that they've got an application form – disabled and abled. There are so many forms out there. And [a barrier is] that web designers, say 'Look how smart I am.' I know how smart you are, but how about making a form or a website that we can use, rather than being an artist . . . (Kevin, Jobseeker)

Kevin pointed out that the multitude of job application forms that employers use constitutes a real barrier for disabled people, as well as the inadequate design of the website and the lack of usability of the processes involved. His suggestion is that employers should standardize their job application forms and recruitment websites in an accessible way for both disabled and non-disabled users. This was also supported by jobseekers with visual impairments. For instance Quentin, who is in his 30s, and has just been offered a job, clarified:

> On some application forms, even in Word, they have formatting where the boxes are white even when you change it [the contrast] . . . The problem [for me] is job specs and PDFs. I rang people [employers] up to ask for an alternative form, [but] never got one . . . (Quentin, Jobseeker)

Even though he had asked for a reasonable adjustment in the form of an alternative application form, the employer did not comply with the reactive duty covered under the Equality Act 2010. This is a major barrier for those disabled jobseekers who are reliant on these adjustments to submit their job application, because without them they are directly excluded from accessing paid employment. Daphne, working for Employer C, advocated that access issues mentioned by disabled jobseekers would only be removed if employers undertake regular monitoring of their technology:

> Get it tested by a disabled user panel. This is the only way to know whether the technology works for disabled people, and they can use it. You can run programs to check it against the World's accessibility guidelines. But the only real way to find it out is to get a disabled user panel to test it for you. (Daphne, Employer C)

Daphne's account suggests that when employers want to challenge the risk that their online recruitment processes are disabling, they could involve disabled users in the co-design of these practices to remove any barriers to application. This was one strategy adopted by employers in this study to make sure that their online recruitment processes are inclusive. This strategy also supports the literature (Lewthwaite, 2014), which suggests that accessibility should be viewed as a relational process that views accessibility as a property of the relation between users and the resource, and acknowledges the unequal power structures that create disability and accessibility.

An alternative option mentioned by jobseekers was that employers could offer applicants the choice to do a telephone application rather than a written job application. This alternative way of recruiting that anticipates any barriers to application was pointed out by Tara, who is in her 60s, has a visual impairment and was employed part-time:

> In the application stage, where you actually find out about the job, I think it would be better if they would do more telephone applications and things like that. So that you can actually speak with somebody, and they could perhaps fill in the form on the other end. That would be quite helpful. And really being a lot more open-minded. Giving people a chance really. (Tara, Jobseeker)

Likewise, Becca who had a visual impairment and learning difficulty advocated that:

> People [should] talk to us more and not [be] singling us out. They [employers] just expect us to go on computers constantly. Sometimes it can be too much. There is no conversation.

> Everything is just on the computer . . . they don't want to use phones anymore; they don't want to talk to people. It is isolating . . . (Becca, Jobseeker)

Both arguments suggest that the online recruitment process should involve human interaction where disabled people can engage with employers or those in charge of the recruitment function, and could request direct support with their job application if required. By giving jobseekers the choice, the online recruitment process could be made more inclusive, especially for those individuals who might struggle to fill in a written online job application. This finding reveals that a spoken way of application can be an alternative approach that can support some individuals with their application.

Adopting Open Recruitment to Challenge Disability Inequality

Echoing the change strategies mentioned above, 'committed' employers argued that recruitment should involve continuous communication with disabled jobseekers throughout the entire process to remove any barriers to application. Caitlyn, working for Employer B, spoke energetically:

> The vacancies are advertised on our website, but rather than asking people to apply on some online system, they can download the application form . . . all the information is available in different formats . . . And you know you literally email it back, it is also mentioned there clearly with that, even if you are struggling in any way, please give us a call. So, all through that process, people are encouraged, if you can't just download the application form, you can contact us. (Caitlyn, Employer B)

Their website has been developed with the requirements of disabled people in mind, and they follow web accessibility guidelines with regular monitoring evaluations. Rather than designing an accessible online application system, which could be an alternative way, jobseekers are encouraged to fill in a job application form in Word (available in accessible formats) and send it back to the employer via email or post. This example shows how recruitment processes can be designed with diverse needs of applicants in mind that offer the flexibility to make further adjustments.

Likewise, Employers A and C also mentioned that they had adopted a policy of 'open recruitment.' Their goal was to actively engage with individuals by establishing trusting social relations through the process by providing them with as much information as needed. Likewise, any job opportunities were widely shared with their networks and accessible job boards. As Daphne put it:

> First, what we do is job analysis. We would analyze the role and write the job description. Clearly following our own best practice guidelines, in terms of inclusive language and terms.

We don't have any desirable criteria, because we don't believe in it, we just have the core criteria. We feel it is really important that the candidate knows as much about the competencies what we will measure to give them the best opportunity to mark their skills. We have a very open documentation about our jobs. We tell them everything. So, it would go up on our website and our careers page, and we would also circulate them through our networks, which is obviously why we get quite a lot of disabled candidates, because we have networks with disabled people. (Daphne, Employer C)

Here Daphne demonstrates the need to be transparent to potential jobseekers by eliminating any skill or attribute that is not relevant for the job, and to advertise through accessible media platforms. The findings suggest that although these employers had sought to anticipate any substantial disadvantage that disabled people might face with the use of technology, the direct contact with jobseekers was seen as vital during the online recruitment process to respond to individual needs. Thus, these organizations recognize that the requirements and needs of every applicant are dependent on their own context and form of impairment.

Conclusion

Taken together, this chapter provides important insights into change strategies advocated by disabled jobseekers and 'committed' employers on how disability inequality embedded in the online recruitment process can be challenged. By adopting the extended social model of disability (Reeve, 2013) and Acker's (2006) conceptual tool of inequality regimes, this study contributes to the scant literature on the negative implications of online recruitment processes.

Firstly, it offers a different insight into the ways that individuals with impairments experience disability in the labor market and in organizations, in particular their engagement with recruitment processes and practices during job searches and applications. The findings demonstrate that with the move to online recruitment processes job seeking has become more complex, in that it involves the use of online application processes, which are not yet fully accessible for disabled jobseekers. As such, some jobseekers face digital exclusion from engaging in job searches online, because of inaccessible technological infrastructure or missing computer training available to the public (Abascal et al., 2016), whereas others who have Internet access encounter accessibility issues.

Secondly, this study demonstrates that barriers in the form of disability inequality also occur within online recruitment practices, and these should be understood within the context of inequality regimes. Building on Ackers' argument that inequality regimes can be challenged, this chapter offers several change strategies that can be adopted by organizations to make their online recruitment practices more inclusive.

The most important change strategy mentioned was for employers to offer training on disability awareness to challenge the stigma attached to the attributes of disabled people by highlighting the real barriers (inaccessible job design) that hinder individuals from being productive workers. Aside from offering internal training to the entire workforce rather than solely to line managers, 'committed' employers also took on the responsibility to enlighten external organizations about the social model of disability to challenge ableist mindsets and organizational practices that produce disability inequality.

In addition to training, it was mentioned that creating barrier-free working environments and challenging the stereotype of lower productivity are vital to foster an inclusive organizational culture where jobseekers feel confident and able to disclose an impairment to receive the right adjustments to fit the job around their needs and requirements. In the UK, government funded sources of advice and training are available to employers, for instance from the EHRC. Yet, given that training on disability awareness is still a voluntary act undertaken by employers, and the Equality Act 2010 still relies on a medical understanding of disability, promoting change to challenge disability inequality within organizations and the wider labor market is highly dependent on further equality intervention. This study suggests that building alliances with organizations that affiliate to the disabled people's movement and endorse the social model perspective, and/or trade unions (Hoque et al., 2014) and other social movements may be a way to educate employers on disabling organizational practices or ableist-mindsets.

Moreover, a variety of perspectives were expressed on which reasonable adjustments could be made to facilitate equal access. These included technological solutions, but also ways of humanizing the use of these online systems. However, under the Equality Act 2010, private sector organizations are still exempt from the requirement to anticipate any barriers to application, and therefore tend to design recruitment processes as one-size-fits-all template rather than acknowledging that the experiences of jobseekers can vary depending on their context and type of impairment. Thus, regular assessment of online application processes is vital to achieve the fullest accessibility for jobseekers, which also requires change efforts from outside the organization by the UK government and/or equality bodies.

Still, as this study shows, change efforts by employers *can* go beyond technological solutions or current legal requirements to show commitment to hiring and retaining disabled workers. 'Committed' employers demonstrate that they were able to challenge discriminatory practices as part of their 'open recruitment' by willingly adopting proactive measures to provide reasonable adjustments and an inclusive workplace culture. This suggests that not only should the duty to provide reasonable adjustments be made mandatory for all employers, but also that governments should implement monitoring procedures to make sure that these legal duties are followed. Given the small-scale size of this study, further research on the negative implications of online recruitment practices in other countries and contexts, and with people who have other impairment types and access issues, is still required. This can help to better capture the full picture of how these organizational practices can be disabling towards disabled people, and how disability inequality embedded within online recruitment processes can be most effectively challenged.

References

Abascal, J., Barbosa, S. D. J., Nicolle, C., & Zaphiris, P. (2016). Rethinking universal accessibility: A broader approach considering the digital gap. *Universal Access in the Information Society*, *15*(2), 179–182. https://doi.org/10.1007/s10209-015-0416-1

Acker, J. (2006). Inequality regimes: Gender, class, and race in organizations. *Gender and Society*, *20*(4), 441–464. https://doi.org/10.1177/0891243206289499

Atheide, D. L., & Johnson, J. M. (1994). Criteria for assessing interpretive validity in qualitative research. In N. K. Denzin & Y. S. Lincoln (Eds.), *Handbook of qualitative research*. Sage.

Bredgaard, T., & Salado-Rasmussen, J. (2020). Attitudes and behaviour of employers to recruiting persons with disabilities. *Alter – European Journal of Disability Research*, *15*(1), 61–70. https://www.sciencedirect.com/science/article/pii/S1875067220300328

Cappelli, P. (2001, March). Making the most of online recruiting. *Harvard Business Review*, 139–146.

Chappell, A. L., Goodley, D., & Lawthom, R. (2001). Making connections: The relevance of the social model of disability for people with learning difficulties. *British Journal of Learning Disabilities*, *29*, 45–50. https://doi.org/10.1046/j.1468-3156.2001.00084.x

Duckett, P., & Pratt, R. (2007). The emancipation of visually impaired people in social science research practice. *The British Journal of Visual Impairment*, *25*(1), 5–20. https://doi.org/10.1177/026461960707177

Easton, C. (2011). Revisiting the law on website accessibility in the light of the UK's Equality Act 2010 and the United Nations Convention on the Rights of Persons with Disabilities. *International Journal of Law and Information Technology*, *20*(1), 19–47. https://doi.org/10.1093/ijlit/ear015

Ehrhart, K. H., Mayer, D. M., & Ziegert, J. C. (2012). Web-based recruitment in the Millennial generation: Work–life balance, website usability, and organizational attraction. *European Journal of Work and Organizational Psychology*, *21*(6), 850–874. https://doi.org/10.1080/1359432X.2011.598652

Equality and Human Rights Commission. (2014). *Equality Act 2010: Summary guidance on services, public functions and associations*.

Hogler, R. L., Henle, C., & Bemus, C. (1998). Internet recruiting and employment discrimination: A legal perspective. *Human Resource Management Review*, *8*(2), 149–164. https://doi.org/10.1016/S1053-4822(98)80002-8

Hoque, K., Bacon, N., & Parr, D. (2014). Employer disability practice in Britain: Assessing the impact of the Positive About Disabled People "Two Ticks" symbol. *Work, Employment and Society*, *28*(3), 430–451. https://doi.org/10.1177%2F0950017012472757

Kitchin, R. (2000). The researched opinions on research: Disabled people and disability research. *Disability & Society*, *15*(1), 25–47. https://doi.org/10.1080/09687590025757

Kulkarni, M., & Gopakumar, K. V. (2014). Career management strategies of people with disabilities. *Human Resource Management*, *53*(3), 445–466. https://doi.org/10.1002/hrm.21570

Lawson, A. (2011). Disability and employment in the Equality Act 2010: Opportunities seized, lost and generated. *Industrial Law Journal*, *40*(4), 359–383. https://doi.org/10.1093/indlaw/dwr021

Lazar, J., Olalere, A., & Wentz, B. (2012). Investigating the accessibility and usability of job application web sites for blind users. *Journal of Usability Studies*, *7*(2), 68–87. http://uxpajournal.org/wp-content/uploads/sites/8/pdf/JUS_Lazar_February_2012.pdf

Lengnick-Hall, M. L., Gaunt, P. M., & Kulkarni, M. (2008). Overlooked and underutilized: People with disabilities are an untapped human resource. *Human Resource Management*, *47*(2), 255–273. https://psycnet.apa.org/doi/10.1002/hrm.20211

Lewthwaite, S. (2014). Web accessibility standards and disability: Developing critical perspectives on accessibility. *Disability and Rehabilitation*, *36*(16), 1375–1383. https://doi.org/10.3109/09638288.2014.938178

Low, J. (2012). Conflict or concert? Extending the Simmelian Triad to account for positive third party presence in face-to-face interviews with people living with Parkinson's disease. *Societies*, *2*(3), 210–221. https://doi.org/10.3390/soc2030210

Moore, K., McDonald, P., & Bartlett, J. (2017). The social legitimacy of disability inclusive human resource practices: The case of a large retail organisation. *Human Resource Management Journal*, *27*(4), 514–529. https://doi.org/10.1111/1748-8583.12129

Oliver, M. (1992). Changing the social relations of research production? *Disability and Society*, *7*(2), 101–114. https://doi.org/10.1080/02674649266780141

Parry, E. & Tyson, S. (2008). An analysis of the use and success of online recruitment methods in the UK. *Human Resource Management Journal*, 18(3),257–274. https://doi.org/10.1111/j.1748-8583.2008.00070.x

Powell, A. (2021, May 24). *Briefing paper: Disabled People in Employment*. https://researchbriefings.files.parliament.uk/documents/CBP-7540/CBP-7540.pdf

Reeve, D. (2004). Psycho-emotional dimensions of disability and the social model. In C. Barnes & G. Mercer (Eds.), *Implementing the social model of disability: Theory and research* (pp. 83–100). The Disability Press.

Reeve, D. (2013). Psycho-emotional disablism. In C. Cameron (Ed), *Disability studies: A student's guide*. Sage.

Scholz, F., & Ingold, J. (2021). Activating the "ideal jobseeker": Experiences of individuals with mental health conditions on the UK Work Programme. *Human Relations*, *74*(10), 1604–1627. https://doi.org/10.1177/0018726720934848

Scholz, F., Yalcin, B., & Priestley, M. (2017). Internet access for disabled people: Understanding socio-relational factors in Europe. *Cyberpsychology: Journal of Psychosocial Research on Cyberspace, 11* (1),Article 4. ISSN:1802-7962

Searle, R. H. (2006). New technology: The potential impact of surveillance techniques in recruitment practices. *Personnel Review*, *35*(3), 336–351. https://doi.org/10.1108/00483480610656720

Thomas, C. (2004). Developing the social relational in the social model of disability: A theoretical agenda. In C. Barnes & G. Mercer (Eds.), *Implementing the social model of disability: Theory and research* (pp. 32–47). The Disability Press.

Trewin, S., Basson, S., Muller, M., Branham, S., Treviranus, J., Gruen, D., & Manser, E. (2019). Considerations for AI fairness for people with disabilities. *AI Matters*, *5*(3), 40–63. https://doi.org/10.1145/3362077.3362086

Miriam K. Baumgärtner, Stephan A. Boehm,
Christoph Breier, and Amit Jain

23 Fostering Disability Inclusion through Evidence-Based Research-Practice Collaborations – Challenges and Key Success Factors

Abstract: In this chapter, we share insights into one of our research-practice collaborations called *Inclusion Champions Switzerland*, in which we work together with different companies and the Swiss Federal Office of the equal treatment of persons with disabilities (EBGB). We first outline how we follow the idea of evidence-based management in approaching the different practice collaborations. Further, we introduce *the St.Gallen Inclusion Index*, which represents our measurement of inclusion, capturing four different dimensions: two on the individual (belongingness, authenticity) and two on the team/organizational level of analysis (synergy, equal opportunities). In addition, we work on different focus projects in each partner company to foster inclusive environments. We present team-based job crafting as one exemplary intervention underlining how a strength focus helps to shift from a disability perspective towards ability management, thereby fostering all dimensions of inclusion. We conclude with summarizing key success factors for establishing effective research-practice cooperation on disability and inclusion.

Keywords: research-practice cooperation, evidence-based management, St.Gallen Inclusion Index, job crafting, strengths use

Why Evidence-Based Research-Practice Cooperation is Important to Foster Disability Inclusion

Today, only few people would doubt the advantages of taking evidence-based decisions in fields such as medicine where it is key to correctly diagnose health challenges, followed by best practice recommendations for their respective treatment (Guyatt et al., 1992). In the field of management, this concept is still less prominent, although advocates such as Rousseau (2006) have pointed to the merits of this approach. As she explains, it is through evidence-based management, that "managers develop into experts who make organizational decisions informed by social science

Miriam K. Baumgärtner, Stephan A. Boehm, Christoph Breier, and Amit Jain,
PwC Switzerland

https://doi.org/10.1515/9783110743647-024

and organizational research – part of the zeitgeist moving professional decisions away from personal preference and unsystematic experience towards those based on the best available scientific evidence" (p. 256). While such evidence can stem from different sources including science, trained experts, or specialist organizations (Briner et al., 2009), research (Rousseau & Barends, 2011) has shown that due to the complexity of the current business environment, there is always a tendency for quick decision making which may not be optimal.

While being crucial for basically all fields of management, we argue that taking evidence-based decisions is particularly relevant for fostering diversity and inclusion in the workplace. Two main reasons account for this assumption. First, the active management of diversity and inclusion (D&I) has become a central element of human resource management practices in many organizations around the world (Boehm et al., 2021; Nishii et al., 2018), calling for effective strategies to foster D&I (Dobbin & Kalev, 2016). Second, managing diversity in general and disability in particular is often strongly influenced by decision makers' own preferences, biases and stereotypes (Baldridge et al., 2018; Brzykcy & Boehm, 2021) which might ultimately lead to decisions based on dogmas, beliefs or even ideology (Pfeffer & Sutton, 2006).

With the increase of workforce diversity, one of the organizational practices that has gained momentum is inclusion (Nishii, 2013; Nishii et al., 2018). Some recent studies (Creary et al., 2020) have taken an evidence-based approach to look at what worked and what did not work for inclusion in the workplace. Industries have also conducted benchmark studies to identify global practices (PwC, 2020). In addition, scholars have tried to analyze both inclusion-enhancing and -hindering factors by conducting systematic reviews and meta-analyses (Bell et al., 2011; Mor Barak et al., 2016). While there has long been discussion about a research-practice gap in diversity management (Bell & Kravitz, 2008; Kulik, 2014), the evidence-based management approach might be a promising strategy to target this gap. Martelli and Hayirli (2018) suggested that evidence variety can ensure capturing contextual, political, and relational aspects and, thus, lead to a better approach.

One of the diversity dimensions that organizations are increasingly focusing on is disability. This growing interest is shared by researchers (Beatty et al., 2019) such as our team at the University of St.Gallen. Core to our and our company partners' ambition to move disability research and practice forward is to take an evidence-based approach, i.e., to engage in joint research-practice cooperation. One of those is "Inclusion Champions Switzerland", a consortium of four Swiss firms (ABB, Hitachi, Novartis, and the Swiss Post) which work together with us and the Swiss Federal Office for the Equal Treatment of Persons with Disabilities (EBGB) to create more inclusive workplaces, particularly for employees with disabilities.

An important foundation of the joint work in this research-practice consortium is the St.Gallen Inclusion Index (SGII) which strives to measure inclusion in a scientifically rigorous manner. We use this tool to analyze the status quo of inclusion in our partner companies and to track progress on the organizations' way to become inclusion champions. In between the measurements, field interventions are conducted which foster employees with disabilities' equity and full participation in the workforce. One of those interventions which we will present in this chapter is a team-based job crafting intervention. Here, we try to leverage inclusion through employees' redesign of their jobs, using their signature strengths (Bakker et al., 2016 Kooij et al., 2017).

Measuring Inclusion – The St.Gallen Inclusion Index (SGII)

The Role of Disability Inclusion

With growing workforce diversity, workplaces bring together people of a variety of backgrounds, attitudes, beliefs, lifestyles, personalities, and abilities. These differences can be a source of both conflict and innovation (Roberson, 2019; Shore et al., 2011; van Knippenberg & Schippers, 2007). Thus, organizations, supervisors and team members must find ways to channel this diversity into a benefit not only for the organization itself but also for its employees. To achieve this goal, organizations must create and foster inclusive work environments in which all employees can thrive (Shore et al., 2018).

Such inclusive environments foster positive team processes and outcomes (De Cooman et al., 2016) such as information processing (Homan et al., 2007), innovation (Qi et al., 2019), productivity (Luanglath et al., 2019), job satisfaction (Findler et al., 2007), and work engagement (Sharma & Sharma, 2015). They reduce potential negative side effects of pronounced workplace diversity by reducing social categorization processes that may otherwise trigger team conflicts, sub-group formation, and discrimination (Boehm & Dwertmann, 2015; van Knippenberg et al., 2004).

This is of particular importance for employees with disabilities. They are often disadvantaged in work settings (Kraus et al., 2018; Schlömer-Jarvis et al., 2022). Due to stigma (Dalgin, 2018) and stereotypes commonly attached to a wide range of disabilities (Cuddy et al., 2007) and prevailing ableist norms in society (Campbell, 2009; Foster & Wass, 2013), persons with disabilities typically face more discrimination than persons without disabilities (Villanueva-Flores et al., 2017). This discrimination harms their personal health and well-being (Krnjacki et al., 2018) and diminishes their socio-economic outcomes (Rollins et al., 2011; Woodhams et al., 2015).

Inclusion is the counterweight to such processes. Truly inclusive workplaces value each employee regardless of disability for who they are and actively work against discrimination, harassment, and unfair treatment (Iwanaga et al., 2018; Shore et al., 2018; Shore et al., 2011). Thus, they help eliminate the disparities between persons with and without disabilities.

Developing the St.Gallen Inclusion Index

Four Dimensions of Inclusion

We understand team inclusion as a process that takes place and effect at two levels: On the individual level, we propose a sense of belongingness (Chung et al., 2020; Jansen et al., 2014) and authenticity (Jansen et al., 2014) as the key dimensions of inclusion. On the team level, synergy (Chung et al., 2020; Dwertmann et al., 2016) and equal opportunities (Dwertmann et al., 2016; Nishii, 2013) are central enablers of inclusive work environments. We integrate these four dimensions in the St.Gallen Inclusion Index (SGII).

Inclusive workplaces must instill a sense of belonginess in every individual employee. Employees should feel not only that they are part of a team but that their team members also value and care for them (Chung et al., 2020; Jansen et al., 2014; Shore et al., 2011). Moreover, authenticity is a key aspect of an inclusive environment. Being authentic means that employees can bring their true self to work and do not have to hide who they are (Jansen et al., 2014). Authenticity relates to self-determination theory (SDT; Deci & Ryan, 1991, 2000), more specifically to the need for autonomy, which can be related to identity. Being authentic means that you reveal who you really are without hiding certain aspects of your true self (e.g., your personality, an invisible disability, etc.). Being authentic implies that group members are allowed to be who they are, which can be either unique, but also similar. Thus, it appeals to both "atypical" (e.g., minority) and prototypical (e.g., majority) group members, which makes this concept broader than valuing uniqueness (Jansen et al., 2014). Creating both a feeling of belongingness and authenticity generates a positive team climate (Grandey et al., 2012): Employees are more satisfied and engaged within their teams (van den Bosch & Taris, 2014) and teams work better together (Connelly & Turel, 2016).

At the team level, synergy is key to harnessing the diversity that employees bring to teams (Dwertmann et al., 2016; Shore et al., 2011). Teams and organizations must listen to, value, foster, and integrate the diverse inputs and perspectives that every person brings to a team (Chung et al., 2020). Doing that increases information elaboration and problem-solving skills in teams and consequently benefits team innovation (van Knippenberg et al., 2004). Rather than just satisfying the need for uniqueness (Shore et al., 2011), inclusion means to build on the unique experiences, insights, and characteristics of employees (Miura & Hida, 2004; Warren et al., 2002) and make them more than the sum of their parts.

The last of the four cornerstones of inclusion is equal opportunity. Teams and organizations must ensure that every employee has fair and equitable access to training, development, pay, promotion, performance review, etc., regardless of their background (Boehm et al., 2014b; Dwertmann et al., 2016; Nishii, 2013). By providing such an environment, all employees have the chance to develop and thrive within their organizations leading to better work attitudes (Sousa et al., 2019), personal well-being (Tuan et al., 2020), and a reduction in workplace discrimination (Boehm et al., 2014a; Shore et al., 2018; Shore et al., 2011). A reporting example of the St.Gallen Inclusion Index is presented in Figure 23.1.

To provide readers with an even better understanding of the SGII, we present some real-life examples of factors fostering and hindering inclusion mapped on the four index dimensions. These examples were extracted from stakeholder interviews and interest group meetings in the consortia organizations. For instance, in all consortia organizations supervisors have been reported to be instrumental in creating a sense of belonging. Especially in the case of disability, an empathetic supervisor was able to bridge the relationships between team members to improve understanding among each other. Conversely, negative attitudes or a lack of understanding of disability have led to the opposite outcomes. Working conditions have also been crucial in fostering or diminishing a sense of belonging. Especially after an accident or an episode of depression, employees found themselves on temporary assignments (between six months and one year). The lack of long-term perspective with their employer and their teams made them hesitant to form strong relationships with colleagues. On the other hand, having that long-term perspective led to the forming of stronger relationships with colleagues and made disability a non-issue in most cases.

As with belongingness, supervisors were also identified as agents of fostering authenticity. Supervisors who communicate openly with team members and show understanding towards employee disability effectively aided employee disclosure towards colleagues. This disclosure then helped to facilitate a better understanding of how and when disability might be relevant to day-to-day work. In creating this open atmosphere, employees with disabilities were actively encouraged to show more of their true self and were less concerned with hiding. On the other hand, supervisors that lacked an understanding of disability have made it significantly harder for employees with disabilities to be themselves. This led to stronger concealing and passing behaviors of employees with disabilities. This was especially pronounced for neurodiverse or psychological conditions.

Examples of fostering synergy within teams (or the organization as a whole) were hard to come by in the stakeholder interviews that we conducted. Participants focused on their relationship with the supervisor or with the company rather than describing team processes or discussions. However, in the job crafting workshops that we describe later, we were able to observe different levels of synergy orientation (or climate) within teams. We could see that in some teams discussions about the crafting plan and team goals were more active and open than in others. The stronger the position of the leader or single outspoken members in these teams, the more reluctant were the other employees to contribute their own ideas, let alone propose something contrary to "popular" opinion. Conversely, in teams in which the supervisor assumed a moderating or reserved position, we observed more individuals voicing ideas, opinions, and suggestions – although even here not everybody participated equally.

No employee in the stakeholder interviews explicitly stated that they were treated unfairly or discriminated against by HR or HR processes. However, there were some instances from which we could deduce that HR processes are not fully fair. For instance, especially after a reintegration process, some employees with disabilities moved from one temporary assignment to another rather than being offered a permanent position or longer contract (e.g., two- to three-year terms). Furthermore, some persons with sensory disabilities reported that they have been overlooked for a position because the respective decision maker had had negative experiences with persons with disabilities. Generally, we also observed a strong deficit focus within certain firms that influenced blue-collar supervisors in particular to be reluctant to offer positions to persons with disabilities. On the other hand, all consortia organizations put notable resources into increasing qualifications of persons in a reintegration process (i.e., persons who have acquired a disability during their tenure with their current employer) by offering them to participate in further education programs that increase their internal and external labor market skills.

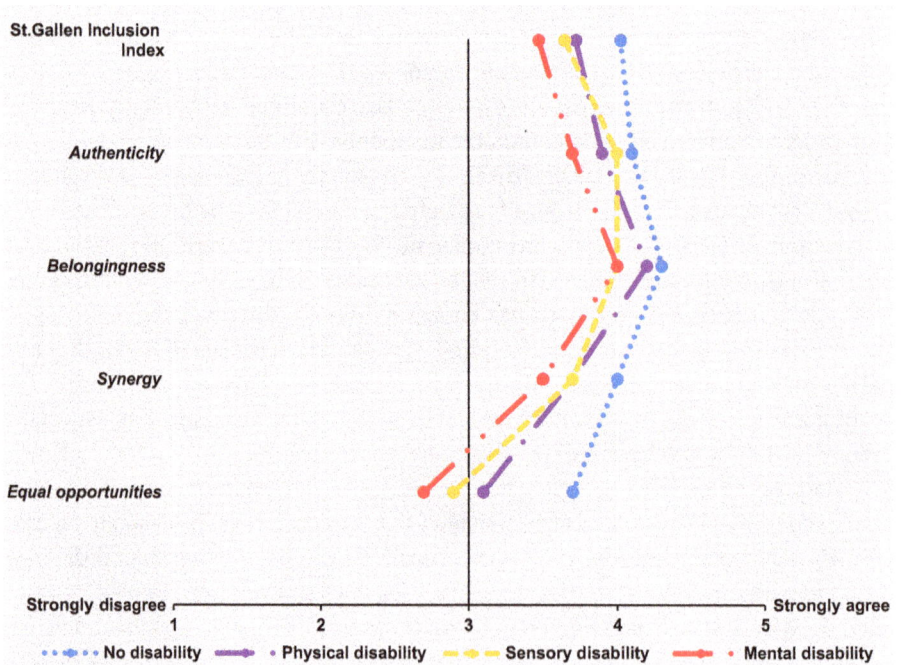

Figure 23.1: Reporting example of the St.Gallen Inclusion Index.

An Intervention to Foster Inclusion: Team-based Job Crafting

In the following, we will present an intervention which we designed for Inclusion Champions Switzerland to improve perceptions of all four dimensions of the SGII. The rationale of a team job crafting intervention is to support organizations in focusing on abilities rather than on disabilities. As a result, employees are encouraged to apply their strengths more purposefully. Focusing on what people can do well is rooted in positive psychology, which is a "science of positive subjective experience, positive individual traits, and positive institutions" (Seligman & Csikszentmihalyi, 2000, p. 5). Interventions that rely on positive human functioning have been shown to increase well-being and performance (Meyers et al., 2013).

Applying Strengths Use in Teams: The Concept of Job Crafting on the Collective Level

Job Crafting, Strengths Use, and the Importance of the Team Context

Job crafting is defined as a form of proactive behavior in which persons initiate a change in their work demands and resources to increase person-job fit (Rudolph et al., 2017; Tims & Bakker, 2010). As such, the efficient use of resources is in the center of the concept. The idea is that people do more of what they are good at and less of what they are poor at or not interested in.

When applying strengths use to organizations, the team context plays a vital role. This is because applying one's own strengths is both enabled and constrained by other team members (van Woerkom et al., 2020). In other words, my own scope of action ends where others come into play. "We can compare this situation to a jazz ensemble in which all musicians are highly skilled and sound fantastic as individuals. When playing together, however, they may sound awful when all individuals decide to play to their own strengths" (van Woerkom et al., 2020, p. 3). Van Woerkom and colleagues (2020) propose that collective strengths use relates to performance via the following mechanisms, which are (1) the collective awareness of different individual strengths, (2) the reliance on and trust in those strengths, and (3) the coordination of working tasks and team roles related to these individual strengths.

Overcoming Deficit Orientation by Practicing Collective Strengths Use

Strengths are defined as characteristics that enable persons to perform well or even at their best (Wood et al., 2011). Compared to the traditional human resources management (HRM) approach targeted at fixing weaknesses, leveraging one's strengths is the only way to get to excellent performance (Buckingham & Clifton, 2001). People with disabilities experience many times that their disability is portrayed in a deficit orientation (Mitra, 2006). Especially the medical model of disability provides deficit-based definitions and perceptions (Haegele & Hodge, 2016). Since persons with disabilities are used to living with certain restrictions and learn a lot about what they cannot do, their confidence in their own abilities may have suffered (Kensbock & Boehm, 2016). Van Woerkom and Meyers (2018) demonstrated the positive effects of a strengths-based intervention, especially for training participants who lack confidence in what they can do. Re-instilling confidence while avoiding putting people with disabilities in the spotlight, but rather treating them as equal members of a team participating in a workshop, seems especially suited to foster inclusion in the whole team. This also relates to work on the discursive disablement of individuals with impairments and the dichotomy of able-bodied/disabled (Jammaers & Zanoni, 2020; Jammaers et al., 2016). Focusing on different strengths within a team, and re-arranging work to fit with these strengths, may be one way to soften this ableist dichotomy by shifting the perspective and focusing on individual strengths that are valuable for particular team processes and working tasks.

Designing a Job Crafting Intervention

Based on van Woerkom et al.'s model (2020), we developed the workshop as a sequence of four different steps, which finally result in writing a concrete plan of to-dos in terms of team crafting activities for the next few weeks. The sequence of our intervention is depicted in Figure 23.2. Two weeks before the workshop, participants get their preparation documents, in which they are asked to do the Reflected Best Self (RBS) exercise (see Roberts et al., 2005 for a detailed description of the RBS exercise). First, participants need to solicit comments from different persons in their work and private environment, asking them to provide specific examples of situations in which their strengths were particularly beneficial. Next, they search for common themes in the feedback, organizing them in a table to develop a clear picture of their strengths. Third, they write a self-portrait that summarizes the feedback. Within the workshop, they do an additional exercise called "appreciation shower", in which they brainstorm strengths they associate with each other within small groups comprising 3–4 persons. Afterwards, they are asked to share their strengths profiles and indicate which of their strengths/interests they aim to use more in their work.

Focusing on these strengths/interests, workshop participants develop specific job crafting strategies (e.g.: "I will initiate project xy to bring in my strength z"). In a first step, they do so individually by using a worksheet that we prepared. Next, they discuss their individual job crafting plans in their teams within the boundaries of their team goals. The team goals have been specified by the team leader in preparation for the workshop. In addition to the performance-related goals, we explicitly asked them to also formulate "social team goals" that focus on team processes, such as "a better onboarding process for new hires" or "better knowledge transfer between team members", which also have performance implications. In this regard, team members can take over informal roles as well. The different roles are assigned in a participative process. Finally, the individual job crafting goals are integrated within an overall team job crafting plan, which aligns with the team objectives.

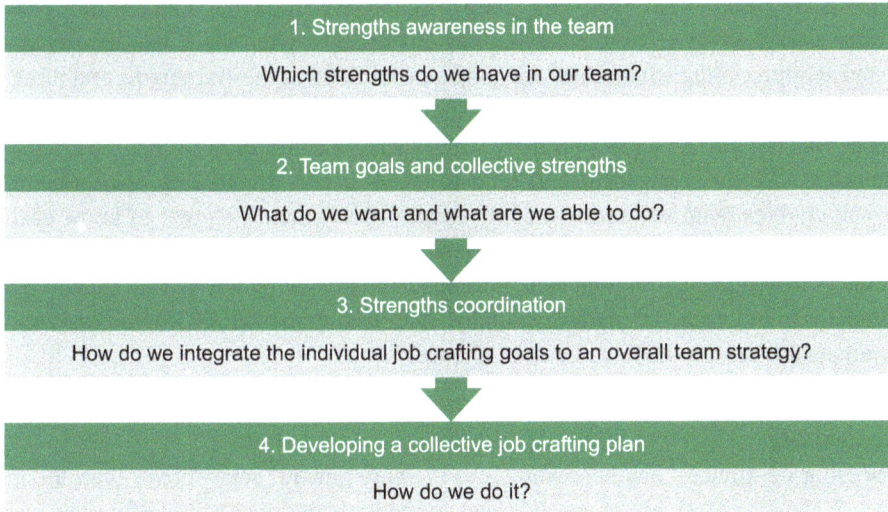

1. Strengths awareness in the team

Which strengths do we have in our team?

▼

2. Team goals and collective strengths

What do we want and what are we able to do?

▼

3. Strengths coordination

How do we integrate the individual job crafting goals to an overall team strategy?

▼

4. Developing a collective job crafting plan

How do we do it?

Figure 23.2: Sequence of the team job crafting intervention.

How the Process of the Workshop Fosters Feelings of Inclusion and Team Climate for Inclusion

As outlined above, we understand inclusion as a combination of authenticity and belongingness at the individual level, and synergy and equal opportunities at the team level of analysis. We propose that the job crafting workshop nurtures all four dimensions in specific ways.

Inclusion on the Individual Level by Fostering Belongingness and Authenticity

During the job crafting workshop, identifying individual strengths in the team is pivotal. The process of appreciating and sharing strengths is likely to foster both acceptance (being the same) and distinctiveness (being different; compare Brewer, 1991). Moreover, we assume that the idea that everyone's strengths contribute to the team's overall strengths portfolio in the pursuit of collective goals further supports the team's willingness to include the individual (Jansen et al., 2014).

Belongingness

"The need to belong is the motivation to form and maintain strong and stable relationships with other people" (Jansen et al., 2014, p. 371). The two cornerstones of belongingness are group membership and group affection. We argue that both are addressed in our workshop since it increases interactions between team members that are targeted at appreciating what others are good at, coordinating these strengths and thinking about how to make team processes more efficient by purposefully using these collective strengths as a team property (van Woerkom et al., 2020). Thus, the interactions are affectively pleasant and tend to create a non-threatening environment, which enables team members to connect with each other. They get to know each other in a different light, learn about their similarities with others, but also about differences in complementing the team portfolio of strengths. By developing trust in the strengths of others or "strengths credibility" (van Woerkom et al., 2020), interpersonal relationships are also likely to be strengthened.

Authenticity

Focusing on abilities has been shown to increase general self-efficacy (van Woerkom & Meyers, 2018). Moreover, it allows individuals to proactively fulfill their personal needs for development (Alderfer, 1969) and for competence (Deci & Ryan, 1991, 2000). Thus, bringing your strengths to work and doing more of what you are good at as well as following your own interests is likely to increase authenticity.

Within the process of the workshop, there is room to share strengths and interests (room for authenticity). Moreover, people are encouraged to be themselves by presenting their individual features and what distinguishes them from others, resembling value in authenticity. By presenting their individual strengths and interests, they show an important part of themselves. By communicating these characteristics, the workshop participants show who they are, and the team acknowledges bringing one's authentic self to work (Jansen et al., 2014).

Increasing Inclusion on the Team Level by Fostering Synergy and Equal Opportunities

Creating collective awareness of individual strengths as well as trust and credibility in using them (compare van Woerkom et al., 2020) is likely to support an environment in which everyone is heard, seen, and treated equally. Moreover, acknowledging the team portfolio consisting of a variety of strengths will make synergy effects of diversity more likely.

Synergy

Synergy diversity climate is defined as "the extent to which employees jointly perceive their organization and/or workgroup to *promote the expression of, listening to, active valuing of*, and *integration of* diverse perspectives for the purpose of enhancing collective learning and performance" (Jansen et al., 2014, p. 1152). By participating in strengths-spotting exercises and talking about diverse strengths, knowledge sharing between workshop participants and insights into their strengths is facilitated. As a result, the various abilities of the team become more apparent ("strengths awareness"; van Woerkom et al., 2020). Team members learn how different group members can contribute to their team goals and develop trust in their strengths ("strengths credibility"). The emerging strengths-based climate is assumed to enable synergy effects of diversity (compare Dwertmann et al., 2016). By coordinating the various strengths, diverse abilities can be used more effectively, and different skills are integrated.

Equal Opportunities

In the workshops, the participants interact on equal terms. Everyone has a seat at the table and is asked to talk about their own strengths, aspirations, and career endeavors. This process highlights that the supervisor and the organization have an interest in all employees' growth and further development which is a key aspect of equal opportunities at work (Nishii, 2013). Further, during the stage of strengths coordination, it is important that the moderator ensures that team members jointly determine how to distribute job tasks and different roles within the team (van Woerkom et al., 2020). Besides task-related roles, informal roles that fulfill social functioning are also ascribed and highlighted. On the one hand, valuing social roles underscores their importance; on the other, explicitly distributing or altering them helps to support a climate of inclusion within the team.

Insights from a Pilot Study

Sample Description and Process

We conducted team crafting workshops in February and March 2021 with eight different teams of one of our partner companies, which consisted of 7–11 members. Overall, 67 employees participated in the training. We had 44 male and 18 female participants (5 did not disclose their gender). The age ranged from 18 to 65 years with a mean of 39.7 years. Within the teams, people with invisible (and mostly non-disclosed) disabilities participated just like any other team member. We trained six white-collar and two blue-collar teams. All the workshops except one with a blue-collar team were conducted online due to the COVID-19 pandemic. The workshops were accompanied by 1–2 moderator/s and 1–2 silent observer/s. The duration of each workshop was 6–7 hours including a one-hour lunch break.

The main objective was to reassign or redesign working tasks within the team based on individual strengths of its members. For an overall evaluation and optimization of the workshop, the participants were asked to respond to a survey at three points in time – before the workshop, one day after, and four weeks later. Moreover, the team leaders were invited to participate in a 30-minute interview to describe their views on and perceptions of the workshop.

Preliminary Evaluation

The survey consisted of both a quantitative and qualitative part with open questions. Overall, the participants reacted very positively to the workshop. The mean value of satisfaction with the workshop was 4.18 (out of 5). They rated the likelihood of recommending the workshop to their colleagues with 7.18 (out of 10). Female participants rated the workshop more favorably than their male counterparts. The participants underlined the added value they perceived in getting strengths-based feedback as well as discussing strengths and how to better integrate them within their working teams. They especially liked the focus on strengths, the appreciative atmosphere in the workshops, and the open exchange with their team members. They mentioned room for improvement concerning the strong orientation towards team goals, leading to a tension with the individual crafting goals, as well as the implementation in their daily working routines. Concerning the measured outcomes such as team cohesion, work engagement, job satisfaction, physical and mental work ability, we observed a slight increase in the means over time. After adapting and optimizing the workshop, it will be offered as a train-the-trainer concept for all employees. As part of this firm-wide implementation of the workshops, a quantitative evaluation will take place with a special focus on the potential impact on inclusion.

Lessons Learned and Conclusion

During our research-practice cooperation in the field of disability and inclusion, we had the opportunity to observe several key success factors for making such projects work which we will share in this concluding paragraph.

Building on Existent Scientific Evidence and Practical Experience

First and foremost, it seems decisive to conduct a structured review of prior knowledge, projects, and activities both in academia and the world of practice. It is one of the cornerstones of evidence-based research to not "reinvent the wheel" but to consider what other scholars and practitioners have done successfully in order to make inclusion work. The growing number of meta-analyses, structured reviews, and comparative case analyses can be used as an ideal springboard for developing one's own initiatives. Both the SGII and our job crafting workshops are examples of this approach as they build on prior scholarly knowledge (e.g., Jansen et al., 2014; van Woerkom & Meyers, 2018).

In addition, already existent corporate initiatives should be considered to secure (top) management support and be compatible with corporate language, culture, and overall goals. For instance, rather than solely relying on input from high-quality research journals, we additionally needed to integrate practice-based input from organizations such as the International Labour Organization and existent business initiatives. Doing this required us as researchers to find the right balance between scientific rigor and the organizational needs for easy-to-implement, easy-to-communicate, and impactful solutions. In addition, such an approach may provide researchers with an excellent opportunity to identify aspects that could easily have been overlooked such as the critical role of internal communication (Pérez-Conesa et al., 2020) or the idiosyncrasies of organizational decision-making processes.

Successful Stakeholder Management

Closely linked to the first point, researchers cannot operate in a vacuum or with limited support from HR to have a sustainable effect on organizational practice. In contrast, durable relationships with top and line management must be developed and fostered. Without those, even the best D&I and disability projects are just a flash in the pan. An especially important role is played by dedicated diversity managers who internally and externally drive the topic (Dobbin & Kalev, 2016). In our experience, these experts are the ideal partners for making disability-related research-practice collaborations work.

Besides leadership personnel and HR, allies play an important role in bringing inclusion to life. In this respect, employee resource groups (ERGs) can become a source of sustainable support at all organizational levels. In our research, this became particularly obvious in one organization where a disability-specific ERG helped us to identify interview partners with disabilities who were willing to share their positive and negative experiences with inclusion, thereby contributing to the improvement of D&I policies. Further, ERGs were instrumental in providing information about the inclusion practices across the globe, helping us to understand and reflect about the cross-cultural aspects of inclusion in our partner organizations. In sum, ERGs are very well suited to reach out to both affected persons and their allies, to collect and synergize input from relevant stakeholders that may otherwise not have been reached, and to disseminate and feed new research insights and adapted processes back into the organization. In this sense, ERGs are instrumental in co-creating insights and implementing new policies for better D&I initiatives within organizations.

The Essential Role of Clear Expectation Management

Finally, as in basically all social situations, communication seems key for project success. This is especially true when scholars want to cooperate with practitioners, as both are often driven by different motives and reward schemes. For instance, while disability researchers have a key interest in measuring everything in the most reliable and valid manner (e.g., with full scales, longitudinal data collections, and access to HR systems data), inclusion practitioners are more interested in keeping the burden for participants low. Concerns regarding anonymity and data security or the potential publication of unpleasant results further complicate the situation. Lastly, time horizons often differ as practitioners strive for short-term interventions and results while scholars are well used to perennial publication loops. To deal with these challenges effectively, project partners should as early as possible set clear criteria for their intended cooperation (e.g., regarding project length, sample size and data access required, publication ambitions, etc.). Further, clear roles must be agreed upon, e.g., regarding the researchers' roles as topic experts and topic owners (who drive the project based on their own research ambitions) versus consultants (who mainly react towards organizations' needs and interests).

This challenge became rather obvious in the beginning of our cooperation as mutual expectations were somewhat unclear, leading to some initial disappointment. From a company perspective, we lacked an oven-ready, easy-to-implement solution to their disability-related challenges. From a research perspective, the company did not provide the field access that might have been necessary to implement a sophisticated research design such as a randomized field experiment. Moreover, as disabilities are often not disclosed, companies do not know which staff members have a disability, complicating access to this employee group (e.g., regarding interviews, etc.). Having discussed expectations openly, we were able to find common ground that satisfied both needs. An open line of communication with a clear contact point (i.e., one or two responsible project owners on each side who regularly meet for a jour fixe) can avert possible conflicts early on. Even more important, intense communication can help to support each other's goals as well as overall project success by increasing visibility and credibility internally (i.e., joint communication of researchers and company partners to top management) and externally (e.g., joint social media posts, joint visits to conferences, etc.).

If researchers and practice partners take these aspects into account, research-practice collaborations can become an extremely efficient and reliable source of new evidence, not only, but particularly in the fields of disability, diversity, and inclusion. Ideally, our short description of Inclusion Champions Switzerland might inspire some international scholars and practitioners to join forces to make working environments more inclusive – one of the biggest, yet most rewarding challenges that our world currently faces.

References

Alderfer, C. P. (1969). An empirical test of a new theory of human needs. *Organizational Behavior and Human Performance*, 4(2), 142–175. https://doi.org/10.1016/0030-5073(69)90004-X

Bakker, A. B., Rodríguez-Muñoz, A., & Sanz Vergel, A. I. (2016). Modelling job crafting behaviours: Implications for work engagement. *Human Relations*, 69(1), 169–189. https://doi.org/10.1177/0018726715581690

Baldridge, D., Beatty, J., Böhm, S. A., Kulkarni, M., & Moore, M. (2018). Persons with (dis)Abilities. In A. J. Colella & E. B. King (Eds.), *The Oxford handbook of workplace discrimination* (pp. 111–127). Oxford University Press.

Beatty, J. E., Baldridge, D. C., Boehm, S. A., Kulkarni, M., & Colella, A. J. (2019). On the treatment of persons with disabilities in organizations: A review and research agenda. *Human Resource Management*, 58(2), 119–137. https://doi.org/10.1002/hrm.21940

Bell, M. P., & Kravitz, D. A. (2008). From the guest co-editors: What do we know and need to learn about diversity education and training? *Academy of Management Learning & Education*, 7(3), 301–308. https://doi.org/10.5465/amle.2008.34251669

Bell, S. T., Villado, A. J., Lukasik, M. A., Belau, L., & Briggs, A. L. (2011). Getting specific about demographic diversity variable and team performance relationships: A meta-analysis. *Journal of Management*, 37(3), 709–743. https://doi.org/10.1177/0149206310365001

Boehm, S. A., & Dwertmann, D. J. G. (2015). Forging a single-edged sword: Facilitating positive age and disability diversity effects in the workplace through leadership, positive climates, and HR practices. *Work, Aging and Retirement*, 1(1), 41–63. https://doi.org/10.1093/workar/wau008

Boehm, S. A., Dwertmann, D. J. G., Kunze, F., Michaelis, B., Parks, K., & McDonald, D. (2014a). Expanding insights on the diversity climate–performance link: The role of work group discrimination and group size. *Human Resource Management*, 53(3), 379–402. https://doi.org/10.1002/hrm.21589

Boehm, S. A., Kunze, F., & Bruch, H. (2014b). Spotlight on age-diversity climate: The impact of age-inclusive HR practices on firm-level outcomes. *Personnel Psychology, 67*(3), 667–704. https://doi.org/10.1111/peps.12047

Boehm, S. A., Schröder, H., & Bal, M. (2021). Age-related human resource management policies and practices: Antecedents, outcomes, and conceptualizations. *Work, Aging, and Retirement, 7*(4), 257–272. https://doi.org/10.1093/workar/waab024

Brewer, M. B. (1991). The social self: On being the same and different at the same time. *Personality and Social Psychology Bulletin, 17*(5), 475–482. https://doi.org/10.1177/0146167291175001

Briner, R. B., Denyer, D., & Rousseau, D. M. (2009). Evidence-based management: Concept cleanup time? *Academy of Management Perspectives, 23*(4), 19–32. https://doi.org/10.5465/AMP.2009.45590138

Brzykcy, A., & Boehm, S. A. (2021). No such thing as a free ride: The impact of disability labels on workplace socialization. *Human Relations, 75*(4), 734–763. https://doi.org/10.1177/0018726721991609

Buckingham, M., & Clifton, D. O. (2001). *Now, discover your strengths*. Free Press.

Campbell, F. K. (2009). *Contours of ableism. The production of disability and abledness*. Palgrave Macmillan.

Chung, B. G., Ehrhart, K. H., Shore, L. M., Randel, A. E., Dean, M. A., & Kedharnath, U. (2020). Work group inclusion: Test of a scale and model. *Group & Organization Management, 45*(1), 75–102. https://doi.org/10.1177/1059601119839858

Connelly, C. E., & Turel, O. (2016). Effects of team emotional authenticity on virtual team performance. *Frontiers in Psychology, 7*, Article 1336. https://doi.org/10.3389/fpsyg.2016.01336

Creary, S. J., Rothbard, N., Mariscal, E., Moore, O., Scruggs, J., & Villarmán, N. (2020). *Evidence-based solutions for inclusion in the workplace: Actions for middle managers*. (May Issue). https://wpa.wharton.upenn.edu/wp-content/uploads/2020/05/Evidence-Based-Solutions-for-Inclusion-in-the-Workplace_May-2020.pdf

Cuddy, A. J., Fiske, S. T., & Glick, P. (2007). The BIAS map: Behaviors from intergroup affect and stereotypes. *Journal of Personality and Social Psychology, 92*(4), 631–648. https://doi.org/10.1037/022-3514.92.4.631

Dalgin, R. S. (2018). The complex nature of disability stigma in employment: Impact on access and opportunity. In S. B. Thomson & G. Grady (Eds.), *Stigmas, work, and organizations* (pp. 55–70). Palgrave Macmillan.

De Cooman, R., Vantilborgh, T., Bal, M., & Lub, X. (2016). Creating inclusive teams through perceptions of supplementary and complementary person–team fit: Examining the relationship between person–team fit and team effectiveness. *Group & Organization Management, 41*(3), 310–342. https://doi.org/10.1177/1059601115586910

Deci, E. L., & Ryan, R. M. (1991). A motivational approach to self: Integration in personality. In R. A. Dienstbier & R. A. Dienstbier (Eds.), *Nebraska Symposium on Motivation, 1990: Perspectives on motivation* (pp. 237–288). University of Nebraska Press.

Deci, E. L., & Ryan, R. M. (2000). The "what" and "why" of goal pursuits: Human needs and the self-determination of behavior. *Psychological Inquiry, 11*(4), 227–268. https://doi.org/10.1207/S15327965PLI1104_01

Dobbin, F., & Kalev, A. (2016). Why diversity programs fail – and what works better. *Harvard Business Review*, July–August, 52–60.

Dwertmann, D. J. G., Nishii, L. H., & van Knippenberg, D. (2016). Disentangling the fairness & discrimination and synergy perspectives on diversity climate: Moving the field forward. *Journal of Management, 42*(5), 1136–1168. https://doi.org/10.1177/0149206316630380

Findler, L., Wind, L. H., & Barak, M. E. M. (2007). The challenge of workforce management in a global society: Modeling the relationship between diversity, inclusion, organizational culture, and employee well-being, job satisfaction and organizational commitment. *Administration in Social Work, 31*(3), 63–94. https://doi.org/10.1300/J147v31n03_05

Foster, D., & Wass, V. (2013). Disability in the labour market: An exploration of concepts of the ideal worker and organisational fit that disadvantage employees with impairments. *Sociology, 47*(4), 705–721. https://doi.org/10.1177/0038038512454245

Grandey, A., Foo, S. C., Groth, M., & Goodwin, R. E. (2012). Free to be you and me: A climate of authenticity alleviates burnout from emotional labor. *Journal of Occupational Health Psychology, 17*(1), 1–14. https://doi.org/10.1037/a0025102

Guyatt, G., Cairns, J., Churchill, D., et al. (1992). Evidence-based medicine. A new approach to teaching the practice of medicine. *Journal of the American Medical Association, 268*(17), 2420–2425. https://doi.org/10.1001/jama.1992.03490170092032

Haegele, J. A., & Hodge, S. (2016). Disability discourse: Overview and critiques of the medical and social models. *Quest, 68*(2), 193–206. https://doi.org/10.1080/00336297.2016.1143849

Homan, A. C., van Knippenberg, D., Van Kleef, G. A., & De Dreu, C. K. W. (2007). Bridging faultlines by valuing diversity: Diversity beliefs, information elaboration, and performance in diverse work groups. *Journal of Applied Psychology, 92*(5), 1189–1199. https://doi.org/10.1037/0021-9010.92.5.1189

Iwanaga, K., Chen, X., Wu, J. R., Lee, B., Chan, F., Bezyak, J., Grenawalt, T. A., & Tansey, T. N. (2018). Assessing disability inclusion climate in the workplace: A brief report. *Journal of Vocational Rehabilitation, 49*(2), 265–271. https://doi.org/10.3233/JVR-180972

Jammaers, E., & Zanoni, P. (2020). Unexpected entrepreneurs: The identity work of entrepreneurs with disabilities. *Entrepreneurship & Regional Development, 32*(9–10), 879–898. https://doi.org/10.1080/08985626.2020.1842913

Jammaers, E., Zanoni, P., & Hardonk, S. (2016). Constructing positive identities in ableist workplaces: Disabled employees' discursive practices engaging with the discourse of lower productivity. *Human Relations, 69*(6), 1365–1386. https://doi.org/10.1177/0018726715612901

Jansen, W. S., Otten, S., van der Zee, K. I., & Jans, L. (2014). Inclusion: Conceptualization and measurement. *European Journal of Social Psychology, 44*(4), 370–385. https://doi.org/10.1002/ejsp.2011

Kensbock, J. M., & Boehm, S. A. (2016). The role of transformational leadership in the mental health and job performance of employees with disabilities. *International Journal of Human Resource Management, 27*(14), 1580–1609. https://doi.org/10.1080/09585192.2015.1079231

Kooij, D. T. A. M., van Woerkom, M., Wilkenloh, J., Dorenbosch, L., & Denissen, J. J. A. (2017). Job crafting towards strengths and interests: The effects of a job crafting intervention on person–job fit and the role of age. *Journal of Applied Psychology, 102*(6), 971–981. https://doi.org/10.1037/apl0000194

Kraus, L., Lauer, E., Coleman, R., & Houtenville, A. (2018). *2017 Disability statistics annual report.* University of New Hampshire.

Krnjacki, L., Priest, N., Aitken, Z., Emerson, E., Llewellyn, G., King, T., & Kavanagh, A. (2018). Disability-based discrimination and health: Findings from an Australian-based population study. *Australian and New Zealand Journal of Public Health, 42*(2), 172–174. https://doi.org/10.1111/1753-6405.12735

Kulik, C. T. (2014). Working below and above the line: The research–practice gap in diversity management. *Human Resource Management Journal, 24*(2), 129–144. https://doi.org/10.1111/1748-8583.12038

Luanglath, N., Ali, M., & Mohannak, K. (2019). Top management team gender diversity and productivity: The role of board gender diversity. *Equality, Diversity and Inclusion: An International Journal*, *38*(1), 71–86. https://doi.org/10.1108/EDI-04-2018-0067

Martelli, P. F., & Hayirli, T. C. (2018). Three perspectives on evidence-based management: Rank, fit, variety. *Management Decision*, *56*(10), 2085–2100. https://doi.org/10.1108/MD-09-2017-0920

Meyers, M. C., van Woerkom, M., & Bakker, A. B. (2013). The added value of the positive: A literature review of positive psychology interventions in organizations. *European Journal of Work and Organizational Psychology*, *22*(5), 618–632. https://doi.org/10.1080/1359432X.2012.694689

Mitra, S. (2006). The capability approach and disability. *Journal of Disability Policy Studies*, *16*(4), 236–247. https://doi.org/10.1177/10442073060160040501

Miura, A., & Hida, M. (2004). Synergy between diversity and similarity in group-idea generation. *Small Group Research*, *35*(5), 540–564. https://doi.org/10.1177/1046496404264942

Mor Barak, M. E., Lizano, E. L., Kim, A., Duan, L., Rhee, M.-K., Hsiao, H.-Y., & Brimhall, K. C. (2016). The promise of diversity management for climate of inclusion: A state-of-the-art review and meta-analysis. *Human Service Organizations: Management, Leadership & Governance*, *40*(4), 305–333. https://doi.org/10.1080/23303131.2016.1138915

Nishii, L. H. (2013). The benefits of climate for inclusion for gender-diverse groups. *Academy of Management Journal*, *56*(6), 1754–1774. http://dx.doi.org/10.5465/amj.2009.0823

Nishii, L. H., Khattab, J., Shemla, M., & Paluch, R. M. (2018). A multilevel process model for understanding diversity practice effectiveness. *Academy of Management Annals*, *12*(1), 37–82. https://doi.org/10.5465/annals.2016.0044

Pérez-Conesa, F. J., Romeo, M., & Yepes-Baldó, M. (2020). Labour inclusion of people with disabilities in Spain: The effect of policies and human resource management systems. *The International Journal of Human Resource Management*, *31*(6), 785–804. https://doi.org/10.1080/09585192.2017.1380681

Pfeffer, J., & Sutton, R. I. (2006). Evidence-based management. *Harvard Business Review*, *84*(1), 62–74. https://hbr.org/2006/01/evidence-based-management

PwC. (2020). *Diversity & Inclusion Benchmarking Survey*. https://www.pwc.com/gx/en/services/people-organisation/global-diversity-and-inclusion-survey/global-report.pdf

Qi, L., Liu, B., Wei, X., & Hu, Y. (2019). Impact of inclusive leadership on employee innovative behavior: Perceived organizational support as a mediator. *PloS one*, *14*(2), e0212091. https://doi.org/10.1371/journal.pone.0212091

Roberson, Q. M. (2019). Diversity in the workplace: A review, synthesis, and future research agenda. *Annual Review of Organizational Psychology and Organizational Behavior*, *6*, 69–88. https://doi.org/10.1146/annurev-orgpsych-012218-015243

Roberts, L. M., Spreitzer, G., Dutton, J., Quinn, R., Heaphy, E., & Barker, B. (2005). How to play to your strengths. *Harvard Business Review*, *83*(1), 74–80.

Rollins, A. L., Bond, G. R., Jones, A. M., Kukla, M., & Collins, L. A. (2011). Workplace social networks and their relationship with job outcomes and other employment characteristics for people with severe mental illness. *Journal of Vocational Rehabilitation*, *35*(3), 243–252. https://doi.org/10.3233/JVR-2011-0575

Rousseau, D. M. (2006). Is there such a thing as "evidence-based management"? *Academy of Management Review*, *31*(2), 256–269. https://doi.org/10.5465/AMR.2006.20208679

Rousseau, D. M., & Barends, E. G. R. (2011). Becoming an evidence-based HR practitioner. *Human Resource Management Journal*, *21*(3), 221–235. https://doi.org/10.1111/j.1748-8583.2011.00173.x

Rudolph, C. W., Katz, I. M., Lavigne, K. N., & Zacher, H. (2017). Job crafting: A meta-analysis of relationships with individual differences, job characteristics, and work outcomes. *Journal of Vocational Behavior, 102*, 112–138. https://doi.org/10.1016/j.jvb.2017.05.008

Schlömer-Jarvis, A., Boehm, S. A., & Bader, B. (2022). The role of human resource practices for including persons with disabilities in the workforce: A systematic literature review. *The International Journal of Human Resource Management, 33*(1), 45–98. https://doi.org/10.1080/09585192.2021.1996433

Seligman, M. E. P., & Csikszentmihalyi, M. (2000). Positive psychology. *American Psychologist, 55*(1), 5–14. https://doi.org/10.1037//0003-066X.55.1.5

Sharma, R. R., & Sharma, N. P. (2015). Opening the gender diversity black box: Causality of perceived gender equity and locus of control and mediation of work engagement in employee well-being. *Frontiers in Psychology, 6*, 1371. https://doi.org/10.3389/fpsyg.2015.01371

Shore, L. M., Cleveland, J. N., & Sanchez, D. (2018). Inclusive workplaces: A review and model. *Human Resource Management Review, 28*(2), 176–189. https://doi.org/10.1016/j.hrmr.2017.07.003

Shore, L. M., Randel, A. E., Chung, B. G., Dean, M. A., Holcombe Ehrhart, K., & Singh, G. (2011). Inclusion and diversity in work groups: A review and model for future research. *Journal of Management, 37*(4), 1262–1289. https://doi.org/10.1177/0149206310385943

Sousa, I. C., Ramos, S., & Carvalho, H. (2019). Age-diversity practices and retirement preferences among older workers: A moderated mediation model of work engagement and work ability. *Frontiers in Psychology, 10*, 1937. https://doi.org/10.3389/fpsyg.2019.01937

Tims, M., & Bakker A. B. (2010) Job crafting: Towards a new model of individual job redesign: Original research. *SA Journal of Industrial Psychology, 36*(2), 1–9. https://doi.org/10.10520/EJC89228

Tuan, L. T., Rowley, C., Khai, D. C., Qian, D., Masli, E., & Le, H. Q. (2020). Fostering well-being among public employees with disabilities: The roles of disability-inclusive human resource practices, job resources, and public service motivation. *Review of Public Personnel Administration, 41*(3), 466–496. https://doi.org/10.1177/0734371X19897753

van den Bosch, R., & Taris, T. W. (2014). Authenticity at work: Development and validation of an individual authenticity measure at work. *Journal of Happiness Studies, 15*(1), 1–18. https://doi.org/10.1080/00223980.2013.820684

van Knippenberg, D., De Dreu, C. K. W., & Homan, A. C. (2004). Work group diversity and group performance: An integrative model and research agenda. *Journal of Applied Psychology, 89*(6), 1008–1022. https://doi.org/10.1037/0021-9010.89.6.1008

van Knippenberg, D., & Schippers, M. C. (2007). Work group diversity. *Annual Review of Psychology, 58*, 515–541. https://doi.org/10.1146/annurev.psych.58.110405.085546

van Woerkom, M., & Meyers, M. C. (2018). Strengthening personal growth: The effects of a strengths intervention on personal growth initiative. *Journal of Occupational and Organizational Psychology, 92*(1), 98–121. https://doi.org/10.111/joop.12240

van Woerkom, M., Meyers, M. C., & Bakker, A. B. (2020). Considering strengths use in organizations as a multilevel construct. *Human Resource Management Review.* https://doi.org/10.1016/j.hrmr.2020.100767

Villanueva-Flores, M., Valle, R., & Bornay-Barrachina, M. (2017). Perceptions of discrimination and distributive injustice among people with physical disabilities: In jobs, compensation and career development. *Personnel Review, 46*(3), 680–698. https://doi.org/10.1108/PR-04-2015-0098

Warren, W. E., Johnson, L., & Zgourides, G. D. (2002). The influence of ethnic diversity on leadership, group process, and performance: An examination of learning teams. *International Journal of Intercultural Relations, 26*(1), 1–16. https://doi.org/10.1016/S0147-1767(01)00032-3

Wood, A. M., Linley, P. A., Maltby, J., Kashdan, T. B., & Hurling, R. (2011). Using personal and psychological strengths leads to increases in well-being over time: A longitudinal study and the development of the strengths use questionnaire. *Personality and Individual Differences*, *50*(1), 15–19. https://doi.org/10.1016/j.paid.2010.08.004

Woodhams, C., Lupton, B., Perkins, G., & Cowling, M. (2015). Multiple disadvantage and wage growth: The effect of merit pay on pay gaps. *Human Resource Management*, *54*(2), 283–301. https://doi.org/10.1002/hrm.21692

List of Figures

https://doi.org/10.1515/9783110743647-025

List of Tables

https://doi.org/10.1515/9783110743647-026

About the Editors

Joy E. Beatty is Academic Department Head of Management and Associate Professor in the College of Business at Eastern Michigan University. Her research focuses on diversity in the workplace, specifically the experiences of employees with disability and chronic illness. Her work has been published in *Human Resource Management*, *International Journal of Human Resource Management*, *Academy of Management Review*, *Group and Organization Management*, and *Journal of Occupational Health Psychology*.

Sophie Hennekam is Professor in Organizational Behavior at Audencia Business School in France. Her research revolves around inclusion, diversity and stigmatized and/or invisible populations at work. She has published in journals such as *Academy of Management Journal*, *Journal of Applied Psychology and Human Relations*.

Mukta Kulkarni is a professor and has held the Mphasis Chair for Digital Accessibility and Inclusion at the Indian Institute of Management, Bangalore. She has published in journals such as the *Academy of Management Journal*, *Human Relations*, the *Leadership Quarterly*, and the *Journal of Organizational Behavior*. She currently serves on the editorial boards of *Human Relations*, *Journal of Organizational Behavior*, and is an associate editor for the *Journal of Management Inquiry*.

https://doi.org/10.1515/9783110743647-027

Index

https://doi.org/10.1515/9783110743647-028